Heart's Flower

The Life and Poetry
of Shinkei

Heart's Flower

The Life and Poetry of Shinkei

Esperanza Ramirez-Christensen

Stanford University Press, Stanford, California 1994

Stanford University Press
Stanford, California
© 1994
by the Board of Trustees
of the Leland Stanford Junior University
Printed in the United States of America

CIP data are at the end of the book

The printing of this volume was
underwritten in part by a grant
from the Japan Foundation.

To my father
who never ceased to wait for the book

Acknowledgments

I should like to take this opportunity to express my abiding gratitude to the mentors who graciously extended their expertise and encouragement through the various periods of my graduate studies and research: Professors Helen Craig McCullough and William H. McCullough at the University of California, Berkeley; Olof Lidin at Copenhagen University's East Asiatic Institute; Edwin Cranston, Howard Hibbett, Itasaka Gen, and Donald Shively at Harvard; and Kaneko Kinjirō at Tōkai University's Japanese Literature Department. The memories of Professor Kaneko's Shinkei and renga seminars in 1979–80, the warm fellowship of his graduate students, the outings to Hakone, Kamakura, and the Ōyama foothills in search of Shinkei's and Sōgi's traces—all were a constant inspiration while writing this book.

I am also grateful to Statens Humanistiske Forskningsråd of Denmark for a grant during the early stages of my work on renga and to the Japan Foundation for a year's dissertation research in Japan. A faculty fellowship from the Mellon Foundation in 1986–87 enabled me to continue with the work reflected in Part Two of this book, and the Office of the Vice President for Research at the University of Michigan helped subsidize its publication.

My colleagues Robert Danly and Ken Itō read the manuscript (along with its projected sequel) and delivered encouraging reports, while Steven D. Carter, a fellow reaper in the renga vineyards—as Helen McCullough used to say—undertook the sober perusal for the Stanford University Press. Thanks are also due to Helen Tartar for tracking the manuscript from Cambridge to Ann Arbor some years later, and to my editor, John Ziemer, for his care and tact in handling it.

E.R.-C.

Contents

Abbreviations

The following abbreviations are used in the text and notes. For complete citations, see under title in the Bibliography, pp. 433–43.

BT	[*Teihon*] *Bashō taisei*
DNCJ	*Dai Nihon chimei jisho*
FGS	*Fūgashū* (seventeenth imperial waka anthology)
Guku	Shinkei, *Guku Shibakusa*
GR	*Gunsho ruijū*
GSIS	*Goshūishū* (fourth imperial waka anthology)
GYS	*Gyokuyōshū* (fourteenth imperial waka anthology)
HD	*Haikai daijiten*
HJAS	*Harvard Journal of Asiatic Studies*
KKS	*Kokinshū* (first imperial waka anthology)
KS	*Kichōkotenseki sōkan*
KT	[*Shimpen*] *Kokka taikan*
KYS	*Kinyōshū* (fifth imperial waka anthology)
MN	*Monumenta Nipponica*
MYS	*Man'yōshū* (first Japanese poetry anthology)
NKBT	*Nihon koten bungaku taikei*
NKBZ	*Nihon koten bungaku zenshū*
NKT	*Nihon kagaku taikei*
Oi	Shinkei, *Oi no kurigoto*
Renju	Kanera, *Renju gappekishū*
RH	*Rengaronshū, Haironshū*
RS	Kidō, *Renga shironkō*
SIS	*Shūishū* (third imperial waka anthology)

SK	*Sōgi kushū*
SKKS	*Shinkokinshū* (eighth imperial waka anthology)
SKS	Shōtetsu, *Sōkonshū*
SKT	*Shinshaku kambun taikei*
SNKBT	*Shin Nihon koten bungaku taikei*
SNKS	*Shinchō Nihon koten shūsei*
SSG	Shinkei, *Sasamegoto*
SSRS	*Shinkeishū ronshū*
SSS	*Shinkei sakuhinshū*
ST	*Shikashū taisei*
STKBS	*Shinsen Tsukubashū* (second imperial renga anthology)
Teikin	Kenzai, *Shinkei-sōzu teikin*
TKBS	*Tsukubashū* (first imperial renga anthology)
Tokoro	Shinkei, *Tokoro-dokoro hentō*
ZGR	*Zoku gunsho ruijū*

Heart's Flower

The Life and Poetry
of Shinkei

Introduction

One of the greatest puzzles in Japanese literary history is the neglect of Shinkei (1406–75), a profoundly acute poet-priest of the medieval period who wielded a decisive influence on the conceptual grounding and artistic development of *renga* (linked poetry). Not even Bashō (1644–94), whose poetry and poetics are amazingly reminiscent of Shinkei's, mentions him, although in *Oi no kobumi* he declared the oneness of his art with that of "Sōgi in linked poetry." Sōgi (1421–1502) was Shinkei's student and friend. An excellent artist and energetic personality, he was instrumental in promoting Shinkei's vision of renga and its central place in Japanese poetic history. Twenty years after Shinkei's death, he compiled the second official renga anthology, *Shinsen Tsukubashū*, and paid homage to his mentor by giving him the highest number of verses there. But nearly two centuries would elapse before Shinkei's deeper vision of renga as a Way, a search for authentic being, would find its proper expression in Bashō, and by then his name had sunk into such obscurity that Bashō himself, at least as far as extant records indicate, would not recognize him as his true precursor.

One reason for Shinkei's obscurity might be his purism. Something about his thought and the whole conduct of his life seems to have distanced him from the popular renga milieu. His other premier disciple, Kenzai (1452–1510), confirms this picture when he writes: "In the Way of renga I humbly look up to the words of this priest as to the teachings of the Buddha." Indeed, if one might speak of a lonely aristocracy of the spirit in Japanese poetry, Shinkei would be its high priest for the intensely pure, lyrical longing for transcendence that is the most marked quality of his sensibility. In an age when anyone who wished to signal his denial of mundane concerns or make his way in the world with relative freedom donned the robes of a monk,

Shinkei stood out by being a practicing cleric with a temple in the capital and a considerable rank to go with it. It is thus impossible to ignore his calling in evaluating his poetic achievement. His priestly duties and his devotion to Buddhist ideals evidently conflicted quite early with his fascination with the craft of words and personal self-expression. Perhaps it was inevitable that he sought to resolve the conflict by boldly identifying the two disciplines in a single Way that has all the loftiness of a religion but is also the hard-won product of an inner struggle waged by a private individual amidst the anarchic conditions of his times.

Shinkei's temple burned in the Ōnin War (1467–77), and he died an exile in the remote foothills of distant Sagami Province before that war's end. For modern readers the subsequent darkness that befell his work has been dispelled to a degree by the publication in 1948 of Araki Yoshio's pioneering study, *Shinkei*. *Shinkeishū ronshū*, a collection of the poet's critical writings edited by Yokoyama Shigeru and Noguchi Ei'ichi, appeared in the same year as the first part of a complete anthology of his works. Four years later, Kidō Saizō produced *Kōchū Sasamegoto kenkyū to kaisetsu*, still the most thorough textual study and commentary on Shinkei's major treatise. In the prose of these pioneering scholars, one senses a feeling of awe toward their subject. In the shock of discovery, Araki went so far as to compare him to a lone peak towering above the vast mountain ranges of Japanese poetry. Kidō characterized his thought as the utmost development of the medieval spirit, and the Muromachi cultural historian Haga Kōshirō ranked him with the Nō artist and theorist Zenchiku (1405–68) as the loftiest representative of Higashiyama aesthetic philosophy.

It was not until the 1970's, however, against the background of a surge of interest in *chūsei* (medieval) literature in general, and renga in particular, that Shinkei studies blossomed. The Japanese are looking beyond the recent past and into the so-called dark ages of their history, seeking to find there the roots of a modern sensibility predating the ideological and institutional feudalism of the Tokugawa period. The gesture seems quixotic, for the Muromachi period was an anarchic age dominated by strong, ambitious, and warlike personalities. Yet it was also in consequence an age familiar with death and mutability, as is apparent in its artistic products, which include some of the most quintessential expressions of existential loneliness, or *sabi*, in the country's history. If there is something modern about the *chūsei* period and a sensibility like Shinkei's, perhaps it lies in the awareness of the fragility of men's works and the anarchy of the human condition. Confrontation with such verities is conducive to the formation of a strong, independent character and an apprehension of the true signifi-

cance of freedom apart from the self-perpetuating myths of an authoritar-
ian power structure.

In the West the German scholar Wolfram Naumann's *Shinkei in seiner
Bedeutung für die japanische Kettendichtung* (The significance of Shinkei
for Japanese linked poetry) appeared in 1967. Based principally on Araki, it
was probably Jacques Roubaud's source for his observations on Shinkei in
Renga: A Chain of Poems, a multilingual sonnet sequence composed by
Octavio Paz, Edoardo Sanguineti, Charles Tomlinson, and Roubaud himself in April 1969. Paz's introduction to this slender volume of poetry,
which marks, according to one review, "the invention of a new kind of
literary discourse," is a fascinating indirect comment on the significance of
renga for the West at the present time. Roubaud quotes Araki on Shinkei's
life thus: "Shinkei's way of life is entirely unknown to us; veiled, it merges
into vagueness, into that tonality of evening light which is in keeping with
renga. Only here and there, like the moon appearing through a break in the
clouds, does a fragment of his existence become visible."

Without dispelling that crepuscular tonality for the harsh light of midday, this book is offered as a somewhat more substantial account of Shinkei's life and works than was possible for Araki in 1948. It is partly the
result of a year's research with Kaneko Kinjirō in 1979–80, just two years
before he published *Shinkei no seikatsu to sakuhin*, now the most authoritative biography of Shinkei. Along with the Shinkei texts themselves, Kaneko's study is the most important source for my own account, although any
errors of interpretation or improper conclusions are solely my respon-
sibility.

The external sources for Shinkei's life are few and fragmentary. By far the
most important for establishing the status of his temple are fifteenth-century
documents in the archives of the Rokuharamitsu Temple in Kyoto. Isolated
references to him occur in such contemporary journals as the *Inryōken
nichiroku* of the Zen temple Shōkokuji, the *Chikamoto nikki* kept by an
official of the bakufu's Administrative Council, Shōtetsu's poetic diary *Sōkonshū*, and the early Tokugawa miscellany called *Keichō kembunshū*,
among others. However, the most revealing sources are Shinkei's own writings: the critical essays, including three extant letters, and renga and waka
poems whose autobiographical implications become apparent when read
against external data. The three *hyakushu* (hundred-poem sequences) from
1463, 1467, and 1471 are especially significant for this crucial period in his
life. Many of the poems are extremely moving and give the modern reader a
near and immediate sense of the man and his age. The renga manuscripts are
equally revealing. Since the texts of *hyakuin* (hundred-verse renga se-

quences) invariably include the date of composition and the names of the participating poets, they are an excellent source for illuminating the renga circles in which Shinkei moved in the various stages of his career. They also reflect on a major part of the contemporary poetic milieu itself. Apart from these hyakuin texts, there exist portions of Shinkei's personal renga collections, among which the *Azuma gekō hokkugusa*, a chronological record of his *hokku* (opening verse of a renga sequence) from 1467 to 1472, is an unrivaled source for his physical circumstances and state of mind during his sojourn in the Kantō region.

Briefly then, the following biography is written around those waka poems, renga verses, and passages in Shinkei's critical essays that are autobiographical in content or implication. The events of his life create a convenient division into two major parts: the Kyoto years, from his early training for the priesthood on Mount Hiei through his residence in the Higashiyama district of the capital, which ended with the outbreak of the Ōnin War in 1467; and the Kantō years, from his departure in the same year through his stay in Shinagawa (in present-day Tokyo), and subsequent retirement in 1471 to Mount Ōyama (in modern Kanagawa), where he died in 1475. The first part comprises the first sixty-one years of his life, which culminated in a measure of fame in the four years before the war; the second part the last eight years in exile in the Kantō, where he became the leading figure in the local poetic circles. The disproportionate space accorded the latter reflects the circumstance that with the significant exception of *Sasamegoto*, his major critical statement, nearly all his prose writings stem from the Kantō years, as do three of the four extant hyakushu, and the *Azuma gekō*. The outbreak of the Ōnin War in 1467 is the crucial boundary in this topography; it interrupted a flourishing career in the capital and turned Shinkei into a refugee deprived of home and position. An earlier crisis in 1462–63 constitutes the other dividing line in his career, since it confirmed him in a determined pursuit of poetry as a Way, a search for existential meaning apart from the uncertainties of material circumstance. It is at this point that Part One, "Heart's Flower: A Shinkei Literary Biography," starts; the crisis presented an excellent, if not strictly chronological, opportunity to evoke a sense of the man himself as well as to sketch the historical background of the age.

My method is to utilize Shinkei's works to illumine the social and mental factors motivating his life; the numerous poems and verses quoted in the biography hence represent an arbitrary selection in terms of literary merit. Some are undeniably excellent, others are aesthetically indifferent, but all are charged with a significance that often transcends the merely personal.

A true valuation of Shinkei's poetic achievement has to be based both on the poems cited in the biography as well as the works translated and analyzed in Part Two, "Gems of the Mind-Heart: A Shinkei Reader." (I have adopted Shinkei's title for his renga collection from the Kyoto years, *Shingyokushū*.) This includes a significant portion of his hokku and *tsukeku* (the lower verse of a linked-verse pair) from the imperial renga anthology *Shinsen Tsukubashū*, presented together with Muromachi-period commentaries on them; two 100-verse sequences from 1467 and 1468; and a selection of 100 waka that I feel manifest the most characteristic aspects of his *kokoro* (mind-heart) and style. In a deliberate decision to let them stand unencumbered, I make no comments on the waka, trusting that my analysis of his poetry in the earlier sections will provide a background for reading them.

Below, for convenience, I present a descriptive list of Shinkei's works; the first source cited under each title is the edition used in this book.

Shinkei's Works

The main surviving corpus of Shinkei's poetry—his renga and waka—consists of his own personal collections from 1463 to 1473. Aside from these, 119 verses appear in the *Shinsen Tsukubashū*, 402 in Sōgi's *Chikurinshō*, and a few hundred more in the records of the renga sessions in which he participated. The extant texts for the sessions held in Kyoto are listed and described in Chapter 3. There are only two extant texts for sessions held in the Kantō; they are described in Chapter 4. With a few notable exceptions, the modern editions of Shinkei's works as listed below have been published without annotations, and therefore present an interpretive challenge to the reader.

I. Personal Renga Collections (unless otherwise noted, all the following works appear in *SSS*)

1. *Shingyokushū* (Gems of the mind-heart collection) or *Shinkei-sōzu kushū* (Bishop Shinkei's verse collection), a selection of the most representative of Shinkei's verses from before the Fourth Month of 1466, that is to say during the Kantō years; 287 hokku and 361 tsukeku on the four seasons, love, and miscellaneous topics.

2. *Shingyokushū shūi*, a supplement to the above; includes 137 hokku composed after 1466.

3. *Shinkei-sōzu hyakku* (100 verses by Bishop Shinkei), a collection of tsukeku on the four seasons, love, and miscellaneous topics. A hokku introduces the verses for each season, making a total of 100 verses.

4. *Shikō Shūa hyakuban renga awase* (Renga contest in 100 rounds by Gusai and Shūa), dated the twenty-fifth day of the Sixth Month, 1468. The work originated in a linked-verse contest in which Gusai (1282–1376) and Shūa (d. 1375?) each appended a tsukeku to the same *maeku* (the upper verse in a linked-verse pair), and Nijō Yoshimoto (1320–88), as judge, marked appropriate points. Later, Shinkei was so impressed by the work that he composed tsukeku to the same maeku. The text is composed of the earlier contest verses and Shinkei's tsukeku. Text in the Seikadō Archives, no. 22 of the *Rengashūsho* manuscript collection.

5. *Renga hyakkutsuke* (100 renga linked-verse pairs), Shinkei's selection of his own tsukeku and the maeku from the preceding item, compiled at the request of the Zen priest Sōgen. Holograph in the Tenri Library.

6. *Shinkei renga jichū* (Shinkei's renga self-annotations), Shinkei's commentaries on the verses in item 5. Text in the Shōkōkan Collection.

7. *Azuma gekō hokkugusa* (Grasses of hokku from the Azuma journey), 210 hokku arranged chronologically according to the four seasons, from the summer of 1467 to the autumn of 1472. This is Shinkei's hokku collection from the Kantō years.

8. *Azuma atari iisute* (Ephemeral compositions in Azuma), 278 tsukeku on the four seasons; dating from 1467 and after, they constitute Shinkei's tsukeku collection from the Kantō years.

9. *Shinkei kushū kokemushiro* (The moss-grown abode: a Shinkei verse anthology), 171 tsukeku illustrative of three major poetic styles: *ushintei* (style of meditation), *yūgentei* (style of ineffable depth), and *mempakutei* (or *omoshiroki tai*; arresting style). Also included are nine hokku illustrative of the *mempakutei*. Date unknown, but definitely postdating item 4.

10. *Shibakusa kunai hokku* (Hokku from the *Wayside Grasses Anthology*), a two-part collection of 636 hokku. The first part contains verses composed before 1467; the second part is the *Azuma gekō hokkugusa* (see item 7). The work is believed to have been part of the *Shibakusa* (Wayside grasses), a sixteen-volume collection of the complete works of Shinkei, compiled by himself, but now partly lost.

11. *Guku Shibakusa* (Humble verses of wayside grasses); also known as *Iwahashi no jō* (*Iwahashi*, first section). A selection of 91 hokku and 132 tsukeku from the *Shibakusa* collection, including commentaries written by Shinkei for his disciple Kenzai during a sojourn in Aizu, Iwashiro Province (Fukushima) in 1470. In *SSRS*, pp. 3–64; variant texts on pp. 65–128, 129–93.

12. *Shibakusa-nai renga awase* (Renga contests from the *Wayside Grasses Anthology*), verses divided into a hokku contest of 50 rounds and a

tsukeku contest of 100 rounds. Undertaken for a Shirakawa monk called Jun'a in the Third Month of 1473.

II. Waka Collections

1. *Gondaisōzu Shinkeishū* (The Bishop Shinkei anthology), three 100-poem sequences, plus another 132 poems on minutely specified topics. The first sequence, divided under the topics of the four seasons, love, and miscellaneous, was composed in 1463 as a prayer offering at the Hachiōji Shrine in Wakayama. The second sequence, similarly divided, was composed between the twenty-fifth and thirtieth day of the Eight Month, 1467. The third, dating from 1468, contains poems on the following topics: flowers, moon, dew, grievances, reminiscences, travel, and Buddhism. Included in *ZGR* 16a: 446.400–419; *ST* 6: 94–105; [*Shimpen*] *KT* 8: 256–63 under the title *Shinkeishū*.

2. *Hyakushu waka* (100 waka), a version of the 1463 sequence above, with Shinkei's own commentaries. In *SSRS*, pp. 317–47, and *Chūsei waka-shū: Muromachi-hen*, *SNKBT* 47: 315–52 under the title *Kanshō hyaku-shu*.

3. *Shinkei-sōzu jittei waka* (Bishop Shinkei's waka in ten styles), 120 poems illustrating the ten styles described by Fujiwara Teika (1162–1241) in his *Maigetsushō* (1219). Probably a part of the *Shibakusa* collection. In *ZGR* 15a: 403. 41–47; and *ST* 6: 106–15. The *ST* edition is based on a variant text from the Ise Shrine Archives and consists of 323 poems; it also includes a *chōka* with an envoi and another 8 poems entitled "The Eight Views of Hsiao-hsiang."

4. *Iwahashi no ge* (Iwahashi, second section), 179 waka with commentaries written by Shinkei for Kenzai during their trip to Aizu in 1470. The companion volume to *Guku Shibakusa* (see item 11 above); the two are collectively known as *Shibakusa kunai Iwahashi* (The *Iwahashi* section of the *Wayside Grasses Anthology*). In *SSRS*, pp. 257–316; the preface and epilogue only are included under the title *Iwahashi no jō, batsu* in Ijichi, *Rengaronshū* 2: 331–39.

5. *Shinkei-sōzu hyakushu* (A hundred-poem sequence by Bishop Shinkei), composed in 1471 to commemorate the thirteenth anniversary of the death of Shōtetsu, Shinkei's waka mentor. In *ZGR* 14b: 397.913–16.

III. Critical Works

1. *Jōhō renga* (Renga by Jōhō), a collection of 100 verse-pairs by Jōhō, a priest of the Tōfukuji, bearing commentaries by Shinkei and a colophon dated the fifteenth day of the Third Month, 1462. The text appears in Shimazu, *Rengashi no kenkyū*, pp. 291–307.

2. *Sasamegoto* (Murmured conversations), Shinkei's major treatise and his most frequently reprinted work; the first part was written in 1463 when he was in Wakayama, and the second part in the capital. A partial translation by Dennis Hirota, incorporating about half of the treatise's 62 sections, appeared in his article "In Practice of the Way: *Sasamegoto*, an Introduction Book in Linked Verse." The forthcoming companion to this book will include my complete translation and study of Shinkei's aesthetic philosophy. Sources and editors for the so-called common-edition line of *Sasamegoto* texts are the following: Kidō Saizō, *RH*; Kido Saizō, *Kōchū Sasamegoto kenkyū to kaisetsu*; Ijichi Tetsuo, *Rengaron shinshū*; Sasaki Nobutsuna, *NKT* 5, under the title *Shinkei shigo*; Hisamatsu Sen'ichi, *Chūsei karonshū*; and Suzuki Hisashi in Haga Kōshirō, ed., *Geidō shisō-shū*. The variant or revised-edition line of *Sasamegoto* texts is represented in *GR* 10: 304, and Ijichi, *Rengaronshū, Haironshū, Nōgakuronshū, NKBZ* 51.

3. *Gikō no eisō Shinkei no tensaku* (Shinkei's critical comments on Sōgi's poetic compositions), Shinkei's commentaries on 114 tsukeku by Sōgi. The manuscript is undated but believed from internal evidence to have been written in or before 1466. In Yunoue Sanae, "*Gikō no eisō Shinkei no tensaku*: honkoku to kaisetsu."

4. *Tokoro-dokoro hentō* (Replies here and there), composed of three letters. In the first, dated the twenty-third day of the Third Month of 1466, Shinkei discusses the historical development of renga, refers to his relationship with his waka mentor Shōtetsu, and appraises the work of contemporary poets like Sōzei (1386?–1455) and Chiun (d. 1448); in the second (date unknown), he points to the *Shinkokinshū* period as the peak of waka history and indulges in some self-laudatory reminiscences; the third, dated the Eight Month of 1470 and addressed to Sōgi, is a critical appraisal of verses submitted by Sōgi for his judgment. In *SSRS*, pp. 194–227; and Ijichi, *Rengaronshū* 1: 305–30.

5. *Shinkei Yūhaku e no hensho* (Shinkei's reply to Yūhaku), a work explaining the mental preparation required of a renga poet and comparing the styles of Gusai and Shūa as seen in each of five corresponding verses from the *Hyakuban renga awase* (see item 4 in the first section). Undated. In Shimazu, *Rengashi no kenkyū*, pp. 308–12.

6. *Hitorigoto* (Solitary ramblings), dating from the Fourth Month of 1468. A critical essay whose opening passage recalls, and is clearly aware of, the *Hōjōki* in its pessimistic view of contemporary conditions. Its focus is the mental attitude required for composing good poetry; the student, according to Shinkei, must train his mind to perceive temporality and value depth and overtones as aesthetic ideals. It includes a brief history of renga

and a discussion of the poetry of Gusai and Shūa, a valuable list of the most famous practitioners of the various arts in the capital before the Ōnin War, and a celebrated panegyric on water in the four seasons. For the text as edited by Shimazu Tadao, see *Kodai chūsei geijutsuron*, pp. 466–78; also in ZGR 17: 497.1126–33, and Hisamatsu Sen'ichi, ed., *Zuihitsu bungaku, Kochū Nihon bungaku ruijū* 3 (1930): 510–25.

7. *Ichigon* (One word), a short and undated manuscript in the Osaka University Archives. It deals with the three basic methods of linking and is believed to have been written for Kenzai. Unpublished; I have relied on a handwritten copy kindly provided by Professor Kaneko Kinjirō.

8. *Shiyōshō* (Notes for private use), presented to the lord of Kawagoe Castle in the Kantō, Ōta Sukekiyo (1411–95; priestly name Dōshin), in 1471. The only work in which Shinkei deals principally with the subject of renga *shikimoku* or rules, if only to censure a literal and slavish adherence to them. He gives 305 items of description and example for *sari kirai*, the rule that forbids the recurrence of similar or closely associated words and images within specified intervals, and 17 items on the procedures for holding a renga session and of recording the verses. In Ijichi, *Rengaron shinshū, Koten bunkō* 113 (1956), pp. 53–98.

9. *Oi no kurigoto* (Old man's prattle), a treatise written in 1471 at the request of the monk at the temple on Mount Ōyama that was Shinkei's final place of retreat. He discusses the history of renga; the styles of Gusai and Nijō Yoshimoto, as well as those of Shūa and Bontō (1349–1427?); and sets forth his concept of the ideal renga poet as one who evinces artistic sensibilities, dedication to the Way as spiritual cultivation, and an attitude of detachment from worldly affairs. The treatise includes a moving description of his mountain dwelling that has been compared to Bashō's *Genjūan no ki*. Along with *Hitorigoto* above, it has been lauded as a fine representative example of medieval *zuihitsu*. For the text as edited by Shimazu Tadao, see *Kodai chūsei geijutsuron*, pp. 410–22; also in *SSRS*, pp. 240–56, under the title *Kokemushiro*.

PART ONE

Heart's Flower

A Shinkei
Literary Biography

CHAPTER I

Prologue: "The Seed of the Heart"

90 Miscellaneous. *A House Amidst Rice Fields*

onozukara	Was he not devoid,
kokoro no tane mo	from the very start, of the
naki hito ya	seed of the heart?
iyashiki ta'i no	Ta'i, rude village amidst
sato ni mumareshi	rice fields, gave him birth.

I was born in the place called Ta'i Village and went up to the capital when I was two. I am all too aware of the fact, while lamenting it in this way.   (*SSRS*, p. 317)[1]

In the spring of 1463 when this poem was written, Shinkei, poet and head priest of Jūjūshin'in Temple in the capital, was visiting his hometown of Ta'i along the Kinokawa River in Nakusa District, Kii Province (Wakayama Prefecture).[2] Here two months later he would write *Sasamegoto*, his most important critical work and today an exemplary document of medieval Japanese thought.[3] The poem is part of a sequence of 100 composed, as he notes in the colophon, "hurriedly as a prayer offering [*hōraku*] while in religious retreat at the Ta'i village shrine." Many other poems in the sequence illumine his personal circumstances at the time. The work, moreover, is unique in including his own annotations (*jichū*) and has since become an invaluable autobiographical source amidst the paucity of external documentary material concerning his life. As will quickly become clear, it also bears the traces of a period of personal crisis for its author, revealing itself as a figurative speech inflected with the stresses of an existence endured more than five centuries ago under a different order of being and thinking, but still eminently readable, as he intended, in our own time and place. For this reading of a life, there is no better place to start than with the 1463 sequence in Ta'i Village, lamented point of origin, fateful "seed" of an absence.

The poem is in fact our only information regarding Shinkei's birthplace. Clearly it alludes to Tsurayuki's famous opening statement in the *Kokinshū* Preface about a different origin: "Japanese poetry has its seed in the human heart, which sprouts into a myriad leaves of words."[4] And doubtless he intends an ironic juxtaposition between this poetic "seed" and that of humble rice plants. It would not be wise, however, to construe from the contextual metaphor that he was born to a family of farmers. The poem was composed on the fixed topic of *denka*—that is, a farmhouse—and utilizes the connotations of the placename Ta'i (lit., "well in the rice fields") to evoke an ignorant rusticity and alienation from poetic privilege. In other words, Shinkei is using the set subject as a context for lamenting his alleged "innate" (*onozukara*) lack of poetic sensibility due to his birth in the rude and lowly (*iyashiki*) countryside in contrast to the refined capital city. That fount of high culture had produced Japan's greatest waka poets heretofore, and they were as a rule of aristocratic origins. Shinkei himself clearly was not. But then ever since he was taken from Kii at the age of two to undergo clerical training on Mount Hiei, he had been living in the capital city of Kyoto and indeed gained a reputation there as a waka and renga poet, along with his considerable social position as head of Jūjūshin'in with the official title of Provisional Major Bishop (*Gondaisōzu*).

An examination of other poems in this sequence will reveal that the self-depreciating tone in the one quoted above was the product of a depressed mood. Nonetheless, its self-ironic humility is somewhat more than a conventional stance. It is a reflection of the high and absolute standards against which he measured himself, as may be seen in the interesting postscript he later appended to the text of the sequence after adding the commentaries: "An ancient has said that even the most excellent poems will become degraded and seem mediocre when expressed in plain language. What shame do I incur in foolishly explaining these crazy poems that are absolutely worthless to begin with!"[5]

Fortunately, despite his conviction that paraphrase diminishes poetry, Shinkei did not therefore desist from it. In fact he wrote comments on some of his other poems and renga verses as well, not to mention his evaluation of other poets' works. They testify to his belief that criticism and interpretation constitute an aspect of poetic activity just as crucial as poetic composition itself. Moreover, apart from fulfilling a pedagogical function, the *jichū* answered to his apparent need for self-explanation. Such is manifest in that significant portion of his surviving waka corpus that has private emotion and biographical circumstance as its material, constituting, as it were, a poetic autobiography. Compared to the style of objective symbolism characteristic of the *Shinkokinshū*, an anthology that he revered, and viewed against the generic impersonality of renga poetry, the autobiographical strain in Shinkei's waka emerges as a particularly distinctive phenomenon. It represents a departure from the formal decorum of mid-classical poetics, a valorization of personal experience that employs the convention of set topics (*daiei*) as a framework or device for self-expression rather than as a subject whose essential nature (*hon'i*) is to be demonstrated.

There are a number of "excellent" poems in the 1463 sequence, and Shinkei's best work may arguably be said to belong to the wholly different mode of objective symbolism established by the *Shinkokinshū* poets. The pieces analyzed below, however, are chosen primarily for their auto-biographical import, for what they reveal of the poet's reaction to the pressure of circumstance as explained by himself.

97 Miscellaneous. *A Distant View*

kyō wa kite	Come today, upon a scene
te ni toru bakari	so poignantly outlined in the haze
kasumu ni mo	I could grasp it in my hand,
fude o zo naguru	this brush—bitterly I fling
wakanoura nami	into the waves of Poetry Bay!

Face to face with the springtime scenery along Waka sea, I am overcome with shame at how uncertain my poetry remains despite the long years I have devoted to it.[6]   (*SSRS*, p. 346)

94 Miscellaneous. *Travel*

isogashi yo	A fretful life—
tabi ni samayou	by endless journeys driven
hodo bakari	to distraction, always,
mono no aware wa	would that I may yet learn
itsu ka shiramashi	the moving power of things.

Forced by circumstances to wander about in the outskirts of the capital, I have become possessed by the dust of the world; blinded by desire, my spirit finds no rest. Amidst the distractions of such travels, predictably even the moving power of things [*mono no aware*] has died in my mind.   (*SSRS*, p. 345)

These two poems open a window onto the psychological state of depression that also generated the lament on his "rude" origins. The reason may be gathered from the commentary to poem 94, in which he speaks of being so absorbed in worldly affairs that the sense of *mono no aware* has deserted him. In Shinkei's critical vocabulary, *mono no aware* in its broad sense of "the moving power of things" is synonymous with the poetic spirit itself, with his view of poetry as a heightened contemplation of life. His sense of inadequacy in poem 97, an expression of angry frustration at his inability to compose a suitable poem on the spring scenery along Wakanoura, was presumably occasioned by the same restlessness. All three poems ultimately bear upon the same complaint: namely, that he was in no position, either socially or spiritually, to cultivate poetry to the degree that he desired. He was not born to the life of genteel leisure; he lacked the mental space to cultivate his sensibilities. Paradoxically the complaint throws into high relief the compelling attraction that poetry exercised upon him, as well as his considerable ambitions in this direction.

Shinkei was fifty-seven in 1463. His priestly rank and office were no mere sinecure but a reward for diligent performance of duties, and no doubt the usual worldly compromises. As late as 1471 when he retired in the hills of Mount Ōyama and wrote his final critical essay, *Oi no kurigoto*, he would still be lamenting the destiny that made the serious, full-time pursuit of poetry impossible for him.

A long time ago I set my heart on this Way [of poetry] and even had occasion to participate in sessions with the old poets and masters of the time. But unfortunately my duties in the Way of Buddhism afforded me no leisure, and even worse, upon reaching the prime of manhood I suffered from an illness for so many years that in the end, despite my desire, all my efforts came to so much water poured through a sieve. Moreover, the persons I relied on for support were early taken from this world, leaving me in such grief that life came to seem even more insubstantial than a phantom vision. My mind became permeated with the sense of things that merely pass without a trace, like the momentary glimpse of a galloping white horse through a gap in the wall, or the trackless flight of birds in the sky.   (*Oi*, p. 412)

The conflict that he apparently experienced between the demands of his priestly calling and his poetic ambitions provides an interestingly realistic counterpoint to the lofty, otherworldly orientation of *Sasamegoto*, in particular to the celebrated unity of the Ways of Buddhism and Poetry enunciated there. Indeed the contradiction—and it was not so much on the plane of ideas as a felt tension between mundane existence and an exalted, poetic mode of being—was most exacerbated in the spring of 1463. As other poems in the sequence will show, Shinkei's presence in Kii during this period was far from an ordinary visit home. In fact he was confronting a crisis that threatened his position as Jūjūshin'in's head priest, the material basis of both his religious and mundane existence.

The very poem that opens the sequence is charged with a personal exigency highly unusual for its topic and formal position as an introduction to the whole.

1 Spring. *Beginning of Spring*

aranu yo ni	Upon a whole new world—
kuremadoinuru	even the darkly vexed struggle
itonami mo	for a means to live,

hitoyo akureba	turned within a night familiar
nareru haru kana	in the dawning light of spring.

This poem should be read with a caesura after the first line, thus: "turned within a night familiar, with the dawning light of spring upon a whole new world." "Darkly vexed" [*kuremadoinuru*] is the oppressiveness one feels under the pressure of earning a livelihood in the world. It describes a state of darkness, not the ending [of the year].[7] (*SSRS*, p. 317)

Become "familiar" and endurable in the fresh new light of spring, the struggle for existence yet casts an ominous gloom over a poem that convention dictates should be an unmixed celebration of the season and unmistakably resonates with the previously cited lament on his humble origins and deprivation of mental space for poetry. Shortly hereafter comes a poem in a strongly elegiac mood that is, to say the least, baffling.

7 Spring. *Plum Blossoms by the Eaves*

ware nakuba	When I am gone,
shinobu no noki no	plum blossoms by those eaves
ume no hana	deep with moss-fern:
hitori niowamu	the sadness of a fragrance
tsuyu zo kanashiki	drifting alone in the dew.

I was imagining the flowers blooming by the moss-deep eaves of my old cottage when I, who have had such joy in them these many years, have vainly passed on in some unknown place. . . . (*SSRS*, p. 319)

"My old cottage" (*Shinkei ga furuya*) refers to his hermitage back in Jūjūshin'in; the annotation suggests that his separation from it at this time is not an ordinary one. A similarly startling intimation of death away from his home in Kyoto shadows the following allegorical poem on cherry blossoms.

17 Spring. *Falling Flowers*

hana naranu	Though no flower
mi o mo izuchi e	this body, to what far corner
sasouran	shall it drift,
midaretaru yo no	in the wake of the spring wind
sue no harukaze	in these tumultuous times?

In this image [of falling flowers] I have expressed my own condition; as driven out by the rife disorders in the capital's outlying areas, I wander here and there in confusion. (*SSRS*, p. 322)

This recalls the previously quoted poem 94 about being distracted by incessant journeys from the sense of *mono no aware*. The one below alludes to his lodgings in the Ta'i village Hachiōji Shrine, where he was in retreat following the disorders in the capital.

28 Summer. *Fifth Month Rains*

kakaran to	Much as I had
kanete omoishi	hoped to hang on within,
kai mo nashi	it avails not:
kaya fuku io no	the rush-thatched hut in
samidare no koro	the dark of the long rains.

Weary of living these many years on the edge of the capital with all its tumult, I desired to spend the rest of my days in some hut of straw in the remote countryside, no matter how rude and lowly. And yet now in the seclusion of this grass hut amidst the long rains, my former spirit dwindles away in misery.[8]   (SSRS, p. 325)

As is well known, the "grass hut" is the symbol of a non-mundane eremetic existence in medieval culture. It is a moving confession that despite his former desire to turn his back on a disordered world and rely upon (*kakaran*) the "grass hut," priest that he was, Shinkei could not at this time endure the lonely isolation of such a life. Perhaps it made a crucial difference that he left not through his own volition but due to straitened circumstances.

29 Summer. *Fishing with Cormorants*

shimatsudori	The cormorant's pain
ukaberu nami no	as it breaks upon the waves
kurushisa mo	off the distant isle,
kuga ni shizumeru	is graved deep in the mind
hito zo shiruran	of the man drowning on land.

In the painful struggles of the bird as it sinks and surfaces, I expressed the pity of my own fallen state [*waga mi no rikuchin*].   (SSRS, p. 325)

This recalls the "darkly vexed" struggle for existence in the opening poem of the sequence and is yet more striking in its tone of despair. Tied with a rope around their necks, the birds were made to dive for fish, which were then retrieved by the fishermen when they surfaced. The rope prevented them from swallowing the fish, an image of forced and unrewarded labor that powerfully figures Shinkei's sense of his own condition. His use of *rikuchin*—it occurs in the *kun*-reading *kuga ni shizumeru* in line 4—is significant, for it is normally used of officials fallen from favor or dismissed from service. The poem below clarifies the nature of his predicament.

95 Miscellaneous. *Lament*

otowayama	Otowa Mountain—
nareshi fumoto no	by those familiar foothills
yado wa arete	my abode goes to ruin;
ima ichigura ni	behind a market stall now
mi o kakusu kana	I hide self from men's eyes.

Here I openly lament my fate. When the old temple where I have lived these many years grew dilapidated amidst the rank reeds and mugwort weeds, there being no one to whom I could turn for help, I wandered out in desperation, staking my life on a rude hovel [*shizuya*] by the wayside, a stall in the marketplace [*ichigura*].   (SSRS, p. 345)

This confirms the location of Shinkei's temple at the foot of Otowa Mountain in the Higashiyama area southeast of the capital. The final two lines convey a startling image. Forced to leave the temple of which he was the head priest, Shinkei is reduced to "hiding" himself in a "stall in the marketplace." It is impossible to determine precisely what this might mean. Is it a mere figure of speech, or did he perhaps engage in commerce to raise funds to restore his temple? The period under consideration is clearly the same as in the poem immediately preceding this in the sequence (quoted above), in which he speaks of being "possessed by the dust of the world." Clearly, the circumstances in which he found himself were painful to his sensibilities both as priest and as poet.

So far, the quoted poems and annotations reveal that Shinkei left Jūjūshin'in due to the disorders in the capital (17, 28) and because the temple itself was in a ruinous state (95). For a while, he led an uncertain existence, staying in a rude hut by the roadside and "hiding" himself in the marketplace. Deprived of the security of his former position, he considers himself fallen in the world (29) and fears that he might die in obscurity away from the capital (7, 17). He also complains of his lack of progress in poetry (97), laments the fading sense of *mono no aware* in his spirit (94), and professes his poetic ambitions doomed from the start by his lowly provincial origins (90). Since these poems were written, according to the colophon, in the last ten days of the Third Month, 1463, we may reasonably infer that they allude to certain events prior to his departure from the capital and that the prayer behind his dedication of the sequence to his home village shrine was that he might overcome his present misfortune.

The precise date of Shinkei's departure for Kii is not known. Extant renga records indicate that he participated in a flower-viewing session at Higashiyama Kurodani on 2.27.1462.[9] Subsequently he reappears in a renga session in the capital on 6.23.1463, just over a month after completing the first part of *Sasamegoto* during the first ten days of the Fifth Month, 1463, at the same Ta'i shrine. This means that the Kii trip occurred sometime between late spring of 1462 and midsummer of 1463.

At this point in Shinkei's life when the force of external events has begun to imperil the very basis of his social and economic position, it will be useful to map out the historical landscape of his age preparatory to examining which of its features brought about the crisis eloquently figured in the 1463 sequence. For this purpose there is no better source than his own portrait of the times in the opening passage of the critical essay *Hitorigoto*. It was written in 1468 in the Kantō the year following the outbreak of the Ōnin War, an event that would permanently alter the course of his career and mark the present crisis as merely a prelude to a greater disaster.

All the world is but a phantom vision; well do I know it, for I have seen before my very eyes the conflagration raging within the three worlds, the seething afflictions without respite.[10] Yet even so, how terrible it is to have been born in the last days of such an utterly degenerate age!

I have clearly seen and heard what has happened these fifty years and more. In all that time there has been no peace over the land.

It was thirty years ago [1438] that all of a sudden disorder broke out in the East. As the months stretched into years, myriads perished, their bodies torn by the sword as men fell upon each other in madness, and still the strife showed no signs of letting up. Shortly thereafter befell that incident in the Akamatsu mansion [1441]; year after year since then, the country has merely tottered along with no help in sight. Even within the powerful clans, selfish quarrels broke out between lord and retainer and among the rank and file, in which men of various stations fell in great numbers. And though they battled day and night, pitting their might against each other in their various territories, nowhere was the outcome ever decisive.

To top it all, the practice arose of issuing edicts called "acts of grace" [*tokusei*], something unheard of in former ages. Year in and year out, the peasants of the countryside would appear from the ten directions and break into the ninefold enclosure, turning the whole city into a den of thieves and striking fear in the people as they endlessly looted for treasures. And thus it came about that the people grew weary, the capital fell into ruin, and of the myriad ways of civilized men nothing remained.

This was the state of affairs when just over seven years ago [1461], there ensued a prolonged drought when not a single tuft of grass grew upon the fields across the land. From the capital and the villages, thousands of starving people, both high and low, wandered out to beg on the wayside, or just sat there till they crumpled over and died. It is impossible to say how many myriads perished in just a single day. The world had turned into a hell of hungry ghosts before my eyes.[11] Long ago in a work called *Hōjōki* [A record of the ten-foot square hut], Kamo no Chōmei recorded the drought that befell in the Angen era [1175–77] when over twenty thousand perished in the capital within a day. A fire arose in the midst of a high wind; starting from around Higuchi-Takakura, it leaped and spread all the way to Nakamikado-Kyōgoku and reduced the city to a heap of ashes. So horrible was this account that I believed it a fabrication until this very day, when all at once it seems that the triple calamities presaging the world's destruction are indeed upon us.[12]   (*Hitorigoto*, p. 466)

The Buddhist metaphor of the world as a burning house, a conflagration of futile passions and suffering, acquires the force of immediacy in Shinkei's account of the deteriorating conditions in the country before the war. It also reflects the medieval consciousness of living in the age of the "degenerate Law" (*mappō*), the third and final stage in the steady decline of human understanding of and adherence to the Buddha's teachings subsequent to his death. One of the most pervasive concepts in the medieval worldview, this *mappō* consciousness implicitly infects Shinkei's dramatic accounts of the sociopolitical anarchy and natural disasters afflicting his age. It will be useful to elucidate the events alluded to here by way of annotating the passage and fleshing out Shinkei's unusual role as a witness to history. Bearing witness to history has not been a recognizable stance for Japanese poets since the ancient days of Hitomaro and Okura in the *Man'yōshū*; here too Shinkei was breaking with a long-established tradition of pure lyricism.

The Ashikaga shogunate that ruled Japan in the Muromachi period (1392–1568) was structurally a coalition of great regional lords (*shugo daimyō*) under the central authority of the Shōgun. Reaching its peak under the third Ashikaga Shōgun Yoshimitsu (1358–1408; r. 1368–94), it continued to wield adequate control during the rule of his two sons, Yoshimochi (1386–1428; r. 1394–1423) and Yoshinori (1394–1441; r. 1428–41), before disintegrating into an impotent pawn in the power struggle among the daimyo during the incumbency of Yoshimasa (1436–90; r. 1449–73).

The rule of Yoshinori in the Eikyō era (1429–41) coincided with Shinkei's coming of age and maturity from age twenty-three to thirty-five. The era came to an abrupt end with Yoshinori's shocking assassination in the Sixth Month of 1441, the Kakitsu Incident to which Shinkei delicately alludes in the foregoing passage, an event marking the turning point in the bakufu's fortunes. Yoshinori was cut down during a banquet at the mansion of Akamatsu Mitsusuke (1381–1441), Lord of Harima (Hyōgo), Bizen, and Mimasaka (Okayama). Mitsusuke was apparently driven to this crime by rumors that the Shōgun was about to dispossess him of the three provinces in favor of his rival and relative, Akamatsu Sadamura. As it turned out, neither party was destined to have these territories. They were awarded to Yamana Sōzen (1404–73), whose punitive forces besieged Mitsusuke's castle in the Ninth Month and caused his defeat and suicide.[13]

The occasion for the party that saw Yoshinori's assassination was ostensibly to celebrate the bakufu's successes in quelling the disorders that had broken out in the Eastern provinces (the Kantō or Azuma region). These had always posed a problem to the central government as the Kantō Kubō, the Shōgun's representative in the East and himself descended from a collateral branch of the Ashikaga, usually harbored an ambition to become Shōgun in Kyoto as well. Mochiuji (1398–1439), the fourth of this line, was no different in this regard. Frustrated in his efforts to be nominated Shōgun instead of Yoshinori, he plotted against the bakufu in 1437 and the following year attacked the stronghold of his own Deputy, the Kantō Kanrei Uesugi Norizane (d. 1455), who was loyal to Kyoto; this is the event Shinkei marks as the beginning of the breakdown of civil order in the East. To chastise him, the bakufu ordered the Uesugi, Imagawa, Takeda, and other Eastern daimyō to move against Mochiuji, who was finally defeated in Hakone and committed suicide the following year, 1439, at the Eianji Temple in Musashi (Tokyo); this was the so-called Eikyō Incident. Matters did not end there, however, as Yūki Ujitomo (1402–41) took up the cause of Mochiuji's sons, and they were not put down by bakufu forces until the early months of 1441. This victory was the ostensible occasion for Mitsu-suke's murderous banquet in the Sixth Month. As we shall see, the disorders in the Kantō were never decisively resolved. They were still raging when Shinkei, driven from the capital by the Ōnin War, went to live there from 1467 until his death in 1475.

Possibly the most overwhelming evidence of the bakufu's rapid decline after 1441 was its total inability to control the internal struggles for succession within the daimyō clans in the quarter century until the Ōnin War. Shinkei clearly had these in mind when he wrote above that "even within the powerful clans, selfish quarrels broke out between lord and retainer and among the rank and file." It was then the practice for daimyō to transmit their entire domain to a single heir, who assumed the headship of the clan upon approval by the Shōgun. Problems arose when the daimyō died without designating an heir or when the heir was too young to maintain his position or was simply unacceptable to his powerful local retainers, who might then proceed to set up a rival candidate. The clan would then split into two, with relatives, senior retainers, and the masses of local samurai aligning themselves with one or the other according to their loyalties or self-interest. For reasons to be discussed later, such internal strife within the Hatakeyama clan had momentous consequences for Shinkei's own circumstances.

It seems reasonable to assume that among the events recounted in the *Hitorigoto* passage, the peasant uprisings known as *doikki* constituted the "rife disorders" (poem 17) that drove him from the capital in 1462 or 1463. These civil riots were particularly frequent in the capital and its environs, as well as in Nara, in the three decades before the war. Unable to meet the excessive interest charged by the moneylenders (the *dosō*), the peasants of Yamashiro and Nara organized themselves under the leadership of local samurai and staged armed revolts in the two cities, with the object of forcing the bakufu to issue the decree of amnesty called *tokusei* (act of grace), the cancellation of debts. To reinforce their demands, they often employed disruptive tactics, such as attacking brokerage houses and destroying pawn receipts. Inevitably undesirable elements would infiltrate their ranks, turning, as Shinkei puts it, "the whole city into a den of thieves and striking fear in the people as they endlessly looted for treasures." Religious institutions, being themselves estate proprietors and commercial agents, were notably not exempt from these depredations. One of the largest of the pre-Ōnin uprisings occurred in 1454, when the peasant leagues of the Yamashina and Daigo Districts destroyed the commercial barrier (*sekisho*) put up by the Tōfukuji, one of the Gozan Zen temples, and marched on to Kyoto to demand an act of grace. Located on the southeastern edge of the city, Shinkei's Jūjūshin'in would have been in the general vicinity of their march to the capital. Records indicate that there were uprisings nearly every year thereafter, sometimes twice a year, or lasting for months, such as those that occurred from the Ninth to the Eleventh Month of 1462.[14] They would have contributed to Shinkei's fleeting desire to renounce the world, to abandon "the capital with all its tumult" for a grass hut in the countryside.

Conditions in Kyoto were further exacerbated by the famines that struck the nearby provinces in 1460–61. Writing in his diary *Hekizan nichiroku*, the Tōfukuji priest Taikyoku noted that already in the Eighth Month of 1459, there were signs of the impending disaster whose effects struck with full force the following year. In the Third Month of 1460, he encountered a woman on her way to the capital with a dead child in her arms. She had wandered from Kawachi Province (Osaka) and reported that the drought there had lasted three years. That summer, long rains fell, resulting in floods and pestilence; people were wearing winter clothes, Taikyoku observes, due to the unseasonably low temperatures. There was a massive famine in the Bishū region, Mimasaka, and Hōki (Tottori) provinces, where it was rumored that starving people were feeding on human flesh. Under these conditions, refugees flocked from the stricken areas into the capital from 1460 to the spring of 1461. In the capital alone, Taikyoku put the dead at 82,000, probably a conservative estimate, since not all the corpses could be counted and buried.[15] Assuming that Shinkei's statement "It is impossible to say how many myriads perished in just a single day" includes the dead in the countryside as well, it would appear that his estimate is not wholly a literary exaggeration.

As suggested earlier, it appears that Shinkei left the capital because the tumult of the peasant uprisings had made living there intolerable and, more to the point, because his temple was in a dilapidated condition. It does not seem proper, however, to conclude that the one was a direct consequence of the other. His commentary to poem 95, for instance, makes no mention of these disorders. In fact some recently discovered documents directly concerning Jūjūshin'in suggest a somewhat different context for his trip to Kii in 1462 or 1463, in addition to illuminating the real reasons that brought about the financial and personal crisis shadowing the Ta'i poem sequence. Belonging to the archives of Kyoto's Rokuharamitsu Temple, these documents consist of five official letters issued by the bakufu to Jūjūshin'in. The oldest, signed by the first Ashikaga shōgun Takauji (1305–58; r. 1338–58) and dated 1354, grants steward's rights (*jitōshiki*) to the temple over estate villages in Kii Province for the performance of religious rites to ensure "peace in the realm" and the bakufu's "enduring military fortunes." The second, issued by Takauji's son Motouji (1340–67) in 1356, enjoins Jūjūshin'in to the devout and thorough performance of rites and confirms its status as a prayer temple (*kigandera*) of the bakufu. The same message is repeated in the remaining three letters, signed respectively by the shōguns Yoshimitsu in 1384, Yoshimochi in 1422, and Yoshinori in 1438.[16]

The dilapidated "old temple" (*furudera*) in Shinkei's commentary to poem 95 is thus revealed to have had a considerable formal status as an official bakufu temple, with a history going back a century to the very beginnings of the Ashikaga shogunate. This explains why he describes his condition in poem 29 as *rikuchin*, a fall from official favor, and measures the height from which he had indeed sunk as the temple's head priest. While there is no evidence to show that he had in fact been dismissed, the facts that the temple had been allowed to deteriorate and that no official support was forthcoming apparently amounted to the same thing in his mind. In this connection, the first document signed by Takauji is specially relevant because it reveals that Jūjūshin'in derived its financial sustenance from its position as steward of estates located in Kii, Shinkei's own province. This means that from 1400, when Kii was included among the domains of the Hatakeyama clan, these lands too would have fallen under their jurisdiction as constable daimyō of the province. Under these circumstances, it would have been natural for the temple, in its own interest, to serve the religious needs of the Hatakeyama along with its functions as a bakufu temple. That this is indeed what happened is borne out by a Muromachi-period lexicon called *Meisū goi*, which gives the following entry under Jūjūshin'in: "Hatakeyama temple, located south of Kiyomizu-zaka in the Higashiyama district of the capital."[17] Particularly after Yoshinori's assassination in 1441, which marked the bakufu's rapid decline until the Ōnin War, Jūjūshin'in would have had to depend on the goodwill and patronage of the Hatakeyama. Its fortunes, in short, were crucially linked to this clan, and it is against this newly discovered background that Shinkei's trip to Kii in 1463, when the temple was in dire financial difficulties, should be viewed.

The Hatakeyama was one of the most powerful daimyō families in the Muromachi period. Apart from Kii, its domains included Kawachi and Izumi (Osaka) and two adjacent central provinces, Nōto (Ishikawa) and Etchū (Toyama), on the Japan Sea coast. Like the Shiba and Hosokawa, it was a cadet branch of the Ashikaga house and shared with these the privilege of occupying the post of Deputy Shōgun (*Kanrei*), the second highest office in the bakufu government. Unfortunately for Shinkei and his temple, the Hatakeyama became embroiled in one of those internal quarrels that he deplores in *Hitorigoto*. These disputes that were to divide the clan and wreak the havoc of war in its territories stemmed from the question of who was to succeed to the powerful family headship after Hatakeyama Mochikuni (1397–1455), Deputy Shōgun in 1442–44, and again in 1449–51. The trouble started when Mochikuni appointed his son Yoshinari (d. 1490) as heir in 1450 in violation of his previous commitment to his nephew and adopted son Masanaga (d. 1493), whom he had placed in line for the headship before Yoshinari's birth. Masanaga had the support of mighty warrior leaders such as Jimbo, Constable of Etchū, whose plot to eliminate Yoshinari was uncovered in 1454 and signaled the outbreak of the war between the two factions. Involving principally areas in Kawachi, Yamato, and Kii, these battles led to no decisive settlement. Moreover, they would later become the arena for a confrontation between Hosokawa Katsumoto (1430–73) and Yamana Sōzen, who were then emerging as the two most powerful political figures of the time. With Hosokawa supporting the claims of Masanaga, and Yamana those of Yoshinari, the Hatakeyama conflict was to escalate into the larger Ōnin War in 1467.

The circumstances just described render it highly plausible that the deterioration of Jūjūshin'in, though perhaps exacerbated by the famines and uprisings in and around the capital, was directly caused by the internecine strife within the Hatakeyama clan. In other words, the temple's income from its lands in Kii had gradually dwindled as the resources of the province were funneled into the war effort. As a matter of fact, there is no lack of contemporary sources connecting the massive starvation of 1461 itself to the warfare within the clans, as warlords forced increasingly greater rice levies upon peasants already burdened by droughts, floods, and consequent bad harvests. One of these is the head priest of the Kōfuku Temple's Daijōin, Jinson (1430–1508), who wrote that "due to the drought in the various provinces last year, and the war disturbances in Kawachi, Kii, Etchū, Echizen, and other places, the people of these provinces flocked to the capital and starved there in great numbers."[18]

Shinkei, as we have seen, left Jūjūshin'in in a state of distraction and was engaged for a time, it would seem, in commercial attempts to raise funds around the capital (poem 95). Perhaps these efforts were not successful, forcing him to go directly to the temple's source of income, Kii Province. There he stayed at his home village's Hachiōji Shrine and composed as a prayer offering the hundred-poem sequence that has so tantalizingly provided the clues to his problems in 1462–63.

The Hatakeyama strife did more than weaken Shinkei's position as head of the clan temple in the capital; other poems in the 1463 sequence reveal that the casualties of the battles in Kii included his own relatives and friends and that his despair at this time sprang equally from a sense of personal bereavement.

47 Autumn. *Moon on the River*

tsuki no mi zo	Only the moon remains
katami ni ukabu	floating in the memory upon
kinokawa ya	Kinokawa River—
shizumishi hito no	pale glistening waves,
ato no shiranami	the blank wake of drowned men.

Among the hundreds and thousands who have drowned and perished in this river due to the disorders in this province were those whom I knew in former days. Often I would walk along the river, gazing at the moon. (*SSRS*, p. 331)

91 Miscellaneous. *Old Hometown*

tachikaeri	Time returns, and
mishi wa kazukazu	the tears fall, less to see
naki yori mo	there had gone so many,
nokori ni au zo	than to come face to face
namida ochinuru	with those who remain.

Due to the more than ten years' disorder in the Ki region, none but a few remain among the people whom I knew in former days. On those rare times when I meet one who has survived, I am overcome with the ineffableness of it all. (*SSRS*, p. 344)

96 Miscellaneous. *Lament for the Past*

naki wa mina	It is long past
utsutsu ni kaeru	since the dead all returned
mukashi nite	to the wholly real;
hitori ima miru	I am left alone, bereft gaze
yume zo kanashiki	upon the dream of the now.

Truly when one comprehends these things, one sees that the dead attain rest in the reality of an original enlightenment without illusions [*mujū hongaku no utsutsu*]. Left behind in the present, weaving delusive thoughts out of various affairs of little consequence—it is I who live in a dream.[19] (*SSRS*, p. 345)

The "more than ten years' disorder in the Ki region" (*Kishū jūyonen no midare*) in 91, and the "disorders in this province" (*kono kuni no midare*) in

47 refer beyond doubt to the Hatakeyama succession disputes, which erupted into open warfare in 1454 and would have been dragging on for ten years by 1463. We do not know the identity of the people whom Shinkei mourns in these poems. However, his sense of utter desolation in 96, his inexpressible feelings in 91 on encountering the few who have survived the conflict, in a word the depth and exigency of personal emotion charging these poems, suggest that he is referring to members of his family and clan, people to whom he would naturally have turned for support in his present predicament. We should recall the passage cited earlier from *Oi no kuri-goto,* "Moreover, the persons I relied on for support were early taken from this world, leaving me in such grief that life came to seem even more insubstantial than a phantom vision. My mind became permeated with the sense of things that merely pass without a trace." Its tone strongly echoes the pervasive sense of unreality in the elegiac poems, a conjunction that suggests Shinkei had the same people in mind in both instances. That is, the persons who were "early taken from this world" were casualties of the protracted battles in Kii and belonged to the local warrior class, Hatakeyama vassals whose business it was to fight wars and die in them, whose deaths in fact left Shinkei feeling wholly alone in 1463, as sequestered in religious retreat at the village shrine, he entrusted his uncertain future into his clan-god's keeping.

98 Miscellaneous. *Shintō Gods*

hitori nao	Alone among all,
waga ujigami ya	could it be, my clan-god has
sutezaran	yet to forsake me?
sarazuba kakaru	In such times had I since
yo ni mo nokoraji	perished, were it not so.

That I have survived till now, even thus wholly cut off from people and the world, must be because, alone among all, my clan-god feels compassion for my state and still protects me against all odds. (*SSRS,* p. 346)

The tone of the poem is a complex one; it simultaneously expresses gratitude at his own survival, a lament at his abandonment by others, and, most hidden but most urgent, a plea for his clan-god's continued protection in overcoming his present misfortune.

The near-decimation of Shinkei's clan meant, in real terms, the loss of influential relatives to look out for his interests—that is, the income from Jūjūshin'in's estates in Kii—and would have rendered him wholly vulnerable to the unpredictable turns of the Hatakeyama conflict. We should consider the poem above in relation to another whose extreme pessimism was doubtless exacerbated by his sense of having been betrayed through loss of patronage as a consequence of the Hatakeyama strife.

86 Miscellaneous. *Pines Along the Bay*

machikouru	Someone waits, longing
hito ari tote mo	for me, you say, but what of it?
nani naran	I have seen the world:
yo wa adanami no	a sea of inconstant waves
mitsu no hamamatsu	flooding the shore pines of Mitsu!

It has been common, since Yamanoue Okura's poem in the *Man'yōshū* which says, "The shore pines of Mitsu / must be waiting and longing," to employ this image thus.[20] Having seen through the reality of my own condition, I cannot but think that even if there were someone awaiting me in the capital, that person too would turn out to be only a dream. (*SSRS*, p. 342)

Grief and despair, a sense of abandonment and betrayal, these emotions as Shinkei bares them before his clan-god are no doubt sincere, yet we should not infer from them that he was wholly without recourse. As Kaneko observes, his warrior clan must have been of some considerable social status in Kii, since not every priest could aspire to promotion to Bishop, a rank second only to that of Abbot, or be appointed to the headship of a shogunal temple like Jūjūshin'in.[21] His staunchest supporters might have perished in the battles, but as head priest of the Hatakeyama and shogunal temple he would have retained some local authority and moral influence. There was also his reputation as a well-known poet in the capital; *Sasamegoto* was written at the request of local renga enthusiasts two months later, and indeed the 1463 sequence itself was annotated for presentation to a friend, or friends, of long standing, seeing that he signed it with his childhood name. Here we have indirect evidence that the commentaries clarifying his dire position had the particular object of mustering sympathy and support for his mission in Kii.

In this connection, it is significant to note that Kii's role in the battles was especially crucial from 1460, when the bakufu, which had heretofore recognized Yoshinari as the legitimate heir, suddenly withdrew its support and appointed Masanaga in his stead. Thus in the Ninth Month of 1460, Yoshinari fled the capital for Kawachi, first taking up a position in Wakae Castle and, when this was overwhelmed by Masanaga's forces, withdrawing to his stronghold on Mount Dake. The ensuing battle of Mount Dake was a protracted one. In 1462 the bakufu even ordered forces from twenty-eight provinces, including a contingent of the Hosokawa, to support Masanaga, but the stronghold proved impregnable to their repeated assaults. Yoshinari's forces, on the other hand, were continually reinforced by men and provisions from Kii Province.[22] It was not until Masanaga succeeded in blocking off the southern route to Kii, Yoshinari's lifeline, that the defense of Mount Dake began to fail. Faced with dwindling supplies, Yoshinari finally admitted defeat in the Third Month of 1463.

That Shinkei's Kii poem sequence is also from the Third Month of 1463 would not then be a simple coincidence, startling though it may be without knowledge of the important Hatakeyama connection. In other words the presence in Kii of the clan's head priest at a most crucial period in the conflict doubtless had more than private significance. What it was precisely is impossible to say. It is clear, however, that the lengthy defense of Mount Dake from 1460 to 1463 would have made heavy demands on the resources of Kii Province and that Jūjūshin'in deteriorated during the same period. Set against this is the positive turn in the temple's fortunes upon Shinkei's return to the capital after the cessation of hostilities. It has been suggested that in the poem below, Shinkei speaks in his official capacity as Hatake-yama head priest and as a loyal son of the clan who has come home to mediate and pray for the resolution of the conflicts tearing it apart.[23]

70 Winter. *End of the Year*

toshi samumi	To render service in
matsu no iro ni zo	the spirit of the pine's greenness
tsukaete wa	in the cold of the year—
futagokoro naki	therein is starkly manifest
hito mo shiraren	a man's singleness of heart.

It is said that the pine tree's stark indifference to circumstance is revealed at year's end, when it remains green against the frosty sky. I was thinking, in connection with the poem's topic, of the saying that the stalwart pine is manifest in the cold season, and the loyal minister appears when the country is in peril.[24]   (*SSRS*, p. 337)

Did Shinkei have himself in mind here as the "loyal minister"? Addressed to clan members by a person of authority, the explanation would have had a purposeful ring, and the poem's valorization of loyalty upheld amidst difficulties resonates against the singularly un-uplifting spectacle of what he would later deplore in *Hitorigoto* as "selfish quarrels . . . between lord and retainer and among the rank and file." Whatever the political nature of his mission in Kii, since his own position and the temple's fortunes were so crucially linked to the Hatakeyama clan, it goes without saying that the cessation of conflict was at the forefront of Shinkei's prayer in that fateful spring of 1463.

100 Miscellaneous. *Auspicious Words*

hitori tada	To sit quite alone,
mi o nagusamuru	finding solace from life
koto no ha mo	in leaves of words,
mitsu no hoka naru	is a pleasure beyond any
tanoshibi ni shite	in all the three worlds.[25]

Coming almost immediately after his desperate plea to his clan-god in poem 98, the close of the sequence suggests that poetry sustained Shinkei through his severe trials at this time. Resonating against the opening poem on the "darkly vexed" struggle for existence and the previously cited construction of mundane affairs as a dream, it confirms the central place of poetry in Shinkei's thought as a mode of being that liberates the mind from illusion and heals the soul from the wounds inflicted by the force of circumstance. Lifting the individual from the illusory hold of origins, "the seed of the heart" would mark not the physical space of an absence but a philosophy of poetry locating its genesis in the inalienable mind-ground (*shinji*) of ultimate reality.

CHAPTER 2

"A Stepchild in the Past, Now an Orphan": Shōtetsu and Shinkei

> sugi no konoma ni Between the cedar trees,
> yuki zo mietaru Glimpses of white snow!
> akesomuru Beyond Yokawa
> yokawa no ochi no the dawn light tints the sky
> hira no yama over Mount Hira.

Someone who has not actually seen this scenery will find it difficult to visualize these verses. The fact is that on the peak of Mount Hira, which is located north of Yokawa, the snow never melts, just as on Mount Fuji. I have merely described the scenery as I was wont to see it for many long years. This is also one style of composing a verse. (*Guku* 144, p. 42)[1]

Shinkei's first appearance in contemporary poetic records was on the occasion of the grand Kitano Shrine Ten-Thousand-Verse (*manku*) Renga in 1433, when he was twenty-seven and already a full-fledged cleric bearing the name Priest Renkai. What were the circumstances of his life after being taken from Ta'i to the capital as a mere child of two? If, as seems likely, his family had early destined him for priesthood at the clan temple, it is most natural to assume that he was already placed at Jūjūshin'in at seven or eight, the usual age when such boys left their homes to formally enter a temple. Subsequently, as may be deduced from the verse and commentary above, he underwent "many long years" (*toshi hisashiku*) of training at the great Tendai monastery of Mount Hiei in the hills northeast of the capital. Yokawa, also called Oku-Hiei, was the innermost of the monastery's three main precincts, located north of the other two to the west and east. From its cedar-covered slopes, one could, as Shinkei states, glimpse the snowy peak of Mount Hira farther north. The course of studies at Hiei normally lasted twelve years, and this would be what *toshi hisashiku* signifies in specific terms.[2]

The decisive influence of this ancient monastery, training ground for Japan's learned prelates through the centuries, on a sensitive young man during the most impressionable period of his mental life can easily be imagined. It was here from his teens to his early twenties that Shinkei began to acquire that considerable knowledge of Buddhist scripture and secular classics, both Japanese and Chinese, so prodigally cited in his own writings, here where the power of the word, or more properly speaking, the mind, would have been impressed upon him. *Sasamegoto* in particular, with its central emphasis on poetic method as a "discipline in the mind-ground" (*shinji shugyō*), bears eloquent testimony to the influence of *shikan* (stillness and insight), the concept and practice of Zen meditation that constitutes, along with Esoteric doctrine, one of the twin foundations of Tendai religious philosophy.[3] But most decisively, by a combination of innate drift and environment, the Hiei years would have fostered in him that cloistered, inviolably purist cast of thought that remains intact and palpable behind his most apparently emotive self-confessions and that would find its highest expression in the "ineffably remote" (*yōon*) quality of his poetry of objective symbolism. Just how memorable these years were is manifest in the verse quoted above, and in at least two other waka poems evoking the scenery of Yokawa. As late as 1467 when the war had driven him from the capital to Musashi in the East, we find him recalling the once familiar mountain peak of Enryakuji, the monastery's main temple, in a verse alluding to a poem by Dengyō Daishi (Saichō; 767–822) to commemorate its founding.

> kumo hiku mine ni   As the cloud banks lift, high on
> tera zo miekeru   the peak a temple lies revealed.
>   omokage ya   Memory traces
> *waga tatsu soma no*   *the timbers that he raised*
>   ato naran   here in image.[4]

By the first year of the Eikyō era (1429–41) when he was twenty-three, Shinkei had already descended from Mount Hiei to take up his appointed life and career as priest of Jūjūshin'in, the temple that he invariably locates, in his poetry, on "the foothills of Otowa Mountain." This site is confirmed in the *Sōkonshū* poem-journal of Shinkei's waka mentor Shōtetsu (1381–1459), who mentions visiting him "in Jūjūshin'in near Kiyomizu Temple" (*Kiyomizudera atari Jūjūshin'in*; SKS, p. 732). In other words Shinkei's temple stood right in the heart of what is now one of Kyoto's most popular tourist spots. Kiyomizu Temple still stands, as does Rokuharamitsuji, in whose archives the Jūjūshin'in documents were discovered. Rokuharamitsuji is located on Matsubara-dōri, just a few blocks from Higashiōji, the main street below Kiyomizu-zaka. It is possible that the documents were deposited there when Jūjūshin'in burned sometime during the Ōnin War. Was it then like Rokuharamitsuji a Shingon temple? *Jūjūshin* itself is commonly taken as a Shingon term for the ten stages in the spiritual development of an aspirant toward full comprehension of the cosmic mysteries. It comes from the "Jūshinbon" chapter of the *Dainichi Sutra*, which was in turn the basis of a famous ten-volume work by Shingon's founder, Kūkai (774–835), entitled *Jūjūshinron*. Yet the evidence that Shinkei trained on Mount Hiei and not Mount Kōya is too strong; moreover, Tendai philosophy was as much rooted in Esoteric or Shingon-related doctrine as in meditation practice. Thus the name Jūjūshin'in itself does not necessarily imply membership in the Shingon sect. In short, it is not possible to make a conclusive sectarian determination at this point.

Just two blocks north of Rokuharamitsuji is the Kenninji, at the time one of the five Gozan Zen temples. It was also connected to the Hatakeyama since Mochikuni, whose successor was to be so violently contested, had a personal sanctuary there. In fact Shinkei's own nephew, the Zen monk Kiyō-shuza, who would also take refuge in the Kantō during the war, was training in the same temple. It is possible that Shinkei had other relatives living nearby who served the Hatakeyama in some capacity, among them those who would perish in the clan's internal strife.

The Eikyō era coincides with the incumbency of the sixth Shōgun, Yoshinori. The fourth son of the great Yoshimitsu, he was originally meant for an ecclesiastical career and was indeed the Tendai Abbot while Shinkei was on Mount Hiei. Yoshinori indirectly figures in Shinkei's biography during this period, the first time when he attended the Bishamon Sermon (*Bishamon-kō*) at Jūjūshin'in on 8.28.1431, as recorded in the contemporary journal *Mansai jugō nikki*.[5] The most important of the rituals regularly performed by Jūjūshin'in in its capacity as a shogunal temple, the Bishamon Sermon has a history going back to the first Ashikaga Shōgun, Takauji. According to the military history *Taiheiki*, Takauji and his son Yoshiakira (1330–67; r. 1358–67) had it performed for them at Iwaya Temple in Tamba in 1351 when they were fleeing the capital.[6] This incident must have set the precedent for the traditional performance of the same ceremony at Jūjūshin'in; it will be recalled that Takauji awarded the temple the Kii estates in 1354 and charged it with praying for "peace in the realm" and the bakufu's "enduring military fortunes." As is well known, the bakufu and the military class in general worshipped the Buddhist deity Bishamon (Skt. Vaiśravaṇa) as a war god and protector of the realm. In sculpture he was portrayed as a fiery warrior dressed in armor, bearing a miniature pagoda on one hand and a spear in the other. Of the Four Heavenly Kings (*shitennō*) who guarded the four directions, Bishamon was considered the most important since he had charge of the north, the direction of the greatest peril in Buddhist cosmology. Hiei was built in the northern hills for this very reason, and within it Bishamon is enshrined in the main temple, Enryakuji, of the Yokawa precinct, where Shinkei trained for his future duties at Jūjūshin'in.

Less than two years following his attendance at the Bishamon Sermon, Yoshinori sponsored the Kitano Shrine Ten-Thousand-Verse Renga (*manku*) on the eleventh day of the Second Month, 1433. This grand event, which marked Shinkei's debut in the field of linked poetry, also heralded the beginning of a renga revival under the leadership of the seven poets—himself among them—who were to dominate the art until the end of the Ōnin War in 1477. The participants were divided into twenty groups: each group composed five hyakuin and was headed by formidable personages like the Shōgun himself; members of the Hosokawa, Yamana, and Akamatsu warrior clans; representatives of the noble Kujō, Ichijō, Nijō, and Hino families; and prominent monks in the service of the bakufu. There is no more impressive evidence of renga's function as a collective ritual and powerful symbol of solidarity than this annual event, which began during Yoshimitsu's time. Jūjūshin'in's special connection with the bakufu is reflected in the rather prominent place accorded Shinkei, a young priest of no rank or, as yet, poetic reputation, on this occasion. He was assigned to the group led by the Middle Counselor Hino Yoshisuke, whose sessions were held in the same Kitano Shrine building as Yoshinori's group. The Hino had become the most influential noble family in the bakufu ever since Yoshimitsu took one of their daughters as consort. This practice was followed by subsequent shōguns including Yoshinori himself, who was married to Hino Shigeko (1410–63), Yoshisuke's sister. Shinkei composed the third verse of the first sequence, right after Yoshisuke's hokku and the *waki* (second verse) by Fujiwara Muneari.

yorozuyo o	Be as holy white pennants
shirayū kakeyo	promising a myriad years—
yaezakura	eightfold cherry blossoms!
Hino-chūnagon	Hino Middle Counselor
midori harumeku	Truly spring-like in their green,
kami no misakaki	the *sakaki* leaves of the gods.
Fujiwara Muneari	Fujiwara Muneari
asahidera	Temple of the morning sun—
terasu miyai wa	in the numinous light the garden
nodoka nite	is raptly tranquil.
Renkai-hōshi	Priest Renkai [Shinkei][7]

Composed in praise of the Kitano Shrine grounds and buildings, among which the Asahi (lit., "morning sun") Temple was the most highly prized, Shinkei's earliest known verse is flawless and already manifests his characteristic style in its combination of wit and a delicately attuned, listening sensibility.

Held nearly every year during the remainder of Yoshinori's incumbency, the Kitano Shrine manku provided a great stimulus to linked-verse activity in the capital. Its grandness of scale was doubtless an impressive display of bakufu power, even while attesting to Yoshinori's enthusiasm for renga, which is confirmed by records of monthly sessions held at the Muromachi Palace and other places.[8] In the field of waka he would also sponsor the compilation of the *Shinzoku Kokinshū*, the very last of the imperial waka anthologies, between 1433 and 1439. Yoshinori directly influenced Shinkei's career one last time by issuing the order, dated 3.15.1438, reconfirming Jūjūshin'in's status as an official bakufu temple.

There are no other datable records of Shinkei's participation in renga or waka sessions in the Eikyō era, which came to an abrupt end, as we have seen, with Yoshinori's assassination in 1441. Quite possibly, he took part in the renga events at Kitano Shrine subsequent to 1433; unfortunately, records of them have not survived. In waka, Eikyō 1 (1429) marks the beginning of that long period of training under Shōtetsu that Shinkei would later describe as a "thirty-years' tutelage" (*misotose no teikin*). And the nostalgic passage in *Hitorigoto* recalling the era indicates that he was an active participant in the capital's flourishing poetic milieu.

Truly until the years of the Eikyō era, the illustrious masters and predecessors of waka and renga still remained in the world, and brilliant poetry gatherings were held at various places. Among the noble houses, those of Ichijō Kanera, the Asukai family, and the two branches of the Reizei; among the warrior houses, those of Hosokawa Mochiyuki, Katsumoto, Dōken, Motoyuki, and Yorihisa, Hatakeyama Yoshitada and Mochizumi, Isshiki Norichika, Takeda Nobukata, Ise Sadakuni and Sadachika, Ogasawara Mochinaga; apart from these, the sessions at the houses of the priests Seigan [Shōtetsu] and Gyōkō. At these different places, monthly meetings, so-called poem-criticism meetings, and various other poetic gatherings were held with countless frequency. . . . I myself participated in them but being untalented and dull-witted derived even less profit than a blind man before red foliage, a cow before lute music. With Priest Seigan in particular I studied continuously for thirty years without retaining anything or acquiring the faintest understanding. Now I can only gnash my teeth in a thousand bitter regrets. (*Hitorigoto*, p. 468)

It is characteristic of the period that most of the names figuring above are of warriors belonging to the deputy shōgun and daimyō class. Comprising the most politically powerful and affluent class throughout the medieval period, these men were also interested patrons and students of poetry in their drive to acquire the high culture that was traditionally the birthright of the now impotent but still prestigious class of court nobles. In poetry, always the art that mattered most, they were represented by the rival Nijō and Reizei families descended from Fujiwara Teika (1162–1241), then as now regarded as the country's greatest waka poet. At this time however, there was no one of exceptional talent among Teika's descendants, and the Asukai family stemming from Teika's contemporary Masatsune (1170–1221) and hereditarily aligned with the Nijō school was acknowledged as the official leader in the waka field. This is evident in the appointment of Asukai Masayo (1390–1452) as the compiler of the *Shinzoku Kokinshū*. Masayo was assisted in this task by the poet-priest Gyōkō (1391–1455), who belonged like himself to the academic Nijō school favored by the Shōgun Yoshinori. Heading Shinkei's list of nobility is Ichijō Kanera, statesman, classical scholar, and the most prominent man of culture in the mid-Muromachi period. A grandson of the distinguished Nijō Yoshimoto, Kanera was active in both waka and renga, frequently participating in Yoshinori's sessions and eventually compiling a twenty-volume renga anthology called *Shingyokushū* (New gems collection) around 1450. In this he was following the impressive precedent set by Yoshimoto in compiling, against the objections of entrenched waka interests, the first imperial anthology of renga, *Tsukubashū* (Tsukuba collection) in 1356.

Shinkei regarded the age of Yoshimoto and Gusai as the first flowering of renga, which declined subsequently, however, in the "middle period," when their aesthetic ideals were rejected in favor of a style centering on verbal wit and rhetorical technique and ignoring the principle of linking through meaning or poetic feeling (*kokoro-zuke*). Basically the contemporary renga revival announced, in effect, by Shinkei in *Sasamegoto* signaled a "return" to the practice of linked verse as a serious art, beyond its continuing popularity as a collective verbal entertainment, and as a social ritual lending grace to a particular occasion whether public or private. The harbingers of this renaissance, according to him, were his older contemporaries Sōzei and Chiun, who "having studied with Shōtetsu for many years . . . were also conversant with waka. It was from this period that the Way of renga, which had for some time lain in a moribund state, began to rise again" (*SSG*, p. 164).

Much has been said about Shinkei's so-called identification of waka and renga. This is not, in my opinion, a real issue. The crucial issue in his mind was the nature of poetry per se, and he had absolutely no doubt that waka, whose centuries-old history peaked in the *Shinkokinshū* age, was its exemplar, whereas in renga the best was yet to come. This is why he thought Sōzei's and Chiun's waka training under Shōtetsu was so decisive in the renga revival. More to the point, Shōtetsu is the figure who looms largest in his own poetic development. It would be no exaggeration to say that Shinkei regarded his mentor with an attitude bordering on veneration.

Again and again in his critical writings, he invokes Shōtetsu as the greatest poet of his age, the sage who rescued waka from its long stagnation subsequent to its golden age in the *Shinkokinshū* (completed 1206) period. Indeed he often implies, from the manner in which he consistently sets up the poetry of the two as models of the highest art, that Shōtetsu is on a par with the great Teika. The character of his regard for his mentor is wholly manifest in this passage from a letter dated 3.23.1466.

Of Priest Seigan [Shōtetsu] the practitioners of poetry have long said that his art is vastly different from that of Tsurayuki and Mitsune in the ancient age, but not a whit inferior to that of Lords Teika and Ietaka. Truly he seems like one of those awesome and miraculous reincarnations of the divine [*gemmyō kidoku no gonja*] that appear but once in a thousand years. What little insight I now possess regarding the language and spirit of waka and renga is due solely to his beneficent light. Once during the monthly poetry meetings at his Shōgetsuan hermitage in the New Year, I composed this poem.

Shintō Gods

sumiyoshi no	The god of Sumiyoshi
kami no mumarete	has been reborn and illumines
yo o terasu	the world of poetry
toki naru kana ya	in these our times—
manabe morohito	Learn, all ye mortals!
	(*Tokoro* I, pp. 204–5)

Viewed in the historical perspective of the whole post-*Shinkokinshū* age, which had produced no comparable achievements in waka since the two anthologies *Gyokuyōshū* (1313 or 1314) and *Fūgashū* (1344–46), compiled by the innovative Kyōgoku-Reizei school in the first half of the previous century, Shinkei's manifestly hyperbolic, rhetorical elevation of Shōtetsu into no less than a reincarnation of the Sumiyoshi deity of poetry is quite understandable. It is also useful to keep in mind that his comments on his mentor, who died in 1459, date from 1463 on, when he was himself engaged in defining renga based on the principles and practice of the *Shinkokinshū* poets and Shōtetsu, and it was imperative to keep his teacher's reputation alive.

By 1429 when Shinkei became his disciple, Shōtetsu was already a major figure in the contemporary poetic milieu, with a social circle encompassing the Hosokawa, Hatakeyama, and other daimyō clans who were his principal patrons and the priestly class in the shrines and temples of the capital. Born to a samurai family in Bitchū (Okayama), he had become a disciple of the Reizei school's foremost spokesman, Imagawa Ryōshun (1325–1420), in his early twenties and was a priest at the Rinzai Zen temple of Tōfukuji sometime in his thirties, a career he soon abandoned, however, in order to devote all his energies to waka composition. Having thus confirmed his vocation, Shōtetsu pursued it with total devotion, doggedly persevering despite a major setback in 1432 when a fire destroyed all his accumulated work of some 27,000 poems in 30 volumes, not to mention notes taken from lectures and manuscript copies of old literary texts. Moving references to this great loss are recorded in his poetry journal *Sōkonshū* (1449–59). The shock of finding years of labor and emotional energy reduced to ashes apparently impressed upon him the tragically ephemeral nature of literary art, at the same time that it steeled his determination to continue as an act of existential choice.[9]

A few years later occurred yet another great disappointment in his shocking exclusion from the imperial anthology *Shinzoku Kokinshū*. As the acknowledged leader of the *jige* (commoner) poetry circles, and on the strength of his own works, Shōtetsu had fully expected to be represented in this major enterprise ordered by Emperor Go-Hanazono in 1433 at the Shōgun Yoshinori's request. Among the factors that may have caused his exclusion, the fact of his non-noble lineage—what Shinkei termed *iyashiki* (lowly) in his own case—coupled with his lack of connection at the time to the highest echelons of the bakufu, is doubtless significant. It is true that the priest Gyōkō was also a commoner, but he was the descendant of the exceptionally famous Nijō poet Ton'a (1289–1372) and in effect the bakufu's poet laureate, even participating in poetry meetings at the court itself; seven of his poems were included in the anthology. Most decisive, however, was Shōtetsu's affiliation with the Reizei school, which Yoshinori regarded with unmistakable disfavor. The Reizei family heir, Tameyuki, had but two poems included despite being an official of the Wakadokoro, and Ryōshun, its most vocal defender, was represented with only one token poem.[10] The official dominance of the orthodox, correct, and academic Nijō school at this time is beyond question. Shōtetsu's prolific genius might impress, but his penchant for highly "unnatural" semantic and syntactic combinations, the minute intricacy, and ineffable ambiguity of both his poetic rhetoric and conception were obviously deemed too radical for the imperial anthology.

His keen sorrow at being thus deprived of the highest official recognition granted a Japanese poet, and what would have been an assured means of posthumous fame, may be read in, among others, a poem composed two months after the anthology's completion in 1439, when accompanied by his disciples, possibly including Shinkei, he made a pilgrimage to the shrine of the god of poetry, Tamatsushima Myōjin, in Kii.

koto no ha o	Among those whose
erabu kazu ni wa	leaves of words are chosen
irazu tomo	I do not count—

| tada kabakari o | yet I pray you look on me |
| aware to mo miyo | with all the more pity! |

(SKS 2298)

Shōtetsu's consciousness of exclusion from official recognition due to the lack of a proper social background and political backing and the perceived strangeness of his language—*SKS* 11208 laments his being regarded as an alien "Chinese" (*Morokoshibito*)—is ironic in view of the fact that he was the country's first major innovative poet of non-noble origins, and the last, along with Shinkei, to do important work in the classical waka tradition.[11]

Writing in a characteristic style of extreme subtlety and concentration, Shōtetsu was well aware that his poems did not conform to the orthodox simplicity approved by official taste, but retained nevertheless a strong confidence in his own talent and abilities. As Shinkei reports in *Oi no kurigoto*, Shōtetsu used to declare, "I might be the last in the line of Lords Teika and Ryōshun, but in poetry I only cherish and inquire directly into the minds of Teika and Jichin. The utterly attenuated [*kudarihatetaru*] heirs of Teika's house, the Nijō and Reizei, hold no attraction for me" (p. 417). This is an illuminating, and devastating, revelation of what the age's greatest poet really thought of his established colleagues. It is also a comment on the entrenched prestige of blood lineage in the waka milieu. Against it *jige* poets like Shōtetsu and Shinkei had to contend and justify themselves by an appeal to the autonomous and transcendent "mind" of past poets from whom they claimed a spiritual descent, a transhistorical relationship of dialogic understanding open only to those able to grasp the true achievement of the *Shinkokinshū* poets.

Shōtetsu is well known for the prodigious energies he devoted to copying and studying classical literary texts. While sheer ambition and the force of arms were constantly changing the power structure of Muromachi society, there was a deep conservative drive to preserve old writing, to commune with past voices before the spectacle of present anarchy. The numerous extant manuscripts that may be traced to Shōtetsu include copies of the *Genji monogatari*, *Ise monogatari*, *Tsurezuregusa*, critical treatises, and individual poem collections, especially those of the *Shinkokinshū* poets Teika, Ietaka, and Yoshitsune. Given his large following among the warrior and priestly classes, his role in the dissemination of the country's classical heritage must be deemed incalculable. It was particularly important for those of his disciples who were like Shinkei to play an active role in the field of renga, to which they brought an aesthetic sensibility and vocabulary learned from the literary tradition. The textual history of some manuscripts bears concrete traces of Shōtetsu's part in this transmission. For instance, an extant *Ise monogatari* copy stemming from 1439 bears a colophon to the effect that it was handed down from Shōtetsu to Shinkei, and the colophon to yet another indicates that the same text was later transmitted by Shinkei to Sōgi, who in turn gave a copy to his disciple Sōchō (1448–1532). There is no more moving reflection of Shōtetsu's intense devotion to literature than the date, 4.25.1459, on his extant copy of the "Kiritsubo" (Paulownia court) chapter of the *Genji*; it reveals that he was still engaged in this task just days prior to his death on 5.9.1459 at seventy-eight.[12]

In his last years, as we know, Shinkei would lament that his priestly duties and a recurring illness prevented him from practicing poetry to his heart's content. Still, surviving records of contemporary poetry meetings after 1441 indicate that he was not exactly inactive in this field. The earliest is the *Hokkekyō jobon waka* dating from 4.10.1442 when he was thirty-six. This is a manuscript of poems on the twenty-eight chapters of the *Lotus Sutra*, composed to commemorate the first death anniversary of the father of Fujiwara Moritaka (d. 1457).[13] The opening-chapter poem was by Gyōkō, the concluding by Shōtetsu, significantly the two leading, and rival, poets of the day. Apart from them and Shinkei, who composed on the sixth chapter, the twenty-eight participants included Shōtetsu's other disciples, of whom we need only mention Shōkō (1412–94), his favorite, and the renga poets Sōzei, Chiun, and Sō'i (1418–85?). The same group participated in the New Year's meeting at the residence of Hatakeyama Kenryō, Master of the Palace Repairs Office and a member of the Nōto Province Hatakeyama, on 1.20.1446. As recorded in Gyōkō's poetic diary, *Gyōkō hōin nikki* (First to Fourth Month, 1446), the topics were assigned by Asukai Masayo, who also acted as reader (*dokushi*), and the poems read aloud by Sōzei as reciter (*kōji*).[14]

The two instances described above indicate that Shinkei participated in the poetic events of the day as a member of the circle around Shōtetsu and that the sessions they attended included the "official" leaders of waka, the Nijō poets Gyōkō and Asukai Masayo. Shinkei's public repute as a waka poet would seem to have reached a high point in his forties, during the Hōtoku era (1449–52), when his work consistently won in a series of poetry contests presided over by Shōtetsu. Our source is the second of his three extant letters. Dating from his final, Kantō period (1467–75), the letter is unique in including a number of self-laudatory reminiscences (*jisan-banashi*) that are a signal departure from his usual modest stance. Perhaps he was allowing himself to indulge in a rare moment of vanity in his old age in the same spirit in which he bade his correspondent, who had apparently submitted a volume of verse for his perusal, to dismiss his criticisms as "the crankiness of a senile old man" (*rōkyō no tanryō*). Or then again, it might be more sound to interpret them in the context of the immediately preceding passage, where he deplores the false modesty of modern poets and laments the decline of that old sense of honor and pride that motivated former poets to record for posterity those occasions that had won them the praise of others.

Among the things that I now recollect with embarrassment is the year when with Priest Seigan as judge, I participated in waka contests along with the major poets of the time and not one of my poems received the losing mark. It was particularly remarkable as that year had an intercalary month, and there were in all thirteen sessions. Apart from these, there were those lively meetings held at Mii Temple's Butchi'in when just about everyone, beginning with Priest Seigan, would come down from the capital. He used to talk about this incident to Shōkō, the present Shōgetsuan; Mochitaka of the Third Rank; and the others, saying teasingly that it must perforce remain forever in my memory, and that my poems were so good it was not possible to win over them. Indeed the whole affair was rather incredible. (*Tokoro* II, pp. 212–13)

Center of the Tendai sect's Jimon faction, the Mii Temple was located just outside the capital to the east, on the plains of Ōtsu near Lake Biwa. The *Sōkonshū* indicates that Shōtetsu's trips there were most frequent between 1449 and 1451, thus these triumphant events must have occurred then. As for that embarrassingly victorious year, it was either 1447 or 1449, since both had an intercalary month. The era of Shinkei's greatest successes in waka apparently also marked the most active phase of his relationship with his mentor. It is significant that the only references to him in the *Sōkonshū* occur in 1450 and 1451.

The first of these, dated 6.24.1450, is a preface to five poems composed "at the residence of the holy man called Provisional Master of Discipline [*gonrisshi*] Shinkei in Jūjūshin'in, Kiyomizu." After quoting the poems, Shōtetsu adds, "People came to mourn the death sometime this spring of his disciple Shinkō and composed a series of poems" (*SKS*, p. 720). The following year, on 2.22.1451, we read: "Among a sequence of fifty poems composed at Jūjūshin'in near Kiyomizu, following the Buddhist rites to commemorate the first death anniversary of Shinkō, disciple of Master of Discipline Shinkei" (*SKS*, p. 723). This Shinkō must be the "young lad" (*warawa*) mentioned by Shōtetsu in a manuscript dated fourteen years earlier, in 1437, which says, "Among poems on ten topics drawn by lot, composed when I visited the temple Jūjūshin'in. A young lad was just then engaged in composing poetry, and people enthusiastically urged me to join in."[15] Shinkō's name appears with Shinkei's in the manuscript of some renga sequences; the lad apparently grew up to be a capable poet, and his untimely demise was mourned as a great loss by the Shinkei-Shōtetsu circle.

The third and last reference to Shinkei in the *Sōkonshū* is dated 10.29.1451.

Provisional Master of Discipline Shinkei asked me to write a poem-inscription on a Chinese scroll painting. I remonstrated repeatedly that it was not an appropriate thing to do, but he said that it was at someone's special request. The painting showed a figure gazing upon flowering plum branches over the water; someone saying that it depicted the "plum blossoms of Western Lake," [I composed this poem].

> yūgasumi
> nishi ni niou mo
> ume ga ka no
> kurenai souru
> haru no sasanami

> Evening haze—
> the glowing in the western sky
> suffuses crimson
> with the scent of plum flowers,
> on the rippling waves of spring.

(*SKS*, p. 743)

Shōtetsu's initial reluctance was due to the fact that it was the practice to inscribe Chinese poems, and not waka, on Chinese paintings, a formality that had to be waived on this occasion, however, since the request must have come from some important personage in Shinkei's circle. The result, at any rate, was rather impressive, an intricately allusive reflection on the painting's visual text, merging its various elements of sunlight, scent, and reflection into a seamless synaesthetic flow.

In view of Shinkei's later adversities, Shōtetsu's references to poetry meetings and Chinese artwork in connection with Jūjūshin'in are useful in showing us glimpses of the thriving and elegant lifestyle at the temple in an earlier day. The head of the Hatakeyama clan, Mochikuni, was Deputy Shōgun at this time (1449–51), and it was still a few years before the outbreak of the turmoil that would eventually imperil Shinkei's position. That said, however, these citations are notable chiefly for not revealing anything of Shōtetsu's attitude to the one among his disciples who would bring his influence to fruition in the field of renga and in whose writings he was to assume such superhuman proportions. In the light of Shinkei's regard, it is remarkable that there are not more references to him in a journal that is an almost daily record of Shōtetsu's poetic activities for the ten years before his death.

As the Shōtetsu scholar Inada Toshinori has observed, Shōtetsu's tone in these passages is singularly distant, particularly in the first where he calls him "the holy man called Provisional Master of Discipline Shinkei" (*Gonrisshi Shinkei toiu hijiri*).[16] The consistent use of Shinkei's official title and the respectful inflection of the verb in *aru hito no waza to nozomu yoshi mōsareshi ni* in the last passage might signal conventional politeness toward a priest of superior rank. Still, it is somewhat peculiar coming from a man whom Shinkei revered as his waka mentor and was moreover twenty-five years his senior. (He was seventy in 1451, Shinkei forty-five.) Here again Inada notes that Shōtetsu never used the expression "the so-called" when referring to his immediate disciples (*chokudeshi*) like Shōkō, who bore the first character of his name and inherited his Shōgetsuan hermitage. From all these we have to conclude that, in his teacher's eyes, Shinkei was just one of his numerous outer circle of disciples among the warrior and priestly classes, neither more nor less.

The matter might have ended there but for the existence of a passage in Shinkei's letter of 1466—directly following the poetic invocation of Shōtetsu as the deity of Sumiyoshi—suggesting that there was rather more than meets the eye in the master-disciple relationship between these two major figures of Muromachi poetry.

While he [Shōtetsu] was alive, there were many things that caused grief between us [*jukkai nado no koto*] concerning the Way. Reflecting upon them now, however, I see nothing that may not be said to be a profound blessing. To his hallowed memory, I address these sentiments.

koto no ha wa	The glow has faded
tsui ni iro naki	from the leaves of my poems,
waga mi kana	from my very being—
mukashi wa mamako	a stepchild in the past,
ima wa minashigo	I am now an orphan.

Such was the degree of his resentment [*kabakari no on'urami*]. But the thirty years' tutelage was truly a great blessing, a wonderful favor upon which I can only look with gratitude, knowing it can never be requited even through many lifetimes across distant kalpas. (*Tokoro* I, p. 205)

Appearing in a letter not intended for public circulation, the aspect of the Shōtetsu-Shinkei relationship revealed here is entirely unimaginable from their other works. Its impact is all the greater from having been written seven years after Shōtetsu's death, when time should have healed any trifling disagreements between them. On the contrary, the very progression of Shinkei's prose is an indication of a silent pool of discord so deep he cannot resist alluding to it twice, and twice endeavor to overcome it through expressions of eternal gratitude. In particular the poem sounds as if he were trying to pacify Shōtetsu's angry spirit by telling him how old he himself has become, how dull and withered his poetry. "A stepchild in the past," with its connotations of exclusion, discloses more than anything else the extent of Shōtetsu's disfavor, confirmed in turn by the clause immediately following the poem, "such was the degree of his resentment." And "orphan" in the poem's last line cannot but acquire an ironic ring in its deliberate juxtaposition with "stepchild" in the preceding.

It is certainly possible that this startling passage reveals no more than a subjective misreading of Shōtetsu on Shinkei's part. It would not be the first time that an admiring disciple has tried to cast the master into a father figure and been frustrated. On the other hand, it is equally possible that Shōtetsu, who attained only to the position of scribe or secretary (*shoki*) in the Tōfukuji and left the priesthood soon thereafter, could not help resenting ecclesiastical rank in someone like Shinkei, twenty-five years his junior and clearly of more than ordinary poetic talent. But it is useless to speculate further on the roots of their conflict; suffice it to say that the tension existed and manifested itself in disagreements "concerning the Way" of poetry. It is rather this area of conflict that must be explored for the light it sheds on the critical questions of the time, in particular the relationship between waka and renga.

Sometime in the Tenth Month when I visited Shōgetsuan [Shōtetsu], he recounted to me the following: "It must have been just recently that the priest called Renkai [Shinkei] composed the lines 'swollen with stormy winds, spits the moon' [*arashi o fukumi / tsuki o haku*]. Spits the moon indeed! It is precisely this sort of thing that will be the ruin of the Way," he muttered over and over again, then continued, " 'Upon the dike at Yokono Field, the mists fall, on the figure yonder, the chill cries of a wild goose' [*yokono no tsutsumi / kiri furite / ochikatabito ni / samuki karigane*]. This is by the same author. It is in the same style. Would that he had simply said 'the figure yonder—' [*ochikatabito ya*] instead!"

Here is a concrete example of the kind of thing that, as Shinkei put it, "caused grief between us concerning the Way." It is a particularly apt instance in that Shōtetsu literally censures Shinkei's lines for bringing on "the ruin of the Way" (*michi no reiraku*). The source for this enlightening piece of information is Tō no Tsuneyori (1401–94), a warrior-poet initially attracted to Shōtetsu but later the disciple of his rival, the Nijō poet Gyōkō. At this time he was still a frequent caller at Shōgetsuan, and the passage is his record of one such visit sometime in the Tenth Month of 1450.[17] The reason for Shōtetsu's overwhelming objection to *arashi o fukumi / tsuki o haku* should be obvious enough. Clearly meant to be in tense juxtaposition, the imagery and diction of these two lines are far too raw, inelegant, and indeed almost vulgar. *Fukumi* (contain, filled with something) by itself is not so offensive, but *haku* (spit, spew, vomit, eject) certainly is, particularly in connection with the moon. The diction, in short, is unrefined, without precedent in the poetic vocabulary of the classical waka tradition, and contrary moreover to Shōtetsu's aesthetic ideal of *yūen*, beauty of a subtle, delicately ethereal quality.

Interestingly enough, it appears that Shinkei did not concur with his mentor's opinion in this matter, for the very poem containing the offensive lines may be found in the *Shinkei-sōzu jittei waka* collection classified "The Stark Style" (*gōrikitei*), and entitled "Winds Before Moonlight."

yū sareba	As darkness falls,
arashi o fukumi	swollen with stormy winds
tsuki o haku	it spits the moon:
aki no takane no	the looming peak of autumn,
matsu samuku shite	pines chill along the crest.[18]

Seen in their proper context and apart from preconceived ideas of acceptable poetic diction, the lines that so offended Shōtetsu seem eminently justified. The poem vividly evokes moonrise on a stormy evening in the mountains. Shinkei concentrates on that particular instant when the moon suddenly comes to view above the pines on the peak. To transmit this powerful impression, he resorts to a radically exaggerated conception in which the moon is seen as having been expelled by the force of the driving winds. The whole point only becomes clear, however, in the last line, where the thin and chill feeling of the pine trees in the glinting moonlight is juxtaposed against the violence of the earlier moment. There is, in other words, a subtle time shift between the first four lines and the last that accentuates the contrast between motion and stillness, the wind's force and the cool weightless disk of the moon.

Shinkei's procedure in this poem is similar to the bold, rough, and powerful brushstrokes of Zen-inspired calligraphy. It also anticipates, several centuries before Bashō-style *haikai*, the use there of unconventional image and diction to transmit the impact of a poetic experience. Although the poem represents only one aspect of his handling of diction, it is nevertheless very much in conjunction with his own dictum in *Sasamegoto* and elsewhere that a poet should practice a variety of styles to enable him to exercise his imagination and to express the essential quality of a particular experience. This was a governing principle in the Reizei school itself, which criticized the Nijō poet Ton'a, for instance, for invariably composing in the same style, and to attack Ton'a was of course to attack his great-grandson and Shōtetsu's rival Gyōkō.[19] Beyond the polemical rhetoric of the Reizei school, Shinkei's advocacy in *Sasamegoto* of pluralism and an unfettered diction is grounded on the Buddhist concept of non-discrimination and the relativity of form. In theory, there should have been no conflict between Shinkei and Shōtetsu; in practice, however, the teacher evidently thought that his student had overstepped the limits that he placed upon freedom of expression.

Shōtetsu's criticism in the second instance, where he quotes Shinkei's poem but without the first line, is quite specific; he thinks *ni* in the fourth line should be *ya*, thus: *ochikatabito ya / samuki karigane*. In analyzing this passage, Inada points out that *ya* would make the last two lines more dependent on the first three and result in a more typical waka-like structural unity. As Shinkei has it, with *ni*, the lower part forms a compact unity syntactically independent of the upper part. In other words, he is employing a poetic syntax similar to that of the clear separation between upper and lower verse in renga, and Shōtetsu disapproved of that. It is true that Shinkei's syntax here, and indeed in many of his waka, is renga-like; however it must be objected that Shōtetsu criticizes this poem for the same reason as the other—"This is by the same author. It is in the same style." It is most likely therefore that just as he disapproved of the radical image of a spewed-out moon, here he is also critical of the literally improbable image of the wild goose's cries *falling upon* the figure on the dike, which is what the locative particle *ni* in *ochikatabito ni* implies. The substitution of the emotive marker *ya* would blur the startlingly direct connection between the bird's cries and the standing figure, dissolving both in the sensation of coldness and rendering the whole image more aesthetically distant and ambiguous. The point is a good one and reflects Shōtetsu's own taste for a hazily floating ambiguity, such as that evoked by the poem on "Plum Blossoms of Western Lake." But what Shinkei manifestly intended to evoke in this case was the chill impact of the bird's cries upon the shadowy figure in the distance, and not just a misty scene.

The difference in the sensibilities of these two poets is not a simple thing to pin down. Both rely upon improbable juxtapositions of words and the slightly disjunctive resonances so produced, a technique learned from Teika and later to be foregrounded in haikai. However, Shōtetsu's characteristic poems are a minutely refined, infinitesimally concentrated contemplation that leaves the mind suspended in a dream-like void, whereas Shinkei's figure an icy, shattering illumination. At their best, both poetries are ultimately founded upon the medieval philosophy of Emptiness (J. *kū*, Skt. *sūnyatā*) but in two modalities as it were. There is, moreover, the important qualification that Shōtetsu's aesthetics was also in the thrall of a nostalgia for the sumptuously ethereal beauty of the vanished world of the *Tale of Genji*, while Shinkei would eventually valorize a wholly distinct aesthetics of the chill and meager.

By 1450 then, about the same period when Shōtetsu was evaluating Shinkei's poems favorably at contests held at Miidera and elsewhere, he had already begun to express dissatisfaction with his radical handling of poetic diction. We do not know how Shinkei reacted to these criticisms. Judging from the fact that he preserved the very poem that provoked his teacher's ire, however, we may assume that he persisted in his own experimentations and showed an independence of mind not easily tolerated in a disciple. If this were indeed the case, it would surely explain his consciousness of being a "stepchild" in Shōtetsu's eyes.

Perhaps the rift widened with time. It is significant that in a poetry contest held on 9.7.1457, just two years before his death, we find Shōtetsu giving the winning mark to the other side in two out of three rounds involving Shinkei. Nearly all the eighteen participants in this contest, the *Buke utaawase*, were disciples of Shōtetsu; although he is named as judge, the decision was apparently reached by majority vote, since in the manuscript the names of the poets who voted for it are listed under each poem. The only round Shinkei won is the very first, in which eleven voted for his piece, while he himself went with his opponent's in accordance with the courtesies of formal procedure. Unfortunately, however, this round has no authentic significance. The position that he occupied, First Round, Left Team, was reserved for the person of the highest social rank in the group, and the victory automatically given it as a mark of honor. Thus apart from disclosing his social precedence, it tells us nothing of what the others thought of his poetry. The two poems of the first round are as follows:[20]

A Snipe in the Rice Fields Round 1

Left, Win

uchishiore	By the hem dragging
wakuru mosuso ni	limp between the foothill grass,
shigi zo tatsu	startled, a snipe rises—
yamada no hara no	across fields of upland paddies,
kiri no yūgure	the dimming mists of twilight.
Shinkei	Shinkei

Right

hito mo naki	The snipe rising
karita no hara ni	from reaped fields of rice along
tatsu shigi ya	the deserted moor—
ono ga aware o	does it also in self-pity
ne ni mo nakuran	raise those haunting cries?
Shia	Shia

Here the subtle originality of Shinkei's procedure stands out against Shia's competent but conventional treatment of the topic. Like the previously quoted poem on moonrise over a stormy mountain, this one presents a sequence of juxtaposed moments: the traveler's flagging steps, a flapping of wings, and the bird's soaring flight until it disappears into the misty evening landscape—a detail seen up close (only the hem of the man's robe is initially mentioned) succeeded by a wide shadowy vista, the two mediated by the bird's sudden appearance and disappearance. The feeling of the poem is evoked by the first line *uchishiore* (turn limp, slack, wilted), which suggests the traveler's loneliness and fatigue and will resonate with the wetness of the mists in the final line. Readers conversant with Saigyō's (1118–90) famous snipe poem, *Kokoro naki*, will recognize this as a brilliant allusive variation on it, one that withholds any expression of *aware* (its necessity is precluded precisely by the existence of the other), locates the snipe in hilly terrain, and concentrates on evoking the moment as a complex of sensations.[21] It will be instructive to present the two rounds where Shinkei lost and speculate on why Shōtetsu preferred the other in each instance.

Ripe Foliage on the Mountain Round 16

Left, Win

shigureyuku	From outlying mountains,
tōyamamoto no	the rain clouds now descend on
hahasohara	the oak-tree plain;
kurenai made wa	will they have dyed it crimson
e ya wa somenuru	after passing through?
Hidechika	Hidechika

Right

somenokosu	The maple leaves you dyed
mine no momijiba	remain vivid on the high peaks,
hisakata no	O rain veering north
yama yori kita no	from far mountains in the sky,
iro na shigure so	fall not in colored streams!
Shinkei	Shinkei

The voting for this round, 5–4, was quite close; Shinkei would have won had Shōtetsu wished it. That he did not, despite the fact that it has a more interestingly complicated conception than the other, is perhaps due to Shinkei's use of manneristic diction in the arresting last line, *iro na shigure so*, a compressed image directly superimposing the scattering crimson leaves upon the falling rain. The resistance to Shinkei's poem in the following round would be of a similar nature.

Praying for a Love Meeting Round 24

Left

hatsuseme ga	Joining with another
aki no tezome no	the single thread dyed deep in
kataito o	autumn's scarlet,
koyoi awase ni	the Hatsuse maid prays tonight,
musubu tsuyu kana	as dew forms on her waiting robe.
Shinkei	Shinkei

Right, Win

kakesoeshi	The cords that I hung
igaki no mishime	as offerings on the sacred hedge,
sue tsui ni	is it a sign my prayer
chigiri arite ya	will come true in the end, that
nabikiauran	they incline to each other so?
Seia	Seia

Here the outcome of the votes, 8–3, was overwhelmingly against Shinkei's poem. And again as in the previous pair, he exhibits greater inventiveness and a more intricate handling of imagery. In this instance, however, the very intricacy tends to fragment the conceptual clarity of the poem (in the original). This is due mainly to its uncontrolled proliferation of double meanings: *awase* signifying "to join together" in conjunction with "single thread" (*kataito*), but also used in the figurative sense of "to cause to meet," and referring to the maiden's "lined robe" when written with the garment radical; *musubu* meaning "to string together," "join two people in love," and "to form" in association with "dew," in turn a metaphor for "tears." The primary emotion remains unrealized, obscured by the punning wordplay. In comparison, Seia's piece, though simpler and less ambitious, has a clear unity of tone and imagery lacking in the other and is more successful.

These instances of Shōtetsu's censure reveal that Shinkei was attempting to strike out in a new direction, toward poetry with a more immediate and startling impact as distinct from the refined aesthetic ambiguity of the *Shinkokinshū* style and the conventional but appealing simplicity of the Nijō school. This is evident in his use of unprecedented turns of expression as well as complex, original conceptions that were not always acceptable to his contemporaries but would have been to an audience reared in the improbable yoking of images in haikai centuries later. In Shinkei's waka collections, one can find other examples of this radical tendency, among them the following.

Autumn Frost

shimo nare ya	Could it be frost?
nete no asake no	Cords round the sleepy flowers
hana no himo	in the morning air,
mijikaku tokuru	undone, oh how shortly
aki no hi no kage	in light of the autumn sun![22]

The essential feeling/thought here is of an ineffable brevity, and it comes into focus in line 4, *mijikaku tokuru* (*shortly* untied/melted), precisely the expression that might strike an orthodox audience as a peculiar combination of terms. *Mijikashi* (short) is primarily a spatial concept, while the action of the verb *toku* (in the sense of both "untie" and "melt") logically requires a temporal modifier like "quickly." Shinkei introduces the classical image of "flower cords" (*hana no himo*) primarily in order to bring out the impression of the temporal brevity of morning frost in a spatial and more immediately experiential sense, although there is also a hint of ephemeral yet seductive sensuality in the image as such.[23] The *rentaikei* inflection of the fourth line, moreover, allows it to modify the autumn sunlight in the fifth line as well, resulting in the subliminal suggestion of a quality— thinness, transparency—that the light shares with the frost it is acting upon. Visually, the sheen of sunlight reflected upon the frost on the surface of the flowers vanishes as the frost dissolves. In this way, *mijikaku tokuru* functions as a kind of joint or node activating the poem's total verbal surface, causing its various elements to slide against each other in an instance of multiplicity of reference that complicates the poem's texture, while evoking the feeling of an ineffable temporality with the immediacy of a concrete sensation.[24]

Village by the Water

shirotae no	Girdling round the evening
nuno ni yūbe o	in a cloth of dazzling white,
makikomete	longingly the river
sarasu hi shitau	laves the declining sunlight
uji no kawashima	along the Uji island shore.[25]

Shirotae no / *nuno ni yūbe o* / *makikomete* ("girdling round / the evening in a cloth / of dazzling white") is, if anything, even more disjunctively startling in effect than *mijikaku tokuru* in the previous piece.[26] Again, the metaphorical figure is elaborated in a sustained, dynamic fashion through a layering of mutually associative semes in the sequence *nuno* (cloth)–*makikomete* (girdling round)–*sarasu* (soak, lave), a series of images that summon to immediate presence, as a visual and tactile sensation, the distant prospect of sunset over Uji island. The use of *shitau* (yearn after, follow) to resonate with *sarasu* (soak, lave) lends overtones, the inwardness of a feeling, to the objective concreteness of the presentation. Like *hana no himo*, *shirotae no* (lit., "of white paper-mulberry"), a stock epithet from the traditional poetic lexicon, is here revitalized within the dynamic context of an almost modernist handling of the poetic image.

The waka analyzed so far in this chapter reveal two aspects of Shinkei's style. One is the disconcertingly direct immediacy, registering almost as a physical sensation, with which the poetic object is *presenced*. This is the effect of such radical turns of phrase as "swollen with stormy winds, spits the moon," "undone, oh how shortly," "girdling round the evening in a cloth of dazzling white," and "laves the declining sunlight." While these poems are not lacking in complexity, they do not have the hazy aura cultivated by Teika, and refined by Shōtetsu, in the *yōen* style of ethereal allure. Things are not perceived through an intricate tracery, a diaphanous veil, but directly confronted by the mind as materially concrete objects in themselves. The second aspect is the barely concealed operation of intellectual wit in these poems. Images are not employed primarily to evoke their beauty and traditional resonances but manipulated intellectually to figure the dynamics of a contemplative experience. It is not the images in themselves but the *process of thinking* that transpires through them that constitutes the poem.

These two aspects, immediacy of sensation and intellectuality, might seem to contradict each other. Yet there is a certain logic in establishing the perceptual materiality of the image in order to deconstruct or transform it under the aspect of temporality. Such a method has affinities with, and is vitally crucial in, renga, a genre that requires disparate elements in contiguous verses to be brought into some sort of dialectical relation. In a poetic tradition wherein bare thought has always been subordinated to, or concealed within, an aura of feeling, aesthetic beauty, and ineffable depth (*yūgen*), Shinkei's waka in this radical mode might be perceived to fail when the intellectuality of wit becomes divorced from feeling, and the ratiocinative process comes to weigh too heavily on the concreteness of the poetic figure. His poetry is at its best when his acuity of mind registers itself in the dynamic figuration of an objective, sensible image, as in the "Winds Before Moonlight" and "A Snipe in the Rice Fields" poems. The romantic, ethereal stuff of dyed threads and Hatsuse maids is not his forte; the somewhat manneristic turns of phrase, "spits the moon" (*tsuki o haku*) and "fall not in colored streams" (*iro na shigure so*), verging on intellectual conceits but held in check by the immediacy of the sensation evoked, are more in conformity with his talent. His best poems, in my opinion, are those in which his native acuity of perception combines with a contemplative depth, and these may be said to fall squarely within the tradition of objective symbolism and *yūgen* established by the *Shinkokinshū* poets.

Shinkei's predilection for double meanings, arresting correlations, and turns of phrase in his waka at this time may be traced to renga practice. Significantly, it is precisely these aspects that drew Shōtetsu's ire. The point is worth noting in view of Shōtetsu's distinct lack of enthusiasm for renga. In an age when this medium had already superseded waka in popularity, there would have been occasions when composing in it became unavoidable even for Shōtetsu. Indeed, a passage or two in his collections suggest that he might have done so.[27] However, there are no known examples of his work in this genre, and neither is he mentioned as participant in the extant records of contemporary renga. This indicates that he consciously refrained from cultivating renga, unlike those of his disciples such as Shinkei who exercised their talent in both mediums. His critical attitude to this form of poetry may be gleaned from a passage in *Nagusamegusa* (Grasses of solace) in which he replies to someone who asked his opinion of it.

It is truly said that in recent years the Way of renga has taken the whole land by storm. Nevertheless it has been blundering in the wrong path ever since its master practitioners all passed away, and now far from being a gathering of people engaged in the proper pursuit of art [*fūga*], I hear that it is more interested in noisy and quarrelsome disputes. Indeed, it must be difficult to get along with such people and participate in their sessions, a state of affairs that Priest Bontō never ceased to deplore. I too thought of studying renga when I was young, but due to my lack of natural talent for it, and then this fearful state of affairs, I kept my distance. Still it might be a good companion for old age.[28]

Clearly Shōtetsu had no good opinion of the renga of his time, which he saw as deviating from the true Way of poetry and whose meetings were rife with disputes. These disputes (*sōron*) most likely involved the interpretation of the renga rules of composition (*shikimoku*) and matters of poetic diction. Along with what he modestly calls his "lack of natural talent," they caused him to "keep his distance." Sounding very much like an explanation for his lack of enthusiasm for renga, the passage also has a faintly condescending ring that is not improved by the final qualification that renga "might be a good companion for old age" (*rōgo no tomo*), as if to say that it was not the proper medium for a poet at the height of his powers. It is interesting to note in this connection that Shōtetsu reportedly praised Sōzei, for many years his waka student but later the most famous renga poet of his time, "for recognizing what suited his talent and limitations and thus reaping honor."[29]

There is no question that Shōtetsu's negative attitude played a role in generating Shinkei's well-known and frequently reiterated declaration that there should be no difference between waka and renga since both belong to the same Way, which is that of poetry. His insistence on a fact in one sense so obvious can only be understood against the background of his attempts to justify renga against Shōtetsu's disapprobation. Ironically, in doing so, he played a major role in formulating the principles that would elevate it to a genre as aesthetically demanding and rewarding as waka. For Sōzei, Chiun, and Shinkei, working with Shōtetsu was an invaluable training in the richly allusive vocabulary and subtle rhetorical techniques of the waka tradition. Linked verse is essentially a verbal art relying on wit and mental agility— that is its basic nature and the source of its unique pleasure. To it Shōtetsu's renga students, these agents of the renga revival among whom Shinkei was the most brilliant, brought what may be called a new artistic intelligence combining wit with delicacy of feeling, a subtle allusive depth seldom seen before in renga's almost two centuries of history. Perhaps when Shinkei wrote those revealing lines in 1466 about his troubled relationship with Shōtetsu, he had already realized that the older man's censure was an instrument that had spurred his own devotion to renga as poetic art and not just mere amusement, so that he could sincerely state that there was "nothing [in it] that may not be said to be a profound blessing."

CHAPTER 3

Rising Star on the Brink of War

The Seven Sages

Sasamegoto from 1463 marks a clear demarcation point in Shinkei's poetic career. Prior to this, certainly until Shōtetsu's death in 1459, he considered himself a waka poet. Nonetheless, he was fascinated with renga's poetic potential and was sufficiently influenced by its distinctive procedure and diction to provoke his teacher's criticism. It could not have been otherwise, given the form's overwhelming popularity, unless one was a purist like Shōtetsu. Indeed, it was mainly in the company of Shōtetsu's outer circle of disciples who were also renga poets that we find Shinkei engaging in linked-verse composition during his teacher's lifetime. These poets were Sōzei (1386?–1455), Chiun (d. 1448), Sō'i (1418–85?), and Senjun (1411–76). Along with Nōa (1397–1471), Gyōjo (1405–69), and Shinkei himself, they are the so-called "seven sages of renga" (*renga shichiken*) whom Sōgi credited with the revival of renga prior to his own career after the Ōnin War. Their practice set Sōgi's own course, and their works were to form the basis of his own criticism. Sōgi preserved their verses in the anthology *Chikurinshō* (Selections from the bamboo grove), compiled sometime before 1476, and again in the second official imperial renga collection of 1495–96, *Shinsen Tsukubashū* (The new Tsukuba collection), in which their work constitutes fully one-fourth of the whole. The name *shichiken* by which they are known in modern scholarship is of later provenance, possibly given by a Genroku-period (1688–1704) renga poet who saw Sōgi's intended analogy between the seven Japanese priests and the famous Chinese Taoist scholars of the Chin dynasty (265–316) who styled themselves "the seven sages of the bamboo grove" (*chu-lin ch'i-hsien*).[1]

The seven sages may be seen as representative figures of Muromachi high culture. Except for Senjun, whose origins have not been established, all came from the warrior class that had officially patronized and promoted renga ever since its early days in the Kamakura period (1185–1333), and they were all priests, either nominally or in actual practice. Moreover, since they were engaged in other careers apart from being renga poets, they are somewhat distinct from the *rengashi*, the professional "teachers of linked verse" like Sōgi and later Jōha (1524–1602)—to mention only two who achieved national prominence—who were as a rule of poor and obscure origins and depended on their skill in this genre to earn a livelihood. The distinction as such is not important on the plane of art, but it is significant from the perspectives of the sociological history of renga and the role of renga teachers in the dissemination of literacy and a national literature among commoners.

The dichotomy between poetry as autonomous art and as source of income, moreover, does not pass unremarked in Japanese literature. Shin-kei deplored those who used renga "solely as a means of livelihood, employing themselves in its vulgarization day in and day out" (*SSG*, pp. 162–63). And Bashō would later express a marked distaste for the commercial aspects of the profession of *tenja* (lit., "one who makes marks"), a renga or haikai teacher who made money from marking people's poetic exercises and presumably had to flatter them to secure their continued patronage. Bashō is reported to have admonished a disciple who wished to become a tenja: "Then you will have to quit haikai. It is very difficult to reconcile haikai and the occupation of tenja. Rather be a beggar than a tenja."[2] His most celebrated declaration of the autonomy of art is of course in *Saimon no ji* (1695): "My poetry is like a stove in summer, a fan in winter; it bucks popular taste and has no practical use" (*BT*, p. 373). But patronage is hardly a negligible issue, even though the figure of the penurious genius is still a compelling image for many.

In Muromachi Japan, patronage meant the bakufu and powerful warrior lords, the upper rungs of the clerical hierarchy, and the emerging mercantile class. The old court aristocrats mattered too, of course, since they were so to speak the original owners of the cultural tradition; they were short of finances but their goodwill and approval invested the aspiring poet with the stamp of authority. Sōgi's mutually advantageous relationship with a scion of the old Fujiwara clan, Sanjōnishi Sanetaka (1455–1537), is well known, as is Jōha's with Sanetaka's son Kin'eda (1487–1563) in a subsequent period.[3] The seven sages were more typical of the Muromachi literati. Their poetic connections came as a matter of course, and like others they began practicing renga both because it was a requisite social accomplishment and because it constituted an aesthetic and philosophical discipline of the inner life, the practice of self-cultivation, which is what culture meant at this time. The public recognition accorded them attests to their preeminence, as does the survival of their verse collections and the manuscripts of sessions in which they appeared.[4] All this is not to say that patronage was not an issue with them; as we saw in Chapter 1, it was a problem for Shinkei by 1462. Whether they practiced renga as a profession or a means of self-cultivation, survival in an age of civil disorder was far from a simple matter for renga poets, even for established literati poets like the seven sages.

Among the seven, Chiun, Nōa, and the youngest, Sō'i, were employed by the bakufu. Chiun, whose secular name was Ninagawa Chikamasa, was awarded the formal court title of Lieutenant of the Right Gate Guards in 1429. He served in the Administrative Council (Mandokoro), the government bureaucracy hereditarily controlled by the powerful Ise clan to whom the Ninagawa had been vassals since Takauji's time.[5] Nōa, or Nōami as he is more commonly known in the art world, was a well-known *sumi-e* painter who served the Shōguns Yoshinori and Yoshimasa as a member of the *dōbōshū*, a group of artists and connoisseurs responsible for the acquisition, appraisal, and display of the Ashikaga shōguns' extensive collection of Chinese paintings and other art objects. Apart from a number of extant paintings attributed to him, Nōa is chiefly known today as the author of important catalogues of the shogunal collection; entries are arranged into artistic groupings that reflect the distinctive mode of exhibiting and appreciating Chinese paintings in palace interiors at the time.[6] Sō'i, secular name Sugihara Katamori, was Constable of Iga Province (Mie) and personal attendant (*kinjū*) of Yoshimasa. Learned in the classics and skilled in archery and horsemanship, he had a reputation for being the exemplary Muromachi gentleman in his twin practice of the literary and the martial arts.

As renga poet, the most famous of the seven at the beginning of Shinkei's career was Sōzei. His secular name was Takayama Tokishige, his official title Popular Affairs Junior Assistant Minister (Mimbu Shōyū). He was also a vassal of the invincible Yamana Sōzen, who was no doubt instrumental in his being named as Master (*sōshō*) or Administrator (*bugyō*) of the Kitano Shrine Renga Meeting Hall in 1448, an appointment indicating the poet's position as leader of linked-verse sessions sponsored by the shōguns, whether at the Kitano Shrine or the Muromachi Palace. Nōa would succeed to the position in 1457, followed by Sō'i in 1471.

Among the seven, Gyōjo most closely resembles Shinkei in being a bona-fide priest. He lived in Mount Hiei's Enryakuji and attained to exactly the same ecclesiastical position: Provisional Major Bishop (*Gondaisōzu*) with the honorary rank of Dharma Seal (*Hōin*). Gyōjo was like Sōzei a Yamana vassal, and the two shared a particularly close friendship of some thirty years' standing. His death by suicide in 1469 suggests that he might have become embroiled in the political complications surrounding the Ōnin War.

Senjun, the other artist in the group, was a master of the art of flower arrangement traditionally practiced by the priests of his temple, the Rokkakudō Chōhōji, founding home of the famous Ikenobō school. He was sometimes called upon to create the floral decorations at the imperial and shōgunal palaces and is credited with defining three basic styles of flower arrangement in a vase; his honorary rank of Dharma Eye (*Hōgen*) is an indication of official recognition of his art. Like Gyōjo, Senjun died violently in the course of the war; Shinkei, who apparently felt closest to him and Gyōjo among the seven, would remember him with nostalgia during the Kantō years.[7]

These, then, were the men who stood at the vanguard of the renga circles in the capital from the Eikyō era till the end of the war in 1477. The most senior among them were Sōzei and Chiun, followed by Nōa, who was nine years older than Shinkei. Gyōjo was Shinkei's senior by one year, while Senjun was five, and Sō'i twelve years younger. All except Sō'i were dead by war's end. Their places as leaders of renga were subsequently filled by Sōgi and his disciples and by Kenzai. It was manifestly Sōgi who bore their influence most and best understood their crucial contribution to the field. As the leading group of renga poets, they composed verses together and in the company of other poet-priests from the shrines and temples of the capital. They also frequently formed the core group in formal meetings sponsored by prominent noble and warrior families and by the bakufu itself. The total number of verses of each one in the *Shinsen Tsukubashū* indicates Sōgi's perception of their relative importance: Shinkei 119, Sōzei 115, Senjun 108, Chiun 66, Sō'i 47, Nōa 42, and Gyōjo 34.

Such are the vagaries of circumstance by which some manuscripts are preserved and others destroyed that for the thirty-year period between Shinkei's debut in the Kitano Shrine manku of 1433 and his trip to Kii in 1463, only the records for thirteen sessions he attended presently exist, and the ones that are dated cluster around the years 1447, 1453, and 1460–62 (see Table 1). They can by no means reflect the true extent of his renga activities. Nevertheless, several other extant sequences from the same period do not include his name, a circumstance suggesting that his attendance at linked-verse sessions before 1463 was comparatively infrequent and that he was interested in making a name for himself more in waka than in renga.

Among the four extant sequences for the year 1447, the first three verses for the one composed in mid-autumn, on 8.19.1447 (item 2 in Table 1), were subsequently included by Sōgi in the *Shinsen Tsukubashū* of 1495.[8]

TABLE I
Extant Manuscripts of Renga Sessions with Shinkei, 1447 to Spring 1462

1. 5.29.1447, *Nanifune hyakuin*. Sōzei 16, Chiun 12, Nōa 10, Ninzei 10, Shinkei 10, Shinkō (Shinkei's disciple) 8.

2. 8.19.1447, *Nanihito hyakuin*. Chiun 20, Ninzei 16, Shinkō 15, Shinkei 13, Senjun 6, and eight other participants.

3. 9.6.1447, *Yamanani hyakuin*. Sōzei 16, Chiun 15, Ninzei 13, Shinkei 12, Senjun 8.

4. 10.18.1447, *Asanani hyakuin*. Sōzei 16, Chiun 13, Ninzei 13, Shinkei 11, Senjun 11, Shinkō 9.

5. Precise date unknown, but before Chiun's death on 5.12.1448, *Yamanani hyakuin*. Chiun 11, Senjun 11, Ninzei 10, Shinkei 10, Shinkō 8.[a]

6. Same general date as 5, *Nanimichi hyakuin*. Sōzei 14, Chiun 10, Nōa 10, Shinkei 10, Ninzei 9, Shinkō 3. Hokku by Sōzei.[b]

7. 3.15.1453 (undated in *SSS*), *Nanimichi hyakuin*. Sōzei 25, Ninzei 20, Shinkei 19, Senjun 19, Gyōjo 16, Motonaga 1.

8. 8.11–13.1453, *Kogamo senku* (Kogamo thousand-verse sequence). Sōzei 164, Ninzei 130, Shinkei 116, Senjun 106, Sō'i 100, Kogamo Yukimoto 97.

9. Precise date undetermined, but prior to Sōzei's departure for Tajima in 1454, *Nanihito hyakuin*. Senjun 18, Sozei 15, Ninzei 12, Shinkei 4. Hokku by Sōzei.

10. Same general date as 9, *Naniki hyakuin*. Sōzei 15, Ninzei 12, Shinkei 12, Senjun 10, Gyōjo 6. Hokku by Sōzei.

11. 10.25.1460, *Ochiba hyakuin*. Shinkei 14, Dempō 10, Hidechika 8, Enshū 7, Chūei 6, Masayori 4; Nichimei 5, Ryuren 9, and seven other participants.[c]

12. 1.25.1461, *Naniki hyakuin*. Shinkei 10, Gyōjo 7, Yorihisa 2, and fourteen other participants.

13. 2.27.1462, *Nanihito hyakuin*. Shinkei 14, Gyōjo 13, Senjun 13, Sō'i 13, and eight other participants. "A session held beneath the flowers in Kurodani, Higashiyama."

NOTE: Unless otherwise indicated, the texts for all Shinkei-related sequences listed here and in Table 2 may be found in *SSS*; however, when a discrepancy arises between *SSS* and Kaneko, *Seikatsu to sakuhin*, regarding the dating of certain sequences or the scores of each participant, I have followed Kaneko, since it is based on the latest textual research.

[a]Unpublished manuscript in the possession of Kidō Saizō, as listed in *RS* 2: 894.

[b]Unpublished manuscript in the Imperial Household Archives, as listed in *RS* 2: 894.

[c]The text of this sequence is available only in the facsimile edition series of renga manuscripts edited by Kaneko, *Renga kichōbunken shūsei*, 4: 559–95.

na mo shiranu	Of unknown name,
kogusa hana saku	tiny grass flowers blooming
kawabe kana	on the riverbank.
Chiun	*Chiun*

shibafugakure no	Hidden in the rank growth,
aki no sawamizu	moor water in autumn.
Shinkei	*Shinkei*

yūmagure	Nebulous twilight—
kiri furu tsuki ni	a snipe calls out as mist falls
shigi nakite	before the moon.
Senjun	*Senjun*

The new renga of the seven sages is manifest here in the precise rendering of an objective scene in a few deft strokes. The vocabulary is classical, the effect evocative. Yet this is not the courtly voice of waka but the rapid, telegraphic diction of a wholly distinct verbal medium: the formal compression of thought and feeling in the integral seventeen- or fourteen-syllable verse, as distinct from the thirty-one-syllable waka poem. In it can already be sensed the beginnings of the cogently terse haiku voice. Chiun, whose delicately austere poetic sensibility is said to most closely approximate Shinkei's among the seven, evokes the quiet beauty of nameless wildflowers in a hokku equally unadorned yet holding much appeal. In later years Shinkei would fondly recall how the older poet had praised his use of the word "autumn," which brings out the meager and still quality of autumn water (as distinct from the rushing profusion of spring waters) through *-gakure* (hidden), in turn an associative echo of *na mo shiranu* (of unknown name) in the hokku. Senjun's third verse points up the deep silence of Shinkei's through the snipe's call, while striking out in a new direction.

kawa no se no	The rushing river's
koe wa iseki no	voice: by the dike wall,
kuina kana	a water-rail.
Chiun	*Chiun*

Chiun's hokku in the session from the previous summer (item 1 in Table 1), from 5.29.1447, is if anything even terser: just two clauses deployed in a relation of equivalence by the particle *wa*, each composed wholly of nominals strung together by the genitive *no*. This flat syntax is vitalized by alliteration and assonance, reminding us that renga was a recited poetry, its words possessing an aurally tactile materiality easy to miss when merely reading the written manuscript. Against this crisp and lucid rhetoric, the point, the ever so slightly disjunctive juxtaposition of two sounds, the rushing of the river and the soft tapping of a rail, emerges more eloquently in being unspoken.

Renga's delight in the play of mind and language is very much in

evidence in the late autumn session from the same year, 1447 (item 3, Table
1), in which Ninzei starts off with a verse that is unabashedly a riddle.

aki no iro	Autumn color
wakaba ni kaeru	turned back to young leaves—
kozue kana	the tips of trees.
Ninzei	Ninzei
midori no matsu ya	Green pines sprouting
kiri no shitamoe	through clouds of mist!
Chiun	Chiun
moshio hi ni	In salt seaweed fire
isoyamagiwa no	along the shore cliff ridge
tsuyu kiete	shrivels the dew.
Shinkei	Shinkei

Chiun proves himself equal to Ninzei's playful challenge in his witty and
imagistically vivid reply: through the dense mists blanketing the autumn-
colored trees, only the tops of the tall green pines are visible, the spring-like
"young leaves" (*wakaba*) of the maeku. Shinkei's *daisan* (third verse) leaves
the playful tone behind; it is a delicately modulated image of dewdrops—
an allusive reference to the mists in the maeku—drying up on the overhanging pine branches on the seacliff as saltmakers burn seaweed below.

sakakiba ni	On the *sakaki* leaves
saku ya yatabi no	blossom in eightfold layers
shimo no hana	flowers of frost.
Sōzei	Sōzei

This bright and aurally lilting hokku from the early winter of 1447 (item
4, Table 1) is a good index to Sōzei's agile wit. It evokes the fresh contrast
between the deep green glossy leaves of the *sakaki* and the whiteness of
frost, here imaged as flower petals. *Yatabi* (lit., "eight times") refers to the
many layers of frost that have fallen on the evergreen leaves through time
without their withering. The use of alliteration and assonance, also marked
in Chiun's hokku in the first sequence, was clearly not uncommon in the
work of the seven sages. As a panegyric to the sacred *sakaki*, the verse
reflects the holding of the session at the Takamatsu Shinmei Shrine, dedicated to the sun goddess Amaterasu (presently located west of Anegakōji
Shinmachi in Kyoto). Two verse-pairs or links from the sequence, one by
Sōzei and the other by Shinkei, appear in *Shinsen Tsukubashū*.[9]
The month following Chiun's death in the Fifth Month of 1448, Sōzei
reached the apogee of his career when he was appointed Renga Master of
Kitano Shrine. In this capacity he collaborated with Ichijō Kanera in writ-
ing the *Shinshiki kin'an* (Proposed modern amendments to the "New
Code"), the 1452 revisions to the renga code of rules established by Nijō

Yoshimoto with the help of the commoner poet-priest Gusai in 1372.[10] In 1450 he collected his verses in the *Sōzei kushū* for inclusion in Kanera's projected anthology of twenty volumes, the *Shingyokushū*. Most probably connected with this enterprise was the renga session on the unusual topic of "the *iroha* syllabary." Shinkei was notably absent from these events, as well as from two 1,000-verse sequences (*senku*) held on 3.12.1452 with the participation of Sōzei, Ninzei, Sō'i, and Senjun, among others, and in the summer of 1452 or 1453. His absence coincides generally with his most active period in waka during the period 1449–52 (see Chapter 2) and follows the death of his disciple Shinkō, a participant in the sessions discussed above, in the spring of 1450. Shinkō's passing was much mourned by the Shōtetsu circle.

After a gap of six years, Shinkei's name surfaces again in a late spring session (item 7, Table 1) on 3.15.1453, headed by Sōzei, who composed the hokku below.

saku fuji no	On the flowering wisteria,
uraba wa nami no	the leaves are lovely sea-tangle
tamamo kana	borne on purple waves.
Sōzei	Sōzei

Sōzei's imaginative wit and dexterity, unsurpassed among the seven poets, are as evident here as in the Takamatsu Shrine sequence. Here the masses of wisteria flowers are imaged as "waves" upon which float the "seaweed" (*mo*) of their leaves. This warrior poet had tremendous natural talent, and his strength and sureness of touch was much admired, although Shinkei was later to deplore the lack of pathos and overtones in his poetry. The sequence is unique in being exclusively by four of the seven sages and Ninzei, except for one verse by Motonaga, the calligrapher and rule expert (*shuhitsu*) for the session.[11] It is also striking that Sōzei himself frequently responds to Shinkei's verses (eight times) and vice versa (six times), an indication that although the former was indeed the acknowledged leader of the renga milieu and composed the highest number of verses here, neither was averse to matching each other's wit.

The two rivals, along with Ninzei, Senjun, and Sō'i, were together again in the autumn of the same year, 1453, for the *Kogamo senku*. Following the standard practice for thousand-verse sequences, this event was held over three days; it was sponsored by Kogamo Yukimoto, an important retainer in Hoki Province (Tottori) of Yamana Sōzen's son Noriyuki. Like Sōzei, Yukimoto belonged to the waka circle around Shōtetsu and could hold his own in a renga session as well, as indicated by his score here (see item 8, Table 1).

The *Kogamo senku* marks one of Sōzei's final appearances in renga sessions in the capital. In the Eleventh Month of the following year, 1454, he was forced to resign his position as Kitano Renga Master and follow his overlord Yamana Sōzen in his retreat to Tajima Province (Hyōgo). Sōzen's arrogance had brought upon him the wrath of the Shōgun Yoshimasa, who accordingly concurred in a plot against him by the Akamatsu and Hosokawa clans. The Akamatsu had understandably been Sōzen's enemies since the Kakitsu Incident of 1441, which resulted in the transfer of their dominions, Bizen, Mimasaka (both in Okayama), and Harima (Hyōgo), to the Yamana. Added to their territories of Hōki, Inaba (both in Tottori), and Tajima on the Japan Sea coast, the acquisition of these three strategic provinces along the Inland Sea meant that the Yamana were now in a powerful position to challenge the Hosokawa dominions in Tamba (Kyoto) and Settsu (Osaka) in the central region, as well as Sanuki (Kagawa) and Awa (Tokushima) on the island of Shikoku. These strategic interests doubtless motivated Hosokawa Katsumoto, Deputy Shōgun from 1452, to support the Akamatsu-inspired plot to attack Sōzen's mansion on a night in the Eleventh Month of 1454. However, Katsumoto also happened to be Sōzen's son-in-law, and it was perhaps this familial relation that caused his sudden change of heart on the appointed night and saved Sōzen's life.[12]

Barely two months after the political disorders that had forced his departure from the capital Sōzei died in Tajima on 1.16.1455. In the Fourth Month of that same year, another central figure in renga, Ninzei, departed for the Kantō after requesting a certificate of his discipleship from his waka teacher Shōtetsu; he was not to return again to the capital. After Sōzei, the post of Kitano Shrine Renga Master was filled by the priest Sōa, a regular member of the sessions at the shogunal palace, shortly thereafter succeeded by another of the seven sages, Nōa, in 1457.

As in the case of Sōzei, the specter of political strife also loomed in Shinkei's horizon in 1454, when the Hatakeyama succession dispute erupted into open conflict. In the Fourth Month of this year Jimbo, Constable of Etchū, rebelled against Yoshinari's official appointment as Hatakeyama head and was killed by forces sent by Mochikuni, the clan's aging leader. Meanwhile, Mochikuni's dispossessed heir, Masanaga, turned to Hosokawa Katsumoto, and his allies to Yamana Sōzen, for aid; thus, both strongmen supported Masanaga in the beginning of the conflict. Some months later, under their combined pressure and due to a newfound dislike for Yoshinari, the Shōgun Yoshimasa reversed his previous decision and ordered him censured. In the Eighth Month fighting broke out between the rival forces in the capital. Surrounded by Masanaga's troops, Mochikuni set his mansion on fire and retired to his personal sanctuary at the Kenninji, not far from the clan temple Jūjūshin'in; Yoshinari fled to Kawachi. Desirous of a peaceful settlement, Masanaga sent his kinsman the Hatakeyama Lord of Awa as envoy to the Kenninji, but Mochikuni refused to receive him and departed from the capital. He died the following year, 1455. Subsequently Yoshimasa again changed his mind—this would not be the last time—and recalled Yoshinari to the headship; this time Masanaga fled to Kawachi. Attempts at reconciliation in the next few years were to no avail. In 1460, as we have seen, Yoshimasa renounced Yoshinari yet another time and ordered Masanaga to chastise him with the support of bakufu troops.

By 1460 therefore, when the next Shinkei-related manuscript after the 1453 *Kogamo senku* appears, his heretofore secure position as head of Jūjūshin'in was already imperiled by the internecine Hatakeyama strife. As for his waka career, it will be recalled that he participated in the *Buke utaawase* contest of 1457 and lost two out of three rounds (see Chapter 2). Two years later, in 1459, Shōtetsu was dead at seventy-eight, leaving him a stranded "orphan" on the shores of Waka Bay and "the Way shrouded in darkness once more" (*SSG*, p. 164).

The *Ochiba hyakuin* (item 11, Table 1) held the following year, 1460, clearly marks Shinkei's emergence as master of a renga session. Significantly, the fifteen participants included five who were like himself former waka disciples of Shōtetsu and participants in the 1457 *Buke utaawase*: Dempō, a Zen priest of the Tōfukuji;[13] the warrior Hidechika who bore the formal title of Lieutenant of the Left Gate Guards; the monk Enshū of the Byōdōbō in Kiyomizudera; Chūei, Constable of Nōto Province (Ishikawa); and Masayori. This event was held as a prayer-offering for the reconstruction of the Honnōji and was sponsored by its head priest Nichimei. The hokku was composed in absentia by the former Regent Ichijō Kanera, the waki by the host Nichimei, and the daisan by Shinkei, who composed the highest number of verses.[14] This will be true of the majority of sessions in which he subsequently figures.

The *Naniki hyakuin* from the First Month of the following year, 1461 (item 12, Table 1), was apparently held at Jūjūshin'in since Shinkei composed the waki as host in reply to the hokku by his guest Hosokawa Yorihisa, Constable of Awa Province, a circumstance worth noting in view of his later role as master of Hosokawa linked-verse sessions. Also a prayer-offering, the formality of the event is indicated by the large number of participants, seventeen in all. It is particularly interesting, in view of his later connections with the Hosokawa camp, that Gyōjo came down from Mount Hiei expressly to attend it. These are the first three verses.

koe zo hana	From tree to tree, sing
kozutai tsukuse	till your voice is all flower,
momochidori	O myriad birds!
Yorihisa	Yorihisa

eda o nokosanu	Ah, for scent of plum blossoms
ume ga ka mogana	close-filling all the boughs.
Shinkei	Shinkei
harukaze ni	In the spring breeze,
kōrikasaneshi	layers of frozen snow, one
yuki tokete	by one, dripping.
Gyōjo	Gyōjo

Impressively minute and exact, the verbal/imagistic linkages here are particularly resistant to translation, and even description. Suffice it to say that *eda o nokosanu* ("not leaving out a single branch"), whose referent is a fragrance, is quite satisfying in response to the truncated syntax of *koe zo hana/kozutai tsukuse*. The same *eda o nokosanu* then acquires a wholly different value in Gyōjo's image of snow dripping wetly from one branch after another. Moving from a future imagined scene to the one right before the eyes, the passage is full of a throbbing expectation in the still chill season before trees bloom.

Spring is again the season in *Nanihito hyakuin* the following year, 1462 (item 13, Table 1), the last extant sequence in which Shinkei figured before departing for Kii. The manuscript bears the brief inscription "A session held beneath the flowers in Kurodani, Higashiyama," whose import will soon become clear.

kyō kozuba	Had we not come today,
mimashi ya yado no	we'd have missed at your lodging,
hanazakari	the flowers at the full.
Gyōjo	Gyōjo
niou sakura no	Anon the cherry blossoms wait,
kaze o matsu koro	glowing before the coming wind.
Shinkei	Shinkei
tsuki wa nao	Still the moon—
kasumeru mine o	over the haze-veiled peak
koeyarade	is yet to rise.
Sō'i	Sō'i
fumoto ni kururu	Dimming over the foothills,
haru no karigane	spring calls of the wild geese.
Senjun	Senjun

A delicately nuanced progression of images, the opening passage also registers the warmly responsive inflections of syntax among four of the five remaining shichiken (only Nōa is absent). Yet when viewed in the light of what we have read in the 1463 Ta'i poems about Shinkei's personal circumstances at this time, the hokku-waki dialogue here becomes charged with a certain allusive urgency. He evidently hosted this session at his "lodging" (*yado*) in Kurodani; Gyōjo says he is glad they came just in time to see the flowers there, and Shinkei replies that yes, it is just before they scatter. When we recall his commentary to poem 95 from 1463, "when the old temple where I have lived these many years grew dilapidated, I wandered out in desperation," this circumstance reveals that at this point he had already left Jūjūshin'in and was staying in Kurodani, some three kilometers north of Kiyomizu-zaka. Furthermore the image of flowers about to scatter before the wind assumes an ominous cast when paralleled with poem 17 (see Chapter 1) in which he employs the same metaphor to express the uncertainty of his own destination "in the wake of the spring wind / in these tumultuous times." In other words, it is almost certain that this session among the surviving seven sages and their friends was held expressly to bid Shinkei farewell before his departure for Kii. Verses 19 and 20 further into the sequence tend to bear this out.

yama tōku	Issuing from the
nagareidetaru	mountain, to far distances it
otowakawa	flows, Otowa River.
Seiroku	Seiroku
sue o miyako ni	To the capital he vows to
chigiru tabibito	return in the end, the traveler.
Keishō	Keishō

The Otowa River flows from Otowa Mountain, on whose foothills Shinkei invariably locates Jūjūshin'in in the context of his poetry (see, for example, poem 95). The Hatakeyama battles were raging in Kawachi, and this year, 1462, the bakufu had ordered forces from twenty-eight provinces, including a contingent of the Hosokawa, to support Masanaga. The traveler might "vow to return to the capital," but Shinkei, as we know, was not certain of surviving his mission in Kii.

Flowers Glowing Before the Wind

In the opening chapter of this biography, I attempted to delve into the nature of the severe crisis confronting Shinkei. Amidst that complicated tangle of highly plausible inferences and arresting speculations, it was always clear that he had fallen from his heretofore secure and even elevated social identity as head priest of Jūjūshin'in. It was not a case of official dismissal; the death of the Hatakeyama leader Mochikuni in 1455 had loosed the conflicting forces vying for succession, and everyone was simply too embroiled in politics and the power struggle to care about the mainte-nance of the clan temple and the fate of its priest.

As dramatically recorded in the Ta'i poem sequence and self-annotations, Shinkei's fall from fortune fostered in him a sense of isolation and even betrayal, due not solely to loss of patronage but also to the untimely deaths of his own relations in the disorders in Kii. As a record of the swindle of time and of a bitterly earned insight into his own bare, unaccommodated condition, the poems and commentary constitute an illuminating personal background for one of *Sasamegoto*'s ground themes, indeed the central theme implicating all the others: "The mind and language of the Way of Poetry are rooted upon a sense of mutability and sorrow for the human condition [*mujō jukkai*]" (*SSG*, p. 139). The doctrine of mutability is ubiquitous in Japanese literature, but it had never before been articulated so explicitly as the primary motivation for poetic composition. Its central place in Shinkei's writing can be explained only by the fact that for him, far from being an abstract principle or mere pious homily, it had all the weight of personal experiences, which reached a critical point in 1462–63. His loss of worldly position would also have played a part in crystallizing his elevated view of poetry as a search for being that is no less authentic than, and is ultimately identified with, the Buddhist path of liberation from mundane passion. In other words, for Shinkei in 1463 poetry had assumed a transcendent significance that it did not necessarily possess when he was insulated within the security of his place in the social hierarchy. As we shall see presently, his fortunes improved considerably on his return to the capital from Kii. But the 1462–63 crisis had done its work, and the greater tragedy of the Ōnin War was to complete his transformation into a quintessential poet of the elegiac voice, and of the chill, still realm of contemplation.

In writing *Sasamegoto*, Shinkei was not only formulating a poetic philosophy. He was also engaged in the no less major enterprise of consolidating the literary history of his age by locating it within the mainstream of Japanese poetic development. The peculiar two-pronged character of his historical and critical approach, which is trained as much on waka as on renga, virtually mirrors his own career until 1463; first as a waka poet under Shōtetsu's tutelage, and then as an emerging leader in renga circles subsequent to the death of Sōzei and Chiun. The place Shinkei gives Shōtetsu in waka history is a central one. He views him as the embodiment of a renaissance of waka's golden age in the *Shinkokinshū* period and invariably quotes a poem by him as a model immediately after one by Teika. The implication is clear that there is a direct line between the two that spans more than two centuries of decline. Furthermore, near the end he also invokes Shōtetsu as the agent of the revival of renga, which had been deteriorating, as he saw it, since its initial efflorescence during the age of Nijō Yoshimoto and Gusai.

The treatise, however, ends on a pessimistic and uncertain note. Shinkei grieves that Shōtetsu's death has plunged the Way into darkness once more and left future generations without guidance. What is more, he chides himself for being obsessed with poetry instead of seeking the path of Buddhist salvation. This last scruple, the perception of a conflict between the poetic and religious pursuits, must have disturbed him, for the supplement, *Sasamegoto* Part Two, he wrote the year after his return to the capital is distinguished by an overwhelming attempt to reconcile the Ways of poetry and Buddhism. Nonetheless, the text written in Kii in the Fifth Month of 1463 was intended as a finished work and may be viewed as his program for a renga revival initiated by Sōzei and Chiun under the influence of aesthetic principles learned from waka and Shōtetsu.

An interesting question is how Shinkei saw his own role in this enterprise. It is not, admittedly, a question whose answer we should expect to find in the treatise; nowhere does he mention or even hint at his own place in the scheme that he has discussed at such length and with such fervor. Rather, we should consider the act of writing *Sasamegoto* itself, his first critical work, as a telling gesture. Its interpretation of literary history, now standard in modern references on the subject, was after all his own conception. It is doubtful that Sōzei or Chiun considered themselves the vanguard of a movement, and, as we have seen, Shōtetsu himself frowned on renga. Indeed, we may go further and state that his presence in the treatise is that of a figurehead and model; the principles that Shinkei chooses to emphasize, and his interpretation of them, are very much his own. Thus it may reasonably be inferred that *Sasamegoto* was a conscious attempt by Shinkei to influence renga's future development toward the high and rigorous ideals that he himself cherished by appealing to the fame and authority of Teika and Shōtetsu. As such, it represents a new awareness of his role as renga poet and critic. This is not to say that he abandoned waka. Far from it. He never ceased to compose in the older genre and maintained to the end his contention that waka was a crucial part of a renga poet's training. But what the age demanded of him was renga and renga criticism, and except for a waka contest in which he acted as judge many years later in the Kantō, all surviving records of his public poetic activities after 1463 consist of renga sessions.

As it turned out, *Sasamegoto* was but the prelude to a brief period of worldly success subsequent to his return to the capital in the summer of 1463, and lasting until the outbreak of the war in the summer of 1467.

During this period he became the leading figure in the poetry sessions held by Hatakeyama Masanaga's eminent ally Hosokawa Katsumoto. What is more, his poetic celebrity was accompanied by the fulfillment of the desperate prayer that he addressed to his clan-god in Kii, the restoration of Jūjūshin'in to its former status as prayer temple of the bakufu and Hatakeyama clan. The traveler who had wandered so far from Otowa Mountain had indeed returned.

Given the wholly depressed mood of the 1463 poems, this sudden positive turn in Shinkei's fortunes must be deemed remarkable, even stunning. It confirms the suggestion made earlier that he was in Kii on a mission to save himself and the temple amidst the perils brought about by the Hatakeyama conflict.

It is not known when he became connected with the Masanaga-Hosokawa faction. The circumstantial evidence presented in Chapter 1 argues strongly for the existence of a link even before his journey to Kii. To someone who had experienced only too well "the darkly vexed struggle / for a means to live" and had had to confront the fate of "the man drowning on land," the harsh realities of the strife-torn age would have been abundantly clear: one either took sides with one of the warring parties or was dispossessed and abandoned to the capricious winds of fortune. Survival for Shinkei had become inextricably linked with factional politics, and it is surely this unpalatable fact that is responsible for the tone of protest that informs some of the poems. The image of fettered cormorants who may not even consume the fruits of their labor in poem 29 is particularly powerful. Its bearing is similar to the one in his tsukeku below (*STKBS* 1267) about a peasant's miserable existence.[15]

aware ni mo	Pitifully he gathers
mashiba oritaku	raw twigs for kindling in
yūmagure	the evening shadows.
sumi uru ichi no	Over the mountains he wends home
kaerusa no yama	from selling charcoal in the town.

Like the cormorants who work for fishermen, this woodcutter cannot himself afford to cook his supper with the charcoal that he makes and sells for a meager subsistence. About this verse, which manifests Shinkei's deep empathy for the difficulties of making one's way in the world, we have Sōgi's testimony that it demonstrates "a kind of significance that was particularly dear to the author" (*kayō [no] kokoro wa, kono sakusha koto ni omou tokoro nari*).[16] The special significance for Shinkei must have had its origins in his 1462–63 crisis. The same concern is manifest in the tsukeku below (*STKBS* 2771).

kokoro arite wa	Heart, when will it ever end,
itsu akashigata	and dawn come to Akashi Bay.
yonayona no	Night after night
tsuri no hi tomosu	the fishing fires are burning
nami no ue	on the dark waves.

In the 10.18.1447 sequence (item 4, Table 1) that is its original source, the maeku alludes to the Akashi Lay Monk in the *Genji* and his worry that his dream of marrying his daughter to a man from the capital might never come to pass.[17] In the context of Shinkei's tsukeku, it becomes a lament on the innately fettered and tragic nature of existence in a world where survival involves the destruction of weaker creatures, the condition symbolized by fishermen nightly plying their murderous livelihood on the waves.

It is a measure of Shinkei's tenacity, and a warning that *Sasamegoto*'s otherworldliness ought not to be taken literally, that he did not now turn his back on society and retire to some "hut of straw in the remote countryside." At a point in his life when it was just as problematic to maintain a foothold in the world as to let go of it, he opted for the first. He remained in the world, caught like everyone else in a morass generated by the consuming human desire for power, seeing through the utter waste and futility of it, and holding fast to his cherished ideal of the true Way (*makoto no michi*), which may be defined as an authentic mode of being through poetry.

Back in Jūjūshin'in a year after his return to the capital, he would be optimistic enough, and perhaps grateful for his recovered fortunes, to set the frail structure of "human feeling" (*hito no nasake*) against the senselessness of the mundane human condition.

Those who would enter the Way must put the ideal of grace [*en*] at the core of their training. Grace, however, is by no means simply a matter of a charming refinement in the diction and configuration of a verse. Rather, it has its source in the heart of a man with but meager worldly desires, one who is keenly aware of the trackless passing of all phenomena and values human feeling so well, he would not begrudge his own life in return for another's kindness. The verses of those whose hearts are adorned, although refined in style and diction, would ring but falsely to the true ear. This is because the mind manifested in such verses lacks clarity. Among the famous old poems and verses esteemed by their own authors, not even rarely do we find any that employs style as a mere ornament. (*SSG*, pp. 176–77)

Shinkei describes beauty as an inner state of being characterized by three conditions. The first two, meagerness of desire and knowledge of impermanence, are clearly related in the sense that a keen awareness of the mutability of all phenomena discourages any strong attachment to them; this is nothing more, or less, than the Buddhist cognition of the illusory character of the psycholinguistic universe. What is given next, however, has

TABLE 2
Extant Manuscripts of Renga Sessions with Shinkei, Summer 1463 to 1466

1. 6.23.1463, *Karanani hyakuin*. Shinkei 14, Gyōjo 12, Senjun 12, Hosokawa Katsumoto 11, Hosokawa Dōken 10, Gensetsu 10, plus five other participants. Hokku by Dōken, waki by Katsumoto.

2. Spring 1464, *Kumano hōraku senku*. Shinkei 109, Senjun 104, Gyōjo 93, Katsumoto 92, Dōken 80, Sōgi 75, Yasutomi Morinaga 65, and others.

3. 12.9.1464, *Nanimichi hyakuin*. Nōa 18, Shinkei 17, Senjun 16, Gensetsu 11, Katsumoto 1, and others.

4. 1.16.1465, *Nanihito hyakuin*. Shinkei 16, Senjun 16, Gyōjo 14, Sōgi 14, Jitchū 9, Gensetsu 9, and five other participants.

5. Precise date undetermined; summer of 1465 or earlier. *Hatsunani hyakuin*. Katsumoto, Shinkei, Senjun, Gyōjo, Sōgi, Gensetsu, Jitchū, Morinaga, and five others (except for Jitchū, all participants in the *Kumano senku* of 1463). Hokku by Katsumoto.[a]

6. Precise date undetermined; autumn of 1465 or earlier. *Nanifune hyakuin*. Senjun 16, Shinkei 14, Gyōjo 14, and eight others. Hokku by Shinkei.

7. 12.14.1465, *Nanifune hyakuin*. Shinkei 13, Senjun 13, Sō'i 12, Gyōjo 11, Sōgi 10, Gensetsu 7, Seiroku 7, Katsumoto 1, and six others. Hokku by Katsumoto.

8. 2.4.1466, *Nanihito hyakuin*. Shinkei 11, Gyōjo 10, Senjun 10, Sōgi 6, and fourteen other participants.[b]

9. Precise date undetermined, but before Shinkei's departure for the East in 1467. *Nanimichi hyakuin*. Shinkei 42, Sōgen 28, Eitaku 24, Riei 4, Kōgyō 2. Hokku by Shinkei.

10. Same general date as 9, *Nanimichi hyakuin*. One of Shinkei's two surviving solo sequences.[c] The hokku: *Kokoro araba / ima o nagameyo / fuyu no yama* ("For the man of feeling / now is the time to gaze at them: / mountains in winter.")

---

[a]Unpublished manuscript, as listed in Ijichi, *Renga no sekai*, pp. 301, 360; see also Kaneko, *Seikatsu to sakuhin*, p. 98.
[b]An annotated edition of this sequence is available in Shimazu, *Rengashū*, pp. 139–72.
[c]For a complete commentary on this solo sequence, see Okamoto, "Shinkei dokugin *Nanimichi hyakuin* shishō."

no logical connection with what precedes it, and involves a leap of faith or moral conviction. Confronted with the meaninglessness of the human condition as such, the poet nevertheless discovers a transcendent value, higher than life itself which is transient, in the expression of and responsiveness to human feeling. In other words, the statement is an affirmation based on a negation, and it is precisely the tension of the contradiction that lends an existential weight—and a moral dimension—to what might seem a flimsy foundation for poetry. Shinkei's ideal poetic mode of being, *kokoro no en*, beauty of the mind-heart, may be translated as "spiritual radiance," the aura emanating from an ideal man who possesses both the chill, penetrating gaze of a Buddhist saint and the compassionate heart of a sensitive human being in the world. "There are," as he explains his hokku below, "many sentient creatures in the world, but among them all man is endowed with the deepest capacity for feeling" (*Guku*, p. 10).

yo ni wa hito	Man's being in the world:
hana ni wa ume no	the radiant glow of plum blossoms
nioi kana	among all flowers.

Shinkei's partiality for plum blossoms reflects their symbolism among Sung literati as an image of nobility of spirit, a pure delicate whiteness that comes into flower after enduring the rigors of icy wind and snow in winter.

Having paused to assess the significance of the pivotal 1462–63 crisis in the development of Shinkei's poetic philosophy, we may now turn back to the narration of his known activities between his successful return to the capital and the outbreak of a greater war that would force another departure, from which there would be neither recovery nor return. For the four-year period 1463–67, there are ten extant renga manuscripts in which he figures (see Table 2). This number is proportionately greater than the thirteen for the fifteen-year period 1447–62, indicating the deep-going poetic commitment already signified by his writing of *Sasamegoto*.

Barely a month after completing that treatise in Ta'i, Kii Province, Shinkei was back in Kyoto leading a session hosted by none other than the Deputy Shōgun, Hosokawa Katsumoto (see item 1, Table 2). In the light of the Hosokawa involvement in the Hatakeyama conflict and Kii's role in the protracted battle of Mount Dake, his presence here so soon after returning from Kii is doubtless politically significant. Katsumoto himself was an enthusiastic poet and had been serious enough in this field to formally employ Shōtetsu as his waka teacher back in 1450. As recorded in the *Sōkonshū*, preface to poems 6618–22, on 11.7.1450, an emissary came from the Hosokawa mansion to the Shōgetsuan with a message from Katsumoto asking Shōtetsu to be the Hosokawa "poetry master" (*kadō no shishō*). When Shōtetsu came to pay his respects the following day, Katsumoto quickly ordered a contract to be drawn up, and five days later he was leading the first of many waka sessions in the Hosokawa mansion.[18] Katsumoto's uncle, the Lay Monk Dōken (d. 1468), secular name Mochikata, also styled as the Director of the Imperial Stables of the Right (*Uma no Kami*), had likewise been a member of Shōtetsu's circle, and two poems by him had been included in the *Shinzoku Kokinshū* imperial anthology. There are twenty references to Dōken in the *Sōkonshū*, second only to Katsumoto's fifty.[19] Given the Shōtetsu connection and the fact that both these personages appear in the previously cited *Hitorigoto* passage on the poetic milieu of the Eikyō era, it is highly possible that Shinkei had known them all along and that this previous connection, coupled with their common involvement with the Hatakeyama, led to his emergence as master of the Hosokawa renga sessions during this period.

The "Kumano Thousand-Verse Prayer Sequence" (item 2, Table 2) was sponsored by Yasutomi Morinaga, an important vassal and deputy (*hikan*) of the Hosokawa in Sanuki Province, Shikoku, and a third-level official in the Popular Affairs Ministry. The time is spring of the following year, 1464; the place the Kumano Shrine in the southeastern tip of Kii Province; and the occasion a *hōraku*, that is, a prayer to petition the god, offer thanksgiving, or both. The need to invoke the Kumano god's blessing can well be imagined. Subsequent to the fall of Mount Dake in the spring of 1463, Hatakeyama Yoshinari and his defeated band had retreated to Kii, with the Masanaga-Hosokawa forces in pursuit. In other words the pacification of Kii was still in progress and would have provided the motivation for this grand votive sequence led by Shinkei and attended by the Hosokawa principals. As Constable of Sanuki, the sponsor Morinaga would have been interested in settling the Hatakeyama conflict because of its disruptive influences on the sea and overland routes from the island of Shikoku to the capital.[20] There appears to be a correlation as well between this session and Shinkei's hōraku poem sequence the previous spring in the Ta'i village collective shrine. Also known as the Hachiōji Shrine, it was one of the stations on the famed pilgrimage route to Kumano.

At this event we find Sōgi participating for the first time in a session involving Shinkei. Sōgi had become a disciple of Senjun around 1457. Though not yet of sufficient importance to be asked to compose the hokku for any of the ten hyakuin here, his presence in such sessions with the rest of the seven sages marks the initial stages of his progress toward the leadership of the renga field subsequent to the Ōnin War.

In the opening passage of the first sequence, Katsumoto, as the most distinguished among the participants, composes the hokku; Morinaga, in his role as host and sponsor, replies with the waki; and Shinkei, as leader of the assembled poets, produces the daisan.

otonashi no	Soundless, the river
kawakami shirushi	upstream is yet manifest—
hana no taki	a cascade of petals.
Katsumoto	Katsumoto
haru yuku mizu zo	Cherry flowers drifting along
sakura nagaruru	the ebbing tide of springtime.
Morinaga	Morinaga
tsuki shiroku	As the moon floats
ukabu kasumi ni	whitely through the haze,
kage fukete	the shadows deepen.
Shinkei	Shinkei

The hokku for each of the ten hyakuin alluded to famous spots and natural features of Kumano; Katsumoto's witty and imagistically lovely hokku, for example, includes a pun on the river Otonashikawa (lit., "soundless river"), which flows by the main Kumano shrine. Similarly Shinkei's hokku for the important tenth and concluding sequence inscribes *nagi no ha* ("beech leaves"), a sacred symbol of Kumano.

umi mo kesa	As the sea this morning,
nagi no ha kasumu	beech leaves motionless in haze:
miyaji kana	the shrine path.

Evoking the pacific calm that is in effect the object of this ritual sequence, the verse exhibits his characteristic handling of objective scene in its simple but skillful suggestion of foreground (beech trees on the shrine path) and background (the Pacific Ocean off the southern coast of the Kii peninsula) in a few economical strokes.

As dilapidated as Jūjūshin'in might have been when he left it in desperation in 1462, there can be no doubt that by the Fifth Month of 1464, Shinkei was living there again. His unusually detailed inscription of his location in the colophon to Part II of *Sasamegoto* reveals as much: "Written in the Fifth Month of the Fifth Year of Kanshō [1464] in Jūjūshin'in, at the foot of Otowa Mountain, east of the Flowery Capital. [seal] Shinkei."[21] He was restored to his old familiar dwelling, at what cost of pain and effort may be gleaned from the 1463 poems, but all finally crowned with resounding success. His celebrity as a renga poet must have been great indeed, for even the Crown Prince summoned him for a session just before his investiture as Emperor Go-Tsuchimikado (1442–1500; r. 1465–1500) in the

Seventh Month of 1464. As may be expected, this signal honor comprises another of Shinkei's *jisanbanashi.*

It was also around this time that the Crown Prince, whose accession was then imminent, summoned me to a renga session, saying that it was being held for my sake. For each and every verse that he composed, he bade me reply with the connecting link. What made the experience particularly awesome was that hearing I would be late for the session, which was scheduled early in the morning, he caused it to be postponed to the afternoon. (*Tokoro* II, p. 214)

Only twenty-two, the Prince evidently summoned Shinkei for a final unencumbered meeting shortly before succeeding to the emperorship with all its formal restrictions. His enthusiasm for renga emerges vividly in this anecdote, where one can almost sense his avid curiosity about how Shinkei would deal with each verse he composed. Long after the poet's death in 1475, this emperor would support the compilation of the *Shinsen Tsukubashū* as a quasi-imperial anthology, and it would include 100 of his verses, only slightly fewer than Shinkei's 119.

The same year, 1464, ends with a session (item 3, Table 2) in which Katsumoto composed only the hokku below, probably sent in absentia.

hitotose ni	In the whole long
osoki hana kana	year, the tardiest flower—
fuyu no ume	plum blossoms in winter.
Katsumoto	Katsumoto

This winter session must have been held at the residence of Gensetsu, the author of the waki. Taking precedence over Shinkei in his capacity as Kitano Renga Master, Nōa composed the third verse, before Shinkei's fourth. The following New Year, 1465, Shinkei, Senjun, and Gensetsu are joined by Gyōjo and Sōgi at a meeting in Osaka (item 4, Table 2).

ume okuru	Sending on
kaze wa nioi no	the plum blossoms, the wind—
aruji kana	master of fragrances.
Shinkei	Shinkei
yadori narekuru	To familiar lodgings it comes,
uguisu no koe	the song of the bush warbler.
Jitchū	Jitchū

Aruji ("master, owner") in Shinkei's hokku is an allusive reference to the host of the session, Jitchū, resident-priest of Keizuian Hermitage in Settsu (Osaka). As a greeting to the host, in effect it praises the flowering plum trees in Jitchū's garden. In turn Jitchū's waki is a warmly welcoming reply that images Shinkei and the other assembled poets as bush warblers come to sing in the fragrant garden. The Heian courtly tradition of verbal and social grace was apparently still very much alive these many centuries later. Although the medieval period was anarchic compared to the halcyon days of the Heian court, clearly poetry still held first place even in the social life of monks, lay monks, and warriors. In his verse collection *Wakuraba* (Aging leaves, 1481 and 1485), Sōgi mentions a "thousand-verse sequence sponsored by the Zen priest Jitchū," rather impressive evidence of this hermit's enthusiastic pursuit of renga.[22]

Shinkei's leading role in Hosokawa-sponsored sessions, so far evidenced by the entries above, is roundly confirmed by the last of his anecdotal reminiscences in the second *Tokoro-dokoro hentō* letter.

Some years ago, the then incumbent Deputy Shōgun [Hatakeyama] Masanaga and his predecessor [Hosokawa] Katsumoto made some rather elaborate arrangements for a flower-viewing session on the same day. The meeting at the former Deputy's was held from daybreak till sundown, at the incumbent Deputy's from evening till the small hours of the night. It is embarrassing to say that I composed the hokku at both places.

chiru o dani	Keep them aloft even
otosu na hana no	as they scatter, O spring breeze
haru no kaze	among the flowers!
Shinkei	Shinkei
kokoro aru ka to	Could it have a heart?
ame zo nodekeki	So gently falls the rain.
Katsumoto	Katsumoto

. . . . .

kimi ga hen	May the springs of
haru no kazu kana	our lord be thus in number:
masagoyama	the bright-sand mountain.
Shinkei	Shinkei
wakamidori sou	Verdant with young green,
matsu zo kodakaki	the stalwart pine trees soar!
Masanaga	Masanaga

Around the same time renga contests started to be held at the mansion of the Deputy Shōgun Katsumoto. Beginning with his uncle the Director of the Imperial Stables [Dōken], prominent people came to participate, and I judged which verses should win or lose.   (*Tokoro* II, p. 213)

Subsequent to the fall of Mount Dake in 1463, Masanaga was ordered by the Shōgun Yoshimasa to return to the capital as the victorious head of the Hatakeyama clan. He arrived in triumph in the First Month of 1464 and was appointed to succeed his sponsor Katsumoto as Deputy Shōgun in the Ninth Month.[23] Thus the sessions recounted in this passage must have occurred in the following spring, 1465. The renga contests at which Shinkei presided as judge would have begun earlier, perhaps shortly after item 1,

Table 2 (6.23.1463). According to *Sasamegoto*, they were a recent phenomenon in the field of linked verse but were crucial to its artistic elevation
through the process of criticism (*SSG*, p. 161). Shinkei's first hokku here is
undoubtedly a veiled request for Katsumoto's help with regard to the failing
clan and bakufu temple Jūjūshin'in, since the latter's reply is so manifestly—and responsively as it turns out—allegorical. The other pair of
verses is particularly arresting in the ways it evokes the triumphant atmosphere of the flower-viewing session held in the spring following Masanaga's appointment to the second highest office in the land. Shinkei's auspicious, congratulatory hokku seems eminently suitable, coming as it does
from the head priest of the Hatakeyama clan temple, while Masanaga's
reply, couched in the metaphor of tall flourishing pines, bespeaks his confidence in his newfound fortune.

With the cessation of the Hatakeyama conflict and Masanaga's appointment as Deputy Shōgun, Jūjūshin'in was restored to its former status as a
shogunal temple, a fact that may be inferred from the holding of the
traditional Bishamon Sermon there this summer.

Following past precedent, the Shōgun decided to present swords and horses to
Jūjūshin'in in connection with the Bishamon Sermon, and he directed the Lord of
Bishū [Ise Sadachika] to transmit this decision to the Deputy Shōgun. Swords . . .
and horses . . . were accordingly sent here, and I handed them over to Jimbo
Shiroyūemon, who had come to collect them. (*Chikamoto nikki*, entry for
6.3.1465)

This enlightening information comes from the journal of Ninagawa Chikamoto (1433–88), son of Chiun or Chikamasa, one of the seven sages, and
like his father an official of the Mandokoro, of which Ise Sadachika (1417–
73) was then the head.[24] The fact that Yoshimasa wished the matter to be
brought to Masanaga's attention suggests that the revival of the official
Bishamon ritual at Jūjūshin'in was due to his application. It is noteworthy,
moreover, that the person who came to collect the shogunal offerings,
Jimbo Shiroyūemon, was a member of the Jimbo warrior clan that figured
as Masanaga's staunch supporters in the Hatakeyama conflict. Two days
later another entry in Chikamoto's journal shows Shinkei himself appearing before the bakufu to acknowledge the ritual gifts: "Jūjūshin'in Shinkei
came to acknowledge the Shōgun's offerings the other day of swords and
horses. He said that his thanks should also be transmitted to the Lord of
Bishū" (*Chikamoto nikki*, entry for 6.5.1465). For the bakufu, Masanaga,
and not least Shinkei himself, this celebration of the Bishamon rite subsequent to the resolution of the Hatakeyama conflict manifestly bore a profound symbolic significance, apart from confirming the temple's traditional

function as religious guardian of peace in the realm and the bakufu's military stability.

Item 8 in Table 2, from 2.4.1466, is the last datable session in which Shinkei participated before the outbreak of the war in the following year.

koro ya toki	Oh, for the seed of
hana ni azuma no	Azuma, pulsating quick with
tane mogana	the season's flowers!
Shinkei	Shinkei
haru ni makasuru	Spring's slow pace its guide,
kaze no nodokesa	tranquil breathes the wind.
Gyōjo	Gyōjo

His hokku is particularly arresting in its reference to Azuma, the East or Kantō region that would be his destination in the following summer. However, the reference here is to Gyōjo's impending departure for the East, where he evidently stayed sometime between the summer of 1466 and spring of 1467. Sōgi, who composed the seventh verse in the first round, also left for the Kantō in the summer or fall of 1466. Shinkei's hokku is based on the popular belief that spring comes from the east, where flowers would consequently bloom earlier than in the capital. Gyōjo's reply acts as a curb to Shinkei's expectant desire: spring's progress in the capital is notoriously slow, and the flowers will bloom in their own time.

An evaluation of the sessions described so far indicates that Shinkei's sphere of renga activity for the period 1463–67 was defined by his connection to the Hosokawa and Hatakeyama clans. Those held exclusively among renga poets and enthusiasts, without Katsumoto's presence, belong to a different order, although there too his position as master is evident in the fact that he almost invariably composes the hokku and the highest number of verses. A notable aspect of his role in the renga milieu as a whole is his apparent absence from sessions sponsored by the shogunal house. In the spring of 1465, for example, renga was held at the Shōgun's Muromachi Palace on the nineteenth of the First Month. The participants included, apart from Yoshimasa himself, high-ranking figures such as Ichijō Kanera, Asukai Masachika (1417–90), Katsumoto, Yamana Sōzen, as well as the other shichiken Nōa, Senjun, Gyōjo, and Sō'i. These four, in particular Gyōjo and Senjun, as well as Katsumoto were, as we have seen, frequent participants in the sessions Shinkei himself led. The same group took part in the renga meeting held during Yoshimasa's famous flower-viewing excursion to Kachōzan on 3.4, and again two days later in Ōharano.[25] In all these celebrated cultural events, considered the most prominent in Yoshimasa's career, Shinkei's name is conspicuous by its absence. It is a curious development when we recall that back in 1433 when he was only twenty-seven, he already had a prominent place in the Kitano Shrine manku sponsored by the previous Shōgun, Yoshinori. Did his religious duties at Jūjūshin'in prevent his joining the others in sessions other than those dictated by the exigencies of the Hosokawa connection? Or was his absence connected to his well-known distaste for the rapid manner of composition that such public events encouraged? Yoshimasa's annual senku at Kitano Shrine belongs to the same category; here too his attendance was quite infrequent, given his considerable poetic reputation.

Whatever might have been the reasons behind his absence, it assumes a certain importance when considered against his view that composing renga is an activity of mental contemplation and his censure of the facile attitude that sees it as mere amusement and verbal exercise. His sweeping denunciation of frivolous poetry in *Sasamegoto* is well known: "Ever since such frivolous versifiers filled the world, the high-mindedness and deep sensibilities intrinsic to the Way as such have disappeared; it has become no more than senseless chatter rolling off the tip of the tongue. . . . No wonder, then, that these so-called thousand- and ten thousand–verse sequences assail the ears from every roadside and marketplace these days" (*SSG*, p. 162).

Regardless of his infrequent attendance at the capital's most famous renga events, however, or his ill-concealed disdain for sessions gathered for sheer entertainment, Shinkei's celebrity during these years is undeniable. The hokku he composed at various meetings were apparently much talked about, since they found their way into one of the primary historical sources of the period, the *Inryōken nichiroku*. This is the journal kept by Kikei Shinzui, a priest of the powerful Zen temple Shōkokuji and a favorite of the Shōgun, therefore in an advantageous position to report on contemporary sociopolitical and cultural events.[26] The references to Shinkei are to be found in four entries for the Second Month of 1466; it will be useful to quote the verses as an index to popular taste.[27] In the entry for 2.5.1466, Shinzui notes down these two hokku.

> ume no hana   Plum blossoms—
> takanu kinu naki   no robe but exudes the incense
> nioi kana   of their fragrance.
>
> . . . . .
>
> tōyama mo   As distant hills in
> kasumu wa yado no   clouded haze, tips of trees float
> kozue kana   above the houses.

A panegyric to the fragrance of plum blossoms permeating the place of composition, the first hokku simultaneously weaves in a playful praise for the gathered guests through the metaphor of incense exuded from their robes. Unfortunately the bright wit and precisely delineated aural structure of this verse is lost in translation. The second is more austere and has the visual effect of an inkwash painting with misty mountains forming a background against which the tops of nearer trees in the place of composition emerge distinctly by contrast; the vantage point would have to be elevated, say the garden pavilion of a hillside temple or mansion on an early spring morning.

The second entry from the following day, 2.6.1466, notes Shinkei's hokku, *koro ya toki,* and Gyōjo's waki from a session held just two days previous (item 8, Table 2), saying that "they were admired by the whole world." In the third entry, 2.17.1466, Shinzui quotes three hokku from the Kitano Shrine Thousand-Verse Sequence held on 2.10, barely a week after the *koro ya toki* sequence; the first is by the Shōgun Yoshimasa, the second by Shinkei, and the third by Gyōjo. Shinkei's is the following.

> hatsuhana ni
> chiru o na mise so
> haru no yuki

> Conceal your falling
> from the year's first flowers,
> O snows of spring!

Following Shinkei's verse, Shinzui adds, "Bandai Matasaburō was present at the session and told me that everyone thought it a remarkable verse." A marvel of allusive indirection, it wittily evokes the delicate beauty of light snowflakes upon plum branches, bare but for the first few white blossoms. The fourth and last reference occurs in the entry for 2.27.1466: "Renkai [Shinkei] composed the following hokku on the seventh day of the First Month":

> sode machite
> seri kōbashiki
> migiwa kana

> Brushed by a sleeve,
> the cool scent of young parsley
> by the water's edge.

The parsley is one of the so-called "seven grasses of spring" (*haru no nanakusa*); excursions to nearby hills to pick them had been an early spring rite since Heian times and reflect upon the occasion for this session as well. Brushed by flowing sleeves—an allusive reference to the members of this elegant excursion, and no doubt their ancient courtly predecessors—the parsley wafts its delicate fragrance in the still cold air along the river.

The combination of wit, fresh sensory perception, and aesthetic refinement manifest in these four hokku are aspects of Shinkei's renga style that apparently appealed to cultured popular taste. The wit is reminiscent of the glancingly oblique manner and conceits of the *Kokinshū* but endowed with a new freshness by its unfailing relevance to the actual context of the session: the scenery and season, the specific occasion, and the members of the group. Like Sōzei before him, Shinkei employs wit in his hokku in a manner dictated by renga's character as a poetry of time and place, in order to render the context of the session in an image of delicacy and loveliness. This is distinct from the comic and satirical uses of wit in haikai and involves a sense of formal decorum that reflects renga's function during the Muromachi period as a social ceremonial, an activity that lends the grace of poetry to a social occasion. For all these reasons, the hokku quoted by Shinzui were widely appreciated at the time, although they do not possess the quality of depth Shinkei himself valued most in poetry.

At any rate, Shinkei's poetic fame during this period would later inspire the following panegyric by the Shōkokuji Zen monk Banri Shūkyū (or Shūku, b. 1428) in connection with his description of Shinkei's nephew, the Kenninji monk Kiyō-shuza: "His uncle Jūjūshin'in composed excellent poetry in the correct waka tradition. The words that he recited at morning would quickly spread to the four directions by evening, causing the price of paper to increase tenfold in the capital."[28] No doubt Banri exaggerates. Taken with the *Inryōken* entries, however, his comment might be said to be a fairly plausible index of the extent of Shinkei's celebrity at this time, which was such that it even reached the ears of the young Go-Tsuchimikado.

Sasamegoto, as noted earlier, signified Shinkei's decision to take an active role in the formulation of the renga aesthetics of his day. The first of the *Tokoro-dokoro* letters, dated 3.23.1466, is in effect a critical essay further developing the ideas introduced in the earlier work.[29] One of its first statements sets forth its theme: "Truly ever since renga became so overwhelmingly popular in recent times it has produced nothing but aberrations" (*Tokoro* I, p. 194). Shinkei then traces renga's historical development according to the tripartite division already familiar from the earlier work: the genre's first flowering in the age of Nijō Yoshimoto and Gusai; the middle, generally stagnant period in the time of Bontō; and the renaissance generated in recent years by Sōzei and Chiun through their studies of waka and classical literature under Shōtetsu. A major departure from *Sasamegoto*'s historical perspective then occurs when the letter launches into a long and overwhelmingly negative evaluation of Sōzei's renga.

You asked me about the poetic style of Priest Sōzei. Truly his verses evince great technical dexterity and a power [*tedari takumi ni yōriki naru tokoro*] that no other poet could rival, and for this reason he was exceptionally famous in his time. But examine his verses carefully and you will find that this poet too was an utterly worldly man [*zokujin*]. At heart he was a warrior ceaselessly exposed to the mundane world of archery, horsemanship, and implements of battle. He lacked a sense of the impermanence and mutability of this world and was without the smallest aspiration in Buddhist learning and spiritual discipline. Was it perhaps due to this deficiency that his verses evince only ingenuity and none of the qualities of ambience, overtones, and pathos [*omokage yojō fubin*]? His love verses are all merely correct and graceless; not one exhibits deep feeling or ineffable depth [*ushin yūgen no mono*]. These are things that Priest Seigan [Shōtetsu] also commented upon time and time again. Among the verses that he collected and submitted for Priest Seigan's inspection in past years [are the following]:

| tachibana niou | Grasses beneath orange blossoms |
| noki no shitagusa | wafting fragrant by the eaves. |

haru kaeri	Spring departs,
hana chiru sato wa	the village of falling flowers
no to narite	turns to wild fields.

The beginning and end of this verse are carelessly rough and leave much to be desired. Someone like Gusai would have responded instead,

yūkaze ni	In the evening wind over
hana chiru sato wa	the village of falling flowers—
hito mo nashi	not one human shadow.

. . . . .

| mi o ba izuku ni | The self—where finds the place |
| sutete okubeki | one can cast it off and settle? |

yo wa tsuraku	Harsh is the world,
mine no iori wa	and lonely, the hut on
sabishikute	the mountain peak.

In this verse too, "lonely" [*sabishikute*] seems quite inferior. Someone like Gusai would have said,

yo wa tsuraku	Harsh is the world, and
mine no iori wa	by the hut on the moutain peak—
matsu no kaze	only the wind in the pines.

. . . . .

ware bakari	Alone among all
mi o ba sutsuru to	I have cast off the self—
omoishi ni	or so I thought.

| ko no moto sabishi | Beneath the trees, lonely, |
| ochikuri no koe | the sound of a falling chestnut. |

This too overtly manifests [the feeling in] "lonely" [*sabishi*], and that is ill-conceived. Again someone like Gusai would have said,

| ko no moto sumi no | Sound of a falling chestnut in |
| ochikuri no koe | a dim corner beneath the trees. |

He would have rendered the loneliness as an ambience of the verse [*ku no omokage*]. (*Tokoro* I, pp. 198–99)

Shinkei's objections to these tsukeku verses by Sōzei are quite clear, and concretely illustrate the basis of his criticism in the *Shinkokinshū* waka aesthetics of ambiguity and depth of feeling. These ideals are ostensively represented here by the Kamakura-Nambokuchō poet-priest Gusai, but the alternative tsukeku were, of course, composed by Shinkei himself. The "roughness" (*ara-arashiku*) of the initial and last lines in the first example refers to the jarringly abrupt shift from "spring departs" to "wild fields," an autumn image. Spring, moreover, is irrelevant since the "falling flowers" can be none other than the orange blossoms of the maeku, and they are a summer image. Yet Sōzei's verse as such is quite ingenious in its two-pronged verbal linkage with the maeku: against *tachibana* (orange blossoms), he juxtaposes *hana chiru sato* (village of falling flowers), an allusion to the chapter of that name in the *Tale of Genji*.[30] He then links up to *shitagusa* (grasses beneath) with *no* (here, "wild field"). It is undeniable however, that such verbal correlations, while evincing a quick wit, remain woodenly uninspired and that "Gusai's" tsukeku connects to the maeku in a more moving, *ushin-teki* fashion. *Yūkaze* (evening wind) animates the "orange blossoms" of the maeku, imaging it as a fragrance stirring in the air, and *hito mo nashi* (rendered as "not one human shadow") completes the evocation of a place abandoned by time but still "fragrant" with memories. In sum, the alternative tsukeku captures the feeling (*kokoro*) and precise tonality of the "Village of Falling Flowers" episode in the *Genji*.

Shinkei's revisions of Sōzei's two other tsukeku eschew overt expression of feeling (the explicit mention of *sabishi*, "lonely") in favor of the allusive ambiguity (*omokage*) of the objective image, that which is evoked by "wind in the pines" (*matsu no kaze*) in the one case, and by "corner" (*sumi*) in the other. His version of the "falling chestnut" verse is indeed a brilliant example of his vision of renga as a symbolist poetry in which the concrete image would function as an objective correlative of an unspoken thought or feeling. It would be a mistake, however, to ignore the conceptual power and forceful diction exhibited by Sōzei even here. Such qualities are essential to the art of linked verse, as Shinkei himself fully demonstrated in his analysis of the structure of the renga link in *Sasamegoto*. And although it is true that allusive indirection and profundity are not Sōzei's strong points, his work is not wholly lacking in them. On the other hand, Shinkei himself, as we have seen, occasionally exhibited a similar forcefulness and power (what he calls *gōriki naru tokoro* in Sōzei) in his waka and was criticized by Shōtetsu for it. Near the end of the letter he apologizes for "nitpicking" by an appeal to the Buddhist practice of debate and criticism (*rongi*), which aims to reveal the enduring principles of the Way and is by no means intended as personal censure. Even the likes of Sōzei and Chiun, he adds, are rare talents that would be difficult to encounter for centuries. The letter ends with the revealing passage about his troubled relationship with Shōtetsu discussed in Chapter 2.

Shinkei's criticism of Sōzei's style is useful in confirming the poetic ideals that he himself valued most. It is also not inconceivably a reflection of his consciousness of being a rival to Sōzei's fame, given the fact that the former was the foremost poet of the Yamana camp, whereas he himself was affiliated with the Hosokawa. Ultimately, however, it should be seen as an indication that although he publicly placed Sōzei and Chiun at the vanguard of a renga renaissance, privately he felt that their poetry still left something to be desired and that the genre's true flowering was still to come.

Shinkei's uncompromising severity when measuring other poets against the lofty standards of the Way is similarly manifest in the manuscript called *Gikō no eisō Shinkei no tensaku* (Shinkei's critical comments on Sōgi's poetic compositions).[31] Consisting of 114 tsukeku submitted by Sōgi for his evaluation, it is a highly valuable demonstration of his acuity as a practical critic as distinct from the philosopher of *Sasamegoto*. His various comments here are manifestly based on two complementary requirements; an exact economy in the handling of poetic diction, and an effective and rigorous linking technique. He faults individual verses for containing more images than necessary for their desired effects and for a tendency toward labored and affected conceptions. In many cases he indicates that the tsukeku merely echoes the imagery of the maeku and results in a tedious redundancy instead of the tense interaction that should characterize the relation between the verses. At one point he apparently loses his temper and declares, "What could a discerning author like you have been thinking of to produce such a verse?" (*kokoro akirakanaru sakusha no kayō no ku asobashisōrō wa nan to yaran omōesōrō*) (p. 26). The beginning of the concluding section is not less formidable for its seeming praise: "Your volume of verses has utterly exhausted all that is possible of interesting styles, and I fear that my judgment has not been equal to the task. It is a remarkable work. However, I should think it deplorable if you were to consider it the level of absolute perfection" (p. 27).

Shinkei's severity with Sōgi is particularly striking when compared to the leniency he displays toward Jōhō, the Tōfukuji priest who submitted 100 verse-pairs for his evaluative commentaries in 1462. There his criticisms are infinitely milder, his praises more ready, and he makes no attempt to set forth definitive principles in the process of his appraisal. Clearly he considered Jōhō an amateur and judged his work accordingly. Sōgi was different. By this time, as the entries from the 1464 *Kumano hōraku senku* onward indicate, he had participated in enough sessions with Shinkei for the older man to be convinced of his talent and status as a professional, someone for whom renga was as serious an art as he himself regarded it.

Sōgi was therefore worthy of thorough instruction and of being initiated into the rigorous disciplines of the Way.

To date, the nature and extent of Shinkei's influence on Sōgi have not been fully studied. This is no doubt due to the fact that whereas Sōgi himself has long been an object of study, the scholarly research on Shinkei, though increasingly prolific and surpassing that on Sōgi in volume, is still a fairly recent phenomenon. Unlike his mentor, Sōgi had no priestly office and duties and could devote himself exclusively to renga and its propagation. In fact he subsequently became the central figure of the poetic world both in the capital and the provinces, and his fame, unlike Shinkei's, endured throughout the Tokugawa period and into the modern century. We do not know how and when the Shinkei-Sōgi association started. We do know that Sōgi was already participating in sessions with Senjun even before Shinkei's departure for Kii, and that, as indicated in Table 2, he was active in sessions led by Shinkei in 1463–66. The *Gikō eisō* manuscript may be viewed as the culmination of their association in the capital, one that would continue, as we shall see, in the Kantō during the war. Of Sōgi's admiration for the older poet there is no doubt. In his first anthology of renga by the seven sages, the *Chikurinshō*, the highest number of verses belong to Shinkei; the same is true of the later official anthology *Shinsen Tsukubashū* of 1495–96, in which Shinkei has a slight numerical superiority over Sōzei. From these it is clear that he considered Shinkei and Sōzei as the greatest among the seven poets.

Any statement regarding the influence of one upon the other must perforce begin by observing that one singular factor unites them; namely, their sense of renga's central place in the development of Japanese poetry and their consequent inscription of this popular but marginalized genre on mainstream literary history. In Shinkei this decisive critical moment is manifested as an aspect of his concept of the "True Way" (*makoto no michi*) of renga, which is based upon the foundations erected by Nijō Yoshimoto and Gusai and encompasses the poetic ideals of the *Shinkokinshū* period as mirrored in Shōtetsu's waka. In turn Sōgi's ideal of the "orthodox Way" (*shōdō*) or style (*shōfū*) reflects Shinkei's concept most significantly in being based upon waka poetic ideals, in particular those of loftiness (*chōkō*), authentic feeling (*ushin*), and ineffable depth (*yūgen*). Furthermore, his perspective on renga history is characterized by the same tripartite division that may be encountered in all of Shinkei's writings.

These coincidences are crucially related to the fact that behind Shinkei's "True Way" concept lay his vision of renga's efflorescence in the face of the vacuum created by Shōtetsu's death and waka's steady decline. Clearly this vision was the inspiration for Sōgi's own compilation of the seven sages' renga as an embodiment of the genre's renaissance and the even greater historical enterprise of preserving their works and his own in an official anthology like the *Shinsen Tsukubashū*. It was an age when imperial anthologies of waka had ceased to be compiled; it was, moreover, unprecedented for a commoner of obscure origins like Sōgi to be appointed editor of an imperial anthology. The grandness of this project, and Sōgi's great ambition to elevate renga's status to that of traditional waka, can only be measured against this background. Thus, an important aspect of Shinkei's influence upon Sōgi was his transmission of his vision of renga's historical mission to the younger man, who carried it out to an extent that Shinkei himself, who died lamenting the dim future of the Way in an anarchic age, could never have foreseen.[32]

Shinkei and the other seven sages are also credited with the creation of the serious and refined renga that Sōgi in his critical writings legislated as the correct, orthodox style, and therefore became established—so great was Sōgi's influence—as the standard for linked-verse composition. This is true with regard to the formation of the essential characteristics of "serious renga" (*ushin renga*): namely, the formal autonomy of the single verse; a linking method, *kokoro-zuke*, based on conception and poetic feeling rather than mere verbal correlations; and an aesthetic of allusiveness and depth. The crucial importance of these three elements in the practice of renga as a serious art was indeed clarified by the poetry of the seven sages and foregrounded and given rational exposition in Shinkei's critical discourse. By requiring a semantic and syntactic closure at the end of each verse, they established the resulting gap in between as the proper site of the link. In doing so, they freed renga from an earlier tendency toward a waka-like structural continuity from upper verse to lower verse. On the other hand, they divorced wit, that essential renga faculty of yoking together disparate elements, from its usual and popular partnership with the comic (that is, from *mushin renga*) and placed it in the service of poetic beauty. This is not to banish wit but to make it serve the purposes of artistic expression and a quasi-religious philosophical contemplation.

The role of the seven sages in the artistic transformation of renga was therefore decisive. It is not clear, however, that there is a direct line from them to the thorough classicism of Sōgi-style, orthodox renga. It is a fact that their understanding of waka aesthetics evolved from their work with Shōtetsu, who belonged to the innovative Reizei school and claimed indeed to be one in spirit with the great Teika. Sōgi, on the other hand, took his waka education where he could find it, and that was often with the dominant and conservative Nijō school. The consequences of this difference remains one of the critical questions yet to be raised and examined in modern scholarship, but it is evident in a certain flattening of effect, a diminution of power from the seven sages' verse styles to that of Sōgi.[33] Kidō Saizō observes, for instance, that when it comes to nature verses, Sōgi occasionally succeeds in evoking a fresh and immediate perception of natural scenery. However, "it may be said that compared to the verses of his predecessors such as Sōzei, Shinkei, and Senjun, in general many have an idealized quality [*kannenteki*] and lack a distinctively individual appeal [*kōseiteki na utsukushisa*]."[34]

It is often said that the true quality of Sōgi's verse emerges only when read within the larger progression of the sequence of which it is a part, whereas Shinkei's is so distinctive that it can hold its own even when read apart from the whole. The difference reflects the fact that it is Sōgi and his immediate disciples who are credited with giving renga its final refinement, which is the smoothly flowing beauty of the progression of the sequence as a whole. This refinement, however, was achieved at the cost of excluding any individualized expression of emotion, an overly exuberant wit, or an unorthodox diction in favor of the harmonious blending of the whole within the idealized realm of the classical waka tradition. This is not what Shinkei had in mind by the "True Way," which is supposed to be the utmost expression of the individual mind itself confronting the verities of nature and existence through the mediation of another's verse and by means of a variety of stylistic modes. And the whole idea of a "correct" style goes against the Reizei principle of pluralism as well as originality of expression. Thus, Shinkei's role in the establishment of an orthodoxy in renga is a literary-historical issue that is particularly resistant to generalization, as befitting a philosophy that valorized poetry as a practice of mental liberation based on an intuition of the emptiness of form.

In the early summer of 1466, Shinkei selected 648 verses from his accumulated compositions to date and sent them to someone who had requested them, possibly one of his Hosokawa patrons. This is known as *Shingyokushū* (Gems of the mind-heart collection), the first part composed of 287 hokku on the four seasons, the second part of 361 tsukeku on the four seasons, love, and other miscellaneous topics. Coming not long before his departure for the East, this definitive collection of his renga until 1466 represents in effect a poetic memento of all his years in the capital.[35]

Already in the Twelfth Month of 1466, the war clouds that would obscure Shinkei's newly risen star were looming on the horizon. Having consolidated his forces in Yamato and Kii subsequent to his defeat in 1463, Hatakeyama Yoshinari suddenly reappeared in the capital after obtaining the Shōgun's pardon through the aggressive intercession of Yamana Sōzen. It was not long before Yamana's espousal of Yoshinari would precipitate a confrontation with his arch-rival and Masanaga's staunch ally, Hosokawa Katsumoto.

The tense political situation was further embroiled by a succession dispute within the shōgunal house itself. In 1465 Lady Tomiko had presented the Shōgun with their first son, Yoshihisa (1465–89); she naturally wished him to be declared heir to the shōgunacy, in spite of the fact that in 1464 Yoshimasa had adopted his younger brother Yoshimi (1439–91) for just that purpose. To protect her son's interests, Lady Tomiko sought the powerful backing of Yamana Sōzen, who in turn saw in this an excellent opportunity for pressing Yoshinari's claims. The combined pressure from his own wife and Sōzen was apparently too much for Yoshimasa. As the year 1467 opened, Masanaga suddenly found himself in disfavor: the Shōgun's traditional New Year's visit to his mansion was canceled, as were his overlordship of the Hatakeyama domains and his attendance in the government. Thus, at a single stroke the bakufu brought the Yamana and Hosokawa to a confrontation from which retreat was impossible.

Perhaps Yoshimasa belatedly realized the gravity of the situation, for he subsequently issued a stern order to the two men to keep out of the Hatakeyama conflict. Given the clear evidence of the bakufu's capitulation to Yamana, however, it was a useless gesture. To further secure his advantage, Yamana arranged for the temporary transfer of Emperor Go-Tsuchimikado to the shōgunal palace. And on the eighteenth day of the First Month, 1467, Yoshinari's troops, with secret aid from Yamana, overwhelmed Masanaga's greatly outnumbered forces in a battle in the Goryō Shrine grounds north of the capital.

The Hosokawas' initial reaction to the Shōgun's order was somewhat different; they did desist from aiding the beleaguered Masanaga. Katsumoto, according to the *Ōninki* (Chronicle of the Ōnin Era), "was not one to confuse the Way of lord and subject."[36] Unlike the Yamana, moreover, the Hosokawa had a long and distinguished tradition of loyal service to the Ashikaga bakufu.[37] On the other hand, the Way of the warrior dictated that Katsumoto come to the aid of an imperiled comrade-in-arms. Indeed, his failure to do so quickly became the object of popular censure. Masanaga's crushing defeat at the Goryō Shrine and the humiliating eclipse of Hosokawa power before the triumphant Yamana were finally to prove intolerable. By the Third Month, Katsumoto's uncle, Dōken, who had earlier restrained him by an appeal to family tradition, tearfully acknowledged that retaliatory action was unavoidable.[38] Thus in the Fifth Month the Hosokawa went on the offensive with an attack on the mansion of a Yamana general. It was in effect the signal for the commencement of the great war.

Subsequently Yoshimasa again reversed his position and allowed Katsumoto the use of the shogunal colors, signifying thereby that his was the loyalist army and Yamana's the rebel. In the Eighth Month Katsumoto purged the shogunal palace of Yamana sympathizers and, just as Sōzen had done at the start of the confrontation, escorted the Emperor and his father there for safekeeping, as a sign that he had the highest legitimate authorities of the country behind him.

Shinkei's reaction to the sudden resurgence of the Hatakeyama conflict is best left to the imagination. Yoshinari's early triumphs in the capital would clearly have made his own position untenable, if not indeed perilous, given his close connections to Masanaga, Katsumoto, and his uncle Dōken—the principals of the Hosokawa camp. His version of the commencement of the war, revealing a detailed knowledge of the alignment of forces on each side, may be read in the following passage from *Hitorigoto*, a continuation of the section quoted in Chapter 1 that ended with the massive famines of 1461.

Could it be that disasters fall thickly on a world already on the brink of collapse? As the preceding year [1467] drew to a close, the disputes between Hosokawa Katsumoto and Yamana Sōzen burst into the open, splitting the country into two factions and plunging it into war. Under this state of affairs, the Emperor and the Retired Emperor set out in procession to the shōgunal palace, and Hosokawa was able to secure their imperial majesties in one place. Among those of the Hosokawa clan who allied themselves with Katsumoto were the Lord of Sanuki [Nariyuki], the Lord of Awa [Katsunobu], his uncle the Master of the Imperial Stables of the Right Division [Dōken], the Lord of Shimotsuke, and all their followers. With him also were the Deputy Shōgun and Lord of Owari, Hatakeyama Masanaga; the Assistant Captain of the Military Guards, Shiba Yoshiharu; Sasaki-Kyōgoku Seikan [Mochikiyo]; Sasaki-Rokkaku Masataka; Priest Akamatsu Jirō [Masanori]; the Master of the Palace Table Office Takeda Nobukata; and others. Yamana's supporters from his clan included the Lord of Sagami [Noriyuki] and the War Ministry Junior Assistant Minister Masakiyo, along with their followers. With him also were the Civil Administration Senior Assistant Minister, Shiba Yoshikado; the Assistant Captain of the Gate Guards of the Right, Hatakeyama Yoshinari; the Assistant Captain of the Gate Guards of the Left, Hatakeyama Yoshinori; the Isshiki clan, the Lord of Mino Toki [Shigeyori]; the Imperial Household Senior Assistant Minister, Rokkaku Masatsuna; Ōuchi Shinnosuke [Masahiro]; Togashi no suke; and others. Beginning with the palaces of the Emperor, the Retired Emperor, and the Shōgun, the Hosokawa surrounded the buildings with fortifications, wide moats, and stockades ten, twenty layers deep. Likewise in the other camp, the mansions of Yamana and his followers were securely fortified. Outside, the temples and shrines of the capital, the homes of nobles, warriors, and commoners were razed to the ground, leaving nothing but vast, blackened fields. All, high and low alike, were thrown into utter confusion and scattered in the four directions, their flight swifter than flowers in a windstorm, red leaves beneath the tree-withering blast. Within the capital, it had become a veritable hell. (*Hitorigoto*, pp. 466–67)

CHAPTER 4

The Sorrows of Exile

1467: Arrival in Shinagawa

Shinkei left the capital on 4.28.1467, subsequent to Dōken's tearful acknowledgment that retaliatory action was unavoidable, but about a month before the Hosokawa offensive against Yamana.[1] His first destination was Ise Province where he made a pilgrimage to the Great Shrine of the Sun Goddess, supreme deity of the war-torn land. A few days later he took ship for Musashi Province (Tokyo) and arrived in Shinagawa, still in the summer of 1467. A hermitage by Shinagawa Bay was to be his home for the next four years. In 1471 the disorders of the battles in the Kantō forced him to move once more, this time to an old temple nestled in the foothills of Mount Ōyama in Sagami (Kanagawa). He died there on 4.16.1475 at the age of sixty-nine, just two years prior to the end of the war in 1477. Fought mainly in the capital and its environs, the war had unfortunately loosed the forces of disorder in the provinces as well, and a lasting peace was to remain an elusive dream for a whole century thereafter.

The evidence of his poetry reveals that to the very end Shinkei considered his life away from the capital a deprivation, a lonely and bitter exile. It could not be otherwise. Kyoto had been his home from infancy. The serene, cedar-covered peaks of Mount Hiei had watched over his youth, he had lived and worked to maintain his temple in the genteel environs of Higashi-yama, and he had in the end become a leading light in the flourishing cultural milieu there. The ancient yet ever new capital city had been, in short, the scene of all those passionate strivings that would or should have come to fruition there. To come away with fresh resolve at sixty-one and develop roots in what was in effect foreign soil was manifestly impossible.

It is not clear, moreover, that he held any specific position at any time during his eight years in the Kantō, certainly nothing comparable to his headship of the shogunal and Hatakeyama clan temple Jūjūshin'in. There is a strong possibility that he was sent by the loyalist Hosokawa army to secure the alliance of the Kantō daimyō, in particular the Uesugi and their senior vassals. His early departure in the Fourth Month for such a specific destination shortly after Dōken's tearful decision and just before the attack itself, his pilgrimage to the Ise Shrine, the pointed reference to Azuma in the 2.4.1466 sequence—all argue for this possibility. But his writings are silent on this score, and his involvement in the political struggle would have been part of what we already know to be his tragic view of survival in an anarchic age. He did make the best of his much reduced circumstances, for otherwise this last stretch of his biography would not need to be written, but his spirit remained in the destroyed capital, and the psychological pressures of exile, coupled with what we know of his frail health, undoubtedly hastened his end.

Hard as the Kantō years were for Shinkei personally and for his shattered dreams of poetic fame and a renga renaissance in the capital, the quality of his literary output from this period presents quite a different story. In fact his greatest poetry was paradoxically a product of these very years of exile. Acuity of wit and perception had always been an abiding characteristic of his sensibility, but to it were now added a luminous freshness inspired by an utterly new landscape and a spare intensity of diction and spirit forged out of suffering. In short his inimitable "chill and meager" (*hieyase*) style came into its own during the Kantō years. This is particularly marked in his renga. His waka, of which we possess three 100-poem sequences from 1467, 1468, and 1471, became more than ever the vehicle for personal lament and poetic autobiography that we saw in the 1463 Ta'i sequence. These poems speak of his unassuaged yearning for Kyoto and his grief at aging in a faraway land. As waka, many are unique in taking for their subject the harsh realities of the times; in their censure of the military class and great moral indignation at the senseless slaughter of war, they constitute a moving mirror and criticism of the age, while simultaneously breaking out of the bounds of what were considered proper "poetical" subjects in the classical waka tradition.

The Kantō period was productive in the area of literary criticism as well; it includes two of the three *Tokoro-dokoro* letters and the critical essays *Hitorigoto*, *Oi no kurigoto*, and *Shiyōshō*. Since his works from these years are a rich mine for his own biography, I shall as before quote liberally from them in the interests of letting Shinkei speak with his own voice. Indeed, of no other Japanese poet can it be said that he has fully taken the measure of his time, borne witness to his age in the character of his poetic voice. Were it for this reason alone, were it only for the breadth and intensity of the human concern manifest in these poems, they would still deserve a singular place in the history of Japanese poetry.

Oi no kurigoto, written shortly after his move to Mount Ōyama in 1471, opens with a reminiscence of the conditions in the capital before his departure and traces his journey until his arrival in Shinagawa. The style of this essay is more consciously literary than *Hitorigoto*; it is written in long, flowing sentences that typically span five to six lines, is clearly influenced by Chinese parallel prose, and is a fine example of the *zuihitsu* genre in the Muromachi period.

A few years ago, turbulent winds and clouds swept the heavens and threw everyone into such a maze of uncertainty that they became oblivious to the light of the turning suns and moons.[2] As darkness crept over the myriad Ways, and even as voices rose here and there to bewail it, the land was suddenly plunged into war.[3] Desperate was the confusion as the realm floundered, and caused the Most High Sovereign and his Consort to move their august palace.[4] The Chancellor and the great ministers, the nobles high and low—lords of the moon and dwellers of the clouds—hid themselves in outlying borders or disappeared into distant lands.[5] Fearful for their lives and with footsteps that faltered, the people followed, scattering in all directions like spring flowers lured by the mountain breeze, autumn leaves laid waste by a chill storm.

And when even the grass blade upon which this lonely dew-life sheltered withered quite away, an acquaintance from Azuma urged me to go and visit the noble peak of Fuji and the village of Kamakura instead of remaining in useless hiding in the capital.[6] Encouraged by his persistence, and wishing at the time to make a pilgrimage to the Great [Ise] Shrine, I thus set out for the East, planning to be away but for a while. From Ise I put my trust in a fisherman with a boat and set out once more, now bobbing softly in the winds and waves of the wide blue sea, now gasping in the smoky spray of the misty sea and sky. Pillowed on the salty seaweed of unfamiliar shores, languishing upon the mugwort mats of unknown isles, I drifted through many nights of restless sleep until, tears falling from weary eyes, we anchored in the bay called Shinagawa in Musashi.

Here I saw the famous sights and began to think of the journey home, but the disorders in the country having steadily worsened, even the far boundaries of Tsukushi [Kyūshū] and the interior of Azuma were now in turmoil, and it became impossible to leave. Upon the unlooked-for rocky coast, then, I built a hut of salt-weed grass and with unfamiliar fisherfolk shared the pillow of waves. Up to five years did I pass suspended as it were within a dream in a temporary lodging.   (*Oi*, p. 410)

The difference between the 1468 *Hitorigoto* passage on the outbreak of the war and this 1471 version is striking. From a distance of four years, the event has undergone a process of poetic restructuring. All the essential facts are there—Yoshinari's sudden reappearance in the capital and Masanaga's fall from office, the long period of unbearable tension as the world waited for Hosokawa's retaliation, their imperial majesties' removal from the palace, and the subsequent flight of nobles and commoners. But they are displaced from the surface of the narrative and subordinated to the demands of a highly rhetorical, unified, and rather moving structure of allusive images. As we shall see, other events recounted here partake of the same process of metaphorical revision.

It is possible to follow the first stages of Shinkei's journey from the capital in the opening poems of the waka sequence that he wrote between 8.25 and 8.30.1467, just three months after his arrival in Shinagawa.[7] Though formally on the theme of spring, these initial ten or so poems significantly have travel as a persistent sub-theme. The first is on crossing the Ōsaka Barrier, the toll station on Ōsaka Mountain east of the capital in what is now Ōtsu-shi, Shiga. The spot had long been a landmark, since all travel between the capital and the Tōkaidō highway passed through it.

1 Spring. *Early Spring on the Barrier Road*

miyako made	All the way to Miyako—
seki no higashi no	leaden garments of the journey
tabigoromo	east of the Barrier,
sora ni yatsusade	while blithely across the sky
kasumu haru kana	floats in haze the springtime.

This is an ungainly poem with a hard rhythm and fragmented syntax, and it is wholly devoid of the courtly aura one associates with classical waka. The first line is a suspended adverbial clause whose significance is postponed until the last two lines, with which it makes a statement bifurcated by lines two and three. The intervention and suspended closure allows a resonant juxtaposition between *tabigoromo* ("garments of the journey") and the unusual fourth line, *sora ni yatsusade*. *Yatsusu* (to make ragged, bedraggled, weak, defeated), here in the negative inflection, is incongruous applied to spring haze, but the very incongruity reveals it as a displaced allusion to the "garments of the journey," itself a metonymic figure for the traveler. Having reached the Ōsaka Barrier, the beginning of the journey east, the weary persona looks back longingly toward the capital (Miyako) through the spring haze, which seems to float all the way back there. The disjunction between the light, free-floating haze, and the leaden, sunken mood of the departing traveler constitutes the emotional node of this complex poem with its resistant wit.

From the Ōsaka Barrier, Shinkei probably continued southward to Awazugahara off Lake Biwa, for the place-name occurs in poem 2, which is about a boat sailing away from the shores of Awazu in the dim dawn haze. Poem 3, "Distant Trees Obscured by Haze," turns out to be a metaphorical evocation of the pine trees in the poet's garden, as sighted from a great distance "through a haze of tears." Poems 4 and 6 below would be from a further stage in his journey southward through Iga to Ise Province.

4 Spring. *Bush Warbler Heard on a Journey*

tare to nenu	Though no one lay
kusa no makura mo	beside me on the grass pillow,
utokarazu	I was not forlorn;
wakaruru nobe no	As I bid farewell to the meadow,
uguisu no koe	the bush warbler's answering call.

6 Spring. *New Shoots by a Farmhouse*

machite tsume	Wait awhile to pick
yukima no nezeri	the parsley between the snow!
asatori no	The morning birds
kōri o tataku	are pecking away at the ice of
haru no oyamada	spring over the hill paddies.

Touched by a lighter wit, an easier rhythm, these two pieces suggest that the sorrow of the journey must have been dispelled by the poet's enjoyment of the scenery along the way. It was already early summer, 4.28, when Shinkei left the capital; consequently the spring season in the opening poems does not literally coincide with the facts. It could not, given the convention of following the natural cycle from spring to winter in the hundred-poem waka sequence. Nevertheless, the persona of the traveler implicit in these compositions—his sorrow at leaving, elation at the natural scenery along the way—is clearly tied to the poet's actual circumstance.

As distinct from waka practice, the rules of composition for hokku required that the season in the verse always coincide with actual fact. Shinkei recorded his hokku for most of the Kantō years in the collection called *Azuma gekō hokkugusa* (Grasses of hokku on the Azuma journey), arranged chronologically from the summer of 1467 to autumn of 1472. The nature of hokku as a poetic evocation of actual time and place ensures its value in providing clues to the poet's circumstances. Thus, from the two hokku below, we learn that it was already the Fifth Month—*satsuki*, the season of the *samidare*, incessant rains of summer—when Shinkei arrived in Ise for the pilgrimage to the Great Shrine.[8]

Prayer Offering at the Great Ise Shrine

427	samidare no	Lower leaves
	shitaba wa mizu no	in summer rain: the oak-
	kashiwa kana	splattered water.
428	tokoyami mo	Of that unmoving darkness
	sazona satsuki no	the very image: rock-fast mountain
	iwadoyama	in the long rains.

Mizu no kashiwa (oak [leaves] on the water) in the first hokku incorporates the double meaning of *mitsu no kashiwa*, the "three-pronged oak leaves" used in divination rites at the Ise Shrine. Oak leaves cast into the river signified luck if they remained afloat, misfortune if they sank. Might Shinkei have had such rites performed on the eve of his mission to the Kantō? Both hokku, we should note, are from prayer-offering sequences held at the shrine. As poetry, the first verse is a dynamic evocation of the lower leaves of the oak trees being plucked off their branches by the downpour and carried down the river. There is a startling ellipsis in the alliterative phrase *samidare no shitaba* (summer rain's lower leaves), which has the effect of superimposing the lower leaves upon the threads of falling rain bearing them down into the river. The topic and contrastive marker *wa* sets off the rest of the verse as a later moment, when the leaves are afloat on the river. *Wa* in other words functions as a hinge bifurcating the verse in two semantic strings resonating against each other.

The second hokku, also featuring a medial caesura, juxtaposes a mythological time of utter unending darkness (*tokoyami*) with the present historical moment. In the ancient chronicles *Kojiki* and *Nihongi*, the Sun Goddess Amaterasu withdrew behind "the heavenly rock-cave door" (*ame no iwa-yado*) in anger over the god Susano'o's sinful polluting of the Harvest Hall, thus plunging the world into total darkness. Shinkei superimposes this mythical significance upon the present gloomy scene of the Fifth Month, season of the long, unending rains now known as *baiu* or *tsuyu*. Again, the sensory evocation of the moment is acute, and the mythical allusion communes with the guardian deity of the land upon the times polluted and darkened by war.

From a harbor in Ise Bay, Shinkei took ship for Shinagawa. The poem below alludes to a night during the sea voyage as the boat carries him ever farther from the capital and the foothills of Mount Otowa.

36 Autumn. *Waiting for the Moon at Sea*

machinareshi	A blank reflection
miyako no yama no	of the hill where I was wont
omokage mo	to await it in Miyako,
tachisou nami ni	wetly glistens the moonlight
nururu tsuki kana	in wake of the departing waves.

The echoing bilabials and slowly rounded vocalics of the aural structure imitate the rolling motion of the waves, and the mutually resonating, polysemic words reinforce the feeling of a poem awash with the empty transparency of memory: moonlight, reflection, water, and tears. The suspension of the referent, the moon, until the last line provides a tense syntactic counterpoint to the hypnotic rhythm of the sounds.

Arriving finally in Shinagawa Bay, Musashi, the Shinkei poetic persona's mingled feelings of relief and wonder at the new landscape are palpable in the following hokku series, which reads like a sequence but is not since these are the first verses of separate sessions. In the last two entries, the feel of newness is penetrated by a sense of lonely, drifting vulnerability.

"In Shinagawa, Musashi"

429	hototogisu kikishi wa mono ka fuji no yuki	Shall I yet marvel to have heard you, cuckoo? Mount Fuji in snow!
430	nagarekite azuma ni suzushi nori no mizu	Borne on the waves to Azuma, a limpid coolness— waters of the Dharma.
431	kokonotsu no shinagawa chigiru hachisu kana	In Shinagawa, the promise of the nine seats on the Lotus Flower.
432	natsu ya aranu tsuki o ukaburu kesa no umi	Can it be summer? setting afloat the moon— the sea of dawn.
433	hiyayaka ni tsuyu shiku take no mushiro kana	Chillingly, the moist dew slowly seeping— the bamboo mat.

The second and third hokku were composed not long after Shinkei's arrival in Shinagawa during sessions at which local poet-priests welcomed him at a temple located beside the bay. These circumstances explain the reference to "waters of the Dharma" (*nori no mizu*), which Shinkei uses here as a figural symbol of Buddhism's lustrating or purifying effects on the soul. Typically, that effect is registered as a sensation of coolness in contrast to the heat of human passions. "Cool" (*suzushi*) itself signals summer in the renga vocabulary, an interesting instance of the occasionally contrapuntal nature of seasonal words in this poetic lexicon. *Nagarekite* should also be read polysemically: first, to allude to himself as one "cast adrift," exiled to far Azuma; second, to mean that the "waters of the Dharma" have accompanied him all the way to this place; and third, to link those waters with the cool waters of Azuma within the fellowship of the Dharma—in this last sense it is a graceful greeting to the welcoming assembly at the temple. The lotus flower hokku following it is of the same nature, and indicates that this temple belonged to the Lotus sect (Hokke-shū) of Tendai.

Apart from no. 431, the predominant images in this summer hokku series are those of water and a sense of coolness. Both are marked items in Shinkei's individual symbolic lexicon. His love for clear, cool waters recalls its sacral significance in Shintō and suggests a felt affinity with the *Man'yō-shū* poets, for whom the mountain streams of sites like Yoshino were a *locus amoenus*, an abiding joy, a nourishment for the body and soul.[9] In Shinkei's sensibility, water also signifies a life-giving source, a wholly positive, maternal space of solace. Equally important, however, is its appearance of colorlessness, a flowing transparency symbolic of Buddhist detachment from the dust of the mundane. In this poetic symbology, limpid water congealing into ice is the inner clarity of contemplation reaching an intense pitch. If water is life, ice is death, a physical death certainly, but more to the point, a dying to worldly passion and illusion, the mind's sheer transcendence of phenomenal reality, including life and death. In this way, Shinkei's aesthetic valorization of the "chill and meager," often expressed in these images of water and ice, the tactile sensations of cool and chill, and a visual transparency, is wholly inspired by Mahayana philosophy, in particular the concept of emptiness and non-dualism.

Among Shinkei's hokku, many are wholly objective images void of any expression of thought or sentiment. Such, for instance is verse 433, which appears to be a pure sensory evocation. This alyrical poetry of pure "objectivity" is indicative of the rejection of meaning, the predicative proposition *about* something, as an unnecessary and illusory enterprise. Non-dualism, among other things, is the erasure of the subject-object distinction; the subject disappears, as it were, into the object, and the reader is directly confronted with the thing as a sensation on the skin, an apparently unmediated presence as the words, being the mere verbal markers of an experience, "disappear" as well. This last hokku resembles later haikai in its choice of a humble unpoetical object, the "bamboo mat," for presentation, and in the use of an exaggerated adverbial, *hiyayaka ni* (chillingly), to modify the soaking action of the dew on the mat. The sense of disproportion or disjunction here represents what might be called a fracturing technique. It is one with Shinkei's other methods of juxtaposition, polysemic layering, and suspension of referent, all of which happen again and again in the space of the gap between two verses in renga and belong to his radical mode in waka.

By a happy chance, the complete sequence of which no. 429 is the hokku has been preserved. It is none other than *Shinkei dokugin Yamanani hyakuin*, the second of Shinkei's two extant solo sequences (for a translation, see Part Two). Although the manuscript is undated, the fact that its hokku heads the Shinagawa, Musashi series in the *Azuma gekō* collection indicates that it was the first sequence the poet composed after his arrival in Shinagawa. The opening verse is an entirely appropriate panegyric on the Kantō region's most renowned sight, Mount Fuji, and reinscribes the age-old wonder at the sight of its snowcapped peak in the midst of summer. Introduced through an arresting juxtaposition with that equally rare phenomenon, the cuckoo's song, Mount Fuji rises sheer and majestic against the background of the clear sky sketched in the tsukeku, a cool clarity that subsequently becomes the dominant motif in the daisan.

hototogisu	Shall I yet marvel
kikishi wa mona ka	to have heard you, cuckoo?
fuji no yuki	Mount Fuji in snow!
kumo mo tomoranu	Not a cloud stops to linger
sora no suzushisa	upon the coolness of that sky.
tsuki kiyoki	So pure the rays of
hikari ni yoru wa	moonlight, the wind is naked
kaze miete	to the eye—the night.

A sense of buoyant elation inspired by exposure to a new landscape is unmistakable in this opening passage, but that is quickly succeeded by the feeling of rootless drifting in verse 4, in which the travel theme makes an unusually early appearance and thereafter recurs with a high frequency in the sequence.[10] Equally significant, given the centrality of water and ice in Shinkei's symbolic system, is the climactic progression in verses 8–9 below from solitude and eremetic tranquillity to the intense pitch of contemplation figured by the congealing of water into ice.

yuku hito mare no	Seldom a passerby's shadow
okagoe no michi	on the road over the hillcrest.
fuyugomoru	Winter-secluded,
fumoto no io wa	the hut below the hill
shizuka nite	rapt in quietness.
kōru bakari no	Chill clarity of the water
mizu zo suminuru	in a moment turning to ice!

The persona of the hermit assumed a dominant significance for Shinkei in the Kantō years, possibly because he was now liberated from the worldly obligations and duties formerly entailed by the headship of Jūjūshin'in. The 1467 waka sequence includes the following three poems suggesting the tranquil solitude of eremetic existence, the realm of "deep thought" (*chinshi*) or intense concentration defined as the site of poetic process and imagination in his critical writings.

25 Summer. *Mosquito-Repellent Stick in the Hermit's Hut*

onozukara	Quietly, beyond
tomosu tsumaki no	the glowing tip of the twig
hitosuji ni	a thin wisp rises,
ka no koe hosoki	frail the cries of mosquitoes
yama no shitaio	in the lone hut on the foothill.

34 Autumn. *Reeds at Early Dawn in the Bay*

mono no ne mo	All the noises of
koe tae tsuki mo	things have ceased, and the moon,
kuraki e ni	dark within the inlet,
hitori koe suru	a solitary voice—
ogi no uwakaze	dim rustle of reeds in the wind.

35 Autumn. *First Cry of the Wild Geese at the Mountain Hut*

yamamoto no	Below the mountain, as
nokiba no yūhi	the sun shrinks along the eaves
kage saete	to a clear cold light,
tamoto ni chikaku	sheer by my sleeve falls
otsuru karigane	the cry of a wild goose.

It has been said that all poetry tends ultimately toward silence, and that is precisely what these three instances of what Shinkei calls in *Sasamegoto* the mode of "ineffable remoteness" (*yōon*) clearly aim to make present.

Rendering the overtly flat syntax of these poems into English is no simple matter. The syntax is dominated by the noun, nouns strung together by the genitive particle *no*; perhaps one or two verbs, adjectives, or adverbials are set against these, but the final line is invariably a nominal phrase. Within this framework, the words are carefully deployed to echo or rub against each other through semantic, as well as phonological similarity or opposition.

The first piece above is a good example. It starts with a solid five-syllable adverbial, *onozukara*, and then divides and settles into two perfectly balanced aural units *tomosu/tsumaki* ending in the genitive *no*. This takes us to their governing nominal *hitosuji*, four syllables marking a modified return to the long first line, plus the singular beat of *ni*, employed here as both enumerative marker and adverbial suffix, and allowing the poem to hang suspended at the end of the third line. Then comes the prominently contrasting rhythm of *ka no koe hosoki*, of syllabic shape 1-1-2-3, which constitutes the main statement, a quickly gathering pulse that settles once again, with the final line, into the balance of a 3-4 rhythm. The aural configuration of the poem is amazingly clean and precise in its modulations, the dryness of the occlusives /k/ and /t/ proclaiming their dominance over the sibilant /s/ and reinforcing the bare austerity of the poetic feeling. Everything in this poem tends toward the sense of *hosoki* (thin, slender)— the glowing twig, the "single line" (*hitosuji*) of smoke rising from it, the cries of mosquitoes, and the hermit's tiny hut at the base of the mountain. It is as if an essential insubstantiality were being analyzed synaesthetically on overlapping sensory dimensions.

Stalking the depths of silence, Shinkei concentrates on listening to the sound of phenomenon at its most reduced and ordinarily inaudible, a stage just barely this side of existence. Such are the cries of mosquitoes in the choking smoke, the rustling of withered reeds in the dimness of pre-dawn, or the shrinking evening light. But this meagerness, this aesthetics of reduction, is no mere absence of substance. Rather it is its distillation into an essence with the hardness of ice or a diamond. The frailness of sound or light is made to resonate against an unspoken vast space of emptiness, the realm of noumenon attained in a meditation that might seem remote but is as close as the trembling of a dewdrop on a leaf when phenomena are seen with the mind's eye, heard with the mind's ear.

Against the eremetic mind figured in these poems, we should compare the following apparently spontaneous and immediate evocations of the Kantō landscape, distinguished like the above by a minute observation, an austere exactitude of diction that renders feeling with the clear outlines of an objective image.

28 Summer. *Summer Grasses in the Field at Evening*

machiwabite	Weary of waiting,
kusaba no sue mo	the grass blades are drooping
yoyo naran	from their tips,
yūgure tōki	so distant the dew of evening
musashino no tsuyu	across Musashino Plain.

44 Autumn. *The Autumn Wind Fills the Plain*

ochikochi no	Near and far
koe mo hitotsu ni	across the bamboo-grass plain,
sasa no ha no	all the myriad voices
hirono ni yadoru	are swept into one wide lodging
aki no yūkaze	for the evening winds of autumn!

These two vivid poems on Musashino Plain both ultimately bring out its vastness, but from two different angles. The first translates a spatial quality into a temporal one: the plain is so wide it takes the evening shadows a long time to traverse it. The poem is rendered appealing through a hint of pathos in the image of parched summer grasses drooping as they wait for the fresh, cool dew of evening; "tips" (*sue*) in line 2 is an associative word for "dew" in the last line. There is a montage-like effect in the shift from the close-up of drooping grass to the wide vista of the plain itself; a clear foreground dissolving into a dusky background. In the second poem, spatial vastness is evoked aurally in the symphonic crescendo of myriads of rustling bamboo grasses, transmitted through the slightly disjunctive concept of the vast plain as a "lodging" for the winds of fall. Both poems evince Shinkei's delight in employing intellectual wit to bring forth a sensory impression in an arrestingly novel way while extracting the essence of the minutely delineated—and therefore difficult—topics.

24 Summer. *Sweet Flag Iris in the Pond at Morning*

niwa no ike no	Upon the new-leaved
karifu no ayame	sweet flag in the garden pond
asagoto ni	each morning
wakiba o shitau	the coolness of dewdrops nestling
tsuyu zo suzushiki	in the hollow of the leaf blades.

"Dew" and "cool"—the feeling depicted here so exquisitely once more reflects upon Shinkei as a lover of cool, clear waters and what they suggest of freshness and vitality. *Shitau* (yearning after, longing), which I have rendered as "nestling," is a rather unusual, and artful, word to use in conjunction with "dewdrops," yet it is precisely the single sign that endows the whole with an undertone of tender pathos, a quality of tactile sensuality, beneath the wholly concrete and objective image.

Shinagawa, the site of Shinkei's cottage, figures in the 1467 waka sequence as well. The poem below plays on the literal meaning of *shina* (quality, kind, degree) in the place-name, and raises an allusion to the famous "rainy night discussion of the qualities" of love and women (*amayo no shinasadame*) in the "Hahakigi" (The broom tree) chapter of the *Tale of Genji*.

16 Spring. *Spring Moon over the River*

ukikage ni	In the wavering light
mukashi ya hito no	did they fathom the nature of love
sadamemashi	in those bygone days?
kasumu amayo no	The moon over Shinagawa River
shinagawa no tsuki	on a hazy night of rain.

It is a fascinating poem suggestive of a certain wistful nostalgia for the refined courtly world and tender sensibilities of the *Tale of Genji*, now even farther than ever from Shinkei in the provincial East. As a comment on the burden of the novel, the implication is that love, that seductive tangle of complications between men and women, is at best ambiguous and beyond determination (*sadame*). If we take *ukikage* as "gloomy light," however, then the suggestion is that the people in the *Genji* did determine love to be a cause of woe. Shinkei's longing for the capital and the Jūjūshin'in, as well as the loneliness of exile, are a dominant strain in the poem sequence, as mirrored in the examples below.

91 Miscellaneous. *Visitors Are Rare in the Mountain Hermit's Hut*

otowayama	Otowa Mountain—
ware dani ideshi	how sad the longing for
koke no to o	that mossy gate
omou mo kanashi	from which even I departed;
tare ga kage sen	Who casts a shadow there now?

97 Miscellaneous. *Lament in the Image of Grasses*

wasureji yo	Cast forever in
nareshi miyako no	the memory, beloved shadow of
kusa no kage	the grass in Miyako—
omowanu nobe no	though I vanish like the dew
tsuyu ni kiyutomo	upon these desolate wild fields.

51 Winter. *Early Winter Rain*

sora ni nomi	How bitter to see it
suguru mo tsurashi	disperse only from the sky—
kaminazuki	upon my sleeves
shigururu sode no	an alien floating cloud still
yoso no ukigumo	rains beneath a wintry moon.

1468: The Heart Is a Desolate Village

"An alien floating cloud" (*yoso no ukigumo*), a wanderer in a strange land upon whose "desolate wild fields" he might perchance expire—such was the Shinkei persona's grievous image of himself and his place of exile just three months after his arrival. No doubt Musashi in 1467 was still far from offering the refinements of culture that he was accustomed to in the capital. The whole eastern region had always been depicted as a backward and remote frontier inhabited by rude warriors in the courtly literature like the *Genji* or *Sarashina nikki*. And perhaps Shinkei even remembered—and feared—the destiny of the renga poet Bontō, Sōzei's renga teacher, who had wandered around the provinces of Azuma and Tsukushi for many years and was widely regarded upon his return to the capital as having lost his poetic sensibility. As Shinkei himself would write in *Oi no kurigoto*:

Toward the end of that period [of Gusai and Shūa] there was Master Bontō, a fine poet who had gained fame at the time, but at forty he came down in the world [*rikuchin no mi ni narite*], abandoned the Way completely, and spent the next twenty years wandering obscurely from the ends of Tsukushi to the remote interiors of Azuma. When he returned to the capital afterward, over sixty years of age, perhaps because the color and fragrance had ebbed from the flower of his diction, and the wellsprings of his mind grown turbid, it was said of him that his grasp of the form had become uncertain, and he neglected all considerations for the maeku [in composing a verse]. Indeed, after all those ruinous years was not the utter decline of his art to be expected? (*Oi*, p. 414)

It is notable that Shinkei uses the same term for Bontō's fall from fortune, *rikuchin*, as he had for his own circumstances during the 1462–63 crisis. Furthermore, like the earlier poet he was now estranged from the capital and condemned to obscurity in Azuma, a condition that undoubtedly made him fear for the decline of his own poetic powers. As a collective art, renga depended upon the quality of the participating poets, and an individual could not expect to perfect his art outside the context of the group. Others who had fled the capital city had not needed to travel too far. Ichijō Kanera, for instance, had merely joined his son Jinson, the powerful cleric of Kōfukuji in Nara, where many other aristocrats followed him and proceeded to amuse themselves with waka and renga sessions, Nō performances, and banquets while the war raged on in the capital.[11]

Distant as Musashi was from the capital, however, it had developed greatly from its primitive image in Heian literature. After all, Kamakura in the neighboring province of Sagami had been the country's administrative capital for nearly a century and a half (1186–1333) and still remained so for the eastern and northern provinces under the Kantō Kubō, an office occupied by a collateral branch of the Ashikaga. The mansions of the military clans and numerous temples, among them those of the Kamakura Gozan, were flourishing centers of poetry, classical learning, and the visual arts in their time. In its early stages in the Kamakura period, renga itself had enjoyed an even greater popularity among the warriors there than in Kyoto, where the court aristocracy viewed the new form with reservations, if not contempt, as a form of plebeian culture.

Moreover, it would have struck Shinkei as a happy coincidence that Reizei Tamesuke (1263–1328), Teika's grandson and founder of the Reizei school, had lived for long periods in the military capital and been the leader in the formation of poetry circles in the Kantō.[12] Tamesuke was also known, from the site of his residence in Kamakura, as Fujigayatsu Tamesuke, and the "Fujigayatsu renga code" (*Fujigayatsu shikimoku*) was formulated under his guidance.[13] In fact, Shinkei himself believed that the *Tsukubashū* poet-monk Gusai he much admired had been a disciple of Tamesuke (*Tokoro* II, p. 211). The significance of these historical and geographical congruences would scarcely have been lost on someone who was so devoted to the principles of the Reizei school and who himself was presently to become a central figure in the resuscitation of the flagging art of poetry in the Kantō. The new role that circumstances thrust upon him may be gleaned from this passage in *Hitorigoto*.

Distant as this world is from the capital, there yet remain a few persons devoted to waka and renga, the "ancient traces," as they call themselves, of the poets of olden days [*inishie no hitobito no kyūseki*]. Now and then they would gather quietly among themselves and discuss poetry. One of them wished to know whether the myriad Ways in the capital were indeed utterly changed from what they used to be, and was particularly interested in the course of renga and waka. I did not feel competent to enlighten him, having utterly forgotten all that I had seen and heard except for the most inconsequential things. But being so insistently questioned time and time again, and keeping in mind the words of an ancient who said that if one does not expose the thoughts in one's breast, one's spleen will swell with frustration, I have decided to reveal here my solitary ramblings on the grass-pillow [*kusa no makura no hitorigoto*], the random fragments of what I have seen and heard in recent times. (*Hitorigoto*, p. 467)

Like his other critical writings from the Kantō years, *Hitorigoto* was written in direct response to requests for instruction by local poetry enthusiasts, a circumstance that clearly indicates the nature of Shinkei's activities during the last eight years of his life. These may be seen as a concrete example of how the exodus of poets and artists from the beleaguered capital contributed to the propagation of high culture in the provinces during the Ōnin War.

To determine more precisely the actual conditions of Shinkei's life in the Kantō, it is logical to begin with the identity of the "acquaintance from Azuma" (*Azuma no kata ni aishireru yukari*) who urged him to go East instead of remaining in hiding in the capital. In *Hitorigoto* he identifies this man by name and inadvertently reveals that the poetic image of a fisherman's boat in the later *Oi no kurigoto* version of his voyage from Ise was in fact a ship sent expressly to take him and his party to Shinagawa: "An acquaintance in the East called Nagatoshi sent a ship to fetch me" (*Azuma no kata ni aishireru Nagatoshi to ieru hito, binsen o okurite*). Kaneko has pointed out that this Nagatoshi is none other than the person identified in the "List of Authors" (*Sakusha burui*) section of the *Shinsen Tsukubashū*, among the group whose verses are designated "anonymous" in the anthology proper, as "Tachibana Nagatoshi: Suzuki. Resident of Musashi Province. 5 verses."[14]

Confirming Shinkei's connections with the Suzuki, an early Tokugawa source for the Keichō era (1590–1615), the *Keichō kembunshū*, includes the following report taken down from an old Shinagawa resident: "A long time ago a wealthy man called Suzuki Dōin lived here. He had a son called Kōjun. Both father and son were fond of the Way of renga and had extensive associations with Bishop Shinkei."[15] This information, along with Shinkei's *Oi no kurigoto*, are cited in a late Tokugawa gazetteer from the period 1810–28, the *Shimpen Musashi fūdokikō*, in the section on Myōkokuji and the Minami-Shinagawa post station. Indeed it lists "the old site of the Suzuki Dōin residence" and "the old site of Bishop Shinkei's hermitage" (*Shinkei-sōzu no anseki*) among the area's famous spots. The poet's local fame had actually survived into the early nineteenth century.

As those who know Hiroshige's *Tōkaidō gojūsan tsugi* (Fifty-three stations on the Tōkaidō Highway) remember, in the Tokugawa period, Shinagawa was the first of the fifty-three post stations on the highway linking Edo (Tokyo) to the old capital, Kyoto. There were actually three Shinagawa stations: Minami-Shinagawa, Kita-Shinagawa, and Kachi-Shinjuku. The one in Minami-Shinagawa was located on the site of the Myōkokuji, a Hokke sect temple founded by a Nichiren disciple from Kamakura in 1285. The Suzuki clan was evidently a generous patron of the temple. The *Myōkokuji engi* recounts that Dōin and other members of the Suzuki had sponsored the construction of the temple's seven halls in fulfillment of a vow made on the occasion of its becoming a branch of the Nichiren head temple in Kyōto, the Myōmanji, and that the project was completed in 1445. An inscription on the temple's Indian bell, dated 12.13.1446, reveals that it was donated by Dōin.

The source of the Suzuki clan's wealth, which was great enough to finance such a major building project for the Myōkokuji, and we might add, to send a ship to fetch Shinkei and his party from Ise in 1467, may be deduced from the content of two official documents. The first, issued by the Kantō Kubō on 11.14.1450, is an order exempting Dōin from the payment of taxes (*kurayaku*) on income from his moneylending transactions. The second is the 1392 register of ships at Shinagawa Harbor, Musashi, which notes that the Suzuki had three *toi* establishments there. *Toi* were commercial agents engaged in the transshipment of goods from provincial port towns to Kyoto and Nara, the major consuming centers at the time. Originally charged with the storage and transport of rice rents from the provincial daimyos' estates, they began to develop as independent brokers and wholesalers, as well as moneylenders, during the Muromachi period. Located in the major ports, they constituted the central elements in the commercial distribution network of the time.[16]

Whether or not the Suzuki Nagatoshi who invited Shinkei to Shinagawa and whose name figures in renga sessions with him thereafter was in fact the lay-monk Dōin, his son Kōjun, or another scion of the clan cannot be ascertained at this time. It is tempting to speculate that Shinkei's friendship with the Suzuki might possibly date from that other major crisis in his life in 1462–63, when it would seem that he engaged in commercial transactions to raise funds for Jujushin'in. At any rate, the data marshaled above strongly suggest that Shinkei's hermitage was located in Minami-Shinagawa's Myōkokuji, of which his hosts were the greatest patrons. Two of the hokku quoted earlier (430 and 431) were doubtless composed in this temple. Number 431 is particularly illuminating in its allusion to "the nine classes of the Lotus seat" (*kuhon no rendai*) promised by the Buddha to the faithful in Paradise in accordance with their various merits. The belief was especially associated with the Lotus sect to which the Myōkokuji and the Suzuki belong. Sōgi's first personal renga collection, the *Wasuregusa* (1473), includes verses that he composed while visiting Shinkei in Shinagawa. In a preface to two of these, "Composed in the hermitage that was Bishop Shinkei's travel lodgings" (*Shinkei-sōzu ryoshuku no bō nite*), his use of the term *bō*, a monk's living quarters, tends to confirm the Myōkokuji as the site of Shinkei's residence in Shinagawa.[17]

It was in the early summer of his second year in Shinagawa that Shinkei wrote *Hitorigoto*. The opening passage (see Chapter 1) recounts the country's deteriorating sociopolitical conditions from the Eikyō Incident of 1438 to the debacle of the Ōnin War in a narrative informed by his bitter conviction that he was living in degenerate days of the Buddhist Dharma, a conviction rendered exigent by his implicit metaphorical vision of contemporary history as a veritable hell. Although the essay includes material on the poetic ideals of renga and a celebrated passage on the beauty of water and ice, the whole is informed by a melancholy awareness that a golden time has passed and that political anarchy has permanently drawn a curtain of darkness over the "myriad Ways" of a civilized society.

Among the objects of his sorrowful reminiscence are the foremost practitioners of the various arts in the capital city before the war: the famous priests who wrote Chinese poetry in the Gozan temples of Nanzenji and Kenninji; the unconventional monk Ikkyū (1394–1481); the *Heike* reciter Sen'ichi Kengyō (d. 1455); the landscape painter Shūbun (fl. ca. 1423–63); and the Nō actors Zeami (1363–1443), his nephew On'ami (1398–1467), and son-in-law Komparu Zenchiku (b. 1405). With Shinkei himself, these celebrated figures are now permanently inscribed in our understanding of the Muromachi age, site of Japan's second cultural flowering subsequent to the splendors of the Heian court. The monk Ikkyū, who wrote poetry as well, is known to have numbered among his numerous followers two of the seven sages, Chiun and So'i, and later Sōgi's disciple Sōchō. The appearance of the names of the Nō actors Zeami and Zenchiku is especially striking, since both were strongly influenced by Buddhist philosophy, notably Zen, in their theoretical exposition of the Nō actor's training and performance. Zenchiku in particular, born only a year before Shinkei himself, has been coupled with him as the most thoroughgoing expositor of a Zen-inspired aesthetic philosophy, doing for Nō what Shinkei did for poetry.[18] It is a measure of Shinkei's keenness of eye, and the breadth of his understanding of quality, that he was fully conscious of the greatness of his contemporaries and immediate precursors even outside his own poetic sphere.

The essay closes with an abbreviated history of renga from the Kamakura period to the renaissance of the prewar years, its final sentence indirectly revealing Shinkei's consciousness of his place in that history and his longing for those old fellow-poets in the capital: "Among the participants in those former sessions were Hōgen Senjun and myself, but separated now by vast distances of mountains and rivers, we have no chance to meet" (p. 475). He could not know that Senjun would be killed in the war disorders in Mino Province (Aichi) in 1476, just a year after his own death, nor could he have had any premonition that another faithful member of his renga group, Gyōjo, would commit suicide in 1469. There can be no doubt, however, that he was profoundly affected by the enforced isolation from the poets with whom he had long shared that special intimacy of mind and heart that a renga session fosters. On this subject, we have Sōgi's statement that "one becomes as intimate as cousins with friends in renga. Indeed one feels a mutual sympathy even with a person one meets for the first time, in the course of exchanging verses with him during a renga session."[19] Shinkei especially valued composing with people of kindred spirit, and the loss of those friends of several years' standing would have been keenly felt.

Thus he was especially excited when toward summer's end he came upon an old manuscript containing verses composed by the ancient poets Gusai and Shūa to the same maeku, with marks assigned by the Regent Nijō Yoshimoto. His copy of this manuscript includes his own tsukeku to the old maeku and is known by the title *Shikō Shūa hyakuban renga-awase* (Renga contest in 100 Rounds by Gusai and Shūa).[20] Dated 6.25.1468, Shinkei's colophon is quite expressive of his elation on discovering such a valuable work and hints as well of the felt lack of stimulating poetic companionship in the provinces.

This is a very rare manuscript showing Gusai and Shūa vying with each other in composing verses [to the same maeku], and the corresponding marks assigned by the Nijō Regent. I was so moved on seeing it that, unable to contain myself, I added my own inferior tsukeku to theirs. An embarrassing thing to do, but I thought it a good means of improving my idle mind in the country [*inaka no tsurezure no kokoro o yashinai*] and as a form of exercise.

Three months later, he copied out only the old maeku and his tsukeku from the collection and sent the abbreviated form, the so-called *Renga hyakkutsuke*, to the Zen monk Sōgen, one of the participants in a session of undetermined date back in the capital (item 9, Table 2).[21] Still later he would append commentaries to his hundred tsukeku, in the manuscript called *Shinkei renga jichū*.[22] The recipient of this last version might have been Sōgi, for he included ten verses from it in the *Shinsen Tsukubashū*. Shinkei's tsukeku are unique in being composed to maeku from a whole century earlier. It is an improbable enterprise, but for the fact that Gusai and Shūa were the two leading lights in renga of the Nambokuchō and early Muromachi periods, when the historical project of elevating the form to serious poetry began. Apart from the text's intrinsic academic interest, Shinkei would have been challenged by the difficulty of inventing yet another tsukeku to a verse that had already been gone over twice by two major poets and pitting his own wit and style against theirs. He was determined to polish his art despite the dearth of suitably challenging partners among the local provincial amateurs.

Only five hokku appear in the *Azuma gekō* for the autumn, somewhat few compared to thirteen for spring, nine for summer, and nine again for winter of the same year. This low number is possibly significant in relation to the overwhelmingly dark mood of the hundred-poem sequence that Shinkei wrote in the first month of autumn. Unlike the poems from the previous summer of 1467, whose composition was motivated by the consciously aesthetic purpose of distilling the essence of some difficult poetic topics, the 1468 sequence has no manifest object other than the wholly personal one of expressing the poet's sorrows. The simple character of the topics attests to this: Flowers 20, Moon 20, Dew 10, Lament 10, Lamenting the Past 10, Evanescence 10, Travel 10, and Buddhism 10. Shinkei has discarded the convention of devoting at least half the poems to the four seasons in favor of singular images and topics of traditionally melancholy significance. His colophon, dated 7.18.1468, unequivocally sets forth the work's cathartic purpose.[23]

I composed this hundred-poem sequence hurriedly within two or three days as a prayer offering and in order to soothe my ailing spirit in exile [*kichū no byōshin*]. Since I wished in particular to express the sorrows in my heart, someone else might find in it numerous inferior poems and careless phrases; in short it is meant to be put away as an offering.

Of particular interest are a number of poems mourning someone dear to the poet, someone on whom he had relied, and whose death might have influenced the pervasive gloom that hangs over the whole sequence and gives it the emotional cast of a memorial. There are, to begin with, these two poems, the first of which makes clear that the departed person was one with whom he had been on familiar terms in the capital.

39 Moon

tomo ni mishi	The image of the moon
miyako no tsuki no	upon which we gazed together
omokage wa	in the capital—
namida nagara ni	despite my tears shall still shine
kumoru yo mo nashi	unclouded in the worlds to come.

40 Moon

sate mo nao	Though clouds still
sakai wa kumo o	bar me from its boundaries,
hedatete mo	yet do I gaze
onaji sonata no	on the same moon as you
tsuki o miru kana	in the realm beyond.

The next pair translated below is shocking in its revelation of a grief so deep as to generate a desire for self-extinction, an urge to forsake the world and disappear into the Void.

52 Lament

tanomitsuru	Sick to follow him
hito no yukue ni	on whom I relied, I yet must not
mi o sutenu	cast this self away—
narai kanashiki	So grievous the vow that binds
sumizome no sode	these priestly black sleeves.

53 Lament

ōsora ni	I would soar off into
tobitatsu bakari	the vast Void of the sky, so
omoedomo	great is my desire—
oi wa hane naki	but old age makes in the end
tori to narinuru	a wingless bird of a man.

In the Travel section, the death of the person on whom the poet relied for support and protection in the capital causes him to despond over his own helpless aging in the distant East and raises anxieties about how long, thus cut off from the familiar city, he can depend upon the hospitality of his Kantō hosts.

81 Travel

mi ni kaemu	The sadness of longing
to omou hito no	to exchange my life for his
yukue o mo	across a distance
kikanu bakari no	so remote no word comes
sakai kanashi mo	of the final way he went.

82 Travel

> tsue to dani
> tanomanu kata mo
> naki oi no
> saka no higashi ni
> mi zo yowarinuru

> With no one to rely on,
> no walking staff to guide me
> in this land
> East of the slope of aging
> have I grown enfeebled!

85 Travel

> itsu made ka
> furusatobito no
> suteobune
> omowanu iso no
> nami o tanoman

> Cast adrift from
> its moorings in the old village,
> how much longer
> can the small boat depend upon
> the waves of an alien shore?

We do not know the identity of this man whom Shinkei mourns with such powerful emotion, and the loss of whose protection made him feel so keenly the fragility of his position in the Kantō. There is a strong possibility, as Kaneko suggests, that this man is none other than Hosokawa Katsumoto's uncle, the lay monk Dōken. Most sources put his death on 10.7.1468, but at least one records it as 2.17.1468.[24] The first date would contradict Kaneko's theory, since the colophon to Shinkei's sequence is dated 7.18.1468. The second date is more encouraging; although it is strange that the news did not reach him until five months later, it was not uncommon during wartime to withhold public announcement of the death of such a leading personage. Poem 81 is also quite apropos in this regard, for there Shinkei laments that the remoteness of Musashi has precluded his hearing of the circumstances of the person's death. There is, moreover, a near congruence between the seventeeth day of Dōken's passing and the eighteenth day of Shinkei's colophon. The fact that he composed the sequence "hurriedly within two or three days" seems to imply that he wishes it to coincide with the day-anniversary (*kinichi*) of Dōken's death. Considering Shinkei's close connections with the Hosokawa in the capital, Dōken's prestige as a poet and respected elder of the clan, and the reference to him in the second of the *Tokoro-dokoro* letters, it seems highly plausible that he is the subject of these memorial poems. Furthermore, if Shinkei was indeed on a Hosokawa mission in the Kantō, Dōken's demise would have brought home the fragility of his position there.

Shinkei's sorrow at the loss of an important patron and friend casts a long shadow and undoubtedly generated the unrelieved darkness of the whole work; one misses those carefully crafted evocations of objective scenery at which he is otherwise so brilliant. And yet the sequence includes some of his most moving poems, and it is doubtful whether waka has ever before or since been employed to bare with such profound and sustained emotion the private griefs of someone trapped in the unfortunate circumstances of his age. The following selections illustrate the content and quality of the whole work; it is best described as a mournful tapestry of images of the moon, flowers, and dew recurring in various contextual registers and revealing an inexhaustible symbolic resonance. Where the 1467 waka sequence distilled the essence of closely delineated topics, this one follows a method, similar to the linking process in renga, of recontextualizing the same image.

With the war in its second year and its end nowhere in sight, the poet's thoughts turn constantly back to the beloved capital and his abandoned home, Jūjūshin'in. Poem 21 in particular implies some premonition of the temple's imminent destruction.

4 Flowers

ko no moto no	Apart from the petals
koke ni ochinuru	falling silent upon the moss
hana narade	beneath the trees,
idenishi yado wa	whose footfall would echo now
tare ka oto sen	in the empty house that I left?

8 Flowers

hitomoto mo	Can flowers still
hana ya wa nokoru	hang on there, even on one tree?
mononofu no	Gracious city in a
arayamaoroshi	tumultuous storm of warriors
sawagu miyako wa	sweeping down its hillslopes.

21 Moon

machinareshi	Remembering how fondly
otowa no yama no	I would wait its rising there,
tsukikage o	my longing follows
katabuku kata ni	the declining light of the
omoiyaru kana	moon over Otowa Mountain.

22 Moon

katare tsuki	Recount it, O moon!
tōki miyako no	Of the piteous fate of the
aware o mo	distant capital
miruran mono o	are you not witness, night
yonayona no sora	after night in a mute sky?

Inevitably the fact of his own homelessness and exile, rendered even more desperate by the probable destruction of Jūjūshin'in, forms the burden of many poems. The dew metaphor in poems 43 and 44 recalls a line quoted earlier from *Oi no kurigoto*: "And when even the grass blade upon which this lonely dew-life sheltered withered quite away." Ultimately transcending private grief, the poems attain the universality of laments for the refugees and exiles of war.

23 Moon

sode no nami	Such is life—
kakete mo shiranu	little knew I that waves should
kono yo kana	engulf my sleeves,
omowanu iso no	while by an alien coast
tsuki o min to wa	I should be gazing at the moon.

43 Dew

oroka ni zo	Foolish it was
kakaru ukimi ni	such a desolate fate as mine
taguenishi	with it to compare—
tsuyu wa kusaba no	In this world the dew at least
yado mo aru yo o	finds a lodging on the leaf blade.

44 Dew

aki no kaze	In winds of autumn
shioru bashō no	the dew clings to the banana leaf
tsuyu yori mo	even as it wilts;
yaburete no yo wa	yet bleaker, this world so torn
oku kage mo nashi	there finds no sheltering shadow.

Shinkei was sixty-two in 1468. He was not terribly old, considering that other renga poets like Gusai, Sōzei, and Sōgi lived to their late seventies and eighties. However, it need scarcely be said that war is a highly unnatural condition and would have taken its toll upon him physically, for he was never of robust health. Even more crucial were its deleterious effects on a mind that was unswervingly trained upon a vision of the human heart (*hito no kokoro*) as the earth's most beautiful flower, and therefore acutely sensitive to the moral debasement of the times. For all these reasons, Shinkei handled the theme of aging with particular immediacy and impact in this sequence. In the poems below, the tone is mainly one of bitter protest, although there is philosophical resignation in 50. An undertone of intellectual irony inheres in all four poems, achieved through a characteristic verbal rhetoric of paradox and tense oppositions, such as present/end, grief/forgetfulness, body/spirit, outside/inside, and the most ironic opposition of all between the weight of a life and the dewdrop in the last poem. This last gets to the very root of the classical metaphor and is to my mind one of the most moving in the language on the dewdrop as essential symbol of *mono no aware*.

64 Lamenting the Past

tadaima o	With no quickening
tare mo oshimade	of regret for the very now,
oroka ni mo	how dumbly
yowariyuku mi no	as the body begins to fail
sue o matsu kana	do we all await the end.

66 Lamenting the Past

nagekashi na	All my wailing
tote mo kainaki	is but impotent against
oi ga mi o	this aging body,
wasururu toki zo	that for the mind's peace
kokoro nodokeki	will exact indifference!

67 Lamenting the Past

sugata dani	Grief is there enough
oi to nareru wa	in the outward aging of the body;
kanashiki o	Undetected by the eye,
mienu kokoro no	must the very spirit within
nani yowaruran	also begin to falter?

50 Dew

tonikaku ni	It all comes to this:
mi no tsurenasa mo	the frailty of the body,
hakanasa mo	the suffering,
nokoru hitotsu no	are in the end only those of
tsuyu no ue kana	one single, pendant, dewdrop.

Perhaps of even greater torment than aging for Shinkei was the fear that the vicissitudes of exile had had a ruinous effect on the further development of his art, and that isolated from superior colleagues against whose skills he could pit his own, his poetry was withering away from lack of nourishment. All these, and the real anxiety that he would die in obscurity without making an enduring mark in the field of his greatest ambition, are implied in the next poem.

60 Lament

koto no ha mo	Even the leaves of poetry,
tabi no fuseya ni	constricted in the low hovels of
otoroete	the journey, wither,
tadorishi hodo no	leaving no mark along the trail
omokage mo nashi	where I have groped so long.

The drying up of poetic sensibility or feeling, what Shinkei calls "the heart's flower" (*kokoro no hana*) below, is synonymous in his mind with physical extinction. This image is a poetic translation of his concept of *kokoro no en*, inner beauty, the radiant emanation of the mind-heart in response to being in the world, a sensibility trained in the knowledge of all phenomena as both ineluctably fleeting (*mujō*) and just as ineluctably real (*jissō*) for the very reason that there is no other reality apart from them. This paradoxical view of phenomena constitutes Shinkei's interpretation of *mono no aware* as the tragic beauty that inheres in all things. In his philosophy, the experiential knowledge of being as both a fullness and an emptiness is the ground of a poetic sensibility; its antithesis is the illusion of permanence or substance which leads to grasping, strife, and blindness to this beauty that is right before one's eyes and is the inalienable being of life itself. It is the responsiveness to this beauty so defined that is "the heart's flower."

20 Flowers

itsu no haru	When comes the spring
kokoro no hana no	when the heart's flower has fallen
furusato ni	to a desolate village,
narite ukimi mo	then may this wretched body too
tsuyu ni kuchimashi	beneath the thick dew moulder.

Just as the heart deprived of poetic feeling is an "old village" (*furusato*), that is, a village abandoned by its inhabitants and fallen to ruin, so is the soul bereft of hope and the numinous vision of human enlightenment symbolized by the moon. Below, Shinkei uses the image of "the moon of the soul" (*kokoro no tsuki*) as a metaphor for a spiritual power lifting one above the darkness of the world and of history, a source of solace.

30 Moon

tachikaeri	It returns—
tsuki wa kokoro no	over the desolate village in
furusato ni	my soul, the moon
mata kono aki mo	shines once again this autumn
sumeru hikari o	with a radiant pure light.

In sorrow, the poet attributes the moral bankruptcy of the age to men's indifference to the moon as a symbol of liberation from the passions that everywhere sow the seeds of dissension and war.

29 Moon

fukenikeri	Diminished utterly.
omou mo sabishi	The thought brings desolation.
miru hito wa	No uplifted gaze—
nuru yo no sora no	while men slept in the world,
tsuki no kokoro o	to the moon-soul across the sky.

The destructive effects of war, its tragic waste of human lives, is powerfully invoked in an arrestingly original variation on the conventional classical image of plants rotting beneath autumn frost.

80 Evanescence

asamashi na	It is too horrible.
midarete no yo wa	Victims of the times' disorder,
aki no shimo ni	all the hard-earned
ukegataki mi o	human destinies lying torn
yaburanu wa nashi	beneath the frosts of autumn.

Buddhism prohibits the taking of all forms of sentient life. Human life is especially sanctified because it is the "hard-earned" (*ukegataki*) result of positive efforts in an earlier, lower stage of existence and holds within itself the potentiality of achieving the highest state, which is that of Buddhahood. Shinkei's censure of "the Way of the warrior" (*mononofu no michi*) employs this allegory of human value to portray the tragedy of untimely, violent death. Moreover, killing and being killed in turn, the warriors would have seemed to him to miss the point in their blind indifference to the very mortality that endows life as such with all the tragic beauty—and dignity—of an ineluctable natural fact.

79 Evanescence

natsumushi no	More absurd even
hi odoru yori mo	than the summer moth dancing
mononofu no	toward the fire,
michi o omou wa	the mind that is inflamed
oroka naruran	with the warrior's way.

However, priest though he was, Shinkei the poet could not ultimately deny the depths of passion and desire that hold a man earthbound, compelling him to seek after power and glory in an endeavor so much more moving because doomed to futility. He recognized with sad irony and wisdom that living is desiring, and that desire terminates only with death.

59 Lament

ōumi o	Though he drank all
nomu tomo nao ya	the vast ocean dry, he would
akazaran	still be dissatisfied—
kagiri naki yo no	a world without bounds in
hito no kokoro wa	the world, this heart of man!

54 Lament

nanigoto mo	That in all things
omoisutetsu to	he has renounced desire:

iu hito mo	the man who says so
inochi no uchi wa	is living a lie, as long as
itsuwari ni shite	life within him breathes.

As if to remind us that its author is in fact a priest, the sequence ends with poems of didactic content that are yet crucially relevant to the times in which he lived.

97 Buddhism

samazama ni	A myriad phenomena,
iro mo katachi mo	yet each has not its own
naki nori o	color or form:
wakezu wa tare ka	without discerning this truth,
yo o mo sukuwan.	who can save the world?

100 Buddhism

tami o nade	A heart that cherishes
mono o korosanu	the people and would never
kokoro yori	kill any creature:
hoka ni satori o	Let no man presume to seek
tare mo tazunu na	enlightenment apart from this.

Poem 97 squarely sets the Buddhist principle of non-discrimination against the fractiousness of the clans, the root cause of the Ōnin War. "Color or form" (*iro, katachi*) is the quality of phenomena as sheer appearance, lacking a core substance or self-nature. Each particular shape or color is a wholly relative manifestation of the particular conditions that gave it birth; it does not belong to the phenomenon as such. This is to "discern" or ferret out the ultimate truth (*nori*) of interdependency and thus "oneness" within the multiple differentiations of phenomena (the verb *waku* has a deliberate, tautly paradoxical resonance here), and should lead to an end to the grasping self-attachment and prejudice that generate all suffering in this world. Yet poem 100 suggests that Shinkei regarded this authentic mental "enlightenment" (*satori*) of the Zen type too elevated an aim within the context of a war imperiling the most basic rules of civilization. Or to put it in another way, knowledge of the truth is but barren wisdom without the compassion that binds all in the tragic beauty of being in this world. The heart's flower, the mind's moon, Shinkei firmly locates the site of poetic practice in *kokoro*, a non-dualism of mind and heart that is truly of this world for having seen through to the emptiness within.

479	meguru ma o	As I recall the time
	omoeba kozo no	gone within a space—last year's
	shigure kana	winter rain.

The first hokku of the winter subsequent to the autumn waka sequence above finds Shinkei's persona emphatically marking his second winter in exile, a prisoner of circumstance wearily noting that the turning time brings no liberation but only the same gloomy confinement. On another level, this brief verse simultaneously inscribes a riddling meditation on the nature of time. It is based on the proliferating senses of *meguru*: the shifting and passing away of time, the motion of an object around its own axis, and a movement away from and then back to the point of origin. Philosophically, what is activated by the polysemic ambiguity is the sense of time itself as an illusion, a mere recurrence of the same ("last year's winter rain"). Time seems to shift away, leaving the weight of a memory in the mind, but it returns as well with the fidelity of the seasons. If the same moment returns, does it not make a mockery of memory, suck off its weight and substance? And is not the winter rain precisely the synecdochic jog that raises the whole apparatus of memory itself, the trace that elicits an identity between now and then precisely through the force of the difference that establishes it as a trace? What is this gap, this interval of space (*ma*), this "room" between a going and a coming that is time?

The elegiac and reflective cast of the waka sequence composed in autumn has left its traces upon some others of the nine hokku for the sessions that Shinkei led the following winter. As a rule, such verses of overtly human concern were barred from the Prelude section (the first 8–10 verses) of a renga sequence. Apart from its poetic nature, a renga session was also a social gathering with its own formal decorum. As a conversation begins with observations about the weather, likewise it was deemed proper to start with wholly seasonal, tranquil verses of objective scenery before going on to the more involved human themes of love, travel, laments, and so on. Thus the two hokku cited below may be said to challenge convention in their allusive reference to the realities of the times.

| 481 | kumo wa nao
sadame aru yo no
shigure kana | There is more fixity
even in the clouds, in a world
of unstill rains. |
| 484 | yuki no oru
kaya ga sueno wa
michi mo nashi | Reeds broken beneath
snow across the plain's horizon:
there is no path. |

Both hokku are a brilliant congruence of spare syntax and powerfully moving emotion that makes a mockery of the at once overdone and crude translation. Verse 481 is now Shinkei's most frequently quoted verse in its character as a monumental epitaph to a warring age. Like the preceding hokku, it is almost "unpoetic" in its diction, concentrating its force in what is left unsaid behind the paradoxical conception. Its verbal structure typically hinges on a comparison between two terms, where the one gains in impact through juxtaposition with the other. Here the disorder of the political situation is heightened by setting it in opposition to the "clouds" that bring the "winter rains" (*shigure*). In the lexicon of classical poetic usage, these rains are specifically understood to come suddenly and as suddenly let up, only to fall again, and yet again; they are therefore an index of unrest and movement. Their coming to seem *sadame aru*—fixed in a regularity, obedient to rule—compared to the times is thus a measure of the tormentingly unpredictable character of the age, and defines it as an anomalous disorder contrary to nature. But the paradox generated by this elliptical syntax does not end there, for the final line reinstates the same rains, but this time as a lyrical evocation of the gloom of the times. Shinkei's use of the *shigure* image is so highly complex as to seem itself unnatural: it is a conceptual metaphor for the civil disturbances, forms one term of the comparison, and is simultaneously present as the scene—overcast, wet, chill—conjuring the darkly depressed tonality of the verse.

As a matter of fact, Sōgi was apparently much struck by this hokku. In ordering the hokku in the *Shinsen Tsukubashū* in 1495, he placed one by himself right after it, so that together the two seem to be communing about the war. This is how they appear in the official anthology.

STKBS 3800. "Presented in the Ōnin era when the country was in the throes of civil war and he went down to the eastern region."

kumo wa nao	There is more fixity
sadame aru yo no	even in the clouds, in a world
shigure kana	of unstill rains.
Gondaisōzu Shinkei	Major Bishop Shinkei

STKBS 3801. "Among hokku on winter rain, composed around the same time, when he was down in Shinano Province [Nagano]."

yo ni furu mo	Time passes, I grow old,
sara ni shigure no	still in fugitive shelters
yadori kana	amidst the unstill rains.
Sōgi-hōshi	Priest Sōgi

Composed two years earlier than Shinkei's, Sōgi's hokku was originally a wholly classical piece on how the winter rains deepen even more (the force of the adverbial *sara ni*) his melancholy awareness of fleeting time while on a journey.[25] By its placement within the context of Shinkei's lament on the war, it gains a new historical exigency and resonance that dictate an interpretation, and translation, different from its former intention. In this editorial gesture of Sōgi's, a dialogic relation is created that is similar to the marvelous effects of contiguity between two verses in renga.

Sōgi preceded Shinkei to the Kantō in 1466. In Musashi in the summer or fall of the following year, 1467, he would have had a glad reunion with his newly arrived mentor from the capital. In 1468 he resumed his travels around the East and at this juncture, winter 1468, had just returned from a trip to Shirakawa Barrier, the boundary to the northern region.[26] He was thus on hand to join Shinkei and local participants in a hundred-verse sequence for which verse 484, *yuki no oru* ("broken beneath snow"), is the hokku. This sequence, *Nanihito hyakuin*, has happily been preserved, providing us for the first time with a picture of the local renga circle around Shinkei in these years (for a translation, see Part Two).

The eleven participants, with their corresponding scores, are Shinkei 19, Sōgi 16, Nagatoshi 12, Norishige 11, Mitsusuke 10, Sōetsu 10, Kaku'a 8, Shun'a 6, Ikuhiro 5, Hōzen 2, and Ken'a 1. Nagatoshi is the same scion of the wealthy merchant family, the Suzuki, who sent a ship to take Shinkei from Ise to Shinagawa in the summer of 1467; he may be regarded as one of the poet's patrons. Norishige was a member of the Ōgo clan, a branch of the ruling Ashikaga based in a town of the same name, Ōgo, in Seta district, Kōzuke Province (Gumma). He was evidently a serious amateur poet, for he later wrote a renga instruction manual called *Ōgo Norishige yoriai* in which he included verses by Shinkei and Sōgi as models for composition. Like Nagatoshi, he would later have five verses anthologized in the *Shinsen Tsukubashū*. His name also figures with other members of this session in an undated manuscript entitled *Ōta Dōkan-tō utaawase*, a local waka contest sponsored by Ōta Dōkan, a senior vassal and deputy of the Kantō daimyō Uesugi. The Ōta were the lords of Musashi Province and Shinkei's patrons as well, as will become apparent later. The holding of such a pioneering poetic event in the provinces may be traced to the tutelage these warriors received from Shinkei, who firmly considered familiarity with the waka tradition a prerequisite for renga composition. Mitsusuke belonged to the Kamata clan and also participated in Dōkan's waka contest. Ikuhiro of the Kurihara family was a deputy of the Chiba clan in Kazusa Province (Chiba). All four warriors hailed from Musashi and the surrounding provinces and were militarily allied with the Ōta, and through them to the Uesugi.

Among the cleric-participants, Kaku'a is most likely the priest of the same name who has two verses in the *Shinsen Tsukubashū*, where he is listed as belonging to the Jishū sect in Echizen Province (Fukui), also Uesugi territory. As may be gathered from the a-suffix (short for Amida) of their names, Shun'a and Ken'a were also Jishū priests. The same probably went for Sōetsu, who hailed from Etchū Province (Toyama) and has three verses in the *Shinsen Tsukubashū*. The link between the Jishū sect and renga practice goes back to the beginning of the art in the Kamakura-Nambokuchō period. At that time, the so-called *hana no moto renga* ("renga under the flowers") were held in the precincts of temples in spring during cherry blossom time. These public events, which were in the nature of a ritual for warding off disease and pestilence, were extremely popular and often led by *rengashi* belonging to the Jishū. Founded by the celebrated mendicant monk Ippen Shōnin (1239–89) in the Kamakura period as an offshoot of the Pure Land sect, the Jishū was a populist religion, and these large-scale renga gatherings undoubtedly provided a fertile ground for their proselytizing activities. The sect's head temple, the Shōjōkōji, was located not far from Musashi in Fujisawa, near Kamakura.

To the modern mind, the military-religious composition of the participants might seem anomalous, but it was typical of the Muromachi cultural milieu. Religious establishments derived strength from their alliance with the military-political power structure, and some of their members actively participated in the central and local governments, usually as advisers. In its nature as a social gathering, a collective activity, the renga session was bound to reflect the social composition of the age; it was just as inevitable that this session was made up of warriors and priests as Bashō's group would later include Edo fish and textile merchants. Both cases point up the value of linked poetry, whether renga or comic haikai, as the arena for the dissemination of classical culture and the making of a national literature, through participatory activity, throughout the centuries before Westernization and the industrial age.

The 1468 winter sequence has that unique interest of showing us Shinkei and Sōgi, the only professional poets in the group, guiding the local amateurs through the mazes of a hundred-verse sequence. There is a common tendency to generalize that Shinkei, although he wrote the most brilliant linked verses (tsukeku) and hokku in the genre's history, is somehow diminished as a renga poet compared to Sōgi at the height of his artistic maturity because he did not express sufficient concern in his critical works for the progression of the sequence as a whole. This generalization confuses the poetry with perceived omissions in the theory and implies that such verses disrupt the smooth flow of the sequence precisely because they are *out*standing, and that Shinkei possessed too distinctive a voice to blend into the collectivity of a session. The unspoken assumption here is that renga ideally aims for a wholly impersonal, harmonious blending that precludes the expressiveness of the individual voice.

This is to judge Shinkei's achievement in renga from a standard shaped by Sōgi's well-bred and consistently refined neo-classical ideal of poetic beauty, one that excludes the arrestingly new, any suggestion of the colloquial or vulgar, the overly difficult or profound. Shinkei's renga vision, on the contrary, places the highest importance on the quality of the *kokoro* that the participant brings to the session, the seriousness with which he grapples with the maeku to make it yield a significance. Linking (*tsukeai*) for him is the dialogic motion of understanding between two minds. The two visions of what renga ideally is differ in very crucial ways. But the point to be made here is that an analysis of the 1468 sequence reveals that whatever else Shinkei's verses might be, they do not disrupt the flow of progression. Indeed, he consistently evinces, by the type of verse that he produces at crucial points in the sequence, a concern for progression both as continuity and as variation. It is true that he occasionally composes verses that hew quite closely to his own personal feelings. Even these, however, are visible only because we know his particular circumstances; they would otherwise pass unremarked in the impersonality of the sequence. The passage from verses 61 to 63 is an example.

arare chiru	As hail beats down
nasu no shinohara	on the bamboo-plain of Nasu,
kaze ochite	the wind falls still.
Norishige	Norishige
kusa no kage o mo	On the open Azuma Road, I seek
tanomu azumaji	shelter in the shadow of the grass.
Nagatoshi	Nagatoshi
minu kuni no	Is the wanderer's fate
tsuchi to ya naramu	to become a clod of earth in
mi no yukue	an unknown country?
Shinkei	Shinkei

The imagistic as well as plot-like progression here is excellent, moving from the wholly objective scene depicted by Norishige to the introduction into this scene of the subjectivity of Nagatoshi's traveler-persona and reaches a climax with Shinkei's dramatic development of that subjectivity. On the level of verbal associations, there are the resonant pairs "hail = shelter," and "plain = grass" from 61 to 62, "shadow of the grass = earth," and "Azuma Road = unknown country" from 62 to 63. The motions of continuity and variation across the three verses have that quality of inevitability possessed by conscious art, yet it does add to our understanding of Shinkei's view of poetry as a response to being in the world that we recognize his verse as a cry from the depths of his private self. As we know, this ominous verse turned out to be prophetic; Shinkei never made it back to Kyoto. His journey did come to an end in Azuma, that "unknown country" of his exile.

The last but one among the nine winter hokku for 1468 is one of a terrible beauty, like the naked, gleaming edge of a blade.

486	hoshi shiroshi	The stars, white.
	karigane kōru	Wild geese cries dripping ice—
	yowa no sora	the sky at midnight.

The piece is in Shinkei's inimitable "chill and desolate" (*hiesabi*) mode and is indicative of a feeling of utter loneliness and isolation, a suppressed nostalgia for something infinitely remote and beyond recovery. This is not a hokku that could have been written at home in Kyoto. It needed the experience of estrangement, exile, uncertainty—all those feelings figured in the waka sequence and other hokku in this chapter—and its tension springs from an open-eyed confrontation with the reality of loss and the futility of nostalgia.

CHAPTER 5

Traveler-Recluse

1469: The Journey to Izu

In the *Azuma gekō* collection the hokku for the years 1469–70 are marked by place-names indicating that Shinkei traveled first south to Izu and Suruga (Shizuoka) and then as far north as Aizu in Iwashiro (Fukushima) during this period. It is possible that he went on other travels during his eight years in Azuma but they are not reflected in his hokku. The collection ends in autumn 1472, a year after his retirement to Mount Ōyama; given his age and frail health, it is unlikely that he undertook other long journeys thereafter. Not that age ever deterred other poets from such protracted journeys. Saigyō (1118–90), one of the illustrious predecessors with whom Shinkei felt a spiritual kinship, was sixty-nine when he set out once more for the northeast, composing along the way the celebrated poem on Sayononaka Mountain in Shizuoka that is quoted in *Sasamegoto*. And Sōgi was all of eighty when he made the arduous trip from the capital to Echigo (Niigata); two years later death would overtake him in Hakone Yumoto, Shizuoka. As is well known, Saigyō and Sōgi were the inspirational models for the most famous poet-traveler in Japanese literature, Bashō.

Shinkei does not belong to this tradition; he did not consciously cultivate travel as a way of life and source of art. We know from *Oi no kurigoto* that he suffered from poor health from his thirties; the same work mentions how the trials of exile broke him down physically. Such a frail constitution could not have borne too well the rigors of traversing long distances on horseback and on foot, the common means of overland travel at the time. For Saigyō as for Bashō, wandering had a religious significance as a demonstration of the original human condition of rootlessness and impermanence; for Sōgi the pilgrimage to *utamakura*, places with literary associations, was a means of communing with the dead spirits of the classical poetic tradition. As the waka sequences quoted so far make abundantly clear, travel for Shinkei was always emotionally colored by a sense of loss and personal deprivation; it remained to the end synonymous with exile.

Oddly enough, a century after him the renga poet Jōha would define this theme in a manner that suggests Shinkei's own experience.

As for the essential nature [*hon'i*] of travel, even at renga sessions in the rustic provinces the poet composes on this topic as if he were a man from the capital. Setting out on the journey, he imagines himself crossing the Barrier on Ōsaka Mountain or floating far away on a boat down the Yodo River. When the ferry weighs anchor for the open sea, he looks back longingly toward the mountains of the capital, and though only a day or two has passed, he feels as if he has traveled for months . . . and begrudges the vast distance he has come.[1]

The statement comes from a period late in renga history, when poetic responses had become stylized to a point when they did not necessarily have to conform with reality—"even at renga sessions in the rustic provinces." Unhappily for Shinkei he was truly a man of the capital, and the essence of the poetic theme of travel as Jōha had learned it from his works had all the force and intractable character of the real.

From the loneliness of exile, now as never before nature provided for Shinkei a release and a solace, not in the sense of being a mirror wherein he might read his own feelings, but simply as a vital presence whose subtlest manifestations he eagerly translated into poetry. We feel this particularly in the frequently recurring images of green foliage and clear waters in much of his work from the Kantō years, images that come to life with a freshness so much more striking when considered against his feelings of inward desolation, what he described in 1468 as his "ailing spirit in exile." As evidenced in the 1468 waka sequence, or in the famous *shigure* hokku among others, Shinkei does often employ natural imagery (dew, moon, flowers, rain, and so on) as an allegorical vehicle for thought and emotion. Indeed, his greatness cannot be appreciated apart from the intensity of the human concern and the strength of the moral passion that emerge from his arrestingly novel use of the allusive weight of these classical images in real-life contexts. But we are concerned at this point with verses that may be designated "pure and objective" in the sense that they have been purged of all overt expressions of the personal and subjective and strike the reader with the impact of an immediate sensation.

Shinkei himself was aware that this poetry constitutes a distinct style, one requiring a high level of mastery. He called it *keiki* or *keikyoku no tai*, "the mode of scene presentation wherein one reads the vital impression of what is seen as such; it belongs to the marvelous realm of the ultimate."[2] Nature has, of course, been a major presence in Japanese poetry from the very start. But as Okami Masao observes, the ancient Japanese intimacy with nature was such that it took centuries for it to emerge as an objective existence set before the gaze and the mind, and as a conscious object of poetic theory.[3] This is clearly distinct from the cosily unexamined relationship between the speaker and nature in much lyric poetry before the *Shinkokinshū* mode of objective symbolism. But it was particularly in the two Kyōgoku-Reizei anthologies of the fourteenth century, the *Gyokuyōshū* and *Fūgashū*, that nature truly became an object of intense, Zen-like contemplation. This same motion, Okami notes, is to be seen in the contemporary arts of black-ink painting (*suibokuga* or *sumi-e*) and the rock garden. In renga, it was Shinkei who first inscribed the value of this objective mode in his criticism and practice. Although it consequently became acknowledged as a basic mode of linking verses, his work in this style remains unrivaled in its immediacy of effect and acuity of perception.

The term "objective" is not of course unproblematic; it raises basic epistemological questions best dealt with in a separate theoretical discussion.[4] Suffice it to say that the clarity and purity of nature's presence in these verses are qualities belonging not so much to the natural object (which is, strictly speaking, indeterminate) as to the sensibility that cognizes it as such, that is to say, the mental state of being of the poet himself. From this point of view, which has the virtue of coinciding with Shinkei's own emphasis on the poem as a state of mind (*kokoro*), and on poetic process as a contemplation, clarity and objectivity signify the overcoming of the private and accidental. Here, in the context of his biography, it means release from the loneliness of exile and the weight of history. Lifted from the personal, emotional, and the mundanely human, Shinkei's poetry of green leaves and pure waters manifests that willed effort toward egolessness and detached concentration that finds its most intense expression in the "chill and thin" (*hieyase*) style, the poetry of transparent ice. Some of the verses and waka quoted heretofore belong to this category, as do many among those cited below, although in varying degrees of concentration.

Spring hokku, 1469

489	tabi no ma ni	Within the space of
	haru o futaba no	a journey, spring has turned—
	wakana kana	a double-leaved shoot.

Just as he had done for the winter of 1468, Shinkei registers his second spring (*futaba no/wakana*, "a double-leaved shoot") in the East with an appropriate hokku; with the summer he will have completed three years of exile. Such overt signs of marking the duration of his estrangement from the capital cease hereafter, eloquent testimony to diminishing hopes.

490	mizu aoshi kiete ikuka no haru no yuki	Limpid green waters— how many days since vanished, the snows of spring.
493	hashi kasumu kawabe ni aoki yanagi kana	By haze-clouded bridge along the river, green the waving willows.
499	tsuyu wakaba haru monofukaki yamaji kana	Dewdrops, young leaves, spring breathing deep within the mountain trail.
502	hana ni chire aoba ga ue no fuji no yuki	Scatter your snow with the flowers, O Fuji, above the greening leaves!
504	hana nokoru yamaguchi shiruki wakaba kana	Flowers remaining, the mountain approach distinct in light young leaf.

It is perhaps impossible to measure the newness of these verses in which nature is presented as a direct perceptual experience instead of being viewed through the beautifully seductive sensibility, and daunting authority, of centuries of a monolithic classical tradition. True, the images—flowers, snow, young leaves—remain those that have been in constant use as indices of the particular season; the conventions of hokku composition ensured that. And there is in fact an allusion to an older poem, *Fūgashū* 36 by Juntoku-in (1197–1242; r. 1210–21), to lend overtones to 490. But all of them nevertheless stand as spontaneous evocations of actual scenery and not of older poetry. Or to put it another way, their concern is to make the object's presence perceptible in the mind. And it is this principle that will inform the method of haiku.

Summer hokku, 1469

505	hitokoe ni minu yama fukashi hototogisu	In that single cry, the depths of unseen mountains —cuckoo!

"The single cry heard on a still day just as it was evoked the mind of a mountain recluse. The hokku was composed in Musashi Plain" (*Guku* 33, p. 11)—thus Shinkei's explanation for his young disciple Kenzai. Readers and scholars alike have frequently noted the high incidence of synaesthesia in his poetry. It is no mere method but the manifestation of a philosophy that eschews the rational separation of the various senses. Again, in the immediately preceding set of verses, "green" is not one singular color but a quality of light modified by and acquiring various textures and shades according to its specific spatial and temporal contexts. The verse above, also appearing in the *Shinsen Tsukubashū* (*STKBS* 3706), is an outstanding example of that hokku style, later to reemerge in Bashō, wherein an immediate physical sensation sets off a spontaneous mental illumination. Here the cuckoo's cry on a summer day, heard in the open plain of Musashi, directly pierces through the veil of ordinary perception and plunges deep into the soul, opening up a cooly limpid space in a sudden moment of liberation. The still depths of the "unseen mountain" imply, as Shinkei says, the depth of mind of the recluse in meditation. The verse itself has a more concentrated power than the others before it; what it figures is the Zen mind of emptiness—heard silence, the still voice.

Continuing into the summer, the following series includes place-names that reveal beyond doubt that Shinkei was traveling in Izu and Shizuoka at this time.

508	aoumi o	Mountain meadows
	shigerikakusanu	burgeoning dense unhidden
	yamabe kana	the blue sea.
509	koe hibike	On the four sides
	yama mo hakone no	of Hakone Mountain let your
	hototogisu	cry resound, O cuckoo!

Anyone who has spent time in the verdant mountains of Hakone on the Pacific Ocean coast in the summer will recognize the kind of setting so freshly evoked in these two verses.

The artful compression of Shinkei's diction, which is easy to forget when relying on translations, is especially apparent here in the novel compound verb *shigerikakusanu*; *shigeru*, the increasing luxuriance of the foliage in summer, naturally glides into *kakusu*, to conceal, but the negative inflection stops us short to reveal, paradoxically, the blue ocean glinting between the dense growth. Through a precise deployment of each verbal element, Shinkei sets in motion an economy of reading that has the materiality of a physical experience. The second hokku incorporates a playful pun on the literal meaning of *hako* (box) in the place-name and imagines the cuckoo concealed within the depths of Hakone mountain as in a box. Punning and the alliterative play in *hibike-Hakone-hototogisu* apparently came easily to this poet; we can well imagine the grins of the locals at such sweet-sounding nonsense. It also reminds us that haikai, or humorous renga, was always in the background, ready to step into the breach should the group and the occasion allow.

Four consecutively numbered hokku, 510–13, reveal that Shinkei had visited the stronghold of the Horikoshi Kubō (Horikoshi Shōgun) Ashikaga Masatomo (1436–91) in Horikoshi, Izu. The third son of the assassinated

Shōgun Yoshinori, Masatomo was recalled from monastic life by his brother, the present Shōgun Yoshimasa in Kyoto. He was sent to the East in 1457 to chastise the rebellious former Kantō Kubō Ashikaga Shigeuji (1434–97), assume leadership in Kamakura, and thus restore order in the eastern provinces. Unfortunately he found it impossible to advance further than Horikoshi (modern Nirayama-chō) in Izu, where he set up camp with the support of the Imagawa clan in neighboring Shizuoka and the powerful Uesugi in Musashi.

510	natsu fukami	In deep of summer
	kaze mo nagoya ga	languid the wind through the
	shitaba kana	under-leaves at Nagoya.
511	yo ni suzushi	High in the East,
	higashi ni takaki	coolly tranquil over the world:
	asazukuyo	the morning moon.

Nagoya in hokku 510 was located in Horikoshi and constituted the eastern flank of Masatomo's defense works. The stronghold bordered on Moriyama Mountain (modern Yokka-machi) to the north and along the Kanogawa River to the west. Hokku 511 was undoubtedly also composed at a session in Horikoshi, for it is so obviously an auspicious formal greeting to Masatomo himself in his office as head of the Kantō government. Reflecting the time when the session started, the image of the morning moon (Masatomo) remaining high in the East (the eastern provinces) over a tranquil world expresses more a wish than a reality, given Masatomo's inability to take over in Kamakura.

512	shigerishi wa	In the thickly sprung
	miyagi no tame no	shrine forest: power of godhead
	yamaji kana	along the mountain trail.
513	kage musubu	As I scoop its image
	shimizu ni samushi	in Shimizu's clear spring, cold
	fuji no yuki	the snow on Fuji.

Hokku 512 and 513 were composed in towns just north of Horikoshi, also under the control of Masatomo's generals. *Miyagi* (shrine trees) in 512 reveals that the sequence of which it was the hokku was composed as a prayer offering at Shizuoka's Mishima Shrine, a center of religious worship for the Kamakura shōguns since the days of Minamoto Yoritomo (1147–99; r. 1192–99). Shinkei's hokku identifies the surging vitality in nature with the Shintō deity; it seems to confirm Motoori Norinaga's analysis of the native religion as a celebration of the forces of life. It also explains the intimate connection between Shintō worship and the warrior class, for whom physical prowess, a sheer vitality, was an essential requirement. In poetry the vital primitive spirit of Shintō lives in the *Man'yōshū*, the ancient anthology praised by Shinkei in *Sasamegoto* for the immediacy and un-adorned quality of its diction (*SSG*, pp. 132, 176). The *Man'yō* poet Akahito was evidently in his mind here in the Kantō, for he alludes to the latter's Mount Fuji *chōka* in the 1467 solo sequence, among others. It would not be surprising if he felt an affinity for this particular poet; both evince a pure sensibility, a kind of numinous sensuality, in their experience of nature that has deep religious roots. This sense of pristine primitivism is significantly present in Zen as much as in Shintō; both are trained on the bare essentials—of the mind-ground in the one, of the life force in the other—beneath all the frippery of the mundane.

Here in Mishima two years later, Shigeuji's forces would attack from the mountains of Hakone, and Sōgi would receive the *Kokin denju* from the warrior-poet Tō no Tsuneyori during lulls in the battles. Shimizu in 513 was situated between Mishima and Numazu.

515	shita tokete	Dripping below
	fujikawa suzushi	on Fuji River the coolness—
	haru no yuki	spring snow.
516	natsu wa kaze	The wind in summer
	sono udohama no	drifting through hempen robe of
	asagoromo	morning on Udohama Beach.

The Fuji River flows west of Mount Fuji and empties into Suruga Bay near Tagonoura, where Akahito once experienced the breathtaking view of Fuji when rowing out from the shore.[5] In an improbable conceit, which has nevertheless an arresting effect, Shinkei imagines the remaining snow on Fuji's lower slopes melting into the river. Udohama on the western coast of Suruga Bay was the farthest point west on Shinkei's itinerary, and this session was most likely held with the Imagawa clan and their retainers. In 518 below, Izu recurs again, but seen from some distance.

518	amagumo wa	Lowering rain clouds—
	izu no takane no	on the high peak of Izu,
	matsu suzushi	the pines are cool.

The absence of any place-name between Shinagawa and Hakone in this hokku series strongly suggests that Shinkei went directly by sea to and from Izu, probably on one of the Suzuki ships that had originally fetched him from Ise in 1467. Furthermore, despite Mount Fuji and the profusion of scenic spots in the area, his journey was not undertaken wholly for the pleasures of sightseeing and poetry. The area from Hakone to Izu and

Suruga was far too significant politically as the headquarters of the Horiko-shi Kubō and his supporters to admit of such a simple interpretation for his trip. It is improbable that his involvement with the key figures in the Hosokawa camp had simply ceased when he left the capital. On the con-trary, his early departure from Kyoto and the rendezvous at Ise with a ship sent by Suzuki Nagatoshi expressly to fetch his group—for we must assume in this scenario that other priests accompanied him—bespeak a certain purposefulness. Kaneko suggests that he came to the Kantō, at least ini-tially, on a political mission for the loyalist army.[6]

In speculating on the nature of that mission, we must note that the route by sea from Shinagawa to Ise and from there overland to Kyoto was vital in the transport of provisions and troops from the eastern region to the Hosokawa army fighting in the capital. It was particularly crucial because the great western daimyō Ōuchi Masahiro (d. 1495), an ally of the Yamana camp, had early taken control of the opposite searoute along the Inland Sea, having arrived with some 2,000 ships off the coast of Harima (Hyōgo) and Settsu (Osaka) on 7.20.1467.[7] As we have seen, Shinkei's connection, the Suzuki, were the major transport agents in Shinagawa. They were also vassals of the Uesugi generals in Musashi, Ōta Sukekiyo (1411–95; priestly name Dōshin) and his son Sukenaga (1432–86; priestly name Dōkan). The Uesugi had heretofore remained loyal to the bakufu and were presumably allied with the loyalist army in the Ōnin conflict. Still, it was crucial for the Hosokawa not only to maintain this advantageous relationship but also to be apprised of any shift in the local power alignments that might threaten their eastern supply route. From this perspective, the location of Shinkei's hermitage right by Shinagawa Harbor and his close association with the Suzuki and, as we shall see, Ōta Dōshin and his son, seem to suggest a role as one of the Hosokawa's unofficial envoys in the Kantō. His visit to the Horikoshi Kubō's seat in Izu and the adjoining Imagawa territory would merely constitute further evidence of it.

There is nothing in Shinkei's writings from the Kantō years to explicitly confirm Kaneko's political mission theory. Neither, for that matter, did Shinkei ever overtly refer to the substance of his relationship with Masa-naga, Dōken, and Katsumoto in the four or five years preceding the out-break of the war. Indeed, as we have seen, his account of his departure from the capital in *Oi no kurigoto*, though it has the conviction of feeling and the ring of poetic truth, deliberately obscures the facts in favor of moving the reader through the power of metaphor. Thus, all our knowledge of his real circumstances has been the product of deductive analysis based on external evidence. Nevertheless, from the severe personal crisis of 1462–63 on, the problem of survival and the search for meaning in an age of civil disturbance, along with a deep yearning for an authentic mode of being through poetry, have been such an exigent undercurrent in his works that we should be doing them a disservice were we to ignore any possibility that might help us to recover from centuries of obscurity the real nature of the tensions from which they sprang.

It was in the late spring of the year of Shinkei's trip to Izu that Gyōjo committed suicide. The event was first recorded some three months later in the *Daijōin jisha zōjiki* entry for 7.11.1469, which gives the date as 3.24.1469, but does not mention where it took place. As mentioned earlier, Shinkei, Senjun, and other poet-priests held a farewell session with Gyōjo and Sōgi before their departure for the Kantō in 1466; this was the session that featured the "seed of Azuma" (*Azuma no tane*) hokku and Gyōjo's waki, which found their way into Shinzui's *Inryōken nichiroku* journal. We next hear of Gyōjo in the New Year's renga at the Muromachi Palace in 1468, and it is clear that he was back in the capital by then. Since he is also known to have traveled to Kyushu at some unspecified date, however, it is impossible to tell whether his suicide occurred in his hermitage on Mount Hiei or somewhere in the provinces. Like Sōzei, Gyōjo was originally a vassal of the Yamana. If, as Kaneko suggests, his Kantō trip was a mission for the Hosokawa army, a conflict of loyalties might have precipitated his suicide. Again, since warriors resorted to this act as an honorable way of confronting imminent defeat, it is equally possible that he was forced to kill himself under enemy siege.

Gyōjo was like Shinkei a high-ranking cleric; the fact that he committed this act despite monastic prohibitions against it (see Shinkei's poem 52, *tanomitsuru*, in the 1468 sequence, Chapter 4) accentuates the tragic anomaly of his situation. No doubt Mount Hiei itself was involved in the Ōnin conflict; the line between religious and political institutions was yet to be drawn at this time, as witness the closeness of the Zen Gozan temples to the bakufu. In short the shocking circumstances of Gyōjo's end can only be attributed to his involvement in the political complications surrounding the Ōnin conflict. It points up once more the difficult conditions under which these Muromachi renga poets practiced their art in the period prior to and during the war. Likewise, it is a chastening reminder that their constant journeying was far from the romantic or purely poetic activity that it is often touted to be.[8] Or to put it differently, their renga, so rarefied, lofty, and well-bred, was in effect a strenuous aesthetic discipline forged out of the violent context of their real lives.

Had Shinkei's object simply been to flee the war, he would not have come to the Kantō. As he wrote himself in the opening passage of *Hitorigoto*, civil disorders broke out here in 1438, when the Kantō Kubō Ashikaga Mochiuji attempted a coup d'état that was not quelled by bakufu forces until 1441. In the wake of Mochiuji's defeat and suicide, the government was run by the Deputy whom he had attacked in the first place, the Kantō Kanrei Uesugi Norizane. Despite the bakufu's request that he stay on, however, Norizane soon retired to a temple in Izu. Subsequently a rapprochement was reached among the contending powers in 1449, by which the late Mochiuji's son Shigeuji was named Kanrei and Norizane's son Noritada his Deputy. Unfortunately harboring a desire to avenge the deaths of his father and brothers, Shigeuji plotted against the Uesugi and their vassals, particularly Nagao Kagenaka and Ōta Dōshin, and finally ended by having his own Deputy, Uesugi Noritada, assassinated in 1454 with the help of the Yūki and Satomi. With this murder the conflict between Shigeuji and the Uesugi erupted anew. Pressed by the former's superior forces, the Uesugi appealed to the bakufu for reinforcements, and in 1455 Yoshimasa ordered Imagawa Noritada to come to their aid. He succeeded in expelling Shigeuji from the official seat in Kamakura and installed another of Norizane's sons, Fusaaki, in his slain brother's place. As previously mentioned, Yoshimasa subsequently sent his brother Masatomo to take over as Kantō Kubō in 1457, but he was unable to advance farther than Horikoshi in Izu and thus became known as the Horikoshi Kubō. Meanwhile, Shigeuji had fled to Koga on the southwestern tip of Shimotsuke Province (Tochigi), where he in turn became known as the Koga Kubō. Masatomo's inability to proceed to Kamakura, just across Sagami Bay from the Izu Peninsula, is evidence that local support for Shigeuji remained strong. The Kantō, in other words, was in a state of war no less insidious than the one in the capital, though less dramatic because the battles were sporadic and spread over a wider territory.[9]

Apart from the Hosokawa connection, the authority of Shinkei's ecclesiastical rank as Bishop, his impeccable culture and learning, and not least his reputation as the most famous renga poet in the capital would in any case have gained him an easy entrée into the highest social circles in the Kantō. It was a time when provincial lords and their vassals were eager to add the grace of the capital city's culture to the wealth and political power that had long been theirs. The Uesugi were especially distinguished for their patronage of literature and learning in their territories and for the welcome they extended to visiting poets, artists, and clerics. Uesugi Norizane, for example, had restored the Ashikaga Academy (in Shimotsuke Province) in 1439 with a considerable endowment of revenues and manuscripts. Patronized hereafter by his descendants, the school became the most important center of Chinese studies and Confucianism outside the capital until the beginning of the Tokugawa period.

A hokku composed by Shinkei in the winter of his trip to Izu in 1469 was almost certainly addressed to the Uesugi deputy in Musashi, Ōta Dōshin. It expressed his appreciation of the latter's promise of protection amidst the civil disturbances in the Kantō, symbolized here as in the 1468 hokku by the image of winter rain (*shigure*).

530	shigururu mo	Though the chill rains
	hitoki no kage no	fall, the promise of a shelter
	chigiri kana	beneath this one tree.

1470: The Journey to Aizu

That the "shelter of one tree" (*hitoki no kage*) amidst the chill rains of war refers to Ōta Dōshin is confirmed by the fact that Shinkei led a thousand-verse sequence sponsored by Dōshin in the Kawagoe Castle in the First Month of the following year, 1470.[10] Fifty-nine years old this year, Dōshin had become a lay monk in 1455 after the battle with Shigeuji in which his young lord, Uesugi Akifusa, perished. Although he still oversaw the defense of the Kawagoe stronghold, he had relinquished the headship of the clan to his son Dōkan and consequently found more time to cultivate Zen and poetry. Dōkan was based in Edo Castle, which he had built in 1457. (This castle, later expanded to become the seat of the Tokugawa shōguns, has survived into modern history as the Imperial Palace.) Dōshin's Kawagoe Castle, in modern Kawagoe City, Saitama Prefecture, was only some thirty-six kilometers southwest of Shigeuji's stronghold in Koga, and one imagines that the atmosphere of the three-day session, from the tenth to the twelfth, was not completely tranquil.

Happily for Shinkei, Sōgi was back in Musashi from a sudden trip to the capital the previous year and could assist him in guiding the local participants in what was doubtless for them an unprecedented poetic marathon. Including Dōshin, there were seven warrior-poets, among them the four who had earlier figured in the winter 1468 hundred-verse sequence. Also participating were a Zen-priest attendant of Dōshin called Chūga; the Lotus sect priest Inkō, who was then visiting from the capital and would join Shinkei in the journey to Aizu this winter; and another priest called Kyōshun, who recent scholarship has proven to be none other than Kenzai, only eighteen years old and newly enrolled as Shinkei's disciple.[11] Long after his teacher's death, Kenzai would become a famous renga poet in the capital, succeeding Sōgi as Kitano Renga Master in 1489 when he was thirty-seven, the youngest person to hold that office. Still a fledgling poet during the *Kawagoe senku* of 1470, he composed the fewest verses during the session, as the following tally indicates: Shinkei 155, Sōgi 126, Dōshin 110, Nagatoshi 97, Chūga 83, Norishige 80, Mitsusuke 73, Inkō 66, Ikuhiro 64, Eishō 54, Yoshifuji 50, Chōhaku 29, Kyōshun 13.

In the first three verses of the opening sequence, quoted below, Shinkei composes the hokku as the renga master for the session, Dōshin the waki in his role as host, and Sōgi the daisan as the next-ranking among the poets present. This formal order of precedence is discarded in the next eight sequences, whose hokku are composed in turn by the other participants. A modified return occurs in the important concluding sequence, for which Dōshin composes the hokku and Shinkei the answering waki. Similarly the image of the flowering plum trees in the gardens of the Kawagoe Castle, evoked in the opening passage below, recurs in the beginning of the closing sequence.

umezono ni	In the plum grove,
kusaki o naseru	a fragrance vitally suffusing
nioi kana	the plants and trees.
Shinkei	Shinkei
niwa shirotae no	A white banner over the garden
yuki no harukaze	snowflakes in the spring breeze.
Dōshin	Dōshin
uguisu no	In the bush warbler's
koe wa toyama no	cry, chill the shadow of
kage saete	yonder foothills.
Sōgi	Sōgi

The images in these first three verses are finely delineated, but there is something unsatisfactory about the contrary progression from Shinkei's truly spring-like hokku to the wintry, chill feeling of Sōgi's daisan. Shinkei's hokku projects the fragrance of the plum flowers as an aura of vitality influencing the other sprouting vegetation; it is also a greeting to the master of these gardens, Dōshin.

Moving from a meadow to a mountain scene, the opening of the second sequence includes a rather beautiful pair by Dōshin and Shinkei that has the effect of a scroll painting.

tōku mite	Gazing far away,
yukeba kasumanu	I see green fields lying clear
aono kana	of the haze.
Sōgi	Sōgi
akuru kozue no	The tranquil color of the treetops
nodokanaru iro	growing apparent in dawn light.
Yoshifuji	Yoshifuji

tsuki usuku	Pale the moon as it
mine no sakura ni	fades upon the flowering cherries
utsuroite	on the peak.
Dōshin	Dōshin
honokuraki e ni	Down the mountain the water falls
mizu otsuru yama.	into the dimness of the inlet.
Shinkei	Shinkei

This is an impressively sustained passage; the tightly compressed diction of the verses by Yoshifuji and Shinkei, in which there is not a single wasted word, is particularly remarkable. Yoshifuji securely captures Sōgi's intention, expressed in *kasumanu* (not hazy) by evoking the image of trees emerging in the dawn light (*akuru*). In turn Dōshin links up to "color" (*iro*) and "treetops" (*kozue*) through the picture of flowering cherry trees in fading moonlight. Shinkei adds a white waterfall below the pale massed flowers and juxtaposes against these the contrasting image of the inlet still wrapped in darkness, in a verse that is both visually beautiful and ineffably remote in effect. In terms of his critical vocabulary, such a verse may be said to be in the *yōon* mode. In general Shinkei's work in the Kawagoe session has a tranquillity and even warmth lacking in his emotional performance in the 1468 winter sequence and suggests that his mood had improved considerably since then.

The *Kawagoe senku* is a literary landmark in various ways. First, it may be seen as a renga recital by the warriors whom Shinkei had been instructing since his arrival in Shinagawa, a grand culmination evincing his role in the revitalization of the flagging art of poetry in the Kantō. In the capital the thousand-verse sequence was commonly sponsored by the shōgun and other ranking daimyō at the Kitano Shrine and elsewhere. The Kantō had but rarely seen a poetic event of such scale since the Kamakura and Nambokuchō periods, and Dōshin was doubtless sensible of that significant fact. Indeed, he and his son Dōkan would go down in history not merely as mighty generals in the Kantō power struggle—something that can only be of ephemeral and banal interest for us now—but more important, as the patrons of Shinkei and Sōgi, men of arms who promoted the art of poetry in the East amidst the disorders and tensions of war.[12]

In Shinkei's biography the *Kawagoe senku* of 1470 is memorable as well in marking the final time that he and Sōgi participated together in a public session. (That is, it is the last extant sequence in which both their names figure, although it is certainly possible that they had other sessions together before Sōgi's final departure for the capital in 1472.) Sōgi also had a hermitage in Musashi, but unlike Shinkei he was frequently away visiting provincial lords and warriors in their castles and battle camps. Since the portrait of Sōgi that emerges in the Kantō is somewhat different from that of Shinkei, it will be useful to trace his activities for purposes of comparison.

Various reasons have been given for Sōgi's long sojourn in the Kantō in the period 1466–72 (interrupted by his return to the capital for some months in 1469), when he was age forty-five to fifty-one. Among them his biographer Ijichi Tetsuo isolates two in particular: his desire to receive instruction from the warrior and Nijō poet Tō no Tsuneyori in the secret traditions of the *Kokinshū* (the so-called *Kokin denju*), and the equally compelling wish to visit and experience places famous for their literary associations.[13] Kaneko suggests a third reason: the successive departures of Sōgi, Gyōjo, and Shinkei for the Kantō between 1466 and 1467 and their possible link with the loyalist army.

It is possible to read all three motives into Sōgi's activities and connections with the warrior clans, which were much more extensive than Shinkei's. His very first renga treatise, the *Chōrokubumi*, was written in the Tenth Month of 1466 while visiting the Nagao clan in their stronghold at Ikago, Musashi.[14] The Nagao were the most powerful retainers of the Uesugi clan's Yamanouchi branch, just as the Ōta were for its Ōgigayatsu branch; together the Nagao and Ōta defended the Uesugi's extensive territories in the Kantō. From Ikago in the following spring, 1467, Sōgi proceeded further north to Kōzuke Province (Gumma) at the Nagaos' invitation and held renga sessions at another camp in Shirai, where the Uesugi were preparing to confront Shigeuji's forces. It was not until the summer or fall of 1467 that he went to Edo, met the Ōta, and had his first reunion with the newly arrived Shinkei in Shinagawa. Sometime in the following year, however, he set off once more, this time to be with Tō no Tsuneyori during his military campaigns in the provinces of Shimōsa and Kazusa (Chiba). Tsuneyori had been ordered here by the Shōgun Yoshimasa in 1455 in order to purge the Chiba clan of rebels and strengthen its alliance with Masatomo in Izu. Tsuneyori, it must be noted, was himself descended from a branch of the Chiba clan, at this time divided, like all the Kantō, between the Shigeuji and Uesugi-Masatomo camps. From Chiba in the autumn of 1468, Sōgi continued north to Hitachi Province (Ibaragi) to view Mount Tsukuba, a mountain legendarily associated with the origins of renga; Nikkō in Shimotsuke Province (Tochigi); and farther north, the Shirakawa Barrier at the invitation of Yūki Naotomo, a strong ally of the Shigeuji faction. The poetic diary *Shirakawa kikō* is a record of this journey.

Back in Musashi in the winter of 1468, as we have seen, he participated in a renga session with Shinkei and the Ōta warrior-poets. Sometime in 1469, he traveled back to the capital and from there found time to compose verses with Ichijō Kanera and his son Daijōin Jinson (the author of the *Daijōin jishi zōjiki*) in Nara in the Seventh Month. Ijichi finds this trip significant in view of the fact that Tsuneyori himself returned to the capital on 4.21.1469 in order to negotiate with Saitō Myōshun (d. 1480) for the return of the Tō estate in Mino Province (Gifu). The Deputy of the ruling Toki clan of Mino and an ally of the Yamana camp, Myōshun had defeated Tsuneyori's brother in Mino during the course of the war and appropriated the Tō holdings there. However, he is reported to have been so moved by poems composed subsequently by Tsuneyori lamenting this misfortune that he gallantly agreed to relinquish them again.[15]

It was the same Myōshun who sheltered Senjun, Sōgi's former teacher and the renga friend for whom Shinkei expressed a yearning in *Hitorigoto*, in his castle in Mino during the war. Unhappily Senjun perished there in 1476, believed to have been killed by the loyalist Ogasawara forces in an encounter with Myōshun and other Yamana troops.[16] Like Shinkei and Sōgi in Musashi, Senjun had been an active renga leader in Mino, where he organized at least three senku sessions—the last, the second *Mino senku*, held on 3.6.1476, just two weeks before his death on 3.20.1476. He was sixty-five. Just what his precise involvement was in the Ōnin conflict is impossible to say; it is somewhat odd that he should have sheltered with a Yamana ally when he was such a regular member of the Hosokawa renga group prior to the outbreak of the war. But no matter. It was, as Shinkei wrote in 1468, a "world so torn / there finds no sheltering shadow (*yaburete no yo wa / oku kage mo nashi*)."[17]

In the winter of 1469, Sōgi was back again in Musashi, composing renga with Shinkei and participating in the *Kawagoe senku* in the spring of 1470. In the first four months of 1471, and again in the Sixth and Seventh months during lulls in the battles at Mishima in Izu, where Tsuneyori was encamped with Masatomo's forces, Sōgi finally achieved one of his compelling motives for coming to the Kantō. In a series of lectures, Tsuneyori transmitted to him the so-called *Kokin denju*, a body of secret teachings regarding the correct interpretation of the *Kokinshū* poems, said to have originated with Teika (this is a matter of dispute) and been passed on to Tsuneyori through his family's hereditary association with the Nijō branch. The content of this body of traditional readings has long been dismissed as negligible by modern scholarship, although that judgment is now under reappraisal. The prestige attached to it then was without question enormous. It invested Sōgi with the symbolic power and authority of the waka classical tradition and may be said to have laid the foundations for his subsequent rise to the leadership of the literary world.[18]

Whether or not Sōgi was on a political mission related to Shinkei's own, his extensive visits and renga sessions with the warrior clans were useful not only in furthering his poetic training but also in establishing powerful connections that would be of practical importance in his personal career. The portrait of Sōgi that emerges from the above account is that of a man of great energy and purpose, someone who had firmly taken the measure of the times and intended to mold his destiny by it. Unlike the seven sages, he came of an obscure background. Possessing neither social rank nor position, he had perforce to employ his poetic ability and later his classical learning as a means of establishing himself in the world. In the process he became the first true professional among the major renga poets of the Muromachi period.

The difference in the pace and character of the two poets' activities in the Kantō during this period should be viewed from the perspective described above. There is, moreover, the matter of their being in two diametrically opposite stages in their lives: Shinkei had already made his reputation in the capital, while Sōgi was at this time still preparing to launch his career. The one had seen the war deprive him of position and home, the other would forge both in spite of it. It appears, in addition, that their sociopolitical attitudes were different. In the Kantō and his later travels as well, Sōgi associated with and was patronized by mutually hostile warrior clans. In other words, the professional and pragmatic artist did not let ephemeral politics dictate who were and were not to be the recipients of his services. For him, renga was above all a métier and universal discipline whose practice was independent of factional considerations. The same principle is apparent in the fact that he sought out the invaluable connection with the Nijō poet Tsuneyori even while receiving poetic instruction from the Reizei poet Shinkei. Such professionalism must be seen as the key to Sōgi's overwhelming worldly success—overwhelming only in view of where he started and apart from his unquestionable talent and prodigious abilities (needless to say not always a guarantee of fame). His was a difficult yet happy victory earned through consummate social skill and discernment, and based upon a sensible appraisal of contemporary political and economic forces and how they might best be employed for the greater glory of his art.

Against the clarity of Sōgi's almost modern professionalism, the ambiguity, even incongruity, of Shinkei's position vis-à-vis society—which is to say warrior society—stands out by contrast. Of his professed attitude there is not the slightest doubt: he disapproved of those who used renga "solely as a means of livelihood, employing themselves in its vulgarization day in and day out" (*SSG*, pp. 162–63). For him the renga session was a gathering of kindred spirits sensible of the vanity of human existence, above considerations of personal glory and worldly profit, and trained solely upon the experience of poetry. Ambiguity arises when one attempts to measure his actual circumstances against such manifestly high ideals, an admittedly problematic and even foolhardy undertaking, given the scarcity of available data. Yet enough has been written up to this point to give the impression of a contradiction between his life, or more accurately, his fate, and the high and noble portrait of the renga poet in *Sasamegoto*. The contradiction came to the fore with the outbreak of the Hatakeyama succession dispute, which necessitated an alliance with the Masanaga-Katsumoto faction and in turn involved him in the Ōnin conflict, if Kaneko is right, as a kind of unofficial envoy for the loyalist army. In short, for all practical purposes his position in the Kantō in relation to warrior society substantially resembles Sōgi's. The crucial difference is that what turned out to be a happy victory in the one case impresses us as an ironic tragedy in the other. That Shinkei himself viewed it as such is evident in the waka poems and autobiographical passages quoted so far; a piece such as the following merely confirms it.

Travel-Lodging Robe

koromode ni	It did not stay,
tsui ni utsusanu	in the end, upon my sleeves—
sumizome no	the ink-dyed mountain
yūbe no yama wa	at evening is as a monk's robe,
waga yado mo nashi	yet finds not my shelter there.

Shinkei's personal tragedy is that he had formally occupied a considerable place in the social structure and been invested with the moral authority symbolized by his priestly calling. Though deprived now of their physical trappings, he could not banish the somewhat aristocratic and purist turn of mind they had fostered and still less conceive of using his connections and abilities, as Sōgi did, to effect a triumphant comeback to the capital instead of ending in obscurity in the Kantō. Politically it is, I believe, not inaccurate to say that he retained a feudal philosophy based on the inviolable relationship between lord and subject and the obligations and duties appertaining to each: the implicitly censorious tone with which he describes the "selfish quarrels" within the warrior clans in *Hitorigoto*'s opening passage suggests as much. There is also a feudal element in the high value he placed upon personal loyalty to someone to whom one owes a debt of gratitude, such a principle as would explain, for instance, his undertaking of a political mission for the Masanaga-Katsumoto faction responsible for Jūjūshin'in's restoration. In other words, he evidently still cherished the ideal of the noble—that is to say, honest and authentic—relationship that should obtain between lord and subject in an age dominated by the opposite, clearly "ignoble" forces of *gekokujō* ("the low vanquishing the high"). And here again his sharply critical mind could not have failed to register the moral contradictions in the positions of everyone involved in the Ōnin conflict.

Faced with political and social anarchy, he did what was necessary to survive and preserve the century-old temple for which he was responsible as head priest. However, close as he was to the reins of power because of Jūjūshin'in's status as a shogunal and Hatakeyama clan temple, he appears to have maintained some distance from them due to that moral fastidiousness everywhere apparent in his prose writings. It is significant, for instance, that except for that single reminiscence in a private letter about composing renga with Katsumoto, Masanaga, and the prospective Emperor Go-Tsuchimikado, those writings make no mention of his political connections. Neither do his personal poetry collections include prefaces that inform us that this poem was composed in the residence of such and such a noble, or that verse in the company of such and such a lord, and so on. Compared to the telling presence of contemporary society names in Shōtetsu's *Sōkonshū* or in Sōgi's *Uraba*, Shinkei's collections stand out by their complete reticence about and disregard for the milieu that he inhabited, as if to say that poetry need not impress through political connection or social pedigree. All this is not in the interest of creating a hagiography for the man; that is neither possible nor necessary. It is merely an attempt, and one dictated by his own lofty attitudes, to distinguish the ambivalence of his relationship to the contemporary power structure in contrast with the genial character of Sōgi's. As a priest and intellectual, Shinkei's victory vis-à-vis the establishment was of another kind, one that necessarily had to assume a moral character, and led him to the self-contradictory position of condemning the actions of the very class on whose patronage he depended.

Interesting as the distinctions in their social backgrounds and attitudes are, however, they did not ultimately matter to the two men, who were brought together by their devotion to the transcendent claims of poetry and their common role in promoting within warrior society the higher values that it represents. Of their association in the Kantō subsequent to the *Kawagoe senku*, we have one final evidence. It is the last of Shinkei's *Tokoro-dokoro hentō* letters, also known as *Sōgi-Zenshi e no hensatsu* (Reply to Zen Priest Sōgi) and dating from the summer of the same year, 1470. From the letter's opening passage, quoted below, it becomes immediately clear that Sōgi had requested an annotated copy of Shinkei's verses, as well as an appraisal of his own recent work.

Worthless as my verses are, I could not resist your request and have written my comments hurriedly and without much judgment on a number that happened to be close at hand; you must consign them to the flames after reading them. Which sort of verse is good and which bad is a matter difficult to establish beforehand; one should simply link up to the maeku according to the actual circumstances at the time [of the session]. Cultivate an elevated spirit [*kokoro o takaku*], a language moving and graceful [*kotoba o en ni*], and guard against the tendency to remain within a single style. That is to say, put aside the desire to produce an eye-catching verse [*ku no omoshiro*] and set your mind instead on quality [*kurai*]. Loftiness [*take*], overtones [*omokage*], and refinement [*shina*] should be your primary considerations. How foolish of me to become carried away by your love for poetry and thus to expose the narrowness of my opinions! Yet I do so only because I believe it is a good training for us both. Regarding your most recent verses, I must say that I find every one of them interesting. However, there are among them a number whose handling is a little uncertain [*obotsukanaki*], and I shall comment on a few of them here.

aki mo nao	Even autumn is yet
asaki wa yuki no	shallow: this evening
yūbe kana.	of snowfall.

To this you added,

mizu kōru e ni	Over the frozen water of the bay,
samuki karigane.	the cold cries of the wild geese.

This verse is somewhat overstated and contrived; it does not connect with the manifest intention and spirit of the hokku. It is desirable when composing the waki and subsequent verses to leave a few things unsaid. To exhaust the images of Water and Winter in this way would make it difficult for the poet of the third verse. It seems to be the common practice when composing verses on say, Autumn, to link up to the maeku by using words like "wild geese," "deer," "dew," and so on, even though the meaning does not actually connect. On the contrary, the verse that truly links up to the maeku from the depths of the poet's mind [*kokoro*] may discard such conventional associations [*engo*] and yet seem fully to connect.   (*Tokoro* III, pp. 214–15)

Shinkei's objection to Sōgi's waki is clear enough: it is "overstated" because it employs too many images of Winter (the redundant *kōru* and *samuki*) and of Water (*mizu, e*) when one for each would have been sufficient; indeed, it might have been better to drop Water altogether. In other words, it is too prodigal with images for a genre that naturally calls for restraint within the single verse in order to leave something over for the next poet. The major thrust of Shinkei's criticism, however, is that the waki does not really link up to the hokku except in a mechanical, "contrived" verbal way, through the Winter topic (i.e., *yuki, kōru, samuki*). Unaccountable as it may seen, Sōgi either missed the point of the hokku or caught it but failed to incorporate his understanding in the verse itself. To recreate the effect of the snowy sky slowly dimming at dusk, he would have had to point up the stillness all around, or the remoteness of the wild geese's cries behind the vague impenetrability of falling snow and darkening shadows.

The letter of 1470 is a valuable document that includes sharp analyses not only of Sōgi's recent work but also of the verses of older poets like Gusai and Sōzei, as well as concise statements of Shinkei's most important critical principles. Here, it is relevant to point out only that it reveals how closely Shinkei with his unrivaled artistic intelligence guided Sōgi's work in its formative stages. As noted earlier, the orthodox or "refined" renga style (*shōfū* or *ushin renga*) of the Muromachi period was mainly, aside from certain crucial differences, their creation. Along with the *Gikō eisō Shinkei no tensaku* from the capital (see Chapter 3), this letter is a compelling evidence that Shinkei also played a crucial role in the development of Sōgi's critical faculties, later to find their most impressive demonstration in his cogent analyses of the seven sages' verses in *Oi no susami* (1479).

The incalculable training that Sōgi derived from his association with Shinkei in the Kantō was clearly equaled by the pleasure and solace the latter felt in providing it. Although his criticism remains as rigorous as in the earlier manuscript, there is in addition a certain warmth in this letter ("carried away by your love for poetry") which indicates that their relationship had deepened amidst the privations of Shinkei's exile. "Since the world does not always conform to our desires, we cannot avoid associating with all sorts of people. However, when it comes to the practice of the various Ways, it is of utmost consequence to have good friends about us" (*SSG*, p. 142). One can imagine how valuable Sōgi's friendship was for the man who wrote those lines. Perhaps they met again after Kawagoe. Unfortunately those occasions could not have been so many. Shinkei left Shinagawa for the trip north to Aizu in the late spring of 1470 and did not return until the late fall or early winter. In the first seven months of the following year, 1471, Sōgi was mainly in Mishima risking life and limb for the *Kokin denju*, while Shinkei retired weary of heart to the foothills of Mount Ōyama. No doubt Sōgi visited him there before starting back for the capital late in 1472, but the *Kawagoe senku* remains today their last sequence together.

Fortunately for Shinkei the same session marked the beginning of a new poetic association with Kenzai. He evidently lost no time in instructing his new disciple. One of the extant *Sasamegoto* texts bears a colophon indicating that he gave a copy to Kenzai on 2.7.1470, barely a month after the grand event at Kawagoe.[19] Moreover, it is almost certain that his trip to Aizu was at his new student's invitation. Aizu in Iwashiro Province (Fukushima) was Kenzai's hometown; he belonged to the Inawashiro family, a cadet branch of the Ashina clan that had ruled the region since the Kamakura period.

We do not know precisely when Shinkei left Shinagawa for the trip north. Among the spring hokku for 1470 in *Azuma gekō* is one that alludes to an impending journey and was probably composed during a renga session to see him off; the reference to himself as a "warbler" recalls Jitchū's similar name for him in the session held in Settsu several years earlier.

543	uguisu mo	With the flowers,
	hana ni tabidatsu	the warbler too sets off to journey
	haruno kana	among spring fields.

It is first among the summer hokku, however, that it becomes clear that he is already on the road. We know for certain that 554 below was composed in Nikkō, because Sōgi later included it in *Chikurinshō* (1665) with the following preface: "On deutzia [*unohana*] flowers, composed when he was living in Azuma and went up to the temple called Nikkō-zan and held a session."

554	unohana ni	Deutzia blooms
	tōki takane ya	on distant towering peaks:
	kozo no yuki	last year's snow!

Nikkō is now a tourist spot famous chiefly for the Tōshōgū, the lavishly decorated shrine erected in the early seventeenth century for the Tokugawa shogunate's founder, Ieyasu. In the Muromachi period the mountains of Nikkō housed a complex of temples, some of them dating from Heian times. Then as now the clear blue waters of Chūzenji Lake to the west formed one of the area's appealing natural scenes.

556	umi kiyoki	Clear the lake,
	wakaba no yama no	glinting between the trees in
	konoma kana	the new-leaved mountain.

Shinkei composed eleven more hokku as he and his party continued north from Nikkō along the Tōzandō Highway. He does not mention the names of the places where they stayed, except for Aizu itself in 567, which is the last of the summer hokku and thus indicates that they did not arrive there till the end of the season. Like the two from Nikkō, these verses are mere impressions of natural scenery, but rendered with a tactile quality that has blithely resisted the weight of intervening centuries.

559	ame aoshi	Green the rain—
	satsuki no kumo no	June clouds clearing in patches
	muragashiwa	the oak-tree grove.
562	tabibito mo	Do they protect
	moru ya miyagi no	travelers too—enjoying the cool
	shitasuzumi	beneath shrine cedars.

565	tsuyu mo hinu	Still wet with dew,
	maki no ha suzushi	the cypress leaves are cool—
	asagumori	a clouded morning.
566	yūdachi wa	Evening shower:
	sugimura aoki	a cool green wake of cedars
	yamabe kana.	the mountain meadow.
567	tsuyu aoshi	The dewdrops, green.
	sara ni tezome no	and even deeper dyed beyond:
	aizuyama	Mount Aizu in indigo.

Finally arriving in Aizu, Shinkei stayed throughout most of the fall and was evidently kept busy holding renga sessions with local enthusiasts, for there are no fewer than twenty hokku in all for the autumn of 1470 in *Azuma gekō*. The first of these evokes a picture of the poet resting in his lodgings after the arduous journey.

568	niikusa no	From my pillow of new-
	makura ni akanu	reaped grass, endlessly inviting:
	hanano kana	fields in fall flower.

Shortly thereafter, as suggested by the context of the two hokku below, he held renga sessions with the Ashina, the ruling daimyō clan of the Mutsu region whose castle was located in the present city of Wakamatsu, Aizu District.

569	ame mo shire	Let the rain too yield
	itsuka o chigiru	the promise of a rich harvest
	aki no kaze	in the winds of autumn!
571	sasamizu ya	Trickling of water:
	niwa o miyama no	in the garden autumn sounds
	aki no koe	the deep of mountains.

Like the *yo ni suzushi* hokku for Ashikaga Masatomo, no. 569 is marked by a formal decorum and auspicious context (the region's bountiful harvest) that reveal it to have been composed at a session with some high personage, in this case either Ashina Morinori or Moritaka (d. 1517), the leaders of the clan. It alludes to the proverb *itsuka no kaze, tōka no ame* ("one windy day in five, one rainy day in ten") about the ideal weather conditions for a good harvest. Number 571, almost certainly composed in the Ashina Castle as well, praises its garden park by saying that its murmuring stream evokes the feel of autumn deep in the mountains.

The young Kenzai, whose family the Inawashiro had a castle by the lake that bears their name, acted as Shinkei's guide in Aizu and was doubtless a participant in all the local sessions. For him Shinkei's sojourn here proved to be a marvelous opportunity to imbibe the master's teachings at first hand. It was at his request, for instance, that Shinkei wrote commentaries to a selection of his own verses (90 hokku, 121 tsukeku) in the manuscript called *Guku Shibakusa*, as revealed by the following colophon.

In the early autumn of the second year of Bummei [1470] in Aizu, the Oshū region, I thoughtlessly wrote these comments at the repeated urging of Kyōshun-daitoku [Kenzai]; they are but of little value.

Traveler-Recluse Shinkei [seal][20]

The modest tone was a conventional feature of authors' colophons at this time, although perhaps more characteristic of Shinkei than of others. The informal character of this self-annotated verse collection is amply borne out by the term *guku* ("my humble verses") in the title; these are not verses Shinkei considered his best or most representative. In fact, the prefatory paragraph suggests that the selection was done by Kenzai, who chose verses he found difficult to understand. Consequently many are of the kind that alludes to older poems, passages in classical tales, and old lore. Obviously intended for a young eighteen-year-old novice, Shinkei's commentaries are simple and aim primarily to illuminate the allusions and the meaning of the verses, as distinct from his more rigorous critical approach in the letter to Sōgi. Since we are all novices like Kenzai in 1470, however, this text remains an invaluable guide to the kind of classical learning required of a renga poet, not to mention the way in which Shinkei intended his verses to be understood.

Iwahashi no ge, the companion volume to *Guku*, consists of Shinkei's commentaries to 179 of his waka, also written for Kenzai and bearing the same colophon plus a long epilogue setting forth his poetic principles.[21] This epilogue was evidently intended to cover both volumes, which are also known by the collective title *Shibakusa kunai Iwahashi*. Since Shinkei held that waka was an important part of a renga poet's training, these two works may be said to constitute a textbook for the beginner, one that he updated occasionally, for it includes a few selections composed subsequent to the autumn 1470 date in the colophon. One more manuscript, very short and undated, remains as an evidence of Kenzai's tutelage; this is the *Ichigon*, precise instructions about the three primary techniques of linking, based on inflectional morphemes (*te ni o ha*); words (*kotoba*)—the autonomous words of the maeku apart from their inflection; and meaning or poetic feeling (*kokoro*).[22] Of these, as might be expected from his whole critical approach, Shinkei sets the highest value on the third.

Great indeed must have been Shinkei's hopes for his new student, given the considerable volume of commentary that he personally wrote for him. Perhaps Kenzai reminded him of Shinkō, the young acolyte in Jūjūshin'in whom he had trained as a poet and whose untimely death was mourned by all the Shōtetsu circle. That was all of twenty years earlier during the halcyon days of Jūjūshin'in's prosperity, long before Shinkei became a "traveler-recluse" (*ryokyaku inshi*) in Azuma. Perhaps too he found pleasure in teaching someone who showed every promise of making renga his career, just like Sōgi and unlike the warrior-poets who formed his circle in Musashi. According to contemporary sources, Kenzai was a child prodigy who had been educated at the famous Ashikaga Academy, the training ground for the talented youth of the eastern provinces.[23] It is interesting to note that like Shinkei he came from a warrior family but chose the priesthood and literature as his profession. His coming under the poet's influence at such a tender age no doubt increased his motivation. It was probably instrumental in his early fame and success in a field requiring so many years of training that it was known as the literature of old men.

Eighteen years later, Kenzai would transmit the lessons learned during his youthful apprenticeship in a manuscript called *Shinkei-sōzu teikin* (Bishop Shinkei's teachings). Its colophon suggests that it was only then, after much intervening experience in the field, that he fully realized their true value.

These notes date from the days of my youth when priest Shinkei taught me the proper mental attitude in renga. Determined at the time not to forget these lessons, I wrote them down and kept the notes until I found them in a drawer recently. Though I took them for granted then, reading them again carefully now I realize how rare and valuable every one of these lessons is. In the Way of renga, I humbly look up to the words of this priest as to the teachings of the Buddha.[24]

Kenzai was thirty-six when he wrote these lines in 1488, just a year away from his appointment as Kitano Renga Master. Young as he was in 1470, he most probably took his old teacher's indulgent attitude toward himself for granted. He was also at this time fortunate to make the acquaintance of Sōgi, who would later help him in the capital and with whom he would collaborate in the compilation of the *Shinsen Tsukubashū*. There is a remarkable coincidence in the fact that the earliest extant record of his renga attendance in Kyoto was at the Kitano Shrine *senku* sponsored by Shinkei's former patron, Hatakeyama Masanaga, at New Year's in 1476.[25] This coincidence, coupled with the fact that he was most active in Hosokawa-sponsored sessions thereafter cannot but suggest the workings of Shinkei's influence in his subsequent career.

Back in Aizu in 1470, teacher and student started back for Musashi in the late autumn. Along the way they stopped at the Shirakawa Barrier marking the boundary between the northern region and the Kantō. The entrance to what was then considered the most remote area of Japan as viewed from the capital, this place was a famous *utamakura*, particularly in connection with a poem by a Heian traveler, the poet-priest Nōin (b. 988), about leaving the capital in the spring haze and reaching this barrier with the autumn wind.[26] Saigyō passed through here in the course of his northern journeys in 1147 and 1186, and in 1468, as we have seen, Sōgi made the pilgrimage that would result in the poetic diary *Shirakawa kikō*. Finally in 1689, overwhelmed by the recollection of all the ancient poets who had gone there before him, Bashō would deplore his own inability to produce a memorable verse in *Oku no hosomichi* (Narrow road to the deep north).[27]

The four hokku composed by Shinkei at the Shirakawa Barrier are not particularly memorable either. Although he does duly register his awareness of Nōin's poem in 584 (see below), he seems to have tossed them off at the mere inspiration of the moment instead of attempting to express his own deep communion with past poets.

582	tsuki shiroshi	White the moon, and
	kawa mo na ni teru	the river illumined as its name
	hikari kana	in streams of light.

Fresh and arresting, this verse clearly revolves around an inspired play of images on the name Shirakawa (lit., "white river"). Evincing that sharpness of wit evident in some of his waka written in the capital, Shinkei goes even further in another Shirakawa hokku, which is pure haikai in its delight in punning.

585	seki mo seki	Barred is the Barrier,
	kozue mo aki no	and autumn's end is on the bare
	kozue kana	branches' end.

Behind the genial wordplay is the image of the Shirakawa Barrier gate stopped up or crammed (*seki*) with the mounds of autumn leaves fallen from the trees. Although it is inconceivable that this is the sort of verse Shinkei had in mind when he wrote in *Sasamegoto* that "double meaning is the life of poetry" (*SSG*, p. 135), it does illustrate his other statement in the same context, namely, that "it is an unskillful practitioner who cannot even compose a punning verse." The impromptu character of renga, it need scarcely be said, demanded a certain facility in the use of the double entendre. Such an understanding is implicit in the contemporary *Chikurin-shō* commentary that says of precisely this hokku by Shinkei that "anyone who can appreciate it will become a skilled renga poet in no time at all."[28]

According to its preface in the *Chikurinshō* (1748), Shinkei composed this hokku "at the castle of the Lay Monk Master of the Palace Repairs Office when he visited the Shirakawa Barrier." The reference is to Yūki Naotomo, the lord of Shirakawa Castle, whom Sōgi himself had visited two years earlier.

The immediately following verse, 584, also appears in the *Chikurinshō* (1749) with the preface, "Composed on his departure from the same place, when people held a session to see him off."

584	akikaze ni	If I start out with
	kaeraba hana no	the autumn winds, Miyako
	miyako kana	in spring flowers.

Conceived as a parallel to Nōin's poem, the hokku voices a mere forlorn hope, since Shinkei never in fact returned to the capital. But the memory of this trip would remain with Kenzai, and he would recall it thirty-one years later when, putting all his subsequent successes in the capital behind him, he returned once more to Aizu to live out his final years.

More than thirty years have passed since I accompanied Bishop Shinkei to see the Shirakawa Barrier. Now as I cross it once more in the first year of Bunki [1501] many thoughts stir in my mind.

kore mo mata	Is this not also
inochi narazu ya	to have borne the weight of
misotose o	a lifetime—
hedatete koyuru	as I cross the mountain barrier
seki no nakayama	bridging thirty years between.[29]

Alluding to the moving poem composed by Saigyō when he came northeast once more at sixty-nine after an interval of thirty-nine years, Kenzai communes with the spirit of his teacher, Shinkei, the poet who had been untimely torn from the capital city to be buried in obscurity in distant Azuma. In this single poem, the spirits of master, disciple, and a still earlier master confronting the passage of time and life merge together through the continuity of an enduring poetic tradition connected with places.

CHAPTER 6

"Bone-Withered Trees"

1471: A Murderous Spring

In 1471, following Shinkei's return from the Aizu journey, civil war erupted anew in the Kantō between the forces of Ashikaga Shigeuji and the loyalist army. The same year marks the final turning point in the poet's life. From his imperiled cottage by Shinagawa Bay in the summer, he would set out for the interior of Sagami Province, seeking a last temporary shelter against the chill rains of war that had dogged his life since the crisis of 1462–63.

Oddly enough, the spring hokku in the *Azuma gekō* evince a tranquillity and even an optimism that contrast sharply with the violence of Shigeuji's attack on Izu late in the Third Month and the despairing poems that Shinkei himself would write in the summer. The hokku that opens the year is quite ironic when viewed in the light of subsequent events.

> 599   nodokeshi na   Over the harbors to and fro,
>   kokonoe yatsu no   tranquil blow the ninefold winds
>   kunitsukaze   across the eight lands!

The winds blowing free and tranquil across "the eight lands" (*yatsu no kuni*) symbolize the pacific amity among the eight provinces of the East, the so-called *Kantō hasshū*: Sagami, Musashi, Awa, Kazusa, Shimōsa, Hitachi, Kōzuke, and Shimotsuke. The auspicious public character of the hokku indicates that it was composed at a session with one of the Kantō's political leaders. This would be Ōta Dōshin, since the same image of calm winds over the Azuma seas recurs in an unusual *chōka* that Shinkei sent, according to its preface, "to the Zen follower Ōta Dōshin as a greeting on the seventh morning" of the New Year, 1471.[1] Composed of thirty-nine lines plus a waka envoi, the poem is strongly reminiscent of the vanished age of Akahito and Hitomaro in its adoption of the persona of a loyal subject addressing his liege in verse. The similarity ends there, however; the language of this *chōka* is far too thin and pale compared to the surging vitality of the *Man'yōshū* poets. Nonetheless, this unique example of Shinkei's work in an antique genre is important because in it he expresses his gratitude to Dōshin for giving him, "a fisherman from the land of Shikishima" (i.e., a poet), a lodging in the midst of his exile. In other words, it must have been Dōshin who arranged for Shinkei's Shinagawa cottage through his vassal Suzuki Nagatoshi. Similarly he would have had a hand in the poet's move this summer to an old temple in Sagami that was, significantly, located near the Kazuya estate and stronghold of the Ōgigayatsu Uesugi.

It was at Dōshin's request that Shinkei wrote the *Shiyōshō* in the Third Month of this year, the only one of his treatises to deal concretely with *shikimoku*, the rules governing the occurrence of similar themes and images in the hundred-verse sequence, and with the procedures involved in holding a renga session.[2] He had already enunciated his theoretical position on this subject in *Sasamegoto*. In his view poetry, as the flower of the mind-heart, cannot be circumscribed by language, much less the predetermined rules governing the procedure of the sequence.

It is said that the way of exercising the rules must depend upon the particular session. These rules represent discriminations made for the sake of convenience upon a base of non-discrimination [*mukaikyū no ue no kaikyū*]; they are in that sense like the prohibitions and precepts in Buddhism. But prohibitions and arguments about doctrine do not yet represent the direct route [*jikiro*] to enlightenment. In the sutras one encounters innumerable instances of license; the reason is that the correct way lies in the ground of the mind itself [*shinji o shōro to suru yue nari*]. Consequently in the work of poets who have attained to the True Way [*makoto no michi*], there are many things that are outside the bounds of rules and standards. (*SSG*, pp. 179–80)

Lest he be misunderstood to be advocating an untrammeled license, Shinkei goes on to qualify this basic principle by saying that rules represent time-proven determinations, a prescriptive guide for attaining goals. One should therefore not be lax in observing them. In other words, rules, as a means (*hōben*) to an end, are essential to the art; they should not, however, be taken so literally as to defeat their purpose and become an end in themselves or, worse, a measure of the quality of the verse and the sequence as a whole. In the *Shiyōshō* he cites a number of concrete instances where a literal application of rules would be undesirable.

With regard to "world" [*yo*], there are practitioners who disapprove of using it [again in the same sequence] without changing from "world" as such to a named world or vice versa.[3] Is this not somewhat foolish? It should be alright to use the same word two or three times if the meanings are different. . . .

The rule that "flower" should occur three times is also taken erroneously in recent times. When in the same sheet, flowers remaining into summer, or the heart's flower, flowers of the waves, cherry [flowers] and so on occur, shouldn't one just let it pass and not count it as one instance of [the three] flowers? To determine three times as absolute is absurd.

About dimorphs with a frequency of two—eaves [noki/nokiba], parting [wakare/wakareji], hut [io/iori], rock [iwa/iwao], etc.—there are those who reject the verse if it does not use the other form of the word; is that not lacking in grace? In this case too one should give way and accept the verse as long as it does not resemble the other. Such instances are too many to count.

There are people who take "mountain path" [yamaji], "boat" [fune], and so on exclusively to mean Travel, but that should depend on the meaning and words of the verse. In waka even when such words are assigned as a topic one does not therefore invariably compose a Travel poem. . . . It all depends on the conception or feeling of the verse itself [ku no kokoro ni yoru beku ya]. But those practitioners who have not thought deeply and closely about this art will not agree.

Love or Laments—there are many verses that span across both, so that it is impossible to distinguish one from the other. Among Love poems too there are those that are wholly in the mode of Laments. So during the session it can happen that in linking up to the maeku the verse will span both [topics], and one must accept it. The heart of Laments [jukkai no kokoro] resides in all the myriad things.   (Shiyō-shō, pp. 54–55)

And so on; the intention behind the words is clear; Shinkei is advocating a reasonable and flexible interpretation of the rules, one that will take account of specific circumstances and not subordinate poetic expression to the dictatorship of the letter. It is a liberal attitude opposed to a mindless adherence to rules.

Rules represent the very possibility of the whole hundred-verse sequence itself as an integral form and as a collective activity. Shinkei's liberalism indirectly raises the critical issue of the generic tension, possibly a latent contradiction, in renga between the parameters of linking and sequence, between the singular and the collectivity. In Shinkei's view, renga is the *expressive* interweaving of several *different* voices, not the monolithic structure of a faceless collectivity subsumed under a linguistic institution. Elsewhere, he had written apropos the common awe for the underachieving heirs of prestigious poetic schools or houses that it is not the house that makes the man but the man that makes the house. Rules are an enabling mechanism; they establish the field and procedures of play, but it is men who play and the way they do it reveals themselves and constitutes the unique expressiveness of renga's poetry.

The two extremes—utter conformity or license—are a sweet path. Shinkei's nuanced attitude of adhering to the spirit of the rule without being bound by its letter was not a popular one, nor was it meant for beginners, as he implies himself in *Sasamegoto* when he warns amateurs against dispensing with training and directly imitating initiates. Similarly here in *Shiyōsho* he requires that the *shuhitsu*, the "referee" whose task—apart from recording the verses—is to ensure the smooth progression of the session, be a man of long experience in the art and of wide understanding of men and the world. This is because his function is to interpret the rules in actual practice, to decide whether or not the verse is acceptable.

Coming not long after his sponsorship of the *Kawagoe senku* of 1470 and all the other sessions that Shinkei must have led for him in Musashi, Dōshin's questions, which led Shinkei to write an untypical treatise (he protests that as a Buddhist recluse he had not felt it proper to make public pronouncements on the issue of rules) confirm this retired samurai general's serious interest in poetry. It is noteworthy that after Shinkei's death, he would welcome the Gozan Zen priest Banri Shūkyū from the capital and hold waka and Chinese poetry meetings, which Shūkyū would enthusiastically report in his *Baika mujinzō*.[4] With his interest in cultivating Zen and poetry, Dōshin was probably for Shinkei in Musashi what Katsumoto's late uncle, Dōken, had been in those prewar years in the capital, a kind friend and patron. Certainly the poet's hokku in this fateful spring have a calm and warmth that recall his verses in the *Kawagoe senku* and that only a feeling of security, or a growing familiarity with life in the Kantō, could have generated. These two are particularly noteworthy.

602	yo ni wa hito	Man's being in the world:
	hana ni wa ume no	the radiant glow of plum blossoms
	nioi kana	among all flowers.
607	yo wa kaze mo	The world and the wind
	ugokanu hana no	in pale splendor stilled
	sakari kana	flowers at the full.

In the Third Month of 1471, shortly after these hokku were written, the winds turned stormy "across the eight lands" as Shigeuji's forces rode forth from Koga to Masatomo's stronghold in Izu. The move apparently caught the loyalist camp unprepared. As the following passage from the *Kamakura ōzōshi* reveals, Masatomo would have been overwhelmed but for timely reinforcements from the Uesugi.

In the Third Month of the third year of Bummei [1471], the forces allied with Shigeuji in Musashi, Shimōsa, and Kazusa fought their way over the Hakone mountains and headed for Mishima in Izu in order to attack Masatomo. Since Masatomo's force was small, he requested reinforcements from Suruga, and with these men he put up a defensive battle at Mishima. But Masatomo's army was unable to get the advantage. They were about to go down in defeat when the Uesugi

Deputy, the Yano Lay Monk of Aki, arrived and joined forces with him. With fresh troops they charged forth into the enemy's ranks. In the ensuing encounter, the leading column of Shigeuji's army, soldiers of the Oyama and Yūki, were vanquished, and the rest fled over the mountains in defeat.[5]

Situated between Koga and Izu, Musashi would have been in an uproar as Shigeuji's forces rode forth to battle and back. The tension both in the Edo and Kawagoe strongholds would have been great as the loyalist camp began preparations for a retaliatory attack on Koga. The siege of Koga Castle, under Nagao Kagenobu, senior general of the Yamanouchi Uesugi, began in the Fifth Month and involved a protracted battle that ended only with the fall of the castle on the twenty-fourth of the Sixth Month. Shigeuji managed to escape, however, and hostilities continued into the following decades, complicated by shifting loyalties among the Nagao and internal strife between the two branches of the Uesugi. The Ashikaga shogunate would never again regain its central authority over the Kantō region; Masatomo remained stuck in Izu, unable to take up the reins of government at Kamakura, and the rebellious Shigeuji was in effect the very last of the Kantō Kubō.

In Shinkei's *Azuma gekō*, the blank space where the summer hokku should have been is eloquent testimony to the confusion of those months when not a single renga session was held. But the poet could not remain silent about these terrible events. They are reflected in the hundred-poem sequence that he composed from the seventh to the ninth day of the Fifth Month, 1471—right in the thick of that bloody summer. Written to commemorate the important thirteenth death anniversary of the single greatest poetic influence in his life, Shōtetsu, it is also the last of his extant waka sequences.[6]

The world that was rapt in the pale splendor of cherry blossoms in hokku 607 and where the sensitive human being was the most radiant creature (602) is utterly transformed in the following poem from the sequence's spring section. It is clearly the same spring, but shadowed now by the violence of intervening events.

10 Spring

ima no yo wa	In these times,
hana mo tsurugi no	even the flowers are thickets
ueki nite	of upturned blades,
hito no kokoro o	and man's heart is impaled to
korosu haru kana.	death in a murderous spring.[7]

The poem's impact lies in the implicit superimposition of human perversity upon the natural order in the image of a gracious spring turned murderous through the distorted passions of men. The emphasis, significantly, is not on physical death as such but on the numbing horror of war, which maims and kills human feeling (*hito no kokoro*). That would be the greatest murder in the eyes of a poet for whom bodily extinction was preferable to the death of the spirit, precisely the source of that radiance which had earlier moved him to write that man was the earth's best flower. *Kokoro* being the source of poetry as well, the poet finds that the violence of the times hinders him from communing with the moon, that symbol of moral clarity in the vocabulary both of literature and Buddhism.

35 Autumn

urameshi na	It is too bitter.
yo wa kurayami no	When I amidst the darkness of
sora no tsuki	the world would sing
nagamu to sureba	of the shining moon in the sky,
mune ni sawagite	a shudder runs through my breast.

No doubt because the sequence is dedicated to Shōtetsu, it includes a number of poems lamenting the death of poetry along with society's decline.

71 Lament

hito o nomi	The poetry of an age
ima wa miru yo no	inhabited solely by men!
koto no ha yo	Say it is mediocre—
tsutanaku tote mo	where is the god before whom
tare ni hajimashi	it need bow in shame?

The word "god" in the translation is suggested in the original by the contrastive juxtaposition between *hito* (men) in line 1 and *tare* (who) in line 5, whose antecedent is clearly "the divine incarnations and poet immortals" (*gonja no kasen*), Shinkei's term for the great *Shinkokinshū* poets and Shōtetsu in *Oi no kurigoto* (p. 415). We will recall that he also extolled the latter as a reincarnation of the god of Sumiyoshi in a letter quoted in Chapter 2. Immediately following this poem is another revealing that he despaired of any possible renaissance of the art even in the future.

72 Lament

koto no ha wa	Since this very age
ima zo mihateshi	has seen the last of the
yo no sue mo	leaves of poetry,
hikobae made mo	shall even future sprouts be
ne o tsukusu kana	stillborn on the blasted trunk?

The immediate proximity of this poem to the preceding and the fact that the whole sequence was a memorial for Shōtetsu again render it highly probable that he was very much on Shinkei's mind here. It is best understood in the light of the following passage near the end of *Sasamegoto*, Part I: "But now that Shōtetsu's influence, which shone like a light from the promontory of a great rock, has been snuffed out, the Way, alas, lies shrouded in darkness once more. Henceforth, though a gifted man may appear in the world, what light can he receive, whose guidance seek, in order to illumine the future generations?" (*SSG*, p. 164).

The true significance of the two poems above is likewise clarified by a set of external factors that would have had a particular exigency for Shinkei. They are related to the fact that the compilation of a new imperial waka anthology, ordered by the Retired Emperor Go-Hanazono with the Shōgun Yoshimasa's encouragement in 1465, had been aborted due to the outbreak of the Ōnin War. The excitement generated in the capital by the announcement of a new anthology to succeed the *Shinzoku kokinshū* of 1439 was considerable. Poetry meetings were held with increasing frequency from 1465, and Asukai Masachika (Masayo's son), the chief compiler, had immediately begun soliciting individual poetry collections for possible inclusion. As stated earlier, Shōtetsu was greatly disappointed by his exclusion from the *Shinzoku kokinshū*. This time around, with the autocratic Yoshinori out of the picture, there was a strong possibility that his poems and Shinkei's would not be overlooked. Tragically, however, all the manuscript contributions were lost in the war fires that destroyed Masachika's residence, then functioning as the Wakadokoro, on 6.11.1467, and the anthology never saw the light of day. There is no doubt that this event was in Shinkei's mind when he wrote the memorial sequence to Shōtetsu, particularly when he states in poem 72 that the age "has seen the last of the leaves of poetry." The final opportunity to include the greatest poet of his time in the official literary history of the age, as a beacon "to illumine the future generations," had been irrevocably lost, and the *Shinzoku kokinshū* was to remain the last of the imperial waka anthologies, an undistinguished end to six centuries of a prodigious poetic tradition. The war dimmed the prospects of renga as well. The *Shingyokushū* (New gems collection), the grand renga anthology which Ichijō Kanera had been in the process of compiling in 1450, was likewise scattered and lost in the fires and looting that destroyed large areas of the capital city.[8]

There is an interesting epilogue to these unfortunate events. In 1489, more than a decade after Shinkei's death, Sōgi discussed plans for a new imperial waka anthology with the influential poet and aristocrat Sanjōnishi Sanetaka (1455–1537); the two went so far as to secure the consent of Asukai Masachika as compiler and editor. For some obscure reasons, this project too was aborted; in its place Sōgi and Kenzai succeeded in bringing out the first quasi-imperial renga anthology after more than a century, the

Shinsen Tsukubashū of 1495. Thus subsequent history confirmed Shinkei's despair about waka's future. Shōtetsu was indeed its last greatest practitioner, and after him, we may add, Shinkei himself. But for the insurmountable accidents of birth and circumstance, both might have revitalized a flagging poetic tradition. As for renga, Shinkei had done his best to elevate it to the status of a serious art not only through his own verses and critical essays but also through his influence on Sōgi and Kenzai. He clearly nourished hopes of a future time when renga would come into its full poetic flower in consonance with the ideals expounded in *Sasamegoto* and elsewhere. The following passage from the Epilogue to *Iwahashi* is quite revealing: "Should the world recover and flourish once more, and a sage of the Way [of renga] appear in the distant future, then the age of the True Way [*makoto no michi*], which surpasses even the ancient period [of Gusai and Yoshimoto], will surely come to pass" (p. 312). The same sentiment is echoed in *Oi no kurigoto* from the autumn of 1471: "Since the Way of waka has been abandoned in recent times, we must at least devote ourselves to the serious study and clarification of this Way [of renga] and in thus preserving a part of waka's teachings and precepts, endeavor to soften the hearts of warriors and rude folk and teach the way of human sensibility [*nasake*] for all the distant ages" (*Oi*, p. 417).

Shinkei's pessimism about poetry's future in the two poems quoted earlier reflects his consciousness of being caught between two ages—one in which waka was dead and renga still to come into its own; the events of a particular war-torn summer doubtless also contributed to his despair. Nevertheless, these passages from *Iwahashi* and *Oi no kurigoto* reveal that his mind had a wider compass and could transcend the darkness of his own time. His vision of renga's aesthetic and, it must be emphasized, worldly efflorescence, was unquestionably accomplished by Sōgi. However, one must look further, to Bashō and his concept of *fūga no makoto* ("the truth of Poetry"), for that deep-going religious search for authenticity that is at the heart of Shinkei's concept of renga as the True Way.

"To soften the hearts of warriors and rude folk and teach the way of human sensibility for all the distant ages" is clearly an ambitious enterprise. Needless to say, the first clause echoes Tsurayuki's *Kokinshū* Preface, with the distinction that what occurs there within a statement of poetry's irresistible power to move the heart-mind is here actively advocated as part of its historic mission. The difference underlines the stark contrast between the character of the Heian and the medieval periods; there can be no doubt that for Shinkei, who lived in an age dominated by military power and war, the necessity for "softening the hearts of warriors" had an urgency it would not have had for Tsurayuki. Indeed, the whole humanistic character of his poetic philosophy, in particular his elevation of the aesthetic into a moral value in his concept of *kokoro no en*, can be viewed quite simply as an imperative response to the times in which he lived. Against its terrible excesses, the greed for power, the senseless destruction and slaughter of human beings—before this numbed and callous surface—he raised the frail structure of feeling or compassion (*nasake*), the capacity to be moved, as a moral imperative in order to recall men from barbarism and into a consciousness of their human state.

Shinkei's most characteristic persona, as a poet of lament (*jukkai*), may also be viewed as an inevitable manifestation of the age. We may well wonder what other authentic response there could have been, what function more relevant for serious poetry in such an age, apart from bearing witness to its sorrow and tragedy. And yet Shinkei's response, inevitable though it might seem to us, was in fact the exception. While the mode of laments has ancient roots in Japanese poetry, it has seldom been enunciated as an implicit moral criticism of a specific historical time and event, so heavy was the weight of the classical lyrical tradition that dictated the vocabulary and themes considered refined enough for use in poetic composition. Shinkei's refusal to be restricted by poetic conventions from making the real circumstances of his times the subject of his poems is noteworthy. To a tradition remarkable as much for the narrowness of its scope as for its extreme subtlety and, occasionally, even profundity, he brought a breadth of perspective and a moral concern that had long been lacking. Other examples from the 1471 memorial sequence illustrate these unique qualities.

22 Summer

aware tote	Take pity, and even
shibashi wa yuruse	for a while, let them be!
tami wa mina	For all the people
kore o inochi ni	life depends upon this season
sanae toru koro	of planting the rice seedlings.

A heartfelt plea that the armed warriors leave the peasants alone to pursue their labor in peace, this poem was doubtless compelled by battle scenes that Shinkei encountered in the countryside this summer. "The season for planting the rice seedlings" (*sanae toru koro*) was in the Fifth Month, right in the midst of the loyalist army's siege of Koga Castle. The real havoc wreaked by the war upon the normal agricultural cycle and the consequent sufferings of the common people (*tami*), who had to feed not only themselves but also the very soldiers disrupting their work, are a set of materials rarely seen in Japanese poetry. Figuring also in the poem below, "the people" had heretofore been considered beneath "poetic" concern.

64 Travel

ajikina ya	It is depressing!
na takaki hito ni	Though you showed the mighty
kuni tami no	the people's sufferings
nageki o miseba	amidst the war-torn land,
yo o ya osamen	would they lay down their arms?

The tone of helpless anger surely springs from bitter experience. Unavoidably involved with the Katsumoto-Masanaga alliance in the capital, and now with the Ōta and Uesugi in Musashi, Shinkei would doubtless have exerted the moral authority of his priestly rank as Bishop to remonstrate with the mighty against the ravages inflicted upon the common people by war. We have seen how he endeavored to secure his own means of livelihood against the internal conflicts within the Hatakeyama clan, only to lose it once more in the greater disorders of the Ōnin War. He was in a sense just as much as the common people a victim of the power struggle among the great lords, since his very survival ultimately depended on their good will and patronage.

The two poems below might be interpreted as a denunciation of the warrior class, but it is probably more accurate to say that Shinkei's censure was directed not at the class itself but at their acts of violence, which have here driven the poet of moon and flowers to almost virulent anger.

83 Evanescence

itsu made no	Do they fancy themselves
yo o hen tote ka	immune to time, these warriors
mononofu no	who send others
hito o ushinai	to their deaths, while driving to
mi o kudakuran	such extremes their own bodies?

84 Evanescence

tsurugi mote	The man who wields
hito o kiru mi no	the sword, slaughtering people,
hate ya tada	shall surely end
shide no yamaji no	as so many chunks of timber
somagi naramashi	cast along Death-Mountain Trail![9]

Contrasting with indignation at the senseless slaughter is profound sorrow and sympathy for the same warriors as Shinkei traces their progress from murderous demons on the battlefield to evanescent smoke back in their hometowns. The two poems below are in effect elegies for the war dead of Azuma that summer.

85 Evanescence

<table>
<tr><td>nobe ni mishi</td><td>Awakening from the</td></tr>
<tr><td>aware mo samete</td><td>horrible sight on the fields,</td></tr>
<tr><td>kuni sato no</td><td>only sadness lingers:</td></tr>
<tr><td>keburi to naru o</td><td>the news of funeral smoke</td></tr>
<tr><td>kiku zo kanashiki</td><td>over village and province.</td></tr>
</table>

65 Travel

<table>
<tr><td>narenureba</td><td>Inured to sorrow,</td></tr>
<tr><td>mata mi ni fukaki</td><td>the heart wells yet again—</td></tr>
<tr><td>nageki kana</td><td>the remains of men</td></tr>
<tr><td>azumaji no tsui no</td><td>who went on their final journey</td></tr>
<tr><td>hito no nagori mo</td><td>along the Azuma Road.</td></tr>
</table>

The theme of exile that was so central in the waka sequences of 1467 and 1468 recurs here, but with less emotional urgency. The following poem suggests the reason for this impression.

26 Autumn

<table>
<tr><td>aki kakete</td><td>By autumn</td></tr>
<tr><td>miyako wa ogi no</td><td>the burning capital had fallen</td></tr>
<tr><td>yakebara ni</td><td>to charred reed fields:</td></tr>
<tr><td>narinishi yado wa</td><td>in my once familiar home now</td></tr>
<tr><td>kaze mo oto seji</td><td>the wind utters not a sound.</td></tr>
</table>

Here it is clear that Shinkei's temple, his home from boyhood until the age of sixty-one, for which he had fought so desperately during the 1462–63 crisis, had been destroyed in the fires of war. Shinkei was in fact the very last head priest of Jūjūshin'in.[10] Dating from the very beginnings of the Ashikaga shogunate in the fourteenth century and dedicated to its preservation, the temple had perforce to share its fate. By 1471 the war began to show signs of subsiding in the capital, as worried daimyō hurried back to their provincial territories to deal with rebellions fomented by their subordinates. But for Shinkei the way back would have been foreclosed by Jūjūshin'in's destruction. Perhaps the prospect of permanent exile generated the sweeping protest in the following poem.

66 Travel

<table>
<tr><td>ukegataki</td><td>What reason was there</td></tr>
<tr><td>yo ni umarete mo</td><td>to have been born into the</td></tr>
<tr><td>nani naran</td><td>hard-earned world</td></tr>
<tr><td>miyako no hoka no</td><td>of men, if I am to become</td></tr>
<tr><td>hito ni nariseba</td><td>to Miyako an utter stranger?</td></tr>
</table>

Confronting the uselessness of a longing without practical hope of fulfillment, the poet finds that he has become inured to exile and homelessness, but then wonders ironically if sorrow driven inward can seem any lesser.

67 Travel

ima wa tada	Left no choice
omoisutsuru o	but to abjure all my longing,
tabi narete	in travel grown
nageki mo usuku	familiar, seems my sorrow
nareru to ya min	to have waned as well?

The last poem in the series formed by poems 65 to 69 revolves around the bitter irony that however long the five years in the Kantō (actually four at this point but it is his fifth summer) seemed, they are in retrospect but a brief interval.

69 Travel

nagekashi na	It breaks my heart.
iku hodo naran	How long has the time been!
itsutose mo	Yet five years are
hitoyo no yume o	but a single night's dream
tabi no yukusue	at the end of the journey.

The dissolution of moral and social order, the concomitant withering of the "leaves of poetry," the destruction of Jūjūshin'in Temple, the death of warriors, of Shōtetsu—all these ultimately resolve themselves into the large theme of evanescence that forms the ground bass of Shinkei's final poem sequence. It surfaces in poems like these.

5 Spring

naki ato o	In his desolate wake,
yowa no harusame	deep in the night the spring rain
tsubutsubu to	drop by halting drop
kataru shinobu no	speaks of a sorrow as it trickles
noki no tamamizu	along my moss-fern eaves.

6 Spring

asajifu ya	In the ruined garden
namida tsuyukeki	moist with the dew of tears
ato toeba	I seek his traces—
munashiki hana ni	among the frail flowers
yūkaze zo fuku	the evening wind is blowing.

46 Winter

okorite wa	A leaping flame
hodo naki yowa no	ere long sinking beneath
uzumibi ni	a mound of ashes
sakaenuru yo no	in the deep of night—
hito o miru kana	man's glory in the world.

44 Winter

mishi wa mina	I saw all, sadly,
aware awayuki	as soft snow from fields dissolve,
kieshi no no	leaving only in
yūkage kusa no	the twilight shadow of the grass
tsuyu o katami ni	gleaming dewdrops in the memory.

Amidst the terrible carnage of the age, Shinkei, ever the priest and poet, holds high the shining altar of the moon.

36 Autumn

tsuki ni aku	Why turns my soul
kokoro no nado ka	yet unsicklied to the moon
nakaruran	eyes that have seen
mina ukikoto wa	all the utmost limits of
mihatenuru yo ni	vileness in this world?

47 Winter

hito no yo wa	In the world of men,
kōri o fumeru	beyond the trampled ice of
katafuchi ni	the river's shallows,
nodokeku sumeru	unsullied shines the moon
tsuki no kage kana	in tranquil pools of light.

Dimming Before the Moon:
Reclusion at Mount Ōyama, 1471–1475

"Yet five years are / but a single night's dream / at the end of the journey": Shinkei's farewell to his life in Shinagawa, Musashi, strongly suggests he intended his move to the foothills of Mount Ōyama to be his final one. Although the war was ending in the capital, it had just started in the provinces, and peace remained an elusive dream. Jūjūshin'in was lost, and at sixty-five he was too weary to go back and petition the requisite powers to have it rebuilt. The *Azuma gekō* hokku collection, our principal source for his renga activities in the Kantō, peters out in the autumn of 1472. *Oi no kurigoto* from the autumn of 1471 is in effect his final critical statement, and in 1473 he would make a final selection of his most representative renga verses. Thus his four years at Mount Ōyama (1471–75) were apparently intended as a period of retirement, a gradual renunciation of worldly ties and concerns as a spiritual preparation for death.

Mount Ōyama is located on the southeastern edge of the Tanzawa mountain range stretching across the central region of Sagami Province (Kanagawa). Also known as Afuriyama, it was then and still is a sacred mountain, believed from ancient times to be the abode of the god who brings rain. An object of religious pilgrimage for wandering ascetics as early as the Kamakura period, it gradually developed as the center of mountain worship and the Shugendō sect in the Kantō region. By the Edo period, the so-called Ōyama Pilgrimage (*Ōyama mairi*) to Afuri Shrine on its peak and the Daisanji Temple just below had become popular among the religious from Edo and the surrounding provinces, particularly during the mountain's festival days from 6.28 to 7.17 in the summer.

Shinkei's abode was on the southeastern foothill, at a place called Ishikura. Whatever his reactions were to the battles that had forced him from his cottage by the thriving harbor of Shinagawa, the deep natural seclusion of Mount Ōyama accorded perfectly with that eremetic lifestyle that had long been for him an object of longing. Such is manifest in his long rhapsodic description of his new surroundings in *Oi no kurigoto*, following the opening passage quoted earlier in Chapter 4. He evidently came to the mountain as to a place of refuge, putting behind him the worldly sorrow and the tragedy in whose service he had long dedicated his poetry.

Up to five years did I pass, suspended as it were within a dream in a temporary lodging. Then to make matters worse, from around the Third Month of this year [1471], battles became more frequent even in Azuma. The din of bows and rattling quivers filled the air as the enemies punished each other until the whole place turned into a living hell, a virtual mountain of blades and forest of swords. Feeling more than ever as if my body would break beneath the anxieties of exile, I yearned for some refuge far beyond the reach of the world's miseries, a crevice between the rocks, a mossy cranny where I could heal my spirit for a while. At last, after some searching I found in the interior of Sagami Province, at a place called Ishikura in the foothills of Mount Ōyama, a temple covered deep with many years' moss.

"In such a place indeed—" I thought, approaching with hesitant steps, and oh, what I beheld was of such wonder that words failed me; it was a realm beyond heaven and earth, such as would surely enchant even the saints and sages who truly love the mountains and find joy in the waters. To the west, solitary peaks towered steeply against the sky, slender pines and cedars stood in long rows along their slopes and hid the slanting sun. A blue cliff some three hundred meters high followed a jagged course down to where I stood, its overhanging ledges overspread with natural mossy beds. All around, the bamboos grew clear green, and from the vague outlines of their foliage at dusk came the quiet murmur of birds. I could almost believe that I had wandered into the gardens of Tzu-yu and Le-t'ien, or the immortal realms into which Wang Chih or Fei Chang-fang had been transported.[11] It was verily a place to soothe the sorrows of old age, heal travel-weariness. Aged with moss was the temple's main hall; its altar platform was sagging, and its cypress-bark roof torn; along the eaves, only ferns and pine seedlings grew to their heart's content. When the wind blowing down from the mountain shook open the doors, the tinkling of the jeweled ornaments drifted through the blinds, and the faint echo of the bell from the distant peak cut clear into one's soul. Nothing at all detracted from the moving quality of the scene.

Near the southern face of the mountain, a branch shrine to the gods of Kumano had been built within the ancient shade of beech and oak trees. In the stillness over the slender mossy path, a godly presence seemed to hover. Outside the gate, cypresses, cedars, and flowering trees stood in rows on both sides, stretching far into the distance. A long river wended its way down, its waters leaping and falling in clear springs laving the moss and washing the shifting pebbles to a gleaming smoothness.[12] Across this stream an old bridge tilted precariously to one side, its steps crooked as wild geese in flight, and I fancied that the fabled bridge over Tiger Ravine in China must have been just so.

Gazing east, one sees bright meadow fields spreading out into the distance where the blue hills rise. All kinds of autumn flowers bloom upon those meadows; glistening with dew at morning, at evening astir with the plaints of insects, they are a sight to break one's heart. To the north a great peak bores through the azure heaven.[13] Smoky clouds and mist would sometimes froth upward to graze the sky, and in the ensuing darkness of falling rain, one feels as if a black dragon had coiled itself around the earth. By those distant foothills, one can see a straw hut in the middle of rice fields, humble eaves huddled together in lone villages; here an old man would be plowing the fields, and there a boy picking the nuts fallen from the trees. The woodcutter sings a rustic ditty as he pulls his oxcart down the hill, and the notes of a grass-reaper's flute as he wends home with his horse echo cold and faint in the distance.

At sunset as I stood lingering on the old bridge, the moon's reflection suddenly appeared on the river, and in the silver waves of its light I felt washed clean of all the dust of the world. Far into the night in the vine-covered cell cave, the sound of the mountain wind shaking the pines tore apart the dream of a myriad forms.[14] Truly the aspects of the scenery move one to feelings too deep for thought, as though one were listening to the night rain of Hsiao-hsiang and Lu-shan, or marveling at the moon over Tung-t'ing Lake.[15]

And so day followed night in rapt contemplation. In the meanwhile, the head priest of the temple began to converse with me about poetry. Not satisfied with studying the flower of the Buddhist Dharma and sitting in Zen meditation before the moon, he is also searching for gems along the shores of Waka Sea with a devotion by no means shallow. After discussing Buddhism by the blue lamplight beneath a crescent moon, he would proceed to record my comments, worthless though they are as the soil from the salt-seaweed or the withered needles of the pine. He questions me with such minuteness it is discomfiting. And so, while wondering at the karma that has brought me here, and unable to refuse him, I respond to his inquiries with references to the Ten Styles and other things of which I know none too well and understand even less. I have no doubt that not one of my words strikes anywhere near the truth of the matter. Nonetheless, apart from the ears of a passing bird or deer, there are none to take offense at such conversations in a moss-grown abode deep in the valley. We are merely unburdening our thoughts as a means of passing a lonely and quiet existence. (Oi, pp. 410–12)

With this essay, Shinkei finally joins the literary-aesthetic and, more important, the philosophical tradition of Taoist and Buddhist recluses living in isolated mountain groves apart from the worldly and profane, pursuing a life of inner freedom and oneness with nature. Here we have left the Confucian realm of poetry as a witness to the moral life of the state, the concept undergirding Shinkei's work in the laments mode. The realm of reclusion inscribed in this essay places it in the history of the *zuihitsu* genre between the *Hōjōki* and Bashō's *Genjūan no ki* (1690).[16] It is one represented in Shinkei's waka by the selections translated in Part Two, "One Hundred Poems," of this book. Some will say that it is in those poems that Shinkei's spirit found its home ground, and they would not be wrong. But these poems are best appreciated against the knowledge of the tensions animating the life. The point is that reclusion defines a mental space held in taut opposition to the pressures of the external world. It is a realm where man knows and confronts his solitude precisely because he has experienced the otherness of the mundane. Reclusion has no meaning apart from this existential tension.

Shinkei clearly felt an affinity with Kamo no Chōmei and his appealing description of his hermitage in the *Hōjōki*, a text whose presence we have already noted in *Hitorigoto*. But the liberal Chinese allusions mark Shinkei's work as a product of its age and indicate that he was as much influenced by the literati ideal depicted in continental poetry, painting, and anecdotal literature. The scenery of the foothills of Mount Ōyama is depicted as the site of an unexpected homecoming after the hardships of war and exile. Here the disembodied spirits of ancient pure "saints and sages who truly love the mountains and find joy in the waters" waited as it were to welcome him into the shared vision of a paradise "beyond heaven and earth"; he feels as if he has "wandered into the gardens of Tzu-yu and Le-t'ien, or the immortal realms into which Wang Chih and Fei Chang-fang had been transported." In the *Meng Ch'iu* (J. *Mōgyū*), Tzu-yu (Wang Hui-chih, d. 388) is depicted as a man who found the duties of public office irksome and insisted on behaving with natural freedom and spontaneity. Once when he was temporarily staying at an abandoned house, he immediately had bamboo trees planted in the garden. Asked the reason for this eccentric behavior, he burst out in song, and pointing to the bamboos replied "How can I live even a day without this dear friend?"[17]

Le-t'ien (J. Rakuten) is the poetic appellation of the T'ang poet Po Chü-i (722–846); although the clear green bamboos in Shinkei's new abode almost certainly called up the reference to Tzu-yu, the source of the allusion to "Le-t'ien's garden" is not clear. However, it is highly probable that Shinkei had in mind the scenery around Po's cottage on Mount Lu (Lu-shan), the great Buddhist center in Chiu-chiang, Chiang-hsi Province. Po was banished to a minor post in Chiu-chiang from 815 to 819, during which his mountain cottage proved to be a great solace. In a letter to a lifelong friend, the poet Yüan Chen (779–831), in 817, he wrote:

This is the second reason for my peace of mind. In the autumn of last year I began making excursions into the Lu Shan and found a spot between the two Forest Monasteries [the Tung-lin and Hsi-lin Temples] just under the Incense-Burner Peak, where the clouds and waters, fountains and rocks were more lovely than at any other place in the mountain. The situation delighted me so much that I built myself a cottage there. There is a group of high pine trees in front of it and a fine cluster of tall bamboos. I have covered the walls with green creepers and made paved paths of white rock. A stream almost encircles it and I have a waterfall at my very eaves . . . everything that has always given me pleasure is to be found in this place. I forget all about going home and would be content to stay here till the end of my days.[18]

Pines, bamboos, and a clear stream around a mountain abode where Po would "be content to stay . . . till the end of my days"—the similarities between these and Shinkei's evocation of his final retreat at Ōyama are striking. Unlike some of the Gozan Zen monks of the period, Shinkei had never been to China. The superimposition of Lu-shan upon a Japanese topography is generated wholly by a sense of kinship—necessarily a self-ironic one—with the minds of the Chinese poets as he encountered them through their writings. It occurs twice more in the *Oi no kurigoto* passage when the crooked bridge over Ōyama River becomes associated with "the fabled bridge over Tiger Ravine" and the experience of hearing the sound of the mountain wind late at night in the eremetic cell, which "moved one to feelings too deep for thought," is compared to "listening to the night rain of . . . Lu-shan" in an allusive reference to Po Chü-i's famous poem.

Hu-hsi, the "Tiger Ravine," was located below the Tung-lin Temple on the slopes of Lu-shan and celebrated for the anecdote known as "the three laughters at Tiger Ravine." The famous monk Hui-yüan (334–416), who lived in the monastery and had never crossed the bridge over the ravine, was once visited by the poet T'ao Yüan-ming and the Taoist scholar Liu Hsiu-ching. On seeing them off, he inadvertently crossed the bridge, and a tiger roared below. Hearing this, the three friends realized that he had just broken his religious vow of never setting foot beyond the monastery and, looking at each other, broke out in peals of laughter. Recorded in the *Lu-shan chi* in 1072, the anecdote of the three laughters was especially popular with the Sung poet Su Tung-po (1026–1101) and his circle of littérateurs and artists.

In Japan the story became a favorite theme in painting and poetry during the Muromachi period, particularly among the Zen monks of the Gozan temples. Simply put, it was taken to signify the intrinsic unity among Buddhism, Confucianism, and Taoism; the spontaneous laughter of the three sages implied freedom from narrow intellectual and formal restraints, as well as the higher all-encompassing principle of non-discrimination.[19] In this sense, Shinkei's allusive reference to the bridge over Tiger Ravine merges with the images of the Buddhist moon and the wind that tears apart "the dream of a myriad forms" in the climactic paragraph that begins "At sunset as I stood lingering on the old bridge, the moon's reflection suddenly appeared on the river, and in the silver waves of its light I felt washed clean of all the dust of the world." Mediated by allusions to a whole literature of reclusion and mental liberation, Shinkei's poetic evocation of a spiritual homecoming traces an inner landscape wholly in contrast to the image of a raging conflagration that opened his account of the history of the age in *Hitorigoto.*

The rest of the essay is a succinct summary and refinement of the critical principles first set forth eight years earlier in *Sasamegoto,* which is as Shinkei intended it. "A long time ago, at the request of some renga amateurs I wrote the two-volume work *Sasamegoto* on just such matters as one should attend to regarding the Way. As this is but a rough summary of those incoherent generalities, strictly speaking it is nothing but tedious prattle" (*Oi,* p. 421). This postscript is the source of the title *Oi no kurigoto* ("Old man's prattle"). Despite Shinkei's tiresome humility, it is a most valuable work because it represents his distillation of the earlier treatise from the perspective of what he had thought and experienced since then. A relevant example is that the "ten virtues" (*jittoku*), which he had formerly held a renga poet should possess, including such factors as learning, calligraphic skill, and even social position, are here reduced to only three: *suki,* a compelling attraction for renga as an artistic pursuit; *dōshin,* dedication to renga as a Way, which is to say as a search for authentic being; and *kanjin,* tranquil solitude. They represent the three essential aspects of Shinkei's concept of renga: as art, as religious philosophy, and as lifestyle.

It need scarcely be said that his description of life in his Mount Ōyama retreat partakes of a certain poetic idealization, as any literary rendering would. In reality the area was not as isolated as we might imagine from *Oi no kurigoto.* As mentioned earlier, it was frequented by the wandering ascetics of the Shugendō sect; the presence of the sacred Kumano Shrine, which Shinkei locates "within the ancient shade of beech and oak trees" where "a godly presence seemed to hover," attests to this fact. This Kumano Shrine was a branch of the one in Kii, which was likewise a popular Shugenja retreat; as noted earlier, Shinkei led a senku there with Hosokawa Katsumoto and Dōken in the old days. Modern scholarship has established that the old moss-covered temple where he lived was the Jōgyōji, built in 1201 through the behest of Hōjō Masako (d. 1225), wife of the first shogun in Kamakura, Minamoto Yoritomo.[20] With such exalted antecedents, the temple would have been maintained and even restored for generations, although it is of course plausible that by 1471 it had, as Shinkei describes it, fallen into a dilapidated state. Rebuilt for the Ōbaku Zen sect in 1683, Jōgyōji existed until 1904, when its main image was transferred to a temple in Odawara.

Barely a kilometer west of the Jōgyōji was the Kazuya-kan, the mansion and stronghold of Ōta Dōshin's overlords, the Ōgigayatsu branch of the Uesugi. It was occupied at the time by Uesugi Masazane (d. 1473) and his heir, Sadamasa (1442–93). The proximity of the temple to the Uesugi mansion confirms what has been suggested earlier, that Dōshin arranged for Shinkei's retirement there. Indeed, some of Shinkei's hokku from the Ōyama years were certainly composed during renga sessions held in the Kazuya Mansion.

In the *Azuma gekō*, the Ōyama period is represented by the last twenty-eight hokku, dating from autumn 1471 to autumn 1472. For a period covering five seasons, they are quite few compared to those of previous years, an indication of the scarcity of renga enthusiasts in the vicinity and further evidence that Shinkei was indeed in retirement. Many of these hokku are fascinating in that the landscape described in *Oi no kurigoto* can be seen refracted through the various seasons and rendered with an immediacy of poetic sensation only occasionally discernible beneath the somewhat ornate surface of the essay's sinified parallel-prose style.

619	kaze orosu	As winds sweep down
	yama matsu aoshi	the mountain, blue the pines—
	yuki no niwa	a snow-heaped garden.

From his first winter in Ōyama, hokku no. 619 is a chill and vivid contrast between the rows of blue pines on the mountain slope and the mounds of white snow deposited by the storm winds on the garden below. The contrastive juxtaposition, effected through a medial caesura, is as typical of Shinkei's procedure as the subtle time shift, in this case from the instant the wind sweeps down the snowflakes on the pine branches in the first two lines to the final still moment achieved with the arrival to line 3. The verse is a simultaneously dynamic and minimalist rendering of the cognitive experience of phenomena through a dialectic of motion and stillness.

621	hana mo mada	Flowers too still
	tōyama komoru	quietly secluded in far mountains:
	yukino kana	a snowy meadow.
622	ta ga sumeru	Behind its boundary
	sakai zo ochi no	what man is dwelling? Yonder
	murayanagi	clump of willows.

Composed in the spring of 1472, these two quietly reflective hokku have a quality of "overtones" (*yojō*) distinct from the wholly stark, objective style of 619. The method of juxtaposition, however, is the same; here it is based on a dialectic of presence and absence. What is present before the eye, the snow-covered fields of early spring in 621, is used to evoke what is absent, the flowers that are still to emerge from their winter seclusion in the mountains. Such as it is, the conception is paradoxical and original; are flowers present somewhere else before their actual appearance? Our knowledge that the poet himself is *also* secluded in the mountains (*hana mo*) lends an indefinable pathos to the verse; he himself is self-absent as it were. But it is the feel of spring's remoteness that is crucial. The remoteness is both temporal (*mada*, "still") and spatial (*tōyama*, "far mountains") yet somehow transcends both to evoke a meditation on the ineffable origin of phenomenal presence: within this space of reclusion (the philosophic associations of *komoru*), there is nothing but the blankness of a reflection on emptiness. The *yojō* quality of 622 is of a more personal kind; it evokes the merest suggestion of a curiosity about other people from the isolation of its author's mountain retreat; what is present, the boundary (*sakai*), evokes a fleeting longing for the warmth of ordinary mundane company and a detached sense of loneliness engendered by the soft swaying of the spring willows.

624	tōumi o midori ni yosuru natsuno kana	Distant sea undulating in a green tide— high fields of summer.
632	sumu hito o iro naru aki no ōyama kana	The men who dwell here lend a color to autumn deep in Ōyama.
633	kiri no ha ni yoru no ame kiku ashita kana	From leaves of paulownia, the sound of the night rain in the still morning.
634	asashio ni tsuki mo tōhiku urawa kana	With the tide of dawn, the moon receding far beyond the widening coast.

Hokku 624 is truly a panoramic view. From his elevated vantage point on Mount Ōyama, the poet looks out upon the vivid green fields of midsummer and the waters of distant Sagami Bay beyond; he then effects a magical connection between background and foreground through a flattening of perspective. The undulating waves of the sea beyond are seen to flow directly into and merge with the greenness of the waving grasses in the foreground.

The same long view appears in 634; the method is also objective, but it is less painterly than "architectonic," and the effect is more evocative: first, because of the arrestingly apt metaphor, "tide of dawn" (*asashio*), for the way the dawn light sweeps up like a tide over the darkness of the night sky, and second, because this same expression in the common sense of "ebb tide" is then made to resound with the action of the pale moon trailing far behind (*tsuki mo tōhiku*) sight, and with the ebbing waves that gradually open up the shoreline (*tōhiku/urawa*). A singular event, dawn, is analyzed into a network of interdependent moments, the appearance of one causing the disappearance of the other. As distinct from the glittering midday brightness of 624, the feeling of this one is dimly subdued, with a certain remote quality engendered by the moon that recedes ever farther from the poet into the realm beyond.

Obviously intended as a greeting to the members of the session, hokku 632 conjures a colorless autumn deep on Mount Ōyama, whose pines and cedars would have been a far cry from the red maple foliage commonly associated with the season. Here Shinkei graciously expresses his appreciation of the company, who make up through the "color" of their poetic sentiment for what is lacking in the austere natural scenery. A second, more "Shinkei-like" reading would take "color" to mean phenomenal form, and the deep, "colorless" mountain recesses as the symbol of the formless realm of noumena that is simultaneously the source of form. On this level, what is being praised is the minds of the men, recluses all, as various external manifestations of the one undifferentiated Buddha-mind.

Hokku 633 is, like 634, a profoundly moving verse, perhaps even more impressive in its masterly technique. Awakening at dawn, the poet listens to the occasional trickle of raindrops caught and left behind on the large leaves of the paulownia trees. It is difficult to pinpoint precisely the appeal of this verse; behind the fresh coolness of a morning after the rain, one senses the mind's ear listening to a soundless voice, the mysterious trace of a phenomenon that came and went unnoticed in the dark of night. It exemplifies the final phase of Shinkei's poetic style: an artlessly (artfully?) simple surface that conceals an ineffable depth (*yūgen*) of feeling or thought that is ultimately beyond the realm of both art *and* thought.

The year after *Azuma gekō* drew to a close, the priest and renga enthusiast Jun'a came to Ishikura from his native Shirakawa up north to visit the ailing Shinkei. Their association most probably dates from the poet's trip to Shirakawa Barrier in 1470. At Jun'a's request, Shinkei made a final selection of his renga verses, the so-called *Jirenga awase* of 3.28.1473.[21] Totaling 300 verses, this collection is arranged as a "personal renga contest": fifty rounds of hokku and 100 rounds of tsukeku. It includes verses composed in the capital and in the Kantō (the latest are from 1472) and undoubtedly reflects what Shinkei himself considered his most representative work. From it Sōgi would later choose 101 for inclusion in the *Chikurinshō* and 35 for the *Shinsen Tsukubashū*, fully one-third of Shinkei's verses in that anthology.

Sōgi himself was back in the capital in 1473, the year that saw the deaths within two months of each other of the chief contenders in the Ōnin War, Yamana Sōzen and Hosokawa Katsumoto. The latter was only forty-three; his influence on Shinkei's renga activities during those last years in the capital and, through his alliance with Hatakeyama Masanaga, on the fortunes of Jūjūshin'in, had been incalculable. In his own way, and to a far greater extent than his rival Sōzen, Katsumoto played a major role as a generous sponsor and enthusiastic amateur in the poetic milieu of the capital.

In the Kantō the death on 11.24.1473 of the Kazuya Mansion's lord, Uesugi Masazane, would have impinged on Shinkei's consciousness with more immediacy. Masazane perished in a battle with Shigeuji's forces at Ikago, Musashi, the same place where Sōgi had written his first treatise seven years earlier. It is almost certain that the *Hokke nijūhappon waka* (Waka on the twenty-eight chapters of the *Lotus Sutra*) sponsored by Ōta Dōkan in the Edo Castle the following spring, 1474, was held as a memorial to Masazane. Dōkan felt the occasion important enough to summon Shinkei, already ailing in 1473, from his Ishikura retreat in order to assign the topics for the poems. As recorded in the waka collection *Ungyoku wakashō*, the participants for this event included Tō no Tsuneyori and Kibe Yoshinori (b. 1434?), a Minatomo warrior from Kōzuke who was also a well-known poet in the Kantō and the capital.[22] A Reizei disciple, he had studied with Shōtetsu and was a good friend of Shinkei's; like Tsuneyori he was at this time encamped with the loyalist forces in Izu. It is possible that Tsuneyori's relationship with Shinkei was not the most cordial. The *Ungyoku wakashō* account of the event, quoted below, suggests that Tsuneyori disapproved of Shinkei's role in the meeting.

When Dōkan decided to have waka on the twenty-eight chapters [of the *Lotus Sutra*] composed at Edo Castle in Musashi, [Kibe] Yoshinori was in Izu, and so he asked Shinkei to assign the topics for the poems. Then Tsuneyori arrived and declared that when the Asukai family was asked to assign the topics during the time of the Lord of Fukōin [the Shōgun Yoshinori], they refused to read them out on the grounds that it was not proper practice. He said further that since the poems would be recited from the lower-ranking upward, the order of the sutra would be reversed, and that such a practice was unknown outside the Reizei family. And so they merely copied out the sutra, composed a few poems, and summoned Yoshinori.[23]

Tsuneyori's objection hinged on the fact that whereas the topics from the first chapter on were assigned in order of descending social rank, the recitation of the poems proceeded the other way, from lower to higher ranks; the order of the sutra would in effect be reversed. In other words, he was concerned about a matter of formal procedure and, more to the point, with the fact that the practice of reading out the poems on the twenty-eight chapters was "unknown outside the Reizei family," that is, not sanctioned by the Nijō-Asukai school to which he himself belonged. As we can see, he won his point, but for Shinkei with his liberal views on matters of rank, rules, and formal procedure, which he thought ultimately extraneous to poetry, such fractious objections were doubtless quite unpleasant, particularly because it would have brought home once again the reality of Nijō dominance in his time. It is, moreover, a strange irony that the same Tsuneyori who had recorded Shōtetsu's criticism of Shinkei's use of radical diction back in 1450 should now, twenty-four years later, be openly challenging his poetic authority in the Kantō.

The circumstances were rather better a few months later on 6.17.1474, when Shinkei acted as judge for a waka contest also held at Dōkan's Edo Castle, but without Tsuneyori. The *Bushū Edo utaawase* (Poetry contest at Edo, Musashi) is the earliest known record of a formal waka contest held in the provinces with local poets as participants.[24] In literary history, it is viewed as an important landmark that signifies waka's coming of age in the East, just as the *Kawagoe senku* had done for renga in 1470.[25] Since both events were held under the leadership of Shinkei, who had himself taught the participants throughout his years in the Kantō, they are the crowning evidence of his major role in the most representative literary development of the Muromachi period—the spread of poetry from the nobility in the capital to the warrior and priestly classes in the provinces. The participants in this contest were, apart from Dōkan and Shinkei, other members of the Ōta family, priests from the nearby temples, and Kibe Yoshinori. Perhaps because he was the judge and sole professional poet in the group, Shinkei gave his three poems the losing mark, an instance of social grace and delicacy so much more striking when we recall his strenuous critical attitude in judging poets of proven caliber, and in contrast to Tsuneyori's fractiousness on the earlier occasion.

Ōta Dōkan formally became a lay monk in 1474 following the death of Uesugi Masazane. As evidenced by his sponsorship of the two poetic events discussed above, like his father, Dōshin, he took a personal interest in the promotion of poetry in Musashi. Said to have been educated by the Zen monks in Kamakura, he was at this period studying waka with Shinkei and would subsequently hold other poetry meetings in his Seishōken Hermitage, as reported by Banri Shūkyū in his *Baika mujinzō*. He was, however, also reputed to be the most capable military general of his time, building the Edo stronghold in 1456 and winning successive victories for the Uesugi in their campaigns against Shigeuji.[26] Unfortunately the power and prestige that he thus garnered for the Ōgigayatsu Uesugi did not sit well with the rival Yamanouchi branch. Its head, Akisada (1454–1510), later instigated the slanders that in turn led Dōkan's overlord, Sadamasa (Masazane's successor), to have him assassinated on suspicion of treason in 1486. The murder took place while Dōkan was staying at the Kazuya Mansion, and he was buried at the Tōshōin, the temple that he had built himself as a chapel for Sadamasa in the Kazuya grounds. It still stands today. In its grounds are Dōkan's moss-grown gravestone and a memorial tablet to Shinkei.

The waka contest at Edo Castle marked Shinkei's final public appearance. On the sixteenth day of the Fourth Month in the early summer of the following year, 1475, his weary years of exile finally came to a close in the Ōyama foothills. He was sixty-nine. Virtually nothing is known of his last hours, nor is it known where he is buried. Unlike Bashō, he did not die surrounded by grieving, faithful disciples. No one has left for posterity the kind of moving account that Sōchō wrote about Sōgi's final moments in Hakone.[27] His achievement, which was at least equal to theirs, lacked popularity, and his life, overshadowed by circumstance, never reemerged into the enduring reincarnations of legend. It was thus a lonely, quiet death, perhaps as befits a man whose spirit represents, according to his first biographer, Araki Yoshio, the loftiest and most desolate peak upon the vast mountain ranges of Japanese poetry.[28]

Written in 1948, Araki's work is more properly speaking a sensitive and extensive appreciation of Shinkei's poetry and criticism rather than a biography per se. I have attempted to piece together the life from isolated external references discovered since then and the autobiographical evidence in Shinkei's own writings. The process of recovery continues. In the archives of the Yūtoku Inari Shrine in Kyūshū, four more hokku have come to light, all bearing the date Bummei 4 (1472) and from their content clearly composed in the winter. Since the *Azuma gekō* ends in autumn 1472, these four represent in effect Shinkei's final hokku, which he was never able to add to that collection.[29] They were, significantly, discovered together with a section of a renga anthology by Ōgo Norishige, one of the warrior participants in the winter 1468 hundred-verse sequence led by Shinkei and Sōgi. The starkly austere and withered (*karabitaru*) sensibility reflected in them recalls the feeling of the poet's final years, apart from confirming his own express opinion that "old age is indubitably the time when the verse that is truly one's own emerges" (*SSG*, p. 162).

koe yowashi	A feeble sound.
kuchiba ni kakaru	Decaying leaves beneath the blow
tama arare	of hailstones.

The crisp sound of hail beating upon the bamboo grass of Musashino is a common image in classical poetry; the difference in sound quality between that and the dull thud they make on sodden, decaying leaves here marks the exact nuance of feeling concealed in this hokku.

shimo no ha wa	Leaves of frost:
aki aokarishi	this branch alone shone green
katae kana	through the autumn.

This hokku cannot but recall Shinkei's numerous rhapsodies on green and gain pathos by comparison. Even on this branch that remained miraculously fresh and green throughout the fall, the winter frost has settled. It is a simple elegy on the sheer will to spiritual clarity finally overcome by mortality and time.

e ya kōru	The inlet about to
sasayaku hodo no	freeze? A rising inaudible murmur
mizu no koe	upon the water.

Like the first hokku, this one is an image concentrated upon the exact quality of a sound that evokes an ineffably remote feeling. More tense than the other (the force of *hodo*), it captures the last extreme moment in the movement toward death, or final silence, through the sound of water about to congeal into ice. *Sasayaku hodo* is paradoxical from a rational viewpoint; it has no counterpart in any sound that we know. Yet it is the brilliant pivot upon which the whole verse turns, and has the effect of magnifying the water's dying whisper so that it begins to reverberate in the mind. The image is similar to the "sound of the mountain" for the dying Shingo in the great novel by Kawabata, a modern author whose mind was still in touch with the Emptiness of medieval philosophy.

tōyama o	Distant peaks of an
sumie ni niwa no	inkwash landscape: in the garden
karegi kana	bone-withered trees.

The final hokku is a concrete representation of Shinkei's point of arrival. Clearly the work of an aged poet reading himself into the foreground (*niwa no karegi*) of a sere, wintry landscape, it is yet wholly objective in all its stark imperturbability. Here near the end all emotion and suffering cease before the clear-eyed contemplation of bare fact.

Perhaps Kenzai was with him to the end; it is certain at least that he was present during Shinkei's last renga session at Ōta Dōshin's Kawagoe Castle, most probably in the spring of 1474 when the poet was in Edo for the memorial for Uesugi Masazane. Kenzai informs us that the following daisan, which Shinkei composed on that occasion, marked "the culmination of his renga in the Kantō" (*Kantō nite renga shitome no ku nari*).[30]

haru no yo nokoru	In the remaining spring night,
shinonome no tsuki	the moon in the dawning sky.
kokoro sae	My very soul
honomeku hana no	a glow enkindled, I lie beneath
kage ni nete	the flowers' shadow.

Why Kenzai chose to designate this as Shinkei's last among all the others that he must have composed for this hundred-verse sequence is evident from its content. The verse is a moving figurative expression of his teacher's undimmed and boundless nostalgia for beauty, which is to say, poetry. We will recall that Shinkei saw *en* or beauty as the heart's flower, a spiritual radiance; here it is expressed as "a glow enkindled" (*honomeku . . . kage*) in the sensitive soul in response to phenomena. A delicate yet ardent glimmer of longing stirs in the poet's soul as he awakens in the shadow of flowers dimly emerging in the half-light of dawn. Evoking the ineffableness of the longing for beauty, this verse is indeed a fitting swan song for Shinkei as pure lyric poet—apart, that is, from his other image as moralist and critic, which is just as essential a part of his poetic achievement.

The flowers of poetic inspiration as imaged in this verse must have been very much in Kenzai's mind when he composed the following hokku by Shinkei's grave seven years after his death.

Composed in the spring of the fourteenth year of Bummei [1482] during a hundred-verse sequence held by the grave of the former Jūjūshin'in, Bishop Shinkei.

chirinishi mo	As for the flowers,
hana wa mata saku	scattered, they bloom once more:
kono yo kana	this our world.[31]

And perhaps some of the members of that last session in the spring of 1474 were also present at Shinkei's grave in another springtime. Five years later Kenzai again led a memorial session, this time for the important thirteenth-year anniversary.

From the hundred-verse sequence invoking the Buddha's name in memory
of Bishop Shinkei's thirteenth death anniversary on the twelfth day of the
Fourth Month, nineteenth year of Bummei [1487].

<table>
<tr><td>natsu no yo no</td><td>Along the trail of a</td></tr>
<tr><td>yumeji sugiyuku</td><td>summer night's dream, the fleeting</td></tr>
<tr><td>tsukihi kana</td><td>suns and moons . . .[32]</td></tr>
</table>

PART TWO

Gems of the Mind-Heart
A Shinkei Reader

Hokku and Tsukeku

This section consists of an annotated selection of hokku and tsukeku by Shinkei mainly from the official renga anthology of 1495, the *Shinsen Tsukubashū*. It generally excludes pieces, mostly hokku, already discussed in the preceding literary biography and devotes greater space to his tsukeku. Muromachi-period commentaries, including Shinkei's own, are translated here as a valuable source for the way the verses were read in their own time. The contemporaneous existence of exegetical and poetic practice in renga is one of its unique aspects and reflects upon the nature of the verse itself as both a reading (of the maeku) and a writing; in that sense it may be said to represent the elevation of hermeneutic practice to poetic art.

Now known as *kochū* or *kochūshaku*, these "old commentaries" were written by renga masters on their own work as well as on that of their famous predecessors. Their aim was practical; it was to instruct their disciples and other aspiring practitioners in the methods of verse composition based on a study of actual models. The ability to establish an effective connection with the maeku was, needless to say, the first requirement for a renga poet. Consequently these exegeses focus on explaining the nature of the link between two verses and only occasionally venture into the realm of aesthetic judgment. They constitute readings that are in effect answers to the implicit question—given such and such a maeku, how did the poet manage to deal with it? In the case of hokku, the primary concern was to clarify the verse's meaning, particularly the way it alludes to the season, place of composition, and specific occasion. This reflects the fact that the inscription of the session's actual context was a formal requirement in composing hokku.

Apart from Shinkei's own self-annotations (*jichū*), the line of commentarial activity on his verses naturally stem from the works of his two foremost students, Sōgi and Kenzai. This is true not only of Shinkei's work but that of the other seven sages as well, for they constituted the model texts for Sōgi's consolidation of the orthodox style. He compiled the *Chikurinshō*, the first anthology of the seven poets' verses, sometime in or before 1478.[1] The following year, 1479, he wrote *Oi no susami*, which gives excellent analyses of 54 selected tsukeku from the *Chikurinshō*, then cites (without individual commentary) 101 verse examples of the ideal style and 110 of a slightly less superior or refined style, all culling from the same anthology.[2] The *Chikurinshō no chū*, Sōgi's annotations on 55 hokku and 347 tsukeku, is undated but believed from internal evidence to be slightly earlier than *Oi no susami*. Sōgi wrote *Yuki no keburi*, on 26 hokku and 88 tsukeku, in 1482, apparently with the intention of giving the verses a more reflective and nuanced reading.[3] The *Chikurinshū kikigaki*, an undated text, is closely related textually to the *Chikurinshō no chū* and may be said to belong to the Sōgi line of transmission as well.

The Kenzai line of transmission is represented by *Chikubun* (Notes on the *Chikurinshō*), brief comments on 246 hokku and 1,192 tsukeku as recorded by a disciple, Kenten, from Kenzai's lectures in 1503 in Aizu.[4] There is also the *Keikandō*, Kenzai's commentaries on 60 tsukeku by the seven sages and Sōgi, classified according to three stages of poetic practice (beginning, middle, and advanced) based on Shinkei's explanations.[5] In addition to these sources, I include comments from other old critical texts when they have something to say on the verse in question. The *Guku Shibakusa*, Shinkei's self-annotations written for the young Kenzai in Aizu, is cited and described in the preceding section. Unless otherwise indicated, the text and numbering of the verses follow Ijichi Tetsuo's abridged, annotated edition of the *Shinsen Tsukubashū* in *Rengashū*. I also give the corresponding number in the complete edition of the *Shinsen Tsukubashū* (*STKBS*) by Yokoyama Shigeru and Kaneko Kinjirō. Selections from the *Chikurinshō* follow the text and numbering in the *SNKBT* edition, and those from Shinkei's own personal collections the *Shinkei sakuhinshū* (*SSS*) edition. My own discussion of the verses utilize the Muromachi annotations as a starting point for analyzing critical issues both in Shinkei's works and in renga in general; it aims to provide the discursive framework by which the specific poetry of the renga link may be appreciated in our own time.

Spring Hokku

205 *STKBS* 3604. "Among hokku on early spring."

yo wa haru to	When all the world turns
kasumeba omou	hazy with springtime, mind is
hana mo nashi	empty of flowers.

Yuki no keburi 3: When spring comes, one naturally longs for the flowers, yet absorbed in the atmosphere of that moment when all the world is hushed in tranquillity and the haze rises to float about everywhere, then one can say that "there is not one thought of flowers [*omou hana mo nashi*]."

Chikubun 1197: Shinkei had a [hidden] intention in this verse. While it is the usual thing to look forward to the flowers when spring comes, there is a satisfaction to be had before them. He is saying that this exceptionally nebulous landscape covered over with haze is not a whit inferior to flowers.

As implied in both the Sōgi and the Kenzai line of old commentaries, the effect of this hokku hinges upon the last clause, *omou / hana mo nashi* (lit., "there is not one thought of flowers"). The statement that the longing for flowers is wholly absent from the observer's thoughts heightens the impact of the haze-veiled scene, which is so tranquil and absorbing that all anticipation of the coming flowers is swept away before it.

The negation *mo nashi* in the last line occurs so frequently in Shinkei's poetic diction as to constitute a distinctive mannerism.[6] He uses it to underscore the impact of what is present by reference to the absence of something else commonly associated with it. An even better example is *Azuma gekō* 469:

musashino ya	Musashino Plain—
kaya ga samidare	dripping reeds in summer rain,
kaze *mo nashi*	motionless the air.

Here the statement of the wind's absence (*kaze mo nashi*) opens the mind wholly and solely to the wetness of the reed stalks and the sound of dripping until it begins to reverberate across the vast space of the plain. This hokku is more effective since all trace of ratiocination has been erased from it. The diction is terser, and the mind so concentrated on the object as to become one with it. One can sense that this is the ultimate point at which Shinkei arrived in his experiments with *mo nashi* within the context of his theory of poetic process in *Sasamegoto* as "deep thought" (*chinshi*) or "a discipline in the mind-ground" (*shinji shugyō*) that aims to destabilize the subject-object dualism.

Araki Yoshio, the first to observe Shinkei's striking use of *mo nashi*, and indeed the first to raise several other critical parameters for the study of his poetry, sees it as an expression of his philosophical aesthetics of the "chill and reduced" (*hieyase*): "Shinkei, who through the symbolism of desolate phenomena had probed the depths of the sense of the chill and icy, the cold and slender, now sought to evoke its utmost limits through the rhetoric of absolute negation [*zenteki hitei*]." After citing twenty-three examples of Shinkei's use of *mo nashi*, he concludes that the expression is a technique "for emphasizing something else on the other side of this absolute negation."[7] This is the same as saying that such verses represent an affirmation based on a negation. It is, I believe, unquestionable that in this Shinkei was influenced by the rhetorical procedures of Buddhist thought, particularly of the Zen kōan, which deliberately baffles logic and confounds reality and illusion in order to show up the relativity of such distinctions.

Some of Shinkei's *mo nashi* verses are in fact rather obscure at first reading.

Azuma gekō 545

asatori no	Morning birds
kasumi ni nakite	crying through clouds of haze,
hana *mo nashi*	there are no flowers.

Guku Shibakusa 17: In the nebulous morning the calls of the birds among the flowers sound tranquil. It means that there *are* flowers. (p. 8)

We have already marked Shinkei's predilection for paradox and the ironic tension created in poetry by the dialectical juxtaposition of terms; the tendency reaches an extreme point here where he expressly states the opposite of what he means. It is obvious why this hokku did not make it into either the *Chikurinshō* or the *Shinsen Tsukubashū*; it is more like a Zen kōan, an esoteric mantra, or a dharani incantation to quell the bifurcating logic of the mundane mind than a poem. And yet it is precisely this gap between presence and absence, this fissure between is and is-not, that is, according to Shinkei himself, the fertile source of the highest kind of poetry. And he did declare that the poem or verse "is the True Word [*darani*] of our country." The feeling of this hokku is similar to the one from the *Shinsen Tsukubashū*, but where the former employs explicit language and mundane reasoning to transmit its meaning, this one deliberately obscures it within a rhetoric of paradox, forcing the reader to shake the words until the truth falls out from the inside, like a seed from a withered acorn. There must, after all, be a compelling reason for saying "there are no flowers" and taking up a whole line in the wholly unprodigal form that is hokku.

206 *STKBS* 3609. "Among hokku on early spring."

chiru o miyo	Watch it scatter!
niwa wa tsuyukeki	the garden dewy-moist
haru no yuki	spring snow.

Chikubun 1208: It says, watch it scatter as snow in the sky.

Kenzai's extremely brief comment gets to the heart of the matter. *Tsuyukeki* is a zeugma modifying both the garden and the snowflakes; the whole point of the verse is to invite appreciation of the spring snow, which melts as soon as it hits the ground. The dynamics of the stages of cognition are interesting: the referent of the verb "scatter" is withheld until the last line, while a new thought—the wetness of the garden—intervenes.

We have seen this technique of suspended reference many times in Shinkei's waka; it fractures the unilinear continuity of the semantic structure in order to bring two thoughts together as a simultaneity rather than a seamless unity. This verse well illustrates the fact that the poetry of hokku, and of the renga link for that matter, consists of a feeling evoked through a cognitive mental process carefully manipulated by the poet. Poetry here is a matter of rendering a familiar sight radically unfamiliar so that it may be seen anew. Yet the point is not so much to render a completed image as such, but rather to initiate an activity of the mind, a mental process provoked by the poet's calculated breaking up of normal syntax through interruption and fragmentation. The image, in short, is not as important as the mental process itself. Shinkei was a poet who could compose "beautiful" verses when necessary, but beauty of an elegant refinement was to him but a futile thing when divorced from moral and existential knowledge, that is to say, from truth, and that is where he most shows himself a product of the medieval period. Poetry as a process of mental cognition, a figuration of the motion of the mind on its way to grasp the object or, more precisely, to show the mediatedness of the object, is not primarily concerned with beauty.

207 *STKBS* 3633. "When people went on a pilgrimage to the Great Shrine [of Ise] and presented as offering a thousand-verse renga sequence."

hi no mikage	Sacred light of the sun
hana ni nioeru	suffusing with a fragrant glow
ashita kana	the flowers this morning.

Azuma mondō: This hokku is reported to be from a thousand-verse sequence religious offering at the Great Ise Shrine. It strikes me as being a wholly perfect hokku. Since ancient times there must have been numerous hokku composed before this August Goddess, but among them all it is doubtful that any could compare with this one.[8]

Chikubun 3148: This hokku is based on the circumstance that the deity is the Sun Goddess. Kenzai said that it lacks a word that would bring out [the honorific prefix] *mi* in *mikage* [rendered as "sacred light"], and that according to Sōgi the author was not particularly attached to this verse.

Chikurinshū kikigaki 347: This is in the spirit of gazing upon the tranquil rays of the Great Goddess Amaterasu's light shining beneficently upon the flowers.

Kenzai's criticism indicates that he expected a greater emphasis on the sacred, beneficent aspect of the sun's light; such would have been the case if Shinkei had ended with *miyai kana* ("the shrine precincts") instead. However, that aspect is already implicit in the double meaning of *kage* as both "light" and "blessing, protection." In opting for *ashita kana* for the last line, Shinkei was emphasizing the softness of the morning light as well as the dewy fragrance of the flowers at that time of day; the attribution of such beauty to the Sun Goddess' beneficence is implicit in the honorific *mi* of *mikage* and the place of composition. It is interesting to note that although Shinkei himself reportedly did not think it special, Sōgi cites it as a model hokku precisely for embodying the essence of the circumstances surrounding its composition. The verse has a formality and grace entirely appropriate for the occasion and demonstrates Shinkei's own dictum in *Sasamegoto* that the style of the hokku cannot be predetermined but must vary according to the circumstances of the session itself.

208 *STKBS* 3656. "Among hokku on flowers."

hana wa tada	The headdress of flowers
kokoro no oi no	only the heart within adorns
kazashi kana	on a withered brow.

Chikubun 1241: The verse treats with irony the sentiment of its foundation poem, the one on the bush warbler sewing the flowers for a hat.[9] One might try hard to resemble the flowers, but there is no hiding [the decline of] one's physical appearance. Thus it says let the heart itself find solace—the intention being to soothe the spirit. This is a verse of which the author was proud, and it is indeed a remarkable one.

Kokoro no oi no / kazashi is an intriguingly unnatural yoking of words; one would have expected *oi no kokoro no / kazashi* ("headdress [i.e., adornment] of the aging heart"), yet that would have reduced the verse to a banal statement. As it is, the inverted syntax forces us to read *kazashi* twice to refer to the heart and to old age separately (*kokoro no kazashi* and *oi no kazashi*). The zeugma-like, compressed verbal construction functions to point up simultaneously the incongruity between flowers and an aged man and the soothing effect, nevertheless, of beautiful flowers upon the tired spirits of an old man. Such are the marvelous effects of a complex thought disciplined into the compressed syntax of hokku as Shinkei was evolving it in his experimentations. Kenzai's remark that "the author was proud" of this verse, taken with his previous observation that he "was not particularly attached" to the *hi no mikage* hokku, seems to confirm Shinkei's manifest liking for the challenge of the difficult. Kyorai, Basho's disciple, would later compose a hokku strikingly similar to this one in spirit, but with the irony modified by the humorous flavor of haikai.

hanamori ya	The flower warden—
shiroki kashira o	drawn to his charges joins
tsukiawase	his white-haired crown.

209 *STKBS* 3667. "Among hokku on flowers."

kinō mishi	The blossoms I saw
hana ka tori naku	yesterday? Murmur of birds
asagasumi	in the mists of dawn.

Azuma mondō: As distinct from the preceding [*hi no mikage* hokku], this one is marked by an inventive skill; its feeling is of a gentle refinement. This and the others may be called the best hokku of our time.   (p. 220)

Chikubun 1258: It says, do they sing among the blossoms invisible in the morning mist?

The "inventive skill" cited by Sōgi refers to the handling of a pair of images, birds and blossoms, that traditionally occur together in poetry and painting. Withholding the flowers from actual presence has the paradoxical effect of recalling their loveliness to memory, and the whole scene of early dawn and floating mists thereby acquires a gentle, evocative quality.

210 *STKBS* 3668. "Among hokku on flowers."

chiru hana ni	In dazzling cascade
asu wa uramimu	of petals now, 'tis no wind to
kaze mo nashi	resent on the morrow.

Guku Shibakusa 20: Resent it as one may, one ends up forgetting how terrible is the wind when the heart is enraptured by the flower petals scattering in glorious confusion. Even though by the following morning, when the flowers are all fallen, no doubt one will blame it for being cold and cruel.   (p. 8)

Chikubun 1259: [An allusion to] the poem, "in a hazy mist the flowers scatter." One gazes at them heedless of tomorrow's regret, so arresting is the present moment.

Here again, Shinkei's technique of bringing together two thoughts to act against each other in the mind is evident. Against present intoxication, he sets the sobering thought of tomorrow, when the wind, having scattered all the flowers, will be blowing again but with a keen sense of regret: this is what the puzzling *asu wa uramimu / kaze mo nashi* (" 'tis no wind to / resent on the morrow") implies. Again, one may blame the wind tomorrow, but the rapture was fully shared by the viewer, and so must the loneliness be as well. It is also possible to read *kaze mo nashi* as "there will be no wind"; in this case the image of a wind that is "invisible" without the whiteness of falling petals becomes paramount. The whole verse is informed by an irony that emerges only by reflecting on what the odd last line really means.

211 *STKBS* 3671. "From renga at Toganoo."

chiru hana no	Even the snow of
yuki sae samuki	falling petals is chill—
miyama kana	deep in the mountain.

Chikubun 1265: One should not suppose that there is real snow before one's eyes here.

According to its preface in the *Chikurinshō*, this hokku was composed "during a session sponsored by Hosokawa Katsumoto at Toganoo." Toganoo in the mountains north of the capital is the site of the Kōzanji, the temple founded by the famous priest and poet Myōe (1173–1232). The effect of this hokku may be described as a juxtaposition of *sabi* and *en*: to a mind disciplined in the renunciation of illusory feelings and passions, the image of pale, fallen petals nevertheless evokes a keen sensation of beauty in the very image of transience. The chill is an affect of renunciation; it opens a chink, quickly suppressed, in the otherwise placid surface of a Buddhist mind. The image of scattering petals is normally one of romantic ethereality; its occurrence with the ontological negation that founds the *sabi* aesthetic of existential loneliness is a primary characteristic of Shinkei's most profound poetry. The following hokku is similar.

Chikurinshō 1639. "From a flower-viewing session at the place called Daigo Jakuseidani."

chiru hana no	So quiet one can hear
oto kiku hodo no	the sound of petals falling—
miyama kana	deep mountains.

Chikurinshō no chū 367: This hokku is especially interesting because it was composed at Daigo Jakuseidani. It says that the deep mountain is so tranquil it feels as if one can hear the sound of falling petals; it is in the mode of giving a heart to flowers. Perhaps it was inspired by the [Chinese] poem that says "Listening to the silence as quietly flowers fall to earth. . . . "

Chikubun 1264: "Listening to the silence as quietly flowers fall to earth . . . ," so it is said, but here the silence is such that one can hear their sound.

Chikurinshū kikigaki 349: This is because it was in the Jakusei valley, in the remote interiors west. [As a poem says] "A fine rain moistens my robe in the vague light, I listen to the silence as quietly flowers fall to earth."

The place-name Daigo Jakuseidani means "valley of the profound tranquillity of the fifth stage," the realm of the wholly illumined mind in Buddhism. Thus, nearly all the texts emphasize how appropriate the hokku is to the place of composition. In Shinkei's lexicon, and no doubt generally at that time, *miyama* (deep mountain) is a sacred site of reclusion, that inner space of profound solitude and tranquillity that is the ideal goal of Buddhist meditation. All the commentaries assume that the hokku is an allusive variation on the line they quote from a Chinese poem, an indication of the currency of Chinese poetry, particularly Zen-inspired Sung poetry, at this time. There is no doubt that Shinkei was a great admirer of the Chinese poets; in his critical writings he encourages renga practitioners to read them particularly for their loftiness of spirit and the "chill and thin" quality of their words, evidence enough that his own valorization of the reduced and attenuated was influenced by his reading of the Sung poets, as was his partiality for the particular symbolism of the plum blossoms. It was the T'ang poet Tu Fu (712–70), however, whom he considered the greatest of Chinese poets; indeed his own persona as a poet of the elegiac mode and witness of the tragedy of his age was crystalized, consciously or unconsciously, I believe, by his sympathetic identification with this poet who lived through the An Lu-shan rebellion.[10]

212 *STKBS* 3673. "Among hokku on falling flowers."

hana ochite	The flowers gone,
ozasa tsuyukeki	bamboo grasses rank with dew—
yamaji kana	the mountain trail.

Guku Shibakusa 18: As long as the flowers remain, even the thick dew on the bamboo grasses quickly disappears in the ceaseless passage of people on the mountain trail. But when the flowers have all fallen and the human shadows gone, upon the grass only the dew remains as thick as before.   (p. 8)

Chikurinshō no chū 368: In the constant coming and going of people when the flowers were in bloom, no dew remained on the bamboo and other grasses beneath them. But now that the flowers have fallen and there are no more sightseers, the dew lies thick on the bamboo grass. In the *Shinkokinshū*:[11]

chiri chirazu	With no one to inquire
hito mo tazunenu	whether or not they scatter,
furusato no	in the old village now
tsuyukeki hana ni	the spring wind is blowing
harukaze zo fuku	on the dew-rank flowers.

Chikurinshū kikigaki 350: When the flowers are in bloom, crowds of people come and roam together, and there is no dew on the bamboo grass. [*SKKS* poem above quoted.]

Shinkei's explanation for the eighteen-year-old Kenzai is certainly thorough, and it is faithfully transmitted and augmented in the two Sōgi-line annotations that follow. Such instances as these give a concrete sense of the pedagogical thrust behind the proliferation of exegetical literature in the Muromachi period, one that saw the ever widening circulation of both classical and contemporary literary texts outside the old aristocracy. Renga is the art of weaving verses together; it is an intertextual poetry as such and also with reference to the whole waka tradition. The commentaries therefore made it a point to inform their audience what old poem or narrative the verse under consideration is alluding to. That the relationship does not have to be one of strict allusive variation is evident here; Sōgi quotes the *Shin-*

kokinshū poem only because its conception and feeling are generally similar to Shinkei's hokku, and perhaps to point out the use of the word *tsuyukeki* (dewy) in a different context. For us it is illuminating to mark in the hokku the extreme compression of renga diction and its necessarily greater degree of allusive ambiguity compared to waka rhetoric. This verse has the same classic simplicity and balance of elements exhibited by the *hi no mikage* hokku; its predominant feeling, however, belongs to the realm of *sabi*.

213 *STKBS* 3677. "Among hokku on spring."

hana ni minu	Unseen among flowers:
yūgure fukaki	the somber depth of evening
aoba kana	on leafy boughs.

Azuma mondō: In this hokku as well, the handling of words is of surpassing excellence, evoking a somber loneliness [*sabishiku*]. One senses here the essence of the author's intention.   (p. 220)

Chikubun 1270: When the flowers were at their height, [one felt that] the twilight was slow to come.

Sōgi's praise of Shinkei's poetic diction here would refer to the extremely elliptical phrase, *hana ni minu* (unseen among flowers), which sets off by contrast the next line, *yūgure fukaki* (evening deep). *Fukaki* in turn functions as a zeugma to modify also the "new green leaves" (*aoba*) in the last line, bringing out both their relative density and their deepening green, compared to the time when there were only white clouds of flowers on the boughs. Sōgi's remark on "the essence of the poet's intention" expresses his perception that the mood of somber loneliness (*sabi*) here constitutes the core of Shinkei's ideal poetic realm.

The *Chikubun* comment does not speak to the essence of the verse; nevertheless, it is useful in understanding the contrast being drawn between the season of the flowers' blossoming and the time thereafter, when the flowers are gone and the boughs coming into thick leaf. Earlier, the whiteness of the cherry blossoms reflected the remaining light so that it seemed that the day was longer and evening came later.

Summer Hokku

Chikurinshō 1660

ame mo mata	Raindrops also
koe naki kiri no	mutely silent, young leaves
wakaba kana	of paulownia.

Chikubun 1280: "Season of paulownia leaves falling in the autumn rain"—rain is of the essence [*hon'i*] of paulownia and such.[12]

This is wholly in the mode of objective scene presentation (*keikyoku no tai*), perhaps the freshest among Shinkei's many styles. Typically it is marked by acuity of perception and a minute concentration of effect. As Kaneko observes, the coming together of spring rain and young paulownia leaves in a circle of mute silence is extremely good.[13] There is at once a sensual feel for the softness of the young leaves, the way they are expanding quietly in the soundless rain, and a tactile sense of how the fine drizzle is absorbed into the broad surface of those leaves. The verse recalls Shinkei's love for clear waters and the color green, signifiers of a pure vitality in nature that lie at the opposite pole of his equally celebrated aesthetics of the chill and withered. The two pieces below are in the same vein. In the first in particular, the image is so precisely yet subtly delineated that one can place the time at midmorning, toward noon.

Azuma gekō 470

tsuyu yowami	Dewdrops wane
hi ni nayutake no	drooping languid in sunlight—
wakaba kana	young bamboo leaves.

Shibakusa kunai hokku 161

natsu fukami	Summer deepens,
kaze kiku hodo no	anon the wind audible
wakaba kana	young leaves.

Guku Shibakusa 34: In the spring season, among the soft leaves one does not hear the sound of the wind, strong though it may be, but when the summer is well under way and the leaves grown, the wind sounds with a faint stirring.   (p. 11)

214 *STKBS* 3699. "Among hokku on summer."

shigeru made	Till new growth is thick
aki no ha kuchinu	autumn leaves unmoldered
miyama kana	the mountain depths.

Chikubun 1283: This means that in the deep mountains the leaves of the past year remain unmoldered until the summer.

The utter simplicity and certitude of the diction of this verse is characteristic of Shinkei's Kantō years, when he gradually discarded the mannered cleverness of many of his poems from the Kyoto period. The earlier tendency toward ratiocinative wit is overcome by conviction of feeling, an authenticity of vision inspired by his new personal experiences as well as the fresh sights of the Kantō region. The profound contrast between the dense summer foliage and the red leaves on the earth, left unaltered from the past autumn—deep in the cold mountains, no one has trampled upon them— constitutes the imagistic node of feeling in this hokku. Between the surging vitality overhead and the silent gleam of fallen leaves below is a vast temporal space heavy with the reality of time, the difference it has wrought, the unspoken thought that those vital green leaves will also meet with autumn. At the same time the green leaves themselves point up the miraculous vital power in the fallen red leaves that have lain unaltered on the earth through winter and spring.

Chikurinshō 1687. "On the Fifth Month rains."

ame aoshi	Green the rain—
satsuki no kumo no	June clouds clearing in patches
muragashiwa	the oak tree grove.

Guku Shibakusa 42: This is the feel of the time when the long rains are finally beginning to clear. All it says is that the clouds are breaking up in patches. It is in the mode of scene presentation [*keikyoku no tai*], which is given over to the feel of a scene just as one sees it at the very moment.   (p. 13)

Azuma gekō 566

yūdachi wa	Evening shower:
sugimura aoki	a cool green wake of cedars
yamabe kana	the mountain meadow.

Guku Shibakusa 43: There are practitioners who think such a verse uninteresting, nothing more than an excuse to say the "evening shower" in the first line. Such a verse presents the fact of the evening shower from beginning to end. The evening shower passes, leaving a trail of greenness in its wake. The "mountain meadow" across which the rain is moving expresses the fact of the rain to the very end. Among Teika's poems is the following; from first to last it overflows with the feeling of spring.   (p. 13)

asa ake ni	In the early dawn,
yukikau fune no	even the look of boats slowly
keshiki made	coming and going
haru o ukaberu	evokes spring in the mind,
nami no ue kana	to float upon the waves.[14]

Shinkei's commentary to this hokku and the one preceding indicates his consciousness of developing a new style that is wholly trained on capturing the feel of an external scene and does not replicate the traditional ways of handling nature imagery in the poetic lexicon. It might be thought that this new method of grasping the object, "the thing itself" (*yūdachi no koto, ame no koto*), was dictated by the hokku requirement of alluding to the place of composition, but one has only to read other examples from the same period to understand that this was not necessarily the case. Thus it may be said that Shinkei showed the direction in which the hokku would later develop into an autonomous art form by Bashō's time. The commentaries reveal that the method is based on a Buddhist ontological approach, in that the object is grasped as its manifestation upon other phenomena. As Shinkei says, "the 'mountain meadow' across which the rain is moving expresses the fact of the rain to the very end." To grasp the rain, one does not focus on the rain as such; one registers its motion, its dynamic interaction with its environment, for it is in the interpenetrability of all phenomena that reality lies.

215 *STKBS* 3706. "Among hokku on the cuckoo."

hitokoe ni	In that single cry,
minu yama fukashi	the depths of unseen mountains
hototogisu	—cuckoo!

Guku Shibakusa 33: That single cry heard on a still day just as it was evoked the mind of a mountain recluse. The hokku was composed in Musashi Plain.   (p. 11)

Chikurinshō no chū 373: This is a verse composed in Musashi Plain. It means that at the very instant when all of a sudden he heard that single cry, his mind became one with the feel of the deep mountains.

Yuki no keburi 8: *Minu yama fukashi* [rendered "the depths of unseen mountains" above] implies that this session was held in a place where there were no mountains. Hearing that unexpected cry, he felt that his own body had become transported to the remote mountain depths.

Chikubun 1294: A hokku composed while in Musashi. It would be uninteresting [were it composed] in a mountainous place. Its feeling is quite profound.

The cry of the cuckoo, heard out in the open plain beneath the summer sun, opens up a deep, fathomless, and cool space symbolic of the mind of a recluse. Piercing through the silence of a hot summer day, the cry is, as it were, a voice from the far side of mundane existence.

Autumn Hokku

Azuma gekō 524

yama no ha ni	Over the mountain rim,
hatsushio wa koe	the first flood tide has crested—
aki no umi	the sea in autumn.

Guku Shibakusa 63: The "first flood tide" of the sea here expresses the fact that the mountain colors have been delayed and are late.   (p. 17)

The "first flood tide" (*hatsushio*) refers specifically to the midautumn flood tide on the fifteenth of the Eighth Month, night of the full moon. The verse presents a dynamic, architectonic handling of visual space that somehow recalls the famous woodblock print of Mount Fuji glimpsed in the trough of a huge, white-crested wave. Here, however, the cresting tide is deliberately employed to at once contrast with (the particle *wa* in line two), and summon through resemblance, the "flood tide" of autumn color that should be flowing over the mountain but is in fact absent.

217 *STKBS* 3751. "Among hokku on autumn."

yanagi chiri	Willow leaves whirl,
karigane samuki	and wild geese's cries strike
kawabe kana	chill the riverbank.

This is marked by a studied simplicity of diction, an elegant internal rhyme, and a measured syllabic cadence (3-2/4-3/3-2) suggesting a slow, stately dance. The chill sensation in the gusts of yellowed willow leaves, the bareness of the trees pointed up by the piercing cries of the wild geese, is indeed striking. What is evoked is the shift of seasons—the willows are going, while the arrival of the wild geese from the north heralds the coming autumn.

222 *STKBS* 3775

kiku ni kesa	Chrysanthemums at dawn—
kumoi no kari no	ah, for the faint calls of geese
koe mogana	in faraway clouds.

Guku Shibakusa 65: It is said that the beauty of autumn is most compelling when wild geese are calling and the chrysanthemums are in bloom.[15] Thus it [the verse] says, if only the wild geese would grace with their calls the chrysanthemums in the dim dawn. (p. 17)

Chikurinshō no chū 390: As the poems say, autumn is in the calls of the wild geese and the flowering grasses; since it is the most interesting period of autumn, this time when the chrysanthemums are in bloom, I would hear the first calls of the wild geese as well—so it says.

Chikubun 1362: The charm of autumn is said to be in the cries of the wild geese while the chrysanthemums are in bloom. Since this is so, I wish to feel the pleasure of hearing the wild geese too.

The aesthetics here is of the "cold and slender" (*samuku yasetaru*) kind: whiteness of chrysanthemum flowers in the dimness of dawn set off by the faint bird cries. Compared to the acute sensation of coldness in the immediately preceding hokku, this one has a more delicately refined beauty.

Chikurinshō 1771

asatsuyu zo	Ah, morning dew.
konoha ni nasanu	Not falling leaves, after all,
sayoshigure	the night rain.

Guku Shibakusa 60: During the night I couldn't distinguish whether it was rain or the leaves, but on waking, I went out and seeing the morning dew realized that it was the rain. (p. 17)

Chikubun 1375: What I thought was leaves in the night was actually the rain, I realized, by the dew.

Okami Masao, with Araki Yoshio one of the earliest students of Shinkei's distinctive poetry, characterizes it as marked by "the shadow of an invisible presence" (*minu omokage*); he refers to those verses, many of which we have seen, where something else is evoked from what is present—vision of flowers in the cries of birds or in the somber depth of evening on leafy boughs, mountain depths in the cuckoo's cry, the unheard sound of falling petals, and here falling leaves in the sound of the night rain. He views these—accurately, I believe, given the nature of Shinkei's theory of poetic method in *Sasamegoto*—as manifestations of a contemplative attitude toward nature and experience, an attitude of listening, of "clarifying the mind's ear," ultimately founded, especially in its chill and withered aspect, on the Zen spirit of emptiness (*kūkanteki na zen no seishin*).[16]

218 *STKBS* 3755

mazu idete	With the early
tsuki ni mataruru	risen moon, bewaited:
yūbe kana	evening dark.

Chikubun 1343 sees the hokku as an allusive variation upon the following poem by Reizei Tamesuke.

kurenu ma ni	Before the dark,
tsuki no sugata wa	the outline of the moon
arawarete	become apparent,
hikari bakari zo	none but the light is now
sora ni mataruru	in the sky bewaited!

It is a pleasure to see Shinkei's clever variation on the foundation poem. The net result is the same, but the outwardly different conceit of waiting for the dark, instead of the light, shows much wit. Indeed Shinkei's conception of waiting for the dark (to see the light of the moon) gives an even greater aesthetic satisfaction. And yet that very satisfaction is based on the allusion to the other poem; the intertextual affect is also the site of pleasure.

Chikurinshō 1733. "On the moon."

kumoru yo wa	Clouded nights
tsuki ni miyubeki	must manifest before the
kokoro kana	moon, the heart.

Guku Shibakusa 62: How one feels about the moon shows the depth or shallowness of one's sensibility; and it is precisely on clouded nights when it is a shame to be indifferent to the moon drifting through [the clouds in] the sky. (p. 17)

Chikubun 1345: It says that it is the very yearning for the moon on a rainy night that shows feeling.

In *Sasamegoto*, Shinkei quotes the *Tsurezuregusa* of Kenkō (ca. 1283–1352) thus: " 'Are we to gaze at the moon and flowers with the eye alone? To lie awake anxiously through the rainy night, and stand before the petal-strewn, drenched shadow of the trees, yearning after what has passed, this indeed. . . .' How profoundly compelling are these words of Priest Kenkō" (*SSG*, p. 178). It was in fact Shōtetsu, Shinkei's waka mentor, who first recognized the value of *zuihitsu* literature and declared the *Tsurezuregusa* and *Makura sōshi* to belong to the same genre.[17] There is no question that Kenkō's *mujō*-based aesthetics, the founding of beauty upon the very fact of phenomena's insubstantiality, struck a deep chord in Shinkei's own poetic sensibility and influenced as well the valorization of *yojō* (overtones), what is left unsaid, in his criticism. This hokku is rather novel in citing a passage from an old essay and in expressing an idea; one imagines the participants of the session must have recognized the allusion with pleasure.

219 *STKBS* 3768. "From a renga in Azuma where he had already spent several years."

tsuki ni koi	A yearning sharpened
tsuki ni wasururu	by the moon, dimming before
miyako kana	the moon: Miyako.

Appearing everywhere most nights of the year, the moon has ever been a symbol mediating between the gazer and the object of his nostalgia, be it the past, a person estranged from himself by time or space, or, as here, a place such as the capital (Miyako), which Shinkei was forced to leave on the eve of the Ōnin War. By its ubiquity the moon is a presence that makes palpable an absence. The same moon, however, is also a Buddhist symbol of empti-ness, its transparent light defining a mental space where nothing leaves a trace. In this sense, the moon represents the renunciation of memory, the nullity of trying to recapture what is ineluctably gone. To gaze at the moon in this way is to liberate oneself from the pain of remembrance; to keep faith with the moon is to find in it a solace for earthly suffering. Training the mind on the empty moonlight itself, the object of nostalgia gradually recedes from memory. Shinkei's hokku is unique in bringing together these dual, contradictory aspects of the symbolism of the moon; the awareness of the duality, moreover, produces a profound ironic tension in the feeling of this verse. Its ultimate meaning lies in the tragic awareness of the emptiness of even the deepest longing.

220 *STKBS* 3769

asashio wa	Ebb tide at dawn:
hisaki kaze fuki	birches tremulous in the wind
hamabe kana	along the widening shore.

Chikubun 1338: The reference is to "beach birches" [*hama hisaki*]; there is a pun on *hi* [in *hisaki*] to mean also that the tide "pulls back." The author thought highly of this verse.

The identity of the tree called *hisaki* is uncertain; modern commentaries and dictionaries identify it with *akamegashiwa* (red-bud oak) or *kisasage*. The tree is famous from the second of Akahito's two envois to the Yoshino chōka (*MYS* 923–25); I have followed the precedent set by previous English translations of Akahito by imaging it as the birch. Although *hisaki* appears as one of the entries in Ichijō Kanera's renga thesaurus *Renju gappekishū*, actual examples of its usage in linked verse are extremely rare.[18] This fact suggests that Shinkei had Akahito's poem in mind when he composed the hokku; in this connection, we should recall that he also alludes to Akahito's chōka on Mount Fuji in verse 2 of his 1467 solo sequence (see below, "Cuckoo"). Here the allusion to Akahito's *MYS* 925 is extremely subtle. Apart from the similar scenery, it is what Gomi Tomohide describes as "the beautifully delicate tremor buried deep beneath his [Akahito's] tranquil poetry" that relates the two poems otherwise so distant from each other in time.[19] In Shinkei's hokku, the poetic tremor is evoked by the faint quivering of the *hisaki* leaves as the cool wind sweeps through them in the fresh morning along the beach. In the *Chikurinshō*, the verse appears with the following preface, "At a lodging near the seashore, when he was down in Azuma"—evidence that it is a composition from Shinkei's Kantō years.

Shibakusa kunai hokku 267

hi ni mukau	Face to the sun,
kiri mo chiri furu	mists settle with the dust
ashita kana	to earth this morning.

Azuma gekō 613

hi ya niou	Effusion of sunlight?
madaki iro koki	how soon the colors have filled
yamabe kana	on the mountain meadow.

Azuma gekō 587

aki no hi no	Cleaving
hikari o wakuru	streams of autumn light—
miyagi kana	shrine cedars.

The sun has somehow not been a major image in traditional waka, and it is a pleasant surprise to discover it in Shinkei's hokku. In particular the sense of the sun's aura (*nioi*) as a vital, energizing force can be sensed in all three pieces above and is possibly indicative of the numinous significance of sunlight in Shintō religious sensibility. It is interesting to note that in Shinkei's waka, it is moonlight that is dominant, for obvious reasons perhaps, given its major place in the whole tradition. At any rate, if one may borrow a Taoist vocabulary, one can say that the sun, pure waters, the vitality of green, of color and light—all these images touched by the living, breathing energy of nature belong to the pole of *yang* in Shinkei's sensibility, whereas the moon and ice belong to the *yin* pole.

Shibakusa kunai hokku 272

yama fukashi	Mountain recesses—
kokoro ni otsuru	falling deep in the soul,
aki no mizu	autumn water.

Guku Shibakusa 51: In tranquil solitude in the mountains, the mind is washed clear in the chilling waters of autumn; thus it says that the inner heart and the water are one in the state of clarity. (p. 15)

Azuma gekō 434

hi o itamu	Worn in the long suns
hitoha wa otosu	a single leaf is falling
kaze mo nashi	in windless air.

Guku Shibakusa 45: It says *itamu ha* [worn, fatigued leaf] because this leaf, which has been deepening in color since the summer, is falling by itself, even before being blown by the wind. (p. 14)

Winter Hokku

Shibakusa kunai hokku 359

koto no ha ni	On my leaves of words,
samuki iro sou	may the winds draw forth
kaze mogana	a cold hue.

Guku Shibakusa 73: Since even the frost turns to ice in the tree-withering wind, it says: may it draw out and vanquish the warm aspects of my poetry. (p. 19)

This allegorical hokku confirms the symbolism of "cold" in Shinkei's poetic criticism and practice. "Cold" and all its associated semes in his critical terminology refer to a poetry ineluctably grounded on an apprehension of impermanence and emptiness and produced through a process of intense mental concentration. In terms of poetic rhetoric, it means a purified diction shorn of all ornament, all desire to impress or seduce through the play of language alone, no matter how brilliant or arresting. A "warm" (*atatakanaru*) diction is one where the words, used inauthentically, interpose themselves between the mind and its object, in contrast to the transparency of the other. "Cold" thus ultimately describes the quality of a poetry that is pure expression, beyond the dichotomy of subject and object.

Shibakusa kunai hokku 397

> yuki usushi
> okabe no take no
> yūzukuhi

> Thin snow:
> through hill-slope bamboos
> the sundown.

Shibakusa kunai hokku 409

> teru hi yoki
> yama no nioi wa
> fuyu mo nashi

> Mountains effulgent
> in sparkling rays of the sun—
> here is no winter.

Shibakusa kunai hokku 361

> sasa kashike
> hashi ni shimo furu
> yamaji kana.

> Bamboo grass shriveled,
> and a bridge gripped in frost:
> the mountain trail.

Guku Shibakusa 78: This is a verse that aims at the true appearance of the mountain trail. Beneath the trees, between the rocks, the low bamboo grasses are wholly wilted and shrunken; only on a single decaying log bridge the frost has iced over. To imagine water here would be absurd and lacking in sensibility.   (p. 20)

A variant of this hokku appears in the *Yamanoue Sōji ki* (1588), which reports that Shinkei composed it at Yoshimasa's request on a tea jar in the shogunal collection called "Abandoned Child" (*Sutego*); the jar had a rough, whitish overglaze that gave the impression of fallen frost. In the same text, we find another reference to Shinkei: "In the renga works of Priest Shinkei, it is said that the style of renga should be withered, shrunken, and cold [*karekashikete samukare to*]. About these words, Jōō always said that the essence of tea should be the same."[20] What might be called Shinkei's aesthetics of reduction, that which is signified by his special use of the terminology of the cold and meager, desolate and withered, refers to a mind that has wholly internalized the Buddhist truths of impermanence and emptiness. On the level of poetic rhetoric, it is manifested in a clarified and economic diction—such as we have been reading in these hokku—a language "reduced" to its absolute bare minimum, without affectation of any kind, eschewing surface beauty or ornament, the better that it may be a transparent medium for the essential quality of the mind and the poetic object.

It is this minimalist aspect of Shinkei's aesthetics that struck a responsive chord in the practice and ideals of *wabicha*. The "chill and withered" realm was there thought to be the ultimate stage of a spiritual practice similar to Shinkei's view of poetic training as a way to arrive at the original ground of the mind and of reality. Formally, this realm is manifest in the deep appreciation of the undecorated, even rough, surface textures and austere design of Bizen and Shigaraki pottery. Such may be gathered in the letter of Murata Jukō (or Shukō, 1422–1502), the founder of *chanoyu* in the second half of the fifteenth century, to his disciple Furuichi Chōin (1452–1508), a warrior priest and minor daimyō from Nara. Significantly, the same Chōin was the recipient of Kenzai's notes on Shinkei's teachings, the *Shinkei-sōzu teikin*.[21] This fascinating coincidence further confirms Shinkei's crucial influence in the major shift to *wabi* aesthetics that occurred in the history of tea after the Ōnin War.[22]

Shibakusa kunai hokku 362

kareshiba ni	On withered brush
shimo no koe kiku	audible the sound of frost
yamaji kana	on the mountain trail.

Guku Shibakusa 79: Deep in winter on the mountain trail, the wholly withered clumps of brush are starkly gripped by frost and give a rustling sound [*soyomeku*] like the wind.   (p. 20)

Shibakusa kunai hokku 375

musubu te ni	Cupped in my hands
nioi wa kobore	a fragrance spilling over—
kiku no mizu	chrysanthemum water.

Shibakusa kunai hokku 376

shitaba yuku	Lower leaves drift
sasamizu samuki	on the rippling water, cold
iwane kana	shadow of the rock.

Shibakusa kunai hokku 382

fukenuru ka	Is it so late?
kawaoto samuki	the river sound is cold—
yūzukuyo	moon-risen eve.

226 *STKBS* 3822. "Among hokku on winter."

ashizutsu no	Sheer as pith of
usuyuki kōru	reed stalk, thin snow icing
migiwa kana	on marsh edge.

Guku Shibakusa 84: *Ashizutsu* is the thin tissue inside the stems of reeds; it expresses a thin transparency.   (p. 21)

Chikurinshō no chū 397: *Ashizutsu* is the thin tissue inside the stems of reeds, so it is being used to express a thin transparency, perhaps according to common practice.

Yuki no keburi 20: *Ashizutsu* is the thinnish white tissue that is found inside the stems of reeds or hollow of bamboos. It is used here wholly to bring out "thin snow" [*usuyuki*]. The mind of this verse embodies the principle of hitting on the right word at the right time.

Chikubun 1413: For *ashizutsu* there are various explanations; one theory has it that *tsutsu* means the interval from one node to another. Again, it is said to refer to the thin tissue inside. This hokku takes the latter meaning.

Chikurinshū kikigaki 372: It is the thin tissue inside the reed stem, thus a pillow-word for "thin" [*usuki*].

Shibakusa kunai hokku 398

kōrikeri	Stilled in ice!
sese o chidori no	shallow pools where plovers
hashirimizu	skimmed the ripples.

Shibakusa kunai hokku 387

hi ya utsuru	Did the sun shift?
konoshita mizu no	on the water below the trees
murakōri	shards of ice.

Shibakusa kunai hokku 426

usuzumi no	Faint inkstroke
mayu ka shigururu	through falling rain
mika no tsuki	eyebrow moon.

227 *STKBS* 3823. "Among hokku on winter."

aki mo nao	Even autumn is yet
asaki wa yuki no	shallow: this evening
yūbe kana	of snowfall.

Guku Shibakusa 90: It says that compared to an evening of deep snow, so lonely [*sabishiku*] and beyond help [*senkata naki*], the autumn dusk is indeed shallow. (p. 22)

Deceptively simple in its spare imagery and the neat balance of its aural structure (*aki- asaki- yuki- yūbe- kana*), this last verse is rendered profound by the sole weight of its intention. Ever since Sei Shōnagon declared that the evening is most moving in autumn (*aki wa yūgure*), a sentiment the *Shin-kokinshū* poets confirmed, the autumn evening has represented one of the waka tradition's deepest symbols. This winter-evening hokku is Shinkei's challenge to and allusive variation on that view. An ink-wash landscape reduced to the barest essentials of black and white, it is one of the pithiest statements on *sabi*—that detached sense of existential loneliness—in Japanese literature before Bashō. Here the aesthetics of reduction is pursued to an extreme point; the terse configuration of the words on the page seems to have no purpose other than its disappearance before the feeling it seeks to convey into the reader's mind. The linguistic surface, in other words, is like "the finger pointing at the moon," a mere instrument, a pure sign wholly dependent on the reader's receptivity.

Shinkei's emphasis on the mind-heart (*kokoro*) over and above language (*kotoba*) in his criticism rests no doubt on necessity: given the extreme brevity of the renga verse, much hinges on the mind of the poet who has to link up to it. But from his philosophical standpoint, it also implies that the truth cannot be encompassed by, nor is it identifiable with, the vehicle of its revelation. And it is precisely for this reason that what is "left unsaid" (*iinokoshi*) has such an important place there. Such a hokku can be taken as a concrete instance of the view expressed in *Sasamegoto* that poetry is a mental transaction, a (nearly) mute transmission from one mind to another (*ishin denshin*).

Shinkei's Tsukeku from the *Shinsen Tsukubashū*, with Commentary

Spring

4 *STKBS* 86

| urasabishiku mo | A loneliness stirring from deep |
| haru kaeru koro | within, days of departing spring. |

moshio yaku	Through clouded haze
keburi ni kasumu	of burning salt-seaweed,
kari nakite	the wild geese call.

Keikandō, Beginning Stage: With regard to *urasabishiku* in the maeku, it occurs in the following poem from the *Kokinshū* [*KKS* 171. Autumn. Anonymous]:[23]

waga seko ga	Blowing back
koromo no suso o	the hem of my husband's robe,
fukikaeshi	*a loneliness*
urasabishiku mo	*stirring from deep within—*
aki no hatsukaze	the first winds of autumn.

Here, however, the tsukeku takes *ura* to mean "bay" and connects to it with "salt-seaweed." Furthermore, it connects to "departing spring" with "wild geese." Such a method of linking in two places at once marks the verse of the beginner. (pp. 130–31)

Chikubun 43: The *ura* in *urasabishiku* is a mere prefix. That it is taken to mean "bay" [in the context of the tsukeku link] illustrates an essential principle in renga.

The three stages of a renga poet. Kenzai means that double-meaning, the polysemic character of language, is basic to renga as *linked* poetry. Kenzai wrote the *Keikandō* in his late years in the Kantō for presentation to Ashikaga Masauji, son of the former Koga Kubō Shigeuji. It illustrates the three levels in a poet's stylistic progression from the beginning to middle to late stages through annotated citation of sixty verses, mostly by the seven sages, though it includes six by Sōgi. That the concept originates with Shinkei is evident in the following passage in the third of the *Tokoro-dokoro* letters, the one addressed to Sōgi:

In general the configuration of a good verse passes through three transformations that correspond to the stage of the beginner, the middle period, and old age. The beginner, still lacking prudence and inner discipline, racks his brains in his dominant concern to produce an interesting, skillfully crafted verse. From the middle period on, his artistic imagination gushes forth; he loses himself in the drifting clouds, whirling snow, and various sceneries, now weaving elaborate figures into his verses, now leaving them unfigured and expansive. His spirit ungathered, his work is excessively beautiful or overly stark, and he finds repose in neither. In old age he cherishes all the ten styles, discarding none; he is deeply conscious of the moving power of things, and a will to observe the Way emerges in his heart.   (*Tokoro* III, pp. 224–25)

In essence, Shinkei's concept of the poet's development is oriented toward a distinct key principle at each stage: namely, skill, artistic imagination, and the Way. The beginner is properly concerned to develop a skillful craftsmanship in composing an interesting verse. Having acquired this basic competence, in the middle stage he is able to articulate his artistic imagination freely in pursuit of whatever his desire dictates at the moment; this is clearly a period of fertile experimentation, in which the poet is trying out various modes in search of his own voice. But it is not until the late stage of old age (*rōgo*) that his art reaches its full maturity, and this is, significantly, not a matter of mere skill or artistic imagination, the key principles of the first two stages, but of existential realization regarding the crucial importance of poetry as a Way, a mode of being trained upon the verities of human existence as understood in Buddhist philosophy. As suggested in the passage, this understanding is characterized by impartiality—"discarding none" of the ten styles—a crucial quality in renga, where one has perforce to relate to various kinds of maeku, animating each one without ignoring its meaning, and using any one of the styles suitable for it. This impartiality implies an overcoming of one's own individual stylistic preferences for the benefit of the sequence as a whole. The other quality that evinces devotion to the Way as such is a profound awareness of the moving power of things (*aware fukaku*), a way of viewing them in all the tragic vitality of their being, and not as mere imagistic devices of art.

It is not possible to measure exactly the extent of Shinkei's contribution to the three-stage formulation illustrated in Kenzai's *Keikandō*. The textual evidence indicates that Kenzai means the reader to understand that he is transmitting his mentor's explanations of the concept. True, it is not immediately clear whether the choice and classification of the verses themselves, and the corresponding commentary on each, may also be attributed to Shinkei.[24] However, as evident in the preceding section on hokku, Kenzai's *Chikubun* is often faithful to the gist of Shinkei's own commentary in the *Guku Shibakusa*, and there is no reason to assume that he would be less than conscientious in the *Keikandō* when consulting his own notes and memory. Therefore it is most reasonable to assume that this work represents the Shinkei-Kenzai line of exegetical transmission on the important subject of the stages of a renga poet's progression toward maturity. As presented in his *Shinkei-sōzu teikin* (Bishop Shinkei's teachings), Kenzai's summary of the three-stage concept sounds like a variation of the formulation in the letter to Sōgi, with the difference that what is couched there as a description is here expressed as instructions to a young disciple.

Mental attitude [*kokoromochi*] may be differentiated into three kinds. During the beginning stage, you must first acquire a verbal facility aimed at composing correctly and gracefully. Then having entered the middle level, you must expand the mind toward the arresting and ineffable, that which entails marvelous transformations, and thus startling the ear and earning people's wonder, compose solely verses that sound attractive. Now having attained the realm of the adept, you acquire a mind to observe the Way; you compose verses like those of a beginner, or then again summon forth the arresting effects of marvelous transformations; now deep, now shallow, you must not become fixed in one direction. This mental attitude is essential. Overtones, aura, the chill and meager [*yojō omokage hieyasetaru koto*] are things that you will come to understand naturally once you have reached the realm of the adept. It is not possible to learn them through instruction. (*Teikin*, p. 1125)

More detailed than the first description, this passage also explains why Kenzai, or Shinkei himself, would take examples from such "adepts" as the seven sages and classify them under the beginning stage, as happens in this link from the *Shinsen Tsukubashū*. For it is precisely the adept who does not discriminate between low and high, but composes solely according to the needs of the particular maeku. Here "the method of linking in two places at once" is one of the basic skills acquired at the beginning stage. It is the ability to work with the conventional associations of the words in the maeku ("departing spring" = "wild geese" that migrate north in spring) and to play on the polysemic character of poetic diction in the process of linking (prefix *ura* = "bay"). (Such a double verbal connection is also known technically as *yotsude*, a four-cornered link.) On the level of poetic effect, the tsukeku is quite subtle in evoking, through a purely objective image, the "loneliness" expressed in the maeku. In particular, the way *ura* is brought out twice, once as the unspoken seme "bay" (where the fisherfolk are burning salt-seaweed) and again as the vague tonal quality or aura of that loneliness (the prefix *ura* signifying "behind, within") as evoked by the remote cries of the geese behind the smoky haze, is rather remarkable.

6 STKBS 156

futatabi wa	To someone who vows
hito to naraji to	never again to be reborn
omou mi ni	as a man.

| tada tsuki ni mede | Only find joy in the moon |
| hana ni kurasamu | and dwell among the flowers. |

Chikurinshō no chū 241: The way the author has figured out how to approach this maeku manifests utmost concentration. He has linked up to it in the spirit of the saying, "To believe that one will become a buddha or be reborn as a god is an empty illusion. All you need do this very moment is to lie beneath the plum blossoms and the moon."

Chikurinshū kikigaki 200: As the saying goes, "Just live in the moment and lie beneath the plum blossoms; attainment of buddhahood and rebirth as a god are all empty illusions." Ignorance or enlightenment are conditions of the mind at birth and there is nothing to be done about it but watch the moon and the flowers. Of all the things in this world of man, there is no thought equal to that of moon and flowers.

Renga entokushō: This verse takes the meaning of the maeku in an unexpected direction. . . . The maeku's "I do not wish to be a man again" means that since this world is such a sea of suffering, I do not want to be reborn in it. [In the tsukeku] this becomes, since one might not be born again as a man, let us pass our days taking pleasure in the moon and flowers while we can.   (p. 125)[25]

Against the Buddhist-inspired view of existence as suffering and the belief in transmigration implicit in the maeku, Shinkei sets the Taoist perspective of mindlessness (*mushin*) or non-action (*mu'i*), which is not, as such, unlike the enlightened Buddhist's realization that transmigration is not to be taken literally but as an ideological device to promote virtue. Kenzai's commentary is more illuminating in pointing out how Shinkei radically inverts the intention behind *futatabi wa / hito to naraji* ("I do not desire to be reborn as a man a second time") to suggest that precisely because this human life does not repeat itself, you must enjoy it while you can. Furthermore, to be one with the moon and flowers is, so to speak, not to be a man but to rise above the mundane human condition of suffering.

8 *STKBS* 204

idete toboso ni	Emerging, he stands by the door,
tsuki o miru kure	gazing at the twilight moon.
hito kaeru	The people gone,
yamaji shizukeki	the mountain path is quiet
hana no moto	in the flowers' shade.

Chikubun 138: This is someone who lives in solitude in the mountains. He retreated indoors while the crowd was about, and now he has come out.

As in the first pair, the handling of the situational or plot-like progression from maeku to tsukeku, as explained in the *Chikubun*, is wholly competent and interesting; this demonstrates the sort of inventive skill, or wit, that is a first requirement in the extemporaneous activity that is renga.

However, on top of it, the verse must be imbued with poetic feeling as well, and this is what Shinkei achieves in the aura of *sabi* that hangs over the link.

12 *STKBS* 250

mada kaze yowaki	The wind is still frail upon
nobe no yūtsuyu	the evening dew in the meadow.
furusato no	In the desolate hamlet
wakaba no ogi ni	white petals are falling
hana ochite	on young-leaved reeds.

Tōfū renga hiji: In renga there are the so-called "empty" words [*kūgen*] and the "real" words [*jitsugen*]; a verse will have any number of both. In linking up to the maeku, one should carefully distinguish the real words in it. Empty words are those used to help complete the verse; it is the way of renga to take these empty words and turn them into real words. For example, to the verse

tamoto ni wa	Its sleeves have been
kiri o kasanuru	moistened in layers of mist—
tabigoromo	this travel robe.

someone composed the following link:

mada kaze yowaki	The wind is still frail upon
nobe no yūtsuyu	the evening dew in the meadow.

This verse connects to the maeku through "evening dew"; the words "the wind is frail in the meadow" are just supplements. Now taking these empty words and making them real, Shinkei linked up to the verse like this:

furusato no	In the desolate hamlet
wakaba no ogi ni	white petals are falling
hana ochite	on young-leaved reeds.

From here, the next poet must in turn take the words "petals are falling" and make them real in his own verse.   (p. 212)[26]

Focusing on "the wind is still frail" (*mada kaze yowaki*) in the maeku, Shinkei brings out, with a concentrated acuity of feeling and method, the gentle frailty of the evening spring breeze in the delicate image of cherry petals softly alighting on the young reeds beneath the trees. The litheness of the breeze is measured exactly in the fact that it has sufficient force to stir the late flowers on the trees but not to scatter the dewdrops on the reeds. The verse as such marks a seamless, barely perceptible transition from the Autumn season of the preceding two verses to Spring; it is also a good demonstration of the impersonal and symbolist lyric poetry of renga at its best.

"Empty words" and "real words": the indeterminacy of the single verse. Sōboku's (d. 1545) commentary in the *Tōfū renga hiji* is significant in offering a theoretical explanation for the linking process based on the concept of "empty" and "real" words. What these terms signify is relative to

the words' function vis-à-vis the link; the real words in a verse are those that directly correlate to the meaning of the maeku. Such is "evening dew" in the maeku to Shinkei's verse; it is the hinge upon which turns the implicit analogy between the "layers of mist" on the travel robe in the *mae-maeku* (the verse preceding the maeku) and layers of dew soaking the meadow in the maeku, unscattered by the frail wind. And it is this frail wind, a mere supplement or "empty words" in the previous link, that now becomes activated and transformed into "real words" through Shinkei's image of young reed leaves as yet too tender to be audible in the breeze. In renga therefore, the isolated verse is wholly ambiguous; it is only within the context of the link that particular words in it become charged with significance, and these words will be different—or if the same will have an altered value—depending on whether the verse is seen through the light of its maeku or its tsukeku. This is the same as to say that center and margin, "true" and "empty," the essential and the supplement, are wholly relative concepts in renga, and linking here consists precisely in playing upon the alterity of the two opposing terms.

16 *STKBS* 270

yume utsutsu to mo	Wavering between dream and
wakanu akebono	reality, the sky before dawn.
tsuki ni chiru	A cascade of petals
hana wa kono yo no	floating in the moonlight—
mono narade	an unearthly sight.

Chikurinshō no chū 47: The flowers scattering in the remaining moonlight of predawn in spring is a sight that breaks beyond the limits of language, one that is not of this world. Therefore one cannot distinguish whether it is real or a dream. [Three poems are cited at this point, all evoking the idea of unearthliness. The third poem, given below, is apparently the source for Shinkei's allusive variation. *Shikishi-naishinnō shū* 110.]

kono yo ni mo	This vision of spring
wasurenu haru no	is such that one forgets
omokage yo	it is of this world:
oborozukiyo no	Pale reflection of flowers
hana no hikari wa	in the hazy moonlit night.

Chikubun 185: In works like the *Tale of Genji*, when people wish to praise something, they say that "it is not of this world" [*kono yo no mono narazu*], meaning that it is like something in paradise. This is a model of a good verse.

This link also appears in Sōgi's *Oi no susami* but without commentary. Nose Asaji speculates that the maeku is probably a Love verse expressing the sense of unreality felt by lovers rudely forced to part at dawn.[27] If that is indeed the case, then Shinkei's tsukeku would be an example of those "marvelous transformations" (*shimpen*) that he speaks of as belonging to the middle stage of poetic development, when the poet allows his artistic imagination free rein. Kaneko observes that Shinkei here evokes the aura of the Buddhist Pure Land (*jōdo*), and this is probably also what Kenzai had in mind by saying that "it is like something in paradise" (*gokuraku no yō nari*).[28]

18 *STKBS* 290

hate wa tada	It is a world where
yoki mo ashiki mo	nothing is ultimately
naki yo ni	good or bad.

| hana chiru ato wa | Even the wind is stilled in |
| kaze mo nokorazu | the wake of scattered petals. |

This is a plain, uncomplicated link but nevertheless notable for the surety and thoroughness with which it deals with the philosophical statement of the maeku. Good and bad are not absolute but temporally conditioned determinations; impermanence is a universal truth applying to moral formulations as well, to evil destroyer as well as helpless victim, and time is the single great leveler. The method of illustrating a general statement with a concrete image is wholly common in renga.

20 *STKBS* 306

| sabishisa tsurasa | To whom shall I speak of |
| tare ni kataran | the loneliness the pain. |

hana otsuru	Even in the days of
koro shi mo ame o	falling flowers, only the rain
yoru kikite	sounds in the night.

A difficult maeku in its emotional tone and emphatic diction. One cannot ignore the twin emotions spelled out so clearly, or the interrogative inflection, without seeming evasive and coldhearted; on the other hand, it will not do to descend to bathos. Shinkei does neither of these things. He rises to the challenge, fully acknowledging the sincerity of the maeku's emotions in a conception that does them justice. The thought of flowers scattering unseen in the night rain accounts for the "pain" (*tsurasa*), and the implicit suggestion that the subject is alone listening to the scene outside responds to the "loneliness" (*sabishisa*) while answering the question "to whom shall I speak" (*tare ni kataran*) in the negative: no visitor comes in the night to share the speaker's burden; what does come is the rain. Technically, the succession of two emphatic particles, *shi* and *mo*, underlines the twin emotions in the maeku by superimposing upon the already melancholy thought of scattering flowers the even more depressing occurrence of the rain hastening them to their end. Renga is in this way necessarily an exercise in the careful weighing of words; it is an art that subjected words to deliberate and minute scrutiny and made the quality of that scrutiny the stuff of its poetry.

22 *STKBS* 318

omou to mo	Parted from me
wakareshi hito wa	though his thoughts still clung—
kaerame ya	will he ever return?
yūgure fukashi	Evening is deep in the hills
sakura chiru yama	where cherry blossoms scatter.

Oi no susami 19: The person who departed is someone who went home after viewing the flowers. The meaning is that although he still longs for the flowers, it is not likely that he will return. If one asks why, it is because the flowers have fallen and the loneliness of evening in the mountain village is too much to bear. This is a way of scrutinizing the mind of another through one's own. (p. 150)

Chikubun 177: The connection hinges on putting oneself in the place of the person [*hito*]. He cannot return since the dusk has grown deep and it is dark. The one from whom he parted is the flowers.

Shadow (omokage). No doubt Sōgi and Kenzai are right in pointing out the breathtaking shift here from a Love to a Spring verse, but the paraphrase of the link sounds rather literal and heavy-handed. The brilliance of this tsukeku lies precisely in what it leaves unsaid, in the way it evokes the shadow (*omokage*) of the situation in the maeku upon the ostensive scene of falling flowers at evening deep in the mountains. The flowers do not exactly replace the woman in the man's thoughts nor does he literally turn into a flower viewer who will not return because of the dark. Rather, the whole scene and the otherwise admirable analysis of the situation in the two commentaries function as objective correlatives of the unspoken thought that he will never return. The tsukeku is a symbolic evocation of a profound feeling of loss; it has that quality of ineffable remoteness (*yōon*), not unrelated to *sabi*, and limned with a clear conviction of the irrecoverability of time, that constitutes the most authentic strain in Shinkei's work and makes him a true poet and not just a craftsman or even artist, as many renga poets are. It is unfortunate that the verse sounds so bland in translation.

24 *STKBS* 342

kokoro ni chigiru	In his heart he makes a vow with
yukusue no haru	departing spring when it returns.
mi no araba	"If this body remains,"
to bakari hana no	is his sole thought, eyes upon
chiru o mite	the scattering flowers.

Chikubun 161: In the falling flowers he finds nothing to reassure him, but "if this body remains," he shall see them again—so he vows in his heart.

Ironic intensification. "In the falling flowers he finds nothing to reassure him"—Kenzai's comment is exactly the point. Shinkei's method here intensifies the urgency of the promise in the maeku through an irony underscored by the polarity between "heart" and "body"; the body does not necessarily honor a vow made in the heart. There is a further paradox implied in the common knowledge that spring will always be true to its annual promise of recurrence, yet the very same spring, in the image of falling flowers, underlines a different "promise" for man.

26 *STKBS* 344

yūbe no kumo o	He gazes through a blur of tears
namida ni zo miru	at the dim evening clouds.
hana mo yo no	Even the flowers,
uree no iro ni	reflecting the hue of infirm
utsuroite	times, turn pale.

Chikubun 835: The evening clouds [in the maeku] are seen as the declining flowers.

The occasion for the tears in the maeku as such is ambiguous, but Ijichi Tetsuo is probably right in reading the evening clouds as a memento of the smoke from someone's cremation; it is not possible to tell exactly without the *mae-maeku*. Ijichi then goes on to note that *yo no uree* refers to sorrow at the passing of a world with the death of a ruler. This tsukeku dates from Shinkei's Kantō period, when as we have seen in the biography, he often used the image of flowers as well as the word *yo* to mourn the tragedy of the times, that is, the Ōnin War, in numerous waka and some hokku.[29] It is most probable therefore that *yo no uree* refers to times *afflicted* by war, and that is how I render the verse. The clouds, seen as traces of cremation smoke in the maeku, become whorls of flowering cherries in the tsukeku, and the tears are shed for the infirmity of the times, as symbolized by those same paling flowers about to scatter. Kenzai's words, "declining flowers" (*hana no reiraku*) are also more appropriate to the intended analogy with a world on the verge of destruction.

Summer

28 *STKBS* 450

kiki zo tsutauru	Echoing through the eras,
kami no sono kami	that ancient age of the gods!
hototogisu	As I lie secluded
hono katараishi	in the mountain, hushed murmur
yama ni nete	of the cuckoo.

Guku Shibakusa 106: This link is based solely on introducing the poem by Imperial Princess Shikishi where she evokes her state as Vestal Priestess [*SKKS* 1484. Miscellaneous]. (p. 28)

hototogisu	Never shall I forget
sono kamiyama no	*the hushed murmur* that drifted
tabimakura	through the sky, *cuckoo*,
hono katalaishi	as I lay secluded in that sojourn
sora zo wasurenu	in *the mountain of the gods*.

Chikurinshō no chū 61: Long ago when the Imperial Princess Shikishi (the third daughter of Emperor Go-Shirakawa) was serving as the Vestal Priestess of the Kamo Shrine, she heard the cuckoo in the sacred mountain. Sometime the following year, having finished her term and descended from the mountain, she composed the following poem recalling the year that had gone. [*SKKS* 1484 above quoted.] Both "mountain of the gods" [*kamiyama*] and "that ancient mountain" [*sono kamiyama*] refer to Kamo Mountain. *Sono kami* in the maeku means "that ancient age"; the tsukeku added the character *yama* [mountain] and interpreted it to mean "that mountain of the gods" [*sono kamiyama*]. As I lie here listening to the cuckoo in the mountain where Imperial Princess Shikishi heard its hushed murmur ages ago, it is like hearing a voice from that age coming down to the present.

Chikubun 234: "It has come down through the eras" [*kiki zo tsutauru*] refers to the cuckoo. Recalling the poem [here quoted] composed by Princess Shikishi after serving as Vestal Priestess, the poet says that he is hearing transmitted to the present the sound from that time.

Asaji 2: This takes from the following poem [*SKKS* 1484 above quoted]. The line *kiki zo tsutauru* is clearly one that is difficult to link up to. Nevertheless, the poet has succeeded in doing so by tying together in his mind the present cry [of the *hototogisu*] and that "hushed murmur ages ago."[30] (p. 318)

Classical pedagogy. As pedagogical texts, one of the main concerns of the Muromachi commentaries was unquestionably to identify the occurrence of classical allusions in contemporary renga. For renga masters, this was no mere passing interest but a project invested with an almost missionary zeal to preserve and transmit intact a dying tradition in an age of political turmoil and social dislocation. The conservative "waka-like" strain in Muromachi renga cannot be understood and appreciated outside this historical context. As we have seen in *Oi no kurigoto*, for Shinkei the practice of renga was a way of "preserving a part of waka's teachings and precepts" in order "to soften the hearts of warriors and rude folk and teach the way of human sensibility for all the distant ages." His real concern, however, was less with traditional rhetoric as such, but with what the courtly poetic sensibility had to teach about a sensitive and compassionate way of viewing phenomena and human relations in an age of armored men with unbridled ambitions. This goes hand in hand with the emphasis everywhere in his writings on *kokoro*, the mind-heart reflected in the poem or verse, over and above *kotoba* or words as such; it is also consistent with his characterization of the most advanced stage of a poet's development as sheer devotion to poetry as a Way, beyond the question of skill in words or brilliance of artistic imagination.

Renga, however, is nothing if not skill in words, and it is precisely this fact that drove Shinkei to focus on *kokoro*; it is all too easy to forget the issue of *expression* (of self and world) in the proliferating play of language encouraged by the very sequential and collective nature of the genre. The language was foreign in the sense that the renga event was a gathering of commoners speaking in the rarefied tongue of court poetry, a centuries-old medium with a weight of accumulated associations, infinitely refined and layered with use, invested with an aristocratic aura and prestige, and for all these reasons fascinating both for the artistic soul and for the *arrivistes* interested in acquiring high culture. Before the so-called poetic revolution inaugurated more than a century later by haikai's rejection of *gago* (refined diction, the language of the belles lettres) and its corresponding institution of colloquial diction (*zokugo*), the courtly heritage was first absorbed into popular consciousness through the agency of orthodox renga and the classical pedagogy of the renga masters. Thus did a politically impotent aristocracy permanently inscribe itself upon history where it most matters, in the living traditions of a national culture, so much so that one of the first Western sociologists of Japan, Ruth Benedict, would characterize it with the symbols of "the chrysanthemum and the sword."

Among renga masters, the most classically oriented was without doubt Sōgi. Particularly near the end, after some forty years of actual practice and exegesis of classical poetry, he seems to have been wholly convinced that the path he had forged for renga was the proper one, quite unaware that within half a century, the refined orthodox style would unravel from sheer exhaustion, and its poor cousin, the formerly marginalized comic haikai, take its place at center stage. "In renga there is no word in any verse that is not from a foundation poem" (*renga wa izure no ku mo honka no kotoba ni arazaru wa haberazu*)—thus Sōgi.[31]

Konishi Jin'ichi early observed the layered intricacy of renga diction, a function of its use of a vocabulary with innumerable precedents in waka, and responsible for the uniquely textural or musical quality of its artistry. When he states further that *honkadori* (allusive variation on an old foundation poem) in renga practice is not typically, as in waka, founded upon the specificity of particular poems, but based more ambiguously upon whole series of poems having similar conceptions or feelings, he is doubtless close to what Sōgi means by the statement quoted above from *Asaji*.[32] Waka exists in renga as a limitless storehouse of precedents for word usages and poetic conceptions that the practitioner activates when he links up to the maeku. Or in Sausurrean terms, the waka lexicon constitutes a *langue*, a complex but recognizable system of semantic and grammatical differentiations into which the poet encodes when he composes the renga verse as a specific instance of *parole* or actual discourse. In practice the waka and the prose literature of past ages are the dictionary of renga discourse. When, as in the verses quoted above, the commentaries cite waka precedents for Shinkei's usage of *urasabishiku* or the unearthly quality of cherry blossoms scattering in moonlight, they are teaching their readers what he meant by in effect citing the relevant entries in the dictionary. Thus "foundation poem" in renga may simply refer to a poem precedent, and not necessarily just a single one. And even in cases where the precedent is singular and specific, as in the allusion to Princess Shikishi's poem in this tsukeku, the "variation" on the foundation poem is minimal compared, say, to Teika's and Shunzei's way of enriching and deepening older poems in their own.

The *Shinkokinshū* poets' allusive variations on *Kokinshū* poems are like powerful translations that, while depending for their existence on the original texts, are so good that they often displace them in the consciousness, particularly where the older poems are of slight quality. This seldom happens in renga. Here, *honkadori* is more like a simple citation than a translation; the original remains intact. What is at stake, rather, is the aptness of the quotation in relation to the maeku, that sense of liberation and pleasure experienced when some well-known cliché suddenly becomes animated within a new, unexpected context. In short, *honkadori* here is wholly an affect of the dynamics of *tsukeai*, a method of animating the maeku through the mediation of an old poem. Princess Shikishi recalls her lonely sacral existence as Vestal Priestess of the Kamo Shrine in the faint cries of the cuckoo that kept her company in the mountain seclusion. Shinkei's persona recalls her recollection in the cries of the same bird in the same hallowed mountain two centuries later, and his experience gains an added, ineffably solemn dimension lent by the communing of two voices across the remoteness of intervening time. This is what *kiki zo tsutauru / kami no sono kami* means, and Shinkei's reading of it is ultimately a meditation on the act of remembrance as an experience of a moment in and out of time.

30 *STKBS* 452

kiku mo mezurashi	'Tis rare indeed that one
kono miyakodori	hears of it, this Capital-bird.
hototogisu	Cuckoo—soaring in
kesa wa otowa no	at last, this very morning
yama koete	over Otowa Mountain.

Oi no susami 24: "Capital-bird" is here taken to mean "bird of the capital." The meaning is that the cuckoo that came this morning over Otowa Mountain is indeed "this bird of the Capital." Here, too, the compositional design of the link [*toria-wase*] is quite impressive. Moreover, the fact that the verse was simultaneously composed in the spirit of the *Kokinshū* poem below is certainly remarkable [*KKS* 142. Summer. Ki no Tomonori. "Composed when he was crossing Otowa Mountain and heard the cry of the cuckoo"]. (p. 151)

otowayama	As I was crossing
kesa koekureba	Otowa Mountain this morning,
hototogisu	of a sudden
kozue harukani	from distant treetops,
ima zo naku naru	the calls of the cuckoo!

Chikurinshō no chū 62: One reads the Capital-bird into place-names like Sumida-gawa, Naniwa, and Horie. It is a bird the size of a snipe, with a red bill and legs. The meaning of this link is that the cuckoo that crossed Otowa Mountain this morning has become a bird of the capital with the rare voice [*KKS* 142 above quoted]. Apart from this poem there are numerous others [that read the cuckoo] in Otowa Mountain.

Deflecting Expectations. Conventional expectations in this instance would dictate linking through an allusion to the "Capital-bird" episode in Chapter 9 of the *Tales of Ise*, where Narihira and his party notice a bird on the banks of the Sumida River in Musashi and are amazed to hear that its name is "Capital-bird." Shinkei wittily departs from the norm by taking the name literally but nevertheless securely links up to the maeku on two counts: through the association between "Capital-bird" and Otowa Mountain, the usual approach to the capital from the east; and between *kiku mo mezurashi* (heard rarely) and "cuckoo." This is what Sōgi means by the "impressive" design of the link. On top of that, he manages to effect a true allusive variation on *KKS* 142: where in Tomonori's poem, the cuckoo is still some distance from the capital, here it has arrived and become, in effect, "a bird of the capital."

Autumn

32 *STKBS* 590

onaji oshie o	It is one and the same teaching
amata ni zo kiku	but heard in a myriad ways.
aki to fuku	Blowing with autumn,
ogi no uwakaze	the wind on the reeds, the storm
yamaoroshi	rushing down the mountain.

Keikandō, Beginning Stage: The wonderful sermons preached by the Buddha in his lifetime were all one and the same teaching, but they were heard in various ways and gave rise to several sects, each with its own interpretation. The verse restates this condition by saying that the wind bodes forth the autumn season in various ways as it rustles softly over the miscanthus grass or storms down the mountainside. (p. 132)

Asaji 35: This way of linking is masterful in simply delineating the meaning [of the maeku]. The message that the same teaching is heard in manifold ways is quite clear. (p. 327)

Figuring concepts. The concept illustrated here is that of "the rain of one flavor" (*ichimi no ame*), preached by the Buddha in the "Medicinal Herbs" chapter of the *Lotus Sutra* in verses such as this:

> Hotoke no byōdō no setsu wa
> ichimi no ame no gotoku naru ni
> shujō no shō ni shitagatte
> ukuru tokoro onajikarazaru koto
> kano sōmoku no
> ukuru tokoro ono'ono kotonaru ga gotoshi

> The Buddha's impartial teaching
> is like rain of a single taste,
> yet it is received variously
> according to the natures of the myriad beings,
> just as grasses and trees
> receive the rain each in its own way.[33]

Shinkei translates the Buddhist parable into the vocabulary of the poetic tradition by marking how the same season, autumn, evokes different feelings in the consciousness according to the nature of the phenomenon it touches.

34 *STKBS* 650

kohagi utsuroi	As the hue wanes on the bush clover
ojika naku michi	along the path, a deer is calling.
susuki chiru	Plume grasses scatter
onoe no miya no	dim the traces of Onoe no miya
ato furite	in the winds of time.

Keikandō, Middle Stage: This verse is in the mode of meditation [*ushintei*]. Instead of linking by means of "meadow" [*no*] as might have been expected, it does so through "old palace" [*furumiya*]. One can also say that the verse belongs to the advanced stage. [*Akishino gesseishū* 1129 below quoted.][34] (p. 136)

takamado no	At Onoe no miya
onoe no miya no	high upon the hill of Takamado,
akihagi o	who think they would
tare kite miyo to	come to see the autumn bush clover,
matsumushi no naku	that the pine insects cry so?

Chikurinshō no chū 97: With Takamado's Onoe Palace, one invariably composes a verse on the bush clover. There is also an Onoe Palace in Minase.[35]

Chikubun 327. In poetry Onoe Palace is associated with both Takamado or Minase. Its exact location is unclear.

Chikurinshū kikigaki 65: This refers to Onoe Palace in Takamado. There is also an Onoe Palace at Minase, which belonged to Retired Emperor Go-Toba. [*SKKS* 1313. Love. "From the Minase Fifteen Poems on Love Poetry Contest." Retired Emperor Go-Toba. First line *sato wa arenu.*]

sato wa arete	The village is in ruins;
onoe no miya no	That evening at Onoe no miya when
onozukara	she kept on waiting
machikoshi yoi mo	on the chance he might yet come—
mukashi narikeri	is now but a thing of the past.

As the *Keikandō* states, the usual link would locate the pink-flowered autumn bush clover in the meadow (*no*); however, the poem by Fujiwara Yoshitsune (1169–1206) can be used as a precedent to establish the link between this image and Onoe Palace. This Onoe Palace, located in the foothills of Takamado Mountain in Furuichi, Yamato Province (Nara), was the detached palace (*rikyū*) of Emperor Shōmu and occurs in some poems in the *Man'yōshū*. By the time of the *Shinkokinshū* poets, as indicated in the quoted poems above, it had become an *utamakura* associated with the theme of recollecting the past.

*The mode of meditation (*ushintei). *Ushintei,* "the mode of meditation," or as Brower and Miner render it in *Japanese Court Poetry*, "the style of conviction of feeling," is identified in Teika's *Maigetsushō* as the realm of the ultimate in poetry. In *Sasamegoto*, Shinkei describes it as poetry "in which the mind has dissolved [*kokoro torake*] and is profoundly at one with the pathos of things [*aware fukaku*]; poetry that issues from the very depths of the poet's being and may truly be said to be his own waka, his own authentic renga [*makoto ni mune no soko yori idetaru waga uta waga renga no koto narubeshi*]" (*SSG*, p. 188). All these characterizations point to an authenticity of feeling and a poetic process involving the utmost concentration, such that any trace of the conceptualizing mind is erased from the surface of the verse and the image-words function only as signs initiating a meditation on phenomena and existence at their deepest level, which is that of *mujo* and emptiness. When Shinkei says that this kind of poetry expresses the poet's authentic voice (*waga uta waga renga*), he does not mean his individual voice, his specific idiolect, if you will. Rather, he means that the voice is truly the poet's own in that it can emerge only from a dynamic process of meditation engaging the mind through and through (*kokoro torake*), and that this direct, personal, and deepgoing experience is an inalienable quality of the poem. No one can imitate it; everyone must undergo the process in order to attain his or her own voice. And that voice, regardless of the poet's specific identity, will then have the ring of authenticity that marks the mode of *ushintei*. The tsukeku above is best appreciated with all this in mind; it is one of Shinkei's best verses in the *Shinsen Tsukubashū*, with a depth and ineffable remoteness that wholly resist translation.

40 *STKBS* 670

shigure no ato no	In the wake of the passing rains
tsuyu zo mi ni shimu	the dew sinks cool into the soul.
mushi no naku	As insects cry in
nobe no tōyama	the meadow tinged in color
iro tsukite	the distant hills.

Keikandō, Middle Stage: Saying that it was a winning verse, he [Shinkei] recited it several times and discussed it at length.   (p. 136)

Oi no susami 25: This links to the maeku by taking "in the wake of the passing rains" to mean that as the remaining traces of the passing rains in the distant hills, the dewdrops in the meadow sink into the soul. Accordingly it says, "As insects cry in / the meadow tinged in color / the distant hills." The linking method is unique, and the verse as such beyond the imagination of most authors. Moreover, it presents the natural scene right before our eyes [*ganzen no keiki nari*]. Given this utterly fresh immediacy, is this not truly an excellent verse?   (p. 151)

Asaji 28: [First sentence same as above.] Therefore it says, "Distant hills beyond the meadow where insects cry." The scene set forth before the eye is truly arresting.   (p. 325)

Chikubun 347: There is a double link here: to "meadow," "dew"; to "passing rain," "tinged in color."

Yuki no keburi 69: The meaning is that in the wake of the rain that blanketed the distant hills, the dew left upon the meadow sinks into the soul. The rains begin to clear and the treetops suddenly emerge tinged with color, while in the dew-wet meadow the insects are crying—does not such a scene truly evoke a feeling that sinks into the very soul?

Perceptual immediacy. Sōgi's enthusiasm for this verse is evident in his multiple commentaries from *Oi no susami* to *Asaji* to *Yuki no keburi*; one wonders if Shinkei's long discussion of it with Kenzai dealt with the same points. In such detailed and surefooted evaluations as these, Sōgi displays the kind of critical acumen that only long practice in the art could have fostered. It is also interesting to note that in the later *Yuki no keburi* version he abandons all talk of method and concentrates wholly on expressing his own empathetic reaction to the verse.

As distinct from the compellingly remote inwardness of the preceding link, this one concentrates on evoking the objective scene as such with that acuity of sense perception that we have often encountered in Shinkei's hokku. The newness of this *keiki* or *keikyoku* mode as a means of linking in renga is evidenced by Sōgi's commentary ("the linking method is unique," "this utterly fresh immediacy"). While using the classical images of the tradition, the verse simultaneously breaks out of their conventionality to summon the vital presence of nature as such, in all its thereness. Not that feeling is absent; the tsukeku is in effect a concrete realization, through sound (the cries of insects) and color, of the scene that "sinks into the soul" (*mi ni shimu*) in the maeku. The whole is framed by the concept of "traces of the passing rain" (*shigure no ato*) introduced there: both the insect cries in the withering, rain-rifled grass and the emergence of autumn tints in the distant hillslopes are manifestations of the cold rains that moved from meadow to hills and are just now lifting from the treetops. This clean surety of touch, this sense of mind stalking mind in a motion of dialogic understanding, constitutes the meaning and the pleasure of what is called *tsukeai* in renga.

42 *STKBS* 706

waga kokoro	My heart,
tare ni kataran	To whom can I speak of it—
aki no sora	The autumn sky!
ogi ni yūkaze	The evening wind upon the reeds,
kumo ni karigane	the wild geese among the clouds.

Keikandō, Advanced Stage: This is a renga beyond words [*gengai no renga nari*]. It expresses wonder, saying that the feeling is such that one cannot speak of it. (p. 142)

Oi no susami 29: This connects to the sense of "to whom can I speak of it" in the maeku by bringing out the inexpressible [*gongo dōdan*] quality of that feeling. The shape of the verse is itself marvelous [*chinchō*], and the style of linking is incomparable [*batsugun*]. Verses such as this lose their effect with frequent use, and poets should by all means exercise discrimination in composing them. (p. 153)

Chikubun 360: In the season of autumn skies, when the evening wind is upon the reeds, and the wild geese trail across the clouds, to whom can I speak of this melancholy—it is beyond my powers to express [*mōsu ni oyobanu*], so it says.

Chikurinshū kikigaki 79: This is an impressively subtle linking technique. [Attempting it] even the adept might fail and end up with a confused logic and discordant effect. Nothing is as insubstantial as the wind and the clouds, and yet the wind has a medium in the reeds, and a natural empathy runs between the wild geese and the clouds. As for myself, to whom can I speak of the feelings [*kansei*] in my heart before such an autumn scene?

"*A renga beyond words.*" By itself this verse is quite unprepossessing, hardly remarkable in its bare enumeration of two parallel images; its "marvel" lies wholly in the unerring accuracy with which it pins down the maeku, like a true arrow hitting its mark. The "incomparable" linking technique here transpires on two levels: first, the twin images concretize the feel of the autumn scene (*aki no sora*) mentioned in the maeku, while simultaneously animating the rhetorical question, "to whom can I speak of it" (*tare ni kataran*), through the unspoken but unmistakable response, "to no one, since it is beyond the power of words to express." On a deeper level, the patterned repetition of the maeku's syntax, "*to whom*" (*tare ni*) in "*to* the reeds the evening wind / *to* the clouds the wild geese" (*ogi ni* / *kumo ni*) has the contrastive, ironic effect of drawing out the profound loneliness of a human subject confronted by the inadequacy of language to express his inner feeling (*waga kokoro*). Formless, the wind is yet visible and audible in the swaying reeds; mere transient vapors, the clouds yet gain in visual presence as the background against which the line of wild geese trace themselves. But for human beings there is only the *medium* of speech, which fails the motions of the heart-mind before such a scene.

The link is ultimately a meditation on the ineffableness of *kokoro*, the sense that there is always that uncloseable gap of a difference between mind and language. It is also a self-commentary on the nature of renga itself as a poetry "beyond words," an art that more than any other can be grasped only in the space between the verses, a paradoxical poetry that inscribes itself by marking the shape of its absence upon the linguistic surface. Sōgi's cautionary warning, that such a simple verse cannot be used too frequently without losing its effect, means that it is easy enough to imitate the syntax, but it takes a master to know when the moment is right and a deep mind to suggest a world of thought in such an apparently "thoughtless" verse.

44 *STKBS* 762

aretaru yado ni	Through the ruinous dwelling
akikaze zo fuku	gusting cold, the autumn wind.
tsuki o tada	Only the moon remains,
uki yūgure no	of the melancholy evening,
aruji nite	sole master.

Yuki no keburi 74: Is it difficult to figure out the way in which this verse connects to the preceding? Does it seem a bit hard to grasp the meaning of the verse as such? In general, is it not so that the moon causes a man to ponder over things, that when he gazes at the moon various thoughts assail him one by one, and that it is precisely because of this that one is advised not to gaze alone at the moon? It is for this reason that the verse refers to the moon as the master of the lonely evening. This poet's attitude was such that he had a profound dislike for verses that link to the preceding in a vague, sloppy manner. Therefore he interpreted and linked up to the maeku in this way. Is this not truly the mind of an incomparable poet?

Chikubun 369: The meaning of the verse is that the evening may be lonely, but with the moon as master, one can find solace.

The "vague, sloppy link." The connection, difficult indeed to grasp at first reading, hinges upon the overt association between "dwelling" (*yado*) and "master" (*aruji*). The ruined house through which the wind blows in the maeku has been abandoned by its owner. Shinkei anchors the ambiguous value of the emphatic particle *zo* in the maeku by taking it to mean that the wind blows *unrestrained* through the abandoned house since it has no master; he then goes on to make the ironic statement that it is the moon that is its sole master, for the reasons that Sōgi explains above and Kenzai briefly amplifies. The evening moon as it illumines an abandoned house summons melancholy thoughts yet ultimately consigns them to emptiness in its transparent rays. "Master" thus means a being with the power to distress as well as to console. As Sōgi observes, Shinkei "had a profound dislike for . . . [the] vague, sloppy [*shitaruki*]" link. A mentally lazy practitioner would have contented himself with underscoring the melancholy feeling in the images of ruinous dwelling and autumn wind, but Shinkei rises to the challenge of the ambiguous *zo* and arrives at the original thought of the moon as master.

Clearly, in renga if one were simply to repeat the conventional sentiments associated with the images, the session would soon deteriorate into sheer monotony. In *Sasamegoto*, Shinkei quotes three verses, in the so-called *yūgen* style, that are "merely steeped in grace and charm," vaguely romantic mood evocations whose effects are indistinguishable from each other. "Verses like these, . . . remaining ever the same though their authors change, are of the type that is highly praised day after day in every renga session" (*SSG*, p. 128). His critique of the common run of renga sessions in his day is aimed precisely at this cavalier, superficial attitude to linking as mere repetition in different terms, without the deep-going reflection that he advocates everywhere in his writings. Significantly, this mental slackness would eventually lead to renga's decline and replacement with haikai.

46 *STKBS* 808

fumu to mo mienu	The path laid with dew-frost
michi no tsuyujimo	bears no mark of trudging feet.
yuku hito mo	The passersby have
shizumaru tsuki no	long stilled as the night
shiroki yo ni	in stark moonlight.

Chikubun 375: This evokes the small hours of the night.

Like the pair on the traces of Onoe Palace, this seamless link is achieved mainly through imagistic progression and a deepening of feeling from one verse through the next. Conceptually the tsukeku is presented as the "reason" for the absence of footprints on the path—the hour is very late, people are fast asleep. But that is really less important than the motion of intensification evoked by the chill reflection of moonlight on the frost of the maeku, a stark, transparent whiteness whose feeling belongs to Shinkei's special poetry of the chill and reduced.

50 *STKBS* 918

aware zo fukaki	It moves the heart deeply—
nobe no yugure	dusk gathering along the moors.
sawamizu o	Wings flapping in
tamoto ni kakuru	chill spray of swamp water,
shigi nakite	a snipe cries out.

Chikubun 453: Sleeves moist with tears are like the snipe wet in the drops of water.

This would also be in the "chill and meager" (*hieyase*) mode in its singular concentration of effect, the terse economic diction that wastes not a single seme in the task of animating the maeku. By itself the verse is a wholly objective image; its juxtaposition with the maeku has the effect of charging the latter's prosaic statement, *aware zo fukaki*, with the force of a visual and tactile sensation, at the same time that it functions as a metonymical detail of the wide evening scenery evoked there. Again, as the *Chikubun* comment explains, the image of the bird may be seen as a metaphorical figure for "sleeves moist with tears," the classical poetic image of a sensibility permeated with a sense of *aware*.

56 *STKBS* 979

ikaru kata ni	Up to how far will it bend,
nabikihatsuramu	yielding to such longing.
musashino ya	Musashino Plain—
kaya ga sue fuku	A sea of plume grass undulating
aki no kaze	in the winds of fall!

Keikandō, Middle Stage: There is nothing concealed here. Exercising the imagination, it is a renga of profound spirit.   (p. 137)

Chikubun 339: The poem *Ikaru sue ni*. [Kenzai refers to the following poem: *SKKS* 378. Autumn. "Among ten poems submitted in Minase." Minamoto Michiteru.]

musashino ya	Musashino Plain—
yukedomo *aki* no	tirelessly I walk, yet see
hate zo naki	no end of autumn;
ikaru kaze no	what sights may it yet disclose,
sue ni fukuramu	wind sweeping over the horizon?

Boundless desire. The referent of the maeku as such is vague, but it is most probably a Love verse in which the subject expresses anxiety about how far her ungovernable desire will lead her. Shinkei effects a brilliantly startling shift to the Autumn theme in a link that pivots around the question of extent posed by the maeku. In effect the scene that he delineates becomes an objective correlative of the limitless, insatiable character of desire. The verb *nabiku* ("to bend, bow, incline"), whose unspoken subject is the heart in the maeku, is displaced in the tsukeku by plume grasses *bending* in the autumn wind; the associative word to *nabiku*, *sue* ("tips," but also "end" in a temporal and spatial sense), also echoes *hatsuramu* in the compound verb *nabikihatsuramu* ([up to how far] will it bend in the end) in the maeku.

When the *Keikandō* declares that "there is nothing concealed" in the link, it means that the verbal associations just described are quite common, and the way in which the shift occurred is unmistakable, that is, after the fact. When it then goes on to commend the verse's imagination and "profound spirit," it is commenting on the originality and depth of thought that translated the maeku's meaning into a landscape suggestive of the limitless delights of the autumn season. This is enabled by the mediation of the *Shinkokinshū* foundation poem, which evokes the vastness of Musashi Plain through the image of the wind sweeping over the far horizon, promising yet more enjoyment to be had in the distance.[36]

58 *STKBS* 1047

kurenuru iro ni	Shifts the wind along the bay
kawaru urakaze	into the dimmed color of dusk.
shimo shiroki	Pale frost on
shii no hayama no	hillslope oak leaves tremulous
aki fukete	in an aging autumn.

Chikubun 488: The color of the undersides of the oak leaves is white. The color of dusk is dark, that of the oak leaves white.

Chikurinshū kikigaki 98: The coming of dusk in the maeku becomes the aging of autumn. The undersides of the oak leaves are white like frost.

An exquisitely executed link, the tonal contrast between the dark background of dusk and the delicate paleness of the "undersides" (*ura*, "bay," in its second unspoken but intended meaning) of the oak leaves blown back (*urakaesu*, a verb suggested by *kawaru*, "shift") by the winds of the maeku evoke a chill sensation indicative of advancing autumn. The way the Miscellaneous maeku is so imperceptibly carried into the thematic frame of Autumn is extremely fine.

Winter

64 *STKBS* 1193.

kariba no kaesa	There's a catch of great prize
emono koso are	on the way back from the hunt!
kururu no ni	Lying in wait for
tsuki o machitoru	the moon, upon the dimming fields
yuki harete	the snow clears up.

Chikurinshō no chū 149: The maeku refers to T'ai-kung-wang [J. Taikōbō], who was the catch obtained by King Wen of the Chou on the banks of the Wei. The tsukeku turns this into a situation in which on the way back from the hunting field, the snow clears up, having waited to catch the moon when it appears. The use of "lying in wait" [*machitoru*] to correspond with "great catch" [*emono*] is of the essence in this link.

Chikubun 557: The way back from the hunting field is a reference to the anecdote about T'ai-kung-wang.

Chikurinshū kikigaki 117: The maeku refers to the anecdote about King Wen obtaining [the services of] T'ai-kung-wang. The tsukeku makes the moon the catch.

The story of T'ai-kung-wang (a title; his name was Lü Shang) is told in the *Shih chi* (Records of the Grand Historian), chapter 32. T'ai-kung-wang, who had turned his back on worldly affairs, was peacefully fishing on the banks of the Wei River when he was discovered by King Wen of the Chou on his way back from a hunting trip. He was straightaway pressed into his service as the long-awaited teacher who would help the Chou put down the Shang and pacify the land. The figural analogy of T'ai-kung-wang to a great "catch" (*emono*) also culls from the *Shih chi* account.

Wit. By a masterful sleight-of-hand, Shinkei banishes the T'ai-kung-wang anecdotal allusion that everyone is expecting—so popular was this historical legend among the literati of the time—and transforms the maeku into a wholly objective Winter verse, while thoroughly capturing the semantic and syntactic inflection of the maeku. In sum, the "catch of great prize on the way home from the hunt" is not Taikōbō but the scene of snow-covered meadows shining whitely beneath the new-risen moon. As Sōgi observes, the tense correspondence between "great catch or prize" (*emono*) and "lying in wait to catch" (*machitoru*) is the pivot of the link; it summons that exact moment when a hunter captures his prey, a dynamics of action superimposed upon the same motion of suddenness with which the falling snow clears up to reveal a pristine whiteness reflecting, that is, "capturing" the moon.

In the *Kokemushiro* collection, Shinkei classifies this verse under the "interesting" (*omoshiroki*) or "arresting" style, which is characterized mainly by a novel, witty conception. This mode does not rank high in his hierarchy of styles, but quickness of wit, it need hardly be said, is a basic requirement in extemporaneous renga. It is a central characteristic that distinguishes it from waka and gives it a dry, analytic character behind all the courtly grace of feeling and aesthetic beauty. It is no accident that it was the preferred medium of warriors and priests.

66 STKBS 1261

sawabe no mizu no	Now far, now close, sound of
ochikochi no koe	water lapping along the moor.

kari zo naku   A wild goose calls!
yuki no kono yo ya   This night of falling snow
fukenuran   So deep . . . ?

Sudden illumination: Shinkei and Bashō. It is interesting to observe
that verses like this, which make no allusion to an older poem or anecdotal
lore, do not surface in the exegetical literature, and equally illuminating to
note that some of Bashō's best hokku and *renku* will have exactly the same
quality of a startling, inward illumination more than two centuries later.
Indeed the similarities in method, critical principles, and philosophic depth
between the two are so specific and far-reaching that Ebara Taizō insists,
despite the scant documentary evidence, that Bashō directly studied Shinkei's mind.[37] That he suppresses any mention of the other, while announcing the oneness of his art with "Saigyō's waka, Sōgi's renga, Sesshū's
paintings, and Rikyū's tea," might conceivably be a case of what Harold
Bloom has called the "anxiety of influence," the Oedipal, psychological
repression of a great precursor-father's power in the mind of a writer
anxious to establish himself.

This possibility is all the more tantalizing in that Bashō's critical principles—*fūga no makoto* (the truth of art), the centrality of *sabi*, the valorization of *nioi-zuke* (linking by "fragrance," i.e., through a mental leap), the
view of poetic process as a self-transcending fusion with the object, and so
on—have definite parallels in Shinkei's poetic practice and critical philosophy, but their major implications were not fully understood in Shinkei's
own time, as may be gathered from the fact that the commentaries presented here do not remark them. It was not until Bashō restated them in the
context of his haikai philosophy and modern scholars took them up as
evidence of the Zen influence in haiku, that they attained the wide recognition they deserve. If we sometimes get the impression that Shinkei was
ahead of his time, while Bashō seemed willfully to reject the "floating
world" of Edo and identify with the stern spirit of the medieval age, it is
precisely due to the remarkable coincidence of these two minds outside the
two centuries that divided them.

The issue of direct influence apart, there is absolutely no question
regarding this intellectual congruence, as anyone who reads both closely
will soon discover. In the matter of linking, consider the quality of this pair
of verses from the *kasen*, "At the Ash-lye Tub" (*Akuoke no*, published
1691).

akuoke no   At the ash-lye tub,
shizuku yamikeri   the dripping is stilled!
kirigirisu   murmur of crickets.
Bonchō   Bonchō

abura kasurite   The oil lamp sputters low
yoine suru aki   dozing in a twilit autumn.
   Bashō   Bashō

In the renga pair, the tranquillity figured by the lapping of the water against the moor bank, advancing, receding, is suddenly stretched taut, distilled as it were into the faint metallic echo of the call of a wild goose from behind the thick blanket of snow, accentuating the depth of the stillness of the night. This movement from a relaxed tranquillity to a concentrated silence is similar to the effect of the link in the haikai pair above, except that the progression occurs in reverse; the tsukeku by Bashō dissolves the tense, resounding stillness of the maeku in the blank image of dozing at twilight. The artistic intelligence is the same in the inwardness of the link, in the stalking of the ineffable dimensions of silence as a cognitive experience registering itself with the acuteness of a sensation. The ineffability is particularly marked in Shinkei's tsukeku in the way it crystallizes "now close, now far" (*ochikochi*), a bipolar image, into a single cry that is sensed as both immediate and remote at the same time.

Elegies

70 *STKBS* 1339

mata yo to iishi   "I will come again," he said,
kure zo hakanaki   Yet another dusk falls, empty.

chiru uchi ni   I gaze, remembering
hito no sakidatsu   him who went before. . . .
hana o mite   The flowers are falling.

Chikurinshō no chū 328: The world of man is even more ephemeral than the flowers. [*KKS* 850. Laments. "Composed while gazing at the flowers on the cherry tree planted by someone who passed away just when it was about to bloom." Ki no Mochiyuki.]

hana yori mo   Man, it turns out, is
hito koso ada ni   even more fleeting than the
narinikere   flowers—now have I
izure o saki ni   seen, having presumed to know,
koimu to ka mishi   who will miss the other first.

Chikubun 1112: The poem "Man is even more than the flowers" is the feeling expressed in the situation of the verse, where the man who said "till we meet again" has passed away.

Mediated by the foundation poem while effecting a variation on it, this verse shifts the context of the maeku from Love to Laments. In the former, the feeling of emptiness (*hakanaki*) is caused by the lover's failure to come at the promised hour of dusk. In the latter the man's absence turns out to be beyond help, since he has passed away. Furthermore, within the context of the link, it is implied that the lover promised to come when the cherries were in bloom; thus their scattering now is filled with a poignant significance for the speaker—this is how Shinkei responds to the maeku's emphatic inflection. Such a link is a particularly clear example of how the maeku in renga always has a double identity, or an indeterminate meaning, until it is fixed by the tsukeku.

72 *STKBS* 1359

chigiri mo yume to	How sad that even a vow
naru zo kanashiki	should turn into a dream!
naki ato ni	I read his letters:
yukusue tanomu	bereft wake of a hoped-for time
fumi o mite	till the end of time.

The tsukeku provides the concrete context by which the maeku's general statement acquires a more compelling, ironic force. The man's passionate vows of fidelity for all time, expressed in his letters, are like a dream now that he is dead. The exact nuance of *chigiri*, which may mean an ongoing intimate relationship, or simply the promise of one, is left ambiguous in the maeku. In the former sense, the verse means that even the closest relationship may be severed and seem dream-like thereafter. Shinkei anchors it to the latter sense, however, while fully responding to the maeku's emphatic inflection: the promise of a union, so deeply longed for, is doubly a dream (*yume to naru zo*) since it was never fulfilled in this life and has now passed forever beyond possibility. The letters are left as paradoxical "traces" (*ato*) of a mere potentiality, something that never was in reality. In this way, linking in renga is like a process of focusing a camera lens to enable the maeku's picture to come through; it is the act of resolving an ambiguity through interpretation.

74 *STKBS* 1361

kiyoki na no mi zo	That only her chaste name remains
nao aware naru	is all the more tragic.
nureginu wa	The sodden clothes:
tsui ni naki yo ni	a slander first revealed to the
arawarete	world when she was dead.

Guku Shibakusa 211: Long ago, I believe it was in Tawarejima Island off the coast of Tsukushi, a woman who wished to get rid of her stepdaughter made her put on drenched clothes to make it look like she had engaged in intimate relations with a fisherman. She then told the girl's father the reason behind the drenched clothes and so was able to eliminate her.   (p. 63)

Chikubun 1117: There was once a couple living in Tawarejima. The mother, hating her stepdaughter, told the girl's father that his daughter had had relations with a fisherman. When the father accused her of lying, she put drenched clothes on the girl and made her go to bed in them. On seeing his daughter thus, the father was convinced and killed her. Afterward she appeared to him in a dream. The verse means that her name was eventually vindicated after her death, but that makes it all the more pitiful.

Chikurinshū kikigaki 300: Long ago in the place called Tawarejima in Chikuzen [Fukuoka Prefecture.], a girl was hated by her stepmother. This stepmother made her put on the drenched clothes of a fisherman and accused her to her father of unchastity. She was then put to death by her father, who later heard the following poem in a dream. [*Ise monogatari shūckū* 336.]

nugikisuru
sono tabakari no
nureginu wa
nagaki namida no
tameshi narikeri

The drenched clothes
forced upon an innocent body
in an evil plot—
have turned into a lesson
in unending tears.

Since then, it is said, false accusations have been expressed through the image of drenched clothes.

Tawarejima is a rock island near the mouth of the Midori River off the coast of Uto District, Kumamoto Prefecture. The place-name and the use of the expression *nureginu kiru* (lit., "wear drenched clothes") to mean "to be falsely accused" occur in a poem in the *Tales of Ise*, section 61. As indicated in all the commentaries above, this figurative expression has its source in an ancient legend about Tawarejima. A good example of the technique of linking through an anecdotal allusion (*honzetsu*), the verse again demonstrates how crucial inflectional particles (*te ni o ha*) and adverbials are in achieving a firm connection with the maeku. These brief words—here, *no mi* (only), the emphatic *zo*, and *nao* (even more)—constitute the bones of a statement, its specific rhetorical force. Their presence makes the task of the tsukeku poet more difficult, and it is therefore a mark of the adept that he confronts them without evasion in his own verse.

78 *STKBS* 1376

koenuru yama ya
hate to naruramu

The mountain is surmounted,
the final boundary reached.

hito no waza
sugureba izuru
mine no tera

The forty-nine days
having passed, they emerge from
the temple on the peak.

Chikurinshō no chū 342: The ritual of sending off a dead man's soul into the next world is called *hito no waza*. When it is held for such high personages as the Emperor, it is called *miwaza*.

Chikubun 1154: *Hito no waza* refers to *chūin*. This period of *chūin* having passed, the mourners leave the mountain temple.

Shinkei renga jichū 57: *Hito no waza* is the name habitually given since the old days to the five periods of *chūin* when the mourners seclude themselves. Therefore the words: "The mountain is surmounted, / the final boundary reached." It is a ritual held in a mountain village temple and such places. The ritual is alluded to in old poems as well. [*SKKS* 764. Laments. "Composed on the death of a woman who had been living with him for many years, when the forty-nine days had ended but he remained in retreat in the mountain." Fujiwara Akisuke.]

hito wa mina	The others have all
hana no miyako ni	to the flowers of the capital
chirihatete	drifted away—
hitori shigururu	I am alone with the autumn rain
aki no yamazato	shrouding the mountain village.

In addition to illuminating poetic and anecdotal allusions and explaining the link, the commentaries elucidated the meanings of words, particularly when they were no longer in current usage, as seems to be the case with *hito no waza* (lit., "a person's deeds"), a term occurring as early as the *Kokinshū*, and equivalent in medieval usage to *chūin* (lit., "the middle darkness"), the forty-nine day period after a person's death when the soul wanders in an indeterminate limbo prior to rebirth in a next existence. During this period, the mourners are in ritual seclusion at a mountain temple, praying for the soul's salvation, keeping it company until it reaches the next world.

The maeku in this pair is a Travel verse; Shinkei implicitly converts it into the journey of the soul in the middle darkness, as shared by his mourners in the mountain temple. *Hate* (the boundary) in the maeku, referring to the final mountain crossing on a long journey, acquires the double sense of a temporal "end" in the tsukeku, where it signifies for the mourners the end of a long period of seclusion, and for the departed soul the entry into another world.

Love

80 STKBS 1399

nageku omoi yo	Bear witness, ye heaven and earth,
ametsuchi mo shire	to the pain of this longing!
kuni to nari	Since land's arising, and
yo to naru yori no	human world's becoming, to love
koi mo ushi	has ever been to suffer.

Chikurinshō no chū 177: This refers to the way of love from the beginnings of heaven and earth, when the two deities [Izanagi and Izanami] appeared and exchanged the first marriage vows.

Chikubun 669: From the drippings from the heavenly spear, the country was formed. The clear substance slowly rose to become the heavens, the impure substance slowly descended to become the earth. The way of love had its beginnings from the very creation of heaven and earth.

Ametsuchi ("heaven and earth") in the maeku called forth the allusion to the creation myth in the *Kojiki* and *Nihongi*, as paraphrased in the *Chikubun* (which seems interestingly to read the heavenly spear as a phallic symbol) and augmented by *Chikurinshō no chū*, which refers specifically to the nuptial rites exchanged by Izanagi and Izanami, the primal couple, in the mythical account. The point of the link, however, is not merely that the very land and humankind were born out of love (according to the mythical account, the Japanese islands arose from the primal deities' divine coupling), but that from that very beginning, "love has been suffering" (*koi mo ushi*). In other words, Shinkei is alluding to Izanagi's terrible grief when Izanami died giving birth to the fire god. So maddened by grief was he that he smote this child and went down to wrest Izanami from the land of the dead. There, however, his very longing drives him to violate the taboo against gazing at her while still in the underworld, and they are condemned to permanent estrangement. This pointed allusion is what gives force to the maeku's impassioned declaration that the very heaven and earth bear witness to (*shiru*, "know, have experience of") the grievous pain of loving.

82 *STKBS* 1415

yukue o towaba	Should one ask my destination,
ikaga kotaen	however shall I answer?
omoiwabi	Wracked by longing,
waga na o kaete	he changed his name to another's
shinobu yo ni	in the secret night.

Chikubun 589: This is on "love borrowing another's name" [*hito no na o karu koi*]. It means, if Captain Kaoru questions me closely, how will I answer him?

Chikurinshū kikigaki 129: While secretly visiting under someone else's name, should someone inquire closely into the matter, what shall I answer? This alludes to the incident in the *Shining Genji* [*Hikaru Genji*] when the Lord of the Military Guards disguised himself as Captain Kaoru and visited [Ukifune].

The maeku as such is a Miscellaneous verse that Shinkei frames in a Love context through an inspired allusion to the incident in the "Ukifune" (Floating boat) chapter in the *Genji* where Niou journeys to Uji in the night and seduces Ukifune by pretending to be her patron and lover, Kaoru.[38] One passage in particular in the description of the fateful Uji journey delves into Niou's feelings of guilt toward Kaoru for his impending betrayal, as he recalls Kaoru's sympathy in the old days when he was courting Nakanokimi in Uji. The same passage mentions his mingled feeling of fear and excitement as he rides toward Uji in a shabby disguise. It is undoubtedly this psychology of fear and guilt that Shinkei is evoking in this link.

84 *STKBS* 1444

akikaze samumi	In the cold gusts of autumn,
yo koso fukenure	the night itself has worn thin.
omoiwabi	As I lay longing-tormented,
yukeba kari naki	the wild geese cried, the moon
tsuki ochite	sank in the sky.

Shinkei renga jichū 25: This is the feeling of being beside oneself in frustrated longing for someone whose heart is cold. This kind of feeling may be discerned too in the old poems. [*SIS* 224. Winter. Tsurayuki.]

omoikane	As beset by yearning
imogari yukeba	I seek my beloved's abode,
fuyu no yo no	in the wintry night
kawakaze samumi	the river wind gusts so cold
chidori naku nari	the plovers are crying.

[*Minishū* 2809. Fujiwara Ietaka.][39]

chidori naku	As plovers cry from
kawabe no chihara	the marsh reeds along the river,
kaze saete	the wind glints chill—
awade zo kaeru	I return, not having met her,
ariake no sora	in the paling sky before dawn.

Chikubun 703: *Omoiwabi* [longing-tormented] is a word used when one should exercise forbearance but is unable to contain oneself. The way in which the deepening of the night is conceived is arresting. He is unable to contain his longing throughout the long night.

Asaji 46: The way in which it evokes the man who is beside himself with yearning, his thoughts wandering futile far into the night, is truly excellent. (p. 330)

The link, as both the later commentaries point out, focuses on *yo koso fukenure* (lit., "how deep has the night grown!"). It conceives the subject of the maeku as a man or woman who has lain awake through the autumn night, beset by intense frustrated desire, suddenly startled out of this self-consuming absorption by the cries of the wild geese and the subsequent realization that the moon has set. The verse echoes the chill self-knowledge foregrounded in the two poems cited by Shinkei himself as precedents. Ietaka's poem, incidentally, is itself an allusive variation on Tsurayuki's. Shinkei's verse is an extremely close, and equally cold evocation of the same experience.

86 *STKBS* 1460

urami aru	Could bitter memory
hito ya wasurete	betray me, that I am again
mataruran	waiting for him?
omoisutsureba	I had cast him from my mind—
ame no yūgure	At dusk the rain is falling.

Chikubun 676: A lower verse conceived in the manner of this one shows skill.

The skill Kenzai praises here refers to the terse simplicity of the fourteen-syllable, two-line lower verse, which nevertheless succeeds in anchoring the thought in the maeku, rendering it more acute and complex. In this link, the involuntary (*jihatsu*) inflection of the verb *matsu* (wait) in the maeku is crucial. Shinkei interprets it to signify a sense of self-disgust: Why am I driven to again yearn for this feckless man though I had firmly renounced him? The rain at dusk is the imagistic correlative figuring the intense loneliness that all unaware creeps upon the subject at that hour when a lover would visit. Her mind inadvertently drops its guard, forgetting his past remissness and feeling only a yearning for companionship amidst the melancholy rains.

88 *STKBS* 1492

karine no toko wa	Sleeping upon a transient bed
yume mo sadamezu	even dreams cannot settle.
hashi chikaku	Along the corner-room
tanomeshi yado ni	lodgings so hopefully chosen,
machifukete	the waiting night dwindles.

Chikubun 614: [The handling of] *karine* is arresting.

The Travel theme signified by *karine* (temporary, brief sleep in unfamiliar surroundings) is maintained in the tsukeku through *yado* (lodgings), at the same time that the Love theme is superimposed as a second layer. In the maeku as such, "dreams cannot settle" (*yume mo sadamezu*) means that on an unfamiliar bed, the traveler's sleep is too restless for any dream to be seen through to the end. In the tsukeku, this "dream" is specified as the hope (*tanomeshi*) of spending the night together. Kenzai's observation that the handling of *karine* is "arresting" (*omoshiroshi*) refers to the witty implication that the corner room, especially chosen for its accessibility, is frequently disturbed by the coming and going of other guests, making sleep and dreams impossible, underscoring the restless feeling associated with *karine*. Furthermore, it is implied that each noise whets the subject's expectation, only to be disappointed again, and yet again, thus pointing up once more "even dreams cannot settle" in the maeku. This is a humorously ironic, almost haikai-*teki* link, quite distinct from Shinkei's usual serious, *ushin* mode of deep feeling. As we have seen in the preceding literary biography, however, Shinkei did not reject even images and conceptions that might be considered unrefined, as long as they achieved a tight link with the maeku.

90 *STKBS* 1552

omou kokoro zo	This yearning heart will be
tōku tsurenuru	beside you, no matter how far!
kawaraji to	Vows of love unchanging
nochi no yo made o	even through worlds to come,
kataru yo ni	in the close-held night.

The tsukeku interprets the ambiguous *tōku* (far) in the maeku as a temporal dimension and suggests an ironic undertone in the marked contrast between the idea of a constancy lasting until the afterlife and the fact that such talk is transpiring in the brief space of the night. The irony is not meant in a sarcastic vein; rather, the third-person observer is moved to a sense of wonder at the psychological force of a passion that drives lovers to believe in a patent illusion.

92 *STKBS* 1554

fukeyuku yowa no	Pain grips the heart, as the
kokorogurushisa	hours dwindle past midnight.
kataru ma no	The moon—within a
tsuki o makura no	passionate space has shifted,
nishi ni mite	west of the pillow.

The sentiment is wholly conventional for the theme, as is invariably the case in renga whose symbolic language is constituted by waka. Lovers bewailing the brevity of the night appear in love poetry from the very beginning, definitely as a conscious motif from the *Kokinshū* on. The point is to render the feeling again with the novel interest of a new conceptual and verbal structure that unexpectedly animates the maeku's words in a specific way. Sometimes the unexpected consists in deflating expectation; the maeku here would usually be read as the pain of lying awake through the night, waiting for one's lover (the *yowa no nezame* motif), but Shinkei transforms it to the pain of swiftly impending separation. There is a sense in which it can be said that renga is at base—prior to any question of poeticity—an analytical interpretive practice, a close investigation into the semantic fields of the maeku's words through the medium of an inventive wit. Keenness of intelligence is foregrounded by the sheer necessity of capturing the maeku's meaning within the brief compass of a fourteen- or seventeen-syllable utterance. The result may not be high poetry; in fact, much renga is undoubtedly minor poetry, judged by Western criteria of greatness. This verse and the preceding, for instance, do not come up to the height, or depth, one has come to expect from Shinkei, but they unmistakably demonstrate the absorbing quality of the renga verse. Terse and analytical, they are exercises in the precise verbal and mental economy of the renga link, a discipline in the efficient dynamics of a new poetic rhetoric.

96 *STKBS* 1586

hito naki niwa wa	In the deserted garden stirs
tada matsu no kaze	only the wind in the pines.
kaeru yo ni	Still she hesitates,
kokorobosoku mo	a forlorn figure in the night
tatazumite	where he heads home.

If evocation of overtly unexpressed feeling (*yojō*) is indeed the poetic moment, as the classical poets from the *Shinkokinshū* period firmly believed, then this verse is unquestionably more "poetic" than the two preceding ones. The way in which the maeku suddenly emerges into significance, as if the words *hito naki niwa* ("deserted garden") and *tada matsu no kaze* ("only the wind in the pines") were all at once charged with tension, is quite subtly handled. We comprehend at once that this woman has just seen her lover off in the waning night, but she remains standing, "hesitating" in the veranda, looking out at the garden long after the other has passed beyond it. The poetic moment or feeling here is expressed by the wind's faint rustling; it delicately figures the furtive wave of longing that momentarily overcomes her at the sound, and underscores the "deserted" quality of the garden.

98 *STKBS* 1588

tanomeokite mo	He leaves me promises to rely on,
nani ni ka wa semu	but what is the use of it all?
inochi o mo	Whether my life will
hito o mo shiranu	endure, or his love, uncertain:
kinuginu ni	this parting at dawn.

Keikandō, Middle Stage: This is a mind that has reflected upon the impermanence of the things of this world and realizes that promises are devoid of substance. (p. 138)

The link is quite close, the technique ratiocinative, but quite impressive in its rhetorical force; in particular the ironic juxtaposition of two incommensurable terms—the duration of a life (hers, potentially shortened by frustration) and the depth of a passion (his, already belied by the emptiness of promises)—is quite effective. Shinkei is certainly projecting an unusually strong-minded woman here, passionate but also cold-eyed.

100 *STKBS* 1616

omoeba ima ni	Pondering, I see that the present
nitaru inishie	to the past bears resemblance.
taene tada	So let us break, cleanly—
mizu shirazarishi	we were naught but utter strangers
naka zo kashi	from the very start!

Guku Shibakusa 117: How could it, from what unbidden moment did the love flowing between us begin to wane? Yet, in explaining it to myself, I see that I must not grieve. Since in the beginning we had never seen or known one another, it is useless to protest if in the end we should return to where we started.   (p. 31)

Chikurinshō no chū 205: This would be in the spirit of the poem [*SKKS* 1297. Love. Saigyō]:

utoku naru	Why resent the woman
hito o nani tote	her growing indifference?
uramuran	Time there was
shirarezu shiranu	when I was to her but
ori mo arishi ni	a stranger, as she to me.

(The gender of *hito* [person] in Saigyō's poem is not clear; I chose the feminine deliberately, although aware that male poets also took on the feminine persona.) One can imagine how the session must have perked up at Shinkei's performance here; the shift from the Miscellaneous maeku to Love—the spontaneous allusion to the conception of Saigyō's waka that securely resolves the puzzle of the difficult, ambiguous proposition that the present resembles the past—is a truly stunning move.

104 *STKBS* 1692

semete wa yoso no	Only come, little enough to ask,
kaesa ni mo toe	on your way home from another!
futamichi no	Even bitterness
urami mo taete	at the twain path lies consumed
koishiki ni	in the fire of longing.

Oi no susami 42, 43:

semete *wa* yoso no	Only come, *little enough to ask*,
kaesa ni mo toe	on your way home from another!
. . . . .	
tsurenaki *mono wa*	*The thing that is* cruelly
inochi narikeri	persistent, is life itself!

In these two verses, the phrases *semete wa* [at the very least] and *mono wa* [the thing that is] constitute the central point where the link must take place. If you do not pay them serious attention, your tsukeku will be vaguely general in outline and will inevitably lack a precise correspondence with the maeku. In response to each of these:

futamichi no	Even bitterness
urami mo taete	at the twain path lies consumed
koishiki ni	in the fire of my longing.
Shinkei	Shinkei

. . . . .

okuyama no	In the deepest mountain
matsu no ha o suki	with only pine needles to chew
koke o kite	and moss to wear.
Sōzei	Sōzei

With these [tsukeku], the crucial words that constitute the site of the link should become clearly perceptible. "Chewing pine needles" refers to food, and "wearing moss" to clothing. That life which survives even such extreme conditions corresponds very well to the phrase "the thing that is cruelly persistent." In composing verses on the four seasons, one can rely on the atmospheric effects of the scenery, so that even if the verse itself is not so minutely conceived, it will nevertheless seem graceful as long as its overall configuration is sound. Of course, it would also be deplorable if it were noticeably at variance with the maeku. Verses on Love, Laments, and Reminiscence, on the other hand, must be composed with precise attention to even the inflectional morphemes [*te ni o ha*] in the maeku. (p. 158)

Keikandō, Beginning Stage: In both waka and renga on Love, it is the practice to evoke an intensely despairing, vulnerable mood. The link with the word *semete* [at the very least] is excellent. This verse is included in both the *Chikurinshō* and the *Shinsen Tsukubashū*. (p. 133)

*Inflectional morphemes (*te ni o ha*).* Sōgi's perspicuity as a critic and teacher of renga is impressively displayed in this lengthy analysis of two verses, the first by Shinkei, the second by the other major poet among the seven sages, Sōzei. He confirms, in effect, what has been observed previously about the importance of "inflectional morphemes" (*te ni o ha*) in the linking process. These apparently include not only *joshi* (syntactic particles) but also *jodōshi* (inflectional suffixes), as well as adverbial expressions that give a specific rhetorical shape to the maeku's diction. As distinct from so-called *kotoba* (nouns, verbs, and adjectives that carry independent semantic values), these morphemes have a purely functional value; they specify how the independent words relate to each other syntactically, and shape the expressiveness of the maeku's utterance. They are therefore frequently decisive, as here in the case of *semete wa* and *mono wa*, in governing the poet's response if it is to attain to the authenticity of a true link. Thus Sōgi calls them *manako no tsukedokoro* (lit., "the eye of the link"), and his whole point is to demonstrate how both Shinkei and Sōzei capture this "eye," the central point where the connection pivots, in their respective responses. To ignore this inflectional node of the maeku's expression results in a failure of connection, a slack, sloppy tsukeku that is wide of the mark, lacking the tight precision that constitutes the economy of an authentic renga link.

Another major point of the *Oi no susami* passage is the distinction drawn, vis-à-vis the subject of inflectional morphemes, between seasonal themes (Spring, Summer, Autumn, and Winter) and the human affairs themes (Love, Travel, Laments, Reminiscence, Buddhism, Shintō). In the former, the images themselves implicitly bear the atmospheric, modal values or feeling tones evolved by centuries of waka composition on just this marked lexicon of the seasons; the rhetorical shape of the verse is not so crucial in these seasonal verses, and the tsukeku may be broadly vague and generalized in the sense of leaving the nominal images themselves to fulfill the function of expressiveness. The human affairs themes, on the other hand, tend to be colored by the poet's subjective, mental experience, and such verses are accordingly more highly inflected in nature. The linking process here should be more minutely (*komakani*) conceived, taking full account of the rhetorical particularity of the maeku as expressed by its inflectional morphemes. The theme of Love in particular, as the *Keikandō* observes, renders an "intensely despairing, vulnerable mood" (*ikahodo mo wabite yowayowa to suru*); it would thus be a violation of what we might call the dialogical authenticity of renga to respond inadequately to such a powerful emotion.

In the first maeku, *semete wa* rhetorically inscribes the measure of the speaker's despair; Shinkei fully takes it into account in his evocation of a woman whose longing is so intense that her very resentment at the man's infidelity (the correspondence between "on your way home from another" and "twain path") crumbles before it, and she is driven to accept even the most minimal (*semete wa*) attention from him. This is perhaps the psychological moment of despairing surrender that the author of the *Gossamer Diary* (*Kagerō nikki*), for instance, refuses to be drawn into, even as she suffers from hearing the noise of Kaneie's carriage before her gate coming and going on his way to another. In the second maeku, *mono wa* underscores the cruel persistence of life, and Sōzei justifies this emphatic force by subjecting the speaker to the extremes of deprivation of a solitary, primitive existence in the mountains, where despite his desire for extinction, his life as a biological organism endures. The implication is that the speaker was driven to renounce the world and life itself due to unhappy experience, only to realize that neither sorrow nor physical deprivation are a match for the elemental vitality of the life force. This is a strikingly novel concept compared to the conventional poetic wisdom that emphasizes life's transience, not its persistence; however, the implicit complaint about existence as a vale of suffering is wholly within the orthodox semantic field of the Laments (*jukkai*) theme.

110 *STKBS* 1764

makura ni hajiyo	Feel shame before the pillow,
shiru to koso ie	For 'tis said to be all-knowing!
madoromu o	What if he who
yume ni toikuru	visits only in dreams, should
hito ya mimu	see me dozing?

Keikandō, Advanced Stage: [*KKS* 676. Love. Lady Ise.]

shiru to ieba	For 'tis said to be
makura da ni sede	all-knowing, I made sure to sleep
neshi mono o	without a pillow—
chiri naranu na no	Still my name, no mere dust,
sora ni tatsuramu	now rises to the sky on rumor?

The third line, a crucial point here, comes to mean "I shall not doze off"—it is a marvelous turn.   (p. 144)

Chikubun 726: Were I sleeping, he who comes to me in a dream, seeing me thus, would blame me for being shallow. Therefore "feel shame before the pillow" and desist from sleeping, it says. "It is said to be all-knowing" means that the person will come to know.

Chikurinshū kikigaki 166: Would he who comes to me in a dream conclude that I have dozed off, forgetful of my longing? Thus it says, "feel shame before the pillow."

The link turns on the speaker's paradoxical quandary, that her lover visits only in dreams, yet she may not go to sleep for fear that he will find her indifferently dozing instead of being beset in wakeful anxiety. The situation is amusing, if we wished to be unfeeling about it, but since this verse is classified under the Advanced Stage in the *Keikandō*, clearly that would not be an appropriate response. What characterizes the late stage is precisely an impartiality of attitude that takes any maeku at all as a serious (*ushin*) utterance and deals with it accordingly; this goes as well for expressions of naiveté, as in this link. Here Shinkei justifies the maeku through what Kenzai calls a "marvelous" (*kimyō*) turn or allusive variation on the *honka*, *KKS* 676 by Lady Ise. In this turn, the third line of the poem, *neshi mono o* (though I slept), is transformed into the implied statement "I shall not doze," and the whole situation changed so that it is not rumor that the speaker fears but the charge of indifference from the lover. In other words, "feel shame before the pillow" (*makura ni hajiyo*) implies, "I shall not take to bed," and the subject of the verb "know" (*shiru*) is not the omniscient pillow of Ise's poem, that intimate sharer of one's most private thoughts, but the man of the speaker's dreams. Here it is well to note that according to popular belief, to see a person in a dream signifies that he/she is thinking of oneself; from this perspective, the speaker's "shame" and consequently the impossibly problematic nature of the situation become more understandable.

112 *STKBS* 1866

kuyashi ya kokoro	Burning with regret, the heart
ajikina no mi ya	within this miserable body!
hitoyo neshi	It was but a night
hito ni asaku mo	I lay with him, and too naively
waga tokete	yielded to passion.

Chikubun 630: This illustrates the longing to meet again the loved one [*aite awazaru koi*]; he beguiled her with many assurances that he would come again and again.

Asaji 54: It is impossible to respond to such a maeku in a simple manner. The sense of the verse itself is plain enough to see, but I cite it to show how it gives full consideration [to the maeku].   (p. 332)

Kenzai zōdan: This verse is from Shinkei's Kantō period. It was composed in a thrice, even before the calligrapher had finished recording the previous verse, and he said that Sōgi spoke of it as an exceptionally marvelous verse.   (p. 402)[40]

Keikandō, Middle Stage: [*Kokin rokujō* 987. "A Mountain Well." Tsurayuki.]

kuyashiku zo	It is too bitter:
kumisometekeru	shallow in the ways of drawing
asakereba	another's heart,
sode no mi nururu	I have only wet my sleeves in
yama no i no mizu	the water of the mountain well.

There are two interpretations to this poem [as it relates to the link]. In the one the speaker regrets having momentarily yielded her heart to the other despite his indifference. In the other, she feels that in cases where the other comes for several nights, one may indeed expect him to remain in one's affections for the repeated demonstrations [of fidelity], but to be thus so attached to him after no more than a single night's meeting is really galling. It is the [rankling] feeling of being unable to yield wholly, and from having yielded all too frivolously. He [Shinkei] said that in renga if one composes in the orthodox mode, one would employ the first interpretation; it is particularly common in the works of the middle period.   (p. 138)

Adequacy of response. "It is impossible to respond to such a maeku in a simple manner" (*kayō no maeku ni wa, naozari ni tsukete wa tsukegataki mono nari*)—that is, the maeku's emotional intensity demands a psychological response that is wholly adequate to it. Sōgi's expressed admiration in the *Asaji* for this tsukeku is confirmed by Kenzai's report, which also incidentally reveals the quickness of Shinkei's response at the actual session. This aspect of his talent is belied in his critical writing by his frequent attacks on the practice of rapid-fire composition, which he felt led to insufficient reflection upon the meaning of the maeku. The most thorough among the commentaries, however, is the *Keikandō*; it details the complex depth of Shinkei's response here, apart from revealing the presence of a foundation poem.

One can only add that the tsukeku fully accounts for the maeku's twin ideas, as clearly presented in its two lines, of bitter regret in the heart (*kuyashi ya kokoro*) on the one hand and the hapless misery of the body (*ajikina no mi*) on the other. In effect, the construction that this was no more than a single night's affair underscores the physical passion into which the subject fell, and which leaves her still in a miserable state of sensual yearning; as may be gathered from the *Chikubun*, this desire for the repetition of an initial singular experience is apparently the meaning of the thematic motif of *aite awazaru koi* (love after a single meeting). *Asaku mo* ("too naively"), on the other hand, precisely accounts for the bitter regret now raging in the subject's heart.

Orthodox and unorthodox readings. An important point to observe in the *Keikandō* passage is its clear recognition of the variability of interpretations of waka employed in renga. It is tempting to see this as a blanket statement on the indeterminacy of meaning, a philosophical stance for which there is ample evidence in Shinkei's *Sasamegoto*. In this instance, however, the distinction being drawn is only that between a simple and a complex reading of Tsurayuki's poem. The first "orthodox" or mundane mode of interpretation (*shōfūtei*) takes it at face value simply as an expression of regret at naively (*asakereba*) surrendering oneself to a man who does not merit such trust, and thus reaping only tears (*sode no mi nururu*, "I have only wet my sleeves") from the experience. The second reading delves into the self-conflicted psychology of the subject, focusing on the ambiguous, complex resonance of *asashi* (lit., "shallow") in the poem as it influences the same term in the tsukeku. This shallowness or naiveté can refer to her gullibility in assuming that one night's meeting is but the prelude to many nights of bliss, or to her ignorance in the ways of drawing another's heart to her own—here taking into consideration the polysemic phrase *kumiso-mete*, which brings together the senses of "drawing" water from the well and "probing" the depths of another's heart and "drawing it out" through a sympathetic response. Similarly, *somu* means both "for the first time"— this is the subject's first experience—and "to be permanently dyed" with love's color.

In sum, Shinkei's reading of the poem, which mediates his response to the maeku, takes the subject's bitter regrets (*kuyashi ya*) to be directed less at the scarce lover than at her own inadequacy of response (*asaku mo*), her easy because inexperienced drifting into physical love without a mature knowledge of the complexity of the human heart, including her own. There is also the implication that superficiality in these matters, the inability to "draw deep" into the bottomless well of love, beyond the easy satisfaction of the senses, can only lead to burning frustration, perhaps to obsession, "the feeling of being unable to yield wholly" and of "having yielded too frivolously" (*yoku tokezu asaku toketaru to iu kokoro*), as the *Keikandō* puts it. There is perhaps a discipline of the heart, just as much as of the body, and to yield or trust fully is a matter of the first.

114 *STKBS* 1904

wakareji ni	A comfort to me
nagusamenishi mo	along the road where we parted,
utsuroite	they are changed.
ouru kuzuba mo	The growing arrowroot leaves also
aki ni au iro	meet with autumn in faded hues.

Asaji 1: This verse culls from the following poem [*SIS* 306. Partings. Anonymous.]:

wasuru na yo	This remember: when upon
wakareji ni ouru	*the growing arrowroot leaves*
kuzu no ha no	*on this road of parting,*
akikaze fukaba	the *autumn* wind comes to blow,
ima kaerikomu	then will I be returning soon.

"A comfort to me" [*nagusamenishi*] refers to the words "then will I be returning soon" [*ima kaerikomu* in the foundation poem]. "Along the road where we parted" [*wakareji ni* in the maeku] summoned the words "the growing arrowroot leaves" [*ouru kuzuba* in the tsukeku]. The arrowroot leaves are things that also change in color when autumn comes. Therefore, although she had found comfort in his promise to return, the message is that he has since changed. The verse uses the foundation poem in a truly interesting way.   (pp. 317–18)

Chikubun 671: It is bad to use direct or plain language in verses on Love. This is based on the spirit of the poem "This remember . . ." [*SIS* 306 quoted]. Through *mo* [also], it becomes a Love verse. It is a truly remarkable use of the foundation poem.

Without the crucial particle *mo*, whose suppressed first referent is the changed heart of the other, the tsukeku would be a purely seasonal verse on Autumn. There is indeed something almost quelling about the swift precision of Shinkei's aim here. The clarity, and deceptive facility, of the move from maeku to tsukeku through the intervention of the *honka* is truly the mark of an adept. In leaps like this, renga becomes as it were a dance of language, a verbal performance powered by the supple sinews of the mind.

116 *STKBS* 1922

omou kokoro zo	Soul mad with longing
sora ni ukaruru	wanders off into the sky.

karasu naku	A crow shrieks—
shimoyo no tsuki ni	before the moon of a frosty night
hitori nete	I lie alone.

Shinkei renga jichū 39: It would be utterly absurd to see this crow as a harbinger of dawn. The verse says, while I lie alone lamenting my fate, deep into the night a lone male crow floats up against the sky, enduring like myself the chill clarity of the moon's rays in the frosty night, and calling to mind a sense of desolation.

Chikurinshō no chū 187: Lying all alone in the cold of the night, taken out of myself in an extremity of longing, my state of mind is equivalent to that crow—such is what "soul wanders off into the sky" [*sora ni ukaruru*] means.

Chikubun 704: One hears of the so-called "mad crows" [*ukaregarasu*].

"The chill and icy": on the brink of madness. An exceptionally arresting verse in Shinkei's "chill and icy" (*hiekōritaru*) mode. The weird appearance of the lone black crow silhouetted against the white moonlight has in it something of the rigorous austerity and intense exaggeration of black-ink paintings inspired by a Zen mind. Longing here is pitched so high as to break beyond the bounds of the human, and even beyond the nostalgic splendor of art, into the realm of madness, the nihility of the abstract. Yet it is held in check at this very extremity and thus evokes a stark tension characteristic of the mind behind Shinkei's poetry of the chill and icy.

This is poetry of extreme desire and extreme deprivation, one that holds before the mind the intense allure and also the wholly vacant transparency of desire. There is, according to Kaneko, but a thin line separating this link from haikai.[41] If I read him right, he refers to the elements of exaggeration and incongruity common to both; the chill and icy would therefore lie precisely in that thin line that holds Shinkei's poetry here poised between an extreme rigor and control on the one hand and the outbreak of the comic on the other. It is poetry, I believe, that is informed by a deep sense of ironic incongruity that refuses to dissolve into, or indulge in, the catharsis of comic laughter, although it is certainly but a step away from cosmic laughter. One can also say that the chill and icy is *sabi*, or existential loneliness, sensed at its most exteme pitch, where it borders on madness.

Travel

130 *STKBS* 2253

ike ni naku	That cry torn from
hitori no oshi o	the lone male duck in the pond:
mi ni shirite	I know it in my body.
tabine kanashiki	Desolate nights of sojourn in
fuyu no yamazato	a mountain hamlet in winter.

Oi no susami 51: The meaning of the link with the maeku is wholly understandable. To deliberately respond to "pond" [*ike*] by means of "mountain hamlet" [*yamazato*] is a measure of the author's utmost efforts. Among Lord Teika's poems is one I believe that also uses the two together. It is true, nevertheless, that the poet would have been capable of making such a link even without the poem. For everything depends upon the reach of the poet's own mind.

Chikurinshō no chū 217: This is about listening to the moving cries of the duck in the pond throughout the night and feeling just as lonely, while spending a night in a mountain village in winter on a journey. It was perhaps inspired by such a poem as this one [*Shūi gusō* 1649. Winter]:

mono omowanu	Let he who feels no
hito no kikekashi	sorrow in things listen!
yamazato no	From the frozen pond
kōreru ike ni	deep in the mountain village,
hitori naku oshi	a male duck weeps all alone.

Yuki no keburi 55: With regard to the method of this verse, it is appropriate enough to have a duck in a mountain village in winter. One might think the existence of a pond there unnatural, but again, why not? Is not the feeling truly desolate and moving? In this author's poetry, and in Senjun's as well, there is a suggestiveness [*omokage*] that hovers about the words of the verses as such. One should read them with the greatest thoughtfulness.

Keikandō, Middle Stage: The linking is not so minute, but it is good. Saying "in a mountain hamlet" [*yamazato*] instead of "in the shadow of the mountain" [*yama-kage*] shows that the poet has given much thought to getting the scene right. The method belongs to the middle stage. Through the sadness of sleeping alone himself, the speaker feels at one with the male duck. It recalls the feeling of the line "Chill the tail of the Mandarin duck, in layers of frost flowers." (p. 137)

Three of the four commentaries observe the unusual placement of the pond in a mountain setting (instead of in the usual lowlands), and the *Keikandō* in particular points out the crucial effect of locating the scene in the "mountain *village*." The implication is that the mountain interior is a lonelier geography than the marshland in the plains, while the word "village" or hamlet underscores the traveler-subject's loneliness amidst the presence of others who, unlike himself, belong there; he is a stranger, the outsider within a tight-knit village community. In other words, the verse skillfully brings out with sharp poignancy the line *mi ni shirite* ("I know it in my body") in the maeku. While Sōgi is wholly justified in saying that Shinkei is capable of making such a connection without the precedent of Teika's poem, Shinkei's admiration for Teika, as expressed in his critical writings, was such that it would be hard to believe that he did not have his poem in mind here.

134 *STKBS* 2325

tsui ni yuku	A temporary lodging
michi no konata no	on this side of the road all
kari no yado	must go, in the end.
yasumishi hodo o	To recover the time he rested,
isogu tabibito	the traveler hastens onward.

Chikubun 816: The "temporary lodging" is the one where the traveler rested.

The maeku is Buddhist in import: this mundane existence is but a "temporary lodging" (*kari no yado*) on the universal road to death and ceaseless transmigration. As Kenzai notes, Shinkei transforms that figurative expression into a literal one, an inn where the traveler spent the night. The point of the link, however, is the almost savage irony generated by the juxtaposition of the two contextual frameworks—one philosophical, the other worldly, such that this unwary traveler who begrudges even the time he lost in sleep is seen to be hastening on to his doom.

136 *STKBS* 2397

satorazuba	Without understanding,
nori no sawari to	would it not become a hindrance
nari ya semu	to the Dharma?
fune ni kaze miru	In the boat, observing the wind
oki no ukigumo	in the drifting clouds at sea.

Chikubun 794: "To understand" [*satoru*] means to carefully observe and discern the wind conditions and such.

As in the previous link, the Buddhist-oriented maeku is transposed into a mundane Travel context, here of a boat about to embark for the high seas. It is important to observe the clouds out at sea and discern from them the lay of the wind, in order to steer the boat safely to its destination. Here *nori*, Buddhist Dharma or teaching, in the maeku is understood as its homonym, the *renyōkei* form of the verb *noru*, to get on a vehicle that will convey one someplace. Still, the double vision inherent in the renga link suggests that the tsukeku can also be seen figuratively: this boat's destination may be "the other shore" (*higan*) of enlightenment, and its passage there can be "obstructed" by the "clouds" of unknowing or ignorance (*satorazuba*). By itself the tsukeku is not Buddhistic in theme; in fact Shinkei's transformation of the maeku into a simple Travel context suggests that his task at this point in the session is to move away from Buddhism. Nevertheless, the effect of contiguity in renga linking is such that the tsukeku inevitably becomes "infected," as it were, with the maeku's theme, so that the tsukeku carries the traces of the former theme in its deep structure in the very process of moving away from it in its surface structure. We should remember that Shinkei himself observed in the *Shiyōshō* that a verse does occasionally straddle two themes at once, and he gave the example of the intimate relation between Love and Laments. The same can easily obtain between Buddhism and Travel.

138 *STKBS* 2431

mata-ne ni nareba	Lying down again, the bed
toko mo natsukashi	is yet warm with memories.
kaeru ni mo	Returning, he seeks
onaji yado toru	along the route he traveled,
tabi no michi	the same inn.

Keikandō, Beginning Stage: This is a model of the beginning stage.   (p. 134)

The situation in the maeku is one wherein a woman has just seen her lover off in the early dawn and goes back to bed (*mata-ne*), wrapped in the memories of the shared night and the scent of the other that still clings to the bedclothes. Shinkei links up to this Love verse by analogically transposing its concept into a Travel framework. On his way back, this traveler stays at the same inn as when he set out, drawn by pleasant memories (*natsukashi* in the maeku) of his earlier sojourn there. The diction of the tsukeku is clear and simple; its meaning is explicit and uncomplicated; the link itself is close, based on the verbal correlatives *mata* (again) = *kaeru* (returning), *onaji* (the same); *ne* (sleep) = *yado* (inn, lodging). It is for these three reasons that Kenzai holds it up as an exemplary verse of the beginning stage; the handling of the maeku is orthodox and competent, and the depth and complexity of the mind-heart are not engaged or at play.

Miscellaneous

140 *STKBS* 2441

chigireru haru no	Upon the promised springtime
omokage mo ushi	memory casts a gloomy shadow.
wakamizu ni	In the young waters,
yuki o kumu made	drawing but whiteness of snow:
mi wa oite	Such has this body aged.

Chikurinshō no chū 238: This means that although one speaks of "young waters" [*wakamizu*], the reflected image of one's hair white as snow makes the springtime gloomy.

Chikurinshū kikigaki 195: The promise was made to last until old age. [*SKKS* 1708. Miscellaneous. "Composed when he scooped mountain water." Priest Nōin.]

ashihiki no	In the water below
yamamoto mizu ni	the foot-dragging mountain,

kage mireba	I stare at my image:
mayu shirotae ni	So aged, the eyebrows
waga oinikeri	are flaxen white.

The shadow of gloom (*omokage mo ushi*) in the maeku is most probably cast by the memory of someone absent, through death or estrangement, with whom the speaker exchanged love vows in a springtime past. In the tsukeku, this "promised springtime" (*chigireru haru*) assumes an altered referent: the "promise" of ever vigorous health signified by the New Year's ritual of scooping the fresh "young waters" from clear springs; similarly, the sense of *omokage* shifts from "shadow" (of a memory) to the old man's "reflected image" on the clear waters. The link is at once seamlessly dexterous and quite moving; it belongs to that realm of ironic pathos known as *aware*. Both verses are on compound topics, Spring and Love in the maeku, and Spring and Laments in the tsukeku. The *honkadori* technique here is in the typical renga mode of simple citation of a precedent poem's concept without overt variation. The tersely compressed yet allusive expression *yuki o kumu made* (lit., "till I am drawing snow") is a good example of renga diction.

142 *STKBS* 2449

waga furusato to	'Tis the birds chirping, as if
tori zo saenuru	to say, "Our own old village!"
ta ga ueshi	Who planted those trees,
kozue no nobe ni	tips lost in the shrouding mists
kasumuran	across the fields?

Oi no susami 13: The old village has fallen to utter desolation, leaving only fields of planted trees, their tips lost in mist, and not a single remembrance of the people who once made their world there. Looking at the birds dwelling familiarly in the treetops, the poet has linked up to the maeku, "It's the birds chirping, 'Our old village,' " by investing it with feeling [*kokoro o irete*]. The design of the verse is arresting [*omoshiroku*], and it is, moreover, moving [*aware*].

Chikurinshō no chū 4: The design of the link is one wherein the old village has become a wild field, and the men who planted the trees are lost in anonymity; there are only the birds in the treetops chirping freely as if in their own old village.

Chikubun 11: What was formerly an old village inhabited by people has been taken over by the birds as their own.

In both the *Chikurinshō* and Shinkei's own collection, the *Shingyoku-shū*, this verse is classified under Spring. It appears under Miscellaneous in the *Shinsen Tsukubashū* presumably because the primary feeling is not seasonal but belongs to the topos of *kaikyū* (remembering the past). *Furu-sato* (old village) in the maeku marks it as a Travel verse; Shinkei connects to it by means of the *kaikyū* theme, while introducing Spring in the image of the mists or haze (*kasumi*).

The design of the link is drawn in sharply incisive lines while accommodating an original conception—this is what Sōgi means by "arresting." It is built around the contrast between the birds singing in the trees and the people who once planted them and are now gone; this dialectical method of evoking what is absent in what is present frequently occurs, as we have seen, in Shinkei's hokku. The gay chirping of the birds, secure in their "own old village" (*waga furusato*) is juxtaposed against the silent enshrouding mists, a metonymical feature of the landscape that simultaneously functions as a symbolic metaphor for the obscurity that has overtaken the former inhabitants of the old village ("who planted those trees"). The passage from maeku to tsukeku is like that of a cheerful, foregrounded scene suddenly stilled and receding back in the mists of time, from where only the faint chirping of the birds echo in remembrance of what has passed; it is the quality of this "passage" that is both arresting and "moving" (*aware*) at the same time, and is the mark of the poet's investment of his heart-mind (*kokoro o irete*, as Sōgi says) in his verbal utterance.

144 *STKBS* 2479

furuki yashiro ni	Season of plum blossoms wafting
ume niou koro	in the silence of the old shrine.
yuki usuki	While through thin snow
hiwada no shinobu	on the cypress-bark eaves, green
katsu moete	the yearning ferns unfurl.

Chikubun 824: In the context of the link to the maeku, this [scene] refers to the shrine; in the verse by itself an ordinary house is meant.

The first gentle stirrings of life in early spring are juxtaposed here with the age of the shrine. The link does not primarily depend on word association, although this is present, but on a tonal allusiveness in which the plum blossoms' delicately wafting scent and the unfurling of the "yearning ferns" (*shinobu* in its double sense) are invested with a faint suggestion of nostalgia for the past. It is another instance of what would later be called linking by fragrance (figuratively) in the Bashō school of haikai.

148 *STKBS* 2607

mada konu kure no	Still to come, already at dusk
aki no hatsukaze	A touch of autumn's first winds.
shitaba chiru	Leaves showering
yanagi ya kari o	from the tips of waving willows—
sasouran	to lure the wild geese?

In the maeku, the emphasis is on the touch of coolness in the wind at dusk, marking the passage of the season from summer to autumn. In the tsukeku, this subtly tactile quality is evoked visually in the leaves floating loose from the tips of the trailing willows; furthermore, the conceit of "luring" (*sasou*) the wild geese who migrate from the north in autumn ties in securely with the phrase *mada konu* (still to come) in the maeku.

150 *STKBS* 2609

mitsu no sakai ni	Through the three worlds blindly
ima zo mayoeru	am I wandering, this very moment!
omowazu no	Soul-struck
tsuki o futsuka no	gaze on the second-day moon,
sora ni mite	in a vast sky.

Asaji 31: This is about a feeling that strikes instantaneously, apart from any logical reason. It shows the bone-deep virtuosity of a keen mind. The second-day moon appears, I believe, in a poem by Priest Jichin. (p. 326)

Sōgi means the poem below, *Shūgyokushū* 4325. "First Love." Priest Jichin.

aru ka naki ka	Is it there, not there?
kokoro no sue zo	how pitiful the trace of this
aware naru	heart that loved:
futsuka no tsuki ni	Faint gleam of *the second-day*
kumo no kakareru	*moon* behind a veil of cloud.

The distant link. The "three worlds" (*mitsu no sakai*) are those of desire, form, and non-form, the totality of the dharmas that constitute the mundane consciousness of existence. "Wandering blindly" (*mayoeru*) refers to the ordinary state of ignorance in which one lives—desires, acts, thinks, according to the viciously mechanistic circular logic of this triple world where the nexus of external phenomena (form) and mind (non-form, i.e, sensations, thoughts) generates desires that, never reaching fulfillment, are doomed to ceaseless repetition. The maeku is in this sense explicitly Buddhist in theme.

On the surface, Shinkei's tsukeku is not as such Buddhist; in fact the "moon" would place it in the topos of Autumn. The apparent lack of verbal semantic relation between the two verses is such that we may characterize the intervening space as Distant (*soku*): an instance where the link, invisible on the linguistic surface (*kotoba*), exists mainly in the deep structure of the mind (*kokoro*). *Soku*, it should be noted, does not refer to a slack link; on the contrary, it is often where the link is most apparently absent that its presence is most perceptible. *Soku* is marked by that sudden tension that grips the mind when the link comes into focus in the sheer act of reading, which in renga more than in any other genre means the act of understanding.

The tsukeku is in effect a symbolic figure, an image as Ezra Pound defined it ("an intellectual and emotional complex in an instant of time"), of the maeku speaker's sudden intuition of his own state of delusion. Once this is understood, then it becomes equally clear how Shinkei has interpreted *ima zo* (this very moment) as that instant of spontaneous illumination—and this is Sōgi's observation as well—when the speaker, gazing at the second-day moon glinting chill and thin in the vast autumn sky, recognizes there the frailty or ungroundedness of his own condition as a creature of circumstance, someone heretofore blind to the very forces holding him in thrall.[42] Such is the power of the image that we sense as well the promise of a greater illumination in the future waxing of this moon; in that sense the present moment of *ima zo* may be characterized as the Buddhist "awakening of the mind" (*hosshin*). The potential fullness of wisdom belongs, however, to the proliferating overtones of the image; the focus of the link itself is that awakening to the perilous frailty of the human condition that is the beginning of wisdom. Incidentally, this image of the thin moon in the vast sky may also be read as a symbolic figure for the religious-philosophical content of Shinkei's mode of "coolness and slenderness" (*yasesamuku*), an aesthetics of mental and rhetorical economy inseparable from a Buddhist philosophy of mind and existence. Sōgi's comment on this verse, that it shows the "bone-deep virtuosity of a keen mind" (*rikon no fūkotsu*), is wholly apt in describing the inspired leap from the maeku to the tsukeku.

154 *STKBS* 2701

tsumadou shika no	The calls of the stag seeking his
koe zo fukeyuku	mate, far into the night wears on.
takasago no	On the waiting pines
matsu ni onoe no	high on Takasago hill falls
kaze ochite	silent the wind.

Guku Shibakusa 158: There is nothing particularly arresting about this verse. I had no other choice since with the maeku the Nocturnal images had already been exhausted, and then of course Takasago is the one place where one reads the deer. In truth I am quite satisfied with the verse as it is, rather than calling upon such colorful images as crimson leaves and [pink] bush clover.   (pp. 43–44)

Chikubun 972: This is a non-predicative verse; it is in the categorical mode. Its feeling is similar to the following poems [*SIS* 191. Autumn. Anonymous]:

akikaze no	With each sweep
uchifuku goto ni	of the cool autumn wind
takasago no	the air sounds
onoe no shika no	with the cries of the deer
nakanu hi wa nashi	daily on Takasago Hill.

[*SKKS* 290. Autumn. "Written along the place depicting Takasago in a screen painting in the Saisho Shitennō Hall." Fujiwara Hideyoshi.]

fukukaze no	The blowing wind
iro koso miene	has no visible color, true—
takasago no	still in Takasago
onoe no matsu ni	already the feel of autumn
aki wa kinikeri	is on the hilltop pines.

The effect of Shinkei's tsukeku is to make the maeku tense in a wonderfully subtle way. By saying that the wind among the pines has died down, in one stroke he evokes the earlier hour when the deer's calls were heard intermittently through the sound of the wind in the pines. This contrasts with the present moment when the wind has stilled (*kaze ochite*) and only the stag's calls, now weaker due to the elapsed time, break the silence. His verse, in other words, points up and justifies the line *koe zo fukeyuku* (lit., "the voice is wearing on," with the emphatic particle *zo*). The passage of time is expressed in the wind's falling off and the deer's faltering voice as the night deepens into silence. Additionally, *matsu* (pines)—conventionally read with its homonym, the verb "waits"—responds to "seeking his mate" in the maeku, imbuing the night itself with a quality of longing, and further underscoring, on the level of feeling, the sense of long duration in the term *fukeyuku*.

Shinkei's own commentary explains how both necessity and personal aesthetics governed his choice of images here. He could not resort to Nocturnal images—say, the moon in response to "night" in the maeku, since their alloted occurrence in this section of the sequence has already been exhausted. "Deer" in the maeku signifies an Autumn theme; to reject the colorful autumnal imagery of crimson leaves and pink bush clover in favor of the "colorless" evergreen pines was not a matter of formal necessity but aesthetic choice; it evinces both his taste for the austerity of *sabi* and his concern for *tsukeai* (linking) as a motion of dialogic understanding. A colorful imagery would have contradicted both the sense and very feeling of the maeku. As for Kenzai's two poem citations, they are apparently meant to give the authority of precedent to the association between the place-name Takasago and "deer"/"pine," as well as the occurrence of all three items in autumn poems. (However, there is no exclusively autumnal image in Shinkei's verse, thus it is classified under Miscellaneous in the *Shinsen Tsukubashū*.)

The construction of the verse as "non-predicative" (*muinaru ku*) and belonging to the categorical mode (*koto shikarubeki tai*) points to Kenzai's awareness of a mode of poetry that does not explicitly assert or express anything notable, but merely names things as they are. In the terminology of Shinkei's criticism, such apparently empty verses would correspond to the *henjodai* mode, which he valorized because they best demonstrate the fact that the poetry of renga does not lie in the isolated verses as such, but in the vital links between them.[43] The following verse is in the same mode.

156 *STKBS* 2737

fuyugare no	In winter-withered
nobe ni sabishiki	fields the color of loneliness
iro miete	apparent.
yūhi no shita no	The glinting line of river
mizu no hitosuji	beneath the dying sun.

Chikubun 865: In the passing hour of the evening light, things look white. An arresting verse.

In the maeku as such "the color of loneliness" (*sabishiki iro*) refers to the withered fields of midwinter, empty of the vitality of green and the vibrant hue of flowers. In the tsukeku this "color of loneliness" over the whole landscape becomes distilled into the chill white glint of the slanting sunlight on the slender river flowing across the fields. In other words, loneliness or *sabi* is symbolically imaged as a cold, "colorless" reflection. The paradox clearly requires a second-order, deep reading whereby "loneliness" becomes equivalent to absence of color—that is, the emptiness of phenomenal form in the Buddhist ontological sense. Loneliness is precisely the momentary yet essential appearance of this "glinting line" of white light before the dark of evening that erases all distinctions among forms. In essence there is only black or white (a polarity reducible to one). Form is not a substance but indeed a "color," not in the sense of applied pigment but of "reflection." Lacking a self-identity, form is only a function, an *effect* (as in "greenhouse effect") of temporality, the vital mutual operation of a network of circumstances. The impersonal loneliness of *sabi*, of which this link is, as it were, a poetic demonstration, is the cognition of this existential truth. A masterly example of the aesthetics of reduction ("distillation" is perhaps the better word) both in its conception and in its intensely spare diction, this is to my mind one of the most brilliant instances of the poetry of the renga link. When the *Chikubun* describes it as "arresting," it is no doubt pointing to all that is implied by the apparent paradoxicality of its difficult wit.

158 *STKBS* 2763

suguru zo oshiki	Gone, how swiftly! The line
kari no hitotsura	of white geese across the sky.
funabito mo	Even the boatman
sao o wasururu	forgets to ply his oar:
aki no umi	the sea in autumn.

Chikubun 474: Even by itself the verse has an arresting conception. The [use of the] word "autumn" is evocative.

As Kenzai remarks, the tsukeku can stand on its own as an autonomous verse due to the effectiveness of its evocation of "autumn"—the way the word is activated through the invention of an efficient context, here of a boatman so absorbed in the scenery that he has forgotten to ply his oar. The nature of that scene of "the sea in autumn" (*aki no umi*) is left to the reader's imagination; the quality of "open-endedness," which is, I believe, the essential aspect of the whole aesthetics of *yojō* or evocation, lies precisely in this suspension of explicit definition, this refusal to trespass on the reader's space. This reserve makes it, if you will, a non-transgressive writing, one that awaits the reader's response to bring it to a provisional closure.

But Shinkei's verse is, of course, itself a response to another. Within the framework set up by the other, we understand that the boatman is lost in a reverie of regret for the line of white geese momentarily outlined in the sky, now gone and leaving it, as well as the mind, a vastly rapt emptiness. In other words, the boatman's absorption in the tranquil seascape and sky was occasioned by that swift passage of white against a limitless blue. Visually the two verses compose, as it were, two frames in a scroll painting or a film. In rhetorical terms, however, the two successive moments are juxtaposed to animate each other; the one inscribing a presence, the other displacing it into the memory as the trace of an absence. That neither presence nor absence registers itself as such, however, but only through the force of the juxtaposition is precisely what governs the dialectics of the interaction of two verses in a renga link.

162 *STKBS* 2613

inaba no kaze no	The sound of the wind in the
oto zo shizumaru	rice stalks suddenly stilled.
furu ame no	Reed-straw hut
ashi no maroya wa	beneath dripping legs of rain:
to o tojite	door shut tight.

Guku Shibakusa 133 (p. 36): It is the practice to call the huts of the keeper of small rice fields and the like *ashi no maroya* [reed-straw hut]; here the name occurs in continuity with *ame no ashi* [legs of the rain]. [*KYS* 173. Autumn. Minamoto Tsunenobu.]

yū sareba	As darkness falls,
kadota no inaba	from the rice stalks by the gate
otozurete	a footfall sounds, then
ashi no maroya ni	rustles over the reed-straw hut—
akikaze zo fuku	the blowing autumn wind!

Chikubun 870: This brings out the feel of "legs of the rain." The poem, "As evening falls, / from the rice stalks by the gate. . . . "

In a succession of montage-like frames similar to the effect of the preceding link, Shinkei here interprets the sudden stillness of the winds in the maeku as the tense, momentary calm before a storm, which has broken out in the tsukeku. The verse is clearly a radical allusive variation on the *Kinyōshū* poem by Minamoto Tsunenobu (1016–97). The fact that it is designated to be in the mode of "ineffable depth" (*yūgen*) in Shinkei's *Kokemushiro* collection (*SSS* 2012) indicates that the link is susceptible to an "uncanny" reading, that is to say, one that registers a sense of the inexplicability of phenomenal occurrence when viewed from an open mind. Winds soughing among the rice stalks, a sudden weird silence, and then the eruption of rain—three moments related only by temporal contiguity. Science may isolate the physical forces interacting to produce the rain and posit a relationship of causation from one moment to the next. But this chain of causation, when logically pursued, extends indefinitely into the past and future, and it is precisely the indeterminacy of this extension in two directions, which must nevertheless determine the present instant, that constitutes the sense of *yūgen*. The link, in other words, brings out the mysterious quality of that pregnant interval that generated the difference or the turn from wind to rain. And it is this uncanny feeling that emerges when we concentrate, meditate upon, the relation between maeku and tsukeku here. In particular its trace is apparent in the *sabi* quality of the image of a lone straw-thatched hut amidst the pouring rain, its shut-in (*to o tojite*), vulnerable isolation, its radical "unrelatedness" to the dripping "legs of rain" crawling all over it. The tactile immediacy of this dripping wet rain and the sense of ineffableness that hangs over the whole scene typify that unusual combination of skin-close objectivity and boundless inwardness that characterizes Shinkei's poetry at its most compelling level.

164 *STKBS* 2821

aramu kagiri ya	It will last for as long as I
ware-hito no michi	live: the way of self and other.
yamazato ni	The lone bridge of
kayou kuchigi no	decaying timber, leading into
hitotsubashi	the mountain village.

In the maeku, "the way of self and other" (*ware-hito no michi*), referring to human interaction with others, is seen as an activity that ends only with one's death. In the tsukeku, *aramu kagiri* (as long as I am), whose implicit subject is "I" in the maeku, acquires an altered referent to become "as long as *the bridge* is." Consequently the sense of the link becomes "as long as the bridge between myself and the mountain village remains, I shall interact with the people there." However, this bridge that enables human communication is already in a state of decay, a detail that points up and simultaneously contracts the idea of extent in the adverbial *kagiri* ("as long as," but also "to the limit of") in the maeku. The feeling behind this link is somewhat ambiguous. But since the speaker is clearly a recluse dwelling up on the mountain, connected to the village in the foothills by a single old bridge, then the tsukeku may be read as an expression of self-ironic vulnerability. A recluse precisely because he has turned his back on mundane human intercourse, the subject nevertheless finds himself momentarily rendered insecure by the thought that the rotting bridge cannot last much longer. In this reading the maeku's construction would be something like "Its days are numbered— / the way of self and other." The prospect of total isolation, in other words, reveals a momentary wavering in the priestly subject's resolution. Again, set against the prior sense of the maeku as such, the appearance of this rift ironically underscores the possibility that the longing for the warmth of ordinary human companionship is so deep-seated it ends only with death.[44]

168 *STKBS* 2877

oku fukaki	To guide me to
michi o oshie no	the teachings, I take the path
tayori nite	deep and remote.
inu no koe suru	Far into the night, the barking
yoru no yamazato	of a dog in a mountain village.

Chikurinshū kikigaki 246: [*GYS* 2257. Miscellaneous. Fujiwara Teika.]

satobitaru	That rustic feeling
inu no koe ni zo	in the barking of a dog
shirarekeru	gives it away wholly:
take yori oku no	the abode of the wise sages
hito no ie'i wa	deep within the bamboo grove.

The maeku follows a procedure contrary to the orthodox practice in Buddhist training, where one studies the teachings as a means of understanding the ultimate principle and attaining enlightenment. Instead this subject proceeds directly along "the way deep and remote" (*oku fukaki michi*)—that is, the path of Zen meditation—and having thus achieved enlightenment, makes that the means (*tayori*) of comprehending the true significance of the teachings. The teachings as embodied in the words of the scriptures first become revealed, as it were, in the light of an achieved wisdom.

Interestingly, Shinkei ignores the Buddhist context of the maeku, choosing instead to interpret "the path deep and remote" in the literal sense of a road in the mountain interior deep in the night. It is possible that with the maeku, the maximum serial occurrence for Buddhism, which is three, had been reached, and it was therefore necessary to shift away from the theme. In the process, the subject implicitly turns into someone who has lost his way in the mountains at night and, suddenly hearing the sound of a dog barking, is reassured there must be a village not too far away. In this amazing revision, the dog's barking is the fateful "guide that teaches" (*oshie no shirube*) or illumines the obscure trail (*oku fukaki michi*) for the lost traveler, leading him out of the maze and into the village. Through the mediation of the *honka* by Teika, this village is understood to be none other than the hidden abode of the sages of the bamboo grove, so that the more esoteric and mysterious implications of the Buddhist maeku is preserved, albeit as a Taoist overtone, in the tsukeku.

170 *STKBS* 2909

mada shiranu	Staking off a place
miyama no oku o	deep within remote mountains
shimeokite	I have yet to know.
maki tatsu niwa no	The dimming shadows of dusk upon
yūgure no iro	the stand of cedars in the garden.

Chikubun 862: This refers to a mountain and stream landscape garden. Since it is in every way like the deep mountains, it is a projection of the mountains I have yet to know.

Like the pair above, this link is not particularly notable. I cite it for cultural interest, for what it reveals of the religious impulse behind the practice and reception of the art of the landscape garden in the Muromachi period. The aim was apparently to evoke the tranquillity of mountain reclusion right within one's backyard, so to speak. The predominance of foliage and evergreen trees over colorful flowering plants in the Japanese landscape garden suggests that the religious-aesthetic ideal of *sabi*, the essential characteristic of medieval poetry, operated here as well. It confirms, moreover, the hold of the ideal of reclusion over the various forms of Muromachi culture.

172 *STKBS* 2913

ame ni ya naramu	Will it turn to rain?
fuku kaze no koe	Voice of the blowing wind.
sue nabiku	From the swaying tops
tanaka no take ni	of bamboos in the rice field,
hato nakite	a dove is crooning.

Chikubun 864: "A dove croons before the rain." In the *Tale of Genji*, there is mention of a so-called house dove crooning from among the bamboos.[45]

Keikandō, Middle Stage: There is a folk saying that the dove calls forth the rain. (p. 139)

This link is somewhat similar to an earlier one on the reed-straw hut in pouring rain. Although it lacks the deep inwardness of the other, it has the same sense of the uncanny, which is here the presentiment of a gathering storm. The "voice of the blowing wind" (*fuku kaze no koe*) in the maeku comes to be the index of an unspecified yet disturbing quality to which the tsukeku gives voice and body through the dynamic image of the faint crooning of a dove amidst the loud creaking of the wildly swaying bamboos. The whole scene is as it were taut with an imminence, an affect of holding at bay the very storm that would dissolve it. The vividly fresh clarity with which a rustic setting is brought forth as a direct experience, apparently unmediated by pastoral poetic precedent, is rare in the history of Japanese poetic materials and their usage.

174 *STKBS* 2941

ishi no ue ni mo	The world, be it in hovel or
yo o zo itoeru	firm stone, turns wearisome.
midarego ni	In that single move
waga ikishini no	at the *go* board I see revealed:
aru o mite	my life and death.

Chikubun 902: He becomes enlightened [about the truth of mundane existence] through winning and losing in *go*.

The sense of world-weariness so openly admitted in the maeku is clarified in the tsukeku as springing from a realization of the arbitrariness of event, of our fate as a creature of ungovernable circumstance. Like winning or losing (here figuratively expressed as "life and death") in the game of *go*, one's luck can always change in a single move. There is no constancy; mutability is the law of mundane existence. As a collective discourse about nature and existence, renga abounds in what even then were doubtless already considered clichés. These have, of course, never prevented anyone from acting contrary to the lessons embedded in them. Various forms of gambling were popular; rapid-composition renga itself was performed for stakes and prizes (one reason why sober practitioners had to distinguish their activity as "serious" or *ushin* renga). The warring of medieval warriors may be said to be the "highest" form of risk-taking, in that they literally staked their lives on it. In short, the mundane attitude—expressed in the cliché, "life is a game"—was more prevalent in medieval culture than is generally supposed from the otherworldly character of the artifacts that have survived from this period. Shinkei's satirical reduction of firm foundation stones to the minuscule black and white stones in a game of chance, the ironic tension in this forced identification of two dimensions, may be said to be a method of registering the truth of a familiar cliché in a strange, new way.

176 *STKBS* 2971

furitsumoru	Foothills beneath
yuki no yamamoto	a deepening pall of snow
kururu hi ni	as twilight falls.
kane hitokoe no	Far away in the cedar grove
ochi no sugimura	the muffled boom of a bell.

In stark contrast to the preceding, this pair is wholly devoid of ideational content on the surface. It clearly belongs to that type of *Shinkokinshū* poetry to which Brower and Miner gave the name "descriptive symbolism." As a poetic method, it shares with some black-ink painting an interest not in phenomena themselves or what they might mean in the semiotic code of iconic conventions but in a quality of contemplation. It is not a poetry of the voice. Rhetorical inflection is here reduced to a minimum; we do not hear a person talking, or sense a subject thinking and feeling. What we do sense is a listening and a gazing, the same non-appropriative and non-intrusive attitude induced by the highly formal yet seemingly natural design of a landscape garden or flower arrangement.

It is not that nothing happens in this link, but all that happens is the inscription of a punctuation or a spacing—in the Derridean sense. The sound of the bell in the tsukeku has the effect of settling the landscape yet deeper beneath the snow and dark of the maeku. A sound punctuates the silence, the silence enables the sound; the space of the difference from maeku to tsukeku has the effect of making the maeku suddenly appear, as when we take a step back, or forward, to focus an image. This sudden coming into appearance of phenomena from the far side of mundane perception, when achieved in a poem through a mind-opening contemplative process, gives it a quality that Shinkei called "ineffable remoteness," and this link is a fine example of it.

182 *STKBS* 3056

kaze mo me ni minu	Invisible as the wind to the eye,
yama no amabiko	the mountain echo from the sky.
monogoto ni	In everything,
tada arinashi o	is and is-not are wholly
katachi nite	a matter of form.

Oi no susami 60: Both the wind and the echo do in fact exist, yet they are at the same time empty of form. Therefore is and is-not are but formal distinctions. "In everything" [*monogoto ni*] means that in these two things [the wind and the echo] one may become enlightened regarding the provisional and empty nature of all phenomena. No doubt the maeku was conceived to link up to the word "call out" [*yobu*] or "answer" [*kotauru*] in the verse preceding it. Is it not a marvelous feat of transformation indeed, to be put in this very difficult position and still come up with such a link as this?   (p. 165)

Chikubun 940: It is difficult to connect to "echo" [in the maeku]. Since it is itself a reply that echoes something in the verse preceding it, it is difficult to connect to the same word again in a different way. Yet the verse does exactly this. It says that like the echo, everything, including human life, has no fixed, determinate existence.

Chikurinshō no chū 289: The echo is a thing whose existence or non-existence is indeterminate. The meaning of the link is that there is the middle truth of True Reality [*chūdō jissō*], apart from the two truths of the empty and the provisional [*kūke*]. Since this echo is something that is different from either the empty or the provisional, it bears a meaning that enlightens us regarding all things.[46]

The commentaries are thorough in explicating the Buddhist view of reality as evoked by Shinkei's inspired response to the difficult image of the "echo" (*amabiko*) in the maeku; Sōgi is particularly admiring. Still, compared to numerous others of the tsukeku so far cited, this one seems wholly didactic and intellectual, lacking in the poetic evocativeness of Shinkei's best work. No doubt such ratiocinative verses have their place in the varied tapestry of rhetorical modes that constitutes the hundred-verse sequence, but read in the context of the isolated verse-pair unit, it is not very appealing, apart from that brief spark of wit basic to the structure of the renga link.

186 *STKBS* 3084

kono kokoro koso	Such a mind is, indeed,
hotoke narikere	that of a Buddha!
midorigo wa	The infant-child
mada omoiwaku	is still free from drawing
koto mo nashi	distinctions.

Chikubun 1033: It is honest and direct, being free of desire.

An unexpected yet thoroughly competent link. Wisdom and compassion characterize the Buddha-mind. Shinkei seizes on the first, particularly its aspect of impartiality (*musabetsu, byōdōshin*), and draws the analogy with the infant's mind in the prelinguistic stage when it has not yet learned the categorical distinctions among phenomena inscribed by the language system and has yet to separate itself as a subject from the other. The analogy is between a true ignorance (the infant child) and an enlightened wisdom (the Buddha): between the beginning and end of a process there is a likeness. The verse may also be read ironically: the infant is still to acquire the knowledge based on illusory—which is to say, conditioned—discriminations. On another level, the infant would not know the distinction between the mind of a Buddha and a layman. In Buddhist training, to reach the end is to realize that one has been there all the time without knowing it. This is to collapse beginning and end, to forget the middle of two points, which is also to erase the whole notion of points.

Kenzai's interpretation is significant as a Muromachi psychological reading that ascribes the mental activity of discrimination to desire. Desire by its very nature signifies a lack that can be filled only by an object; thus Lacan, for instance, posits it precisely as that which is constitutive of the Subject. That is, the primary separation between subject and object arises from desire. It is worth noting, in this connection, that Freud recognized an all-embracing "primary ego feeling," of which our present ego is but a shrunken residue, that corresponds "to a more intimate bond between the ego and the world about it."[47] But he was skeptical about pointing to this primary sense of oneness with the universe as the origin of religiosity, choosing instead to see it as no more than the infant's feelings of helplessness and longing for the father (why not for the mother, one might ask).

Shinkei's view on this issue is not revealed by the link above, for it rests on an analogy, and the ontological status of a trope is a problematic one. His task was to illumine *in what way* the infant may be said to be like a buddha, not to propose a primordial origin for the wisdom of non-discrimination. We are aware that the aim of Zen practice is to attain (return?) to the Original Mind, and a childlike spontaneity or lack of calculation has been, in Buddhism, Taoism, and Christianity, celebrated as one of the characteristics of saints and sages. This is all, however, an outgrowth of Kenzai's reading, and in renga there are only readings powered by desire, a desire above all to interrogate the prior text, cause it to reveal itself for an instant before the revelation in its turn becomes a question in an endless chain of signifiers whose signified or referent is constantly being displaced, from one verse to the next, in a series of desire-generated differentiations marking the tense vibrant space of the many between the one of the "infant-child" and the Buddha.

188 *STKBS* 3088

> sa mo araba
> are tote nado ka
> isoguran

> "If it be so,
> so be it!" Having said thus,
> why the hurry?

| hikari no kage zo | For the shadow trails the light, |
| hito o omowanu | implacably, indifferent to men. |

Asaji 59: Here, too, the manner of linking is clear. The way in which the author has linked up to this maeku demonstrates mastery. The maeku requires great care, for it is truly a difficult one to handle. Such a response—the verse as such—sounds nice and easy, but is not the sense [of the link] arresting?   (p. 333)

Hikari no kage (lit., "the shadow of the light") is a reference to *kōin* (light-and-shadow), an allegorical term for time, as in the proverb *Kōin ya no gotoshi* (Time is like a [swift] arrow). Sōgi's commentary is admirably precise and to the point, and confirms Ijichi's observation that Shinkei's move here shows a seemingly "artless virtuosity" (*musōsana tsukeai no takumisa*). The contradiction posed by the maeku is indeed difficult to resolve, for it forecloses precisely that sense of stark resignation suggested by the declaration, "If it be so, so be it!" Shinkei's solution is to read the resignation as a willful, angry resolve, while retaining the maeku's starkness of inflection by introducing the idea of the equal implacability of the march of time. *Precisely because* (this is the force of *zo*) time does not stop for man, because night follows day as inexorably as light casts a shadow, one must make haste (*isogu*) before the dark falls; this is the altered sense of *sa mo araba are*. Such is the thin line that divides passive resignation and an active resolution.

190 *STKBS* 3096

waga mi ni nitaru	The pathos of that aging body
oi no awaresa	bears to myself a resemblance.
iro mienu	Undetected by the eye,
kokoro mo hate wa	the spirit too, in the end,
yowarikite	begins to falter.

Guku Shibakusa 189: The situation in the maeku, which compares another person and myself, is transformed to mean that like my body, even my spirit, has aged, becoming weaker.   (pp. 53–54)

Oi no susami 56: The aging in the maeku refers to someone else. The point of the link, "bears to myself a resemblance," turns on the spirit. There are these two things: body and spirit. The decline of the body is indeed plainly visible to the eye, but the spirit is something that is not outwardly manifest. This is true, and yet when one has aged, the spirit itself weakens even as the body—such is the idea by which the link is achieved.   (pp. 163–64)

Chikubun 938: A marvelous verse. Since the spirit also becomes exhausted, it resembles the body in its aging.

Yuki no keburi 65: "Bears to myself a resemblance" in the maeku refers to someone else's aging. The method of linking specifies the resemblance to lie in the spirit. The deterioration of the body is something visible to the eye. The spirit is not outwardly visible, but the fact that it nevertheless also declines is cause for sadness.

This verse recalls Shinkei's poems on aging discussed in Part One. The proliferation of commentary, all of them excellent and thorough, indicates the moved response elicited by this verse that hews uncomfortably close to the reality of aging, and evokes contrapuntal echoes, within English poetry, to Shakespeare's raving old king and Dylan Thomas's "Do not go gentle into that good night." Is the denial of aging in some Western traditions to be ascribed to the dominance of the heroic strain in them? To what extent is the heroic allied with a primal fear of death, and what effect does an unreflective complicity with this cultural value have on contemporary society's rejection of such weak creatures as old people and children? What is the price for our mean-hearted and cowardly denial of the reality of time?

It is not that Japanese culture shows no traces of a shrinking before the fact of extinction. The ancient chronicles give a precise record, in the story of Izanagi's descent to Yomi, of the fear and abhorrence that marked man's primal encounter with a rotting corpse. Indeed Shintō's most important ritual, that of purification (*misogi*, *harae*), originates from Izanagi's therapeutic act of washing away in the river the pollution that adhered to him from the contact, a process that unleashed, ironically enough, both the forces of good and evil in the world. There is no permanent recovery from the taint of knowledge.

Here death is not finally conquered or erased but merely kept at a distance (the "warding off" of *harau*). It was no doubt Buddhism with its ringing insistence on impermanence that brought death back to the foreground of human observation. The *Heike* in effect tells us that the medieval warriors' reaction to this homily was much like that figured in link 188: the obstinately stalwart resolution of "If it be so, so be it!" It did not befit the heroism of warriors to "go gentle into that good night." One does not wait dumbly for death's coming; one rushes headlong to pit the vitality of life against its dark foe—this is also the ideology that informs Mishima's life and writings, in particular his view, expressed through Isao in *Runaway Horses*, that history is real and happens only and precisely because some men courageously dare to challenge the status quo with the greatest thing they have to lose, their lives. That is, history, which is the unfolding of a narrative in time, is the dynamic inscription of a difference upon the deadening sameness or inertia of abstract time. To defy death is also to know the full weight of time in the sense of making it real.

Yet the *Heike*'s own overarching agenda is apparently not history as heroic narrative but the didactic theme announced by its opening passage on the evanescence of human achievement (*shogyō mujō*) and the inevitability of the drift from power to impotence (*jōsha hissui*). Its potent instrument for transmitting this message is the rhetoric of *aware*, pathos, whose influence on Japanese culture has been so deep and extensive that tough-minded writers like Mishima conceived a veritable, though possibly misguided, disgust for it. It persists in contemporary cultural products, most notably television dramas of all genres, whether heroic, mock-heroic, romantic, or humorous, and may be said to constitute the most durable strain in popular culture, although its origins in the Heian period were decidedly aristocratic.

Shinkei, in his poetry, and expressly in his critical writings, sought to inculcate *aware* as the most appropriate response to both the mundane and the metaphysical limitations of the human condition in that sole, certain middle ground between the "mindless" states of an infant-child and a buddha. The verse above is merely one expression of this attitude. It refuses the idealism that would stake the deathlessness of the heart-mind (*kokoro*) as a bulwark against Izanami's rotting body (*mi*). The mind's dwindling responsiveness to life's sound and fury is also of the body (*waga mi ni nitaru*); these are, unfortunately, not two, not separate. In Shakespeare, love brings the maddened king to a sober acceptance of death. The stoic grace of *aware*, which is ultimately nothing more, or less, than an empathetic response to temporality, or the presence of death in life, fulfills much the same function in Japanese culture.

192 *STKBS* 3106

yowaku nariyuku	Ineffably growing fainter—
yamakaze no sue	the wake of the mountain wind.
kane tōki	With the remote echo of
sato ni wa yume ya	the bell over yon village, dreams—
nokoruran	do they yet linger?

Chikubun 944: This was the fifth verse on the first page [of a hundred-verse sequence]. Sōgi felt that it was an especially fine one.

The subliminally faint tremor of the wind as it dies down in the mountain is evoked twice in the tsukeku; first, in the remoteness of the booming bell's echo as it drifts in from the distant village in the foothills, and second, in the imagined traces of the dreams there. The time is clearly at dawn, and the point of view would have to be understood as that of a priest or recluse dwelling in the mountains. The link is, for all the minutely close tonal relation among the images, extremely subtle. It turns around the distance between the priestly mind, which is—or strives to be—liberated from the illusory, and the mundane mind that is still caught in the thrall of dreams.

This distance, syntactically marked by the contrastive function of *wa* in *sato ni wa* (lit., "as for the village"), is said to be great (*kane tōki / sato*). The tolling of the temple bell, allegorically the signal of an "awakening," sends back only a distant echo from the village, while in the mountain the wind, which both stirs up and scatters dreams, is dying down. But ironically this distance between the mundane and supra-mundane is reduced in the very gesture of inscribing it. In the very act of wondering about the dreams of a world—or rather the "dream world"—he has renounced, the priestly subject shows himself still susceptible to a certain mind-wandering or drift, slippage. In this sense the faint tremor of the dwindling wind in the maeku becomes charged with significance as the "prefiguration" of a yearning for the dream even as it vanishes. The link is in effect a meditation on the ineffable mystery of desire, the longing for something as elusive as the trace of a dream.

198 *STKBS* 3296

kanashi ya sate mo	Such sorrow this! What reason then
nani mumarekemu	was there to be born at all?
saki no yo o	In the world before,
mireba namida no	I seek, and find no "I"
nushi mo nashi	weeps these tears.

Keikandō, Advanced Stage: The maeku is taken to mean "seeing that everything is in essence empty [*honrai kū*], what then is that which became myself?" The interpretation of the word *nani* ["why," "what reason" in the translation] is of utmost importance here. Since the subject "I" does not exist, what is the thing that was born? The verse is simple compared to the emotionally involved maeku, but its mind [*kokoro*] is limitless.   (p. 144)

Chikubun 1090: This is about the root source of life-and-death. Seeking in the world before, one finds no distinction between good and bad. These tears flow from a mind that makes the distinction.

As may be gathered from Kenzai's exegesis, the link is based on the radical transformation of *nani*, "why" in the maeku, to mean "what" in the tsukeku, so that "What reason was there to be born?" suddenly assumes the wholly different cast of "What is there in the previous world that gave birth to my sorrowful life in this one?" Both readings of *nani*, however, ask the question of the cause or reason and origins of existence, although only rhetorically in the maeku as such. Shinkei's reply is ironic: there is nothing and no one in the previous world that is the cause and source of these tears; *nushi* is used here in the philosophical and grammatical sense of "subject," while retaining its common senses of "master, owner." The response is given from the level of impartiality, a perspective that transcends the mundane belief in karmic causation and the dualisms of subject and object, this world and anterior worlds. All the dharmas are at base empty, there is no*thing* causing these tears, they are in that sense unreal. Or to put it in the language of the *Chikubun*, existence as such is neither painful nor pleasurable. It is the mind itself that draws the distinction.

Returning now to the maeku within the context of the tsukeku's response, we should note how the force of *kanashi ya* ("sad" + emotive particle *ya*) gains in depth and complexity from this new perspective. In the maeku as such, the sorrow is caused by disappointment, the frustration of mundane desire. Now it is caused by the realization that this sadness has no true basis (*nushi mo nashi*), that suffering is illusory, the product of an unenlightened mind, and that existence itself has no original, determinate ground.

At its highest level, *aware* is the tragic pathos generated by this dialectical awareness that suffering *does* in fact exist on the mundane level, where experience confirms its truth, but its existence cannot rationally be founded on firm ground and is therefore illusory. When registered as a sense of existential loneliness, an awareness of the "subject-less" (*nushi mo nashi*) impersonality of the dharmas, *aware* is more appropriately called *sabi*. The austere loneliness of *sabi* that informs what we sense to be a characteristically medieval poetic is born of the stark knowledge of the absence of comfort; at its extremity, this knowledge generates Shinkei's distilled poetry of the "chill and icy." Again, when the mind, acknowledging its own poverty, becomes open to the bottomless depth and elusively shifting margins of phenomena, that awareness is registered as *yūgen* (ineffable depth) or in Shinkei's terminology, *yōon* (ineffable remoteness). All these terms, from *aware* to *yūgen*, signify modes of aesthetic-philosophical responses to the tension between desire (for the security of presence, permanence, substantiality) and knowledge of its groundlessness. They spring from that middle ground (*chūdō*) between the is (*ke*) and is-not (*kū*) that establishes and undercuts both in the very same stroke and constitutes, according to Tendai philosophy, the true "ground" of being.

Shinkei Alone and with Other Voices: Two Hundred-Verse Sequences

The two hyakuin translated and analyzed in this section have already been introduced in Part One within the context of Shinkei's literary biography. The two are chronologically proximate: "Cuckoo" (*Hototogisu*), the solo sequence, was composed shortly after his arrival in Shinagawa, Musashi (Tokyo), in midsummer of 1467, and the second, "Broken Beneath Snow" (*Yuki no oru*), dates from the winter of the following year, 1468, by which time a local renga group had consolidated around him. Together the two texts provide an excellent opportunity to hear Shinkei alone and then as one among several voices and to observe thereby the clear difference between these two events. (For translations, without commentary, of both texts, see the Appendix.)

Given the common understanding of renga as an impersonal code-bound art that has no place for individual self-expression, it would seem anomalous to describe the 1467 solo sequence as a long integral lyric poem figuring the state of a distinct sensibility at a particular point in time. But that is what Shinkei's dokugin is. In other words, in his hands the renga sequence composed by one individual shows its real possibilities as an expressive lyric poem. We are made to see that the formal conventions of the genre—the use of a special poetic lexicon and predetermined themes, and the grammatical rules of frequency, duration, and intermission governing them—constitute in themselves a language like any other. This language can be spoken, particularly in the case of solo composition, in order to express the pressures of real circumstance upon an individual human destiny. And that expression here is as always tied to the act of interpretation, the will to understand and translate an impersonal language in the light of one's own experience.

The expressiveness of the 1467 sequence, what distinguishes it from other solo or collective sequences, lies in a number of distinct yet mutually resonant modalities of feeling that remain in the memory and become akin to the work's signature in the reader's mind. There is to begin with a distinct sense of self and phenomena in a state of drift. It is signaled by the unusually early introduction of the Travel theme in verse 4 and its subsequent high frequency in the first half of the sequence: by verse 58, it has been sounded no less than five times. This is a remarkable statistic, especially in view of the fact that it will recur only once thereafter, in 87. It argues for the theme's immediate urgency for the author and reflects his recent arrival in Shinagawa after a long sea voyage from the Ise coast and the Kyōto–Ise journey preceding it. Yet this sense of implacable drift breaks beyond the topos of Travel. The windswept clouds in the chill rays of moonlight in link 2/3, formally a pair of purely seasonal verses, belong to the same modality. It infects the ostensive Love theme of 13/14, shadows 18 (Autumn + Laments), 21/22 (Spring), and 37 (Miscellaneous, with its image of a ship sailing away), surfaces with clarity in 75 (Laments, a statement about the utter absence anywhere of a place of rest and refuge), and reaches a climax in 85 (Autumn), which resembles 2/3 except that the focus is on the harrowing sound of the wind scouring the autumn sky.

Related to the drift leitmotiv is the remarkably high frequency of the lexical category Waters in this sequence; it occurs all of six times, and mostly in extended runs of three or four verses each time. This is significant in comparison, say, with the 1468 hyakuin, where Waters occurs in the occasional isolated verse three times and only once in a series of three units. And when we include items like "dew," "tears," "mist," and "rain," which do not belong to the Waters category but are alike in their wetness, its special place in this work (and indeed in the whole of Shinkei's poetic symbology) emerges as a distinct characteristic. Although obviously correlated to the drift motif when it occurs in the thematic context of Travel, the sensation of wetness has two other registers in the work. It may, like the dew laving the moss in 35, or spring rain finely infusing the plants in 95, connote a gracious nurturing power, in contrast to the "parched rice" of the impoverished in 62, or the summer heat overcoming a traveler in 58/59. Moreover, the cool clarity of water is also a positive image of spiritual refreshment and transcendence of the mundane. But the wetness of dew and rain also figures a sense of vulnerability, the feeling of being exposed to and overcome by circumstance. Such is the modality of the feeble cries of insects in the rain-rifled grass of verse 6, the sleeves drenched in oar spray in 12 and glistening in dew-tears in 31, the lone fisherman's hut "dripping in saltspray" in 49, the boat hurtling past in the swollen currents of 91, and so on.

At its most extreme, where the mind unflinchingly confronts the fact of its own existential vulnerability, the modality of wetness shifts over into that of a chill, piercing transparency—of moonlight in 3 and 84/85, of ice in 10, of the wind in 99/100.

Yet a third resonant leitmotiv sounds the somber tone of loneliness and loss; this is already familiar to us from the numerous elegiac waka cited in Part One. In this sequence it is most palpable in the aura of ineffable remoteness, both spatial and temporal, that hangs over a great many of the verses. There is the last light flickering out from the bush clover branch of 7, followed by the deserted road of 8, and the winter-secluded hut in 9. Waves never meet in 13, time shifts implacably in 15, and cherry blossoms fall in obscurity in 20/21, where *mono sabishiki zo* ("an utter loneliness in things") verbalizes the motif as an existential condition. The motion of the poet's mind from 29 to 35 is particularly arresting. From 29, where the war-ruined capital is imaged as an old village inhabited only by the harsh winds, the traveler persona awakens to an uplifting vision of Mount Hiei, guardian of the nation's peace (32/33), only to note the failure of that moral vision in present reality (34), and subsequently seek solace in the beneficence of waters in 35. Verse 68, on the sadness of greening leaves after the white splendor of flowers, is introduced by a maeku of inward turmoil, 72 mourns the irrecoverable setting of the Buddhist moon of the soul, and link 87/88 details the obliteration of a path leading back to the past. In sum the 1467 sequence is unified by a sensibility playing upon the finite, mutually correlated modalities of drifting, vulnerability, loneliness, and loss. These motifs constitute its particular expressiveness beneath the always already inscribed, impersonal thematic fields of the renga genre, and mark its contingency, the temporal character of its speech within historical time.

To read the 1468 collective sequence after Shinkei's lyrical interior "monologue" is like emerging into the broad light of day and listening to a conversation among friends involved in a common project that is none other than the hyakuin itself. True, Shinkei is still incorrigibly recording the tragedy of his age; the hokku, as I explain in the commentary, may be read as a lament on the times' moral disorder, and the acute sense of drifting in the earlier piece reappears in his tsukeku in 62/63 and 90/91. But this time he is predominantly a man conversing with other men, and also a renga master ensuring through the unspoken hints in his own verse that the sequence keeps moving along in new directions and, through allusions to older poems and prose literature, that it achieves variety and textural density. It is not surprising, for instance, that he most often initiates the shift into a new theme: ten times compared to Sōgi's eight, Nagatoshi's six, Kaku'a's five, and so on in descending order. Similarly, it is he who first introduces an allusion to an older poem in verse 25, a move accompanied by a simultaneous breathtaking shift from Summer to Love. He plants the significant terms, *kumo to naru* ("turn into a cloud"), that would raise the specter of the goddess of Fuzan legend in link 39/40; *awaii* ("millet rice") in his verse 45 is calculated to evoke the famous Taoist anecdote of the dream of Han-tan; he inspires Sōetsu's allusion to the "robe of feathers" motif in 63/64, which in turn leads to the image of Kaguyahime (from *Taketori monogatari*) in 65. In this way, the 1468 sequence concretely shows us Shinkei in the public role of renga master, one that is often neglected because of the modern perception of his strikingly distinctive poetic voice compared with other renga poets, celebrated or otherwise.

That said, it must be recognized that we will not find in this Musashi hyakuin the beauty of sequence that Sōgi and his disciples Shōhaku and Sōchō will demonstrate in the "Three Poets at Minase" two decades later. Nor is it appropriate to look for the sustained passages of finely modulated and movingly expressive lyricism found in Shinkei's dokugin. Needless to say, the quality of a session is a function of the nature of the group itself. A consistent artistry of sequence is difficult to achieve with so many participants, and there are eleven in this case. An essential factor in Sōgi's later success in perfecting the artistry of the renga sequence as a whole, as Kidō Saizō has observed, was his training of close and immediate disciples of notable ability like Shōhaku and Sōchō (*RS* 1: 448). The long association of these three produced the artistic kinship and mutual understanding that marks the Minase sequence.

In Musashi in the winter of 1468, on the other hand, we have no less than three types of participants: Shinkei and his disciple Sōgi were in effect visiting poets from the capital; Nagatoshi, Norishige, Mitsusuke, and Ikuhiro were local Eastern samurai; Kaku'a, Shun'a, and Ken'a were Jishū monks, as was in all probability Sōetsu; about Hōzen, we know nothing at all (see Chapter 4). The wonder is not that this mixed company did not produce a distinctly artistic sequence but that the work is as good as it is. Not that anyone among the group was a rank amateur. Kaku'a and Sōetsu in particular seemed to have a competent grasp of the classical poetic language, and the warriors made up in arrestingly fresh conceptions for what they lacked in aesthetic refinement and proved themselves competent and interesting participants, especially in the latter half of the session.

Were one to sum up the particular appeal of the 1468 Musashi sequence, it would lie in the genial spectacle of the pure lyric poet Shinkei interacting with the robust personalities of the Kantō, assisting in that process of "softening the hearts of stern warriors" that he saw as poetry's mission, particularly in his war-torn age. Again, as in the case with the preceding dokugin, its appeal lies in its very temporality: the historic fact that present and future renga master are performing together in a session (it is fascinating, for instance, that Sōgi responds to fully eight out of Shinkei's seventeen verses, a high number considering the several other participants); that this is one of the few extant works from this time involving leading poets in a provincial milieu; and that Musashi, later to blossom into Edo and Tokyo, is the actual setting of the session and indeed surfaces in the verses themselves. There is, finally, the palpable sense of a conversation among several voices, each one bringing to bear upon the verse at hand a different mind and point of view, working each in his own way with the common formal language of the genre in the very act of speaking it.

There are four manuscript copies of the 1467 solo sequence, all dating from the late Edo period. The best among them is the copy made by Nankyoku Enshū sometime in the Bunka era (1804–18) and deposited in the Osaka Temmangū Shrine archives. It is the text included in the definitive edition of Shinkei's renga, *Shinkei sakuhinshū* (*SSS*), and is used in this translation. The *SSS* text of the 1468 sequence is also from the Osaka Temmangū Shrine and done by the same copyist during the same period. Although I have used it in the main, I have supplied two words missing in verses 17 and 18 of this text from the Itsukushima Jinja Nozaka-gūjike Text, which is Kaneko Kinjirō's main source in *Shinkei no seikatsu to sakuhin*. Similarly I have preferred to use the Nozaka Text version of verses 10 (*yowaki hikage* instead of *kohagi ga kage* in the Temmangū Text), 21 (*tōmi . . . chirite* for *hiromi . . . ochite*), 28 (*shiite* for *shirite*), 74 (*ume* for *hana*), and 96 (*manabu* for *mukau*) for the principal reason that these variants are better from the logic of linking and sequence, slight though the differences are. Though of earlier provenance, being a copy from the late sixteenth century, the Nozaka Text is also clearly corrupt in several places and requires in its turn to be collated with the Temmangū version. In short, it is not possible to state definitively which is the more accurate of the two.

The commentaries that accompany the translation are based on the work I did for the Shinkei seminars with Professor Kaneko many years ago. They are collated with his later definitive reading in *Shinkei no sakuhin to seikatsu* and further modified by my thinking on renga in the course of reflecting on Shinkei's thoughts on the subject. Following accepted practice, I note the theme and principal lexical categories for each verse and list the conventional word associations (*yoriai*) between verses where they are present. My primary concern, however, has been to go beyond formal categories and elucidate as precisely as possible the specific nature of the link between contiguous verses, as well as to trace the path of a movement across a series of verses, where it is discernible.

As is well known, and this is Shinkei's central critical tenet, the poetry of renga does not lie in the individual verses but in the relation between them. To put it strictly, one reads, not the verses themselves, but the charged space between them. Elsewhere I have described the poetry of linking as that instant when the maeku suddenly becomes charged with significance through the action of the tsukeku. The tsukeku is akin to a switch that sends an electric current running from itself to the maeku and then back again. Or it might be understood as a catalyst that triggers a chemical reaction in the configuration of the preceding verse. For instance, the links in verses 3–5 of the 1468 sequence are uncomplicated and for that very reason provide a good illustration of what I mean. Verse 3 is purely a description of a wintry night scene along the river; Kaku'a's tsukeku instantly makes that scene perceptible to the senses; he translates it to a complex of sensations. "Listening" (*kikeba*) actualizes the cry of plovers in the maeku, and "night wind drifting past my pillow" renders its winter night as a chill sensation on the skin. Verse 4, in other words, repeats verse 3 but with a difference, and it is in this palpable sense of a difference wherein lies the poetry of the link. It shows us that the gap between the verses has a real functional value; it is a charged space wherein one may read the operation of a mind or sensibility. In turn Norishige translates the tactile sensation of cold in link 3/4 to the olfactory perception of a fragrance in the air. In doing so, he activates the "wind" in the maeku as the bearer of a scent that drifts in from one knows not where. In this link 4/5, the verb *kiku* in its auditory sense drops out of consciousness to be replaced by its other sense of "to smell." Similarly we are transported instantly into the thematic field of Spring; at this point the Winter tonality of link 3/4 has also dissolved from the plane of consciousness.

In isolation, verse 4 of this three-verse series is indeterminate. Although it makes literal sense, it has no significance; it is an ambiguous utterance waiting to be *read*, a muteness wanting a voice to make it *speak*. This reading, this speaking of the maeku, is the tsukeku. The blankness of the single renga verse is here clearly evidenced by the fact that verse 4 has one value in connection with its maeku and another in the light of its tsukeku: within the context of the former, it refers to the chill of the winter wind sensed through the cries of the plovers; with the latter, it means a light spring breeze faintly scented with flowers.

In his classic book on poetry, Owen Barfield locates the site of our aesthetic pleasure in a poem in "a felt change of consciousness" that occurs on our first encounter with it. Significantly, he is at pains to make us understand that this phrase be taken with some exactitude. He does not mean merely that the poet enables us to see the world in a new way through another's eyes; he refers quite specifically to "the actual moment of change," that instant on reading the poem when we pass "from one plane of consciousness to another" through the power of the poet's imagination as concretized in the poem's specific diction.[1] It is not the one plane or the other as such that triggers the poetic experience but the *passage* between them. This is if anything even truer in renga in which neither the single verse nor the sum of the 100 verses constitutes the poem itself; the verses are there, as it were, to trace the invisible but palpable *passages* between them. In other words, we find here a peculiar genre that has apparently isolated the site of poetic pleasure and instituted its refinement and expansion through no less than ninety-nine minute turns of consciousness. Closer to our own time, Roland Barthes has also located "the pleasure of the text" in the discontinuities that open up between or among distinct planes of language, consciousness, orthodoxy and paradox, and so on, in one and the same work.[2] Locating the bliss of reading in the close attention to the seam, the fault, the interstices in the fabric of the text, Barthes's book recalls the Japanese *zuihitsu* in the simultaneous promiscuity and ellipticality of its discourse. It is indeed itself a kind of renga and can be read with profit as a sort of radical introduction to what is most essential about it.

Historically however, all this has been said before by Kenkō in the celebrated statement that in all things it is the beginnings and endings—that is, the transitions from one state to another—that are most moving. *Mujō* (temporality), the single most powerful idea in medieval Japanese culture, is always apt to be invested with a sense of melancholy. Nijō Yoshimoto saw renga with its ever shifting boundaries as a literary demonstration of the principle and thereby a means of attaining salvation.[3] It is possible, however, that the overwhelming popularity of renga practice had equally as much to do with the pleasure generated by temporality itself.

"Cuckoo"
A Hundred-Verse Solo Sequence
Composed by Shinkei in Musashi in the
Summer of Ōnin 1 (1467)

1	hototogisu	Shall I yet marvel
	kikishi wa mono ka	to have heard you, cuckoo?
	fuji no yuki	Mount Fuji in snow!

First Fold, Front. Summer: *hototogisu* (cuckoo). Mountains: *Fuji*. Named Place: *Fuji*. Falling Phenomena: *yuki* (snow).

Shinkei's elation at his first encounter with the Kantō landscape may be sensed in the buoyant quality of the first three verses of this sequence. The encounter is fittingly celebrated by the opening panegyric on the region's most renowned geographic feature, Mount Fuji. An extremely well-turned-out and inspired hokku, it fulfills the seasonal requirement through the image of the cuckoo, bird of summer, whose song is cherished because heard so rarely. The elliptical terseness of the diction conceals a comparison of two terms and a favoring of the last; it may be paraphrased at length thus: "Here in the Kantō, I heard the rare call of the cuckoo and marveled greatly, but what is that compared to the noble peak of Fuji, snowcapped even in the midst of summer? Full of wonderful sights indeed is the Kantō, but Mount Fuji is the greatest of them all!" The verse is a witty, fresh rendition of the "land-praising song" (*kunibome uta*), one of the most ancient modes of Japanese poetry. Indeed Shinkei's consciousness of joining the ancient *Man'yōshū* bards in their praise of Mount Fuji presently becomes manifest in the second verse.

1	hototogisu	Shall I yet marvel
	kikishi wa mono ka	to have heard you, cuckoo?
	fuji no yuki	Mount Fuji in snow!
2	kumo mo tomaranu	Not a cloud stops to linger
	sora no suzushisa	upon the coolness of that sky.

Summer: *suzushisa* (coolness). Rising Phenomena: *kumo* (cloud).

It must be a pleasure for readers to recognize the allusion here to Akahito's famous chōka, *MYS* 317, on Mount Fuji, in particular the last four lines in the following passage:

Fuji no takane o	When we gaze up
ama no hara	upon the heavenly plain
furisakemireba	at the lofty peak of Fuji,
wataru hi no	the light of the crossing sun
kage mo sakurai	is obscured,
teru tsuki no	the rays of the shining moon
hikari mo miezu	become invisible,
shirakumo mo	*even the white clouds*
iyukihabakari	*dare not traverse it*
tokijiku zo	*and no matter the season*
yuki wa furikeru	*it is white with fallen snow.*

The verse maintains the summer seasonal theme through the word *suzushisa* (coolness), which brings out the effect of the snow in the hokku, and the freshness of the sky, in which Fuji's snowcapped peak rises sheer and majestic in the almost cloudless blue sky. The link is comprehensible without knowledge of Akahito's chōka of course, but the allusion adds a dimension of sublimity lent by an age-old poetic tradition.

2	kumo mo tomaranu sora no suzushisa	Not a cloud stops to linger upon the coolness of that sky.
3	tsuki kiyoki hikari ni yoru wa kaze miete	So pure the rays of moonlight, the wind is naked to the eye—the night.

Autumn: *tsuki* (moon).

Traditionally the third verse perceptibly moves away from the first two. Thus while Shinkei maintains the sweeping panoramic view of the sky—now without Mount Fuji—he shifts to a different time and season and images bathed in the utter clarity of autumn moonlight. The luminosity of the evening is brought out in the radical diction of *yoru wa / kaze miete*, signifying that the night, normally dark, is wholly illuminated, so transparent that even the wind, though invisible, is apparent to the eye. In the context of this verse alone, this is an unnatural and exaggerated turn of phrase, of the kind Shinkei employs to transmit the precise quality of an intense poetic vision. In the context of the link with verse 2, however, *kaze miete* alludes to the clouds blown away by the wind; that is to say, the wind is "visible" in the wisps of cloud trailing across the illuminated sky.

3	tsuki kiyoki hikari ni yoru wa kaze miete	So pure the rays of moonlight, the wind is naked to the eye—the night.
4	yume odorokasu aki no karifushi	Startled, dreams fall away: a transient sleep in autumn.

Autumn: *aki* (autumn). Travel: *karifushi* (transient, temporary sleep).

Here occurs a major shift in mood; from the heightened elation of the first three verses, the poetic persona is, as it were, recalled to his condition as a homeless exile. Significantly, the moment of awakening coincides with the unusually early introduction of the Travel theme. Awakened from dreams by the streaming moonlight and the wind in 3, the persona now finds himself in some makeshift wayside lodging. Continuing into verse 6, this new mood is one of pathos and lonely vulnerability.

4	yume odorokasu aki no karifushi	Startled, dreams fall away: a transient sleep in autumn.
5	okimasaru tsuyu ya yadori ni fukenuran	Dew soaking deep about my lodging, is the night so far advanced?

Autumn: *tsuyu* (dew). Travel: *yadori* (lodging). Word Association: *karifushi* = *yadori*.

As distinct from the situation in the preceding link, here in link 4/5 it is the wetness of the thick dew that startles the traveler awake, intruding upon his dreams. The two situations evoke and mutually contrast distinct sensations: the first is sharp, instantaneous, and luminous; the second is of a chill moistness slowly penetrating. The subtle distinction thus generated by juxtaposing the same unit, verse 4, against two contexts (3 and 5) well illustrates the generic nature of renga as a poetry of montage and the kaleidoscope rather than one of linear plot development. Each verse signals a turn, a twist, a rearrangement, of elements into a new poetic image.

5	okimasaru	Dew soaking deep
	tsuyu ya yadori ni	about my lodging, is the night
	fukenuran	so far advanced?
6	mushi no ne yowaki	Grass clumps in the passing shower
	kusa no murasame	the insects' voices are frail.

Autumn: *mushi* (insects). Falling Phenomena: *murasame* (passing shower). Word Association: *tsuyu = murasame*.

As readers of Japanese poetry will know, the image of dewdrops in the maeku carries a hint of tears, which in this case alludes to the traveler's lonely vulnerability. That same feeling now becomes projected upon the objective image of unseen insects crying in the rain-rifled grass that functions in effect as their "lodging"; similarly, the dewdrops of the maeku are modified as those left by the "passing shower." Seemingly distant, this link is actually quite close in that it falls in with the maeku in a seamless integrity of poetic feeling. The method of bridging that distance between the traveler and the insects, man and his environment, is the typical one of analogy. Indeed, if one were to distill all the manifold ways of linking one verse to the next in renga, it will be seen that they are all based on the rhetoric of the metaphor. The method recalls the operation of poetry in the Heian lyrical narrative, where metonymical details in the setting turn to metaphors in the poems composed by the characters.

6	mushi no ne yowaki	Grass clumps in the passing shower
	kusa no murasame	the insects' voices are frail.
7	hagi ga e no	On the bush clover branch,
	shitaba nokorazu	the lower leaves flicker out in
	kururu no ni	the darkening meadow.

Autumn: *hagi* (bush clover).

The sense of pathos (*aware*) in the passage from 4 to 6 now gives way to the mood of impersonal loneliness known as *sabi*. It creates here a modal and aesthetic continuity among such thematically diverse verses as this final one in the Autumn series 3–7, verse 8 (Miscellaneous), and verse 9 (Winter). On the meadow where insects are crying in the wet grass, evening gradually settles, a process represented in the small focused image of the last light flickering out from the lower leaves of a bush clover branch.

Professor Kaneko finds *kururu* ("darkening with the dusk") in this verse unnatural in conjunction with its adverbial modifying clause *shitaba nokorazu* (lit., "with no lower leaves remaining," that is to say, "all the way down to the lowest leaves"). He implies that it was most likely a scribal misreading of *karuru* ("withering"), and that is how he interprets the verse. Accordingly, the link would hinge on the shower in the maeku scattering the withered bush clover leaves, the "grass" where the insects would now be crying. Such a link however, "though intricately minute, is labored [*kudoi*]" (*Seikatsu to sakuhin*, p. 273). The "withering" version is indeed unsatisfactory in dwelling too much on the pathos of the insects—on top of being wet, they would be left without a lodging in this case, and so I have chosen to adhere to the letter of the text as preserved. While unusual, the combination *shitaba nokorazu / kururu* is not so much unnatural as arresting and compelling; it is the sort of slightly dissonant expression Shinkei occasionally resorted to in order to transmit the exact nuance of a poetic image. Moreover, he would doubtless have pointed to a kind of precedent in *KKS* 260, an Autumn poem by Tsurayuki whose last two lines are *shitaba nokorazu / irozukinikeri*, "[Mount Moru] has wholly taken on color, down to the lowest leaves." Whereas Tsurayuki evokes the gradual coloring of the autumn mountain until it is wholly bright, Shinkei traces the opposite process, following the sunlight declining in the meadow until it flickers out from the lower leaves, leaving the whole in darkness.

| 7 | hagi ga e no shitaba nokorazu kururu no ni | On the bush clover branch, the lower leaves flicker out in the darkening meadow. |
| 8 | yuku hito mare no okagoe no michi | Seldom a passerby's shadow on the road over the hillcrest. |

Miscellaneous. Mountains: *oka* (hill).

We move away from the meadow and up along the hill road where no one passes. A completely still and empty scene at dusk, it has a finality or aspect of closure that suggests its position as the end of the Prelude, the introductory passage to the whole sequence.

| 8 | yuku hito mare no okagoe no michi | Seldom a passerby's shadow on the road over the hillcrest. |

9	fuyugomoru	Winter-secluded,
	fumoto no io wa	the hut below the hill
	shizuka nite	rapt in quietness.

First Fold, Back. Winter: *fuyugomoru* (winter-secluded). Mountains: *fumoto* (foothill). Dwellings: *io* (hut).

The Miscellaneous verse 8 by itself is non-seasonal, and it comes to function as a transition to the Winter theme here; the *sabi* mood, however, remains the same. The linking method consists principally of deploying elements into a spatial arrangement, as in a painting. Along the empty hillcrest road of the maeku, the eye comes upon an isolated hut nestled on the foothills of some mountains farther up in the background. It can be assumed that the maeku is meant to be the view as seen by the hermit from his hut.

9	fuyugomoru	Winter-secluded,
	fumoto no io wa	the hut below the hill
	shizuka nite	rapt in quietness.
10	kōru bakari no	Chill clarity of the water
	mizu zo suminuru	in a moment turning to ice!

Winter: *kōru* (turn to ice). Waters: *mizu* (water). Word Association: *fuyu* = *kōru*.

In striking contrast to the calm placidity of the maeku, this verse sets up an image of intense, concentrated power. The chill clarity of water about to freeze over links up to 9 not only as a Winter image, understood to be a pond or a stream by the hut but, more important, as an objective correlative of the hermit's mental power at the utmost stage of concentration when the mind becomes wholly empty and still, congealing into the Void that is the object of its meditation. This is an unparalleled example of the "chill and thin" (*hieyase*) mode that manifests Shinkei's poetic sensibility at its deepest, most intense level. It is also a noteworthy poetic demonstration of his famous homage to water in all seasons in the following passage from *Hitorigoto*, his 1468 critical essay:

Indeed nothing is as profoundly moving, or as refreshingly clear, as water. The water of spring makes the heart tranquil, stirs memories, and is somehow achingly appealing. In summer it feels chillingly cold at the source of limpid rivers or by the bank of a spring. And the mere sound of autumn water is enough to brace and clarify the soul. Again, nothing is as alluring as ice. Amidst the reaped rice fields at morning, the thin transparency of water turned to icicles along the eaves of ancient cypress-bark roofs, the look and feel of the dew that has frosted on the grasses and trees of withered fields—are they not arresting and compelling? (p. 469)

10	kōru bakari no	Chill clarity of the water
	mizu zo suminuru	in a moment turning to ice!
11	uchishiore	Swiftly wilting
	asakawa wataru	as I cross the morning river:
	tabi no sode	sleeves of travel.

Travel: *tabi no sode* (sleeves of travel). Waters: *asakawa* (morning river).

The Waters imagery introduced in 10 continues here and through verse 13 in the first of six such passages in the whole sequence. Such a high frequency is one of the distinguishing features of this work; it attests to the special place of water in Shinkei's symbolic lexicon and evokes as well, when it occurs as here in a Travel context, the immediate personal circumstance that this sequence was composed shortly after his long sea voyage from the Ise coast to Shinagawa (Tokyo), a journey that would turn out to be a permanent exile from his temple home in the capital city, Kyoto.

It is somewhat problematic to define precisely the link between 10 and 11. The obvious way would be to transpose the water in 10 to the morning river of 11; the verse would then be about the keenly tense sensation of crossing the icy river on foot in the morning. But as Kaneko observes (p. 275), such a reading is contradicted by the word *uchishiore*—which means "droop or wilt," like delicate flowers in a hot sun, or "become damp and weak," lacking in energy. In other words, a rift in poetic logic would open up between the two verses.

Shinkei is demonstrably a poet with an acute sense for the nuances of poetic language, and therefore we must presume that he intended the link to be read in another way. I believe that apart from the close association between "water" and "river," no other semantic and situational similarity is intended between the two verses, nor are they intended to fall together in an integral unity of feeling. The only way to read this would be as an instance of the *soku* or Distant Link based principally on sensibility and conceptualization rather than the usual plot-like associations from one verse to the next. In short the contradiction or stark contrast between 10 and 11 is in fact the point of the link. We are presented as it were with two juxtaposed and opposite processes: water congealing into ice, and crisp fabric crumpling with moisture. The one is an image of intensifying power, the other of its depletion. Circumventing word association and plot continuity, such a distant link between apparently disparate terms challenges us to find the abstract idea that would set them vibrating in relation to each other. It is in fact no different from *shinku* or the Close Link except in being almost wholly invisible.

11	uchishiore	Swiftly wilting
	asakawa wataru	as I cross the morning river:
	tabi no sode	sleeves of travel.
12	sao no shizuku mo	Drenched in the oar spray—
	kakaru funamichi	taking passage on a boat.

Travel: *funamichi* (lit., "ship-road"). Waters: *funamichi*. Word Association: *sode* (sleeve) = *sao no shizuku* (drops of oar spray); *kakaru* (hang upon, adhere to).

The link hinges upon the transformation of the journey on foot to one by boat. Or to put it more strictly, *wataru* (cross), itself ambiguous in the maeku, becomes specified here as a crossing by boat. Simultaneously the pathos of the wilted sleeves, evoking in this context both the physical and emotional strain of the journey, is intensified by concretely imaging them this time as drenched in the oar spray. Compared to the preceding, this link is quite close.

12	sao no shizuku mo	Drenched in the oar spray—
	kakaru funamichi	taking passage on a boat.
13	motometsutsu	Waves that ever seeking,
	yoru se mo shiranu	never meet in a single current—
	naka wa ushi	the torment of loving.

Love: *naka wa ushi* (the relationship between lovers is painful). Waters: *se* (current of the waves).

In one single dramatic yet smooth move, Shinkei shifts into the Love theme by transforming the waves, an obvious metonymical adjunct to the situational frame of the maeku, into a metaphorical image for the failure of lovers to come together. In this new context, the drops of spray in the maeku also become a metaphor for tears, and the emotional fatigue there is redefined as one of suffering frustration, the strain of a desire that finds no relief.

13	motometsutsu	Waves that ever seeking,
	yoru se mo shiranu	never meet in a single current—
	naka wa ushi	the torment of loving.
14	wakare no koma wa	The departing horse would not be
	hiki mo kaesazu	stayed, restrain it as I would.

Love: *wakare* (parting).

A flashback to the moment of the lovers' parting, the verse is about the inevitability of separation; taken with the maeku, it is also about the impossibility of repeating that single meeting, of recalling what has passed.

The horse has departed, it will not turn back, and the waves are left to drift forever out at sea.

| 14 | wakare no koma wa
hiki mo kaesazu | The departing horse would not be
stayed, restrain it as I would. |
| 15 | utsuriyuku
toki o koyoi no
urami nite | Each hour, as
it shifts, is yet more
bitter this night. |

Love: *urami* (bitterness).

The departing horse in the maeku now becomes identified with the allegorical figure in the common saying that time flits by as swiftly as "a galloping horse glimpsed through a chink in the fence" (*hima o yuku koma*). One might try to stop it, like the horse in the maeku, but to no avail. The persona waits for her lover, but only the time comes and goes, each passing hour (*utsuriyuku toki*) leaving only a diminishing expectation and an ever greater deposit of resentment. That she cannot arrest the passing moments (*hiki mo kaesazu*, "restrain it as I would") and postpone her disenchantment is the point of the link. Seemingly pointless and difficult by turns, it comes out to be rather wonderful when one has puzzled it out.

| 15 | utsuriyuku
toki o koyoi no
urami nite | Each hour, as
it shifts, is yet more
bitter this night. |
| 16 | chigiri ni wataru
ariake no tsuki | Holding to its promised course,
the moon in the paling sky. |

Autumn: *ariake no tsuki* (remaining moon at dawn). Love: *chigiri* (vow, promise).

Primarily an Autumn seasonal verse, this sounds the Love theme solely through the word *chigiri*, which refers to the lover's "promise" in conjunction with the maeku. In the verse as such, however, *chigiri* points to the "fixed" course of the moon in the sky through the night; it has traversed the sky as ordained and now remains in the paling dawn sky. The lover, however, has not come as promised; he has been false to his vows, leaving the woman to wait out the empty hours with only the faithful moon for company until the dawn. *Chigiri*, therefore, is the pivot upon which the link turns; the contrast between the two situations, one natural, the other human, one demonstrating fidelity, the other its absence, sharpens with irony the persona's feelings of "bitterness" (*urami*).

| 16 | chigiri ni wataru
ariake no tsuki | Holding to its promised course,
the moon in the paling sky. |

17	yo no naka ya	Such is our world:
	kaze no ue naru	dewdrops teeming in the meadow
	nobe no tsuyu	before the wind.

Autumn: *tsuyu* (dew). Laments: *yo no naka* (the mundane world). Falling Phenomena: *tsuyu.*

Leaving the Love theme behind, Shinkei now employs the same image of the moon's fidelity to a fixed course, which gives it the aspect of permanence, to thematize the opposite, wholly transient character of our human existence. He sets against the tranquil presence of the moon the myriad dewdrops gleaming on the meadow grass at dawn but soon to be scattered by the wind. The contrast is enforced by the spatial juxtaposition of celestial moon and terrestrial dew and meadow, and by the ironic consciousness that both are in fact following their own distinct "preordained" destinies.

17	yo no naka ya	Such is our world:
	kaze no ue naru	dewdrops teeming in the meadow
	nobe no tsuyu	before the wind.
18	mayoiukaruru	Groping astray in mountains
	kumokiri no yama	obscured in mist and cloud.

Autumn: *kiri* (mist). Laments: *mayoi* (delusion, ignorance). Mountains: *yama* (mountain). Rising Phenomena: *kumo, kiri.*

Moving from meadow to mountains, the poet continues the allegorical mode of presentation in the maeku with a restatement of the human condition. Whereas the former focused on mutability, this one images worldly existence (*yo no naka*) as a state of wandering delusion, the darkness of a soul lost in endless craving. Such a Buddhist allegorical reading of *kumokiri* (mists and cloud) is a conventional one in renga and waka, as well as in the Nō plays. Like the dew in the maeku, the mists and clouds as such are momentary, elusive phenomena, apt to be dispersed by the wind, yet there is irony in the fact that man takes them, in his ignorance, to be real.

18	mayoiukaruru	Groping astray in mountains
	kumokiri no yama	obscured in mist and cloud.
19	naku tori no	Birds cry,
	kozue ushinau	losing their treetop perches
	hi wa kurete	as sunlight sinks.

Miscellaneous.

In the mountain the sunlight is extinguished from the treetops, and in the ensuing darkness the birds cry in consternation and alarm. Delineating a wholly objective scene, this verse impacts on the maeku by activating the line *mayoiukaruru* ("groping astray") on the plane of sound, giving a pathetic cast to the cries of the birds as they grope about for their perches in the dark.

19	naku tori no	Birds cry,
	kozue ushinau	losing their treetop perches
	hi wa kurete	as sunlight sinks.
20	mono sabishiki zo	An utter loneliness in things—
	sakura chiru kage	shadow of scattering cherry.

Spring: *sakura* (cherry).

Within this wholly new context, the same bird cries take on a subtly different cast. They become more distant, a faint sound heard in the background, delicately accenting the mood of vacant and grey loneliness, or *sabi*, that occupies the poetic foreground. *Ushinau* (lose), whose object was "treetops," now comes to refer to the loss of the cherry flowers among which the birds had been disporting themselves. Birds and flowers constitute, of course, an irresistibly linked pair in Japanese and Chinese painting.

20	mono sabishiki zo	An utter loneliness in things—
	sakura chiru kage	shadow of scattering cherry.
21	furusato no	As for springtime in
	haru o ba tare ka	the old village, who would come
	toite min	to see it?

Spring: *haru* (spring). Dwellings: *furusato* (old village).

Mono sabishiki (vague loneliness) becomes redefined as arising from the location of the cherry trees in an old abandoned village. The splendor of their blossoming, and the lonely beauty of their scattering, transpire in a vacuum with no one to appreciate them. Loneliness refers, then, to the absence of human response; the underlying thought is that of transient and wasted beauty.

21	furusato no	As for springtime in
	haru o ba tare ka	the old village, who would come
	toite min	to see it?
22	kasumi hedatsuru	Through impenetrable haze
	kata wa shirarezu	one would not know the way.

Spring: *kasumi* (haze). Rising Phenomena: *kasumi*.

The link here is quite obvious: to the rhetorical question in the maeku, this is certainly one sort of response. The whole, however, would gain in poetic depth if one read the obscuring haze as an allusion to the distancing effects of time. Such a reading would, it seems to me, felicitously bring out the essential character of the image of the "old village" (*furusato*) in the maeku, apart from having a precedent in another tsukeku by Shinkei himself in the *Shinsen Tsukubashū* (see no. 142, *ta ga ueshi*, in Section I above). In Kaneko's reading, this is a Travel verse in which the old village of the maeku turns into the traveler-persona's hometown. His vision cut off by the haze, he gazes toward his hometown uncertain of the way back to it and feels a pang of homesickness. Such a reading also invests the link with more interest and appeal, but I feel it is problematic to posit a traveler-persona here. The point of view of both 21 and 22 seems to be that of an impersonal third-person narrator or observer, not that of a persona involved in any dramatic action. The question is whether the poetic sentiment is one of an elegiac longing for the past, or for one's originary place. Ultimately no doubt the one may be said to be a symbolic correlative of the other.

22	kasumi hedatsuru	Through impenetrable haze
	kata wa shirarezu	one would not know the way.
23	musashino wa	Across Musashi Plain
	kayou michi sae	even the daily round takes
	tabi ni shite	one on a journey.

Second Fold, Front. Travel: *tabi ni shite* (on a journey).

Musashi Plain is so vast, the houses so few and far between, that even a simple trip in the course of daily business feels like a journey. (This sounds like an actual impression made by Musashi upon Shinkei, who was used to the shorter distances and confined terrain of Kyoto.) And when the thick haze blurs this vast, uniformly featured landscape, it is all too easy to lose one's way.

23	musashino wa	Across Musashi Plain
	kayou michi sae	even the daily round takes
	tabi ni shite	one on a journey.
24	nagameshi ato no	Before my gaze hills receded
	tōki yamakage	into the shadows far behind.

Travel: *ato no tōki* (the far distance left behind).

Reinforcing the impression of the vastness of Musashi Plain, this verse evokes the long time it takes to traverse it by saying that the hills before one's eyes gradually recede into the shadowy distance behind, as one moves on toward one's daily destination; the experience is like going on a journey (*tabi ni shite*).

| 24 | nagameshi ato no | Before my gaze hills receded |
| | tōki yamakage | into the shadows far behind. |

25	waga mi yo ni	Bitter to find
	omowazu henuru	the years have passed her by,
	toshi wa ushi	all unawares.

Laments: *mi* (one's self, one's life), *yo* (the world), *henuru toshi* (the years that have passed).

Signaling an exciting shift after the near-linear, cumulative progression from 22 to 24, Shinkei here translates the image of vast spatial distance in the maeku into a temporal one, as the numerous years that have passed the persona by without her being aware of it. In diction and conception, the verse itself and the link with *nagameshi* (gazed upon) in the maeku are an unmistakable allusion to Ono no Komachi's poem, *KKS* 113:

hana no iro wa	Faded now the glow
utsurinikeri na	on the flower, *while vainly*
itazura ni	*I passed the years,*
waga mi yo ni furu	*gazing lost upon a world* in
nagameseshi ma ni	the dark of the long rains.

In the context of the link, the hills in front of the traveler, which eventually recede into the distant shadows behind him, turn to the future years facing Komachi's persona in her youth, which in time become the "distant shadows" (*tōki . . . kage*) of her past. *Nagameshi* (gazed upon) in the maeku takes on the second meaning of "brooded upon" here, and *omowazu* (suddenly, catching one unawares) brings out the woman's realization that she has wasted those years in brooding introspection while the vibrant bloom of her beauty faded—a whole life has passed her by without her marking it. In this way the technique of alluding to old poems in renga is a kind of paradigm for the method of linking itself, which may be described as the continuous displacement of the referent, or the progressive manipulation of the maeku's context. The maeku is transposed into a new framework through the *honkadori* device, while the old poem instantly or momentarily acquires a new past as it were by being cited within a new context.

25	waga mi yo ni	Bitter to find
	omowazu henuru	the years have passed her by,
	toshi wa ushi	all unawares.

| 26 | hakana ya inochi | So fleeting this breath of life, |
| | nani o matsuran | for what does it wait? |

Laments: *inochi* (life).

This verse is in effect a comment on the situation in the maeku. Looking back upon the years of her past, the persona feels as if they have glided away in a dream, fleetingly. Now on the threshold of old age, she wonders what else life could hold in store, except more of the same unenlightened drifting. The underlying viewpoint here is as Kaneko observes, the Buddhist idea that a life devoid of spiritual aspiration is one lived in illusion, no more substantial than a dream.

26   hakana ya inochi   So fleeting this breath of life,
      nani o matsuran   for what does it wait?

27   yasaki ni mo   Right in the arrow's path
      tsumadou shika wa   still the deer, searching for
      tatazumite   its mate, hesitates.

Autumn: *shika* (deer).

Another startling contextual shift so soon after that of 24/25; Komachi's persona, the subject of the earlier link, here turns into a deer. This dramatic, tension-filled juxtaposition suddenly activates the second line of the maeku, "for what does it wait" (*nani o matsuran*), through the figure of the deer hesitating right before the arrow's path; it also lends a concrete dimension to the maeku's first line, "So fleeting this breath of life" (*hakana ya inochi*). The perilous moment on the brink of life and death gains an added richness and depth when we dwell on the detail that it is his great longing for his mate that has driven the deer into this crisis. In the way it sets the splendor of longing against the certainty of death, the verse is a signal departure from the Buddhist view of love as an illusion. Or again, we might say that its ineffable depth is owing precisely to the Buddhist teaching that love is ultimately a vain delusion.

27   yasaki ni mo   Right in the arrow's path
      tsumadou shika wa   still the deer, searching for
      tatazumite   its mate, hesitates.

28   akikusa shigemi   Through the rank autumn grass
      shiranu hitokage   dim glimmer of a human shadow.

Autumn: *akikusa* (autumn grasses).

Shinkei develops the situation above by shifting to the other end of this confrontation, to the hunter wielding bow and arrow. We seem to feel the deer's fearful start as it senses but does not clearly see a human shadow among the dense, tall grasses. The atmosphere at this moment becomes eerie and uncanny; the link is made not only through a plot-like progression but more important, through a poetic evocation of mood that would later become known in Bashō school haikai as *nioi-zuke* (linking by fragrance), a late variant on the whole aesthetics of *yojō* or suggestiveness that is fore-grounded in Shinkei's poetics and itself constitutes the basis of renga as poetic art.

28	akikusa shigemi	Through the rank autumn grass
	shiranu hitokage	dim glimmer of a human shadow.
29	furusato ni	In the desolate hamlet,
	nowaki hitori ya	the field-cleaving wind alone
	kotauran	echoes in answer.

Autumn: *nowaki* (lit., "field-cleaving," i.e., typhoon, gale). Travel: *furusato* (old village). Word Association: *akikusa = nowaki*.

In this new link, it is a traveler who senses or thought he saw a human shadow among the swaying tall grasses, but when he called out, there was no answer but the whistling of the wind. This vague, eerie presence, coupled with the stormy wind cleaving the rank grasses, combine to reinforce the ghostly atmosphere in this deserted village long abandoned to the elements, its inhabitants either dead or gone elsewhere. The passage from 27 to 29 is quite vivid visually; the handling of the three successive moments evokes the method of montage in film. We are presented with three related frames, each reinforcing the other to suggest a half-emerging narrative in which the feeling of some crucial scenes are quite specific but the plot itself is still undecided, to be provided, perhaps, by the reader.

29	furusato ni	In the desolate hamlet,
	nowaki hitori ya	the field-cleaving wind alone
	kotauran	echoes in answer.
30	karine no tsuki ni	A time of wakeful thoughts upon
	mono omou koro	a transient bed beneath the moon.

Autumn: *tsuki* (moon). Travel: *karine* (transient sleep).

Here the old village becomes the object of the persona's thoughts as he lies wakeful beneath the moon, traveling away from home and yearning for his family and friends there. Sadly, however, his thoughts encounter no human response, only the sound of the ravaging wind there (*nowaki hitori ya / kotauran*). To better understand this link, we should note Kaneko's observation (p. 285) that this "old village," now interpreted as the persona's hometown, must refer to Kyoto. Its desolate aspect evokes none other than the ruined city during the Ōnin War, the same that turned Shinkei himself into an exiled traveler and refugee in the Kantō.

30	karine no tsuki ni	A time of wakeful thoughts upon
	mono omou koro	a transient bed beneath the moon.
31	sode nurasu	On sleeves wet
	yamaji no tsuyu ni	with dew on the mountain trail
	yo wa akete	glistens the dawn.

Autumn: *tsuyu* (dew). Travel: *yamaji ni yo wa akete* (dawn on the mountain trail). Falling Phenomena: *tsuyu*. Word Association: *tsuki* (moon) = *tsuyu*.

Shinkei now locates the traveler along a mountain trail, adds the detail of the dew to evoke tears glistening in reflected moonlight, and activates the phrase *mono omou koro* (time of wakeful thoughts) by specifying the coming of dawn. That is, he suggests that the persona has been rapt in disturbing thoughts through the night until the dawn, which finds his sleeves all damp with dew/tears. Both sentiment and image are classic and wholly conventional; this is an unprepossessing *yariku* (lit., "sending-on verse") whose object is simply to move the sequence along.

31	sode nurasu	On sleeves wet
	yamaji no tsuyu ni	with dew on the mountain trail
	yo wa akete	glistens the dawn.
32	kumo hiku mine ni	As the cloud banks lift, high on
	tera zo miekeru	the peak a temple lies revealed.

Buddhism: *tera* (temple). Mountains: *mine* (peak). Rising Phenomena: *kumo*.

The simple maeku now reveals itself to be the prelude to a kind of epiphanic moment. Awakening at dawn with tear-stained sleeves, the traveler gazes up at the peak, where the clouds are just drifting away to reveal a temple. The emphatic *zo* clearly expresses his surprise at this revelation; against the depressed mood signaled by tears, it should be understood as containing a positively reassuring, bracing influence. The careful arrangement of the various details of the landscape, along with the evocation of mood, has a natural, inevitable quality that makes this a rather exquisite link.

32	kumo hiku mine ni	As the cloud banks lift, high on
	tera zo miekeru	the peak a temple lies revealed.
33	omokage ya	Memory traces
	waga tatsu soma no	the timbers that he raised—
	ato naramu	here in image.

Buddhism: *waga tatsu soma* (the timbers that I raise). Mountains: *soma* (timbers).

One of the most moving moments in this whole solo sequence, this verse gives an extraordinarily intimate sense of the man behind the impersonal poetic mask, as he longingly traces in the contours of the temple the remembered image of Enryakuji, the temple on Mount Hiei where he had undergone twelve years of priestly training before being assigned to the Jūjūshin'in in Higashiyama, whose head priest he eventually became. From this perspective, one can read an autobiographical undertone in the Travel verses from 29 until this point.

The allusion to Enryakuji is embodied in the second line, which is taken from the poem composed by Mount Hiei's founder, Dengyō Daishi (Sai-chō), upon the temple's construction.

SKKS 1921. "Composed when he built the Main Hall [Enryakuji] of Mount Hiei." Dengyō Daishi.

anokutara	Hark, ye Buddhas
sammyaku sambodai no	of perfect wisdom, unparalleled
hotoke-tachi	and compassing all:
waga tatsu soma ni	Confer your invisible powers on
myōga arasetamae	*the timbers that I raise here!*

Commemorating the founding of Mount Hiei as a religious center in En-ryaku 7 (788) when Saichō was only twenty-one, this famous poem is also cited in the *Wakan rōeishū, Ryōjin hishō*, and Shunzei's treatise, *Korai fūteishō*. Within the context of the link, the emphatic force of *zo* in the maeku now comes to express the poet's profound emotion at the unexpected evocation of a fond memory from his now vanished existence in the capital.

33	omokage ya	Memory traces
	waga tatsu soma no	the timbers that he raised—
	ato naramu	here in image.
34	yomogi ga shima no	Immortal Island: not one tree
	hana no ki mo nashi	flowers amidst the rank growth.

Spring: *hana* (flower). Word Association: *soma* = *yomogi* (mugwort weed, rank growth).

Yomogi ga shima has at least two connotations. *Yomogi* as such is the mugwort weed; one of the representative wild plants in the classical poetic lexicon, it usually connotes a neglected garden or a house in a ruinous condition. It is the central image, for instance, in the *Tale of Genji*'s "Yomo-gyū" (Wormwood patch) chapter, about the impoverished Hitachi Princess. The association between "mugwort" and "timber" in the maeku is based on poems like the one below.

GSIS 273. Autumn. Sone Yoshitada.

nake ya nake	Cry on, you crickets,
yomogi ga soma no	cry on in *the mugwort weeds*
kirigirisu	*corded thick as timber*—
sugiyuku aki wa	for the passing of autumn
ge ni zo kanashiki	is wholly sad indeed.

Yomogi ga shima (lit., "island of mugwort"), however, so inelegant in name, also refers to Mount Hōrai (Ch. P'eng-lai), the fabled mountain-island paradise where Taoist immortals dwell, as well as to the island country of Japan itself.

Here Shinkei employs all these connotations of *yomogi*. The tone of the verse as such is clearly elegiac. In the maeku, momentarily elated at the memory of Mount Hiei, the persona envisions it, and by extension the islands of Japan itself as the immortal abode of wise sages, Mount Hōrai (*yomogi ga shima*). However, returning to present reality, he sees that what is before him is in fact no more than a ruinous weed-choked place where "not one tree flowers" (*hana no ki mo nashi*). The lament can only be properly understood as an evocation of the war-torn country; not improbably, Shinkei might have been remembering that Hiei was established to protect the nation from evil influences, but the "invisible powers" invoked by Dengyō Daishi in the poem have apparently withheld their blessing. The contrast being drawn is that between the remembered vision (*omokage*) of a tranquil ideal realm and the present national reality. "Flower," as has been noted previously in Shinkei's biography, connotes the grace and beauty of a moral sensibility in Shinkei's poetry; its maiming in the depredations of war is the primary image in the poem *ima no yo wa* from the spring of 1471 (cited in Chapter 6). Another poem, "Lament Drawn by Flowers" from *Shinkei's Waka in Ten Styles*, confirms the place of flowers in his criticism of his times.

	fuke arashi	Blow, winds of storm!
	chirasu bakari no	in a world bent only on
	yo no naka ni	tearing asunder,
	fuku kotowari no	where finds there a single
	hana ya nakaran	stirring flower of truth.
34	yomogi ga shima no	Immortal Island: not one tree
	hana no ki mo nashi	flowers, amidst the rank growth.
35	haru fukami	Deep into spring,
	midori no koke ni	dewdrops trickle on
	tsuyu ochite	the greening moss.

Spring: *haru* (spring). Falling Phenomena: *tsuyu*.

In a startling turnabout, we leave the dark tonality raised by the ironic juxtaposition of miraculous vision and disappointing reality in link 33/34. Here 34 acquires a purely descriptive cast in conjunction with 35, yet another instance of the fact that in renga, the verse as such is ambiguous until fixed by a neighboring context. It is late spring, the flowers all fallen ("not one tree flowers") in the now luxuriantly verdant island, a process represented by the pure image of dewdrops laving the moss, heightening its greenness. The allusion to Japan as Mount Hōrai in the maeku is reinstated; nature as such, perceived in all its rich and bountiful beauty, suggests the blessed abode of the Taoist immortals.

35	haru fukami	Deep into spring,
	midori no koke ni	dewdrops trickle on
	tsuyu ochite	the greening moss.
36	iwa kosu mizu no	Blurring to a murmur—sound of
	oto zo kasumeru	water coursing over the rocks.

Spring: *kasumeru* (hazy). Waters: *mizu* (water).

This verse is equally appealing in its attitude of rapt contemplation of nature. It immediately recalls the moss of the maeku, which must be upon these rocks. "Deep," which modifies the spring season in the sense of "late, advanced" and is associated with "moss" and "green" in the maeku as well, here acquires a new context: the sound of the mountain stream is softened by the thick carpet of moss, and similarly the waves are broken up into droplets of dew laving it—*zo* being in effect the signal that we should associate the thick moss and blurred sound. Introducing the second Water passage in the sequence, this link eloquently recalls Shinkei's rhapsody on water in *Hitorigoto*: "The water of spring makes the heart tranquil, stirs memories, and is somehow achingly appealing." Along with the sensation of a moist greenness, spring water in Shinkei is symbolic of the pure vitality of life; it also connotes a nurturing, solacing power.

36	iwa kosu mizu no	Blurring to a murmur—sound of
	oto zo kasumeru	water coursing over the rocks.
37	isogakure	As the waves recede
	nami ni ya fune no	behind the shore cliffs is that
	kaeruran	a ship sailing away?

Second Fold, Back. Miscellaneous. Waters: *nami* (waves), *fune* (ship), *iso* (rocky coast).

In a sweeping move that opens up the pictorial vista of this poetic painting scroll, Shinkei relocates the detail of a mountain landscape in the maeku to the craggy seacoast. As the waves pull back, blurring to a murmur upon the rocks, the persona gazes out to sea at a ship receding in the distance. Referring to a sound in the maeku, *kasumeru* is here interpreted visually. Tonally, this verse shares with the preceding a sense of the vacant, suspended tranquillity characteristic of spring in the classical poetic vocabulary.

37	isogakure	As the waves recede
	nami ni ya fune no	behind the shore cliffs is that
	kaeruran	a ship sailing away?
38	waga omoine no	In sleep restless with desire
	toko mo sadamezu	the bed yields no place to settle.

Love: *omoine* (sleep broken by yearning thoughts).

The vanishing ship has no direct relation to the sleepless persona whose eye momentarily registers it here, but it somehow reinforces the intensity of the yearning that keeps her tossing restlessly in bed—a motion, moreover, that evokes the waves of the maeku. The link is subliminal, yet no less effective; it is also instructive on the subject of thematic shifts in renga in demonstrating how the Love theme can be introduced into a wholly descriptive verse.

38	waga omoine no	In sleep restless with desire
	toko mo sadamezu	the bed yields no place to settle.
39	yume ni dani	Were it only in a dream
	ikani mien to	could I but somehow see him—
	kanashimite	she pleads in sorrow.

Love: *yume* (dream).

The depth of the persona's desolation may be gauged by the paradoxical logic of her situation. She seeks to assuage her longing for an absent lover by dreaming of him at least, but that very longing drives out sleep and dreaming. Thus she is trapped in a state of restless frustration from which there is neither escape nor relief, an intolerable physical sensation ("the bed yields no place to settle") so acute the mind cannot overcome it.

39	yume ni dani	Were it only in a dream
	ikani mien to	could I but somehow see him—
	kanashimite	she pleads in sorrow.
40	kakotsu bakari no	Only resentment forms on the
	tamakura no tsuki	pillowing arm, the empty moon.

Autumn: *tsuki* (moon). Love: *kakotsu* (blame, resent); *tamakura* (pillowing arm).

The "pillowing arm," symbolic of the intimacy of lovers, acquires a paradoxical intensity due to the absence of the other, a human absence marked by the cold, transparent rays of moonlight. Highly elliptical yet precise, the verse imagistically distills the sense of desolation in the maeku; it also brings out the utter futility of feelings of resentment against an absent object.

40	kakotsu bakari no	Only resentment forms on the
	tamakura no tsuki	pillowing arm, the empty moon.
41	ajikinaku	For these sobs
	musebu ya aki no	of despair, is not autumn alone
	toga naran	to blame?

Autumn: *aki* (autumn).

The object of resentment now shifts to the autumn season itself, whose most moving feature is the moon, as the long-suffering persona is finally reduced to sobs (*musebu*) of despair. This move does not detract from the reader's impression that the dark emotional tonality has become too pervasive at this point in the sequence; this is in fact the fourth verse in the same vein. Still, there is psychological acuity in the underlying observation that a person at the end of her tether, inner resources exhausted, will blame any irrelevant thing in her despair. In other words, the verse is a comment about the subject's loss of mental control; blaming the season is a measure of her helpless predicament.

41	ajikinaku	For these sobs
	musebu ya aki no	of despair, is not autumn alone
	toga naran	to blame?
42	uezuba kikaji	Unplanted, they would be dumb,
	ogi no uwakaze	the reeds soughing in the wind.

Autumn: *ogi* (reeds).

This plainly contradicts the rhetorical question posed in the maeku: autumn, now represented by the sound of the wind over the withered reeds, is not melancholy as such but thinking makes it so. Having "planted" the grasses herself, she is the cause of her own condition. In effect the verse is a metaphorical affirmation of the pathetic fallacy in that nature does not constitute the cause and source of feeling but only its language. The root of feeling is "implanted" in the human heart itself; but for that fertile ground, nature would be virtually silent in the sense of expressing nothing.

This verse is not original with Shinkei. It appears in the first official renga anthology from 1356–57, the *Tsukubashū* (1116, Miscellaneous, by Sugawara Nagatsuna) as the tsukeku in the following pair:

ukikoto mo	Autumn comes, letting
ware to shirubeki	me know myself the cause
aki naru ni	of my own misery.
uezuba kikaji	Unplanted, they would be dumb,
ogi no uwakaze	the reeds soughing in the wind.

This tsukeku was originally composed for a thousand-verse sequence held sometime in the Bunna era (1352–56), and there its maeku, quoted below, was somewhat different from the *Tsukubashū* version.

ukikoto wa	Unending the gloomy
kokoro ni taenu	thoughts in the heart—
aki naru ni	for it is autumn.

It is interesting to examine which of the three maeku, including Shinkei's, sets off the same tsukeku most effectively. Clearly, the original version is quite weak, doubtless the reason why it was revised for inclusion in the official anthology. The second, much improved version crisply activates the tsukeku; Shinkei's version, similarly effective, is slightly more subtle in being indirect ("Is autumn alone to blame?"), thus increasing the impact of the image of reeds sounding in the wind.

The question of why Shinkei should include another's composition in his own solo sequence is an interesting one, given his strictures against plagiarism in *Sasamegoto*. There he concedes the possibility of coincidental similarity, innocent of copying, between two verses by different contemporary poets. But then he also quotes two hokku by himself side by side with similar versions by other poets as an instance of plagiarism. In the case of the *Tsukubashū* verse here, we might speculate that he had forgotten its original provenance and it had joined the latent fund of verses in his poetic imagination. But since it is given in exact fidelity to the *Tsukubashū* text, with no attempt whatsoever to conceal its source by modifying a word here and there, it is more likely that he intended it to be recognized as such and was interested in demonstrating how it acquires a different cast when placed against a different maeku. It is significant to note that in the *Hyakuban renga awase* (Renga contest in 100 rounds, dated 6.25.1468), Shinkei responded to a similar urge to pit his skill against the *Tsukubashū* poets of a century earlier by composing his own tsukeku to the original maeku from a contest in which Gusai and Shūa, with Nijō Yoshimoto as judge, vied with each other in composing the better tsukeku. In short, the inclusion of *Tsukubashū* 1116 in this solo sequence is best seen as a quotation from an older source, which a modern poet modifies by giving it a new maeku and tsukeku—a new context, in other words, in the manner of *honkadori*.

42	uezuba kikaji	Unplanted, they would be dumb,
	ogi no uwakaze	the reeds soughing in the wind.
43	haru o nao	Still now, a memento
	wasuregatami ni	of that indelible spring—
	sode hosade	sleeves that will not dry.

Spring: *haru* (spring).

In the verse itself, wet sleeves evoke sorrow at spring's passing. In relation to the maeku, however, they are a "memento" (*katami*) of a past spring when the persona wet her sleeves planting the reeds, the same that now in autumn move her to tears. In other words, within the context of the link, this spring season does not exist in the narrative present but only in the memory. The circumstance that made that spring so "difficult to forget" (*wasuregatami*) is suggested in the next verse. Here we should note the clever way Shinkei found to shift to Spring by conceiving it as a flashback in time from the autumnal present of the maeku.

43	haru o nao	Still now, a memento
	wasuregatami ni	of that indelible spring—
	sode hosade	sleeves that will not dry.
44	kasumi ada naru	The sadness in the wake
	ato no awaresa	of the vanished haze.

Spring: *kasumi* (haze). Rising Phenomena: *kasumi*.

Wet sleeves are now ascribed to sorrow at the ephemerality (*ada naru*) of that symbol of spring, the haze. *Ada*, however, also means "fickle, inconstant," and therefore suggests a fleeting love affair that ended in the subject's abandonment.

44	kasumi ada naru	The sadness in the wake
	ato no awaresa	of the vanished haze.
45	awayuki no	In the thin snow
	kieyuku nobe ni	dissolving in the meadow
	mi o shire	is my fate revealed.

Spring: *awayuki* (thin snow). Laments: *mi*. Falling Phenomena: *awayuki*.

The link is based on a simple parallelism between the ephemeral haze and the easily melted spring snow, an analogy only heightened by the contrastive juxtaposition of rising and falling phenomena. The new element is in the subject's predictable reading of the same evanescent nature in her own existence.

45	awayuki no	In the thin snow
	kieyuku nobe ni	dissolving in the meadow
	mi o shire	is my fate revealed.
46	hito mo tazunenu	The fragrance of plum flowers
	yado no ume ga ka	draws no visitor to the abode.

Spring: *ume* (plum blossoms). Dwellings: *yado* (abode, house).

The elusive fragrance of plum blossoms wafting in the empty air, unappreciated by anyone, is also an image of transience, but the feeling that emerges from the verse is primarily that of loneliness or *sabi*. Kaneko observes that although plum blossoms have a frequency value of five in a standard sequence, Shinkei has condensed them all into this single outstanding occurrence, a fact that indicates their special personal significance for him. Below I quote a waka he composed in 1463, along with his own commentary, to suggest that the image of plum blossoms wafting their fragrance in vain is associated in Shinkei's poetic imagination with the pathos and fear of his own obscure end. In other words, this image in conjunction with the last line of the maeku (*mi o shire*, "my fate revealed") reflects his consciousness of the possibility that a similar fate awaited him.

ware nakuba	When I am gone,
shinobu no noki no	plum blossoms by those eaves
ume no hana	deep with moss-fern:
hitori niowamu	the sadness of a fragrance
tsuyu zo kanashiki	drifting alone in the dew.

I was imagining the flowers blooming by the moss-deep eaves of my old cottage when I, who have had such joy in them these many years, have vainly passed away in some unknown place.

This was written in 1463 when he was forced to abandon Jūjūshin'in, his "old cottage" in the capital and was staying in Kii Province. Now four years later, in an exile that would prove permanent in the Kantō, we find him using the same image in the same way. No doubt the conjunction between the plum blossoms' fragrance and an enforced banishment from the capital was inspired by the famous poem by Sugawara Michizane, *SIS* 1006: Miscellaneous Spring, "While gazing toward the plum blossoms of his home when he was banished [from the capital]."

kochi fukaba	When the east wind blows,
nioi okoseyo	send your fragrance from afar,
ume no hana	O flowers of the plum—
aruji nashi tote	Forget not the springtime
haru o wasuru na	though your master is gone.

46	hito mo tazunenu	The fragrance of plum flowers
	yado no ume ga ka	draws no visitor to the abode.
47	kakureiru	Where I live hidden in
	tani no toyama no	the valley, the mountain's shadow
	kage sabite	deepens with time.

Laments: *kakureiru* (living in hiding, as a recluse). Mountains: *tani* (valley), *toyama* (foothills).

The "abode" (*yado*) in the maeku now becomes specified as a hermit's cottage in an isolated mountain valley. *Kage sabite* ("the shadow deepens with time") is an arresting turn of phrase to render his consciousness of the many lonely years he has spent there; its deeply somber mood of *sabi* heightens by contrast the wafting, elusive fragrance of the plum blossoms.

47	kakureiru	Where I live hidden in
	tani no toyama no	the valley, the mountain's shadow
	kage sabite	deepens with time.
48	keburi sukunaku	Meager the hearthsmoke
	miyuru ochikata	rising off in the distance.

Miscellaneous.

In a typical move in the delineation of landscape in renga, Shinkei sketches the view as seen from the valley abode. From the mountain hamlet in the distance, the rising hearthsmoke looks as sparse as the rustic peasants' means. A *sabi* grayness and austerity unites the distinct lives of commoners and their recluse observer.

48	keburi sukunaku	Meager the hearthsmoke
	miyuru ochikata	rising off in the distance.
49	shio taruru	Dripping in saltspray
	suzaki no ama no	at the far end of the sandspit:
	hanareio	a lone fisher's hut.

Miscellaneous. Waters: *suzaki* (sandspit). Dwellings: *hanareio* (a hut off by itself).

From the mountains, the landscape now shifts to an open coastal scenery, focusing in particular upon a single fisherman's hut at the tip of a long, narrow sandspit projecting out at sea. Such scenery, which would be unknown in Kyoto, recalls that at this time Shinkei was living by Shinagawa Bay. Apart from the counterpoint between mountain and sea imagery, a contrast is also being drawn between the scant smoke rising in the air, and the saltspray dripping down the fisher's hut. This last image, *shio taruru*, is particularly arresting in the way it precisely evokes a concrete tactile sensation. A beautiful scene lent pathos by the suggestion of a harsh existence wholly exposed to the elements, this begins the third Water passage in the sequence.

49	shio taruru	Dripping in saltspray
	suzaki no ama no	at the far end of the sandspit:
	hanareio	a lone fisher's hut.
50	toma fuku fune ni	With the sedge-roofed boat,
	nami zo naraeru	the white cresting waves align!

Miscellaneous. Waters: *fune* (boat), *nami* (waves).

While sustaining the painterly mode of the maeku, this verse has left pathos behind and is wholly concerned with visual design. It gives the impression of a dynamic scene—waves cresting high and white in rows about the sedge-roofed boat, momentarily arrested by the observing eye into an ordered pattern, and has the satisfying aesthetic appeal of an *ukiyo-e* print. Along with this visual beauty, there is a specifically verbal wit in *naraeru* (learn, copy, model oneself upon), which transmits the idea that the cresting waves are "patterning" themselves after the triangular shape of the boat's roof.

| 50 | toma fuku fune ni | With the sedge-roofed boat, |
| | nami zo naraeru | the white cresting waves align! |

51	furu yuki ni	Companionless amidst
	tomonaki chidori	the falling snow, the plover
	uchiwabite	calls out in sorrow.

Third Fold, Front. Winter: *yuki* (snow), *chidori* (plover). Waters: *chidori*. Falling Phenomena: *yuki*.

The poet now blurs the visual clarity of the seascape with a screen of falling snow, accentuating the whiteness of the cresting waves, and pointing up the whole with the lone figure of a plover crying on the cold, white shore. The brilliant shift into Winter is accompanied here by the introduction of lyrical pathos or *aware*.

51	furu yuki ni	Companionless amidst
	tomonaki chidori	the falling snow, the plover
	uchiwabite	calls out in sorrow.
52	hitori ya nenan	Alone can I drift off to sleep—
	sayo no matsukaze	night astir with the pine winds.

Love: *hitori-ne* (sleeping alone).

The cries of the lone plover turn to the rustling of the wind in the pines as heard by a woman awaiting her lover; her heart gives a slight tremor at the sound, indicating her uncertainty as to whether she can endure sleeping alone through such a night. The metaphorical association between lone plover and woman is quite clear, as is the semantic contiguity of *tomonaki* (companionless) and *hitori* (alone). It would be poetically unappealing, I believe, to fuse the two visual frames—one wintry, the other miscellaneous as to season—for that would result in a redundancy of image (and sounds). It would be contrary, moreover, to Shinkei's own teachings about economic precision in the matter of poetic diction, the need to have "a keen sense for discriminating which words in the maeku ought to be adopted and which discarded" in the process of linking (*SSG*, p. 124). Thus I read the link here as Distant: the only thread running between the two verses is a sense of lonely deprivation; the image of the plover is not in the present frame but has been transformed into a metaphor for the lonely woman.

52	hitori ya nenan	Alone can I drift off to sleep—
	sayo no matsukaze	night astir with the pine winds.
53	towarezuba	Unvisited,
	mi o ikani sen	what shall I do with myself?
	aki no sora	the empty autumn sky.

Autumn: *aki no sora* (autumn sky). Love: *towaru* (be visited).

The idea of being visited corresponds of course to the "waiting" implied by the second meaning of *matsu* (pine trees, wait) in the maeku, and a shift to Autumn is accomplished with the image of the woman gazing vacantly at the autumn sky. Otherwise, compared to 51/52, this is a plain and Close link in that the verse merely expands on the sentiment already given in the maeku, and there are no other shifts in referent.

53	towarezuba	Unvisited,
	mi o ikani sen	what shall I do with myself?
	aki no sora	the empty autumn sky.

54	tanomeokitsuru	So much and long dependent upon:
	tsuki no yūgure	this evening of moonrise.

Autumn: *tsuki* (moon). Love: *tanomeoku* (rely upon, trust).

In the autumn sky, the moon has risen, it is evening, the time when the woman's lover promised to come. As she gazes at that moonlit sky, she is taken with anxiety as to what she would do with herself (*ikani sen*) should he fail her. Another Close link, but the effect is more striking than that of 52/53; the sense of classic rightness in both the diction and conception is quite satisfying.

54	tanomeokitsuru	So much and long dependent upon:
	tsuki no yūgure	this evening of moonrise.

55	tsurenaku mo	Indifferent he might be,
	tsuyu no nasake wa	yet a dewdrop of pity must
	arinubeshi	lodge in his heart?

Autumn: *tsuyu* (dew). Love: *tsurenashi* (cold, indifferent, cruel), *nasake* (feeling, pity, compassion).

Still anxiously awaiting a man who has not come at the appointed time, the woman is now clutching at the smallest straw, relying upon an assumption that although he has proven himself indifferent to her, nevertheless he might still come out of charity. Such is the depth of her obsession, or desperation.

This ends the Love passage beginning with 52 and immovably fixed upon the pathetic figure of an anxiously waiting woman. Such a view of love as experienced by the female seems quite cruel, and it is certainly feudal. Yet it is the conventional view in the imperial waka anthologies and has the weight and authority of the Heian romantic narratives as well, in particular the *Tale of Genji*, required reading for aspiring renga poets as for the waka poets before them. Shunzei, for instance, declared during the "Poetry Contest in 600 Rounds" that "the poet who has not read the *Genji* is much to be deplored" (*NKBT* 74, p. 442), and Shinkei himself counted that work as among those exhibiting a "refined diction and behavior of appealing sensibility" (*SSG*, p. 132). Is it possible that for the male renga poets the traditional mythos of the female love experience was symbolic of their own deep, frequently frustrated desires, whether sexual or otherwise? We cannot explain the persistence of the Love theme, so conceived, in Japanese poetry until the nineteenth century except by presuming that it gave the male poets an opportunity to dwell upon and thus relieve, through the code-bound, formal, and acceptable language of poetry, the pressures and anxieties of repressed individual will in a feudal society.

| 55 | tsurenaku mo
tsuyu no nasake wa
arinubeshi | Indifferent he might be,
yet a dewdrop of pity must
lodge in his heart? |
| 56 | sode ni shigure no
susamajiki koro | Days of chill autumn showers
piercing through my sleeves. |

Autumn: *shigure* (incessant rain), *susamaji* (chill). Falling Phenomena: *shigure*.

In the context of the link, the chill wetness of this wholly seasonal verse is an objective correlative to the maeku persona's emotional state. The man's indifference and the now apparent futility of the self-deceiving thought in the maeku (that theoretical ounce of charity) affect her like the incessant, chill autumn showers. There is a subliminal ironic contrast as well between the meager "dewdrop of pity" (*tsuyu no nasake*), which turns out to be nonexistent, and the chill pouring rain that cruelly assaults her spirit. This is a dramatic, psychologically acute link.

| 56 | sode ni shigure no
susamajiki koro | Days of chill autumn showers
piercing through my sleeves. |
| 57 | yama fukami
yuki no shitamichi
koekanete | In mountains deep
under snowdrift the trail
is hard to follow. |

Winter: *yuki* (snow). Travel: *yamagoe* (mountain crossing). Falling Phenomena: *yuki*. Mountains: *yamagoe*.

The persona whose sleeves are wet with rain now becomes a traveler impeded by the extreme adverse conditions in the snow-covered mountains. The two verses are linked by a parallelism between two figures suffering exposure to the harsh elements of distinct seasons; there is a contrapuntal effect, however, in the fact that the maeku image is properly read symbolically, while the tsukeku describes an objective situation. That is to say, the maeku evokes the tonality of the feeling of the tsukeku's persona.

| 57 | yama fukami
yuki no shitamichi
koekanete | In mountains deep
under snowdrift the trail
is hard to follow. |

58   iwao no kage ni   A traveler lies prostrate
        fuseru tabibito   in the shadow of a great rock.

Travel: *tabibito* (traveler).

The progression from 57 to 58 is obvious: the traveler, plodding in the snowbound mountain trail, is overcome with fatigue and has fallen in the shelter of a huge rock. The shift in point of view from the subjectivity of the traveler himself in 57 to an impersonal narrator here is highly effective and dramatic. It demonstrates how the manipulation of point of view is one more parameter operating in the progression of a renga sequence.

58   iwao no kage ni   A traveler lies prostrate
        fuseru tabibito   in the shadow of a great rock.

59   natsu zo uki   Summer goes hard—
        mizu ni hitoyo no   ah, for a night on a rushmat
        mushirokaze   fanned by the seabreeze.

Summer: *natsu* (summer). Travel: *hitoyo no mushirokaze* (one night on the rushmat in the breeze). Waters: *mizu* (water).

The fallen traveler is now conceived as having been overcome by the summer heat in the hills and dreaming of the seashore with its cool breezes. The suddenness of the shift from the cold of winter in the preceding link to the heat of summer here is quite bracing and impressive. Here begins the fourth Water passage.

59   natsu zo uki   Summer goes hard—
        mizu ni hitoyo no   ah, for a night on a rushmat
        mushirokaze   fanned by the seabreeze.

60   e no matsu ga ne ni   A fishing boat moored to the roots
        tsunagu tsuribune   of a great pine tree in the cove.

Miscellaneous. Waters: *e* (cove), *tsuribune* (fishing boat).

The sense of tranquil ease and relief in the maeku's vision becomes concretely realized here as we imagine a man lounging in the fishing boat, enjoying the delicious wind stirring the pine branches. The visual scene as such may be appreciated aesthetically, suggesting as it does a detail from a landscape painting of the Southern School.

60   e no matsu ga ne ni   A fishing boat moored to the roots
        tsunagu tsuribune   of a great pine tree in the cove.

61   kurekakaru   As the dark gathers along
        naniwa no ashibi   Naniwa Bay, reed fires are lit
        takisomete   one after another.

Miscellaneous. Waters: *Naniwa*. Named Place: *Naniwa*.

From the detail in the maeku, the visual perspective widens to include the long shoreline of Naniwa Bay (Osaka) in a panning motion suggestive of the cinema camera. There is also a filmic quality in the evocation of the small fires lighting up here and there in the gathering dusk. The easeful delight in the preceding link shifts here to the somber tonality of *sabi*.

61	kurekakaru	As the dark gathers along
	naniwa no ashibi	Naniwa Bay, reed fires are lit
	takisomete	one after another.
62	kareii isogu	Hurrying with the parched rice—
	koya no awaresa	the pathos in the hovels.

Miscellaneous. Dwellings: *koya* (hut, hovel).

The reference to the humble fare of the fishermen's families along the coast, their lack of means and leisure, would stem from Shinkei's own observation of the daily life of the peasant poor during his travels. Compassion for the poor and defenseless (here, *koya no awaresa*, "the pathos in the hovels") is no doubt a conventional sentiment in a Buddhist priest, but Shinkei's biography indicates that it was a moral conviction born of personal experience (see Chapter 3). Indeed the importance of *sabi* in his work must be viewed as the artistic inscription of a clear-eyed recognition of deprivation, whether material, social, or existential.

62	kareii isogu	Hurrying with the parched rice—
	koya no awaresa	the pathos in the hovels.
63	wabinureba	Bewailing fortune,
	namida shi sosogu	he weeps copious tears upon
	karagoromo	the once splendid robe.

Laments: *wabinureba* (bewailing fortune). Word Association: *kareii* (parched rice) = *Karagoromo* (Chinese, i.e., splendid, robe).

The frugal meal in the maeku now becomes an aspect of the much reduced circumstances of a former aristocrat. As readers of the *Tales of Ise* will recognize, the fixed association between "parched rice" and "Chinese robe" has its source in Section 9 of that Heian classic. There the courtier hero, depressed by his failures in the capital, travels east in search of a place to live. At Yatsuhashi in Mikawa Province, his party stops by a marsh to have a meal and he composes the following poem, which so moved his companions that "their tears fell upon the *parched rice* until it swelled."

karagoromo	As a *Chinese robe*
kitsutsu narenishi	worn softly familiar was
tsuma shi areba	my wife to me—
harubaru kinuru	my heart is weary, thinking
tabi o shi zo omou	how far away I have come.

Shinkei's verse is an instance of *honzetsu*, a technique of linking through allusion to an episode in a well-known prose work; it is similar to the *honkadori* method of alluding to a famous poem. Here, the sorrowful figure of Narihira in the *Tales of Ise* is like an evocative shadow casting an ambiguous light upon the present persona whose situation is vaguely similar. The difference, that this man is actually wearing a "Chinese robe"—it is not a metaphor—merely points up the apparent aim of the *honzetsu* device, which is to superimpose upon the present scene an intertextual reference, in order to enrich its feel and texture.

63	wabinureba	Bewailing fortune,
	namida shi sosogu	he weeps copious tears upon
	karagoromo	the once splendid robe.
64	urami narikeri	Become this bitter resentment:
	hito no itsuwari	the treacherous words of a man.

Love: *urami* (resentment), *itsuwari* (lie, deception). Word Association: *wabi* = *urami*.

The maeku's miserable state is revealed to be due to a man's deceitfulness in the past. This negative experience has ruined her, robbed her of all interest and hope for the future, and so she harbors a deep-seated resentment against him. The shift to a female persona would seem to be signaled by *urami*.

Although I have followed Kaneko's reading, in turn based on Ichijō Kanera's placement of both *urami* and *itsuwari* in the thematic field of Love (*Renju* 899), it seems to me possible to read this verse within the maeku's framework of Laments. That is, the "lie" for which the persona bears the man a deep grudge would be a false accusation of treason, which led to the former's fall from courtly society and a miserable existence. I mention this alternative interpretation because of Shinkei's known objection to a wholly code-bound reading in which a verse's meaning is governed by the presence in it of certain thematically predetermined words. Instead of considering words in isolation, he advocated attention to its integral message, which is here simply grievous resentment at a man's deception. He also said that it can happen that a verse will straddle two thematic fields, particularly in the case of Love and Laments (see Chapter 6). This verse could very well be such an instance.

64	urami narikeri	Become this bitter resentment:
	hito no itsuwari	the treacherous words of a man.
65	waga shiranu	For an affair of which
	koto nomi yoso ni	I knew naught, my name grew
	na no tachite	notorious to others.

Third Fold, Back. Love: *na no tachite* (become the subject of rumor; acquire a bad name).

The man's deceitfulness (*itsuwari*), which one assumed to be a matter of his faithlessness in the preceding link, turns out to be something else again here: he has been spreading false rumors about intimate relations with her, a slander to ruin her name. If we go by the alternative reading of 64 in the preceding link, it is first here, in 64/65, that the thematic frame definitely shifts from Laments to Love. Read this way, the shift becomes more dramatic.

65	waga shiranu	For an affair of which
	koto nomi yoso ni	I knew naught, my name grew
	na no tachite	notorious to others.
66	toishi sono yo wa	That night you came to me:
	yume ka utsutsu ka	Was I dreaming? Was it real?

Love: *toishi* (visited); *yume* (dream).

To preclude confusion, it must be said at once that the matter of slander in the preceding link is now wholly irrelevant to this one, which centers around the dream-like quality of one single night of love, the feeling immortalized in Section 69 of the *Tales of Ise*, to which this verse makes a clear allusion. In that episode, the Priestess of the Ise Shrine appeared before the erstwhile hero sometime before midnight, left again before three, then sent him this poem after dawn.

kimi ya koshi	Came you to me, or
ware ya yukikemu	might I perhaps have gone to you?
omōezu	I cannot fathom it—
yume ka utsutsu ka	*Was I dreaming? Was it real?*
nete ka samete ka	Was I sleeping? Awake?

The verse makes no specific reference to the identity of its speaker; from the context of the *Ise* story and the poem above, it could be either Narihira or the priestess (*kimi ya koshi*). In connection with the maeku also, the same is true, since both would have had to bear the brunt of scandal. What is pertinent to note here is that Shinkei is playing, somewhat disingenuously to be sure, upon the very ambiguity concerning the reality of that night. If it were indeed a dream, then both parties can claim to be wholly innocent; in particular, *waga shiranu / koto nomi* (lit., "something of which I am ignorant") is made to artfully resonate against *omōezu* ("I cannot fathom it") in the poem of the priestess. When even I cannot tell whether it was a dream or real, what basis can there be for such rumors? This link is distinguished by a humorously ironic wit in the psychological reversal operating between maeku and tsukeku.

| 66 | toishi sono yo wa | That night you came to me: |
| | yume ka utsutsu ka | Was I dreaming? Was it real? |

67	kaerusa wa	On the way back,
	kokoro mo madoi	my heart was in a turmoil,
	me mo kurenu	blinded my eyes!

Love: *kaerusa* (the way back); *madou* (to be deluded, confused).

The persona being evoked here is Narihira, and the speech in the maeku would have to be his as well in the context of the link. Coming away from that "incredible" tryst, he is so overwhelmed that he cannot think or see clearly ("blinded my eyes"), and is therefore unable to decide whether or not it actually happened. The allusion is to Narihira's reply to the poem by the priestess quoted earlier:

kakikurasu	*I wander delirious*
kokoro no yami ni	*through the roiling darkness*
madoiniki	*within my heart—*
yume utsutsu to wa	*Was it a dream? Reality?*
koyoi sadameyo	*I beg you decide, tonight!*

Shinkei's method here of responding to an allusion to one poem by citing another, albeit from the same episode in the *Tales of Ise*, is rather unusual but highly effective.

67	kaerusa wa	On the way back,
	kokoro mo madoi	my heart was in a turmoil,
	me mo kurenu	blinded my eyes!

| 68 | aoba kanashiki | Sad the greening leaves on |
| | hana no yamakage | hills lately white with flowers. |

Spring: *hana* (flowers). Mountains: *yama*.

Definitely a Distant link; the shift from delirious passion to heartbroken regret for the vanished cherry blossoms is utterly amazing. A Distant link, it must be noted, does not indicate a loose connection but rather a subtle, unexpected one. Conventional word associations are usually absent in it or, if present, do not begin to explain the move from one verse to the next. *Kaerusa* ("on the way back") is the clue to the linking transition here; it is reinterpreted to mean the persona's "return" from viewing the flowers at their height, which is to say, just before their certain scattering. Yet the verse as such is set later in the season, when the trees are beginning to teem with green foliage. The force of *kaerusa*, in other words, exists only in that wide gap that the reader must bury to read the connection. The "sadness" (*kanashiki*) is at the recollection of the flowers' splendor, which has left not a trace in the greening leaves. In this new context the inner turmoil (*kokoro mo madoi*) in the maeku becomes redefined as the helplessness one feels at the inevitable passing of something beautiful. The link is informed by passion—for love in the maeku, for beauty in this verse.

68	aoba kanashiki	Sad the greening leaves on
	hana no yamakage	hills lately white with flowers.
69	mizu ni uku	Across the water
	tori no hitokoe	the floating note of bird cry
	uchikasumu	turns hazy.

Spring: *kasumu* (be hazy). Waters: *mizu* (water), *uku tori* (floating bird).

The bird cry floating hazily across the water is a wholly objective image, but it takes on a delicate hint of pathos in connection with the maeku's sadness at the vanished flowers. Another effect of the juxtaposition is to bring out the quality of vague, gentle nostalgia in the maeku: the image of the flowers (*hana no . . . kage*) formerly so vivid to the eye turns nebulous and ineffable in the memory, like a cry floating through haze. As in the preceding case, we have here a Distant link based neither on a plot-like continuity nor on a synecdochic alignment of details in a single visual plane, but solely upon poetic sense and concept. The fifth Water passage begins here with a note of tranquillity recalling the second such passage at the end of the front page of the second fold.

69	mizu ni uku	Across the water
	tori no hitokoe	the floating note of bird cry
	uchikasumu	turns hazy.
70	fune yobau nari	Someone calling out to the boat—
	haru no asanagi	Calmness of a spring morning.

Spring: *haru* (spring). Waters: *fune* (boat).

The bird cry turns to the voice of someone calling out to a boat on the water. The link is Close; both are metonymical features of a wholly relaxed and tranquil spring morning scene. Like the bird cry, the man's voice sounds remote as it drifts across the hazy air over the water.

70	fune yobau nari	Someone calling out to the boat—
	haru no asanagi	Calmness of a spring morning.
71	omoshiroki	Entranced by the
	umi no higata o	wide curving beach at ebb tide,
	osoku kite	he was slow to come.

Miscellaneous. Waters: *umi no higata* (the sea at ebb tide).

The gracefully curving beach at ebb tide is so appealing that the person taking his morning walk slows down to appreciate it. His elation and sense of well-being before the scenery, we may imagine, caused him to call out gaily to the boat in the distance as another might playfully throw a stone across the water. It is a delicate and satisfying link.

| 71 | omoshiroki
umi no higata o
osoku kite | Entranced by the
wide curving beach at ebb tide,
he was slow to come. |
| 72 | tsuki no irinuru
ato wa shirarezu | Once the moon has set, nothing
remains to trace its passage. |

Autumn: *tsuki* (moon).

Along with the graceful line of the coast at low tide, we now momentarily glimpse the pale outline of the moon as part of the scene that so captivated the persona in the maeku. But the verse itself evokes a later moment, when "the moon has set" (note how the perfective suffix *nu* activates *osoku kite*, "slow to come," in the maeku), and the viewer, first noting its disappearance, is struck with a sense of the ineffableness of things, how the moon is visible to the eye at one moment and in the next wholly absent and leaving no trace of its earlier presence (*irinuru / ato wa shirarezu*). This Distant link contrasts the elation of the maeku with the bereft feeling that succeeds it. There is an unspoken gap in time that exists only in the space between the two verses but must be read in order to make the link comprehensible.

| 72 | tsuki no irinuru
ato wa shirarezu | Once the moon has set, nothing
remains to trace its passage. |
| 73 | kuraki yori
kuraki o omou
aki no yo ni | In the autumn night,
imaging the path out of darkness
into deeper darkness. |

Autumn: *aki no yo* (autumn night). Buddhism: *kuraki yori kuraki* (from darkness into deeper darkness). Word Association: *tsuki* (moon) = *kuraki yori kuraki*.

The moon of the maeku now turns into the Buddhist "moon of the mind-heart" (*kokoro no tsuki*). The darkness that ensues after its setting (*tsuki no irinuru / ato*) is read as "the long night of ignorance" (*mumyō chōya*), the state of samsaric delusion in which sentient creatures wander through karmic cycles of birth and death, passing from one realm of suffering to another until enlightenment is attained. The link itself is unmistakably an allusive variation and reading of the famous poem by the Heian poetess Izumi Shikibu:

SIS 1342. Laments. "Composed and sent to Priest Shōkū." Masamune's Daughter, Shikibu.

kuraki yori	*Out of darkness*
kuraki michi ni zo	*into yet deeper darkness* is the
irinubeki	path *I must enter—*
haruka ni terase	Shed your rays from afar, O *moon*
yama no ha no *tsuki*	verging on the mountain crest!

In Shinkei's reading the moon hovering on the mountain crest of Izumi's poem has set, plunging the world into the utter darkness of suffering delusion, so that her plea gains in urgency and despairing pathos. One senses in this reading the *mappō* (latter days of the Buddhist Dharma) consciousness that strongly informs medieval literature, and Shinkei's own writing with it. The poem *fukenikeri* (quoted in Part One, Chapter 4), which laments the setting of the Buddhist moon before man's moral indifference, provides substantial insight into this particular link.

73	kuraki yori	In the autumn night,
	kuraki o omou	imaging the path out of darkness
	aki no yo ni	into deeper darkness.
74	kiri furu nozato	Mist falls on the meadow village,
	kumo no yamazato	Clouded the mountain village.

Autumn: *kiri* (mist). Rising Phenomena: *kiri, kumo*.

The semantic content and rhetorical doubling in the verbal structure of "out of darkness into deeper darkness" (*kuraki yori kuraki*) are here reproduced on the plane of concrete visual image; the link is essentially a translation of one set of terms into another. Mists and clouds also constitute a metaphor for the darkness of ignorant delusion, emphatically seen here as a universal condition (*nozato / . . . yamazato*). Formally and conceptually, the link is wholly Close.

74	kiri furu nozato	Mist falls on the meadow village,
	kumo no yamazato	Clouded the mountain village.
75	mi o yasuku	Nowhere a refuge,
	kakushiokubeki	not a moment's respite for
	kata mo nashi	the tired spirit.

Laments: *mi o kakusu* (live in hiding, i.e., from the mundane world).

Even in the remote countryside—the meadow and mountain hamlets of the maeku—where one would expect to find a tranquil refuge from mundane suffering, the darkness of unknowing reigns. Such a verse is profitably read against the background of Shinkei's prose account of his wanderings as a refugee from the Ōnin War in the opening passage of his 1471 critical essay *Oi no kurigoto*; it evokes his sense of homeless drifting, of being hounded by circumstance, and, most of all, a deep weariness of spirit, which resonates here as well. "Mists and clouds" would then allude to the spiritual darkness that breeds war.

75	mi o yasuku	Nowhere a refuge,
	kakushiokubeki	not a moment's respite for
	kata mo nashi	the tired spirit.
76	osamare to nomi	"Cease this tumult!" That is all
	inoru kimi ga yo	I pray for in my Lord's reign.

Laments: *osamare to inoru* ("Cease this tumult," I pray).

A series of Close links started from 73 and will continue until 77, in contrast to the predominance of Distant links in the passage before. Hounded by the restless tides of war, unable to find shelter anywhere, the maeku persona is driven to scream, so to speak, to the warring forces to pacify themselves in that singular verb in the imperative, *osamare*; this is like commanding the turbulent waves to calm down or snarling dogs to be still. With the reference to the war-torn reign of the then Emperor Go-Tsuchimikado (r. 1465–1500), private lament widens to implicate the public sphere. In the summer of 1464, just prior to his coronation, this emperor did Shinkei the signal honor of summoning him for a renga session. The encounter, fondly remembered in one of the poet's three extant letters, lends a specifically personal character to this public prayer.

76	osamare to nomi	"Cease this tumult!" That is all
	inoru kimi ga yo	I pray for in my Lord's reign.
77	kami no tame	For he is a god,
	michi aru toki ya	the times may yet come to bend
	nabikuran	to the right Way.

Shintō: *kami* (god).

As indicated in the translation, I have chosen to render the first line *kami no tame* ("for he is a god") as a reference to the divine nature of the Emperor (*kimi*) in the maeku; that is to say, because he is a god, the time must come when the Way will be observed, and peace restored to the troubled realm. It may, however, be taken in a more general sense thus: "by the grace of the gods, the time must come. . . . " Kaneko paraphrases the sense of the link in this way: "Since it is precisely in times when the Way of worshipping the gods is properly observed that the world is at peace, I pray to the gods for peace in His Majesty's reign." In this reading, the primary link is from "pray" in the maeku to "gods" here, and the governing idea is that worshipping the gods constitutes the way of civil order. One wonders, however, why Shinkei did not then write *kami no michi / aru tame toki ya /*

nabikuran. The distinction between the two readings is a minor one, since both are based on the same Shintō political-religious ideology that is as old as the *Man'yōshū,* an anthology for which Shinkei demonstrably felt an affinity. Even in the medieval period, this ideology was closely bound up with the Japanese sense of nationhood. The idea that the Emperor's divinity empowers him to influence the times toward peace fits in well with the allegorical image of subjects bowing in homage to the sovereign in the following verse.

77	kami no tame	For he is a god,
	michi aru toki ya	the times may yet come to bend
	nabikuran	to the right Way.
78	kaze no mae naru	The grasses bowing their heads
	kusa no suezue	in serried ranks before the wind.

Miscellaneous. Word Association: *nabiku* (bend) = *kusa* (grasses), *sue* (tip, head).

Nabiku in the maeku, whose referent or subject is "the times" (*toki*), is displaced here by grasses with their tips or "heads" bending in the wind. The image is clearly a metaphor for the pacified times anticipated in the maeku, when the unruly, warring subjects would be "bowing" in reverence before the immanent divine power of the sovereign. This power, as we know from the *Man'yōshū,* is conventionally imaged as a pacifying "divine wind" (*kamikaze*) and is especially invoked when the country is in peril. For all these reasons, this link must be said to be very close indeed.

78	kaze no mae naru	The grasses bowing their heads
	kusa no suezue	in serried ranks before the wind.
79	fuyu no no ni	Seeing dewdrops
	koboren to suru	about to spill over in
	tsuyu o mite	the winter meadow.

Remaining-Trace Fold, Front. Winter: *fuyu no no* (winter meadow). Falling Phenomena: *tsuyu* (dew).

Suezue, the "tips" of the blowing grasses in the maeku, come into focus yet again with the addition of dewdrops upon them, while simultaneously undergoing a semantic shift to signify the temporal "end" of those same grasses now withered by winter. In the verse itself, the "end" is expressed in the momentarily stilled image of the dewdrops about to spill over (*koboren to suru*), but in the context of the link, the precise nuance of the reduplicative *suezue* (the distant final end) is captured in the cumulative effect of the advancing season, as daily the autumn wind spilled the dewdrops over and over again, until the present moment in winter, when the grasses have all shriveled. Such is the minute intricacy of the work of words, and the bounty hidden in the empty spaces, in Shinkei's renga. This link and the following are slightly Distant.

| 79 | fuyu no no ni
koboren to suru
tsuyu o mite | Seeing dewdrops
about to spill over in
the winter meadow. |
| 80 | harawaji mono o
koromode no yuki | I could not brush them away—
the snowflakes upon my sleeves. |

Winter: *yuki* (snow). Falling Phenomena: *yuki*. Word Association: *tsuyu* = *koromode* (sleeves).

Koboru (spill over) in the maeku becomes charged here by juxtaposition with *harau* (brush off), a tense conjunction further pointed up by their contrastive potential-mode suffixes -*mu* and its negative, -*ji*. The dewdrops, moreover, are now to be understood as teardrops in conjunction with "sleeves." Seeing dewdrops about to spill in the meadow, the persona is brought to mind of her own tears spilling on her sleeves, a memory so personally moving that now as snowflakes fall upon those same sleeves, she cannot find the heart to brush them away. The diction of this verse, which functions as a transition from the objective to the subjective emotional plane, is quite detailed in configuration in relation to the maeku, but its conception is perhaps a bit labored and unnatural. The coupling of external nature and human emotion in a wave of pathos, usually carried off in such a seemingly natural manner in Japanese poetry, is not wholly successful in this otherwise technically arresting verse.

| 80 | harawaji mono o
koromode no yuki | I could not brush them away—
the snowflakes upon my sleeves. |
| 81 | tsumorikuru
hito yue fukaki
waga omoi | Gathering ply on ply,
because of him my anguish grows
still deeper. |

Love: *hito yue no omoi* (a yearning caused by someone).

Tsumorikuru (pile up in layers) is clearly associated with "snow" in the maeku, while modifying the persona's deepening anguish in the verse as such. In the context of the link, the snow, which is now a metaphor for her attachment or obsession, has become so deep she cannot, even if she would, "brush it away." The link is close, and more successful in translating the objective image than the preceding.

| 81 | tsumorikuru
hito yue fukaki
waga omoi | Gathering ply on ply,
because of him my anguish grows
still deeper. |
| 82 | ikuyo ka tada ni
akashihatsuran | How many more nights shall see
the end of these useless dawns? |

Love: *tada ni akasu* (spend a useless night).

Still the pivot of the link here, *tsumorikuru* now signifies the accumulated nights the persona has spent alone. The design of the link is constituted by the binary opposition between the series of empty nights from the past up to the present moment and the haunting vision of the similarly empty nights stretching into the future. The moving effect of the verse lies precisely in this setting up of two quantities against each other—one already weighed in the anguish of experience, the other still a yawning space in the mind but already shadowed with the foreknowledge of futility. The fact that the ironic opposition is posed rhetorically as a question is also highly effective; it is perhaps the most expressive use of the interrogative mode in this whole sequence. That its full effect is only to be realized in relation to the maeku demonstrates the unique poetry of renga.

82	ikuyo ka tada ni akashihatsuran	How many more nights shall see the end of these useless dawns?
83	aramashi o nezame sugureba wasurekite	Hopes of release, held in wakeful moments, slide into forgetfulness.

Laments: *aramashi* (hopes for the future).

Aramashi signifies the persona's hopes of escaping from the cycle of desire and suffering through spiritual discipline. Felt most keenly in the wakeful moments of dawn, such a hope is eventually forgotten as the day advances and he or she is caught again, willy-nilly, in the grip of mundane desire. Whereas in the previous link verse 82 refers to amorous desire nightly frustrated by the lover's non-appearance, in this link it refers to religious aspiration repeatedly betrayed by a weak resolve. *Tada ni* (uselessly, vainly) in the maeku is the pivot of this impressive major shift; the passage seems to be building toward a climax.

83	aramashi o nezame sugureba wasurekite	Hopes of release, held in wakeful moments, slide into forgetfulness.
84	tsuki ni mo hajizu nokoru oi ga mi	Shameless before the lucid moon, the remnants of an aging life.

Autumn: *tsuki* (moon). Laments: *oi ga mi* (an aging life).

The desire to renounce a banal mundane existence repeatedly aborted for lack of resolve, the persona has now merely grown old, his spiritual potential unrealized, his mind grown indifferent to the inner purity symbolized by the Buddhist moon (*tsuki ni mo hajizu*), except in moments of fearful wakefulness (*nezame*) like this one, which, unfortunately, "soon slides into forgetfulness." Here the progression of feeling recalls a similar passage in verses 48–50 of the "Three Poets at Minase" sequence to be composed by Sōgi and his disciples two decades later.

84	tsuki ni mo hajizu	Shameless before the lucid moon,
	nokoru oi ga mi	the remnants of an aging life.
85	fuku kaze no	Harrowing, the sound
	oto wa tsurenaki	of the wind sweeping through
	aki no sora	the autumn sky.

Autumn: *aki no sora* (autumn sky).

The climax of the passage of self-reflection initiated in 82, this is one of those wholly objective images that take on human significance only through their contiguous position in relation to the situational field of the previous verse. It is a particularly fine example of the topological nature of renga poetry, which is like a chemical reaction that occurs on the basis of the verse's specific position within a pair, and eventually in a series, and then in the sequence as a whole. Here the cruel (*tsurenaki*) sound of the wind is an objective correlative of the aging persona's own fearful consciousness, as he nears his end, of his utter alienation from the hope of salvation signified by the moon. In the context of the link, moreover, *nokoru* (remaining) in the maeku reverberates with and suggests an image of remaining clouds dispersed by the wind scouring the autumn sky.

85	fuku kaze no	Harrowing, the sound
	oto wa tsurenaki	of the wind sweeping through
	aki no sora	the autumn sky.
86	mukaeba yagate	In a while, right before my eyes
	kiyuru ukigiri	the floating mists have vanished.

Autumn: *ukigiri* (floating mists). Rising Phenomena: *ukigiri*.

Sight is joined to sound as the whistling wind becomes visualized as a force rending apart the floating mists of comfortable illusions, leaving only the vast open sky of autumn (*aki no sora*), here a symbol of the Void. Forcibly stripped of all illusions and confronted with this emptiness, the ordinary mind senses it as cruel and harrowing, which is a measure of its own inadequacy before it. This link is in Shinkei's inimitable "chill and thin" style.

86	mukaeba yagate	In a while, right before my eyes
	kiyuru ukigiri	the floating mists have vanished.
87	michi wakuru	On the fine sand
	masago no ue no	the trail of footprints
	uchishimeri	moistens over.

Travel: *michi wakuru* (tracing a path).

Kaneko reads the link to mean that the mists obscuring the traveler's vision as he plods on gradually clear up, until he can clearly see the path without going astray. As indicated in my translation, I read the path over the sand (*masago no ue*) as a trail of footprints that become moistened over (*uchishimeri*), that is, flattened out and effaced, in the wetness along the beach. I feel it is more striking, poetically, to see a subliminal parallel between the mists that vanished (*kiyuru ukigiri*) before the persona's eyes in the maeku and a trail that dissolves as he follows it here. A disappearance occurs in both cases, but they involve different phenomena and processes. The link is forged not through the unity of a narrative progression (the mists are not necessarily in the same temporal and visual frame as the tsukeku's trail on the sand), but solely through an inner metaphorical juxtaposition. Thus it could be characterized as Distant, and similar to what Bashō would call "linking by fragrance" or evocative resonance.

87	michi wakuru	On the fine sand
	masago no ue no	the trail of footprints
	uchishimeri	moistens over.
88	furuki iori zo	Still the ancient hermitage
	namida moyōsu	causes the tears to well.

Laments: Remembering the Past: *furuki iori* (ancient hermitage).

Uchishimeri (moistens over) translates here as the welling up of tears (*namida moyōsu*) at the sight of an ancient hermitage long empty of its inhabitant. Similar moments occur several times in the *Narrow Road to the Deep North*, when Bashō pays a pilgrimage to the former abodes of hermits. Moreover, the dissolving footprints in the maeku subtly reverberates against *furuki* (old) here, evoking as it does the process of dissolution through time. A long time has passed, "effacing" the life that used to inhabit this shelter, but its trace, the ancient hermitage, still has the power to move the mind-heart. This would be the significance, I think, of the emphatic and contrastive *zo* in the context of the link.

88	furuki iori zo	Still the ancient hermitage
	namida moyōsu	causes the tears to well.
89	tachibana no	The orange-blossom tree
	ki mo kuchi noki mo	is rotting with age, and the
	katabukite	eaves are sagging.

Summer: *tachibana* (orange blossoms). Laments: Remembering the Past: *noki . . . katabukite* (eaves sagging).

In contrast to the subtlety of the preceding, this link is obvious and unremarkable; it expands upon the ruinous age of the hermitage in the image of the rotting tree in the garden ("orange blossoms" are conventionally associated with remembrance of the past) and the sagging eaves. Such a straightforward, thoroughly visible link also constitutes one method in renga, and it is useful in creating a variety of poetic effects. It is not, however, Shinkei's characteristic manner.

| 89 | tachibana no
ki mo kuchi noki mo
katabukite | The orange-blossom tree
is rotting with age, and the
eaves are sagging. |
| 90 | tou hito mare no
samidare no naka | Hardly anyone calls, through
the long dark rains of June. |

Summer: *samidare* (rainy season in summer, modern *baiu* or *tsuyu*).

The scene of ruined hut and garden now becomes enveloped in a mood of dim and timeless loneliness through the evocation of the poetic associations around *samidare*, the monthlong rains that fall continuously from June to July, an overcast and melancholy season. The orange blossoms in the maeku also come to life as a fragrance wafting in the drenched atmosphere, evoking romantic associations that belong to the dimly remembered past of the famous *Kokinshū* poem (no. 139, *satsuki matsu*) and allusions to it in later poetry and prose. Here begins the sixth and final Water passage in the sequence; it ends with another rain image in verse 95.

| 90 | tou hito mare no
samidare no naka | Hardly anyone calls, through
the long dark rains of June. |
| 91 | se o hayami
yūkawabune ya
nagaruran | In the swift current,
was that boat cast adrift upon
the evening river? |

Miscellaneous. Waters: *se* (current), *kawabune* (riverboat).

Only the image of the *samidare* rains falling in the deserted space is taken up in this link, which leaves behind the associations from the past in the maeku. The observing eye notes how swift and swollen the river has become due to the long, incessant rains and wonders if the empty boat drifting past was cut loose from its moorings by the force of the current. The link is more Distant than Close.

| 91 | se o hayami
yūkawabune ya
nagaruran | In the swift current,
was that boat cast adrift upon
the evening river? |
| 92 | tomaranu nami no
kishi o utsu koe | The incessant sound of
waves pounding the shore. |

Miscellaneous. Waters: *nami* (waves), *kishi* (shore).

In a close link, the force of the current in the maeku is translated here into an auditory image. As Kaneko suggests, the word *tomaranu* (incessant, without stopping) echoes *nagaruran* (flowing past, drifting) in the upper verse; although it refers primarily to the pounding sound of the waves in the verse itself, it also activates the image of the wayward boat hurtling swiftly past in the maeku.

92	tomaranu nami no	The incessant sound of
	kishi o utsu koe	waves pounding the shore.
93	yamabuki no	Yellow mountain roses—
	chirite wa mizu no	with each petal shower the water
	iro mo nashi	turns, colorless.

Remaining-Trace Fold, Back. Spring: *yamabuki* (yellow mountain roses; Japanese kerria). Waters: *mizu* (water). Word Association: *kishi = yamabuki*.

Couched in the paradoxical language of a riddle or a Zen kōan, this verse by itself apparently means that the yellow petals outspread on the water are so vivid that the water itself suddenly loses its color, that is, becomes muted and dim. By calling attention to the absence of one term in *mizu no / iro mo nashi* (lit., "the water has no color"), the verse enhances the profuse presence of the other term, the vivid loveliness of the yellow petals themselves.

In connection with the maeku, "the water has no color" is meant to invite a contrastive juxtaposition with the proposition that "the water has a voice" (*mizu no koe ari*), as may be deduced from the sound of waves pounding the shore (*nami no / kishi o utsu koe*) in the maeku. Furthermore, through the mediation of the conventional poetic lore that the color of the *yamabuki* is like that of the yellow dye extracted from the berries of the *kuchinashi* (gardenia or cape jasmine), commonly written as the ideographic pun "no-mouth," they were conventionally imaged as mute. Thus another hidden proposition in this link is that in contrast to the water, which has a voice but "no color," the roses have a color but no voice.

The playfulness of the method here is certainly more characteristic of comic *haikai no renga* than the refined *ushin renga* later to become epitomized by the work of Sōgi and his disciples. It is interesting to note, indeed, that the common association between *yamabuki* and *kuchinashi* apparently originates from *Kokinshū* poem 1012 by Monk Sosei, which is classified under the "Eccentric Poems" (*haikai no uta*) section in that anthology. There is no doubt that Shinkei loved and was skillful in the play of wit, punning, and double meaning that is ultimately the very life of renga poetry itself, since a verbal art of linking transformation is impossible without it. Still, as this verse illustrates, he made it a point not to indulge in wit for its own sake but to serve his equal love for poetic beauty, for the precise, vivid, and simultaneously subtle image.

Speaking of subtlety, I have so far followed Kaneko and presented the link here as based on the contrast between the vividness of a sound and the equal but mute vividness of a color. However, I wonder if Shinkei did not intend the link to turn also on the word *tomaranu* (incessant, without stopping) in the maeku. That is to say, *chirite wa mizu no / iro mo nashi* ("with each petal shower the water / turns, colorless") might also mean, that each time the petals fall, they glow vividly for a moment on the water before disappearing within the trough of the cresting wave as it folds over against the riverbank, leaving the water "colorless" again. Personally, I prefer this reading since it focuses in a precise yet subtle manner on the dynamics of the moment and in effect transposes upon the visual plane the incessant pounding of the waves (their coming and going) against the shore of the maeku. As a link not based wholly on verbal correspondences but more on the conceptual dynamics of the image, I find it tighter and more satisfactory. The imagistic progression from verse 91 to 93 is somewhat reminiscent of the following poem from the *Shinkokinshū*.

SKKS 160. "Presented for a Hundred-Poem Sequence during the reign of the Cloistered Sovereign Horikawa [r. 1087–1106]." Provisional Middle Counselor [Minamoto] Kunizane

	iwane kosu	Hurtling over rocks,
	kiyotakigawa no	the Crystal Falls River
	hayakereba	flows *so swift*,
	nami orikakuru	*the waves* are cresting back upon
	kishi no yamabuki	*the mountain roses on the shore.*
93	yamabuki no	Yellow mountain roses—
	chirite wa mizu no	with each petal shower the water
	iro mo nashi	turns, colorless.
94	yae oku tsuyu mo	The eightfold dewdrops also
	kasumu hi no kage	a hazy shimmer in sunlight.

Spring: *kasumu* (be hazy). Word Association: *yamabuki* = *yae-* (eightfold, many-layered).

"Eightfold," while evoking the profusion of dewdrops, recalls by association the manifold petals of the yellow mountain roses in the maeku. The muted glimmering of a myriad dewdrops in the overcast atmosphere also activates *mizu no / iro mo nashi*, the muted color of the water, by analogy. The linking method, a typical metonymical progression from one aspect of a scene to another, by blurring the surrounding vegetation and the air in a cloud of haze, again brings out the vividness of the flowers. In contrast to the focus on dynamic motion in the preceding link, this one evokes a mood of still tranquillity. Such a juxtaposition between motion and stillness (*dō* and *sei*) is later to become a typical move in Bashō school haiku and *renku*.

94	yae oku tsuyu mo kasumu hi no kage	The eightfold dewdrops also a hazy shimmer in sunlight.
95	harusame no komakani sosogu kono ashita	The spring rain is seeping finely over all, this morning.

Spring: *harusame* (spring rain). Word Association: *tsuyu = ame*.

"Seeping finely over all" (*komakani sosogu*) momentarily brings to vivid life, by association of cause and effect, the profuse dewdrops of the maeku, at the same time that the scene widens to include all that the eye can see on a hazy, tranquil morning of soft spring rain. Keeping in mind the appeal that water and other images of moisture had for Shinkei, one senses in this scene the grace and nurturing power of the rain that seeps into all the grasses and trees. It recalls the "Medicinal Herbs" chapter of the *Lotus Sutra*, in which the Buddha's all-encompassing wisdom and compassion is likened to a thick cloud (*mitsu'un*) spreading over all, a fine rain infusing everything with life.

95	harusame no komakani sosogu kono ashita	The spring rain is seeping finely over all, this morning.
96	omoikudaku mo kinuginu no ato	A heart is breaking into shards in wake of the dawn's parting.

Love: *omoikudaku* (torn in anguish); *kinuginu* (parting of lovers at dawn).

This verse marks a startling major shift from the beneficent tranquillity of the seasonal maeku to the now familiar mood of anguish connected with the Love theme; the link is Distant. The connection hinges on *komakani* (finely, minutely), which is here echoed in *omoikudaku*, a compound verb coupling *omou* (think, feel, yearn), and *kudaku* (shatter into tiny pieces, like china). Thus the objective image in the maeku comes to express a subjective state of mind, and in a marvelous transformation, the tranquil threads of spring rain now seem like needles spreading a fine pain in the woman's heart as she stares desolately out at the spring morning scene after her lover's departure. The verse captures both the bereft feeling as well as the indefinable anxiety close upon the moment of parting after a night of shared intimacy. It ends the absorbing run of minutely conceived links that began in 92.

96	omoikudaku mo kinuginu no ato	A heart is breaking into shards in wake of the dawn's parting.
97	koishisa no nakute sumu yo mo aru mono o	Surely there are worlds where one can live free of this yearning.

Love: *koishisa* (yearning, desire).

From here to verse 99 is a series of broadly conceived, generalized statements on the human condition that are closely linked by the logic of reason. Given the unbearable anguish of 96, the desire for release from desire and all its attendant suffering is thoroughly understandable. *Sumu* (to live) is also being used in its other sense, "clear, transparent," that is, without the pollution of desire.

97	koishisa no	Surely there are
	nakute sumu yo mo	worlds where one can live free
	aru mono o	of this yearning.
98	ikani shite ka wa	But how can I ever find
	kokoro yasumen	the way to quiet my mind?

Laments: *kokoro yasumen* (pacify, make tranquil the heart-mind).

Although it is possible to attain to a higher realm of liberation from desire—that is in effect the sum of Buddhist teaching—the way of mental discipline required to arrive there is difficult to follow. Perhaps because he was a priest and accustomed to reflect upon the darker depths of the human heart, Shinkei had taken a realistic measure of the deep-seatedness of desire. Two poems on Lament from his 1468 hundred-poem sequence may be taken as an illuminating commentary on the burden of the present link.

ōumi o	Though he drank all
nomu tomo nao ya	the vast ocean dry, he would
akazaran	still be dissatisfied:
kagiri naki yo no	a world without bounds in
hito no kokoro wa	the world, this heart of man!

nanigoto mo	That in all things
omoisutetsu to	he has renounced desire:
iu hito mo	the man who says so
inochi no uchi wa	is living a lie, as long as
itsuwari ni shite	life within him breathes.

Buddhism might preach with certitude the existence of "a world / . . . free of this yearning" (*koishisa no / nakute sumu yo*) but human experience shows that there is seemingly no end to the sea of *samsara*, that the desiring heart of man constitutes in itself "a world without bounds" (*kagiri naki yo*), which only death might conceivably destroy.

| 98 | ikani shite ka wa | But how can I ever find |
| | kokoro yasumen | the way to quiet my mind? |

99	tsukiyo ni mo	On moonlit nights, and
	tsuki o minu yo mo	even nights blotted of the moon,
	fushiwabite	I lie disconsolate.

Autumn: *tsuki* (moon).

Again the connection with the maeku, and indeed with the two poems cited, is clear. The most representative expression of the effect of the autumn moon on the heart is probably this poem from the *Kokinshū* (*KKS* 184, Autumn, Anonymous).

konoma yori	I see the moon's rays
morikuru tsuki no	dripping between the trees
kage mireba	and know that autumn,
kokorozukushi no	that heart-consuming season,
aki wa kinikeri	is once more upon us.

Why the presence of the moon (*tsukiyo ni mo*) should stir such longing thoughts in the beholder's gaze is best left to the imagination. Why its absence (*tsuki o minu yo mo*) should stir a yearning as well is all too clear. At any rate, against the theoretical possibility of its cessation, Shinkei sets the immovable certitude that to live is to desire; the human heart seems constitutionally addicted to it. Moreover, that desire in its boundlessness seems wholly incommensurate to its object, remaining constant despite the object's presence or absence, and thus ultimately beyond fulfillment.

99	tsukiyo ni mo	On moonlit nights, and
	tsuki o minu yo mo	even nights blotted of the moon,
	fushiwabite	I lie disconsolate.
100	kaze yaya samuku	About the rice-warden's pallet,
	inaba moru toko	The chill of the wind deepens.

Autumn: *inaba* (lit., "rice-place," rice granary or rice fields ripe with grain).

The sequence ends, after the vainly enlightening generalizations in the preceding three verses, in Shinkei's chill and thin mode and the final link is Distant. Verse 100 is in effect a final evocative and distilled image of the human condition of everlasting toil and sorrow beyond consolation. Moving imperceptibly but inexorably from autumn to the chill of winter, it is a somber, open-ended closure that simultaneously points the way to another beginning of the manifold circles of desire and suffering, and beauty, nature, and time, that is existence as the medieval renga poets inscribed it in their poetic scrolls.

"Broken Beneath Snow": A Hundred-Verse Sequence Composed by Shinkei, Sōgi, and Others in Shinagawa, Musashi, in the Winter of Ōnin 2 (1468)

1	yuki no oru	Reeds broken beneath
	kaya ga sueno wa	snow across the plain's horizon—
	michi mo nashi	there is no path.
	Shinkei	Shinkei

First Fold, Front. Winter: *yuki* (snow). Falling Phenomena: *yuki.*

Shinkei's hokku is manifestly no more than an objective image of a pathless, snow-covered landscape in winter. It conforms to the emerging conventions of the important first verse in citing the actual season of composition as its primary topic, and in its wholly autonomous formal shape—in renga the hokku, above all, must be able to stand on its own. It has one controversial aspect, however, and that is the unmistakable undertone of lament that informs it, particularly the strongly emotive final line with its negative inflection, *michi mo nashi* ("there is no path"). Composed in Musashi Plain in the second year of the Ōnin War, the verse is in fact a metaphor of the times; the image of heaps of reeds broken under the weight of snow all across the plain suggests a wasted battlefield, and the absence of a path implies the moral bankruptcy of the age, in that *michi* may also be interpreted as "the Way." The rule that nothing inauspicious or emotional should disturb the tranquillity of the Prelude section has yielded here to the pressure of circumstance, yet in the magnitude of the view it unfolds before the eye and the depth of emotion it evokes, this hokku attains to a sublimity rare, because difficult, in a three-line seventeen-syllable poem.

1	yuki no oru	Reeds broken beneath
	kaya ga sueno wa	snow across the plain's horizon—
	michi mo nashi	there is no path.
	Shinkei	Shinkei
2	yūgure samumi	Not a moving figure in sight
	yuku sode mo nashi	across a frozen twilight.
	Sōgi	Sōgi

Winter: *samumi* (cold).

Sōgi's second verse is a model of its kind in the way it maintains the scenery introduced by Shinkei, while enhancing its bleak mood. "Cold" naturally echoes "snow" in the hokku, and *yuku sode mo mizu* (lit., "not a moving sleeve is seen") is quite closely connected to *michi mo nashi* ("there is no path") both in syntax and semantic significance. As may be gleaned from its technical name, *waki* (lit., "alongside," that is, "a companion verse"), the second verse follows alongside the hokku as a kind of accompaniment; there should not be a visible gap between the two but a harmonious blending. In its simple, unassuming character, Sōgi's verse in effect tranquilizes the ever so subtle yet poignant lament in the hokku by fusing it within an impersonal feeling for the wintry and deserted twilight scene.

2	yūgure samumi yuku sode mo nashi Sōgi	Not a moving figure in sight across a frozen twilight. Sōgi
3	chidori naku kawara no tsuki ni fune tomete Norishige	As plovers cry along the river shallows, a boat glides up beneath the moon. Norishige

Winter: *chidori* (plovers). Waters: *kawara* (shallow riverbed), *fune* (boat). Word Association: *samumi* = *chidori naku* (plovers crying).[4]

This is not so apparent in the translation, but the bleak tonality of the first two verses breaks down completely here: the poetic landscape, heretofore still and deserted, instantly becomes cluttered with images: crying plovers, the river, a boat anchoring, the moon. True, the *daisan* (third verse) should signal a definite shift and strike out in a new direction, but Norishige overshoots the mark; the distance is too wide between 2 and 3. Nevertheless, if we ignore the imperfect execution and focus on the intended link, we see that the chill rays of moonlight evoked by the verse echoes "cold" in the maeku; the boatman is wholly alone on the riverbank, there are no other "moving figures," only the cries of the plovers and the luminous moon. Still, the verse as such links only slackly to its maeku.

3	chidori naku kawara no tsuki ni fune tomete Norishige	As plovers cry along the river shallows, a boat glides up beneath the moon. Norishige
4	kikeba makura o suguru sayokaze Kaku'a	Listening, I feel the night wind drifting past my pillow. Kaku'a

Miscellaneous.

Kaku'a compensates for the crowded effect of the maeku with a simple verse. Having anchored his boat, the speaker senses the wind drifting over his pallet within, interspersed with the calls of the plovers.

4	kikeba makura o suguru sayokaze Kaku'a	Listening, I feel the night wind drifting past my pillow. Kaku'a

5	sakurabana	Cherry blossoms—
	sakuran kata ya	already in flower yonder?
	niouran	a wafting fragrance.
	Nagatoshi	Nagatoshi

Spring: *sakurabana* (cherry blossoms).

Although marred by the aural and inflectional redundancy of *sakura-bana / sakuran . . . / niouran*, Nagatoshi's verse manages to deftly introduce the Spring theme by imagining the scent of cherry blossoms carried by the wind of the maeku. The turn is effected by reinterpreting the verb *kiku* (to listen) in the maeku in its other sense of "to smell" (usually said in conjunction with incense and perfumes), thus generating the verb *niou* (waft a fragrance) in the third line.

5	sakurabana	Cherry blossoms—
	sakuran kata ya	already in flower yonder?
	niouran	a wafting fragrance.
	Nagatoshi	Nagatoshi
6	haru ni okururu	Spring comes late to the village
	yamakage no sato	in the mountain's shadow.
	Sōetsu	Sōetsu

Spring: *haru* (spring). Mountains: *yama* (mountain). Dwellings: *sato* (village).

The scent of cherry blossoms, now interpreted as the glowing of their color (the other sense of *niou*), recedes further in the imagination as Sōetsu introduces a mountain village where spring comes later than in the plains. Dwelling in the mountain's shadow, the speaker expresses a nostalgic anticipation of the flowers' bright splendor. Poetically, this splendor held only in the mind sharpens by contrast the remote, lonely atmosphere of an isolated hamlet.

6	haru ni okururu	Spring comes late to the village
	yamakage no sato	in the mountain's shadow.
	Sōetsu	Sōetsu
7	kane kasumu	Hazy booms the bell
	onoe no kikori	on the peak where a woodsman
	tomo yobite	calls out to his fellows.
	Mitsusuke	Mitsusuke

Spring: *kasumu* (hazy). Mountains: *onoe* (peak). Rising Phenomena: *kasumu*. Word Association: *kikori* (woodsman) = *yamakage* (mountain's shadow).[5]

A clear spatial contrast is being drawn between the peak of the mountain, where the woodsmen are preparing to descend after finishing the day's work, and the village below ("in the mountain's shadow"), where they live.

The verse is notable in evoking the feeling of an everyday scene among common people, an unusual occurrence in the courtly waka tradition and revealing the country origins of the samurai participants here. The "haziness" of the temple bell's booming is particularly effective in summoning the feel of the warming air in early spring, compared to its clear tones in winter.

7	kane kasumu	Hazy booms the bell
	onoe no kikori	on the peak where a woodsman
	tomo yobite	calls out to his fellows.
	Mitsusuke	Mitsusuke
8	kaeru ka kumo no	Will it return as well?
	nokoru hitomura	The cloud bank left behind.
	Hōzen	Hōzen

Miscellaneous. Rising Phenomena: *kumo* (cloud). Word Association: *kasumu* = *kumo* (cloud).

The link between the sounds of the woodsmen's departure and the word "return" (*kaeru*) is clear. In the verse itself, "return" refers to the "cloud left behind" (*kumo no nokoru*), hanging on the peak of the maeku; in this context it means "disperse." This simple image enhances the slow, vaguely nebulous atmosphere of the spring dusk of the maeku.

8	kaeru ka kumo no	Will it return as well?
	nokoru hitomura	The cloud bank left behind.
	Hōzen	Hōzen
9	harekumoru	Now clear, now clouded
	ame sadamenaki	in rain, the restlessly shifting
	aki no sora	autumn skies.
	Shun'a	Shun'a

First Fold, Back. Autumn: *aki* (autumn). Falling Phenomena: *ame* (rain).

Will the remaining cloud disperse, clearing the sky, or will more clouds darkly gather, bringing back the rain? How uncertain is the autumn weather. The Miscellaneous, seasonally neutral maeku emerges as a perfect transition between the Spring season of verses 5–7 to Autumn here. It is particularly illustrative of how in renga, the same image (here, the clouds) acquires a wholly different value within a changed context, and the link generates, as Shinkei conceives it in *Sasamegoto*, a continual process of recontextualization, what in modern terms would be called displacement.

9	harekumoru	Now clear, now clouded
	ame sadamenaki	in rain, the restlessly shifting
	aki no sora	autumn skies.
	Shun'a	Shun'a

| 10 | yowaki hikage zo
tsuyu ni yadoreru
Ken'a | Feeble the gleam of sunlight
lodging motionless in the dew.
Ken'a |

Autumn: *tsuyu* (dew). Falling Phenomena: *tsuyu*. Word Association: *ame* (rain) = *tsuyu*.

With the emphatic particle *zo*, a clear contrast is drawn between the restlessly "shifting" (*sadamenaki*) sky on the one hand and the frail stillness of the sun's reflection as it "lodges" (*yadoreru*) in the dew. This juxtaposition of motion and stillness is a notable method of linking in renga. By itself and in connection with the maeku, this single verse by Shun'a is quite impressive. The dew is understood to be from the rain mentioned in the previous verse.

| 10 | yowaki hikage zo
tsuyu ni yadoreru
Ken'a | Feeble the gleam of sunlight
lodging motionless in the dew.
Ken'a |
| 11 | sasa no ha ni
mushi no ne tanomu
no wa karete
Shinkei | Even as insects cry
pleading in the bamboo grass,
the meadow withers.
Shinkei |

Autumn: *mushi* (insects). Word Association: *tsuyu* (dew) = *mushi*, *no* (meadow).

The primary connection hinges on the evocation of the word "feeble" (*yowaki*) in the maeku, which comes to lend its pathos to the declining insects and vegetation here. Similarly, *yadoreru*, "lodges, dwells," reverberates against the insects' imminent loss of their "shelter" as the meadow plants wither with advancing autumn. A beautifully seamless link.

| 11 | sasa no ha ni
mushi no ne tanomu
no wa karete
Shinkei | Even as insects cry
pleading in the bamboo grass,
the meadow withers.
Shinkei |
| 12 | makura omowanu
yowa no matsukaze
Sōgi | Indifferent to my lonely pillow,
wind in the pines at midnight.
Sōgi |

Love: *makura* (pillow). Word Association: *sasa* (bamboo grass) = *makura*.

Omowanu (indifferent, unsympathetic) links up to the meadow of 11 that withers *despite* the plea of the insects, but in verse 12 as such, the reference is to the wind whose harrowing sound exacerbates the loneliness of the persona who lies awake at midnight, having waited in vain for one who did not come. In effect, Sōgi translates the maeku into a metaphor for his persona's state of mind, even while it remains a metonymical adjunct of the present scene. The faint chirping of insects in the grass and the soughing wind in the pines combine to evoke the sadness of ephemerality in both the insect and human worlds. Another good link between Shinkei and Sōgi.

12	makura omowanu	Indifferent to my lonely pillow,
	yowa no matsukaze	wind in the pines at midnight.
	Sōgi	Sōgi
13	yume yo nado	Dreams, unbidden
	hito koso arame	you come to others, then why
	itouran	shun me?
	Norishige	Norishige

Love: *yume* (dream). Word Association: *makura* (pillow) = *yume*.

An elliptical diction is characteristic of renga, but this one is particularly difficult in its abbreviated second line, *hito koso arame* (lit., "there are indeed people . . ."). Its effect is to draw out the irony of a situation in which the one who is most eager to see her beloved in a dream is unable to do so. "Indifferent" (*omowanu*) in the maeku and "shun" (*itou*) here are synonymous; within the context of the link, the wind is understood to have broken into the persona's dream, though that is not necessarily apparent in the verse's diction, wherein the agent of "shun" is wholly the "dream." For this reason, Kaneko detects a misstep here, a "gap" (*zure*), in Norishige's manner of linking. Nevertheless, since the wind in connection with dreams is conventionally seen as a disruptive force, it is also possible that Norishige was depending on the sheer magnetic effect of contiguity to signal the association.

13	yume yo nado	Dreams, unbidden
	hito koso arame	you come to others, then why
	itouran	shun me?
	Norishige	Norishige
14	kakute mo kokoro	So be it, but still the heart
	nao ya matamashi	would wait, even so.
	Mitsusuke	Mitsusuke

Love: *matsu* (wait).

Within the context of the link, the logical object of "wait" would be the "dream" of the loved one, but in the verse itself, it would be the man himself. He clearly "shuns" her in not coming to her even in a dream, since in ancient belief a person who longs for someone appears in the latter's dream. The verse is essentially an expression of desperate yearning against the certitude of loss, and that is what Sōetsu picks up in the next link.

14	kakute mo kokoro	So be it, but still the heart
	nao ya matamashi	would wait, even so.
	Mitsusuke	Mitsusuke

15	kono mama no	"We part, for the last
	wakare to iite	time," he said, and left me thus
	ideshi yo ni	in this world of night.
	Sōetsu	Sōetsu

Love: *wakare* (parting). Laments: *ideshi yo* (left the mundane world).

Given the situation revealed in this verse, where the lover does not come because he has said goodbye for the last time and renounced the world of desire itself, the maeku gains a greater force of despair. This pair highlights the procedure of reading in renga, which always involves a doubling back to the maeku in order to comprehend the tsukeku in its light. *Kakute mo* ("so be it, but") in particular acquires a new tension of meaning through Sōetsu's introduction of the speaker's real circumstance; this night of waiting turns out to be a permanent condition.

15	kono mama no	"We part, for the last
	wakare to iite	time," he said, and left me thus
	ideshi yo ni	in this world of night.
	Sōetsu	Sōetsu
16	kumo ni mo ato wa	Even its traces have vanished
	taenu yamamichi	in the clouds: the mountain path.
	Kaku'a	Kaku'a

Miscellaneous. Mountains: *yamamichi* (mountain path). Rising Phenomena: *kumo* (clouds).

The point of view shifts here to the man who left society for a life of reclusion in the mountains. In verse 16, the referent of "traces" (*ato*) is the path obscured by clouds; in relation to 15, however, "traces" refers metaphorically to the memory of the mundane existence, including the world of love, that the persona has rejected; this is a good demonstration of the typical operation of polysemic reference in renga. The path between two opposed existences has been obliterated, thus enforcing the permanence of the parting (*kono mama no / wakare*) in 15, yet the very observation suggests that the speaker is not yet wholly immune to a nostalgia for the past. The shift in perspective here infects the maeku in such a way that it should be read as: "We part, for the last time," I said, and left her and the world.

16	kumo ni mo ato wa	Even its traces have vanished
	taenu yamamichi	in the clouds: the mountain path.
	Kaku'a	Kaku'a
17	sewashinaki	Restive in
	shiba no io ni	the brushwood hut, the years
	toshi o hete	have passed.
	Nagatoshi	Nagatoshi

Laments: *toshi o hete* (pass the years). Dwellings: *shiba no io* (brushwood hut).

The speaker has not attained the utter tranquillity in solitude that he expected. Nevertheless, while enduring his restlessness at the constricted lifestyle in the brushwood hut, he finds that the time has lengthened into years, and he is now wholly cut off from the world by the isolating clouds (*kumo ni ato wa / taenu*) up the mountain crest where he dwells.

17	sewashinaki	Restive in
	shiba no io ni	the brushwood hut, the years
	toshi o hete	have passed.
	Nagatoshi	Nagatoshi
18	shigure kanashiki	Sad the falling rain in
	fuyu no kuregata	the dim winter twilight.
	Ikuhiro	Ikuhiro

Winter: *shigure* (intermittent rain, either in autumn or winter), *fuyu* (winter). Falling Phenomena: *shigure*.

The passing years of solitude have not dimmed the hermit's human sensibility, in particular to the moving quality of the rain on cold winter evenings. The sense of *sabi* or impersonal loneliness here is best understood within the philosophical context of eremetism.

18	shigure kanashiki	Sad the falling rain in
	fuyu no kuregata	the dim winter twilight.
	Ikuhiro	Ikuhiro
19	sode nurenu	How would it be, were
	tsuki no tabine mo	sleeves wet only with moonlight,
	ikanaran	these nights of sojourn?
	Sōgi	Sōgi

Autumn: *tsuki* (moon). Travel: *tabine* (travel-sleep). Word Association: *shigure* (rain) = *nuru* (wet).

An ironic rhetorical question serving to reinforce the tonality of the maeku, while subtly shifting the thematic context to Travel. The verse projects a situation contrary to the actual one, where the persona's sleeves are in fact wet both with rain and tears. In the poetic tradition, travel is always done alone (in stark contrast to the modern Japanese practice of it as a group activity, which completely misses the essential nature of travel as an experience of human rootlessness and solitude). The conjunction between eremetism and travel in renga is influenced by the Buddhist symbolism of existence as a temporary dwelling (*kari no yado, kari'io*). Sōgi's construction of the link is quite satisfying in its ironic indirection.

19	sode nurenu	How would it be, were
	tsuki no tabine mo	sleeves wet only with moonlight,
	ikanaran	these nights of sojourn?
	Sōgi	Sōgi

20	kaeru miyako zo	Mind on returning to the capital,
	aki o wasururu	one *can* be oblivious to autumn.
	Shun'a	Shun'a

Autumn: *aki* (autumn). Travel: *kaeru miyako* (returning to the capital). Word Association: *tsuki* (moon) = *aki*.

A general statement as such, the verse should be read as a comforting reminder to the traveler of 19: I understand, traveling in autumn is sad enough to make one weep, but think how glad you will be on your return to the capital. Note the typical ellipsis *aki o wasururu*, "forget the autumn"; it is not necessary to specify its melancholy, for, in the waka tradition since the *Kokinshū*, autumn has ever been known as a "heart-consuming" season (*kokorozukushi no aki*).

20	kaeru miyako zo	Mind on returning to the capital,
	aki o wasururu	one *can* be oblivious to autumn.
	Shun'a	Shun'a
21	no o tōmi	So broad the plain,
	taorishi kusa no	the wildflowers I plucked have
	hana ochite	since fallen.
	Shinkei	Shinkei

Autumn: *kusa no hana* (wildflowers). Travel: *no o tōmi* (so distant the plain).

The plain is so vast that at some point, the wildflowers I had plucked as I traveled through it have withered and fallen. The plain's expanse may be measured by the span of time that elapses while crossing it, and the temporal space is in turn concretely defined by the blooming, then withering, of the fields. In this arresting link, Shinkei contrasts the feeling of anticipation at journey's beginning (when one's mind is focused on the destination, and one may "forget" the loneliness of autumn in delight at the profusion of wildflowers blooming in the meadows) with the loneliness the persona feels in gazing at those same flowers, withered now, across the vast expanse that still separates him from the capital. In effect, the verse restores the melancholy evoked by autumn and suggests that it is as inescapable as the passing of time itself. Thought, a conscious anticipation, has not as long a span; only time remains, defeating any enthusiasm or delight.

21	no o tōmi	So broad the plain,
	taorishi kusa no	the wildflowers I plucked have
	hana ochite	since fallen.
	Shinkei	Shinkei
22	kawaru yadori zo	At these shifting abodes,
	tou hito mo naki	no one ever comes to call.
	Kaku'a	Kaku'a

Travel: *kawaru yadori* (different or changing lodgings).

"Shifting" or "changing" (*kawaru*) resonates with the fallen flowers (*hana ochite*) of the maeku, and the flowers' absence becomes lack of companionship here. The journey across the vast plain is now imaged as a lonely series of transient sojourns from one inn to another.

22	kawaru yadori zo	At these shifting abodes,
	tou hito mo naki	no one ever comes to call.
	Kaku'a	Kaku'a

23	aramashi no	It's enough to invite
	hodo koso sasoe	a long-cherished vision: deep
	yama no oku	mountain recesses.
	Norishige	Norishige

Second Fold, Front. Laments: *aramashi* (hopes or wishes, usually frustrated).

In renga, *aramashi* usually refers to an abiding wish to renounce mundane existence for a higher life as symbolized by that persistent image of spiritual aspiration in medieval literature, the hermit's hut in the mountains. For obvious reasons, however, that wish seldom comes to fruition, and the desire signaled by *aramashi*, which is no more than a grammatical inflection, "would it were so," is usually better rendered as "what might have been." Traveling in the mountains, the persona is brought to mind of his long-standing desire, and the maeku then comes as an afterthought: were he in fact to "change" his abode and move to the mountains, no one would come to visit, he might never endure the loneliness there. The maeku would then read: "At my changed abode / no one would ever come to call." The emphatic *koso* underlines the powerful attraction of the mountains for the speaker, but the equally emphatic *zo* of the maeku means that fear of solitude is a strong deterrent to a higher life.

Kaneko's reading is slightly different and also interesting. "While talking about our plans to flee the world for the deep mountains, we encouraged one another [in the idea], but were I actually to change my abode for one there, no one would come to visit anymore. Such is the way of the world" (*Seikatsu to sakuhin*, p. 343). This reading takes a conversation among friends as the subject of *sasou* (invite, attract, draw towards) and *hodo* as signifying a temporal duration ("*while* conversing about . . . ") rather than a degree. The extreme ellipsis of the diction makes interpretation difficult, but Kaneko is undoubtedly right within the context of the link; I offer mine as a variant reading.

23	aramashi no	It's enough to invite
	hodo koso sasoe	a long-cherished vision: deep
	yama no oku	mountain recesses.
	Norishige	Norishige

24	hatsu hototogisu	In the wake of the passing shower,
	suguru murasame	the first calls of the cuckoo!
	Nagatoshi	Nagatoshi

Summer: *hototogisu* (cuckoo). Falling Phenomena: *murasame* (passing shower).

"Cuckoo" and "passing shower" constitute an associative pair in the verse itself. The affinity, which is marked in the waka vocabulary, is based on the observation that this bird likes to sing out in the wake of a shower. Again, the cuckoo makes its home in the remote mountains, and its call is heard so rarely in town and city that as an image in renga it may occur only once in a sequence.

The link may be paraphrased thus: "In the stillness after a shower, suddenly the call of a cuckoo is heard. Such is that voice that it transports my spirit to the deep, remote mountains." Its feeling recalls one of Shinkei's famous hokku: *Hitokoe ni / minu yama fukashi / hototogisu* ("In that single cry, / the depths of unseen mountains— / cuckoo"). Here the link is very fine indeed, not only in lyrical feeling, but also from the perspective of the uniquely renga-like effect by which a word or words in the maeku suddenly become charged with a new meaning within a changed context. In this instance, *sasou* is pinned down in the sense of "summon up, conjure, transport [the mind]." Of course, it is imperative in this reading to note that the persona who hears the cuckoo is not in fact in the mountains.

24	hatsu hototogisu	In the wake of the passing shower,
	suguru murasame	the first calls of the cuckoo!
	Nagatoshi	Nagatoshi
25	urameshi na	They hurt me.
	konu yo amata ni	Again, the unvisited nights
	mata narite	drag on, too many.
	Shinkei	Shinkei

Love: *urameshi* (bitter, hurting).

By itself the verse expresses a woman's grief for the continued absence of her lover. He came once, after subjecting her to many anxious nights of waiting, but since then, *once again* (*mata*), he has stayed away several nights running. In the metaphorical doubling that constitutes renga's specific poetry of the link, the image of the cuckoo is superimposed upon that of the lover as the "object" of the persona's emotion. For many nights, she had been waiting in anxious expectation for the *first* cry of the cuckoo, but after that single time, *once again* the bird has remained silent. The weight of the link bears centrally on the word *hatsu* (first) in the maeku, which suddenly becomes intensified through *mata* (again) in Shinkei's verse. That single cry of the bird and that single visit by the other, and all the waiting

before and since, fall into a taut connection through this seemingly in-
nocuous semantic juxtaposition. This masterly link that simultaneously
marks a breathtaking shift to the Love theme is clearly an allusive variation
on *SKKS* 214, Summer, by Fujiwara Ietaka:

ikani semu	I know not what to do—
konu yo amata no	Too *many the unvisited nights,*
hototogisu	*cuckoo*—yet, when I
mataji to omoeba	would wait no longer, suddenly,
murasame no sora	the *passing shower* in the sky!

Apart from transposing the *honka* into a Love context, Shinkei's link effects
an intricate variation through a reversal of its situation. In the former, the
cuckoo is still to come; in the latter, it has come and gone.

25	urameshi na	They hurt me.
	konu yo amata ni	Again, the unvisited nights
	mata narite	drag on, too many.
	Shinkei	Shinkei
26	makura no shiran	Depressing too to think my pillow
	hitorine mo ushi	knows of my sleeping alone.
	Sōgi	Sōgi

Love: *makura* (pillow); *hitorine* (sleeping alone).

The conventional conceit that the pillow, that intimate accessory, is
omniscient about one's true situation and thoughts is reflected in such a love
poem as Lady Ise's *KKS* 676, *shiru to ieba*, quoted in the tsukeku section.
The verse focuses on the misery of feeling oneself unloved and someone
else—the pillow personified, knowing it. A simple, predictable link that
does not quite do justice to the rhetorically crucial words (*amata ni, mata*)
in Shinkei's verse, it functions mainly to move the sequence along within the
thematic field of Love.

26	makura no shiran	Depressing too to think my pillow
	hitorine mo ushi	knows of my sleeping alone.
	Sōgi	Sōgi
27	kokoro dani	When this very heart,
	omoiyowareba	weakened by longing, can hold
	naki mono o	no more.
	Sōetsu	Sōetsu

Love: *omoiyowaru* (weakened by longing).

Focusing on the persona's loss of control and its self-exposure, this
verse, taken with the maeku, suggests the reason for the pillow's coming to
know her utter misery. The concept behind it is similar to a poem by

Princess Shikishi about the force of a desperate, hidden longing, *SKKS* 1034, Love, "On secret passion, one in a sequence of 100 poems."

	tama no o yo	O jewel-strand of life,
	taenaba taene	if you would break, break quickly!
	nagaraeba	for hanging on and on,
	shinoburu koto no	I will soon be too frail
	yowari mo zo suru	to hold locked this passion!
27	kokoro dani	When this very heart,
	omoiyowareba	weakened by longing, can hold
	naki mono o	no more.
	Sōetsu	Sōetsu
28	namida wa shiite	Still the tears would fall,
	nao ya ochinan	defying reason, all the more.
	Shinkei	Shinkei

Love: *namida* (tears).

The link with 28 is clear, and close—this is in fact the third close link in a series from 26. The adverbial *shiite* (obstinately, defying reason) charges with irony the first and last lines in the maeku, *kokoro dani / naki mono o* (lit., "even though the heart is not"). The logic (or ironic illogic) of the link yields: although the weakened heart is depleted and *can hold* no more, yet fall the tears, against all reason, even more. The Temmangū Text has *shirite* (know) instead of *shiite* here, producing a different but even more involved logic:

kokoro dani	When this very heart,
omoiyowareba	weakened by longing, can hold
naki mono o	no more.
namida wa shirite	Tears, do they know it so,
nao ya ochinan	and fall all the more.

Shinkei's use of the word "know" in this other version violates the rule against repetition of the same lexical item in close proximity. "Know" occurs in verse 26, "my pillow *knows*," and Sōgi's tsukeku below also includes it, "who would *know*." As we know (again!) from his critical works, Shinkei frowned on a slavish conformity to the rules that the concrete circumstances involved. Nevertheless, as Kaneko observes, it is most probably due to the occurrence of the same word three times in short intervals that in the Nozaka Text *shirite* has been emended to *shiite*. In the *shirite* version, the irony lies along a different path of reasoning: I know that I have yielded all my heart to passion, and it is this very knowledge of my weakness that makes me weep. In effect, I weep because I am weak, and weep *the more for knowing (shirite nao)* myself so weak. So precise, and yet so complex, are the effects of the smallest adverbials and verbal shifts in renga diction.

In renga it is apparently the Love theme that inspires the most involuted turns of reasoning, the most intricate nuances of emotion; these are often accompanied by a sense of irony. Doubtless Love refers to the emotion between men and women, but almost incidentally, as it were. It seems important to point out that, as a major theme in renga, Love has a more comprehensive significance and represents all deep-seated desire and attachment, the dynamic impetus of action as well as the single, essential source of human suffering. Renga poetry may be seen as having two basic foci: nature, the external world, which is always depicted through the temporal perspective of the four seasons; and human affairs (*jinji*), in which desire or yearning constitutes the primary experience. Deep and persistent, never fulfilled, ever frustrated; cause of rancor toward the other, of insecurity and a bad conscience, as well as the occasion for self-analysis and knowledge, Love is the topos corresponding to all that is implied by "civilization and its discontents" as Freud analyzed it in European society. For this reason, it is understandable that the poet-priests of renga should see in the theme a persistent challenge and a weighty subject matter. In it they were perhaps reading and writing their own frustrated desires, their religious conviction—for they were ineluctably of their time—that desire is suffering, and their equally firm, but thoroughly human, experience that desire nevertheless constitutes the very fabric of the only reality that most of us will ever know.

28	namida wa shiite	Still the tears would fall,
	nao ya ochinan	defying reason, all the more.
	Shinkei	Shinkei
29	kimi ga yo o	Who would know of
	tare shirakawa no	those bygone times, the currents
	tagitsunami	swirling on White River?
	Sōgi	Sōgi

Remembering the Past: *kimi ga yo* (lit., "the times of our lord").

Following Shinkei's lead in introducing *honkadori* into the sequence in verse 25, Sōgi now effects a link through *KKS* 830, Laments, "Composed on the night when the former Chancellor [Fujiwara Yoshifusa] was laid to rest by the White River," by Priest Sosei:

chi no *namida*	The crimson of blood,
ochite zo tagitsu	*my tears fall, swirling with the*
shirakawa wa	*currents of White River—*
kimi ga yo made no	a name now laid to rest with
na ni koso arikere	*the vanished times of our lord.*

Those "times of our lord" were so long ago that no one would remember them now, although the Shirakawa (lit., "White River") still flows, as then, in swirling currents.[6] With the maeku, the reading becomes: those days are beyond memory, but these tears, as if possessed of a knowledge of their own, are *still* falling now as then. *Nao* (still more), an adverb of degree in the maeku as such, acquires the temporal force of "still, yet" in Sōgi's interpretive link, which simultaneously moves the sequence away from the preceding series of close links and shifts to a new theme.

29	kimi ga yo o	Who would know of	
	tare shirakawa no	those bygone times, the currents	
	tagitsunami	swirling on White River?	
	Sōgi		Sōgi
30	furuki sakura no	So lonely, the scant shade	
	kage zo sabishiki	of the aged cherry tree.	
	Ikuhiro		Ikuhiro

Spring: *sakura* (cherry).

The area around Shirakawa was famous for its cherry blossoms and the so-called "six *shōji* temples" (*rokushōji*), among them the Hosshōji, built by Retired Emperor Shirakawa in his detached palace there, and the Saishōji of Retired Emperor Toba (r. 1107–23). In all likelihood, the verse is alluding to a particular cherry tree in the grounds of the Saishōji that figures in a poem by the *Shinkokinshū* poet Asukai Masatsune (1170–1221). Masatsune was also one of the most skilled kickball (*kemari*) enthusiasts among Go-Toba's courtiers, and his poem refers to the cherry that marked the northeast corner of the kickball court at Saishōji.[7]

SKKS 1455. Miscellaneous. "The cherry tree at the Saishōji Temple had long stood as one of the tree-bases for kickball. When he heard that the aging tree had been toppled by a storm, he ordered some courtiers to transplant another cherry tree where the old had been. Coming before anyone else to see it, he recalled how for many years and up until this past spring he had stood familiarly in the shade of the old tree, and composed this poem."

narenarete	Fondly through all
mishi wa nagori no	the years, how could my gaze know
haru zo to mo	it held the memento of
nado *shirakawa no*	a final springtime, *the shade*
hana no shitakage	*of the flowers at Shirakawa.*

The ghostly "shade" of Masatsune's aged cherry in this poem casts an allusive reflection upon this verse, a distant link to the maeku's reference to Shirakawa and the past lives that inhabited it.

30	furuki sakura no	So lonely, the scant shade
	kage zo sabishiki	of the aged cherry tree.
	Ikuhiro	Ikuhiro
31	amata heshi	After many years, only
	haru no mi tsuraki	the springtime, poignant as ever
	kusa no to ni	by the grass-hut door.
	Nagatoshi	Nagatoshi

Spring: *haru* (spring). Dwellings: *kusa no to* (grass-hut door).

Nagatoshi presents a hermit who finds that although he has been able to endure the trials of reclusion through the years, spring alone (*haru no mi*) still retains the power to pain him, to pierce through his mental detachment. Within the context of the link, "*by* the grass-hut door" marks the location of the maeku's "aged cherry tree," and the tree becomes the objective correlative of the aging persona's feelings in springtime. Here the "loneliness" beneath the cherry's shade alludes not to a bygone time but to the fact that it has become so old and exhausted it puts out fewer and fewer blossoms each spring. It is this implicit image of a few lovely blossoms on a gnarled old tree that figures the subject's complex feeling of poignancy. Furthermore, when *haru no mi* is read as "the body in spring," another layer of suggestion appears, and the focus would be on the persona's aging body in contrast to the plants burgeoning outside his door.

31	amata heshi	After many years, only
	haru no mi tsuraki	the springtime, poignant as ever
	kusa no to ni	by the grass-hut door.
	Nagatoshi	Nagatoshi
32	kasumu to mo naku	So cold the wind in the mountains,
	samuki yamakaze	the haze is barely able to form.
	Norishige	Norishige

Spring: *kasumu* (be hazy). Mountains: *yama* (mountain).

The haze, sign of spring's arrival, is caused by the warmer air, but here in these mountains the temperature is so cold it does not form. The "cold wind" tenses up the phrase "body in spring" in the maeku—the aged body feels the coldness more than ordinarily in the poignant season of spring. Kaneko observes that the verse, however, fails to recreate or respond to the singular force of *nomi*, "only," in the maeku. In that sense, the link may be said to be a bit slack.

32	kasumu to mo naku	So cold the wind in the mountains,
	samuki yamakaze	the haze is barely able to form.
	Norishige	Norishige

33	yuki harau	Distantly, a figure,
	ochikatabito no	sleeves brushing off the snow—
	sode kiete	melts away.
	Shinkei	Shinkei

Winter: *yuki* (snow). Word Association: *kasumu* = *sode* (sleeve). Falling Phenomena: *yuki*.

Shinkei picks up on the distant perspective already suggested in the maeku and, in a delicately quick turn sensible only in that blank space between the verses, suggests that the haze, "barely able to form" (*kasumu to mo naku*), has turned back to snow in that uncertain transition between late winter and early spring. In verse 33, it is the figure of the traveler, here imaged metonymically as a sleeve fluttering in the cold wind, that vanishes (*kiete*) in the whirling snow. In the context of the maeku, however, the reference is to the barely formed haze that dissolves, dispersed by the "cold wind" that brought the snow.

The link focuses on a moment arrested briefly within the ebb and flow of things, their coming into and passing out of existence as figured here by the traveler, the haze, and the snow. It has that ineffably remote (*yōon*) quality Shinkei himself valued, and it is characteristic of classical poetry that focuses upon the mystery of the appearance and disappearance of phenomena in the flow of time. The more doggedly and delicately the poet attempts to capture the fleeting moment, that exact instant when presence becomes absence or vice versa, the closer does he approach the heart of things as understood in the philosophy of emptiness.

33	yuki harau	Distantly, a figure,
	ochikatabito no	sleeves brushing off the snow—
	sode kiete	melts away.
	Shinkei	Shinkei
34	kareno ni takaki	High above the withered plain,
	akatsuki no kane	the booming of the dawn bell.
	Sōgi	Sōgi

Winter: *kareno* (withered field).

Clearly inspired by Shinkei's maeku, Sōgi follows up with an equally impressive verse that links to it by a contrastive juxtaposition. The figure dissolves from the horizon of vision in the snowy dimness of pre-dawn, and in a while the temple bell announcing the dawn echoes high above the lightening plain. Where all was nebulously remote in the previous moment, now all is gauntly visible on the withered plain from which the snow has cleared. The transition between the two moments, that pregnant pause between the dissolution of the one and the coming into appearance of the other, is unspoken, but it has to be felt for the link to be properly appreciated. A truly fine example of renga as high poetry, and as a poetry of the gap, the charged pause, the interval.

34	kareno ni takaki	High above the withered plain,
	akatsuki no kane	the booming of the dawn bell.
	Sōgi	Sōgi
35	ariake no	Chillingly clear,
	kage ya sayaka ni	the form of the remaining moon
	fukenuran	has aged.
	Kaku'a	Kaku'a

Autumn: *ariake* (remaining light of the moon at dawn).

Kaku'a proves himself equal to Sōgi's maeku. He maintains its open and wide vista by focusing on the white clarity of the remaining moon in the cloudless sky of dawn. The succession of images—the booming echo of the bell rising in the sky, and then the entrance of the moon into the field of vision—is, I think, quite inspired. This passage of three impressive links from 33 to 35 is characterized by a precise economy of diction and depth of feeling that Shinkei called the "chill and thin" mode.

A word about the handling of seasons in renga seems appropriate here. As apparent in the change from spring to winter in 33 and from winter to autumn here in 35, seasonal progression does not follow the natural cycle but shifts alogically from one season to another according to the internal necessities of the sequence as it evolves and the rules of intermission and duration that govern it. In other words, in renga time does not follow the mundane calendar but a formal aesthetic one, as influenced by the fortuitous dynamics of the specific session. Time is not an objective chronology but an experience in the round; what is at issue is a feeling for the essential nature or *hon'i* of phenomena as movement and appearance grasped through the temporal dimension of the seasons. The isolated renga verse is, formally speaking, indeterminate. Thus it is possible for it to signify in two temporal registers according to context, as the snow in 33 is spring snow in conjunction with its maeku but winter snow when linked to its tsukeku. The same is true of the dual seasonal character, wintry and autumnal, of the "remaining moon" here. No doubt these seasonal transitions unmediated by a Miscellaneous verse are difficult to handle and therefore interesting, but they merely underline the basic ambiguity of renga diction and the fact that this is a poetry of gaps and spaces, a kind of readerly writing. As in a kaleidoscope, the picture changes at every turn, but it is the way in which the practitioner achieves that turn that bears watching. Indeed, one could say that in renga the picture is not really visible unless one has "observed" the turn.

35	ariake no	Chillingly clear,
	kage ya sayaka ni	the form of the remaining moon
	fukenuran	has aged.
	Kaku'a	Kaku'a
36	uchinuru yado no	Night after night of autumn
	yonayona no aki	in sleep-hushed lodgings.
	Mitsusuke	Mitsusuke

Autumn: *aki* (autumn). Travel: *yado* (lodging).

A simple verse counting the long nights spent in various travel lodgings in autumn, Mitsusuke's tsukeku reveals its true significance in relation to its maeku: awakening each dawn in a different lodging, I see the remaining moon more chillingly, and more clearly, each time, as the season ages and gradually I forget mundane attachments and draw ever closer to the spirit of travel. On the symbolic plane, the pallid clarity of the moon in the maeku is seen as the ultimate stage of a progressive meditation on the true human condition.

36	uchinuru yado no	Night after night of autumn
	yonayona no aki	in sleep-hushed lodgings.
	Mitsusuke	Mitsusuke
37	yama fukami	In mountains so deep
	ine moru hita no	audible the clatter of pipes
	oto wa shite	guarding the rice stalks.
	Nagatoshi	Nagatoshi

Second Fold, Back. Autumn: *ine* (rice stalks); *hita* (wood clappers).

Something like the old Japanese equivalent of the scarecrow, *hita* (lit., "board for pulling") is a device set out in the rice fields to scare away birds and animals. Also called *naruko* ("crying child"), it consists of narrow bamboo pipes suspended on boards and attached to a rope, in such a way that the pipes clatter when the rope is pulled. No doubt because it serves its purpose best when the plants are heavy with the ripening grain, it is an autumn image, as are the rice stalks themselves.

The location of the lodgings in the maeku is here specified as a farming village in the mountains, where the deep silence of the night is broken by the hollow clapping noise of the *hita*. As the nights pile on, his sleep often interrupted by this noise, the traveler's sensitivity to the essence of autumn is increasingly sharper. The verse as such is quite appealing in its evocation of rusticity but the handling of the link is not very effective; Nagatoshi's bald diction does not sustain the pathos of the maeku on the level of poetic tone.

37	yama fukami	In mountains so deep
	ine moru hita no	audible the clatter of pipes
	oto wa shite	guarding the rice stalks.
	Nagatoshi	Nagatoshi
38	tsuraki wa sate mo	Even here is no respite
	yamu toki mo nashi	from the painful toil.
	Shun'a	Shun'a

Laments: *tsuraki* (painful, harsh).

Sate mo, which I have rendered "even here," is a clear reference to the maeku's mountain location—"even here" in the remote hills far from the rat race, so to speak, the harsh toil of the struggle for existence asserts itself. Interrupting the farmer's rest, the sound of the wooden clappers comes to represent the labor involved in ensuring the harvest after all the toil of planting.

38	tsuraki wa sate mo	Even here is no respite
	yamu toki mo nashi	from the painful toil.
	Shun'a	Shun'a
39	kumo to naru	Indelible memory
	hito no katami no	of someone become a cloud—
	sode no ame	rain on my sleeves.
	Shinkei	Shinkei

Love: *katami* (memento, traces); *sode no ame* ("rain on sleeves," i.e., tears).

Another startling thematic shift by Shinkei, who transposes the pain of *tsuraki* into the context of Love and death. The smoke of cremation at the other's funeral rose to join the clouds (*kumo to naru*), which now fall as rain and tears upon the sleeves we once shared—such is her memento. *Sate mo*, "even here" in the maeku is reinterpreted as "even now"; even now when she is long gone, there is no end to my suffering. Her indelible memory is this incessant rain of tears upon my sleeves.

Kumo to naru ("turn into a cloud"), along with the rain image, is an unmistakable allusion to a famous anecdote in the preface to the *Kao-t'ang fu* by Sung Yü (290–223 B.C.) in the *Wen hsüan*. It recounts that when the King of Ch'u was on an excursion in Kao-t'ang, the heavenly goddess of Mount Wu (Wu-shan) appeared before him while he was dozing and he made love to her. When the goddess departed at dawn, she said: "You may find me in the high slopes on the southern face of Mount Wu, changed into a morning cloud at dawn and become the rain falling at dusk."[8] The poetic motif of "the dream of Wu-shan" (J. *Fuzan no yume*) was an inspiration to medieval Japanese poets from Teika to Shōtetsu and Shinkei. Shōtetsu evoked it to illustrate the *yūgen* mode in the *Shōtetsu monogatari*, and Shinkei himself used it as a metaphorical image of the "ineffably remote" (*yōon*) style in *Sasamegoto*.[9] Murasaki Shikibu alludes to it in a poem exchange in the "Aoi" chapter of the *Tale of Genji*, and the famous anecdote of Narihira's brief, dream-like encounter with the Ise Priestess may have been inspired by this same Chinese legend. Its abiding appeal doubtless lay in the ethereality of the meeting, the essential mystery of love, which is as fleeting and empty as clouds and rain, yet has the power to hold the mind in thrall. In sum it belongs ineluctably to the medieval aesthetics of presence and absence, and of emptiness. As Kaneko observes, in introducing such a Chinese poetic allusion, Shinkei here was exercising his role as a learned guide and teacher to those participants of the session who were still amateurs in the images of classical poetry. At the same time, the allusion lends an ironic and tragic overtone to the whole link, in the implication that an all too real suffering is rooted upon the ephemerality of a dream.

39	kumo to naru	Indelible memory
	hito no katami no	of someone become a cloud—
	sode no ame	rain on my sleeves.
	Shinkei	Shinkei
40	yume yori hoka wa	What else, apart from the dream,
	nani o tanoman	is there left to rely on?
	Sōetsu	Sōetsu

Love: *yume* (dream).

With the word "dream," Sōetsu happily signals his recognition of Shinkei's erudite Chinese allusion. On the first level, it connects to the maeku thus: now when she is dead and an actual meeting rendered impossible, what else can I *hope for* except that she visit me in dreams? On the second level where the anecdotal allusion takes effect, the link would go like this: now when she has joined the clouds, what else can I *rely upon* apart from that unforgettable dream of love whose reality is evidenced by its indelible traces, these tears upon my sleeves? This last reading projects the bereft king as poetic voice or subject and resonates with the rich ambiguity of the "dream of Wu-shan" motif.

40	yume yori hoka wa	What else, apart from the dream,
	nani o tanoman	is there left to rely on?
	Sōetsu	Sōetsu
41	chiru hana ni	In the scattering flowers
	tsurenaki oi o	I find solace, midst callously
	nagusamete	lingering old age.
	Sōgi	Sōgi

Spring: *hana* (flowers). Laments: *oi* (old age); *yume no yo* (life as dream, in the context of the link).

Sustaining the twists and turns that enliven this passage of the session, Sōgi takes "dream" from the romantic context of Love in the preceding two verses and views it from a philosophical standpoint. Life itself is an insubstantial dream; in that truth, which is manifest even now in the flowers scattering before my eyes, I take comfort from the callousness (*tsurenaki*) of old age, this life that persists despite my weariness. From this perspective, the maeku would read: "What else, apart from the truth that this life is but a dream, is there left to rely on?"

As evidenced by the importance of Heian social rituals celebrating people's birthdays after forty, longevity was undoubtedly desired. Even then, however, a tenacious clinging to life was felt to show a lack of sensibility, and in the medieval period, as we know from Kenkō's *Tsurezuregusa* and its influence upon Muromachi literati, such a sentiment became dominant. The categorical observation, that it is precisely because phenomena are ephemeral that they have the power to move us, may be said to be the basis of the medieval aesthetics of *aware*. Spiritual grace and beauty, no less than morality, is here grounded on the wholly human, experiential knowledge of death and mutability. Still, Sōgi's verse is a wholly unexpected turn after the high-flown, emotionally involved tone of the preceding two; everyone must have perked up in attention and fallen into a mood of bracing sobriety.

41	chiru hana ni	In the scattering flowers
	tsurenaki oi o	I find solace, midst callously
	nagusamete	lingering old age.
	Sōgi	Sōgi
42	haru no kokoro wa	The heart that looks on spring
	mukashi ni mo nizu	is not now what it was of old.
	Ikuhiro	Ikuhiro

Spring: *haru* (spring). Laments: *mukashi* (former times; of old).

Ikuhiro's verse is in effect a comment on the attitude reflected in Sōgi's. Whereas in the days of one's youth, one could feel only a poignant regret for the falling flowers, now in old age one can gaze upon them with calm equanimity as a comforting example of one's own mortality. The difference is between the fear and the acceptance of death.

42	haru no kokoro wa	The heart that looks on spring
	mukashi ni mo nizu	is not now what it was of old.
	Ikuhiro	Ikuhiro

43	sumu yama wa	Living in the mountains,
	hi mo nagakarade	the days do not seem long—
	okuru mi ni	body engaged in chores.
	Mitsusuke	Mitsusuke

Spring: *hi nagashi* (days are long). Mountains: *yama* (mountains).

(Again, Mountains; we are now almost halfway into the sequence and have seen Waters but once, quite a contrast with Shinkei's solo sequence.) The change from former days (*mukashi*) and the present in the maeku is here redefined as a shift of residence from town to mountains. The spring days, conventionally sensed as long, do not seem so to me here, where each day is taken up with the various physical chores necessary to sustain life in wholly uncultivated surroundings. The implication is that the subject has abandoned the refined existence of the capital city, where one could enjoy the long spring days at one's leisure. Mitsusuke was also the author of verse 7 on woodsmen winding up the day's work in the mountains; might he have been impatient with aristocratic conceits?

43	sumu yama wa	Living in the mountains,
	hi mo nagakarade	the days do not seem long—
	okuru mi ni	body engaged in chores.
	Mitsusuke	Mitsusuke
44	hata utsu mine no	Plowing the fields, gathering
	shiba o oritsutsu	brushwood on the peak.
	Nagatoshi	Nagatoshi

Spring: *hata utsu* (plowing the fields). Mountains: *mine* (peak).

A simple link enumerating the concrete tasks that engage the subject of the maeku, making him feel that even the long spring days are short (*hi mo nagakarade*).

44	hata utsu mine no	Plowing the fields, gathering
	shiba o oritsutsu	brushwood on the peak.
	Nagatoshi	Nagatoshi
45	aware ni mo	Pitifully, he hastens
	awaii isogu	to make a fire for the frugal
	hi o takite	bowl of millet.
	Shinkei	Shinkei

Autumn: *awaii* (millet meal).

Shinkei sustains the topic of a humble and harsh existence, bringing out in particular its poverty—the subject cannot afford rice—and its lack of leisure in the word *isogu* ("hasten"). There is a shift in point of view, however, as the speaker is obviously not himself a peasant but an observer moved to compassion by the poverty of that class. As in 39, Shinkei introduces an image, *awaii isogu*, "hurries [to make] millet rice," calculated to summon an anecdotal allusion (*honzetsu*) to the "dream of Han-tan" in the following verse, in the interest of enlivening the session. Poetic and anecdotal allusions were a means of generating variety and enriching the aesthetic texture of the sequence, but, needless to say, they required a degree of learning in the participants.

45	aware ni mo	Pitifully, he hastens
	awaii isogu	to make a fire for the frugal
	hi o takite	bowl of millet.
	Shinkei	Shinkei
46	makura hodonaki	Barely an interval on the pillow,
	tsuyu no karifushi	the traveler's sleep on the dew.
	Sōgi	Sōgi

Autumn: *tsuyu* (dew). Travel: *karifushi* (transient sleep, usually on a journey).

The peasant in the maeku becomes a traveler whose sleep is quickly broken by his unfamiliar makeshift bed close to the elements. Awakening, he quickly boils millet for a simple breakfast before going off again. "Pitifully" (*aware ni mo*) refers to the primitive circumstances of this journey, but its effective force really emerges on the plane of the anecdotal allusiveness of the millet image.

This anecdote has its source in the T'ang tale *Chen chung chi* (J. *Chin-chūki*) and is variously known in Japanese literary citation as *kōryō issui no yume* or *awaii issui no aida* ("a dream seen in the space of a pot of millet boiling over"), *Kantan no yume* ("the dream at Han-tan"), or *Kantan no makura* ("the pillow at Han-tan"). While staying at an inn in Han-tan, a youth called Lu Sheng (J. Rosei) fell asleep on a pillow borrowed from the Taoist wizard Lü-weng (J. Ryo'ō) and dreamed a whole life as a rich and celebrated man in the capital. Awakening, he was shocked to find that while he was living a lifetime in the dream, the interval that had elapsed was in fact so brief that the millet simmering in the pot by his bed was not even cooked yet. It is said that through this dream, Lu Sheng was instantaneously enlightened about the evanescence of glory and the frailty of human existence.

In Sōgi's verse, *makura hodonaki*, "barely an interval on the pillow," is a terse elliptical response to "millet" in Shinkei's maeku, and the pathos of *aware* there comes to refer to the evanescence of Lu Sheng's dream of glory in Han-tan.[10]

46	makura hodonaki	Barely an interval on the pillow,
	tsuyu no karifushi	the traveler's sleep on the dew.
	Sōgi	Sōgi
47	megurikinu	It has come round again,
	furusato ideshi	the midnight moon when I left
	yowa no tsuki	the old village.
	Norishige	Norishige

Autumn: *tsuki* (moon). Travel: *furusato* ("old village," one's hometown; it may indicate the capital if one is from there; also, an old village encountered on a journey). Word Association: *tsuyu* (dew) = *tsuki*.

Verse 47 expresses a conventional sentiment of longing for one's home-town. The moon that shone that midnight when I left my village, having completed one revolution along its fixed course, has come round again; I have now spent a full year away from home on a lonely journey. However, the linking context places primary emphasis on how "swiftly" that year has gone (*hodonaki*, "barely an interval" in the maeku), as if it were no more than a dream seen in a temporary lodging on a journey. As often in renga, the link is more interesting than the isolated verse as such. Here it renders time ambiguous and comments on how memory collapses a long duration into the space of a brief interval; in this sense the dream at Han-tan is no more than a dream within the dream of life itself.

47	megurikinu	It has come round again,
	furusato ideshi	the midnight moon when I left
	yowa no tsuki	the old village.
	Norishige	Norishige
48	wasurenu mono o	I have not forgotten, but
	hito ya wasuren	has she perhaps done so?
	Nagatoshi	Nagatoshi

Love: *wasuru* (to forget).

The moon is the same as when I departed, and so am I—still faithful to the one whom I left in my hometown—but what of her? The longing for the hometown, a subordinate theme in the preceding link, here becomes the primary one; it is expressed as a sense of insecurity regarding one's roots and relationships while away from home. Nagatoshi is alluding to Fujiwara Yoshitsune's poem below, *SKKS* 941, Travel, "Composed when people presented poems on the topic 'Traveling Beneath the Moon' during the Ten Moon-Poems Contest held at the Waka Bureau."

wasureji to	Light of a memory
chigirite ideshi	*we vowed never to forget*
omokage wa	*as I departed—*

> miyuran mono o   does it touch her gaze still,
> *furusato no tsuki*   *the moon over the old village.*

Nagatoshi's verse is rather blunt in expression, but the allusion to this *honka*, which specifies the function of the moon in the link, gives it a more delicate undertone.

48	wasurenu mono o hito ya wasuren Nagatoshi	I have not forgotten, but has she perhaps done so? Nagatoshi
49	kawaraji no sono hitofude o inochi nite Shinkei	That single letter saying, "I shall not change," I cling to as my very life. Shinkei

Love: *hitofude* (letter).

The connection is clear. Shinkei intensifies the uncertainty of the maeku, gives it a dramatic edge of desperation, for the persona's raison d'être (*inochi nite*) rests on no more than a promise of fidelity inscribed on a piece of paper. Kaneko notes a shift in point of view to that of a woman. No doubt he is right, since according to poetic and social convention, it is the woman who waits. As has been observed earlier, this is less important than the fact that in Japanese classical poetry, we find male poets reading their hopes and desires in the female situation.

49	kawaraji no sono hitofude o inochi nite Shinkei	That single letter saying, "I shall not change," I cling to as my very life. Shinkei
50	hakanaki ato to miru zo kanashiki Mitsusuke	To see it but an empty trace— I am bereft twice over! Mitsusuke

Love: *hakanaki ato* (empty, ephemeral trace).

The link deepens the emotion of the maeku and lends it even greater ironic force by exploding the desperate hope expressed there. That vow of fidelity has proven to be, finally, groundless. The hope for the future expressed in the letter has now become a thing of the past—the "trace" (*ato*), that is, literally speaking, the lover's handwriting (*hitofude*), proved to be without reality. The force of the emphatic *zo*, which I have rendered "twice over," refers to the fact that the speaker suffers a double loss: that of the lover's hoped-for fidelity and her very reason for existence (*inochi nite*). The force, indeed, is greater if *hakanaki ato* is interpreted to mean that the lover has died, and that is what I suggest in the translation; Sōgi interprets it the same way in his tsukeku below.

50	hakanaki ato to	To see it but an empty trace—
	miru zo kanashiki	I am bereft twice over!
	Mitsusuke	Mitsusuke
51	chitose to mo	"A thousand years," they
	iishi ya itsu no	prayed, when might it have been?
	tsuka no matsu	Pine tree by the grave mound.
	Sōgi	Sōgi

Third Fold, Front. Elegy: *tsuka* (grave mound).

"A thousand years" (*chitose*) is directly associated with the long-lived pine but refers also by ironic contrast to the much briefer lifespan of the person buried in the grave; the irony is enforced by the double entendre in *tsuka no matsu* ("pine tree by the grave mound"), which can also be read *tsuka no ma* (an instant). Indeed the same pine tree that was planted in durable memory of the deceased, an "evergreen" trace, is the ephemeral or "empty trace" (*hakanaki ato*) in the maeku. Destroyed by the elements, the tree itself has proved as fleeting as the person it was meant to commemorate, thus lending force to *miru zo kanashiki* (rendered "bereft twice over" in the translation).

Kenkō's *Tsurezuregusa* includes a passage that might have inspired Sōgi: "but in the end, even the *pine tree* that groaned in the storm winds is broken into firewood before it reaches its alloted *thousand years*, and the *old grave* is plowed up and turned into rice land. *How sad it is that even this last memento of the dead should vanish.*"[11] One of the "Nineteen Old Poems" in the *Wen hsüan* contains a similar passage: "Emerging from the city gates I gaze straight ahead, / and see nothing but hills and burial mounds. / Old graves have been plowed into rice fields, / and their pines and oak trees splintered for kindling. / Only the pale willows filled the air with their sighs, / piercing with a myriad sorrows the heart."[12] Perhaps Kenkō himself was influenced by these lines when he wrote the passage in the *Tsurezuregusa*. Sōgi in turn demonstrates his effective study of old classical writing by his adept use of it in this link. As previously mentioned, it was in Shōtetsu's circle that the value of old *zuihitsu* like the *Tsurezuregusa* and Sei Shōnagon's *Makura sōshi* first came to be appreciated. This is evident in Shinkei's *Sasamegoto*, which cites Kenkō and praises his aesthetic philosophy, and now in this allusion by Sōgi, Shinkei's renga disciple.

51	chitose to mo	"A thousand years," they
	iishi ya itsu no	prayed, when might it have been?
	tsuka no matsu	Pine tree by the grave mound.
	Sōgi	Sōgi
52	kokoro ni hikeru	A memory pulling at the heart,
	funaoka no haru	springtime at Funaoka Hill.
	Shinkei	Shinkei

Spring: *haru* (spring). Named Place: Funaoka. Word Association: *matsu* (pine) = *hiku* (pull).

Drawn by Sōgi's excursion into the classical past, Shinkei echoes his "when might it have been?" by evoking the old associations around Funaoka, a hill in Murasakino north of Kyoto. It was the custom among Heian courtiers to hold the "pine-*pulling*" ritual there on the first Rat day of the year as part of the New Year's festivities, the so-called *nenohi-asobi*. This practice of pulling up pine seedlings to ensure longevity, an instance of sympathetic magic, is reflected in the following poem from the *Fubokushō* I, "Day of the Rat," by Minamoto Tsunenobu.

ne no hi shite	As we hold the Rat Day
yowai o noburu	the span of our lives to prolong
funaoka wa	*on Funaoka hill,*
matsu no chitose o	are gathered and piled high
tsumeru narikeri	*the thousand years of the pine!*

More specifically, what *"pulls* at the heart" (*kokoro ni hikeru*) about Funaoka is not only that it was the scene of longevity rituals but was also a gravesite, as we read, again, in Kenkō: "On some days certainly, many more than one or two are seen to their graves at Toribeno, Funaoka, and other mountainsides, but never a day passes without a single funeral."[13] The effect of this simple verse is to heighten with moving irony the mortality figured in Sōgi's image of a grave mound by conjoining it with the auspicious significance of the pine-pulling ritual. It also ties the maeku to a specific place and shifts the season to Spring. Interestingly, this is the only occasion in the whole sequence where Shinkei links up to a verse by Sōgi; in all the other instances where they are paired, it is the other way around. This case is so singular one wonders if no one else could come up with an appropriate link and so it fell to Shinkei to step into the breach.

52	kokoro ni hikeru	A memory pulling at the heart,
	funaoka no haru	springtime at Funaoka Hill.
	Shinkei	*Shinkei*
53	kasumi sae	Even the haze is
	tsuki wa akashi no	gloomy, this sad drifting beneath
	ukimakura	the bright Akashi moon.
	Nagatoshi	*Nagatoshi*

Spring: *kasumi* (haze). Travel: *Akashi no ukimakura* (drifting pillow at Akashi). Named Place: Akashi. Word Association: *oka* (hill) = *Akashi*.

(Waters finally reappear after a long absence.) Famous place-names (*nadokoro, meisho*) constitute a marked category in the renga lexicon due to their literary and historical associations, as we have just seen above and see here with the evocation of Genji's exile on the Akashi coast. The link with the maeku, however, is at once so mechanical and then so involved it is difficult to grasp, and thus gives an impression of slackness. On the evidence of the *Renju*, entry 86, "hill" and "Akashi" make an associative pair based on a passage in the "Akashi" chapter that recounts how on the night of the violent storm that drove Genji from his imperiled lodgings at Suma and into the safer haven of Akashi, his protector, the Lay Monk of Akashi, "had arranged for his daughter and her women to move [from the coast] to a house in the *hills*." Funaoka (orthographically, "ship" and "hill") in the maeku therefore becomes the hills of Akashi in this verse, and "ship" in the place-name understood to be the one that miraculously appeared during the storm to transport Genji from Suma to Akashi. Furthermore, this boat "pulls at the heart" (*kokoro ni hikeru* in the maeku) of Genji, that is, compels him, because its mysterious arrival in Suma tallies with a dream he had while wallowing in a reverie of hopelessness. In the dream, his father's ghost takes his arm and pulls him up, urging him to leave Suma for his safety. This is all very interesting in explaining the shift from Funaoka to Akashi, but the verse itself is obscure in diction and therefore conception. It is an attempt to evoke Genji's feeling of hopeless drifting in exile—*ukimakura* containing the common double meaning of "gloomy" and "floating," and is best appreciated as an echo of the following poem by Genji in the "Akashi" chapter.[14]

	tabigoromo	In travel garments
	urakanashisa ni	muffling in sadness the heart,
	akashikane	the nights are long
	kusa no makura wa	until the dawn, and barren,
	yume mo musubazu	the grass pillow, of dreams.
53	kasumi sae	Even the haze is
	tsuki wa akashi no	gloomy, this sad drifting beneath
	ukimakura	the bright Akashi moon.
	Nagatoshi	Nagatoshi
54	moshio no toko ni	Farewell calls of the wild geese,
	kari kaeru koe	upon the pallet of salt-seaweed.
	Sōgi	Sōgi

Spring: *kari kaeru* (wild geese departing). Waters: *moshio* (salt-seaweed). Dwellings: *toko* (bed, pallet).

Retaining the coastline geography of the maeku through "salt-seaweed," Sōgi also accentuates its feeling by introducing the calls of the wild geese as they migrate back to the north in spring. The subject's identity is ambiguous; by the unavoidable association evoked by sheer contiguity, it can be imagined to be Genji, and then again it may be just an anonymous fisherman. The very indeterminacy makes possible a transition away from the world of the novel.

54	moshio no toko ni	Farewell calls of the wild geese,
	kari kaeru koe	upon the pallet of salt-seaweed.
	Sōgi	Sōgi
55	hitoyo no mi	Sleepless in
	kareru tomaya ni	the sedge-grass hut he rented
	nezame shite	for only a night.
	Shun'a	Shun'a

Travel: *hitoyo kareru* (rented for one night). Dwellings: *tomaya* (sedge-grass hut).

Apart from the semantic proximity of lexical items in connection with those in the maeku—pallet = hut/night; salt-seaweed = sedge-grass—and the implication that the sleepless persona hears the calls of the wild geese, the verse seems only slightly connected. Nor does it advance the sequential progression very much. As such, and in connection with the preceding, it lacks the poetic chemistry springing from *kokoro*, for all the firm clarity of its semantic design.

55	hitoyo no mi	Sleepless in
	kareru tomaya ni	the sedge-grass hut he rented
	nezame shite	for only a night.
	Kaku'a	Shun'a
56	ukimi no ue zo	There is cause enough for tears
	namida soinuru	in this miserable life.
	Sōetsu	Kaku'a

Laments: *ukimi* (miserable self, life, or lot).

The sequence remains bogged down in the feelings of gloom introduced in 53 with "drifting / gloomy pillow" (*ukimakura*) and recurring here with "miserable life." The new, potentially interesting element in the maeku, "for only a night" (*hitoyo no mi*) falls by the wayside, although it could have advanced the sequence in another direction. The sense of stagnation becomes quite noticeable at this point.

56	ukimi no ue zo	There is cause enough for tears
	namida soinuru	in this miserable life.
	Kaku'a	Kaku'a
57	tarachine no	The added pain
	omou o miru mo	of seeing the anxiety
	kurushiki ni	in my parents' eyes.
	Sōetsu	Sōetsu

Laments: *tarachine no omou* (parents' anxiety).

Finally, Sōetsu releases the session from stagnation by a skillful interpretation of the maeku focusing on the inflectional effect of *zo*, which I
render as "cause enough." A miserable lot is bad enough (*ukimi no ue zo*),
but the added knowledge that it is causing my parents anxiety and grief is
truly hard to bear (*tarachine no . . . mo*). Sōetsu in this way skillfully brings
out the impact of the emphatic *zo* in the maeku in his own response. At this
point the sequence quickens with life again, a sense of forward motion that
will not slacken again until the final verse.

57	tarachine no	The added pain
	omou o miru mo	of seeing the anxiety
	kurushiki ni	in my parents' eyes.
	Sōetsu	Sōetsu
58	ima kon tote mo	This world do I renounce, though
	sutsuru yo no naka	death come this very moment!
	Norishige	Norishige

Laments: *sutsuru yo* (renounce the world).

In verse 58, the urgent motivation for renouncing the world is the
knowledge that death, the crucial event determining one's next existence,
may come "this very moment" (*ima kon*) and one must assure the salvation
of one's soul. In the context of the link, however, the first motivating force is
the misery and suffering of a mundane existence. By cultivating inner
wisdom, the persona releases not only himself but his anxious parents from
this suffering.

58	ima kon tote mo	This world do I renounce, though
	sutsuru yo no naka	death come this very moment!
	Norishige	Norishige
59	tsumi aru o	Yet knowing my sins,
	mukae no kuruma	to meet the Vehicle of the Law
	osoroshi na	fills me with terror.
	Shinkei	Shinkei

Buddhism: *tsumi* (impurity, sin).

Shinkei sets *mukae no kuruma* (lit., "the carriage [come] to fetch me")
in tense juxtaposition with *ima kon* ("come this very moment") in the
maeku, turning the urgency of renunciation into the tension of fear, as the
persona worries how his sins will be reckoned before the Vehicle of the Law.
This last image is an allusion to the parable of the burning house in the
Lotus Sutra, where the Buddha saves the children, absorbed in their play
inside, from the conflagration by telling them about the three fabulous
carriages that awaited them outside.[15] Here, the persona is fearful that his
sins may disable his hopes for salvation as symbolized by the coming vehicle

or carriage, and that he may be condemned forever to the "burning house" that is mundane existence as seen in Buddhist literature. That fear raises the urgency of renunciation expressed in the maeku.

59	tsumi aru o	Yet knowing my sins,
	mukae no kuruma	to meet the Vehicle of the Law
	osoroshi na	fills me with terror.
	Shinkei	Shinkei
60	mikari no kaesa	Riding home from the royal hunt—
	no mo hibiku nari	the very fields seem to resound.
	Sōgi	Sōgi

Winter: *kari* (hunting). Word Association: *tsumi* (sin) = *kari*.

Sōgi effects a quick and startling major shift into a purely descriptive mode following the emotionally involved passage from 56 to 59. The Buddhist vehicle of redemption turns into a grand carriage with outriders, taking a party home from the hunt; the referent of the respectful prefix in *mikari* may also be shōgunal or of the daimyō class. The fear and trembling of the maeku is for the "sin" of taking animal life committed by these men.

60	mikari no kaesa	Riding home from the royal hunt—
	no mo hibiku nari	the very fields seem to resound.
	Sōgi	Sōgi
61	arare chiru	As hail beats down
	nasu no shinohara	on the bamboo-plain of Nasu,
	kaze ochite	the wind falls still.
	Norishige	Norishige

Winter: *arare chiru* (hail falling). Named Place: Nasu. Falling Phenomena: *arare*.

Following Sōgi's lead, Norishige produces a wholly descriptive verse that skillfully animates *no mo hibiku* ("the very fields resound") through the auditory image of hail pattering on the bamboo grass. The hunting party has passed on, the wind is still, and there is only the unnaturally loud sound of hailstones on the dry bamboo blades: a concentrated, impactful image.

The Kantō geographical setting, Nasu in northern Shimotsuke Province (Tochigi Prefecture), brings the sequence close to the home of these Eastern warrior-participants and, of course, to Musashi itself, where the session is being held. Nasu, anciently known for its hunting fields, was, as readers of the *Tale of the Heike* will recall, the hometown of the Minamoto warrior Nasu no Yoichi, the long-distance archer who successfully shot down the fan attached to the Heike boat as it bobbed up and down on the waves, in one of the memorable episodes in that work. Nasu was also the site of the "life-killing stone" (*sesshōseki*) in the Nō play of that title, and the stone would later figure in Bashō's *Narrow Road to the Deep North*. A precedent for the image of hail on the bamboo-grass field of Nasu is this vivid poem by Minamoto Sanetomo (1192–1219), Teika's poetry student and the last Minamoto shōgun, assassinated in his prime (*Kinkaishū* 217, KT 29698).

mononofu no	As warriors reach back
yanami tsukurou	into the arrows in their quiver,
kote no e ni	on their raised gauntlets,
arare tabashiru	hailstones recoil with a patter
nasu no shinohara	on the bamboo-grass plain of Nasu.

It is quite likely that Norishige, amateur poet and warrior who belonged to the Ōgo clan based in the neighboring province of Kōzuke (Gumma), intended an allusion to this poem by another warrior-poet as a *honka* to his verse.

61	arare chiru	As hail beats down
	nasu no shinohara	on the bamboo-plain of Nasu,
	kaze ochite	the wind falls still.
	Norishige	Norishige
62	kusa no kage o mo	On the open Azuma Road, I seek
	tanomu azumaji	shelter in the shadow of the grass.
	Nagatoshi	Nagatoshi

Travel: *Azumaji* (Azuma Road). Named Place: Azuma.

Nagatoshi introduces the figure of a lone traveler on the open, wintry plain, forced to shelter among the grass from the falling hail. "Azuma Road" falls in with Nasu Plain in the maeku and continues the local Kantō setting of this passage, while "*shadow* of the grass" (*kusa no kage*) logically emerges from "bamboo grass" above as a metonymical adjunct. The verse as such draws out the sense of vulnerability latent in the maeku's objective scene.

62	kusa no kage o mo	On the open Azuma Road, I seek
	tanomu azumaji	shelter in the shadow of the grass.
	Nagatoshi	Nagatoshi
63	minu kuni no	Is the wanderer's fate
	tsuchi to ya naran	to become a clod of earth in
	mi no yukue	an unknown country?
	Shinkei	Shinkei

Travel: *minu kuni* (unseen [alien] country). Grievance: *mi no yukue* (the end/destination of life or self).

The feeling of vulnerability rises to a poignant pitch as Shinkei's persona contemplates death on the road in Azuma, "the unknown country." Given the coincidence with the session's actual location, and Shinkei's real situation at this time as a traveler in the Kantō from the capital, there is no doubt that he is reading himself into this verse.[16] Yet its resonance is such that it would have spoken equally to the warrior-participants of the session, members of the Ashikaga-Uesugi alliance to whom death away from their hometowns was always a concrete possibility, given the state of civil war in the Kantō at this time. Technically, "clod of earth" (*tsuchi*) is a metonymical adjunct to "shadow of the grass" (*kusa no kage*) and continues the satisfying chain of mutually resonating imagistic details starting from verse 60. The Nozaka Text has *tama* (spirit, shade) instead of *tsuchi* in this verse; I follow the Temmangū Text because *tsuchi* is in my opinion more effective poetically in the links with verses 61 and 63.

63	minu kuni no	Is the wanderer's fate
	tsuchi to ya naran	to become a clod of earth in
	mi no yukue	an unknown country?
	Shinkei	Shinkei
64	hate mo kanashiki	Pitifully sad is the end,
	amatsu'otomego	ethereal maiden of the sky.
	Sōetsu	Sōetsu

Miscellaneous.

Sōetsu brings in the word *hate* (end) in association with Shinkei's *yukue* (destination) above, thus bringing to a close the passage begun in 60. The subject of the maeku's lament for a possible death in alien surroundings here becomes the *amatsu'otomego* (maiden of the sky), image of an ethereal creature set in a tense and tragic juxtaposition with "clod of earth" in the maeku. In effect Sōetsu opens up a whole new realm of associations with the story immortalized in the Nō play *Robe of Feathers* (*Hagoromo*). In the play, a fisherman steals the robe of feathers of a Heavenly Maiden who has come down to earth. Unable to return to the sky without it, she is in danger of dying and becoming permanently mired on earth. As the signs of earthly suffering begin to appear on her, happily the fisherman relents and returns her feathery robe, and she performs a beautiful dance for the earth in thanksgiving. A hauntingly lyrical symbolic play, *Robe of Feathers* is one of the most enduring pieces in the Nō repertory.

The first line of the verse, *hate mo kanashiki* ("pitifully sad is the end"), evokes the imminent death or "decay of the angel" (*tennin gosui*—the title, incidentally, of the last novel in Mishima's final opus). This is marked by five signs: her crown of flowers withers, her heavenly robe becomes dirtied with the dust of the earth, sweat pours from her armpits, darkness descends upon her flickering eyes, and she loses pleasure in her heavenly home.[17] The following passage in Arthur Waley's rendering of the play is particularly evocative of the link between 63 and 64 as it focuses on the tragic contrast between the earthy and ethereal.

Angel: Like a bird without wings,
            I would rise, but robeless
Hakuryo: To the low earth you sink, an angel dwelling
            In the dingy world.
Angel: This way, that way,
            Despair only. . . .
Chorus: Then on her coronet,
            Jewelled as with the dew of tears,
            The bright flowers drooped and faded.
            O piteous to see before the eyes,
            Fivefold the signs of sickness
            Corrupt an angel's form.[18]

The way Sōetsu translates the idea of exile and an earthly death in Shinkei's verse into the Heavenly Maiden legend is a truly inspired move, showing imagination and lyrical feeling. Kaneko also cites another version of the Hagoromo legend in the Tango *fudoki*, in which one of a group of eight angels has her robe of feathers stolen and, unable to return to the sky with the others, is condemned to wander the earth.[19]

64   hate mo kanashiki   Pitifully sad is the end,
        amatsu'otomego   ethereal maiden of the sky.
                    Sōetsu   Sōetsu
65   omokage no   Her shimmering image,
        tsuki ni koishi mo   the moon draws all his yearning,
        ato nakute   yet is it void of trace.
                    Mitsusuke   Mitsusuke

Third Fold, Back. Autumn: *tsuki* (moon). Love: *omokage* (image, shadow, reflection; trace, wake, memory).

Mitsusuke continues within the realm of tale and legend introduced by Sōetsu, while effecting a shift of referent to another heavenly maiden, Kaguyahime, the Shining Princess in the *Tale of the Bamboo-Cutter* (*Taketori monogatari*). She spends some years on earth, forming attachments to her foster parents and the Emperor, but in the end returns to her true home in the moon. "Pitifully sad is the end" (*hate mo kanashiki*) would then refer to the parting scene in the tale, when Kaguyahime dons the heavenly robe of feathers and ascends to the moon escorted by the resplendent creatures who had come to fetch her. The subject of the sentiment in the verse is the emperor; the imagery poetically evokes the shimmering radiance of Kaguyahime's being, as well as the romantically ephemeral, and ethereal, relationship between the two.

65	omokage no	Her shimmering image,
	tsuki ni koishi mo	the moon draws all his yearning,
	ato nakute	yet is it void of trace.
	Mitsusuke	Mitsusuke
66	hitodanome naru	Hope leaps at a rustling sound—
	kosu no akikaze	bamboo blinds in the autumn wind.
	Norishige	Norishige

Autumn: *akikaze* (autumn wind). Love: *matsu koi* (waiting love, in concept).

Norishige repeats the same movement of yearning expectation, then deflation, in the maeku's verbal configuration: a stirring in the bamboo blinds causes the persona, now a woman, to momentarily think that her lover has come, but it is only the sound of the autumn wind. A precisely drawn image, the verse fills the maeku's third line, *ato nakute* ("void of trace") with a new significance in this changed context. Hope leaps, then dies, leaving no trace, like the autumn wind that stirred the blinds and gave rise to hope in the first place.

66	hitodanome naru	Hope leaps at a rustling sound—
	kosu no akikaze	bamboo blinds in the autumn wind.
	Norishige	Norishige
67	shitamomiji	Crimson-dyed lower leaves
	tare ni wakeyo to	part to make a path for whom—
	midaruran	swaying all tremulous.
	Sōgi	Sōgi

Autumn: *momiji* (crimson leaves).

Sōgi continues, with an added richness through the image of crimson leaves trembling in the wind, the mood of ethereal courtly romance begun in 65. Resonating with the image of the wind-stirred blinds (*kosu no akikaze*) in the maeku, the swaying of the trees' lower foliage (*shitamomiji . . . midaruran*), now colored with the autumn, becomes an objective correlative for the emotional state of a woman waiting for her lover; the specific term, *shitamomiji* (crimson lower leaves), moreover, delicately evokes a lady's flowing hem and sleeves as glimpsed beneath the swaying bamboo blinds of the maeku, at the same time that it suggests the hidden, repressed quality of her longing. The verse is rich with the subtle mystery of the Heian romance.

67	shitamomiji	Crimson-dyed lower leaves
	tare ni wakeyo to	part to make a path for whom—
	midaruran	swaying all tremulous.
	Sōgi	Sōgi
68	kururba kaeru	As darkness falls, the mountain
	yama zo harukeki	of my home recedes yet farther.
	Kaku'a	Kaku'a

Miscellaneous. Mountains: *yama* (mountain).

Kaku'a effects a linking contrast between the brightly colored leaves swaying by the persona's feet and the shadowy mountain in the distance; we have left the Love theme behind. The colored lower leaves of the maeku still function as a symbol, but of a different "excitement"—this persona's feelings of anxiety about the long distance he has yet to traverse in the dark before reaching home. Here around me, the bright leaves are discernible, as if to make a path for someone, but all is dark farther on.

68	kurureba kaeru yama zo harukeki	As darkness falls, the mountain of my home recedes yet farther.	
	Kaku'a	Kaku'a	
69	yuku kata mo isa shirakumo o naka ni mite	Uncertain too of the way ahead, he sees the white clouds massed between.	
	Shinkei	Shinkei	

Travel: *yuku kata* (the way ahead).

Shinkei deepens the anxiety in the maeku simply by adding the detail of thick clouds hovering between the traveler and his destination. Through the contrastive juxtaposition of *kaeru* (return) and *yuku* (go), he also places the persona in a real impasse: dusk finds him far from the mountain of his home, while before him, the way ahead is further obscured by clouds. By this contrast, Shinkei shifts the context in such a way that instead of being on his way home, the persona is traveling away from it. The way ahead obscure, he looks back to where he started, but that point too has receded in the dark. In this link, the emphatic *zo* in the maeku and *mo* (also) here are made to carry the load of the signifying contrast in an outwardly simple yet quick and skillful turnabout.

69	yuku kata mo isa shirakumo o naka ni mite	Uncertain too of the way ahead, he sees the white clouds massed between.	
	Shinkei	Shinkei	
70	suginuru tori no kasukanaru koe	Faint sound of birdcall flitting swiftly past.	
	Shun'a	Shun'a	

Travel: *suginuru* (went past). Word Association: *kumo* (cloud) = *tori* (bird).

This verse is most effective when the traveler is understood to be walking beneath the obscuring clouds of the maeku. Uncertain of his direction, he suddenly hears the faint calls of a bird as it flits swiftly past him overhead. The concentrated auditory image impacts upon the maeku as an accent: the sound coming from nowhere and disappearing into the unknown way ahead sharpens the isolation of the traveler within the obscuring clouds. This is a poetically satisfying link.

70	suginuru tori no	Faint sound of birdcall
	kasukanaru koe	flitting swiftly past.
	Shun'a	Shun'a
71	tabibito no	With the dawning light,
	koyuru sekito no	the barrier-gate opens for
	akuru yo ni	the crossing traveler.
	Nagatoshi	Nagatoshi

Travel: *tabibito* (traveler), *sekito* (barrier-gate).

Here the fleeting birdcall is heard by the traveler as he prepares to cross the barrier-gate in the faint light of dawn. Kaneko observes that the link, based on the semantic similarity between *suginuru* (went past) and *koyuru* (cross over), effects no great variation from the maeku, and that the "faint calls" (*kasukanaru koe*) of the bird do not come to life in this verse. It is true that the aural image is not as startling and satisfactory here as in the preceding link. Nevertheless, the time, which is specified as early dawn when the night has just begun to lift, seems to me to enhance the birdcall to some degree, as if it were a harbinger of the light. Furthermore, the configuration of the scene, with the barrier-gate just before the traveler, while the bird itself has already passed it overhead, is not without poetic appeal in the disjunction of pace and movement suggested by two kinds of "crossings."

71	tabibito no	With the dawning light,
	koyuru sekito no	the barrier-gate opens for
	akuru yo ni	the crossing traveler.
	Nagatoshi	Nagatoshi
72	tomo o ya matan	I think I'll await a companion
	iwagane no michi	at the foot of the craggy trail.
	Sōetsu	Sōetsu

Travel: *michi* (road, trail).

Within sight of the barrier-gate, the traveler decides to rest a while and wait for someone to accompany him in climbing the rocky trail up to it. Given the Kantō setting of the session, Sōetsu most probably had the Hakone mountain pass in mind here. The link consists of the now familiar technique of adding metonymical details—here, the path between the crags—in the course of developing a narrative.

72	tomo o ya matan	I think I'll await a companion
	iwagane no michi	at the foot of the craggy trail.
	Sōetsu	Sōetsu

73	ki no shita o	Here in the shadow of
	hatsuyuki nagara	the trees, the first snow patches
	kieyarade	have yet to dissolve.
	Mitsusuke	Mitsusuke

Spring: *hatsuyuki* (first snow of the year; spring snow). Falling Phenomena: *yuki*. Word Association: *tomo* (companion, friend) = *yuki*.

In the classical vocabulary, "first snow" refers to the light snowflakes that fall in early spring and dissolve quickly in the warming air; here in the cold shadow of the deep mountains, however, they remain whitely on the ground without melting.

In its visual design of white splotches of snow against the dark and still bare, gnarled branches of ancient trees, the verse has the aesthetic quality of an ink-wash painting. Semantically, "have yet to dissolve" (*kieyarade*) subtly resonates against the maeku's "I think I'll await a companion" (*tomo o ya matan*) to suggest a new reading: I am thinking of waiting for a companion to share the beauty of this scene of white snow patches in the shadow of the aged trees.

"Companion" or "friend" (*tomo*) makes an associative pair with "snow" here through the mediation of the lines from a poem by Po Chü-i, "Sent to Yin Hsieh-lu," inscribed in Japanese literature through their citation in *Wakan rōeishū* 734, under "Associating with Friends": "Forsaken by [former] companions in the zither, poetry, and wine, / I long for you most when the snow, the flowers, and the moon are in their season."[20] The sentiment behind the link in this instance, one that recurs in various contexts in Japanese classical sources, was summed up by Kawabata Yasunari in his Nobel Prize acceptance speech:

When we see the beauty of the snow, when we see the beauty of the full moon, when we see the beauty of the cherries in bloom, when in short we brush against and are awakened by the beauty of the four seasons, it is then that we think most of those close to us, and want them to share the pleasure. The excitement of beauty calls forth strong fellow feelings, yearnings for companionship, and the word "comrade" can be taken to mean "human being."[21]

As evidenced by the central place of *aware* in Shinkei's aesthetics as well, in the traditional Japanese sensibility cherished even by a modern writer like Kawabata, the sense of beauty is never divorced from the human condition. Indeed it is what binds people in a common human sympathy.

The currency during the Muromachi period of the lines from Po Chü-i may be observed also in a linked-verse handbook from 1494, *Renga yoriai* (Renga word associations). An entry in this text explains that to "friend," one links the number "three" to refer to "the three friends" (*sanyū* or *mitsu no tomo*), which are variously, the zither, poetry, and wine; snow, moon, and flowers; or pine, bamboo, and plum.[22]

73	ki no shita o	Here in the shadow of
	hatsuyuki nagara	the trees, the first snow patches
	kieyarade	have yet to dissolve.
	Mitsusuke	Mitsusuke
74	katsu saku ume ni	Yet sweet is the morning dew as
	niou asatsuyu	one by one plum blossoms unfurl.
	Shinkei	Shinkei

Spring: *saku ume* (blossoming plum). Word Association: *kiyu* (dissolve, vanish) = *tsuyu* (dew).

Shinkei maintains the aesthetic orientation of the maeku by evoking the classic combination of snow and plum blossoms, traditionally the earliest flowers of the year. The verbal pivot of the link is carried by *katsu*, meaning "one after another" in verse 74. In the context of 73, however, it registers as "on the other hand"; in this sense it activates *nagara* ("while . . . ") there: while the first snow has yet to dissolve, on the other hand, the plum blossoms are already unfolding one after another. The tone of the link has a delicacy and cool freshness that together constitute one of Shinkei's signature styles. The scent of plum blossoms has a noble delicacy poetically enhanced by the coolness of remaining white snow and the ineffable effect of *katsu* here as an adverbial evoking, in slow motion as it were, the very unfurling of the petals in the fresh dew.

74	katsu saku ume ni	Yet sweet is the morning dew as
	niou asatsuyu	one by one plum blossoms unfurl.
	Shinkei	Shinkei
75	haru no no ya	Ah, the spring meadows—
	narenu sode o mo	even the sleeves of strangers
	kawasuran	brushing each other.
	Norishige	Norishige

Spring: *haru no no* (spring meadow).

From the subtle poetry of 74, Norishige shifts to a livelier mood suggesting the carefree gladness, the sense of release from winter bondage brought on by spring. The scene is of people enjoying spring and its flowers in the meadow, much as the Japanese hold "flower-viewing" (*hanami*) parties even now under the cherry blossoms. "Sleeves of strangers / brushing each other" is delicately suggestive of romance, and subliminally of the unfurling petals in the maeku.

75	haru no no ya	Ah, the spring meadows—
	narenu sode o mo	even the sleeves of strangers
	kawasuran	brushing each other.
	Norishige	Norishige
76	kasumi shiku e ni	On the bay overhung with haze
	fune kayou miyu	boats seen gliding to and fro.
	Sōgi	Sōgi

Spring: *kasumi* (haze).

Sōgi's poetic camera pans away from the meadow to take in the larger, distant, and tranquil view of the bay overspread with haze, through which boats can be seen silently gliding past each other—a motion that subtly repeats, with a difference, the close image of sleeves brushing one another in the maeku.

Here ends the generally tranquil mood begun in verse 70, a passage characterized by a consciously aesthetic orientation and painting-like scenes, evocativeness, and subtle poetry. As such, it contrasts with the complex, emotionally involved, and depressed mood of several of the preceding passages.

76	kasumi shiku e ni	On the bay overhung with haze
	fune kayou miyu	boats seen gliding to and fro.
	Sōgi	Sōgi
77	kokoro naki	For the man devoid
	hito no yūbe wa	of feeling, the dimming evening
	munashikute	holds nothing.
	Sōetsu	Sōetsu

Laments: *kokoro naki* (lit., "lacking a heart-mind").

Contemplating the tranquil seascape of the maeku, Sōetsu locates it temporally at dusk and states that for someone without sensibility, such a scene holds no significance, is *munashi* (in vain, empty, useless). This is merely an indirect way of saying that the evening scene is a deeply moving sight, but that quality is a function of the beholder's *kokoro*; the gaze is contemplative and enabled by the operation of the mind-heart. The classical overtones of this verse are unmistakable; it resonates with allusions to older poems using the vocabulary of *kokoro ari* or *kokoro nashi* and of *aware*.

77	kokoro naki	For the man devoid
	hito no yūbe wa	of feeling, the dimming evening
	munashikute	holds nothing.
	Sōetsu	Sōetsu
78	susumuru kane o	Hear the infinite sadness in
	aware to mo kike	the lesson of the booming bell.
	Shinkei	Shinkei

Buddhism: *susumuru kane* (the bell signaling and promoting apprehension of the Buddhist truth).

The ensuing discourse between two priests turns inevitably Buddhist as Shinkei introduces the tolling of the temple bell at evening and enjoins the hearer to recognize there, and respond with *aware*, to the central lesson of *mujō*, the "mutability" of human existence. *Kokoro naki* is more specifically delineated here as the absence not only of feeling as such, but of a sensibility founded upon a sense of *mujō*. What is at issue is *aware* in its medieval sense as a sensitive and compassionate responsiveness to things in their sheer temporality, a concept formally inscribed in poetic criticism by Shinkei himself in *Sasamegoto* and elsewhere.

A possible *honka* for the link between evening, the bell, and *aware* as a feeling of sadness is a poem by Priest Jakuzen in the *Shinkokinshū*.

SKKS 1956. Buddhist Poems. "On [the lines] 'the day has ended, my life approaches its dissolution,' one in the sequence of 100 Buddhist Poems that he presented to various people."[23]

kyō suginu	This day has ended;
inochi mo shika to	and soon too shall this life—
odorokasu	in the mind-bracing
iriai no kane no	booming of the evening bell,
koe zo kanashiki	echo of an infinite sadness.

In another possible honka for the link, *Fūgashū* 2036 below, the connection between the uselessness (*munashi*) of the evening for the man devoid of sensibility, as expressed by the maeku, and Shinkei's allusion to the lesson of the evening bell, is much clearer.

FGS 2036. Buddhist Poems. Priest Kyōshō. "On the spirit of [the words] 'unperceiving and unknowing, unalarmed and unafraid.' "[24]

	odorokade	Unmoved as ever,
	kyō mo munashiku	yet another day has drawn
	kurenu nari	to a useless close;
	aware ukimi no	the pathos of drifting souls as
	iriai no sora	the evening bell fades in the sky.
78	susumuru kane o	Hear the infinite sadness in
	aware to mo kike	the lesson of the booming bell.
	Shinkei	Shinkei
79	sakazuki o	Passing the sake cup
	megurasu madoi	in a happy circle, the night
	oshiki yo ni	ends too soon.
	Nagatoshi	Nagatoshi

Remaining-Trace Fold, Front. Miscellaneous.

In an impressive shift marking the entry into the Fourth Fold, the final movement of the sequence, Nagatoshi transposes Shinkei's maeku into the context of an all-night party. As friends and guests enjoy each other's company with talk and wine far into the night, the tolling of the temple bell breaks upon their consciousness, calling to mind the passing time (*oshiki yo*), the brevity of joy, and their own mortality. Here *aware* gains a sharper poignancy; the reality of time is experienced unexpectedly, precisely because it had been forgotten in the pleasures of companionship and wine.

79	sakazuki o	Passing the sake cup
	megurasu madoi	in a happy circle, the night
	oshiki yo ni	ends too soon.
	Nagatoshi	Nagatoshi
80	koto no ne nokoru	The zither's notes linger on
	ariake no sora	with the moon in the paling sky.
	Sōgi	Sōgi

Autumn: *ariake* (remaining light, of the moon at dawn).

Sōgi links up to the maeku by focusing on the expression *oshiki yo*, a night cherished and regretted in its passing, and by analyzing it into two metonymical details—the notes of the *koto* (zither) and the clear autumn moonlight—that come to represent what has been enjoyed. In the paling night, the last notes still echo in the hearts of the listeners, who would have wished the music would never end, while the moon remains momentarily in the sky before it too is taken by the dawn light. The way in which *nokoru* (remaining, lingering) activates *oshiki* (cherished and regretted) in the maeku is subtle and fine indeed; it is a movingly delicate turn, a moment caught and held for a while in its passing.

80	koto no ne nokoru	The zither's notes linger on
	ariake no sora	with the moon in the paling sky.
	Sōgi	Sōgi
81	kie mo senu	Lamenting his body that
	mi o wabihito no	would not melt, hapless man
	aki fukete	in deepening autumn.
	Ikuhiro	Ikuhiro ·

Autumn: *aki* (autumn). Humanity: *wabihito* (hopeless, unfortunate person fallen in the world, living in reduced circumstances). Word Association: *koto* (zither) = *wabihito*.

Nokoru (remain, linger) becomes the verbal pivot of the link as Ikuhiro gives it a new turn in the synonymous expression *kie mo senu* (does not melt or disappear), whose referent, however, is a man's body. Depressed, kept awake by endless thoughts of his misfortune, a man bitterly regrets the persistence of his own life as the long night pales and the melancholy autumn ages. Where "lingering" in the previous link was to be cherished, here it is to be decried. Otherwise, this link is somewhat slack and mechanical because trained principally on the verbal. The conventional association between "zither" and "hapless person" is based on the following *Kokinshū* poem.

KKS 985. Miscellaneous. Yoshimine Munesada [Bishop Henjō].
"Composed and sent to a dilapidated house from where he had heard a woman playing the zither, when he was down in Nara."

wabihito no	Thinking, as I gaze,
sumubeki yado to	of the *hapless person* that
mirunabe ni	must dwell in this house,
nagekikuwawaru	a *zither* sounds from within
koto no ne zo suru	to add to the mournfulness.

Apart from the mechanical verbal link between the two terms above, the *kokoro* of the poem itself does not come to life in Ikuhiro's verse, so that it cannot be called a *honka* in the sense of the *Shinkokinshū* usage of this technique. Nonetheless such is the power of the empty space in renga *tsukeai* that the allusion imparts to the link an ambiguous evocativeness that need not be further specified.

81	kie mo senu	Lamenting his body that
	mi o wabibito no	would not melt, hapless man
	aki fukete	in deepening autumn.
	Ikuhiro	Ikuhiro
82	kumokiri ikue	Ply on ply, the cloudy mists over
	sumeru yamazato	the mountain village where I live.
	Sōetsu	Sōetsu

Autumn: *kiri* (mist). Rising Phenomena: *kumokiri*. Word Association: *kie* (melt, disperse) = *kiri*.

The hapless man in the maeku is imaged here as living in an isolated mountain village covered by mists and cloud. Such an image reinforces the depressed tonality of the maeku and alludes, it seems to me, to Prince Hachi's reclusion in the mist-covered *mountain village* of Uji in the *Tale of Genji*. Prince Hachi, victim of political misfortune and also of a personal tragedy in his wife's early demise and the burning of his mansion in the capital, is a classic case of a *wabihito*, a man fallen from society and living in isolation and straitened circumstances. In the "Hashihime" (Lady of the bridge) chapter, he composes a poem whose last two lines echo the words *kie mo senu* / *mi* in the maeku; furthermore, the prose passage that follows makes the link between the *wabihito* image and a mist-covered mountain village clear.

mishi hito mo	She who dwelt
yado mo keburi ni	beside me, my home, all
narinishi o	have turned to smoke;
nani tote waga *mi*	to what end does *this body*
kienokorikemu	remain, unmelted, behind?

Such longing consumed him, for he had nothing left to live for. To his abode surrounded by *range upon range of mountains,* no one came to visit. . . . As he passed the days and nights gazing on peaks where the morning *mists* never lift. . . .[25]

Sōetsu's handling of *honka* and *honzetsu* here as a linking technique is rather good.

82	kumokiri ikue	Ply on ply, the cloudy mists over
	sumeru yamazato	the mountain village where I live.
	Sōetsu	Sōetsu
83	samidare wa	The long June rains:
	mizu no koe senu	not a valley but resounds with
	tani mo nashi	the swollen waters.
	Shinkei	Shinkei

Summer: *samidare* (monthlong rains in summer). Falling Phenomena: *samidare*. Waters: *mizu* (water).

In a barely perceptible move that suddenly transports us into summer, Shinkei responds with an inspired piece on the natural scenery. Imagistically sharp, the verse brings into vivid life the layers of clouds and mists over the mountains of the maeku (*kumokiri ikue* / . . . *yamazato*) by redefining them into the dense clouds that bring the constant, long rains of the Fifth Month (*samidare* is modern *baiu* or *tsuyu*, the rainy season from June to July), swelling the streams and rivers all over the valley. The poetic effect of the verse, it seems to me, gains more power and interest if *sumeru* ("dwelling, living in") in the maeku is read as the homonymous verb, also in its stative inflection, meaning "clarified, purified." The layers of clouds, having fallen as rain over a long period, have lifted from the mountain village, the sky is clear, now only the swollen torrents resound all over the mountain in the aftermath of the long rains. Read thus, the link becomes more arresting, and the scene itself rendered with a fresh and bracing, *sugasugashii* tone that is one aspect of Shinkei's poetic sensibility. Moreover, the passage from 81 to 83 acquires a symbolic dimension when *kumokiri* in 82 is interpreted as the Buddhist "clouds and mist" of religious unknowing in association with the *wabihito* of 81. The dispersal of these clouds would then evoke the spiritual exaltation that is the feeling one instinctively senses in 83. In this reading, the maeku would read: "Ply after ply, the clouds and mists / now *clearing* from the mountain village." It is noteworthy, in this connection, that in *Sasamegoto* Shinkei cites a verse by Gusai similar in imagery to his tsukeku here and that he classifies it under the symbolic mode.[26]

83	samidare wa	The long June rains:
	mizu no koe senu	not a valley but resounds with
	tani mo nashi	the swollen waters.
	Shinkei	Shinkei
84	nagare no sue ni	At the mouth of the swift current,
	ukabu mumoregi	a buried tree floats into view.
	Hōzen	Hōzen

Miscellaneous. Waters: *nagare* (current, flow).

Hōzen skillfully translates the aurality of Shinkei's image of resounding torrents into a tactile and kinetic force so strong it has pried loose a long-buried tree stump (*mumoregi*) along its course and propelled it all the way down to the river's mouth. Here ends the three-verse passage of objective description of natural scenery marked by a dynamic vividness. Norishige returns to human affairs (*jinji*) themes in the next verse, which ends the first half of the movement on the face or front of the Fourth Fold, the Remaining-Trace Fold (*nagori no ori*).

84	nagare no sue ni	At the mouth of the swift current,
	ukabu mumoregi	a buried tree floats into view.
	Hōzen	Hōzen
85	au se ni mo	Hide it I would not,
	yoshi ya kakotaji	could we but meet, in spite
	natorikawa	of Rumor River.
	Norishige	Norishige

Love: *au se* (lit., "meeting shoals"). Waters: *se, kawa* (river). Named Place: Natorikawa ("Rumor River"). Word Association: *mumoregi* (buried tree) = *se*, Natorikawa.

The maeku motif of the sudden exposure of what is deeply hidden, as imaged in the "buried tree," is transformed into the possible exposure of a hidden love. The force of the river's current becomes a metaphor for the power of a repressed passion, which is such that it would risk exposure and gossip for a single meeting with the beloved. The *yoriai* pair *mumoregi = se, Natorikawa* has its source in *KKS* 650, Love, Anonymous.

> *natorikawa*　　　　Were the *buried tree*
> *seze no mumoregi*　　to float into view upon the

arawareba	*shoals of Rumor River,*
ikani semu to ka	what did I think to do, lost in
aimisomekemu	the rapture of that first tryst?

In Norishige's verse, the situation is one wherein the persona has not in fact achieved even a first tryst, and the expressed indifference to rumor is in contrast with the anxiety mirrored in the *honka*. In this way, the verse may be said to be a true allusive variation on the foundation poem.

85	au se ni mo	Hide it I would not,
	yoshi ya kakotaji	could we but meet, in spite
	natorikawa	of Rumor River.
	Norishige	Norishige
86	yoso ni morenan	My unassuaged hue become apparent
	iro zo monouki	to others—that would be misery!
	Shun'a	Shun'a

Love: *moreru iro* (lit., "a hue leaking out," i.e., a hidden passion exposed).

Shun'a develops the logic of the maeku in the following manner: if we could meet or had in fact met, I would not care if the affair became known to others, but what would really pain me is that they should discover my hidden, unrequited longing, the truth that you do not deign to meet me. The reasoning turns, it would seem, on a point of pride or the desire for personal satisfaction. I can endure the rumor if we were in fact having an affair, but the exposure of this unassuaged love is a different matter altogether. The force of the emphatic *zo* turns on this linking contrast between the two hypothetical situations.

86	yoso ni morenan	My unassuaged hue become apparent
	iro zo monouki	to others—that would be misery!
	Shun'a	Shun'a
87	kaimami mo	Leaving gaps naked
	arawa to ashi no	to the eye, the hedge of
	ha wa karete	reed leaf shrivels.
	Shinkei	Shinkei

Winter: *ashi no ha karete* (reed leaves wither). Love: *kaimami* (glimpse through gaps in the hedge).

Shinkei brings the motif of exposure, which began in 84, to an apparently simple, yet allusively rich ending with another vividly sharp picture that has the primary purpose of shifting to the new theme of Winter. The image is of a small, poor hut surrounded by a miscanthus hedge that has shriveled, exposing the shabbiness of its interior to the onlooker. In effect, the verse specifies the concrete situation in which the persona of 86 finds himself or herself, with *yoso ni morenan* ("apparent to others") reverberating in the image of the gaping hedge; and *iro*, "color, hue," usually alluding to love-longing, acquiring here its second sense of "form, appearance." In this context, the maeku becomes an expression of the persona's feelings of shame at the poverty of his/her surroundings, and may be rendered thus: "Evidence of my poverty bared / to others—that is too wretched!"

Kaneko detects a delicate evocation of the destitute life of the reed cutter (*ashikari*) along the Naniwa shore, in the famous legend of that name.[27] Apart from the appropriateness of the setting, the link brings out in particular the reed cutter's complex feeling of mingled shame and longing for his former wife, forced by their destitution to seek her fortune in the capital, where she eventually becomes a nobleman's wife, though still emotionally attached to her former husband. She seeks him out, he hides from her, and it is his feeling of mortification at her discovery of his unchanged poverty that is brought out by this link. The pathos of this old legend has clearly appealed to authors and readers for centuries down to our time, as witness Tanizaki's novella *Ashikari* and Higuchi Ichiyō's reworking of the tale in the short story "Jūsan'ya" (The thirteenth night).

87	kaimami mo arawa to ashi no ha wa karete Shinkei	Leaving gaps naked to the eye, the hedge of reed leaf shrivels. Shinkei
88	fuyu wa sumarenu sumika to o shire Mitsusuke	In winter, I would have you know, this abode is not to be endured. Mitsusuke

Winter: *fuyu* (winter).

Mitsusuke simply gives voice to what is already concretely illustrated in the maeku; he directly expresses the feelings of the unfortunate inhabitant of the hut, bringing out its nakedly unprotected character, open as it is to the harsh elements in winter.

88	fuyu wa sumarenu sumika to o shire Mitsusuke	In winter, I would have you know, this abode is not to be endured. Mitsusuke
89	miyako ni wa yuki mezurame ya ono no yama Sōgi	In the Capital City, they cherish the rare snow, but here in Mount Ono! Sōgi

Winter: *yuki* (snow).

Sōgi locates the unendurable wintry abode of 88 in snowy Mount Ono and thereby signals a clear allusion to Section 83 of the *Tales of Ise*. There, Narihira travels from the capital to visit his former patron Prince Koretaka.

Disappointed by his meager prospects in society, the prince had become a monk living in a hermitage at Ono, "where the snow was quite deep, since it was at the foot of Mount Hiei," as the *Ise* text says. Within this anecdotal context, verses 88 and 89 are to be understood as words spoken by the lonely prince to the man who used to be his companion in the refined, courtly activities of his former life.

89	miyako ni wa	In the Capital City,
	yuki mezurame ya	they cherish the rare snow, but
	ono no yama	here in Mount Ono!
	Sōgi	Sōgi
90	shigure ni tsuki no	Piercingly chill the moonlight
	kage mo susamaji	in the wake of the sudden rains.
	Kaku'a	Kaku'a

Autumn: *tsuki* (moon), *susamaji* (piercingly chill).

Shigure, written with the ideographs "time" and "rain," are the rains that suddenly fall and as suddenly cease in the change of season from late autumn to early winter. Here it is best to place the time in autumn, since the moon as such and the term *susamaji* are both indices of this season in renga. In the context of the link with 89, Kaku'a says in effect that living in remote Ono is just as unendurable in autumn as in winter. The verse as such, in isolation, is impressively stark; however, the link with 89 is general, not minute or close. Such a method of merely adding new elements to the maeku instead of activating or transforming it is also one way of linking, and characterizes the run from 88 to 90.

90	shigure ni tsuki no	Piercingly chill the moonlight
	kage mo susamaji	in the wake of the sudden rains.
	Kaku'a	Kaku'a
91	kogarashi no	Swept adrift
	sora ni ukaruru	across the storm-scoured sky,
	aki no kumo	the clouds of autumn.
	Shinkei	Shinkei

Autumn: *aki no kumo* (clouds of autumn). Rising Phenomena: *kumo*.

Once more tightening the sequence after the slackness of the preceding run, Shinkei responds to 90 with an equally stark verse that animates its *susamaji* feeling in the image of clouds set nakedly drifting in the "tree-withering storm" (*kogarashi*) that swept across the sky. The moment captured here is the interval between the intermittent rains of the maeku, when the moon appears starkly clear, illuminating the moving clouds before the sky darkens again in rain. It is a masterly link in the way it tenses up the maeku and brings the two verses together in an integral, seamless node of feeling (*kokoro*), the mode of "the single, undulating line" (*hitofushi ni iinagashitaru*) or of "monochromatic integrity" (*mono isshiki ni*) in Shinkei's critical vocabulary. It is also worth noting that like 63, this verse has a certain autobiographical dimension; the image of storm-swept clouds suggests Shinkei's poetic projection of his situation as a refugee in the Kantō region, helpless before the shifting tides of the Ōnin War.

91	kogarashi no	Swept adrift
	sora ni ukaruru	across the storm-scoured sky,
	aki no kumo	the clouds of autumn.
	Shinkei	Shinkei
92	kari mo uchiwabi	Lonesome too the wild geese
	kure wataru koro	flitting in the dusk shadows.
	Mitsusuke	Mitsusuke

Autumn: *kari* (wild geese).

The tension of the preceding link dissolves into a softer, more generalized melancholy as Mitsusuke shifts into the classic modality of an autumn evening. Against the now dimming clouds of the maeku, he points up the white silhouettes of the wild geese as they fly, crying, across the sky. The contrast between this link and the preceding demonstrates how the same verse, here 91, can acquire a wholly different cast within a new context; it illustrates again the open, ambiguous, or provisional character of the single verse in renga. Thus ends the front of the Fourth Fold, in the minor key.

92	kari mo uchiwabi	Lonesome too the wild geese
	kure wataru koro	flitting in the dusk shadows.
	Mitsusuke	Mitsusuke
93	mi ni kagiru	Not I alone
	namida naraji to	weep these tears—
	nagusamete	I solace myself.
	Norishige	Norishige

Remaining-Trace Fold, Back. Love: *namida* (tears). Word Association: *kari* (wild geese) = *namida*.

An uncomplicated link based on the conventional associative pair indicated above, and competent in the way it responds to the particle *mo* (also) in the maeku through *mi ni kagiru . . . naraji* (lit., "not limited to myself")— that is, the wild geese know sorrow as well. The source of the *yoriai* pair is *KKS* 221, Autumn, Anonymous:

nakiwataru	Are they *tears* dropped
kari no *namida* ya	by the *wild geese* as they flew,
ochitsuramu	crying, across the sky—
mono omou yado no	the dew on the bush clover
hagi no e no tsuyu	about my brooding abode.

The link, in other words, is made more interesting through the allusion to the sentimental conceit in the *Kokinshū* poem; possibly the pleasure of inscribing such an allusion and having the other participants recognize it was more important in this case than the sentiment itself.

93	mi ni kagiru	Not I alone
	namida naraji to	weep these tears—
	nagusamete	I solace myself.
	Norishige	Norishige
94	shina koso kaware	Desire takes various forms, yes,
	yo wa ukarikere	but 'tis all one world of misery!
	Nagatoshi	Nagatoshi

Love: *shina* (kinds, degrees), *yo* (the world, here, of love). Laments: *ukiyo* (miserable world).

The words *ushi* (miserable, depressing) and *ukiyo* are classified under Laments in *Renju* 900, but given the sense of the maeku and the allusion to the *shina sadame* section in the "Hahakigi" (Broomtree) chapter of the *Genji* here, the main theme is probably Love. Still, one can only agree with Shinkei's observation that it is not always possible to distinguish between Love and Laments, since the one tends naturally to slide into the other.[28]

As distinct from link 92/93, where the speaker finds "solace" in the thought that even nature partakes of sorrow like his, here the comfort is to be found in the more philosophical attitude that love or, more properly, desire, dooms everyone, not only the maeku's persona, to suffering. The ranks and degrees, the circumstance and object, of each attachment might change (*shina koso kaware*), but the misery is all the same; desire in all its varied manifestations redounds to one result. One wonders if this allusion to the *Genji* implies Nagatoshi's judgment that the novel is indeed beguiling in its depiction of various forms of love but it is ultimately one long tale of woe.

This verse initiates a passage of content-oriented discourse running until 96; in 97 Sogi shifts to the mode of "objective" description, which continues until 99, and the sequence ends, appropriately, in the auspicious spirit of verse 100.

94	shina koso kaware	Desire takes various forms, yes,
	yo wa ukarikere	but 'tis all one world of misery!
	Nagatoshi	Nagatoshi
95	me no mae ni	Awake and be amazed:
	aru o odoroke	the six realms of illusion are
	mutsu no michi	right before your eyes!
	Sōetsu	Sōetsu

Buddhism: *mutsu no michi* (the six realms).

The maeku concept that all variety is a function of one and the same becomes translated here into the Buddhist principle of non-dualism; all phenomena are but provisional aspects of one ultimate principle. The so-called "six realms or worlds" (better known in its *on*-reading, *rokudō*)—of hell, hungry ghosts, beasts, demons, humans, and heavenly beings—through which one allegedly transmigrates according to the degree of one's merits, or lack of same, belong to the world of ignorant desire, which is all "one world of misery." These six worlds are not anywhere else but here, "right before your eyes" (*me no mae ni / aru*); you have only to look into yourself and all around you to see that everyone suffers, whether in castle or hovel. When you have, through spiritual discipline, attained enlightenment, you will see that these distinctions are all illusory.

95	me no mae ni	Awake and be amazed:
	aru o odoroke	the six realms of illusion are
	mutsu no michi	right before your eyes!
	Sōetsu	Sōetsu
96	manabu mo utoki	The principle of poetry remains,
	uta no kotowari	despite all one's study, obscure.
	Shinkei	Shinkei

Miscellaneous.

(The Temmangū Text has *mukau*, "face, confront," instead of the "study" [*manabu*] in the Nozaka Text; in this case the two verbs are synonymous in that both are actions by a subject vis-à-vis an object, and Shinkei's point is that this is not the way to understand things.) In the passage from 94, which has successively touched upon the large topoi of Love, Laments, and Buddhism, Shinkei now adds the theme of poetry in a characteristic statement: "the principle of poetry" (*uta no kotowari*), that is, its truth, which is founded on emptiness, cannot be understood only through diligent study; it requires as well an intuition generated by direct personal experience, that is, through the way of Zen meditation. Technically, the implicit link here is between the maeku's "six worlds" and the so-called "six principles" (*rikugi*) of poetry. Better understood as the six modes of poetic expression, the concept represents a theory of poetic types that Shinkei defines and illustrates in section 35 of *Sasamegoto*. The point of the link is that like the concept of various worlds in Buddhism, the idea of categories in poetry will not lead one to its essential nature, which transcends, while encompassing, these. Like the truth of Buddhism, poetic truth is "right before your eyes" (*me no mae ni aru*), it only needs an open, infinitely expansive mind to grasp it. In both poetry and Buddhism, and as we know Shinkei's criticism fuses the two, categorical distinctions have only a provisional reality; the point is to leap right into the source, that is, the Original Mind, "the ground of the mind" (*shinji*) or the ultimate *kokoro* itself, and experience it directly. Given Shinkei's philosophy, the link from Buddhism to poetry at this juncture in the sequence is indeed revealing of its author.

96	manabu mo utoki	The principle of poetry remains,
	uta no kotowari	despite all one's study, obscure.
	Shinkei	Shinkei
97	ura tōku	Remotely mysterious
	tamatsushimayama	across the bay, Isle of Jewels
	uchikasumu	enveloped in haze.
	Sōgi	Sōgi

Spring: *kasumu* (be hazy). Named Place: Tamatsushima. Word Association: *uta* (poetry) = Tamatsushima.

Another impressive link between the two leading poets of the group; it is almost as if Sōgi is reading Shinkei's mind in evoking here the ideal of ineffable depth, or profound ambiguity, called *yūgen*. He links to the poetry theme through the place-name Tamatsushima (lit., "Island of Jewels"), shrine of the god of poetry Tamatsushima-myōjin. Located on the coast of Wakanoura in Kii Province (Wakayama), it was the object of sacred pilgrimage by contemporary poets.[29] Along with that of two other poetry deities, the gods of Sumiyoshi and Kitano, the worship of Tamatsushima as the divine fount of poetic inspiration was very active in the medieval period. *Ura tōku*, which I have rendered "remotely mysterious across the bay," puns on *ura* as both "bay" and "interior/underside" (as opposed to surface). And of course it resonates with *utoku* (obscure, remote, difficult) in the maeku, restating Shinkei's statement on the difficulty of grasping the essence of poetry by saying that it is subtle and profound, and so alluding to the ideal of *yūgen*.

With this verse, Sōgi simultaneously converts Shinkei's philosophical discourse into a concrete image, in effect shifting to a tranquil mood in anticipation of the session's imminent end.

97	ura tōku	Remotely mysterious
	tamatsushimayama	across the bay, Isle of Jewels
	uchikasumu	enveloped in haze.
	Sōgi	Sōgi
98	haru shiru oto no	Spring is audible in the sound:
	yowaki matsukaze	soft murmur of the pine breeze.
	Kaku'a	Kaku'a

Spring: *haru* (spring).

Kaku'a maintains the maeku's objective and tranquil mode, merely contrasting the near perspective of pine trees along the bay with Sōgi's distant view of the haze-covered island across the water.

98	haru shiru oto no	Spring is audible in the sound:
	yowaki matsukaze	soft murmur of the pine breeze.
	Kaku'a	Kaku'a
99	hana ni nomi	With the flowers alone
	kokoro o noboru	breathes the heart at ease
	yūmagure	this glimmering dusk.
	Mitsusuke	Mitsusuke

Spring: *hana* (flowers).

The spring-like feeling in the soft murmur (*oto no yowaki*) of the pine breeze is translated here into the equally gentle stirring of white cherry blossoms. The breeze is so delicate, as if it cherishes the fragile blooms, that the heart can remain tranquil (*kokoro o noboru*), free from the anxiety that they might scatter. This reading takes *haru shiru . . . kaze* in the maeku to mean literally that "the wind knows it is spring," and so blows only faintly. By itself, the verse evokes the stillness of a spring dusk, when the mind-heart is wholly vacant, taken out of itself as it were by a rapt contemplation of the white flowers in the growing evening.

99	hana ni nomi	With the flowers alone
	kokoro o noboru	breathes the heart at ease
	yūmagure	this glimmering dusk.
	Mitsusuke	Mitsusuke
100	sakari naru mi zo	May it span through long years,
	yowai hisashiki	this life at its glorious height.
	Ikuhiro	Ikuhiro

Miscellaneous.

The session ends typically with an auspicious verse, here, congratulating the participants or, as would be more likely, the host of the gathering, for the fullness of his years, and wishing him an even longer life. The wish is beautifully rendered in the image of the cherry blossoms which are themselves now at the height of their flowering.

Total Number of Verses: Shinkei 19 Sōgi 16 Nagatoshi 12 Norishige 11 Mitsusuke 10 Sōetsu 10 Kaku'a 8 Shun'a 6 Ikuhiro 5 Hōzen 2 Ken'a 1

One Hundred Poems

I close the "Reader" with a personal selection of one hundred poems highlighting the salient characteristics of Shinkei's aesthetic sensibility. Whereas the biography culled from four dated hyakushu, with their eloquent autobiographical resonances, these poems are mostly from two comprehensive collections not used earlier (except for three pieces). A few among them, such as "Moon on the Mountain" and "Winter Rains in the Old Village," do recall the mode of laments thematized in the biography, but many are wholly impersonal evocations of scenery.

The impersonality cannot be understood apart from the attitude of contemplation or "deep thought" (*chinshi*) that Shinkei required of serious poetry. Nor can one neglect the crucial influence of Zen meditation on medieval poetic practice. It is palpable in the trance-like state in which a scene—the event—registers itself with a clarity and immediacy beyond mundane perception, and so requiring from the reader a like concentration. Again, many of the poems evoke a sense of the ineffableness of phenomena, their coming into and trailing out of the perceptual field through an interrelation whose remote beginning and end are beyond rational calculation. To thus stalk the interstices of things, to simultaneously incise and dissolve their solidity, is also to use language against itself, to stalk the silence that trails the verbal like a shadow.

As for the rest, readers of Japanese will undoubtedly register Shinkei's terse and fragmented renga-like idiom, his fondness for the doubleness of the zeugma, his occasionally unpolished (even awkward) syntax, and radically fresh conceptions. I have tried to follow the dictum "less is more" in translation, but have frequently broken it in order to transmit more than the nothing that would result from the pieces that were beyond my powers.

From *Bishop Shinkei's Waka in Ten Styles*[1]

The Style of Meditation (*Ushintei*)

Flowers in the Old Village

fukaki yo no	In deepest night
noki no shinobu ni	about my moss-grown eaves
tsuyu ochite	dew falls,
hana ni kasumeru	a hazy shimmer on the flowers,
ariake no tsuki	shadow of the lingering moon.

Fireflies

hotaru kie	The fireflies dimmed,
noki no shinobu no	along my yearning-moss eaves
shitatsuyu ni	the hanging dewdrops
hikari soiyuku	slowly follow the light as
shinonome no sora	dawn streaks the eastern sky.

Old House in Moonlight

yado fukaki	In a house deep
yomogi ga tsuyu ni	within rank weeds the moon
tsuki fukete	ages with the dew,
munashi kuruma ni	fleeting, on the carriage—
nokoru omokage	the shadow of a memory.

Moon on the Mountain

mate shibashi	Stay a while longer,
waga itsuwari no	O moonlight hovering on
aramashi o	the mountain crest,
susumuru yama ni	recalling me to what I once
kakaru tsukikage	desired with a lying heart!

Crimson Foliage

susuki chiru	As reed plumes scatter
kareno no ue no	through white mists of dawn
asagiri ni	upon withered fields,
nokoru mo usuki	hanging on but faintly, a tinge
mine no momijiba	of red leaves on the peak.

Mountain Rose in Winter

miru mama ni	While I gaze out
hana no hoka sae	on a scene empty of flowers
yamabuki no	in the gloaming dusk,
iro ni nariyuku	distant huts turn the color
yūgure no yado	of molten mountain rose.

Moon in Late Autumn

aki no yuku
kokoro mo sazona
susuki chiru
kareno no ue ni
hosoki tsukikage

Departing autumn
bares here its very soul—
upon shriveled fields
of scattering plume grass,
gaunt silhouettes in moonlight.

Winter Rains in the Old Village

kono yo yori
furinuru yado no
sayoshigure
ukimi o koke no
shita ni kiku kana

Cast off by the times,
my ruined abode on this night
of chill rains—
does it hear my desolate soul
beneath the silent moss . . .

The Bell on a Frosty Night

shirotae no
shimotsu izumo no
koe fukete
miyako no yume ni
sayuru kane kana

White as purest cloth,
frost glistens in the echoing
silence at Izumo,
as a dream of the beloved city
chills in the clear cold bell.

Traveler Crossing a Bridge

tanomishi wa
yo o hayakawa no
ukihashi ni
hitori tadayou
ato no tabibito

The sum of my hopes:
along the floating bridge of
the times' swift river,
a lone figure falters on the
dwindling journey's trail.

A Receding Feeling at Dawn

yoyo no yume
tou wa kokoro no
sue kiete
tomoshibi aoki
akatsuki no ame

Nightly reaching out
in the wake of a dream, soul
as a wick dwindles,
a lamp flame flickering green—
the rain falling in the dawn.

Style of Ineffable Depth (*Yūgen*)

Pure Waters of Spring

yama takami
yuki no shitamizu
kasumu nari
ochikuru koe mo
kiyoki haru kana

In mountains high,
water pooling under the snow
hazes over in clouds,
while down below drips cool and
clear the sound of springtime.

Water Rail

yamazato wa
mizu no hibiki mo
kasukanaru

Mountain hamlet—
as the water murmurs faint
as the moonlit shadow

sugima no tsuki ni
kuina naku nari

behind the cedars comes
the soft tapping of a rail.

Mosquito Fires

kurekakaru
sueno no ie'i
uchikemuri
kayari ni kasumu
mori no hitomura

In the growing dusk,
the huts on the field's edge
turn to a murky shadow,
as mosquito fires draw a filmy
haze before the shrine grove.

Insects at Dawn

yowa no mushi
koe no chigusa no
iro nagara
hana ni nariyuku
shinonome no niwa

A myriad colors
in black of midnight, the
insects' voices
slowly turn to flowers, as
dawn glides over the garden.

Deer in the Evening Mountain

yūgure wa
tōzakariyuku
yama no ha o
nokiba ni kaesu
saojika no koe

As evening settles,
receding far in the distance,
the mountain's outline
returns close beside my eaves
in the voice of the wild deer.

A Wild Duck

oyamada ya
akatsuki samumi
naku kamo no
tsubasa kakikumoru
tsuki wa shigurete

Upland rice paddies—
a wild duck cries in the
coldness of dawn,
wings roiling the shadows
beneath the raining moon.

Hail in the Night

koboretsuru
arare wa sugite
fukaki yo ni
hitori oto suru
noki no matsukaze

Shattering the sky,
the hailstones passed on, and
far into the night—
alone the sound of the wind
brushing the pines by my eaves.

Remaining Wild Goose over the Inlet

fukenikeri
katabuku tsuki mo
tōki e no
kōri ni otsuru
kari no hitokoe

Deep is the night.
As the moon declines along
the frozen surface
of the distant inlet falls
the sheer cry of a wild goose.

Love in Winter

okiizuru
yume mo kareno no

In the parting wake
of dawn on withered fields

kinuginu ni	the dream too casts
omokage samuki	a shadow cold as the moon
yama no ha no tsuki	above the mountain ridge.

The Arresting Style (*Mempakutei*)

Bush Warbler

yuki wa mina	The snows wholly
koe yori tokete	from its voice melted away,
uguisu no	the warbler, with the
iro ni kusaki mo	plants and trees bursts forth,
nareru haru kana	in the colors of springtime!

Plum Blossoms in the Night

kokoro naki	A bird of no-mind
tori zo uguisu	indeed, the bush warbler—
yomosugara	all the night long
nioeru ume no	within the wafting scent of
hana ni nenuran	plum blossoms, sweetly asleep!

Flowers by the Travel Inn

fuke arashi	Blow, winds of storm,
mata ya nezaran	again sleep would fail me
kasumu yo no	on this hazy night,
tsuki no tamakura	arm pillowing but moonlight,
hana no samushiro	fallen petals a cold sward.

Frogs in Spring Meadow

kawazu naku	Where frogs croak on
tanomo no kogusa	the field face, so tender the
sue yowami	tips of the tiny plants,
koe ni wakaba no	each cry scatters in alarm
tsuyu mo midarete	the dew on the young leaves.

Moon on the River

konoma moru	Through trees drenched
tsuki ni kawaoto	with moonlight, the river sound
sayo fukete	is hushed with night;
fune ni hito naki	only an empty boat stirs in a
uji no yamakaze	drifting wind from the Uji hills.

Evening Fog on the Inlet

tomoshibi mo	As the wavering flame
hosoe no hashi no	at the narrow inlet's point
yūgiri ni	through evening fog,
mukai no mura ya	the barking of a dog echoes
inu no koe shite	from the dark hamlet beyond.

Morning After a Typhoon

asa madaki	In the gray dawn
mushi ni tsuyu kau	there is no plant with dew
kusa mo nashi	to feed the insects:
yowa no nowaki no	ravaged garden in the wake of
niwa ni midarete	a field-cleaving night storm.

Still Garden in Frost

ogi no ha zo	When did the reed leaves
hitori ochinuru	crumple up, all on their own—
shimo no niwa	Frost garden
fukeyuku tsuki wa	beneath a starkly aging moon:
kaze mo soyogazu	stilled in motion the wind.

Snow in Moonlight

yuki omoru	Weighed with snow,
toyama no kozue	the boughs on the foothills
shita orete	crack from below, and
machiaezu izuru	straining at the wait breaks out,
tsuki no sayakesa	so dazzling white, the moon.

Woodcutter on the Road at Dusk

takigi toru	Gathering kindling
ochi no yamabito	yonder the woodsman seems to
isogu nari	quicken in motion,
yūgure hakobu	as the dusk is borne aloft on
kane no hibiki ni	the dimming echoes of the bell.

Mountain Hermit's Water

waga tame ya	Is it for my sake—
kakehi ni ukete	receiving on the bamboo trough
matsu no ha mo	the pine needles also
koke no iori ni	I carry into the mossy hut,
hakobu yamamizu	with the mountain water.

The Style of Balanced Harmony (*Reitei*)

Haze over the Searoute

suma no ura ya	The coast of Suma?
kokorozukushi ni	Departing on a boat, weary of
funade seshi	heart, that storied past
mukashi mo tōku	withdraws yet farther in the
kasumu nami kana	nebulous wake of the waves.

Bush Warbler by the Hermit's Hut

haru to dani	Even in springtime,
hito ya oto senu	one hears not from people here

yamakage no
take no to akuru
uguisu no koe

in the mountain's shadow,
the bamboo gate opens at dawn
to the bush warbler's song.

Remaining Snow in the Valley

hito no mi ka
tani no shibahashi
haru no kuru
ato dani miezu
fureru shirayuki

It's not only people—
brushwood bridge in the valley:
even the marks of
spring's arrival are hidden,
beneath a white snowfall.

Clouds in Summer Hills

kono yūbe
yama no ha kiyoki
samidare no
nagori suzushiki
tsuki no usugumo

This evening how pure
the outline of the hills after
the summer rains,
their traces cool in wisps of
cloud lined with moonlight.

Crickets After a Rain

murasame wa
sugi no ha kumoru
yamamoto no
yūhi ni yowaki
higurashi no koe

Passing shower:
from clouded cedar boughs on
the mountain base,
feeble the cries of cicadas
in the dusky evening light.

Shintō Dances in Deep Night

fukuru yo no
shimo ni mo karezu
kirigirisu
niwabi ya nuruki
mori no shitagusa

In the chill frost of
advancing night unwithered
the chirp of crickets;
garden torches warmly damp
on the shrine grove underbrush?

Moonlight Like Snow

orefusu mo
yuki ya wa omoki
nowaki seshi
kusaki no ue no
aki no tsukikage

All crumpled and torn—
would snow have been so heavy?
In the typhoon's wake
upon the plants and trees,
reflection of the autumn moon.

Hidden-Love Tryst

honokanaru
mayu no nioi mo
yosome uki
neya ni somukuru
tomoshibi no kage

A delicate perfume,
your dimly drawn brow seems to
shy from people's eyes,
as the lamp flame that flickers
away from the bed curtains.

Love in Repeated Nights of Waiting

tsurenashi na
iku mikazuki ni

It is too cruel—
how many nights has waxed

utsururan
chigirishi mama no
ariake no kage

the crescent moon,
while a vow remained stilled
in its meager light at dawn.

Herons Along the Inlet

uchisosogi
mizu mo yurugazu
furu ame no
hosoe ni kasumu
sagi no hitotsura

As it drizzles, barely
rippling the water, the rain
hangs a hazy veil
over the line of white herons,
along the slender inlet shore.

The Lofty Style (*Chōkōtei*)

Plum Blossoms Deep in the Night

fukaki yo no
ume no nioi ni
yume samete
kosu makiaenu
sode no harukaze

Trailing a scent of
plum blossoms deep in the night,
the dream dissolves—
barely lifting the reed blinds,
spring breeze along my sleeves.

Hunting by Torchlight

tomoshi suru
nobe no saojika
natsu no yo mo
mi ni shimo fureru
yume wa miyuramu

The stag in the glare
of torchlights across the fields—
even in the summer night
must feel itself chilled in
a dream of fallen frost.

The Evening Shower Clears

iroiro no
kuchiba nagarete
miyamaji wa
ishihara takaki
yūdachi no ato

From a myriad trees,
a whirling of dead leaves deep in
the mountain trail, then
high and bare the rocks loom—
sheer wake of the evening shower.

Dew on the Summer Grass

yamazato no
yūkage kusa ni
tsuyu ochite
konu aki fukaki
higurashi no koe

Gloaming on the grass
in the mountain village, dew
falls, still to come,
anon autumn wells deep within
the clear tones of the cicada.

Dew at Dawn

yogareyuku
yomogi ga sue no
tsuyu samumi
ariake no niwa ya
tsuki no furusato

The dew is so cold
on the tips of the mugwort grass
as the night shrivels,
the garden seems transfigured—
a desolate village of the moon.

Hail on the Roof

waga io no
noki no sugifuki
sue kuchite
tsutau arare no
koe zo mijikaki

Along the eaves of
my cottage, the cedar shingles
decay at the ends,
a patter of hail abruptly
plunged in emptiness.

Moon in the Mountains in Winter

miyamakaze
konoha fukimaku
koe taete
koke no mushiro ni
tsuki zo fukeyuku

The sound of the wind
swirling the dead leaves falls
silent in the hills, as
deep in the mossy swards sinks
the spent rays of moonlight.

Old Mountain Monkey

yo zo fukaki
kozue yori nishi ni
tsuki ochite
yokawa no mine no
saru no hitokoe

Deep is the night.
As the moon glides down behind
the treetops to the west,
the piercing cry of a monkey
high on the slopes of Yokowa.

The Intricate Style (*Nōtei*)

Swallow

sode chikaku
irikuru tsubame
ochikata ni
kaeru ha hayaki
kosu no hatakaze

Tripping in close
by my sleeves, the swallow
in a split flash
of wings whirled back yonder:
blinds quivering in empty air.

Love in the Lamp Flame's Image

machifukete
izureba neya ni
kage zo sou
namida ni fukashi
yowa no tomoshibi

Waiting-spent, I
come out of the bedroom, and
its shadow follows,
looming large through my tears,
the lamp flame at midnight.

The Style of Lessons for Humanity (*Bumintei*)

The Flowers Swift or Late

tameshi uki
kono yo ni sakite
sue no tsuyu
moto no shizuku to
hana zo ochiyuku

Blooming in the world,
a virtual image of its sorrow,
as the dew from treetop
or boughs dripping down low,
fall the flowers, everywhere.

Wind in the Mountain Cottage

yūmagure
nokiba no yama zo

Vagueness of dusk—
the mountains by my eaves

iro mienu	dissolve in form,
matsu wa arashi no	yet the vanished pines remain
koe ni nokorite	in the voice of the moving wind.

Unfolding a Scroll, Learning the Past

makisuteshi	Brushing live moths away
uchito no fumi ni	from long forgotten scrolls of
sumu mushi o	holy and secular writing,
harau tamoto ni	I find upon my sleeves
tsuyu zo koboruru	the dew of tears brimming over.

The Style of Singular Conception (*Issetsutei*)

Falling Leaves

taema naku	Rather than the
sasou kaze yori	ceaselessly drawing wind,
tada hitoha	but a single leaf
kokoro ni otsuru	falling within the soul—
yama zo shizukeki	the utter quiet of mountains.

Hailstones on Bamboo

yo o samumi	The night is so cold
sawagu to kikeba	it sounded like cries of alarm,
muratori wa	village birds—
negura no take ni	upon their roost in the bamboos,
chiru arare kana	the crisp patter of hailstones.

Grass Hut in Rain

okiidete	Getting up I cast out
waga morisutsuru	into a midnight gloom that
yowa mo ushi	would not be barred:
ame o aruji no	the frail grass hut in
kusa no kariio	the grip of the falling rain.

Wind in the Reeds

yūmagure	In the dusky shadow
konomoto susuki	of the trees the autumn wind
sumizome no	stirs among the reeds
sode tou iro no	in shades drawn to the color
akikaze zo fuku	of my ink-dyed monk's sleeves.

The Style of Valuing the Old (*Sonkotei*)

Wind Over the Autumn Rice Fields

kari nakite	Wild geese cry,
akikaze samumi	and so cold the gusts of autumn
waga yado no	over the hill paddies
yamada no yanagi	about my hut, the willows shed
shita wa chiru koro	from their tips a golden shower.

Winter Moon over the Mountain Cottage

yamazato wa	In the cries of
yamome karasu no	the lone crow echoing in
nakigoe ni	the mountain village,
shimoyo no tsuki no	one senses the piercing rays
kage o shiru kana	of the frosty night moon.

The Stark Style (*Gōrikitei*)

Mosquito-Repellent Fire Next Door

naraisumu	Of long habit inured,
shizuya no kahi no	humble folks' mosquito fires
utsuriga ni	send an acrid scent with
sode ni urusaki	a humming din about my sleeves—
tabi no karifushi	this restless bed on a journey.

Summer Bamboo

natsu zo naki	It cannot be summer—
saeda kirisute	dripping through freshly cut
take no hi ni	pipes of bamboo,
mizu wa shirakasu	the water is chillingly white
yama no shitakage	in the mountain's shadow.

Summer Sun

terinikeri	Brightness explodes!
natsu no sueno no	From the far end of the summer
asahikage	fields, the morning sun
kusaba o yoru no	leaves not one drop of night dew
tsuyu mo nokosade	on the glowing leaves of plants.

Winds Before Moonlight

yū sareba	As evening falls,
arashi o fukumi	swollen with stormy winds
tsuki o haku	it spits the moon:
aki no takane no	the looming peak of autumn,
matsu samuku shite	pines chill along the crest.

Mostly from an Untitled Collection[2]

Hearthsmoke over a Distant Village

nagaresu ni	Rowing up to the
obune kogisute	rippling sandbar, he discards
kemuri tatsu	the boat for the village
irie no mura ni	by the inlet where smoke rises:
kaeru tsuribito	a fisherman returning home.

Pines by the Eaves

fukikudaru
arashi ya mine ni
  yowaruran
fumoto no noki o
uzumu shirakumo

In the gusting descent
down from the peaks, did the
  storm exhaust itself?
eaves piled with white clouds
at the foot of the mountain.

Mountain Abode

sumeba ya na
tou hito mare no
  mizu kiyoku
kozue furitaru
yama no shitaio

Ah, to dwell where
people seldom visit, and pure
  the water streams
from the time-dimmed treetops
to the cottage on the foothill.

Cicada in the Forest

watatsumi no
nami ya utsusemi
  koegoe ni
sawagu nagisa no
mori no shitakaze

From out at sea,
the swollen wave crashes in
  a din of cicada voices,
as along the shore the winds
glide in beneath the forest.

Smoke over a Distant Village

taedae no
michi mo keburi mo
  hi kurureba
musubōreyuku
sue no yamamoto

Dwindling, the trail,
the smoke, as evening settles,
  merge into a darkness
choking the inmost recesses
of the farthest foothills.

Wind in the Willows

asamidori
sora wa kasumite
  furu ame no
yanagi ni haruru
niwa no harukaze

Greenness at dawn:
with the falling rain the
  clouded sky lifts
from the willows, as a spring
breeze stirs across the garden.

Travel-Lodging Robe

koromode ni
tsui ni utsusanu
  sumizome no
yūbe no yama wa
waga yado mo nashi

It did not stay,
in the end, upon my sleeves—
  the ink-dyed mountain
at evening is as a monk's robe,
yet finds not my shelter there.

Morning Flowers

yamazakura
iro mo nioi mo
  uchishimeri
hana ni chirasanu
haru no asatsuyu

Deep mountain cherries:
a rosy tint drenching in
  fragrance the air
unruffled upon the flowers
still dews of a spring dawn.

Lovers' Parting in the Image of Flowers

kinuginu no
iro minu yowa no
michishiba ni
yukue kasumeru
hana no ka mo ushi

From the wayside plants,
hidden in deep night as the
afterglow of a tryst,
the scent of blossoms clouds
in sadness the homeward path.

Rice-Seedling Beds

asatsuyu no
okabe no sanae
wakite matsu
midori zo takaki
haru no nawashiro

Pushing up through the
morning dews on the hillslope
the young shoots await,
so keen in their green,
the rice seedlings of spring!

Deutzia Flowers

nami ya koru
shii no wakaba no
urakaze mo
nao shirotae no
mine no unohana

As a wave cresting,
the baywind as it blows back
the young oak leaves
surges to a gleaming white—
deutzia blooms high on the peak.

Cuckoo

hitokoe wa
aoba yori idete
aoba yori
iro koki ono no
yamahototogisu

That single cry
issuing from green leaves
cast a verdure
yet deeper over the meadow,
cuckoo from the mountains.

Deutzia Flowers in Their First Bloom

yūzukuyo
kasumi mo niou
kage nare ya
sakiizuru ochi no
mine no unohana

Moon-risen evening:
even the haze seems perfumed
in its reflection—
faint white drift of deutzia
afloat on the mountain crest.

Farm Birds

murasuzume
ochiho o hirou
sato no ko no
tamoto ni sawagu
aki no yamakaze

A flock of sparrows:
picking at the fallen grain
beside the farmchild's
sleeve, scatter in alarm—
as autumn gusts from the hills.

Mosquito-Repellent Fires

kayari taku
sora ni susukete
yūzukuyo
hikari kasumeru
shizu ga yamazato

Burning mosquito fires
smudge with soot the evening sky,
and the rising moon
spreads in a filmy haze over
the rustic mountain village.

Deutzia Flowers

kumo no nami
koete mo kiezu
iwagane ni
yoru shiranami ya
kishi no unohana

Is it a white wave
drawn to the cloud-wave that
rolled past, leaving it
clinging to the rocky crag?
deutzia blooms along the beach!

Evening Shower

ochikata ni
furikuru kumo no
ashi hayami
yuku hito sasou
yūdachi no sora

Off in the distance
the dripping cloud approaches
on feet so swift
they draw the traveler forward
beneath the evening-shower sky.

Love, a Listening

tamadare mo
hedatete kakeshi
chigiri sae
kareyuku koe no
okufukaku naru

The love we vowed across
a barrier greater than jeweled
blinds, even so turns
distant as your voice, to echo
deep in the recesses of my mind.

Moon on the Waves

shiranami no
kage wa sawagite
ashi no ha no
tsuyu ni zo fukuru
aki no yo no tsuki

A tremor disturbs
the sheen on the white waves,
as on the reed leaves
the moon deepens with the dews
in the autumn night.

Quail by the Inlet

hi kurureba
irie o tatete
kusagakure
fushimi no nobe ni
uzura naku nari

As darkness falls,
from along the curving inlet
a quail wings off,
its voice a secluded echo in
the deep grass of Fushimi moors.

Autumn Frost

shimo nare ya
nete no asake no
hana no himo
mijikaku tokuru
aki no hi no kage

Could it be frost?
Cords round the sleepy flowers
in the morning air,
undone, oh how shortly,
in light of the autumn sun!

Distant Sound of the Fulling Block

ochikochi no
sue wa hakarete
kusagoromo
utsu koe nabiku
nobe no akikaze

Fathoming the
margins of near and far,
garment of grass—
the pounding beat wavers in
the autumn wind over the meadow.

Warbler

furu yuki ni
musubōrenuru
uguisu no
naku ne fukitoke
nobe no harukaze

Thick smothered
in the falling snow, the song
of the bush warbler,
in your melting breath set free,
O spring breeze in the meadow!

Frost on the Bridge

asa madaki
mine no kakehashi
kasumu nari
ochikatabito ni
shimo mayouran

In the early dawn
the bridge hanging from the peak
is clouded in haze;
as the distant figure below
uncertain seems the frost.

Dwelling in Tranquillity

tomo to seshi
kokoro ya yama o
idenuran
manako ni utsuru
noki no matsukaze

The mind I had made
a companion, has it gone away
from the mountain?
reflected on the empty eye,
pine winds along the eaves.

Willows Along the River

midarenuru
yanagi no kami no
kushidagawa
toku koso mizu no
haru no asakaze

Along Combfield River,
the tangled willow strands
loosen in waves
as the melted waters glide in
the breezes of a spring morning.

Enjoying the Evening Cool in Summer

sumizome no
tamoto ni usuki
miyamakaze
tsuki ni suzu fuku
yūgure no sora

Lightly stirring
along my ink-black sleeves
deep in the mountain,
winds blow cool the faint disk
of the moon in the evening sky.

Voices of Insects Beneath the Hedge

iro mienu
hana koso nakere
yūgure no
magaki ni niou
mushi no koegoe

In truth the hue
on the flowers is apparent—
in the shadowed dusk
the dim hedgerow is fragrant
with a myriad insects' voices.

Hearing the Cuckoo

hototogisu
suginishi koe o
nokosu kana
kururu fumoto no
sugi no murakumo

The cuckoo—
left its cry behind as
it flew past:
stilled cloud on the cedar grove
as evening dims on the foothills.

Clouds at Dawn by the Sea

> akenuru ka
> matsu no hagoshi ni
> hiku kumo no
> nami ni wakaruru
> ano no tōyama

> Apparition of dawn:
> the clouds slowly brush off
> the tips of the pines,
> departing in waves from the sea—
> the distant peaks of Mount Ano.

Plum Tree on Journey's Path

> kurenai wa
> iro mo susamaji
> hitoe ni zo
> aware mo tomaru
> ume no shitakage

> Crimson, the hue
> braces chill the mind;
> single-petaled,
> arresting all pathos—
> shade of the plum tree.

Autumn Mist over the Ancient Ferry Crossing

> kumo kudari
> kiri furu ama no
> tatsu no nada
> sanagara fune o
> makeru nami kana

> Clouds descend, and
> mists rain down from the heavens
> at Dragon's Crossing—
> where soon the boat is tossing
> in the grip of the coiling waves.

Bush Warbler on the Neighbor's Bamboo

> nakagaki o
> ware ni hedatezu
> yukiore no
> take no hazutau
> uguisu no koe

> Heedless of
> the hedge in between, from
> snow-bent leaves
> of bamboo reaching out
> to me, the warbler's call!

Cloud on Evening Mountain

> hitori nomi
> koke no tobira ni
> irikuru mo
> kumo wa oto senu
> yūgure no yama

> My sole guest,
> even in entering the moss-grown
> doors makes no
> sound of footfall, cloud on
> the mountain at sundown.

Moon on the Mountain

> murasame no
> haruru mo matanu
> tsukikage o
> sode ni machitoru
> yama no ha no tsuki

> Not waiting till
> the raincloud has passed off,
> the gleaming rays
> are caught on its sleeve—
> mountain ridge at moonrise.

Sky Dimming in Snow over the Inlet

> murakamome
> ashi no ha shiroki
> yuki no e ni
> iro wakareyuku
> yūgure no sora

> A flock of seagulls—
> whitely from among the reeds
> on the snowy inlet,
> a blankness slowly recedes
> into the dimming evening sky.

Epilogue

Summer is the most appropriate season to visit the site of Shinkei's final abode in the Ōyama foothills. It is even better when the *samidare* rains are falling. From the Odakyū Line's Isehara station, Ishikura is a mere fifteen minutes' ride on the bus headed for the mountain. One gets off at the Ishikurabashi intersection and follows a small wooden sign marked *Shinkei-zuka* (The Shinkei grave mound). Across a hedge of purple and white azaleas, one leaves the main road and enters a narrow dirt trail between rice fields stretching fresh and emerald green beneath a rain-clouded sky. The still reflection of young rice plants on the water-flooded paddies is cool and startlingly clear. Farther up, the sound of a stream gurgling between the rocks is increasingly louder as one approaches an old stone bridge just around the bend. The Ōyama River has its source up in the mountain, where it creates some lovely waterfalls before flowing southeast to Ishikura. From here it meanders on a southerly course for some ten miles and finally empties into Sagami Bay. This is the same "long river whose leaping springs laved the moss and washed the shifting pebbles to a gleaming smoothness" in *Oi no kurigoto*. Here in a farmer's private land its waters have remained fresh and clear. The crooked wooden bridge where the poet used to linger at dusk, waiting for the evening moon to rise, must have been hereabouts.

Today there is not a soul abroad. Still splattering on the dirt road, the rain seems to vanish in the greenness of the rice fields. The farmer is not there, and only a long silence follows the peal of the doorbell to his house with its gleaming blue rooftiles. Around the back then, one follows a short hillside path between slender young bamboos into what is evidently a persimmon grove. Shoes sinking into the soft wet earth, one attempts to walk amidst the rank undergrowth of mugwort weeds and here and there some stray blue dayflowers. Small hard persimmons lie scattered about on the brown earth, each one a round green head set in the middle of a stiff four-petaled collar. The old site of the Jōgyōji Temple, there is nothing here to mark the final dwelling of the man whom a local inhabitant, dead these many years, reported having heard described by his own grandfather as *Nippon ichi no utayomi* ("the greatest poet of Japan"). Now in the closed silence within the grove, only the sound of rain comes dripping long and slow through the trees. On the mugwort leaves dewdrops glisten pale in the dark.

Outside the rain is pouring harder. The great peak of Mount Ōyama to the north is completely hidden behind clouds. They drift and change formation incessantly as one watches. Once in a while the outlines of taller mountains are tantalizingly discernible. On a higher hill behind the grove there is an ancient burial mound known in the local oral tradition as Shinkei's grave. Here on clear days one can glimpse the glinting waters of Sagami Bay far in the distance. If the local tradition is indeed correct, then it was here that Kenzai and the others gathered in the spring of 1482 to compose the hundred-verse memorial sequence.

Barely a kilometer east of Ishikura lies the old site of the Uesugi Kazuya Mansion where Shinkei used to hold renga sessions and Ōta Dōkan was murdered more than a decade later. But all this, including Ishikura, used to be Uesugi territory. Now it is principally a residential area, a pleasant walk between flowering hedges, and now and then large tracts of open land planted to vegetables. Across a peanut field dotted with yellow flowers, one notices a small shrine dedicated to the Ōta clan. It gives one pause, and summons a reflection on the role of ancestor worship in the preservation of local history.

Of the buildings in the old Kazuya estate, only the Tōshōin Temple survives, though not of course in its original structure. It is situated beside a bamboo grove, which is all that is visible from the main road. One enters the temple along a modest avenue lined with plum trees. Here on the twenty-first of April 1974, renga scholars, poets, and local historians held a memorial on the five-hundredth anniversary of Shinkei's death, perhaps the very first since Kenzai himself passed away. Lectures were delivered, and in a not unfitting tribute, a hundred-verse haikai sequence composed. To further mark the occasion, another recently recovered piece of Shinkei's writing was exhibited for the first time. It consisted of two fragments from a lost manuscript, mounted together as a *kakemono* of the type that might have hung in the alcove of a tea-ceremony room. The right half of the text was in Shinkei's own hand and was clearly the beginning of a hundred-poem sequence. The left half was a colophon written by a certain Sōyū.[1]

Hundred-Poem Waka Sequence
Spring. 20 Poems. *Shaku* Shinkei.

urameshiku	Upon this world—
nigoru wa tsuchi to	this earth of dross congealed
nareru yo no	from a finer sky,
hito no kokoro ni	bitterly the heart of man now
kasumu haru kana	shrouds in haze the springtime.

These eight volumes are in the hand of Major Bishop Shinkei. He had them sent from the place called Ishikura in Sagami Province, bidding me to keep them as a remembrance (*katami*). But as the infirmities of old age weigh heavier upon me day by day, I hereby bequeath them to Kōyū, whose skill and enthusiasm for poetry are unparalleled. They include eight of sixteen volumes.
Bummei 9 [1477]. Second Month. Thirteenth Day. Sōyū [seal]

Alluding to the creation myth in the *Nihongi*, where the earth is said to be the result of gross or impure matter sedimenting from the purer air, Shinkei's poem on the tragedy of the human condition was doubtless motivated by the Ōnin War and composed sometime during his Kantō exile. The colophon itself is strangely moving. Written by Sōyū just two years after Shinkei's death, it evokes the poet's last days in Ishikura, when he evidently set his manuscripts in order and, among others, had sixteen volumes sent to Sōyū in the capital. According to this colophon the complete works, the *Shibakusa* collection, of which extant texts comprise isolated parts, must originally have been at least sixteen volumes in all; eight that made up the waka section were sent to Kōyū, and eight consisting of renga and perhaps treatises remained with Sōyū. Of Sōyū we know that he was enough of a renga poet to have two verses included in the *Shinsen Tsukubashū*, where he is identified as "Inadoko, Lord of Hyūga [Miyazaki], ally of the Hosokawa."[2] He is doubtless the Inadoko Motonari who figures in a contemporary Gozan source that describes how he devoutly collected Hosokawa Katsumoto's letters to himself, had the *Lotus Sutra* engraved on their backs, and sections mounted as a decorative handscroll in memory of his lord.[3] As we have seen in the cases of Ōta Dōshin and Dōkan, it was the practice for vassals to enter religious life at the demise of their lord. Thus Inadoko Motonari would have become Priest Sōyū at Katsumoto's death in 1473 and probably did not long survive the infirmities of which he wrote in the colophon of 1477. At any rate the fact that Shinkei entrusted his works to him testifies to the weightiness of their relationship and confirms once more the poet's own close connections with the Hosokawa clan. As for Kōyū, the "unparalleled" poet whom Sōyū deemed worthy of inheriting Shinkei's manuscripts, no clue exists as to his identity, except that the use of the honorific in the colophon indicates a person of high social rank.

An exact reproduction of the Shinkei manuscript fragment described above may now be viewed at the Tōshōin. Likewise mounted as a *kakemono*, it was commissioned from a calligrapher by the temple's head priest, Mr. Adachi Hisao. Also a local historian at the Isehara City Office, Mr. Adachi had researched the documents that established the Jōgyōji as the site of the poet's final abode. The local Kantō poetic tradition to which Shinkei, Sōgi, and then Kenzai contributed ages ago evidently still survives, a tiny but well-tended garden amidst a world as dark and tattered now as it ever was in their time. The priest-historian talks with modest enthusiasm about the activities of the local haikai club and a projected lecture series on Shinkei and Ōta Dokan right here at the Tōshōin.

It is getting on toward dusk. The rain has ceased. Beneath the trees in the garden the evening shadows soften the grating newness of the large stone tablet erected in the poet's memory in 1974. The bamboo grasses that have been planted below it gleam a dark green.

> kusa no kage o   On the open Azuma Road, I seek
> tanomu azumaji   shelter in the shadow of the grass.
>
> minu kuni no   Is the wanderer's fate
> tsuchi to ya naramu   to become a clod of earth in
> mi no yukue   an unknown country?

Across from the memorial stone stands the far smaller, moss-grown stupa of Ōta Dōkan's grave. Thus after five-hundred years the poet-priest and the warrior whose divergent paths had crossed in Azuma faced each other once more. Both had lived and died under the shadow of a war-torn age to which the lines carved out on the stone remain the epitaph.

> kumo wa nao   There is more fixity
> sadame aru yo no   even in the clouds, in a world
> shigure kana   of unstill rains.

> Minamiyana, Hatano
> Kanagawa
> Summer 1980

Appendix

The Two Sequences Without Commentary

"Cuckoo"
A Hundred-Verse Solo Sequence
Composed by Shinkei in Musashi in the
Summer of Ōnin 1 (1467)

First Fold, Front

1   hototogisu   Shall I yet marvel
         kikishi wa mono ka   to have heard you, cuckoo?
         fuji no yuki   Mount Fuji in snow!

2   kumo mo tomaranu   Not a cloud stops to linger
         sora no suzushisa   upon the coolness of that sky.

3   tsuki kiyoki   So pure the rays of
         hikari ni yoru wa   moonlight, the wind is naked
         kaze miete   to the eye—the night.

4   yume odorokasu   Startled, dreams fall away:
         aki no karifushi   a transient sleep in autumn.

5   okimasaru   Dew soaking deep
         tsuyu ya yadori ni   about my lodging, is the night
         fukenuran   so far advanced?

6   mushi no ne yowaki   Grass clumps in the passing shower
         kusa no murasame   the insects' voices are frail.

7   hagi ga e no   On the bush clover branch,
         shitaba nokorazu   the lower leaves flicker out in
         kururu no ni   the darkening meadow.

8   yuku hito mare no   Seldom a passerby's shadow
         okagoe no michi   on the road over the hillcrest.

First Fold, Back

| 9 | fuyugomoru
fumoto no io wa
shizuka nite | Winter-secluded,
the hut below the hill
rapt in quietness. |

| 10 | kōru bakari no
mizu zo suminuru | Chill clarity of the water
in a moment turning to ice! |

| 11 | uchishiore
asakawa wataru
tabi no sode | Swiftly wilting
as I cross the morning river:
sleeves of travel. |

| 12 | sao no shizuku mo
kakaru funamichi | Drenched in the oar spray—
taking passage on a boat. |

| 13 | motometsutsu
yoru se mo shiranu
naka wa ushi | Waves that ever seeking,
never meet in a single current—
the torment of loving. |

| 14 | wakare no koma wa
hiki mo kaesazu | The departing horse would not be
stayed, restrain it as I would. |

| 15 | utsuriyuku
toki o koyoi no
urami nite | Each hour, as
it shifts, is yet more
bitter this night. |

| 16 | chigiri ni wataru
ariake no tsuki | Holding to its promised course,
the moon in the paling sky. |

| 17 | yo no naka ya
kaze no ue naru
nobe no tsuyu | Such is our world:
dewdrops teeming in the meadow
before the wind. |

| 18 | mayoiukaruru
kumokiri no yama | Groping astray in mountains
obscured in mist and cloud. |

| 19 | naku tori no
kozue ushinau
hi wa kurete | Birds cry,
losing their treetop perches
as sunlight sinks. |

| 20 | mono sabishiki zo
sakura chiru kage | An utter loneliness in things—
shadow of scattering cherry. |

| 21 | furusato no
haru o ba tare ka
toite min | As for springtime in
the old village, who would come
to see it? |

| 22 | kasumi hedatsuru
kata wa shirarezu | Through impenetrable haze
one would not know the way. |

Second Fold, Front

| 23 | musashino wa
kayou michi sae
tabi ni shite | Across Musashi Plain
even the daily round takes
one on a journey. |

24	nagameshi ato no tōki yamakage	Before my gaze hills receded into the shadows far behind.
25	waga mi yo ni omowazu henuru toshi wa ushi	Bitter to find the years have passed her by, all unawares.
26	hakana ya inochi nani o matsuran	So fleeting this breath of life, for what does it wait?
27	yasaki ni mo tsumadou shika wa tatazumite	Right in the arrow's path still the deer, searching for its mate, hesitates.
28	akikusa shigemi shiranu hitokage	Through the rank autumn grass dim glimmer of a human shadow.
29	furusato ni nowaki hitori ya kotauran	In the desolate hamlet, the field-cleaving wind alone echoes in answer.
30	karine no tsuki ni mono omou koro	A time of wakeful thoughts upon a transient bed beneath the moon.
31	sode nurasu yamaji no tsuyu ni yo wa akete	On sleeves wet with dew on the mountain trail glistens the dawn.
32	kumo hiku mine ni tera zo miekeru	As the cloud banks lift, high on the peak a temple lies revealed.
33	omokage ya waga tatsu soma no ato naramu	Memory traces the timbers that he raised— here in image.
34	yomogi ga shima no hana no ki mo nashi	Immortal Island: not one tree flowers, amidst the rank growth.
35	haru fukami midori no koke ni tsuyu ochite	Deep into spring, dewdrops trickle on the greening moss.
36	iwa kosu mizu no oto zo kasumeru	Blurring to a murmur—sound of water coursing over the rocks.

Second Fold, Back

37	isogakure nami ni ya fune no kaeruran	As the waves recede behind the shore cliffs is that a ship sailing away?
38	waga omoine no toko mo sadamezu	In sleep restless with desire the bed yields no place to settle.
39	yume ni dani ikani mien to kanashimite	Were it only in a dream could I but somehow see him— she pleads in sorrow.

40   kakotsu bakari no   Only resentment forms on the
         tamakura no tsuki   pillowing arm, the empty moon.

41   ajikinaku   For these sobs
       musebu ya aki no   of despair, is not autumn alone
         toga naran   to blame?

42   uezuba kikaji   Unplanted, they would be dumb,
         ogi no uwakaze   the reeds soughing in the wind.

43   haru o nao   Still now, a memento
       wasuregatami ni   of that indelible spring—
         sode hosade   sleeves that will not dry.

44   kasumi ada naru   The sadness in the wake
         ato no awaresa   of the vanished haze.

45   awayuki no   In the thin snow
       kieyuku nobe ni   dissolving in the meadow
         mi o shire   is my fate revealed.

46   hito mo tazunenu   The fragrance of plum flowers
         yado no ume ga ka   draws no visitor to the abode.

47   kakureiru   Where I live hidden in
       tani no toyama no   the valley, the mountain's shadow
         kage sabite   deepens with time.

48   keburi sukunaku   Meager the hearthsmoke
         miyuru ochikata   rising off in the distance.

49   shio taruru   Dripping in saltspray
       suzaki no ama no   at the far end of the sandspit:
         hanareio   a lone fisher's hut.

50   toma fuku fune ni   With the sedge-roofed boat,
         nami zo naraeru   the white cresting waves align!

Third Fold, Front

51   furu yuki ni   Companionless amidst
       tomonaki chidori   the falling snow, the plover
         uchiwabite   calls out in sorrow.

52   hitori ya nenan   Alone can I drift off to sleep—
         sayo no matsukaze   night astir with the pine winds.

53   towarezuba   Unvisited,
       mi o ikani sen   what shall I do with myself?
         aki no sora   the empty autumn sky.

54   tanomeokitsuru   So much and long dependent upon:
         tsuki no yūgure   this evening of moonrise.

55   tsurenaku mo   Indifferent he might be,

	tsuyu no nasake wa arinubeshi	yet a dewdrop of pity must lodge in his heart?
56	sode ni shigure no susamajiki koro	Days of chill autumn showers piercing through my sleeves.
57	yama fukami yuki no shitamichi koekanete	In mountains deep under snowdrift the trail is hard to follow.
58	iwao no kage ni fuseru tabibito	A traveler lies prostrate in the shadow of a great rock.
59	natsu zo uki mizu ni hitoyo no mushirokaze	Summer goes hard— ah, for a night on a rushmat fanned by the seabreeze.
60	e no matsu ga ne ni tsunagu tsuribune	A fishing boat moored to the roots of a great pine tree in the cove.
61	kurekakaru naniwa no ashibi takisomete	As the dark gathers along Naniwa Bay, reed fires are lit one after another.
62	kareii isogu koya no awaresa	Hurrying with the parched rice— the pathos in the hovels.
63	wabinureba namida shi sosogu karagoromo	Bewailing fortune, he weeps copious tears upon the once splendid robe.
64	urami narikeri hito no itsuwari	Become this bitter resentment: the treacherous words of a man.

Third Fold, Back

65	waga shiranu koto nomi yoso ni na no tachite	For an affair of which I knew naught, my name grew notorious to others.
66	toishi sono yo wa yume ka utsutsu ka	That night you came to me: Was I dreaming? Was it real?
67	kaerusa wa kokoro mo madoi me mo kurenu	On the way back, my heart was in a turmoil, blinded my eyes!
68	aoba kanashiki hana no yamakage	Sad the greening leaves on hills lately white with flowers.
69	mizu ni uku tori no hitokoe uchikasumu	Across the water the floating note of bird cry turns hazy.
70	fune yobau nari haru no asanagi	Someone calling out to the boat— Calmness of a spring morning.

71	omoshiroki umi no higata o osoku kite	Entranced by the wide curving beach at ebb tide, he was slow to come.
72	tsuki no irinuru ato wa shirarezu	Once the moon has set, nothing remains to trace its passage.
73	kuraki yori kuraki o omou aki no yo ni	In the autumn night, imaging the path out of darkness into deeper darkness.
74	kiri furu nozato kumo no yamazato	Mist falls on the meadow village, Clouded the mountain village.
75	mi o yasuku kakushiokubeki kata mo nashi	Nowhere a refuge, not a moment's respite for the tired spirit.
76	osamare to nomi inoru kimi ga yo	"Cease this tumult!" That is all I pray for in my Lord's reign.
77	kami no tame michi aru toki ya nabikuran	For he is a god, the times may yet come to bend to the right Way.
78	kaze no mae naru kusa no suezue	The grasses bowing their heads in serried ranks before the wind.

Remaining-Trace Fold, Front

79	fuyu no no ni koboren to suru tsuyu o mite	Seeing dewdrops about to spill over in the winter meadow.
80	harawaji mono o koromode no yuki	I could not brush them away— the snowflakes upon my sleeves.
81	tsumorikuru hito yue fukaki waga omoi	Gathering ply on ply, because of him my anguish grows still deeper.
82	ikuyo ka tada ni akashihatsuran	How many more nights shall see the end of these useless dawns?
83	aramashi o nezame sugureba wasurekite	Hopes of release, held in wakeful moments, slide into forgetfulness.
84	tsuki ni mo hajizu nokoru oi ga mi	Shameless before the lucid moon, the remnants of an aging life.
85	fuku kaze no oto wa tsurenaki aki no sora	Harrowing, the sound of the wind sweeping through the autumn sky.

86	mukaeba yagate kiyuru ukigiri	In a while, right before my eyes the floating mists have vanished.
87	michi wakuru masago no ue no uchishimeri	On the fine sand the trail of footprints moistens over.
88	furuki iori zo namida moyōsu	Still the ancient hermitage causes the tears to well.
89	tachibana no ki mo kuchi noki mo katabukite	The orange-blossom tree is rotting with age, and the eaves are sagging.
90	tou hito mare no samidare no naka	Hardly anyone calls, through the long dark rains of June.
91	se o hayami yūkawabune ya nagaruran	In the swift current, was that boat cast adrift upon the evening river?
92	tomaranu nami no kishi o utsu koe	The incessant sound of waves pounding the shore.

Remaining-Trace Fold, Back

93	yamabuki no chirite wa mizu no iro mo nashi	Yellow mountain roses— with each petal shower the water turns, colorless.
94	yae oku tsuyu mo kasumu hi no kage	The eightfold dewdrops also a hazy shimmer in sunlight.
95	harusame no komakani sosogu kono ashita	The spring rain is seeping finely over all, this morning.
96	omoikudaku mo kinuginu no ato	A heart is breaking into shards in wake of the dawn's parting.
97	koishisa no nakute sumu yo mo aru mono o	Surely there are worlds where one can live free of this yearning.
98	ikani shite ka wa kokoro yasumen	But how can I ever find the way to quiet my mind?
99	tsukiyo ni mo tsuki o minu yo mo fushiwabite	On moonlit nights, and even nights blotted of the moon, I lie disconsolate.
100	kaze yaya samuku inaba moru toko	About the rice-warden's pallet, The chill of the wind deepens.

"Broken Beneath Snow"
A Hundred-Verse Sequence
Composed by Shinkei, Sōgi, and Others
in Shinagawa, Musashi, in the Winter of Ōnin 2 (1468)

First Fold, Front

1   yuki no oru   Reeds broken beneath
     kaya ga sueno wa   snow across the plain's horizon—
     michi mo nashi   there is no path.
              Shinkei   Shinkei

2   yūgure samumi   Not a moving figure in sight
     yuku sode mo nashi   across a frozen twilight.
              Sōgi   Sōgi

3   chidori naku   As plovers cry along the
     kawara no tsuki ni   river shallows, a boat glides up
     fune tomete   beneath the moon.
           Norishige   Norishige

4   kikeba makura o   Listening, I feel the night wind
     suguru sayokaze   drifting past my pillow.
             Kaku'a   Kaku'a

5   sakurabana   Cherry blossoms—
     sakuran kata ya   already in flower yonder?
     niouran   a wafting fragrance.
           Nagatoshi   Nagatoshi

6   haru ni okururu   Spring comes late to the village
     yamakage no sato   in the mountain's shadow.
             Sōetsu   Sōetsu

7   kane kasumu   Hazy booms the bell
     onoe no kikori   on the peak where a woodsman
     tomo yobite   calls out to his fellows.
           Mitsusuke   Mitsusuke

8   kaeru ka kumo no   Will it return as well?
     nokoru hitomura   The cloud bank left behind.
             Hōzen   Hōzen

First Fold, Back

9   harekumoru   Now clear, now clouded
     ame sadamenaki   in rain, the restlessly shifting
     aki no sora   autumn skies.
             Shun'a   Shun'a

10   yowaki hikage zo   Feeble the gleam of sunlight
     tsuyu ni yadoreru   lodging motionless in the dew.
             Ken'a   Ken'a

11   sasa no ha ni   Even as insects cry
     mushi no ne tanomu   pleading in the bamboo grass,
     no wa karete   the meadow withers.
           Shinkei   Shinkei

12	makura omowanu yowa no matsukaze Sōgi	Indifferent to my lonely pillow, wind in the pines at midnight. Sōgi
13	yume yo nado hito koso arame itouran Norishige	Dreams, unbidden you come to others, then why shun me? Norishige
14	kakute mo kokoro nao ya matamashi Mitsusuke	So be it, but still the heart would wait, even so. Mitsusuke
15	kono mama no wakare to iite ideshi yo ni Sōetsu	"We part, for the last time," he said, and left me thus in this world of night. Sōetsu
16	kumo ni mo ato wa taenu yamamichi Kaku'a	Even its traces have vanished in the clouds: the mountain path. Kaku'a
17	sewashinaki shiba no io ni toshi o hete Nagatoshi	Restive in the brushwood hut, the years have passed. Nagatoshi
18	shigure kanashiki fuyu no kuregata Ikuhiro	Sad the falling rain in the dim winter twilight. Ikuhiro
19	sode nurenu tsuki no tabine mo ikanaran Sōgi	How would it be, were sleeves wet only with moonlight, these nights of sojourn? Sōgi
20	kaeru miyako ni aki o wasururu Shun'a	Mind on returning to the capital, one *can* be oblivious to autumn. Shun'a
21	no o tōmi taorishi kusa no hana ochite Shinkei	So broad the plain, the wildflowers I plucked have since fallen. Shinkei
22	kawaru yadori zo tou hito mo naki Kaku'a	At these shifting abodes, no one ever comes to call. Kaku'a

Second Fold, Front

23	aramashi no hodo koso sasoe yama no oku Norishige	It's enough to invite a long-cherished vision: deep mountain recesses. Norishige
24	hatsu hototogisu suguru murasame Nagatoshi	In the wake of the passing shower, the first calls of the cuckoo! Nagatoshi

25	urameshi na konu yo amata ni mata narite Shinkei	They hurt me. Again, the unvisited nights drag on, too many. Shinkei
26	makura no shiran hitorine mo ushi Sōgi	Depressing too to think my pillow knows of my sleeping alone. Sōgi
27	kokoro dani omoiyowareba naki mono o Sōetsu	When this very heart, weakened by longing, can hold no more. Sōetsu
28	namida wa shiite nao ya ochinan Shinkei	Still the tears would fall, defying reason, all the more. Shinkei
29	kimi ga yo o tare shirakawa no tagitsunami Sōgi	Who would know of those bygone times, the currents swirling on White River? Sōgi
30	furuki sakura no kage zo sabishiki Ikuhiro	So lonely, the scant shade of the aged cherry tree. Ikuhiro
31	amata heshi haru no mi tsuraki kusa no to ni Nagatoshi	After many years, only the springtime, poignant as ever by the grass-hut door. Nagatoshi
32	kasumu to mo naku samuki yamakaze Norishige	So cold the wind in the mountains, the haze is barely able to form. Norishige
33	yuki harau ochikatabito no sode kiete Shinkei	Distantly, a figure, sleeves brushing off the snow— melts away. Shinkei
34	kareno ni takaki akatsuki no kane Sōgi	High above the withered plain, the booming of the dawn bell. Sōgi
35	ariake no kage ya sayaka ni fukenuran Kaku'a	Chillingly clear, the form of the remaining moon has aged. Kaku'a
36	uchinuru yado no yonayona no aki Mitsusuke	Night after night of autumn in sleep-hushed lodgings. Mitsusuke

Second Fold, Back

37	yama fukami ine moru hita no oto wa shite Nagatoshi	In mountains so deep audible the clatter of pipes guarding the rice stalks. Nagatoshi

38	tsuraki wa sate mo yamu toki mo nashi Shun'a	Even here is no respite from the painful toil. Shun'a
39	kumo to naru hito no katami no sode no ame Shinkei	Indelible memory of someone become a cloud— rain on my sleeves. Shinkei
40	yume yori hoka wa nani o tanoman Sōetsu	What else, apart from the dream, is there left to rely on? Sōetsu
41	chiru hana ni tsurenaki oi o nagusamete Sōgi	In the scattering flowers I find solace, midst callously lingering old age. Sōgi
42	haru no kokoro wa mukashi ni mo nizu Ikuhiro	The heart that looks on spring is not now what it was of old. Ikuhiro
43	sumu yama wa hi mo nagakarade okuru mi ni Mitsusuke	Living in the mountains, the days do not seem long— body engaged in chores. Mitsusuke
44	hata utsu mine no shiba o oritsutsu Nagatoshi	Plowing the fields, gathering brushwood on the peak. Nagatoshi
45	aware ni mo awaii isogu hi o takite Shinkei	Pitifully, he hastens to make a fire for the frugal bowl of millet. Shinkei
46	makura hodonaki tsuyu no karifushi Sōgi	Barely an interval on the pillow, the traveler's sleep on the dew. Sōgi
47	megurikinu furusato ideshi yowa no tsuki Norishige	It has come round again, the midnight moon when I left the old village. Norishige
48	wasurenu mono o hito ya wasuren Nagatoshi	I have not forgotten, but has she perhaps done so? Nagatoshi
49	kawaraji no sono hitofude o inochi nite Shinkei	That single letter saying, "I shall not change," I cling to as my very life. Shinkei
50	hakanaki ato to miru zo kanashiki Mitsusuke	To see it but an empty trace— I am bereft twice over! Mitsusuke

Third Fold, Front

51	chitose to mo iishi ya itsu no tsuka no matsu <div align="right">Sōgi</div>	"A thousand years," they prayed, when might it have been? Pine tree by the grave mound. <div align="right">Sōgi</div>
52	kokoro ni hikeru funaoka no haru <div align="right">Shinkei</div>	A memory pulling at the heart, springtime at Funaoka Hill. <div align="right">Shinkei</div>
53	kasumi sae tsuki wa akashi no ukimakura <div align="right">Nagatoshi</div>	Even the haze is gloomy, this sad drifting beneath the bright Akashi moon. <div align="right">Nagatoshi</div>
54	moshio no toko ni kari kaeru koe <div align="right">Sōgi</div>	Farewell calls of the wild geese, upon the pallet of salt-seaweed. <div align="right">Sōgi</div>
55	hitoyo no mi kareru tomaya ni nezame shite <div align="right">Shun'a</div>	Sleepless in the sedge-grass hut he rented for only a night. <div align="right">Shun'a</div>
56	ukimi no ue zo namida soinuru <div align="right">Kaku'a</div>	There is cause enough for tears in this miserable life. <div align="right">Kaku'a</div>
57	tarachine no omou o miru mo kurushiki ni <div align="right">Sōetsu</div>	The added pain of seeing the anxiety in my parents' eyes. <div align="right">Sōetsu</div>
58	ima kon tote mo sutsuru yo no naka <div align="right">Norishige</div>	This world do I renounce, though death come this very moment! <div align="right">Norishige</div>
59	tsumi aru o mukae no kuruma osoroshi na <div align="right">Shinkei</div>	Yet knowing my sins, to meet the Vehicle of the Law fills me with terror. <div align="right">Shinkei</div>
60	mikari no kaesa no mo hibiku nari <div align="right">Sōgi</div>	Riding home from the royal hunt— the very fields seem to resound. <div align="right">Sōgi</div>
61	arare chiru nasu no shinohara kaze ochite <div align="right">Norishige</div>	As hail beats down on the bamboo-plain of Nasu, the wind falls still. <div align="right">Norishige</div>
62	kusa no kage o mo tanomu azumaji <div align="right">Nagatoshi</div>	On the open Azuma Road, I seek shelter in the shadow of the grass. <div align="right">Nagatoshi</div>

63	minu kuni no
	tsuchi to ya naran
	mi no yukue
	       Shinkei
		Is the wanderer's fate
		to become a clod of earth in
		an unknown country?
		       Shinkei

64	hate mo kanashiki
	amatsu'otomego
	       Sōetsu
		Pitifully sad is the end,
		ethereal maiden of the sky.
		       Sōetsu

Third Fold, Back

65	omokage no
	tsuki ni koishi mo
	ato nakute
	       Mitsusuke
		Her shimmering image,
		the moon draws all his yearning,
		yet is it void of trace.
		       Mitsusuke

66	hitodanome naru
	kosu no akikaze
	       Norishige
		Hope leaps at a rustling sound—
		bamboo blinds in the autumn wind.
		       Norishige

67	shitamomiji
	tare ni wakeyo to
	midaruran
	       Sōgi
		Crimson-dyed lower leaves
		part to make a path for whom—
		swaying all tremulous.
		       Sōgi

68	kurureba kaeru
	yama zo harukeki
	       Kaku'a
		As darkness falls, the mountain
		of my home recedes yet farther.
		       Kaku'a

69	yuku kata mo
	isa shirakumo o
	naka ni mite
	       Shinkei
		Uncertain too of the way
		ahead, he sees the white clouds
		massed between.
		       Shinkei

70	suginuru tori no
	kasukanaru koe
	       Shun'a
		Faint sound of birdcall
		flitting swiftly past.
		       Shun'a

71	tabibito no
	koyuru sekito no
	akuru yo ni
	       Nagatoshi
		With the dawning light,
		the barrier-gate opens for
		the crossing traveler.
		       Nagatoshi

72	tomo o ya matan
	iwagane no michi
	       Sōetsu
		I think I'll await a companion
		at the foot of the craggy trail.
		       Sōetsu

73	ki no shita o
	hatsuyuki nagara
	kieyarade
	       Mitsusuke
		Here in the shadow of
		the trees, the first snow patches
		have yet to dissolve.
		       Mitsusuke

74	katsu saku ume ni
	niou asatsuyu
	       Shinkei
		Yet sweet is the morning dew as
		one by one plum blossoms unfurl.
		       Shinkei

75	haru no no ya narenu sode o mo kawasuran Norishige	Ah, the spring meadows— even the sleeves of strangers brushing each other. Norishige
76	kasumi shiku e ni fune kayou miyu Sōgi	On the bay overhung with haze, boats seen gliding to and fro. Sōgi
77	kokoro naki hito no yūbe wa munashikute Sōetsu	For the man devoid of feeling, the dimming evening holds nothing. Sōetsu
78	susumuru kane o aware to mo kike Shinkei	Hear the infinite sadness in the lesson of the booming bell. Shinkei

Remaining-Trace Fold, Front

79	sakazuki o megurasu madoi oshiki yo ni Nagatoshi	Passing the sake cup in a happy circle, the night ends too soon. Nagatoshi
80	koto no ne nokoru ariake no sora Sōgi	The zither's notes linger on with the moon in the paling sky. Sōgi
81	kie mo senu mi o wabihito no aki fukete Ikuhiro	Lamenting his body that would not melt, hapless man in deepening autumn. Ikuhiro
82	kumokiri ikue sumeru yamazato Sōetsu	Ply on ply, the cloudy mists over the mountain village where I live. Sōetsu
83	samidare wa mizu no koe senu tani mo nashi Shinkei	The long June rains: not a valley but resounds with the swollen waters. Shinkei
84	nagare no sue ni ukabu mumoregi Hōzen	At the mouth of the swift current, a buried tree floats into view. Hōzen
85	au se ni mo yoshi ya kakotaji natorikawa Norishige	Hide it I would not, could we but meet, in spite of Rumor River. Norishige
86	yoso ni morenan iro zo monouki Shun'a	My unassuaged hue become apparent to others—that would be misery! Shun'a

87 kaimami mo
    arawa to ashi no
    ha wa karete
            Shinkei

Leaving gaps naked
to the eye, the hedge of
reed leaf shrivels.
            Shinkei

88 fuyu wa sumarenu
    sumika to o shire
            Mitsusuke

In winter, I would have you know,
this abode is beyond endurance.
            Mitsusuke

89 miyako ni wa
    yuki mezurame ya
    ono no yama
            Sōgi

In the Capital City,
they cherish the rare snow, but
here in Mount Ono!
            Sōgi

90 shigure ni tsuki no
    kage mo susamaji
            Kaku'a

Piercingly chill the moonlight
in the wake of the sudden rains.
            Kaku'a

91 kogarashi no
    sora ni ukaruru
    aki no kumo
            Shinkei

Swept adrift
across the storm-scoured sky,
the clouds of autumn.
            Shinkei

92 kari mo uchiwabi
    kure wataru koro
            Mitsusuke

Lonesome too the wild geese
flitting in the dusk shadows.
            Mitsusuke

Remaining-Trace Fold, Back

93 mi ni kagiru
    namida naraji to
    nagusamete
            Norishige

Not I alone
weep these tears—
I solace myself.
            Norishige

94 shina koso kaware
    yo wa ukarikere
            Nagatoshi

Desire takes various forms, yes,
but 'tis all one world of misery!
            Nagatoshi

95 me no mae ni
    aru o odoroke
    mutsu no michi
            Sōetsu

Awake and be amazed:
the six realms of illusion are
right before your eyes!
            Sōetsu

96 manabu mo utoki
    uta no kotowari
            Shinkei

The principle of poetry remains,
despite all one's study, obscure.
            Shinkei

97 ura tōku
    tamatsushimayama
    uchikasumu
            Sōgi

Remotely mysterious
across the bay, Isle of Jewels
enveloped in haze.
            Sōgi

98 haru shiru oto no
    yowaki matsukaze
            Kaku'a

Spring is audible in the sound:
soft murmur of the pine breeze.
            Kaku'a

99   hana ni nomi   With the flowers alone
        kokoro o noburu   breathes the heart at ease
        yūmagure   this glimmering dusk.
                    Mitsusuke   Mitsusuke

100   sakari naru mi zo   May it span through long years,
        yowai hisashiki   this life at its glorious height.
                    Ikuhiro   Ikuhiro

Reference Matter

Notes

All citations from Shinkei's works both in the text and Notes refer to the first title given under each entry in the "Shinkei's Works" section of the Introduction. The numbering of poems from imperial anthologies and other collections follows [*Shimpen*] *Kokka taikan* unless another source is cited. For complete author names, titles, and publication data for works cited in short form, see the Bibliography, pp. 433–43. For the abbreviations used here and in the text, see pp. xi–xii.

Chapter 1

1. From Shinkei's *Hyakushu waka*. Here as with Shinkei's three other hundred-poem sequences, I have numbered the poems consecutively from 1 to 100 for convenience. The text used in *SSRS* is the poet's holograph of 1463, now in the archives of the Tenri Library; it is in the form of a handscroll and includes his own comments in red ink. I have also consulted the text annotated by Araki Hisashi in *SNKBT* 47 under the title *Kanshō hyakushu*. Also from the Muromachi period and now in the Kyoto University Library, it is a copy of a later variant manuscript believed to have been sent off to someone by Shinkei. Although there is some variation in the wording of the comments between the two texts, their content is generally the same.

2. The name Ta'i is no longer in current usage, and Nakusa is now part of Kaisō District.

3. Shimazu Tadao (*Rengashi no kenkyū*, p. 143) calls *Sasamegoto* "the most outstanding poetic treatise of the medieval period," representing, along with Zeami's Nō drama treatises, the heights of medieval Japanese thought.

4. *Yamato uta wa, hito no kokoro o tane to shite, yorozu no koto no ha to zo narerikeru* (*KKS*, p. 49).

5. Quoted in Kaneko, "Seikatsu-ken," p. 2; see also in *Kanshō hyakushu*, p. 352. This singular postscript appears only in the Kyoto University Text, which is signed "Tsuruwaka," Shinkei's childhood name. Kaneko (ibid., p. 8) suggests that its unusual use here is an indication that the *jichū* were originally written for a person or persons with whom Shinkei had been familiar since childhood.

6. Wakanoura (lit., "Waka Bay") is located in modern Wakayama City; it was from ancient times an *utamakura*, a place with poetic associations, due to the name and the presence there of the Tamatsushima Shrine dedicated to the deities of poetry, Wakahirume no mikoto and Sotoorihime. The Kinokawa River, on whose banks Ta'i was located, emptied into Wakanoura.

7. Shinkei's poem is probably an allusive variation on the following poem by Saigyō (1118–90), GYS 2060, "On the topic 'thoughts at the end of the year.'" According to Araki Hisashi (*Kanshō hyakushu*, p. 315), Saigyō composed it when he was living in a hut in Higashiyama after withdrawing from society.

toshi kureshi	That press of work
sono itonami wa	with which the year ended
wasurarete	is all forgotten,
aranu sama naru	and now I busy myself
isogi o zo suru	in a whole new way!

8. Araki Hisashi reads *kakaran* in line 1 as an elision of *kaku aran* ("would be like this"); I take it as the verb *kakaru*, "lean on, rely on." An example of the latter usage is verse 22, by Sōgi, in the *Minase sangin hyakuin*: Oi no yukue yo / nani ni kakaran, "Old age goes before me! / What shall I lean on?" (Ijichi, *Rengashū*, p. 349).

9. Dates are here given according to the old lunar calendar, which is more than a month later than our own, and are in the format month.day.year.

10. "The conflagration raging within the three worlds" (*mitsu no sakai hi no naka ni shite*) is a Buddhist metaphor for the imperiled state of sentient beings caused by the illusory realms of desire (*yokkai*), form (*shikikai*), and the formless (*mushikikai*). Also known as "the burning house of the three worlds" (*sangai no kataku*), the metaphor stems from the famous parable in Scroll 2, Chapter 3, of the *Lotus Sutra* recounting how a great man lured his children from the burning house by promising them that rare carriages, i.e., the Buddhist "vehicles," awaited them outside.

11. "A hell of hungry ghosts" (*gakidō*) is one of the six states or worlds (*rokudō*) into which a being is reborn according to the merits or demerits of his former existence; they are the world of hell (*jigoku*), hungry ghosts, beasts (*chikushō*), demons (*ashura*), human beings (*ningen*), and heavenly beings (*tenjō*). Occupying the second lowest state, the "hungry ghosts" (Skt. *preta*) were imaged in literature and the visual arts as naked, emaciated creatures with swollen stomachs and needle-thin throats that condemned them to perpetually unsatisfied hunger and thirst, particularly since everything they imbibed instantaneously turned to fire in their mouths. Since the "hungry ghost" image was possibly originally inspired by the sight of victims of famine and pestilence, Shinkei's evocation of it here is especially apt.

12. "The triple calamities presaging the world's destruction" (*ekō massei no sansai*) refers to the disasters wrought by fire, water, and wind during the age of the world's dissolution. *Ekō* is the third of the four kalpas or cosmic ages from the world's creation and duration of existence to its final nihility.

13. See the account of the Kakitsu Incident in Varley, *The Ōnin War*, pp. 65–70.

Varley's work is one of my principal sources for understanding the political and economic forces at work during Shinkei's age.

14. This event is noted in Suzuki, *Ōnin no ran*, p. 205.

15. See entries for 3.16, 6.3, and 6.5.1460, and 2.30.1461 in the *Hekizan nichiroku*, pp. 303, 313, 336. This journal covers the years 1459–63 and 1465–68. See also Suzuki's discussion (pp. 1–6) of Taikyoku's account of the famine.

16. Ishihara, "Jūjūshin'in kō"; the official letters to the temple are quoted in ibid., p. 2, from a facsimile of the *Rokuharamitsuji monjo* in the Shiryō Hensanjo. Ishihara's article is to date the sole authoritative study on the status of Jūjūshin'in.

17. Quoted in Ishihara, p. 3.

18. Quoted in Suzuki, p. 8, from the journal *Daijōin jisha zōjiki*. A scion of the Fujiwara's Ichijō branch, Jinson was the son of the eminent statesman Ichijō Kanera (or Kaneyoshi, 1402–81), who served as Regent three times in his career. The Daijōin was the main temple of the great Fujiwara clan temple in Nara, the Kōfukuji.

19. The second sentence of the commentary in the *SSRS* text is somewhat obscure; I have followed the *Kanshō hyakushu* version (p. 350) in rendering it.

20. *MYS* 63. "Composed by Yamanoue Okura when he was in China and thinking of his homeland."

iza kodomo	Come, my men,
hayaku yamato e	let us swiftly to Yamato!
ōtomo no	In Ōtomo
mitsu no hamamatsu	the shore pines of Mitsu
machikoinuran	must be waiting and longing.

(Kojima et al., *Man'yōshū*, NKBZ 2: 97) The embassy to China embarked from Mitsu Bay (also known as Naniwazu) in Ōtomo, the ancient name for present-day Osaka. Incorporating the last two lines of *MYS* 63, Shinkei's poem is an allusive variation on Okura's; it is more complex and has a tone of near cynical despair at variance with the other.

21. Kaneko, "Seikatsu-ken," p. 5.

22. According to the *Chōroku Kanshō ki*, Masanaga's forces consisted mainly of samurai bands from Yamato (Nara), and Yoshinari's followers came from Kawachi and Kii. This historical work is primarily a record of the Hatakeyama clan during the Chōroku (1457–60) and Kanshō (1460–66) eras and is thus an excellent source for the succession dispute; see *GR* 16: 375.233–43.

23. See Ishihara, p. 4.

24. Possibly an allusion to *KKS* 340. Winter. Anonymous. "From the Empress's Poetry Contest in the Kampyō era [889–98]."

yuki furite	It is in the season
toshi no kurenuru	when the year draws to a close
toki ni koso	beneath falling snow
tsui ni momijinu	that the pine reveals itself
matsu mo miekere	unaltered in hue to the end.

Like this *KKS* poem, Shinkei probably also had in mind the following passage from the *Rongo* (Analects): "The Master said, In the cold of the year—only then do we come to know that the pine and cypress are the last to wither" (*Rongo*, p. 214).

25. As Shinkei explains it, "three" (*mitsu*) in the poem, by which he means "the three worlds" (*mitsu no sakai*), refers to two distinct sets of fortune found there: to be born with unimpaired vision and hearing, a man and not a woman, and live into old age; or then again, to be free of the encumbrances of property, money, and family. In other words, the solace to be derived from composing poetry is beyond mundane happiness (*SSRS*, pp. 346–47).

Chapter 2

1. All references to the *Guku shibakusa* are to the Bummei 11 (1479) manuscript copy in *SSRS*, pp. 3–64.

2. Kaneko, *Seikatsu to sakuhin*, p. 32. He bases the twelve-year figure on information in the *Sange gakushōshiki* (Prescribed forms for mountain-priest students), a work by Mount Hiei's founder, Dengyō Daishi (or Saichō, 767–822), describing the system of education that he established there for the Tendai priesthood.

3. In China the concept and practice of *shikan*, established by Tendai's founder Chih-i (538–97), predated the rise of Zen in the eighth century. Similarly in Japan, Zen as such did not become a major sect until the thirteenth century. On Hiei, Chih-i's monumental treatise on *shikan* meditation, the *Makashikan* (The great stillness and insight), had long been a basic text, along with his commentaries on the *Lotus Sutra*. By Shinkei's time, it is not clear that a strict distinction was made between the Tendai and Zen practice of meditation; Zen teaching is at any rate abundantly reflected in his critical writings.

4. *SKKS* 1921. "Composed when he built the Main Hall of Mount Hiei." Dengyō Daishi.

anokutara	Hark ye Buddhas
sammyaku sambodai no	of perfect wisdom, unparalleled
hotoke-tachi	and compassing all:
waga tatsu soma ni	Confer your invisible powers on
myōga arasetamae	*the timbers that I raise here!*

(Kubota Jun, ed., *Shinkokin wakashū zenhyōshaku*, 8: 456; all citations and poem numbers from the *Shinkokinshū* refer to this edition.) The verse-pair is from Shinkei's 1467 solo sequence, one of the two hyakuin translated in Part Two of this book.

5. *Mansai jugō nikki* in *ZGR*, suppl. vol. 2: 870b.285. The Shingon ecclesiastic Mansai (1378–1435) was Abbot of the Daigoji and Sambōin. A nephew or adopted son of the Shōgun Yoshimitsu, he exercised considerable influence in the inner circles of the bakufu during the rule of both Yoshimitsu and Yoshinori and was known as "the black-robed minister." Also an enthusiastic renga practitioner, his name frequently appears in records of sessions sponsored by Yoshinori. His journal covers the period 1411–35.

6. *Taiheiki 3, NKBT 36:* 120.

7. *Kitano-sha ichimanku gohokku waki daisan narabi ni jo*, p. 335. This manuscript record includes only the first three verses of each of the twenty sequences, plus a preface by Ichijō Kanera.

8. See the "Rengashi nempyō" entries for the years 1428–41 in Kido Saizō, *RS*, 2: 887–91. Kidō's two-volume work is the principal and most up-to-date modern source for renga history.

9. See *SKS* 1737 and preface to 1734; also the Preface to the whole journal on p. 532. The *Sōkonshū* is Shōtetsu's most extensive poem collection; in the *ST* edition, it includes 11,238 poems in 15 volumes arranged chronologically from 1414 to 1459, except for the undated volumes 4–6 and 15. Covering a period of forty-five years until his death, it was compiled posthumously from his manuscripts by his closest disciple Shōkō, with a preface written by Ichijō Kanera in 1473. Extensive prose passages explaining the circumstances of the poems' composition provide valuable autobiographical material as well as a substantial picture of the contemporary milieu.

10. Inada, *Shōtetsu no kenkyū*, pp. 69–70. This monumental, 1,332-page study is today the main secondary source for Shōtetsu's works and biography.

11. For other poems revealing Shōtetsu's feelings regarding the *Shinzoku Kokinshū*, see *SKS* 2129, 2293, 2296, 5055.

12. Inada, *Shōtetsu no kenkyū*, pp. 106, 109–10. English rendering of chapter titles from the *Tale of Genji* are adopted from the Edward Seidensticker translation.

13. Manuscript in the archives of the Imperial Household, Kunaichō Shoryōbu; described in Inada, *Shōtetsu no kenkyū*, pp. 986–89.

14. *Gyōkō hōin nikki*, pp. 453–54.

15. *Eikyō kunen Shōtetsu eisō*, p. 520, preface to poem 84; this is a manuscript of 117 poems composed from the First to the Seventh Month of Eikyō 9 (1437); 3 are by other authors.

16. Inada, *Shōtetsu no kenkyū*, pp. 221–22.

17. From the *Tōyashū kikigaki* (Notes from the eastern plains), p. 354. This work is a collection of poetic anecdotes that Tsuneyori heard from Shōtetsu, his waka teacher Gyōkō, and other fellow poets and friends. Although it includes entries from as early as 1427 and as late as 1456, the greater part is concentrated around the four-year period 1449–52. Its title alludes to Tsuneyori's surname, Tō ("east"), and his official position as Constable of Kōzuke (lit., "upper plain") Province (Gumma Prefecture) in the East.

18. *Shinkei-sōzu jittei waka*, p. 47. Also *ST* 6: 115, no. 315.

19. Ton'a established the particular Nijō line of transmission of which Gyōkō was the contemporary representative. A priest of warrior lineage—his father was Constable of Shimotsuke Province—his orthodox mode of graceful simplicity won him a place in court poetry circles and in the five imperial anthologies that appeared during his lifetime. His reputation became firmly established in 1364, when he was appointed to finish the task of compiling the *Shinshūishū* upon the death of its original editor, Fujiwara Tameaki. He was the first *jige* poet to be thus honored. His personal poem anthology, the *Sōanshū* (Grass-hut collection), was later criticized by

Imagawa Ryōshun and Shōtetsu for being too conservative, but it wielded a great influence then and subsequently, so much so that the very title of Shōtetsu's own *Sōkonshū* (Grass-roots collection) doubtless reflects his sense of rivalry with this *jige* poet so honored in his own time. Ton'a's fame was perhaps even greater after his death: nineteen of his poems were included in the *Shinzoku Kokinshū* imperial anthology from which Shōtetsu was excluded. Since Gyōkō's authority and high connections ultimately derived from Ton'a, to criticize him was tantamount to questioning Gyōkō's own position.

20. The text of *Buke utaawase* is in Inoue, *Chūsei utaawaseshū to kenkyū 3*, pp. 62–73.

21. Saigyō's poem is *SKKS* 362. Autumn.

> kokoro naki
> mi ni mo aware wa
> shirarekeri
> shigi tatsu sawa no
> aki no yūgure

> Even to a self
> empty at heart is disclosed
> a moving power—
> From the marsh a snipe rising
> in the autumn twilight.

22. Poem 88 (numbering mine), *Gondaisōzu Shinkeishū*, p. 417; number 388 in the *ST* and *KT* editions. The *ST* text includes an orthographic error: *ami* (net) instead of *himo* (cord, thread).

23. *Hana no himo* (flower cord) or *hana no shitahimo* (flowers' undercord) is a metaphor both for a tightly furled flower, that is, a bud, and the cords of a woman's undergarment. For its usage in poetry, see, e.g., *SKKS* 84 and *Kokin rokujō* 4: 3356.

24. In a perceptive early article on Shinkei's waka, "Shinkei no waka hyōgen no tokusei: gengo no jūsō kōyō," Inada Toshinori analyzes the effects of this type of polysemic "layering" in Shinkei's waka diction. He points out that it is different in nature from the traditional use of puns (*kakekotoba*) and associative words (*engo*) in waka, and characterizes it as a technique of deploying two or more objects in the same spatial frame and showing how they mutually shift and develop temporally.

25. This poem by Shinkei is interestingly cited in the *Tokihide-kyō kikigaki* (Lord Tokihide's notes, p. 17) as an example of a kind of obscure poetry called *miraiki*. A collection of anecdotes on such topics as poetic diction and mental attitude, this work was written by Nishinotōin Tokihide (1531–66) in 1559 and transmits the poetry and ideas of Shōtetsu, Shinkei, and Shōkō.

26. Inada ("Shinkei no waka hyōgen no tokusei," p. 42) observes that *makikomeru* has no single precedent in all the twenty-one imperial waka anthologies, and that the only known use of it is in a poem by Shunrai (1055–1129) in his personal anthology, *Samboku kikashū* (ca. 1128). The poem is no. 364 on the lotus flower, *tamamizu o*, in *KT*.

27. See, e.g., *Sōkonshū*, colophon to a hundred-poem sequence composed in the Kasuga Shrine in Hotoku 3 (1451), p. 562; *Eikyō kunen Shōtetsu eisō*, preface to poems 105 and 110, pp. 511–12.

28. *Nagusamegusa*, p. 121.

29. As reported in *Ungyoku wakashō* (a poetry collection dating from 1514), p. 177.

Chapter 3

1. The Genroku renga poet is Saijun in his two-volume critical work from 1692, *Renga hajakenshō*, as cited in Saitō, *Chūsei renga no kenkyū*, pp. 147–48.

2. As reported in the *Ishijarishū* (1724), *BT*, p. 700.

3. For English-language sources on Sōgi, see Carter, "Three Poets at Yuyama," and *The Road to Komatsubara*; and Miner, *Japanese Linked Poetry*. On Jōha, see Keene, "Jōha," and Miner, pp. 49–56. In Japanese, a good single-volume sociohistorical account of the *rengashi* phenomenon is Okuda, *Rengashi: sono kōdō to bungaku*.

4. Aside from the previously mentioned Muromachi anthologies, the extant individual verse collections of the shichiken are gathered in a modern edition in Kaneko and Ōta, eds., *Shichiken jidai renga kushū*. This includes the six poets apart from Shinkei, whose renga collections are gathered separately in *SSS*.

5. For the most complete presentation to date of documentary materials relating to five of the seven (excluding Shinkei and Sōzei), see Ishimura, *Waka renga no kenkyū*, pp. 196–303. Kido appraises their renga styles in *RS* 1: chap. 7, "Chūkōki no renga." The most detailed biographical study of Sōzei is Kaneko, *Shinsen Tsukubashū no kenkyū*, pp. 117–89.

6. For an enlightening study on the significance of Nōa's work in the assimilation and transformation of Chinese aesthetics in Japanese painting, see Weigl, "The Reception of Chinese Painting Models in Muromachi Japan." On Nōa as shogunal connoisseur, see Nakamura, "Gyobutsu gyoga mokuroku no senja Nōami ni kansuru ikkōsatsu."

7. Mention should also be made of Ninzei (fl. 1429–55), a priest of the Kenshōin and a waka student of Shōtetsu's, whose name frequently appears in renga meetings with Sōzei, Chiun, and Shinkei. See Ishimura, pp. 239–49. Although as active in the contemporary renga milieu as the seven sages, Ninzei subsequently fell into obscurity, possibly because Sōgi did not hold him in high regard. He is not among the poets anthologized in the *Chikurinshō*, and there are but twelve verses by him in the *Shinsen Tsukubashū*.

8. An annotated edition of this sequence may be found in Shimazu et al., *Chikurinshō*, pp. 373–400, under the title *Bun'an yonen Chikamasa-tō Nani hito hyakuin*.

9. An annotated edition of this sequence may be found in Kaneko et al., *Renga haikaishū*, pp. 124–46. For a translation, see Hare, "Linked Verse at Imashinmei Shrine."

10. The set of rules set down by Nijō Yoshimoto with Gusai's help in 1372 is known as the "New Renga Code" (*Renga shinshiki*) or "New Code of the Ōan Era" (*Ōan shinshiki*). For this original version, along with Kanera's proposed revisions and additions in 1452, and the later comments by Sōgi's disciple Shōhaku in 1501, see Carter's complete translation of the renga code in *The Road to Komatsubara*, pp. 41–72; see also his Introduction on pp. 33–40.

11. For an annotated edition, see Shimazu, ed., *Rengashū*, pp. 106–35. Among extant manuscripts, two have the title *Honka renga* and provide the foundation poem or waka presumably alluded to in each verse. The source for many of the

poems, however, is unknown and leads Shimazu to speculate that they were in fact composed later, on the inspiration of the verses, and not the other way round. This late inversion of the *honkadori* method is certainly unorthodox and novel. Commentary on some of the verses is also available in Okamoto, *Shinkei no sekai*, pp. 218–37.

12. See Varley, pp. 85–86, for the nature of the Hosokawa-Yamana conflict and the circumstances surrounding the 1454 plot against Sōzen, and pp. 71–75, for the shift in the power balance among the shugo daimyō clans as a result of the Kakitsu Incident of 1441.

13. Dempō is the same person as the Jōhō who submitted a hundred verse-pairs for Shinkei's comments in the manuscript called *Jōhō renga*, dated 3.25.1462; text in Shimazu, *Rengashi no kenkyū*, pp. 291–307.

14. The text of this sequence is available only in facsimile edition in Kaneko, ed., *Renga kichōbunken shūsei*, vol. 4.

15. Unless otherwise specified, all citations and numbering of verses from *STKBS* are from Yokoyama and Kaneko, eds., *Shinsen Tsukubashū: Sanetaka-bon*. The abridged annotated edition in Ijichi, ed., *Rengashū*, has also been consulted for reference; it includes only the verses by the seven sages plus Sōgi, Kenzai, Shōhaku, and Sōchō.

16. In *Oi no susami*, p. 156; this work consists of Sōgi's commentaries to selected verses of the seven sages from the *Chikurinshō* anthology.

17. In his commentary to this sequence, Kaneko (*Renga haikaishū*, p. 135) reads a pun on the name Akashi, Genji's place of exile, and *akashi* in the sense of "reveal," an allusion to the Akashi monk's confession to Genji of his high hopes for his daughter. Isolated from its context in the sequence, the maeku as such in *STKBS* is ambiguous. Thus Ijichi (*Rengashū*, p. 254) interprets it as the thought of a man burdened by a secret love he may not reveal, and his reading of Shinkei's tsukeku is also different. My rendering, which centers on the difficult coming of the dawn (the operative pun is *akashigata*) takes account only of what the maeku becomes in the light of Shinkei's tsukeku.

18. *SKS*, pp. 725–27. The preface to poems 6673–75 mentions that from 11.27.1450 on, people came to the Shōgetsuan to congratulate him on this signal honor.

19. Evidently, Shōtetsu's association with the Hosokawa was of long standing, dating as far back as the Ōei era (1392–1428) during the time of Mitsumoto (1378–1428), Dōken's father and Katsumoto's grandfather. See Inada, *Shōtetsu no kenkyū*, p. 116.

20. Kaneko, *Seikatsu to sakuhin*, p. 94.

21. Colophon to the Kokemushiro Text of *Sasamegoto*, in the archives of the Ise Shrine. This text is a copy dating from the Muromachi period and consists only of Part II; quoted in *RH*, p. 24.

22. Preface to verse 1701 in *Wakuraba*, *SK*, p. 196.

23. Suzuki, p. 205.

24. See *Chikamoto nikki*, *Zoku shiryō taisei* 10: 315, for the entries quoted here. The Ninagawa were hereditarily appointed to the position of Mandokoro-dai due to their connection as deputy of the Ise clan, which headed that office.

25. Kaneko, *Seikatsu to sakuhin*, p. 98, has 2.6 as the date of the Ōharano excursion; Kidō (*RS* 2: 900) has 3.6, as does Varley (p. 119), who translates the *Inryōken nichiroku* entry for 3.4.1465 describing the famous shogunal outing to Kachōzan just two days previous.

26. The Inryōken was an office within the Shōkokuji's Rokuon'in, whose head priest (at this time Shinzui) was charged with keeping a record of matters relating to the bakufu's administration of Zen temples. The portions of the journal written by Shinzui cover the years 1435–66.

27. The Shinkei-related entries quoted below may be found in the *Inryōken nichiroku*, 134: 594–604 *passim*.

28. From Banri's Chinese poetry and prose collection, *Baika mujinzō*, ZGR 12b: 338.967, in the section *Kiyō-shuza wain no jo*. According to Banri, Kiyō was born in Kii, began studying for the priesthood at the Kenninji while still a child, and was well known for his pleasing conversation and eloquent speech. When the war broke out in 1467, he went to live at the Kamakura Gozan temple of Kenchōji. Still later he moved to Edo under the patronage of the Lord of Musashi, Ōta Dōkan (who figures in the latter part of this biography). Banri was also staying in Edo from 1485 to 1488, and it was there that he met Kiyō.

29. The recipient of this letter is unknown, but for reasons too complex to discuss here, Kaneko (*Seikatsu to sakuhin*, p. 108) believes it was most probably Hosokawa Katsumoto or his uncle Dōken.

30. See the exchange of poems between Genji and Reikeiden, one of the late emperor's former ladies, in the "Hana chiru sato" (Village of Falling Flowers; called "The Orange Blossoms" in the Seidensticker translation) chapter of the novel (*Genji monogatari*, 2: 148–49; Seidensticker, *Tale of Genji* 1: 217). The verbal/imagistic link between "village of falling flowers" and "orange blossoms" in the verse-pair culls from it.

31. For the text, see Yunoue, "Gikō no eisō Shinkei no tensaku."

32. In the chapter called "Sōgi no shōfūron" in *Shinsen Tsukubashu no kenkyū*, and the article "Shinkei no makoto no michi," Kaneko discusses the critical content of Sōgi's "orthodox style" and Shinkei's "True Way" concept, but he has still to arrive at a definitive answer to the problem of how the critical principles of one bear upon the other.

33. Here it should be noted that "verse" or "verse style" in renga refers primarily to the tsukeku in relation to its maeku, not to the individual verse as such, unless it is the hokku that is under consideration. Thus a verse by a particular renga poet always appears with its maeku, which is understood to be by someone else. Most anthologies of renga contain individual links from various sessions, not whole hundred-verse sequences.

34. *RS* 1: 452–53.

35. Text in *SSS*, pp. 34–69.

36. *Katsumoto kunshin no michi magawazaru hito nari* (*Ōninki*, p. 262).

37. The Hosokawa were among Takauji's strongest allies in his struggle to consolidate the bakufu's power against the dissident forces of the Southern Court. Katsumoto's ancestor Hosokawa Yoriyuki (1329–92) is justly famous for holding the government together upon the death of Yoshiakira in 1368, when the future

Shōgun Yoshimitsu was only ten. As Deputy Shōgun from 1367 to 1379, Yoriyuki instituted the structure of fiscal and administrative policies upon which Yoshimitsu's reign could flourish. See Varley, pp. 50–58.

38. *Ōninki*, pp. 262–66; trans. Varley, pp. 165–69.

Chapter 4

1. Shinkei noted the date of his departure, 4.28.1467, in the colophon to a copy of the *Kokinshū* (now in the Tenri Library) that he made in Shinagawa in autumn of the same year, for he had left his library in the capital. The colophon is quoted in Kaneko, *Seikatsu to sakuhin*, p. 116.

2. *Utsuriyuku tsukihi no hikari o mo wasure*—that is to say, forgot the passage of time due to anxiety and suspense.

3. "The myriad Ways" (*yorozu no michi*) refers to the various practices—political, economic, social, and cultural—that make up the fabric of a functioning civilized society; their abandonment brings darkness and anarchy.

4. As mentioned already in the *Hitorigoto* passage at the end of Chapter 3, the imperial family moved to the Shōgun's Muromachi Palace for safety and as a matter of political expediency, in order to signify official backing of the Hosokawa camp.

5. "Lords of the moon and dwellers of the clouds" (*gekkei unkaku*). More commonly known as *kugyō*, "lords of the moon" is a Sino-Japanese figure for the country's highest officials in the first three court ranks: the Chancellor (*Daijōdaijin*), the Ministers of the Left and the Right (*Sadaijin, Udaijin*), and the Major and Middle Counselors (*Dainagon, Chūnagon*). "Dwellers of the clouds," also *tenjōbito*, refers to officials and nobles of the fourth and fifth ranks who were likewise allowed attendance at the court. In this official cosmological metaphor, the Emperor himself was imaged as the sun.

6. The dewdrop on a blade of grass is a metaphorical image that Shinkei frequently employed to refer to his fragile living conditions during the Ōnin War. The withering away of the sheltering grass blade suggests that it had become unsafe for him to remain in Jūjūshin'in. The temple was too closely associated with the Hosokawa-Masanaga faction and might even have been used as a base camp.

7. The text used in the translations below is the one included in *Gondaisōzu Shinkei shū*, *ZGR* 16a: 446.405–10. The corresponding poem numbers in the *ST* 6 edition are 101 to 200, pp. 94–100. The numbering is the same in *KT* 8: 258–60.

8. For the text of the *Azuma gekō hokkugusa*, see *SSS*, pp. 26–33. The numbers preceding each hokku are those of *SSS* Sec. I, in which the verses are numbered consecutively through six separate collections.

9. I am alluding here to the article by Edwin Cranston, "The River Valley as *Locus Amoenus* in Man'yō Poetry."

10. The statement that the appearance of the Travel theme in verse 4 is unusually early is based on my reading of other Muromachi-period sequences. It is confirmed by Shinkei's contemporary Ichijō Kanera in his *Renga shogakushō* (Notes for renga beginners): "In modern times, just as in the front [of the first fold or sheet], one does not, in the first two verses of the back, employ verses on Love,

Laments, Famous Places, and so on" (text in Ijichi, *Rengaronshū*, 2: 298). In other words, the norm was wholly seasonal themes in the first eight verses (the Prelude or *jo* section), as well as in the first two verses of the Development (*ha*) section. For the formalities of renga sequence structure and the renga manuscript, see Miner, pp. 58–85, and figs. 1 and 2.

11. Inoue Muneo, *Chūsei kadanshi no kenkyū*, 2: 196. Inoue's three-volume work on the history and composition of waka poetry circles in the capital and provinces in the medieval period is the standard source on the subject.

12. Ibid., pp. 14–16. Tamesuke resided in Kamakura from around 1292 in order to persuade the Kamakura bakufu to award him the Hosokawa estate (in Harima Province) whose ownership he was disputing with the heirs of his half-brother Nijō Tameuji (1222–86), the founder of the Nijō school. See Brower and Miner, *Japanese Court Poetry*, pp. 344–56, for an account of the family disputes surrounding Teika's material and poetic heritage.

13. In his treatise *Tsukuba mondō* (Tsukuba dialogues), written sometime in the period 1357–72, Nijō Yoshimoto credits Tamesuke with the codification of renga rules in Kamakura: "In Kamakura Lord Tamesuke published the so-called Fujigayatsu Code under the pen name Hokurin" (*RH*, p. 101). Tamesuke's mother, the nun Abutsu, was also known as Hokurin Zenni from her former place of residence in Kyoto, the Jimyōin Hokurin. For Tamesuke's role in Kamakura renga, see Kidō, *RS* 1: 201–2.

14. Six extant manuscripts of the *Sakusha burui* are included in the *Shinsen Tsukubashū* text edited by Yokoyama and Kaneko. For the quoted entry on Nagatoshi, see p. 376. An invaluable source for the social and geographical composition of the renga poets included in the anthology, the *Sakusha burui* was originally compiled in accordance with a request made by the court sometime between the completion of the anthology's first and second drafts in 1495. See Kaneko, *Shinsen Tsukubashū no kenkyū*, pt. II, chap. 4, for its textual history.

15. Quoted in *DNCJ* 2: 227, entry on "Myōkokuji." All subsequent citations from primary sources on the subject of the Suzuki and the Myōkokuji are as quoted in Kaneko, *Seikatsu to sakuhin*, pp. 124–26.

16. For studies of the growth of *toi* establishments in Kyoto and the provinces, see Toyoda and Sugiyama; and Morris. The commercial development traced in the two articles can be read profitably as a background for understanding the business activities of the Suzuki at this time.

17. *SK*, p. 18, preface to verse 256.

18. See Haga, *Higashiyama bunka*, p. 180, where Zenchiku and Shinkei are said to represent "Higashiyama culture at its loftiest level."

19. In the critical essay *Yodo no watari*, p. 294.

20. Text in the Seikadō Archives, no. 22 of the *Rengashūsho* MSS collection. Colophon quoted in Kaneko, *Seikatsu to sakuhin*, p. 136; see also the colophon to *Shinkei renga jichū* in *SSS*, p. 251. For a study of selections from this work, see Okamoto, *Shinkei no sekai*, pp. 238–75.

21. *SSS*, pp. 96–103.

22. *SSS*, pp. 231–51.

23. The colophon and poems from the 1468 waka sequence, quoted below, are translated from the text in *ZGR* 16a: 446.410–13. Poem nos. 201–300 in *ST* 6: 100–102 and in *KT* 8: 260–61.

24. Sources cited in Kaneko, *Seikatsu to sakuhin*, p. 135; the 2.17.1468 date appears in the third of the Hosokawa genealogical accounts in *ZGR* 5b: 114.

25. For this point about the chronological priority of Sōgi's hokku and the significance of his placing it after Shinkei's in the *Shinsen Tsukubashū*, see Saitō, *Chūsei renga no kenkyū*, pp. 208–12.

26. Sōgi's diary *Shirakawa kikō* is a brief record of this journey and includes the text of a hundred-verse sequence, the *Shirakawa hyakuin*, held on 10.22.1468. For an annotated edition of the prose section, see Kaneko, *Sōgi tabi no ki shichū*, pp. 9–26. The diary has been translated in Steven Carter, "Sōgi in the East Country: *Shirakawa kikō*."

Chapter 5

1. From Jōha's treatise *Shihōshō* (Notes on attaining the treasure), written for the country's military leader, Toyotomi Hideyoshi, in 1585. Ijichi, *Rengaronshū* 2: 235.

2. From the Hokuni Bunkō *Sasamegoto* text, as quoted in Kaneko, *Seikatsu to sakuhin*, p. 194.

3. Okami, "Shinkei oboegaki: aoi to keikyoku to minu omokage," p. 270.

4. I am preparing a separate volume on Shinkei's philosophy and criticism; it will include a complete translation of *Sasamegoto*.

5. *MYS* 318, the *hanka* to Akahito's famous Mount Fuji *chōka*, *MYS* 317. See commentary to verse 2 of Shinkei's 1467 solo sequence, "Cuckoo," in Part Two for his allusion to this poem.

6. Kaneko, *Seikatsu to sakuhin*, pp. 143–44.

7. Suzuki, pp. 61–62.

8. George Sansom (p. 263) states that renga poets "at times, no doubt, also acted as spies and gave the warlords news from other territories." Renga scholars themselves have remarked on the freedom with which the *rengashi* traveled across mutually hostile territories—thanks to the warlords' enthusiasm for poetry—and on the opportunity, as a social gathering, the renga session afforded for collecting and exchanging information. To my knowledge, no Japanese scholar has yet gone so far as to ascribe to them an occasional role as secret agents but that could be a case of reserve.

9. For a wider perspective on the war in the Kantō, see Sansom, pp. 195–200, 241–42.

10. Text in *SSS*, pp. 392–426. The information below regarding the participants is based on Kaneko, *Seikatsu to sakuhin*, pp. 146–47.

11. Kyōshun's identity was uncovered by Yunoue Sanae's research, as presented in "Kenzai to Kyōshun."

12. See, e.g., the entries for Ōta Sukekiyo and Ōta Dōkan in the *Nihon rekishi daijiten* 2: 251–52. They also figure as such in Inoue's literary history of the medieval poetic milieu (see vol. 2 [*Muromachi zenki*]: 229–31, 302–4).

13. Ijichi, *Sōgi*, pp. 85–88, 100–102.

14. The following account of Sogi's activities in the Kanto is summarized from ibid., pp. 60–102.

15. Ibid., pp. 86, 98; Inoue, 2: 232.

16. Ijichi, *Sōgi*, p. 125; also *RS* 1: 417.

17. From poem 44, *aki no kaze*; see Chapter 4.

18. According to Inoue (2: 234, 239, 241–42, 298), Tsuneyori was far from being a central or influential figure in waka circles in the capital during his lifetime. His celebrated reputation was a product of subsequent periods, a reflected glory from his famous disciple Sōgi, and had the effect of elevating the latter's own poetic pedigree (p. 242). There is no doubt that the prestige of the *Kokin denju* itself owed much to Sōgi's success in disseminating the value of the old teachings. His record of Tsuneyori's lectures, including his own comments on them, is known as the *Kokin wakashū ryōdo kikigaki* (Notes on two transmissions of the *Kokinshū*).

19. The colophon in question appears at the end of Part I of the Tenri Library Text, in Kidō Saizō, ed., *Kōchū Sasamegoto kenkyū to kaisetsu*, p. 83. See also Kaneko, *Seikatsu to sakuhin*, p. 149, for an interesting exegesis illuminating Shinkei's playful use of a nonexistent date in the colophon.

20. Text in *SSRS*, pp. 3–64.

21. In *SSRS*, pp. 257–316; the preface and epilogue only also appear in Ijichi, *Rengaronshū* 2: 331–39.

22. Unpublished manuscript in the Osaka University archives; I have relied on a handwritten copy kindly provided by Professor Kaneko.

23. Kaneko, *Kenzai*, pp. 18, 22.

24. *Shinkei-sōzu teikin*, p. 1126.

25. In *Kenzai*, Kaneko takes New Year 1475 as the date of this event based on information in Kenzai's personal renga collection in four volumes, the *Sono no chiri*. The *ZGR* text of *Sono no chiri* (p. 761), however, gives Bummei 8 (1476) as the date of the senku sponsored by Masanaga at the Kitano Shrine. Kidō (*RS* 1: 461) thinks 1476 is the more accurate, since Kenzai was still in Mino in the Eleventh Month of 1475, when he participated in a senku with Senjun and others; moreover, it would have been natural for him to leave the Kantō only after Shinkei's death in the summer of 1475.

26. *GSIS* 518. Travel

miyako o ba	When I left,
kasumi to tomo ni	the haze was just rising
tachishikado	over the capital—
akikaze zo fuku	across Shirakawa Barrier now
shirakawa no seki	the autumn wind is blowing.
Nōin-hōshi	Priest Nōin

The *Goshūishū* was ordered by Emperor Shirakawa in 1075 and completed in 1086.

27. For Bashō's impressions of the Shirakawa Barrier and the poetic anecdotes associated with it, see *Oku no hosomichi*, sections 12–13, pp. 350–51.

28. *Kono hokku nado o omoshiro to omowan toki, haya sono hito wa, renga no jōzutarubeshi* (Yokoyama, *Chikurinshō kōchū*, p. 98, comment to verse 389).

29. From Kenzai's waka anthology *Kanjinshū*; the poem is no. 338 in the *ST*

text. It is an allusion to Saigyō's famous *toshi takete* poem, *SKKS* 987, translated below.

SKKS 987. Travel. "Composed when he came to the vicinity of Azuma." Priest Saigyō.

toshi takete	Now full of years,
mata koyubeshi to	did I ever think then that I
omoiki ya	would cross it once more?
inochi narikeri	O Mountain-Amidst-the Night,
sayononakayama	a lifetime do I bear here!

Chapter 6

1. Text in *ST* 6: 115, poem 324.

2. *Shiyōshō* text in Ijichi, *Rengaron shinshū*, 1: 53–98.

3. Examples of "named world" (*na no yo*) are "floating world" (*ukiyo*), "the world of love" (*koi no yo*), "the afterworld" (*nochi no yo*).

4. Banri came to Edo in 1485 and stayed at a hermitage built for him in the Edo Castle grounds by Dōkan. Because the hermitage was situated within a plum grove, he called it the *Baika Mujinzō* (Inexhaustible treasure-trove of plum flowers), and named his Chinese poetry and prose collection after it. Banri remained in Edo for two more years after Dōkan's death in 1486, enlivening Dōshin's poetry sessions and associating with Shinkei's nephew Kiyō and the Zen monks of the Kamakura Gozan temples. Katsumori, *Ōta Dōkan*, pp. 114–15; see also note 28 to Chapter 3 above.

5. *GR* 16: 382, 514–15. The *Kamakura ōzōshi* is a Muromachi military chronicle recounting the civil wars and political conditions in the Kantō during the years 1379–1479, in particular the power struggle between the Ashikaga Kubō and the Uesugi, and the exploits of their major generals, the Yūki, Chiba, and Ōta.

6. Text of the 1471 Shōtetsu memorial sequence in *ZGR* 14b: 397.913–16.

7. I have followed Kaneko's reading (*Seikatsu to sakuhin*, p. 162) of poem 10, *korosu* ("kill") in line 5 as distinct from *utsusu* ("reflect") in the *ZGR* text; the former is more powerful in connection with *tsurugi* ("sword") in line 2. The poem includes an allusion to *tōzan kenju* ("a mountain of blades, trees of swords"), a Buddhist image of the tortuous geography of Hell; Shinkei uses it again in *Oi no kurigoto*, written in autumn of the same year.

8. "Sometime after the compilation of the renga anthology *Tsukubashū*, it began to fall into obscurity; thinking this deplorable, I would occasionally remember to record the verses of our own time, collecting as much as I could, until I had copied down twenty volumes under the name *Shingyokushū*. But these too were lost, torn and scattered, no one knows where." From Ichijō Kanera's instruction book on renga linking, *Fude no susabi* (Solace of the brush), written in 1469 at the Kōfukuji in Nara, where he took refuge during the war. This passage continues the description of how early in the war, mobs of looters broke into the building housing his library and destroyed several hundred volumes of Chinese and Japanese books that had been transmitted in his family for ten generations. Text of *Fude no susabi* in Ijichi, *Rengaronshū* 1: 281–303; quoted passage on p. 284.

9. "Death-Mountain Trail" (*shide no yamaji*); according to popular Buddhist belief, the souls of the dead are condemned to cross a steep mountain presided over by the Ten Kings of Hell, who subject them to various forms of torture as punishment for their sins. The *Sutra of the Ten Kings* mentions that at the southern gate of Death Mountain, the skin and flesh of the victims are torn apart, and their bones crushed until the marrow oozes out. This probably suggested the graphic image of dismemberment in Shinkei's poem.

10. In 1480, five years after Shinkei's death, a certain Ryōshō-shōnin applied to the Tōji Temple for permission to build in its grounds a hall to house the destroyed Jūjūshin'in's main image (*honzon*) until such time as the temple itself could be rebuilt. The request was denied, however, and Shinkei's much-lamented abode passed permanently from history ("Jūjūshin'in kō," p. 5).

11. Tzu-yu and Le-t'ien are identified later in the text. Wang Chih of the Chin dynasty (265–419) is the protagonist of a famous Taoist tale. While cutting trees on Shih-shih Mountain, he became absorbed in watching two boys playing chess. When he came to, he found that the handle of his axe had rotted and several hundred years had passed in the space of half a day. Verse 545 in the *Wakan rōeishū* alludes to this tale (*Wakan rōeishū*, p. 189).

Fei Chang-fang, a native of Ju-nan District in the Later Han dynasty (25–220), is likewise a Taoist hero. Leaping into a wine jar with an old sage, he discovered a wondrous realm built of precious stones, where one could partake of the finest wine and delicacies. Later the old man gave him a stick with which to master the gods and demons of earth, and he became famous as a healer (*Mōgyū*, 2:669–70, 852–53; see also *Wakan rōeishū*, verse 540, p. 188). The Fei Chang-fang anecdote appears in Japanese narrative literature (*Konjaku monogatari*, *Soga monogatari*, and *Gikeiki* among others) in various versions. In *Konjaku monogatari* 10:14, he learns the methods of Taoist magic and is transported to the immortal realm of Hōrai (Ch. P'eng-lai) in a dream.

12. "A long river" refers to Ōyama River, which has its source in the mountain and empties into Sagami Bay.

13. "A great peak" refers to Mount Ōyama, which rises to an altitude of 1,253 meters. The rain image in the following sentence was inspired by the mountain's legendary reputation as the abode of the rain god.

14. "The dream of a myriad forms" (*shikisō no yume*): in Buddhism the visible phenomenal world as apprehended by the mundane mind has only a provisional or conditional existence, and the distinctions that make things seem as they are have neither substantial nor transcendental reality. They are in that sense an unreal "dream." This Buddhist principle of non-discrimination, or emptiness, is the subject of poem 97, *samazama ni*, in Shinkei's 1468 waka sequence (see Chapter 4), and is likewise a grounding concept in *Sasamegoto*.

15. "The night rain of Hsiao-hsiang" (*Hsiao-hsiang yeh-yu*) and "the [autumn] moon over Tung-t'ing Lake" (*Tung-t'ing ch'iu yüeh*) are two of the so-called Eight Views of Hsiao-hsiang, the scenic area along the banks of the Hsiang River, which empties into Tung-t'ing Lake in Hunan. Lu-shan is in the adjacent province of Chiang-hsi to the east; Shinkei is alluding to Po Chü-i's famous poem, "Staying Alone in My Grass Hut, Listening to the Night Rain on Lu-shan," a melancholy

evocation of his lonely exiled existence in contrast to the splendor of his friends' life back in the court at Ch'ang-an. Two lines from this poem appear in the *Wakan rōeishū* (verse 555, p. 191) and have since echoed through the pages of Japanese literature from Sei Shōnagon to Bashō.

16. Araki Yoshio (*Shinkei*, p. 25 on) was the first to observe that *Oi no kurigoto* is a work equal to and belonging to the same literary tradition as Chōmei's *Hōjōki* and Bashō's *Genjūan no ki*. In an early standard source for Japanese literary history, Ishizu Naomichi, writing on the development of the *zuihitsu* genre in the late medieval period, confirms Araki's evaluation. He goes further to observe that among the "literary-critical essays" (*bungakuron-teki zuihitsu*) of this period, which would include the *Kōun kuden, Shōtetsu monogatari,* and Sōgi's *Oi no susami,* among others, "Shinkei's *Sasamegoto, Hitorigoto,* and *Oi no kurigoto* are preeminent not only in their deep-going search for beauty and lofty contemplation of human existence; they are also a demonstration of a rich aesthetic sensibility, and may be considered models of the literary-critical essay" (Ishizu, p. 428).

17. The *Meng Ch'iu* (J. *Mōgyū*) is a T'ang collection of anecdotes about historical and literary figures that had been enormously popular in Japan since the Heian period. Tzu-yu or Wang Hui-chih was the son of the celebrated Chin dynasty calligrapher Wang Hsi-chih (321–79). The elegant practice of referring to bamboos as "this dear friend" (*kono kimi*) arises from this anecdote. See *Mōgyū* 1: 432–33.

18. Trans. Waley, *Life and Times of Po Chü-i*, p. 120.

19. For a study of the influence of this theme in the cultural milieu of Muromachi Japan, see Rosenfield, "The Unity of the Three Creeds."

20. Karaki, "Shinkei-zuka." However, it was Adachi Hisao who first established the Jōgyōji as the site of Shinkei's "old temple" in his article "Shinkei kyoseki to Jōgyōji-seki ni tsuite," *Isehara shiwa* 4 (Feb. 1968); cited in Kaneko, *Seikatsu to sakuhin,* pp. 163, 166.

21. Text in *SSS,* pp. 104–21, under the title *Shibakusa-nai renga awase.*

22. For Kibe Yoshinori, see Inoue, 2: 183–85.

23. *Ungyoku wakashō,* pp. 192–93. This work is a collection of poetic anecdotes and poems by its author Junsō and by other poets both ancient and contemporary. The text's editors, Shimazu and Inoue, conclude from internal evidence that Junsō (obviously a pen name) was a former warrior general who lived for many years in Edo and subsequently retired to Shimōsa (Chiba). He was a friend of Kibe Yoshinori and was quite knowledgeable about Tō no Tsuneyori, Shinkei, Sōgi, and other well-known figures of the contemporary Kantō *bundan* (literary milieu).

24. Text in *GR* 9: 209.668–71.

25. Inoue, 2: 230.

26. Katsumori Sumi's detailed single-volume biography, *Ōta Dōkan,* is also a useful account of the political conditions in the Kantō in the fifteenth century.

27. See *Sōgi shūenki* (A record of Sōgi's final days). For an annotated version, see Kaneko's *Sōgi tabi no ki shichū,* pp. 103–25.

28. Araki, *Shinkei,* Preface, p. 1.

29. The four hokku are cited in Kaneko, *Seikatsu to sakuhin,* pp. 168–69.

30. Yokoyama, *Chikurinshō kochū,* p. 149; the verse in question is *Chikurinshō* 129.

31. From Kenzai's renga collection, *Sono no chiri*, p. 762. The hokku hinges on the contrast (*hana wa*) between the flowers that return each spring and the departed Shinkei.

32. Ibid., pp. 762–63.

Section I

1. All references to the *Chikurinshō* follow the numbering of the verses in the Shimazu et al. edition, *SNKBT* 49 (1991). Note, however, that Hoshika Sōichi, ed., *Kōhon Chikurinshō* (1937) was the only available printed edition heretofore, and all pre-1991 Japanese studies referring to the anthology cite the numbering there.

2. References to *Oi no susami* are to the text edited by Kidō Saizō in *Rengaronshū* 2, pp. 137–86; I have numbered the verses consecutively for convenience in citation. For textual commentary, see Nose Asaji, "*Oi no susami* (Sōgi rengaronsho) hyōshaku."

3. For the dating and internal textual relationships among these three Sōgi-line *Chikurinshō* commentaries, see Kaneko, *Renga kochūshaku no kenkyū*, pp. 36–38.

4. For the texts of *Chikubun*, *Chikurinshō no chū*, *Yuki no keburi*, and *Chikurinshū kikigaki*, see *Chikurinshō kochū*. Citations of them in this book follow Yokoyama's numbering there.

5. Text of *Keikandō* in Ijichi, *Rengaronshū* 2: 127–46.

6. According to Yamane Kiyotaka ("Shinkei no hyōgen: 'mono mo nashi' o megutte"), this expression occurs 17 times in the *Kokinshū*, 27 in the *Shinkokinshū*, 89 in the *Tsukubashū*, and 91 in the *Shinsen Tsukubashū*. Furthermore, in the seven sages' verses in the *Chikurinshō*, Shinkei and Chiun use it twice as often as the other five, and Shinkei's manner of using it is distinct from all the others.

7. Araki Yoshio, *Shinkei*, pp. 243–44, 247.

8. *RH*, p. 220. Sōgi wrote the *Azuma mondō* (Azuma dialogues) for renga enthusiasts in the Sumidagawa area of Musashi in 1470. It is his most important treatise, marking the beginnings of his project of defining the orthodox renga style based on the work of Sōzei, Shinkei, and the other seven sages.

9. The foundation poem (*honka*) Kenzai refers to is:

KKS 36. Spring. "Composed when he broke off a spray of plum blossoms."
The Higashisanjō Minister of the Left [Minamoto Tokiwa].

uguisu no	The warbler, 'tis said,
kasa ni nuu chō	sews them into a hat—
ume no hana	blossoms of the plum,
orite kazasamu	I'll pluck and adorn my head,
oi kakuru ya to	surely they will hide my age?

10. "Among Chinese poets Tu Fu may be said to have sung a lifetime of sorrow" (*SSG*, p. 139).

11. The poem is *SKKS* 95. Spring. In the spirit of "flowers in the old village." Former Abbot Jien.

12. "Days of peach blossoms opening in the spring breeze, / Season of paulownia leaves falling in the autumn dew"—these two are among the lines from Po Chü-

i's *Ch'ang hen ko* (J. *Chōgonka*; Song of everlasting sorrow) that appear in the *Wakan rōeishū*, verse 781, p. 252. Kenzai's text may have had "rain" instead of "dew," or he could be remembering wrong; Shinkei also has "rain" in *Sasamegoto* (*SSG*, p. 178).

13. Kaneko, *Seikatsu to sakuhin*, p. 249.

14. *Shūi gusō* 109, where the first line is *asanagi ni* ("in the dawn calm"). References to the *Shūi gusō*, Teika's poetic anthology, refer to the text edited by Kubota Jun, *Fujiwara Teika zenkashū*.

15. Shinkei might have had in mind this poem in *Ise monogatari* 68 (*NKBZ* 8:90):

kari nakite	When wild geese call and
kiku no hana saku	chrysanthemums bloom, autumn is
aki wa aredo	just fine, but how good
haru no umibe ni	'tis to dwell in Sumiyoshi Beach,
sumiyoshi no hama	beside the sea in springtime!

16. Okami, "Shinkei oboegaki," pp. 275–79, 284.

17. Kubota Jun, *Saigyō, Chōmei, Kenkō*, pp. 173–74. See also Shōtetsu's remarks on Kenkō and *Makura sōshi* in *Shōtetsu monogatari*, pp. 187–88; and Brower, trans., *Conversations with Shōtetsu*, pp. 95–96.

18. *Renju gappekishū*, entry for *hisaki* (registered as *hisagi*), no. 324.

19. As cited by Kubota Jun in his commentary to Akahito's poem in *SKKS* 641.

20. *Yamanoue Sōji ki*, pp. 56, 97. Takeno Jōō (1502–55) transmitted the ideals of the tea cult's founder, Murata Jukō (1422–1502), and was the teacher of the famous tea master Sen Rikyū (1522–91). Yamanoue Sōji (1544–90) in turn studied with Rikyū for twenty years and the *Yamanoue Sōji ki* is his record of the ideals, practice, and famous implements of tea, as secretly transmitted from Jukō down to Rikyū. Sōji also notes that it was Nōami (Nōa, one of the seven sages) who first recommended Jukō and the practice of tea to the Shōgun Yoshimasa (pp. 51–52).

21. See *Jukō, Furuichi Harima-hōshi ate no isshi*. The letter, which deals with the proper mental attitude in attaining to the highest in tea, is also known as *Kokoro no shi no fumi* (A letter on the mind-heart's teacher).

22. For Shinkei's role in the development of *wabicha*, see, e.g., Murai Yasuhiko, "The Development of *Chanoyu*," esp. pp. 21–23; and Haga Kōshirō, "The *Wabi* Aesthetic," esp. pp. 212–15.

23. The fourth line in modern printed texts of the *Kokinshū* is not *urasabishiku mo* but *uramezurashiki*, evoking a feeling not of loneliness but pleasure at the clear coolness of the first autumn winds after the humid heat of summer. Kenzai is probably quoting a variant *Kokinshū* text.

24. This qualification is made by Kidō Saizō in *RS* 1: 469. In general Kidō believes that Kenzai, in transmitting Shinkei's teachings, was not necessarily faithful to them but interpreted and altered them in his own way. See also Kidō, *Kōchū Sasamegoto*, p. 298. On the other hand, Kaneko ("*Keikandō* no shochūgo-kan," in *Shinsen Tsukubashū no kenkyū*, pp. 190–207) demonstrates that the *Keikandō* does represent Shinkei's classifications and commentary. My own reading is that although Kenzai might have altered, and inevitably so, Shinkei's wording and

emphases in his various treatises, he is faithful to the main thrust of his mentor's poetic philosophy, that his attitude of mind was clearly early inspired by the other, and his works like *Shinkei-sōzu teikin* are in fact fascinating in revealing other facets and applications of Shinkei's main principles as he discussed and illustrated them orally during Kenzai's tutelage in the Kantō.

25. The *Renga entokushō* was written by Kenzai for the great western daimyō Ōuchi Masahiro when he was visiting Yamaguchi between late 1490 and into the New Year; one of its colophons states that it represents "a transmission from Shinkei to Kenzai." Ōuchi Masahiro was one of the most affluent daimyō of his time, having amassed great wealth from the China trade. A great patron of the arts, he also invited Sōgi to Yamaguchi in 1480, Sesshū painted his famous Long Scroll there in 1486, and it was through his strong recommendation and support that the *Shinsen Tsukubashū* came about; it includes seventy-five of his verses. Kenzai's 1490 trip to Yamaguchi was in connection with the anthology's compilation; he would return there in the Ninth Month of 1495 to show the completed manuscripts to the dying Masahiro and subsequently write the diary *Ashita no kumo*, an account of Masahiro's death and funeral, including memorial hyakuin held daily after his death from the eighteenth to the end of the Ninth Month.

26. The *Tōfū renga hiji* (Secrets of the renga style of our time) is a comprehensive renga instruction manual written by the master Sōboku (d. 1545) for his son and poetic heir Sōyō (d. 1563). Sōboku studied renga with Sōgi's disciples, Sōchō and Sōseki (1474–1533), and in turn became the leading renga master after their deaths. As he puts it in his colophon to the *Tōfū renga hiji*, "This volume does not wholly issue forth from my own lips and mind; it is a record of the words of Sōzei, Shinkei, Sōgi, Kenzai, Sōchō, and Sōseki" (p. 228). In that sense, the work may be viewed as a record of the accumulated practical wisdom of the generations of renga masters who had molded the orthodox renga style.

27. Nose, "*Oi no susami* hyōshaku," p. 494.

28. Kaneko, *Seikatsu to sakuhin*, p. 202. He also cites the verse as an example of that aspect of Shinkei's lyricism that may be called sincerity, a profundity of feeling (*shinjō*) that draws us into the deepest layer of the poetic realm. This realm is commonly known as *yūgen*, but in Shinkei's terminology the appropriate term is *yōon*, a quality of "ineffable remoteness" we have seen among the waka translated in the literary biography and in a few of the preceding hokku. In *Shinkei*, Araki refers to this quality as *yūin*, an "ineffable echo"; Okami Masao implies the same realm in his term for it, "unseen presence" (*minu omokage*).

29. The verse appears in the *Azuma atari iisute* (no. 76), a collection of Shinkei's tsukeku from the Kantō years; see *SSS*, p. 179.

30. *Asaji*, written in 1500, is Sōgi's last critical work. It deals with the subject of *honka*, poem-allusions, and *honzetsu* (anecdotal allusions to prose literature) as methods of linking and illustrates these with 72 examples from the seven sages, Kenzai, Shōhaku, and others. The second part also illustrates the conventional associations attached to famous place-names (*meisho*) from some 39 provinces by citing poem-examples, without commentary. Page citations refer to the text edited by Kidō Saizō in *Rengaronshū* 2; I have numbered the verse-examples for convenience.

31. From the opening passage of *Asaji* (p. 317), where Sōgi underlines the overwhelming importance of learning to use allusions in the training of a novice.

32. Konishi, "Renga-teki sekai no keisei to tenkai," esp. pp. 66–67.

33. Sakamoto Yukio and Iwamoto Yutaka, trans., *Hokkekyō*, 1: 282.

34. The *Akishino gesseishū*, composed of some 1,600 poems, is the personal poetry collection of the *Shinkokinshū* poet Fujiwara Yoshitsune (1169–1206); *Akishino gessei* (clear moon on autumn bamboo grass) is part of his pen name. The KT text of the poem has a different last line: matsumushi no *koe*.

35. The Onoe no miya in Minase, Mishima County, Osaka, was the detached palace of the Retired Emperor Go-Toba; it would become famous as the setting for the *Minase sangin hyakuin* (Hundred-verse sequence by three poets at Minase), composed by Sōgi, Shōhaku, and Sōchō in 1488 as a prayer-offering dedicated to Go-Toba at the Minase Shrine, which stood at the old site of his palace.

36. The poem, by no means a simple one, is explained in Kenzai's *Jisankachū* and also in the *Shinkokin nukigakishō*, which is believed to transmit Shinkei's commentary on some 116 *Shinkokinshū* poems. In the latter, Kenzai writes: "This has been transmitted in several poetry houses as a distinctive poem. In Musashi Plain, the bush clover, the maiden flower, and various other flowers bloom, dew falls, the insects cry, and so on; no matter how far one walks, there are the same affecting sights and sounds. Finally, when one is ready to lodge at the very end of the plain, what might be the affecting things yet to be found there— so one wonders in imagination. The spirit of the poem is one of enjoyment of nature [*fūryū no kokoro*]. This commentary is transmitted in a work bearing [Fujiwara] Tameie's annotations" (quoted in Kubota, *Zenhyōshaku*, 2: 399).

37. Ebara, "Shinkei to Bashō." Shinkei's name does not occur in Bashō's writings, but isolated passages from *Sasamegoto* are cited in other contemporary haikai criticism, evidence that his work was not unknown among haikai poets at the time. As we now know, "the old site of Bishop Shinkei's hermitage" was one of the famous places listed in a couple of Edo gazetteers; it is inconceivable that Bashō was unaware of the work of one of Sōgi's mentors.

38. Ijichi in the headnote to this verse (*Rengashū*, p. 245) says it refers to Niou's seduction of Nakanokimi in the guise of Kaoru. Since that incident happens much earlier, in the "Hashihime" (Lady of the bridge) chapter, and with Kaoru's cooperation, it would contradict the sense of the link. Perhaps "Nakanokimi" in the note is a misprint for "Ukifune."

39. The *Minishū* is the individual anthology of the *Shinkokinshū* poet Fujiwara Ietaka (1158–1237); it includes some 2,850 poems and was compiled in 1245 by Kujō Motoie.

40. The *Kenzai zōdan* (A miscellany of Kenzai's lectures) is a collection of Kenzai's teachings about waka and renga; it includes anecdotes reminiscing on Shinkei, Sōzei, Sōgi, and the compilation of the *Shinsen Tsukubashū*, as well as commentary on the poetic lexicon. Dating from after Kenzai's return to the Kantō in his late years, it was recorded there by his disciple Kenjun.

41. Professor Kaneko made this observation during a Shinkei seminar, in response to my remark that the feeling of the link approximates the effect of the stark brushstrokes of certain *sumi-e* paintings.

42. In the lunar calendar, the moon is at the full on the fifteenth of each month; thus the "second-day moon" is very thin and insubstantial indeed.

43. For Shinkei's discussion of the structure of the link and the character of the *henjodai* verse, see *SSG*, pp. 156–59, 173–75; for an analysis of this *Sasamegoto* passage, see Ramirez-Christensen, "Renga janru ni okeru 'imi' no isō," esp. pp. 137–43.

44. It should be noted that Ijichi (*Rengashū*, p. 254) reads the maeku differently, in particular *ware-hito no michi* as *ware hito no michi*, thus: "For as long as I live, I at least shall hold fast to and practice the way of man to the fullest extent" (*ikiteiru kagiri wa, semete jibun dake de mo hito no fumiokonau michi o tsukushi, mamorō*). His construction of the link then becomes, "though the bridge may be rotting, as long as it remains, it will serve [the way of] man." A different syntactic reading of the maeku's second line leads then to a Confucian, rather than Buddhist, construction. My reading is based on *ware-hito no michi* ("the way of self and other"), as in *oya-ko no michi* ("the way of parent and child"), although *hito no michi* is of course also a possibility. I also give more weight to *yamazato ni kayou . . . hashi* ("the bridge . . . leading to and from the mountain village") as a pointed response to "the way of self and other" in the maeku. The existence of two possible constructions here is evidence above all of the fascinating character of renga as a genre that more than any other foregrounds the activity of reading itself.

45. Kenzai is referring to the scene in the "Yūgao" (Evening face flower) chapter, when alone with his dead lover in the deserted mansion, the grief-stricken and terrified Genji hears the weird cooing of a dove outside. No doubt it is the portentous quality of the link that evoked the "Yūgao" scene in Kenzai's mind.

46. The Tendai concept of the three truths (*santai* or *sandai*) refers to three ways of viewing phenomena. They are "empty" (*kū*) in lacking an unchanging core, and "provisional" (*ke*) in having nevertheless a temporal existence; the truth of the "middle way" (*chūdō*) names the ineffably indeterminate nature of phenomena as both real and unreal, or neither, at the same time. The link here is an allegorical illustration of the concept.

47. Freud, *Civilization and Its Discontents*, p. 15.

Section II

1. Barfield, *Poetic Diction: A Study in Meaning*, p. 52.
2. See Barthes, *The Pleasure of the Text*.
3. In Yoshimoto's treatise *Tsukuba mondō* (pp. 82–83), in answer to the question of whether renga practice can be a means of attaining religious enlightenment.
4. The *yoriai* or conventional word association between "cold" and "plovers crying" culls from a poem by Tsurayuki (*SIS* 224. Winter).

omoikane	As beset by yearning
imogari yukeba	I seek my beloved's abode,
fuyu no yo no	in the wintry night
kawakaze *samumi*	the river wind gusts so *cold*
chidori naku nari	the *plovers are crying.*

5. This *yoriai* pair is noted in *Renga tsukeai no koto* (entry 112, p. 218), a renga word association "thesaurus" of anonymous authorship. Although of much smaller scale than Kanera's *Renju*, it includes items excluded there and is believed to typify the more common sort of renga dictionary in the medieval period.

6. The Shirakawa River has its source in the valley below the Shiga Pass; it joins the Kamo River in the vicinity of Gion. The area along its banks in the eastern section of the capital was also known as Shirakawa. Yoshifusa's villa there later became the detached palace of the retired Emperor Shirakawa (r. 1072–86).

7. The other tree-bases of the *kemari* court were the willow in the southeast corner, the pine in the northwest, and the maple in the southwest.

8. *Wen hsüan* X, *Kokuyaku kambun taisei* ed., 2: 1–2.

9. *Shōtetsu monogatari*, p. 232, where the poet cites the *Guhishō* recounting of the tale, which ends with the statement: "It is this mode of gazing at the morning clouds and the evening rain that is called the *yūgen* style." For a translation of the Wu-shan passage, see Brower, *Conversations with Shōtetsu*, pp. 161–62. See also *Sasamegoto*, p. 179.

10. In *Oku no hosomichi* (p. 364), Bashō alludes to the same anecdote in the opening line of the section on Hiraizumi, where the hunted hero of the Gempei Wars, Minamoto Yoshitsune, made his last stand and the northern Fujiwara were destroyed for harboring him: *Sandai no eiyō issui no uchi ni shite* ("the glory of three generations in the space of a moment's dream").

11. Keene, trans., *Essays in Idleness*, chap. 30, p. 31 (my italics); the Japanese text is *hate wa arashi ni musebishi matsu mo chitose o matade takigi ni kudakare, furuki tsuka wa sukarete ta to narinu. Sono kata dani nakunarinuru zo kanashiki* (*Tsurezuregusa*, pp. 118–19).

12. *Wen hsüan* XV, *Kokuyaku kambun taisei* ed., 2: 464; 88 (Chinese text).

13. Keene, *Essays in Idleness*, p. 120; *Tsurezuregusa*, pp. 203–4.

14. In the *NKBZ* text of the *Genji*, the passages cited here are in 13: 219, 224, and 237.

15. However, it is also possible that *mukae no kuruma* refers to the carriage of Emma, King of Hell, who comes to fetch the dead and metes out punishment or reward according to their deeds. Emma is a well-known figure in popular belief and the visual arts.

16. See Part One, Chapter 4 above for similar poems composed by him earlier in the year.

17. This information on "the five marks of a heavenly maiden's decay" (*tennin no gosui*) is cited from the *Ojōyōshū* in the headnote to *Hagoromo* in *NKBZ* 33: 354.

18. Waley, trans., *Nō Plays of Japan*, pp. 220–21.

19. See *Nagu no yashiro*, one of the Tango province *fudoki*, in *NKBT* 2: 466–69.

20. *Wakan rōeishū*, p. 239.

21. From the translation of *Utsukushi Nihon no watakushi* by Seidensticker, *Japan, the Beautiful, and Myself*, pp. 68–69.

22. Kidō and Shigematsu, *Renga yoriaishū to kenkyū*, 1: 124, entry 193.

23. According to Kubota, the cited lines of the poem's topic are from the second

volume of the *Shutsuyō-gyō* (*Zenhyōshaku*, 8: 519). This is a 30-volume sutra composed of verses, hymns, and allegorical tales in prose illustrating Buddhist teachings. The poetry section is believed to stem from the *Hokkukyō* (Pali *Dhammapada*), the oldest Buddhist text, compiled around the third or fourth century B.C. (Mizuno, *Butten kaidai jiten*, p. 66).

24. This citation is from the *Hiyubon* (Parables) chapter of the *Lotus Sutra*, the passage where the Buddha explicates the parable of the burning house, and the Thus-Come-One's role as the father who rescues the children from their mindless play in the conflagration that is mundane suffering. "It is in the midst of such various woes as these that the beings are plunged, yet they cavort in joy, *unaware, unknowing, unalarmed, unafraid*, neither experiencing disgust nor seeking release. In this burning house of the three worlds they run about hither and yon, and, though they encounter great woes, they are not concerned" (Hurvitz trans., p. 61; italics mine). The poem's author, Priest Kyōshō (or Keisei, 1189–1268), was a son of the Regent and *Shinkokinshū* poet Gokyōgoku (Fujiwara) Yoshitsune. A Tendai priest, he traveled to Sung China in 1213, and has ten poems in the *Fūgashū*.

25. *Genji*, 16: 118–19. For the narrative and symbolic context of the poem, see Ramirez-Christensen, "Operation of the Lyrical Mode," pp. 22–27.

26. *SSG*, p. 160, section on "the six modes of poetry." Gusai's verse is *samidare wa / mine no matsukaze / tani no mizu* ("The long June rains: / pine winds across the peaks, / the valley streams!"). Kidō (in headnote 4) speculates that it might have been influenced by a hymn by Dengyō Daishi that reads the sound of the valley streams and mountain wind as manifestations of the Buddhist truth of the nondualism of phenomena and ultimate reality. By using the verse to illustrate the symbolic mode, Shinkei implies a similar significance.

27. See *Yamato monogatari* 148, *SIS* IX, *Gempei jōsuiki* 36, *Konjaku monogatari* 30, the Nō play *Ashikari*, and Tanizaki Jun'ichiro's tale of the same title. The story clearly had a wide distribution.

28. The remark is made in his treatise *Shiyōshō*, quoted in Part One, Chapter 5 above.

29. See, e.g., Shōtetsu's poem-prayer to the Tamatsushima deity, *koto no ha o*, in Part One, Chapter 2 above.

Section III

1. The source used for the translations is *Shinkei-sōzu jittei waka*. I have also consulted the text in *ST* 6: 106–15.

2. The source text is the final untitled collection in the *Gondaisōzu Shinkeishū*, pp. 413–19. It corresponds to poems 301–432 in *ST* 6: 102–5 and *KT* 8: 261–63.

Epilogue

1. The text of the mounted scroll fragment is also quoted in Kaneko, *Seikatsu to sakuhin*, pp. 174–75.

2. Entry 237 in the *Sakusha burui* section of the *Shinsen Tsukubashū*, p. 409.

3. The source is the *Hoan kyōka zenshū* in Tamamura, *Gozan bungaku shinshū*

1: 223. Dating from 1472 on, this work is a Chinese poetry and prose collection by Osen Keisan (1429–93), one of the last luminaries of Gozan literature. A poet-priest of the Shōkokuji, he was like Shinkei a beneficiary of Hosokawa Katsumoto's patronage and was in fact asked by Motonari to copy out one of the *Lotus* chapters for the memorial handscroll.

Bibliography

Primary texts and sources cited by acronyms are listed under their titles. Abbreviations are as listed on pp. xi–xii. Unless otherwise noted, place of publication for Japanese-language sources is Tokyo.

Araki Yoshio. *Shinkei*. Sōgensha, 1948.

Asaji (Low rushes) by Sōgi. In Kidō Saizō, ed., *Rengaronshū 2. Chūsei no bungaku*, 1st series, 14: 315–75. Miyai Shoten, 1982.

Aston, W. G., trans. *Nihongi*. Tokyo: Charles E. Tuttle, 1972.

Azuma gekō hokkugusa (Grasses of hokku from the Azuma journey) by Shinkei. In *SSS*, pp. 26–33.

Azuma mondō (Azuma dialogues) by Sōgi; ed. Kidō Saizō. In *RH*, pp. 207–37.

Baika mujinzō (Inexhaustible treasure-trove of plum flowers) by Banri Shūkyū. In *ZGR* 12b: 338.789–1013.

Bakhtin, M. M. *The Dialogic Imagination*, trans. Caryl Emerson and Michael Holquist. Austin: University of Texas Press, 1981.

———. *Speech Genre and Other Late Essays*, trans. Vern W. McGee. Austin: University of Texas Press, 1986.

Barfield, Owen. *Poetic Diction: A Study in Meaning*. Middletown, Conn.: Wesleyan University Press, 1973.

Barthes, Roland. *The Pleasure of the Text*, trans. Richard Miller. New York: Farrar, Straus and Giroux, 1975.

[*Teihon*] *Bashō taisei*, ed. Ogata Tsutomu et al. Sanseidō, 1959.

Brazell, Karen, and Lewis Cook, trans. "The Art of Renga." *Journal of Japanese Studies* 21.1 (Winter 1975): 33–61.

Brower, Robert, trans., with introduction and notes by Steven D. Carter. *Conversations with Shōtetsu* (*Shōtetsu Monogatari*). Ann Arbor: University of Michigan, Center for Japanese Studies, 1992.

Brower, Robert, and Earl Miner. *Japanese Court Poetry*. Stanford: Stanford University Press, 1961.

Buke utaawase. In Inoue Muneo et al., eds., *Chūsei utaawaseshū to kenkyū 3. Mikan kokubun shiryō,* 3rd series, 16: 62–73. Mikan Kobubun Shiryō Kankōkai, 1970. Also in *KT* 10: 348–49.

Bushū Edo utaawase (Poetry contest in Edo, Musashi). *GR* 9: 209.668–71. Also in *KT* 10: 349–50.

Carter, Steven D. *The Road to Komatsubara: A Classical Reading of the Renga Hyakuin.* Cambridge, Mass.: Harvard University Press, 1987.

———. "Sōgi in the East Country: *Shirakawa kikō.*" *MN* 42.2 (Summer 1987): 167–209.

———. "Three Poets at Yuyama: Sōgi and *Yuyama sangin hyakuin,* 1491." *MN* 33.3 (Autumn 1978): 241–83.

Chan, Wing-tsit, trans. and comp. *A Sourcebook in Chinese Philosophy.* Princeton: Princeton University Press, 1963.

Chikamoto nikki (The diary of Ninagawa Chikamoto, comp. 1465–86). *Zoku shiryō taisei* 10–12. Kyoto: Rinsen Shoten, 1967.

Chikubun [Kenzai's notes on verses from the *Chikurinshō*]. In *Chikurinshō kochū,* pp. 133–305.

Chikurinshō. In Shimazu Tadao et al., eds., *Chikurinshō.* SNKBT 49. Iwanami Shoten, 1991. Also Hoshika Sōichi, ed., *Kōhon Chikurinshō.* Iwanami Shoten, 1937.

Chikurinshō kochū, ed. Yokoyama Shigeru. *KS* 2. Kadokawa Shoten, 1969.

Chikurinshō no chū [Sōgi's annotations on verses from the *Chikurinshō*]. In *Chikurinshō kochū,* pp. 31–100.

Chikurinshū kikigaki [a *Chikurinshō* commentary]. In *Chikurinshō kochū,* pp. 307–89.

Chōroku Kanshō ki (Record of the Chōroku and Kanshō eras). In *GR* 16: 375.232–46.

Cranston, Edwin. "The River Valley as *Locus Amoenus* in Man'yō Poetry." In Japan P.E.N. Club, ed., *Studies in Japanese Culture,* 1: 14–37. 1973.

Dai Nihon chimei jisho, ed. Yoshida Tōgo. 8 vols. Fūzambō, 1971.

Derrida, Jacques. *Margins of Philosophy,* trans. Alan Bass. Chicago: University of Chicago Press, 1982.

———. *Of Grammatology,* trans. Gayatri Spivak. Baltimore: Johns Hopkins University Press, 1976.

———. *Writing and Difference,* trans. Alan Bass. Chicago: University of Chicago Press, 1978.

Ebara Taizō. *Renga. Ebara Taizō chōsakushū* 2. Chūō Kōronsha, 1979.

———. "Shinkei to Bashō." *Nihon bungeiron no sekai* 17.10 (Oct. 1942): 289–311.

Eco, Umberto. *Semiotics and the Philosophy of Language.* Bloomington: Indiana University Press, 1984.

Eikyō kunen Shōtetsu eisō. In *Chūsei III. ST* 5: 517–22. Meiji Shoin, 1974.

Freud, Sigmund. *Civilization and Its Discontents,* trans. James Strachey. New York: W. W. Norton, 1961.

Fude no susabi (Solace of the brush) by Ichijō Kanera. In Ijichi Tetsuo, ed., *Renga-ronshū* 1: 281–303. Iwanami Shoten, 1953.

Fūgashū. In Tsugita Kasumi and Iwasa Miyoko, eds., *Fūga wakashū. Chūsei no bungaku,* 1st series, 4. Miyai Shoten, 1974.

Fukui Kyūzō. *Renga no shiteki kenkyū.* Yūseidō, 1969.

Genji monogatari. In Abe Akio et al., eds., *Genji monogatari.* 6 vols. NKBZ 12–17. Shōgakkan, 1970–76.

Gikō no eisō Shinkei no tensaku (Shinkei's critical comments on Sōgi's poetic compositions) by Shinkei; ed. Yunoue Sanae. In "Gikō no eisō Shinkei no tensaku: honkoku to kaisetsu." *Renga haikai kenkyū* 45 (Aug. 1973): 22–31.

Gondaisōzu Shinkei shū. In ZGR 16a: 446.400–19. Also in ST 6: 94–105 and KT 8: 256–63 under the title *Shinkeishū.*

Guku Shibakusa (Humble verses of wayside grasses) by Shinkei. In *SSRS,* pp. 3–64.

Gunsho ruijū, comp. Hanawa Hokiichi. 24 vols. Tōkyō Naigai Shoseki, 1928–37.

Gyōkō hōin nikki (Diary of Dharma Seal Gyōkō). In *Chūsei III. ST* 5: 451–58. Meiji Shoin, 1974.

Haga Kōshirō. *Chūsei bunka to sono kiban. Haga Kōshirō rekishi ronshū* 4. Shibunkaku Shuppan, 1981.

———. *Higashiyama bunka.* Hanawa Shobō, 1962.

———. "The *Wabi* Aesthetic Through the Ages," adapted and trans. Martin Colcutt. In H. Paul Varley and Kumakura Isao, eds., *Tea in Japan: Essays on the History of Chanoyu,* pp. 195–230. Honolulu: University of Hawaii Press, 1989.

———, ed. *Geidō shisōshū. Nihon no shisō* 7. Chikuma Shobō, 1971.

Hall, John Whitney, and Jeffrey Mass, eds. *Medieval Japan: Essays in Institutional History.* Stanford: Stanford University Press, 1974.

Hall, John Whitney, and Toyoda Takeshi, eds. *Japan in the Muromachi Age.* Berkeley: University of California Press, 1977.

Hare, Thomas W. "Linked Verse at Imashinmei Shrine: *Anegakōji Imashinmei Hyakuin,* 1447." *MN* 34.2 (Summer 1979): 169–208.

Hashimoto Fumio et al., eds. *Karonshū.* NKBZ 50. Shōgakkan, 1975.

Hayashiya Tatsusaburō. *Chūsei bunka no kichō.* Tōkyō Daigaku Shuppankai, 1953.

Hekizan nichiroku. Vol. 26 of [*Shintei zōho*] *Shiseki shūran.* 43 vols. Kyoto: Rinsen Shoten, 1967–68.

Hirohata Yuzuru. *Chūsei injabungei no keifu.* Ōfūsha, 1978.

Hirota, Dennis, trans. and intro. "In Practice of the Way: *Sasamegoto,* an Introduction Book in Linked Verse." *Chanoyu Quarterly* 19 (1977): 23–46.

Hisamatsu Sen'ichi, ed. *Nihon bungakushi: chūsei.* Shibundō, 1955.

——— and Nishio Minoru, eds. *Karonshū, Nōgakuronshū.* NKBT 65. Iwanami Shoten, 1961.

Hitorigoto (Solitary ramblings) by Shinkei; ed. Shimazu Tadao. In Hayashiya Tatsusaburō, ed. *Kodai chūsei geijutsuron,* pp. 464–78.

Hōjōki by Kamo no Chōmei; ed. Kanda Hideo. In Kanda Hideo et al., eds. *Hōjōki, Tsurezuregusa, Shōbōgenzō zuimonki, Tannishō.* NKBZ 27: 27–49. Shōgakkan, 1971.

Hokkekyō (Lotus sutra), trans. Sakamoto Yukio and Iwamoto Yutaka. 3 vols. Iwanami Shoten, 1976.

Hurvitz, Leon, trans. *Scripture of the Lotus Blossom of the Fine Dharma.* New York: Columbia University Press, 1976.

Hyakushu waka [the 1463 waka sequence with Shinkei's own commentary]. In *SSRS*, pp. 317–47.

Ichigon (One word) by Shinkei. Unpublished MS in the Ōsaka University Archives.

Ijichi Tetsuo. "Kitano shinkō to renga." *Shoryōbu kiyō* 5 (Mar. 1955): 32–41.

———. *Renga no sekai.* Yoshikawa Kōbunkan, 1976.

———. *Sōgi.* Seigodō, 1943.

———, ed. *Rengaron shinshū. Koten bunkō* 113. Koten Bunkō, 1956.

———. *Rengaronshū.* 2 vols. Iwanami Shoten, 1953, 1956.

———. *Rengashū. NKBT* 39. Iwanami Shoten, 1960.

Ijichi Tetsuo et al., eds. *Haikai daijiten.* Meiji Shoin, 1972.

———. *Rengaronshū, Nōgakuronshū, Haironshū. NKBZ* 51. Shōgakkan, 1973.

Imoto Nōichi et al., eds. *Matsuo Bashō-shū. NKBZ* 41. Shōgakkan, 1972.

Inada Toshinori. "Muromachi-ki no waka ni okeru rengateki hyōgen: Rengashi no waka o chūshin ni shite." In Kaneko Kinjirō-hakase Kokikinen Ronshū Henshū Iinkai, ed., *Renga to chūsei bungei,* pp. 149–65. Kadokawa Shoten, 1977.

———. "Shinkei no waka hyōgen no tokusei: Gengo no jūsō kōyō." *Chūsei bungei* 45 (Nov. 1969): 33–51.

———. *Shōtetsu no kenkyū.* Kazama Shoin, 1978.

——— et al., eds. *Chūsei bungaku no sekai.* Sekai Shisōsha, 1984.

Inoue Muneo. *Chūsei kadanshi no kenkyū.* 3 vols. Meiji Shoin and Kazama Shobō, 1961–72.

——— et al., eds. *Chūsei utaawaseshū to kenkyū. Mikan kokubun shiryō,* 3rd series, 16. Mikan Kokubun Shiryō Kankōkai, 1970.

Inryōken nichiroku. Dai Nihon Bukkyō zensho 133–37. Bussho Kankōkai, 1912.

Ise monogatari, ed. Fukui Teisuke. In Katagiri Yōichi et al., eds., *Taketori monogatari, Ise monogatari, Yamato monogatari, Heichū monogatari. NKBZ* 8: 133–244. Shōgakkan, 1972.

Ishihara Shizuko. "Jūjūshin'in kō." *Renga haikai kenkyū* 49 (1976): 1–9.

Ishimura Yasuko. *Waka renga no kenkyū.* Musashino Shoin, 1975.

Ishizu Naomichi. "Zuihitsu." In Hisamatsu Sen'ichi, ed., *Nihon bungakushi: Chūsei,* pp. 428–39. Shibundō, 1955.

Itō Kei et al., eds. *Chūsei wakashū: Muromachi-hen. SNKBT* 47. Iwanami Shoten, 1990.

Iwata Tatsushi. "Shinkei no sakuhin ni miru nendaiteki hensen." *Gengo to bungei* 39.9 (1964): 37–48.

Jōhō renga. In Shimazu Tadao, *Rengashi no kenkyū,* 291–307. Kadokawa Shoten, 1969.

Jukō, Furuichi Harima-hōshi ate no isshi (A letter addressed to the Harima Priest Furuichi by Jukō). In Haga Kōshirō, ed., *Geidō shisōshū. Nihon no shisō* 7: 271–76. Chikuma Shobō, 1971.

Kamakura ōzōshi. In *GR* 16: 382.473–518.

Kaneko Kinjirō. *Renga kochūshaku no kenkyū.* Kadokawa Shoten, 1974.

———. *Rengashi Kenzai denkō. Kokugo kokubungaku kenkyū sōsho* 9. Ōfūsha, 1977.

————. "Shinkei no fūga ishiki." *Bungaku, Gogaku* 90 (June 1981): 45–60.

————. "Shinkei no makoto no michi." *Shōnan bungaku* 11 (Mar. 1977): 1–8.

————. "Shinkei no seikatsu-ken." *Risshō joshidaigaku kokubun* 1 (Mar. 1972): 1–10.

————. *Shinkei no seikatsu to sakuhin. Kaneko Kinjirō renga kōsō* 1. Ōfūsha, 1982.

————. "Shinkei no shochūgo-kan." *Kokugo to kokubungaku* (June 1956): 1–10.

————. *Shinsen Tsukubashū no kenkyū.* Kazama Shobō, 1969.

————. *Sōgi tabi no ki shichū.* Ōfūsha, 1976.

————. *Tsukubashū no kenkyū.* Kazama Shobō, 1965.

————. "Yoshimoto rengaron no kotsu, koppō, koppū." *Gengo to bungei* (Mar. 1959): 26–31.

————, ed. [*Renga kichōbunken shūsei kinen ronshū*] *Renga kenkyū no tenkai.* Benseisha, 1985.

————. *Renga kichōbunken shūsei.* 10 vols., plus 4 suppl. and 2 indexes. Benseisha, 1978– .

Kaneko Kinjirō and Ōta Takeo, eds. *Shichiken jidai renga kushū.* Kadokawa Shoten, 1975.

Kaneko Kinjirō et al., eds., *Renga haikaishū. NKBZ* 32. Shōgakkan, 1974.

Kaneko Kinjirō-hakase Kokikinen Ronshū Henshū Iinkai, ed. *Renga to chūsei bungei.* Kadokawa Shoten, 1977.

Kanjinshū by Kenzai. In *Chūsei IV, ST* 6: 536–47. Meiji Shoin, 1976.

Kanshō hyakushu [the 1463 waka sequence with Shinkei's own commentary], ed. Araki Hisashi. In *Chūsei wakashū: Muromachi-hen. SNKBT* 47: 315–52. Iwanami Shoten, 1990.

Karaki Junzō. "Shinkei-zuka." *Bungaku* 36.7 (July 1968): 845–47.

Katsumori Sumi. *Ota Dōkan. Nihon no bushō* 26. Jimbutsu Ōraisha, 1966.

Keene, Donald. "Jōha, a Sixteenth-Century Poet of Linked Verse." In George Elison and Bardwell L. Smith, eds., *Warriors, Artists, and Commoners*, pp. 113–31. Honolulu: University of Hawaii Press, 1981.

————, trans. *Essays in Idleness.* New York: Columbia University Press, 1967.

Keikandō by Kenzai. In Ijichi Tetsuo, ed., *Rengaronshū* 2: 128–46.

Kenzai zōdan (A miscellany of Kenzai's lectures). In Sasaki Nobutsuna, ed., *Nihon kagaku taikei* 5: 390–425. Kazama Shobō, 1977 [1957].

Kichōkotenseki sōkan. 13 vols. to date. Kadokawa Shoten, 1968– .

Kidō Saizō. "Kenzai to Sōgi: *Shinkei-hōin teikin* no seiritsu o megutte." In Kaneko Kinjirō, ed., *Renga kenkyū no tenkai*, pp. 59–79. Benseisha, 1985.

————. *Kōchū Sasamegoto kenkyū to kaisetsu.* Rokusan Shoin, 1952. Published in new ed. as *Sasamegoto no kenkyū.* Rinsen Shoten, 1990.

————. *Renga shironkō.* 2 vols. Meiji Shoin, 1973.

————. "Yoriai, tsukeaigo gikō." *Nihon joshi daigaku kiyō: bungakubu* 29 (Mar. 1980): 1–8.

———— and Shigematsu Hiromi, eds. *Rengaronshū* 1. *Chūsei no bungaku*, 1st series, vol. 2. Miyai Shoten, 1972.

———— and Shigematsu Hiromi, eds. *Renga yoriaishū to kenkyū.* 2 vols. Toyohashi-shi: Mikan Kokubun Shiryō Kankōkai, 1978, 1979.

Kitano-sha ichimanku gohokku waki daisan narabi ni jo. In Kunaichō Shoryōbu, ed., *Renga I. Katsuranomiyabon sōsho* 18. Nara: Yōtokusha, 1957.

Kodai chūsei geijutsuron, ed. Hayashiya Tatsusaburō. *Nihon shisō taikei* 23. Iwanami Shoten, 1973.

Kojiki. In Ogihara Asao and Kōnosu Hayao, eds. *Kojiki, Jōdai Kayō. NKBZ* 1. Shōgakkan, 1973.

[*Shimpen*] *Kokka taikan,* ed. Shimpen Kokka Taikan Henshū Iinkai. 10 vols. with separate indexes. Kadokawa Shoten, 1983–92.

Kokinshū. In Ozawa Masao, ed., *Kokin wakashū. NKBZ* 7. Shōgakkan, 1971.

Konishi Jin'ichi. " 'Hie' to 'yase.' " *Bungaku, Gogaku* 10 (Dec. 1958): 12–29.

———. "Renga-teki sekai no keisei to tenkai." *Kokugo to kokubungaku* 27.10 (Oct. 1950): 62–71.

———. *Sōgi. Nihon shijinsen* 16. Chikuma Shobō, 1971.

Kubota Jun. *Saigyō, Chōmei, Kenkō.* Meiji Shoin, 1979.

———, ed. *Shinkokin wakashū zenhyōshaku.* 9 vols. Kōdansha, 1977.

Kurokawa Yōichi, ed. *To Ho* [Ch. *Tu Fu*]. 2 vols. *Chūgoku shijin senshū* 9–10. Iwanami Shoten, 1957.

Makashikan, ed. and trans. Sekiguchi Shindai. 2 vols. Iwanami Shoten, 1966, 1967.

Mansai jugō nikki. 2 vols. ZGR suppl. vols. 1–2: 870a–b.

Man'yōshū, ed. Kojima Noriyuki et al. 4 vols. *NKBZ* 2–5. Shōgakkan, 1971.

McCullough, Helen Craig, trans. *Kokin Wakashū: The First Imperial Anthology of Japanese Poetry.* Stanford: Stanford University Press, 1985.

———. *Tales of Ise.* Stanford: Stanford University Press, 1968.

Minase sangin hyakuin (Hundred-verse sequence by three poets at Minase) by Sōgi, Shōhaku, and Sōchō. In Ijichi Tetsuo, ed., *Rengashū. NKBT* 39: 343–66. Iwanami Shoten, 1960.

Miner, Earl. *Japanese Linked Poetry.* Princeton: Princeton University Press, 1979.

Mizuno Kōgen et al., eds. *Butten kaidai jiten.* Shunjūsha, 1977.

Mōgyū (Ch. *Meng Ch'iu*), ed. Hayakawa Mitsusaburō. 2 vols. *SKT* 58–59. Meiji Shoin, 1973.

Monzen (Ch. *Wen hsüan*), ed. Kokumin Bunkō Kankōkai. 3 vols. Kokumin Bunkō Kankōkai, 1921–22.

Morris, V. Dixon. "Sakai: From Shōen to Port City." In John Whitney Hall and Toyoda Takeshi, eds., *Japan in the Muromachi Age,* pp. 145–58. Berkeley: University of California Press, 1977.

Murai Yasuhiko. "The Development of *Chanoyu*: Before Rikyū," trans. H. Paul Varley. In H. P. Varley and Kumakura Isao, eds., *Tea in Japan: Essays on the History of Chanoyu,* pp. 3–32. Honolulu: University of Hawaii Press, 1989.

Nagashima Fukutarō. *Chūsei bungei no genryū.* Kyoto: Kawara Shoten, 1948.

Nagusamegusa (Grasses of solace) by Shōtetsu. In *GR* 15: 334.117–24.

Nakamura Hideo. "Gyobutsu gyoga mokuroku no senja Nōami ni kansuru ik-kōsatsu." *Tōkyō Kokuritsu Hakubutsukan kiyō* 7 (1971): 157–205.

Naumann, Wolfram. *Shinkei in seiner Bedeutung für die japanische Kettendichtung. Studien zur Japanologie* 8. Wiesbaden: Harrassowitz, 1967.

Nihon kagaku taikei, ed. Sasaki Nobutsuna. 10 vols. Kazama Shobō, 1956–63.

Nihon kagaku taikei, ed. Sasaki Nobutsuna and Kyūsojin Hitaku. 15 vols. Kazama Shobō, 1977–81.

Nihon kokugo daijiten, ed. Ichiko Teiji et al. 20 vols. Shōgakkan, 1972–76.

Nihon koten bungaku taikei, ed. Takagi Ichinosuke et al. 102 vols. Iwanami Shoten, 1956–68.

Nihon koten bungaku zenshū, ed. Akiyama Ken et al. 51 vols. Shōgakkan, 1970–76.

Nihon rekishi daijiten, ed. Nihon Rekishi Daijiten Henshū Iinkai. 12 vols. Kawade Shōbō, 1968–70.

Nihon shoki, ed. Sakamoto Tarō et al. 2 vols. *NKBT* 67–68. Iwanami Shoten, 1965, 1967.

Nitta Masaaki. *Tendai tetsugaku nyūmon*. Daisan Bummeisha, 1977.

Nose Asaji. "*Oi no susami* (Sōgi rengaronsho) hyōshaku." In *Renga kenkyū*, pp. 379–559. *Nose Asaji chōsakushū* 7. Shibunkaku Shuppan, 1982.

Oi no kurigoto (Old man's prattle) by Shinkei; ed. Shimazu Tadao. In *Kodai chūsei geijutsuron*, pp. 410–22. Iwanami Shoten, 1973.

Oi no susami by Sōgi; ed. Kidō Saizō. In *Rengaronshū* 2. *Chūsei no bungaku*, 1st series, vol. 14: 137–86. Miyai Shoten, 1982.

Okami Masao. "Mono: dashimono, monokise, hana no moto renga." *Kokugo kokubungaku* 24.2 (Feb. 1955): 31–36.

———. "Shinkei oboegaki: aoi to keikyoku to minu omokage." *Kokugo kokubun* 22.9 (Sept. 1947): 266–86.

Okamoto Hikoichi. "Shinkei dokugin *Nanimichi hyakuin shishō*." *Ritsumeikan bungaku* 403–11 (Jan.–Sept. 1979): 4 pts.

———. *Shinkei no sekai*. Ōfūsha, 1973.

Okazaki Yoshie. *Bi no dentō*. Kōbundō Shobō, 1940.

Oku no hosomichi (Narrow road to the deep north) by Bashō; ed. Imoto Nōichi. In *Matsuo Bashō shū*. *NKBZ* 41: 341–86. Shōgakkan, 1972.

Okuda Isao. *Rengashi: sono kōdō to bungaku*. *Nihonjin no kōdō to shisō* 41. Hyōronsha, 1976.

Ōninki. In *GR* 16: 376.252–97.

Paz, Octavio; Jacques Roubaud; Edoardo Sanguineti; and Charles Tomlinson. *Renga: A Chain of Poems*. New York: George Braziller, 1971.

Philippi, Donald L., trans. *Kojiki*. Tokyo: Tokyo University Press, 1968.

Ramirez-Christensen, Esperanza. "The Essential Parameters of Linked Poetry." *HJAS* 41.2 (Dec. 1981): 555–95.

———. "The Operation of the Lyrical Mode in the *Genji monogatari*." In Andrew Pekarik, ed., *Ukifune: Love in the Tale of Genji*, pp. 21–61. New York: Columbia University Press, 1982.

———. "Renga janru ni okeru 'imi' no isō: Shinkei no tsukeairon o megutte." In Kaneko Kinjirō, ed., *Renga kenkyū no tenkai*, pp. 133–54. Benseisha, 1985.

Renga entokushō by Kenzai. In Ijichi Tetsuo, ed. *Rengaronshū* 2: 116–26. Iwanami Shoten, 1956.

Rengaronshū, Haironshū, ed. Kidō Saizō and Imoto Nōichi. *NKBT* 66. Iwanami Shoten, 1961.

Renga shinshiki (The new renga code), ed. Okami Masao. In *Yoshimoto rengaron-shū* 1, pp. 7–23. Koten Bunkō, 1952. Also in Yamada Yoshio and Hoshika Sōichi, eds., *Renga hōshiki kōyō*, pp. 25–93. Iwanami Shoten, 1936.

Renga shironkō by Kidō Saizō. 2 vols. Meiji Shoin, 1973.

Renga shogakushō (Notes for renga beginners) by Ichijō Kanera. In Ijichi Tetsuo, ed., *Rengaronshū* 2: 287–310. Iwanami Shoten, 1956.

Renga tsukeai no koto (On renga linking). In Kidō Saizō and Shigematsu Hiromi, eds., *Rengaronshū* 1, pp. 204–20. Miyai Shoten, 1972.

Renju gappekishū by Ichijō Kanera. In Kidō Saizō and Shigematsu Hiromi, eds., *Rengaronshū* 1, pp. 26–202. Miyai Shoten, 1972.

Rongo (Ch. *Lun-yü*), ed. Yoshida Kengō. *SKT* 1. Meiji Shoin, 1980 [1960].

Rosenfield, John. "The Unity of the Three Creeds: A Theme in Japanese Ink Painting of the Fifteenth Century." In John Whitney Hall and Toyoda Takeshi, eds., *Japan in the Muromachi Age*, pp. 205–25. Berkeley: University of California Press, 1977.

Saitō Yoshimitsu. *Chūsei renga no kenkyū*. Yūseidō, 1979.

———. "Karon kara mita Shinkei, Sōgi no rengaron." *Renga haikai kenkyū* 11 (Mar. 1956): 19–27. Reprinted in idem, *Chūsei renga no kenkyū*, 191–207. Yūseidō, 1979.

Sansom, George. *A History of Japan, 1334–1615*. Stanford: Stanford University Press, 1961.

Sasamegoto (Murmured conversations) by Shinkei; ed. Kido Saizō. In *RH*, pp. 119–204. *NKBT* 66. Iwanami Shoten, 1961.

Seidensticker, Edward, trans. *Japan, the Beautiful, and Myself (Utsukushi Nihon no watashi* by Kawabata Yasunari). Tokyo: Kōdansha, 1969.

———. *The Tale of Genji*. 2 vols. New York: Alfred A. Knopf, 1977.

Shibakusa-nai renga awase by Shinkei. In *SSS*, pp. 104–21.

Shihōshō (Notes on attaining the treasure) by Jōha. In Ijichi Tetsuo, ed., *Rengaron-shū* 2: 231–59. Iwanami Shoten, 1956.

Shikashū taisei, ed. Wakashi Kenkyūkai. 7 vols. Meiji Shoin, 1973–76.

Shimaji Daitō, ed. *Kanwa taishō Myōhōrengekyō*. Meiji Shoin, 1914.

Shimazu Tadao. "*Kenzai zōdan* oboegaki." In Kaneko Kinjirō, ed., *Renga kenkyū no tenkai*, pp. 81–100. Benseisha, 1985.

———. *Renga no kenkyū*. Kadokawa Shoten, 1973.

———. *Rengashi no kenkyū*. Kadokawa Shoten, 1969.

———, ed. *Rengashū*. SNKS 33. Shinchōsha, 1979.

Shinchō Nihon koten shūsei. 48 vols. Shinchōsha, 1976–89.

Shingyokushū (Gems of the mind-heart) by Shinkei. In *SSS*, pp. 34–69.

Shingyokushū shūi by Shinkei. In *SSS*, pp. 69–74.

Shinkei sakushinshū, ed. Yokoyama Shigeru. *KS* 5. Kadokawa Shoten, 1972.

Shinkeishū ronshū, ed. Yokoyama Shigeru and Noguchi Ei'ichi. Kisshōsha, 1948.

Shinkei-sōzu hyakushu (A hundred-poem sequence by Bishop Shinkei [the 1471 memorial to Shōtetsu]). In *ZGR* 14b: 397.913–16.

Shinkei-sōzu jittei waka (Bishop Shinkei's waka in ten styles). In *ZGR* 15a: 403.41–47; also in *Chūsei IV, ST* 6: 106–15.

Shinkei-sōzu teikin (Bishop Shinkei's teachings) by Kenzai. In *ZGR* 17b: 497.1120–26.

Shinkokinshū. In Kubota Jun, ed., *Shinkokin wakashū zenhyōshaku.* 9 vols. Kōdansha, 1977.

Shin Nihon koten bungaku taikei. 100 vols. to date. Iwanami Shoten, 1989– .

Shinoda Hajime. *Shinkei. Nihon shijinsen* 28. Chikuma Shobō, 1987.

Shinsen Tsukubashū. In Yokoyama Shigeru and Kaneko Kinjirō, eds., *Shinsen Tsukubashū: Sanetaka-bon. KS* 4. Kadokawa Shoten, 1970. Abridged annotated edition in Ijichi Tetsuo, ed., *Rengashū. NKBT* 39: 177–341. Iwanami Shoten, 1960.

Shinshaku kambun taikei, ed. Uchida Sennosuke et al. 114 vols. plus 1 suppl. Meiji Shoin, 1960– .

Shirakawa kikō (Journey to Shirakawa) by Sōgi. In Kaneko Kinjirō, ed., *Sōgi tabi no ki shichū,* pp. 9–26. Ōfūsha, 1976.

[Shintei zōho] Shiseki shūran, ed. Kondo Heijō et al. 43 vols. Kyoto: Rinsen Shoten, 1967–68.

Shiyōshō (Notes for private use) by Shinkei. In Ijichi Tetsuo, ed., *Rengaron shinshū,* pp. 53–98. *Koten bunkō* 113. Koten Bunkō, 1956.

Shōtetsu monogatari, ed. Hisamatsu Sen'ichi. In Hisamatsu Sen'ichi and Nishio Minoru, eds., *Karonshū Nōgakuronshū,* pp. 165–234. *NKBT* 65. Iwanami Shoten, 1961.

Shūi gusō. In Kubota Jun, ed., *Fujiwara Teika zenkashū.* 2 vols. Kawade Shobō, 1985, 1986.

Sōgi kushū, ed. Kaneko Kinjirō and Ijichi Tetsuo. *KS* 12. Kadokawa Shoten, 1977.

Sōgi shūenki (A record of Sōgi's final days) by Sōchō. In *GR* 22: 521.773–77. Annotated ed. in Kaneko Kinjirō, *Sōgi tabi no ki shichū,* pp. 103–25. Ōfūsha, 1976. Also in Tsurusaki Hiroo and Fukuda Hideichi, eds., *Chūsei nikki kikōshū. SNKBT* 51: 449–61. Iwanami Shoten, 1990.

Sōkonshū by Shōtetsu. In *Chūsei IV, ST* 5: 532–870. Meiji Shoin, 1976.

Sono no chiri by Kenzai. In *ZGR* 17b: 487.736–845.

Suzuki Ryōichi. *Ōnin no ran.* Iwanami Shoten, 1973.

Takagi Masakazu, ed. *Haku Kyo'i* [Ch. *Po Chü-i*]. 2 vols. *Chūgoku shijin senshū* 3–4. Iwanami Shoten, 1958.

Taketori monogatari (Tale of the bamboo cutter), ed. Katagiri Yōichi. In Katagiri Yōichi et al., eds., *Taketori monogatari, Ise monogatari, Yamato monogatari, Heichū monogatari. NKBZ* 8: 51–108. Shogakkan, 1972.

Tamamura Takeji, ed. *Gozan bungaku shinshū.* 8 vols. Tōkyō Daigaku Shuppankai, 1967–81.

Tanaka Yutaka. *Chūsei bungakuron kenkyū.* Hanawa Shobō, 1969.

Tōfu renga hiji (Secrets of the renga style of our time) by Sōboku. In Ijichi Tetsuo, ed., *Rengaronshū* 2: 210–28. Iwanami Shoten, 1956.

Tokihide-kyō kikigaki (Lord Tokihide's notes) by Nishinotōin Tokihide. In *ZGR* 17a: 464.11–18.

Tokoro-dokoro hentō (Replies here and there) by Shinkei. In *SSRS,* pp. 195–227. Also in Ijichi Tetsuo, ed., *Rengaronshū* 1: 305–30. Iwanami Shoten, 1956.

Tōyashū kikigaki (Notes from the eastern plains) by Tō no Tsuneyori, ed. Sasaki Nobutsuna. In *NKT* 5: 329–89. Kazama Shobō, 1977.

Toyoda Takeshi and Sugiyama Hiroshi. "The Growth of Commerce and the Trades." In John W. Hall and Toyoda Takeshi, eds., *Japan in the Muromachi Age*, pp. 129–144. Berkeley: University of California Press, 1977.

Tsuji Zennosuke. *Nihon bukkyōshi*, vol. 6: *Chūsei-hen no go*. Iwanami Shoten, 1970.

Tsukuba mondō (Tsukuba dialogues) by Nijō Yoshimoto, ed. Kidō Saizō. In *RH*, pp. 69–106.

Tsukubashū. In Fukui Kyūzō, ed., *Kōhon Tsukubashū shinshaku*. 2 vols. Waseda Daigaku Shuppanbu, 1936, 1942. For an abridged edition, see Ijichi Tetsuo, ed., *Rengashū*. *NKBT* 39 (1960): 39–174. Iwanami Shoten, 1960.

Tsurezuregusa (Essays in idleness) by Kenkō; ed. Nagazumi Yasuaki. In Kanda Hideo et al., eds., *Hōjōki, Tsurezuregusa, Shōbōgenzō zuimonki, Tannishō*. *NKBZ* 27: 85–285. Shōgakkan, 1971.

Ungyoku wakashō, ed. Shimazu Tadao and Inoue Muneo. In *Koten bunkō* 248. Koten Bunkō, 1968.

Varley, H. Paul. *The Ōnin War: History of Its Origins and Background with a Selective Translation of the Chronicle of Ōnin*. New York: Columbia University Press, 1967.

—— and Kumakura Isao, eds. *Tea in Japan: Essays on the History of Chanoyu*. Honolulu: University of Hawaii Press, 1989.

Wakan rōeishū, ed. Kawaguchi Hisao. *Wakan rōeishū*. *NKBT* 73. Iwanami Shoten, 1965.

Waley, Arthur. *The Life and Times of Po Chü-i*. New York: Macmillan, 1949.

——, trans. *The Nō Plays of Japan*. New York: Grove Press, 1957.

Weigl, Gail Capitol. "The Reception of Chinese Painting Models in Muromachi Japan." *MN* 36. 3 (Autumn 1980): 257–72.

Wen hsüan. See *Monzen*.

Yamada Yoshio. *Renga gaisetsu*. Iwanami Shoten, 1937.

—— and Hoshika Sōichi, eds. *Renga hōshiki kōyō*. Iwanami Shoten, 1936.

Yamagishi Tokuhei, ed. *Hachidaishūshō*. 3 vols. Yūseidō, 1960.

Yamane Kiyotaka. "Shinkei ni okeru chōkaku hyōgen." In Kaneko Kinjirō-hakase Kokikinen Ronshū Henshū Iinkai, ed., *Renga to chūsei bungei*, pp. 135–48. Kadokawa Shoten, 1977.

——. "Shinkei no hyōgen: 'mono mo nashi' o megutte." In *Chūsei bungei: gojūgokinen ronshū*, pp. 50–68. Hiroshima: Hiroshima Chūsei Bungei Kenkyūkai, 1973.

Yamanoue Sōji ki, ed. Kuwata Tadachika. In Sen Sōshitsu, ed., *Chadō koten zenshū* 6: 49–116. Kyoto: Tankōsha, 1956.

Yodo no watari (The Yodo crossing) by Sōgi. In Kidō Saizō, ed., *Rengaronshū* 2. *Chūsei no bungaku*, 1st series, vol. 10: 281–96. Miyai Shoten, 1982.

Yoshida Ayao. *Fujiwara Teika kenkyū*. Shibundō, 1975.

Yoshikawa Kōjirō and Ogawa Tamaki, eds. *Chūgoku shijin senshū*. 18 vols. Iwanami Shoten, 1958–61.

Yuasa Kiyoshi. *Shinkei no kenkyū*. Kazama Shobō, 1977.

Yuki no keburi by Sōgi. In Yokoyama Shigeru, ed., *Chikurinshō kochū*, pp. 103–32. *KS* 2. Kadokawa Shoten, 1969.

Yunoue Sanae. "*Gikō no eisō Shinkei no tensaku*—honkoku to kaisetsu." *Renga haikai kenkyū* 45 (Aug. 1973): 22–31.

————. "Kenzai to Kyōshun." In Kaneko Kinjirō-hakase Kokikinen Ronshū Henshū Iinkai, ed., *Renga to chūsei bungei*, pp. 60–83. Kadokawa Shoten, 1977.

Zoku gunsho ruijū. 71 vols. Zoku Gunsho Ruijū Kanseikai, 1931–33.

Zoku Shiryō taisei, ed. Takeuchi Rizō. 22 vols. Kyoto: Rinsen Shoten, 1967.

Character List

Afuriyama 雨降山・阿夫利山
aite awazaru koi 逢不逢恋
Aizu 会津
Akamatsu Mitsusuke 赤松満祐
akamegashiwa 赤芽柏
Akishino gesseishū 秋篠月清集
Amaterasu 天照
amayo no shinasadame 雨夜の品さ
　だめ
Anegakōji Imashimmei
　hyakuin 姉小路今神明百韻
aoba 青葉
Asaji 浅茅
Asanani hyakuin 朝何百韻
Ashikaga Masauji 足利政氏
　　　　Masatomo 政知
　　　　Mochiuji 持氏
　　　　Motouji 基氏
　　　　Shigeuji 成氏
　　　　Takauji 尊氏
　　　　Yoshiakira 義詮
　　　　Yoshihisa 義尚
　　　　Yoshimasa 義政
　　　　Yoshimi 義視
　　　　Yoshimitsu 義満
　　　　Yoshimochi 義持
　　　　Yoshinori 義教

Ashina Morinori 蘆名盛詮
　　　　Moritaka 盛高
ashi no maroya 蘆の丸屋
Ashita no kumo あしたの雲
ashura 阿修羅
Asukai Masachika 飛鳥井雅親
　　　　Masatsune 雅経
　　　　Masayo 雅世
Azuma atari iisute 吾妻辺云捨
Azuma gekō hokkugusa
　吾妻下向発句草
Azuma mondō 吾妻問答
Baika mujinzō 梅花無尽蔵
Banri Shūkyū 万里集九
Bashō 芭蕉
batsugun 抜群
Bishamon-kō 毘沙門講
Bontō 梵灯
bugyō 奉行
Buke utaawase 武家歌合
bumintei 撫民休
Bun'an yonen Chikamasa-tō Nani-
　hito hyakuin 文安四年親当等
　何人百韻
Bushū Edo utaawase 武州江戸歌合
buun chōkyū 武運長久
byōdōshin 平等心

Chen chung chi (J. *Chinchūki*)
枕中記

Chih-i (J. *Chigi*) 智顗

Chikamoto nikki 親元日記

Chikubun 竹聞

Chikurinshō 竹林抄

Chikurinshō no chū 竹林抄之注

Chikurinshū kikigaki 竹林集聞書

chikushō 畜生

chinchō 珍重

chinshi 沈思

Chiun (Ninagawa Chikamasa)
智蘊(蜷川親当)

chōka 長歌

chōkōtei・take takaki tai 長高体

Chōrokubumi 長六文

Chōroku Kanshō ki 長禄寛正記

chūdō jissō 中道実相

Chūei 忠英

Chūga 中雅

chūin 中陰

daiei 題詠

Daigo Jakuseidani 醍醐寂静谷

Daijōin jisha zōjiki 大乗院寺社雑
事記

daisan 第三

daisōzu 大僧都

darani 陀羅尼

Dempō 伝芳

Dengyō Daishi (Saichō)
伝教大師(最澄)

denka 田家

dōbōshū 同朋衆

doikki 土一揆

dokugin 独吟

dōshin 道心

dosō 土倉

Eikyō kunen Shōtetsu eisō 永亨九年
正徹詠草

ekō massei no sansai 壊劫末世の三災

emono 獲物・得物

en 艶

Enryakuji 延暦寺

Enshū 円秀

Fei Chang-fang (J. *Hichōbō*) 費長房

fubin 不便

Fude no susabi 筆のすさび

fūga no makoto 風雅の誠

Fūgashū 風雅集

Fujigayatsu shikimoku 藤谷式目

Fujiwara Teika 藤原定家
          Yoshitsune 良経

Funaoka 船岡

Furuichi Chōin 古市澄胤

Fuzan no yume 巫山の夢

gago 雅語

gakidō 餓鬼道

ganzen no keshiki 眼前の景色

gemmyō kidoku no gonja
玄妙奇特の権者

gengai no renga 言外の連歌

Genjūan no ki 幻住庵記

Gensetsu 元説

Gikō no eisō Shinkei no tensaku
祇公の詠草心敬の点削

Gondaisōzu Shinkei shū
権大僧都心敬集

gongo dōdan 言語道断

gōrikitei 強力体

Guhishō 愚秘抄

Guku Shibakusa 愚句芝草

Gusai (or Kyūsei) 求済

Gyōjo 行助

Gyōkō 堯孝

Gyōkō hōin nikki 堯孝法印日記

Gyokuyōshū 玉葉集

Hachiōjisha 八王子社

hama hisaki 浜楸

hana no himo 花の紐

Han-t'an 邯鄲

harae 祓

Hatakeyama Kenryō 畠山賢良

Masanaga 政長

Mochikuni 持国

Yoshinari 義就

Hatsunani hyakuin 初何百韻

hatsushio 初潮

Hekizan nichiroku 碧山日録

henjodai 篇序題

Hidechika 毗親

Hiei 比叡

hiekōritaru 冷え氷たる

hieyase 冷え痩せ

Higashiyama 東山

hikan 被官

hi no mikage 日の御影

Hino Yoshisuke 日野義資

Hirayama 比良山

hitofushi ni iinagashitaru 一筋に云流
したる

hito no waza 人の業

Hitorigoto 独言

Hoan kyōka zenshū 補庵京華前集

hōben 法便

hōgen 法眼

hōin 法印

Hōjōki 方丈記

Hokkekyō 法華經

Hokke nijuhappon waka 法華二十八
品和歌

hokku 発句

hon'i 本意

honkadori 本歌取

Honnōji 本能寺

honrai kū 本来空

honzetsu 本説

Hōrai (Ch. P'eng-lai) 蓬莱

hōraku 法樂

Horikoshi Kubō 堀越公方

Hosokawa Dōken 細川道賢

Katsumoto 勝基

Mitsumoto 満基

Yorihisa 頼久

Hosshōji 法勝寺

Hōzen 法泉・宝泉

Hsiao-hsiang yeh-yü 瀟湘夜雨

Hu-hsi 虎溪

Hui-yüan 慧袁

Hyakuban renga awase 百番連歌合

hyakuin 百韻

Hyakushu waka 百首和歌

Ichigon 一言

Ichijō Kanera (or Kaneyoshi) 一条
兼良

ichimi no ame 一味の雨

Ikago 十五子

Ikenobō 池の坊

Ikkyū 一休

Imagawa Ryōshun 今川了俊

Inawashiro 猪苗代

Inkō 印孝

Inryōken nichiroku 蔭涼軒日録

Ise Sadachika 伊勢貞親

Ishijarishū 石舎利集

Ishikura 石蔵・石倉

ishin denshin 以心伝心

issetsutei・hitofushi naru
tai 一節休

Iwahashi no ge 岩橋下

Iwahashi no jo 岩橋上

Jakuzen 寂然

jichū 自注

jige 地下

jigoku 地獄

Jimbo 神保

Jimbo Shiroyūemon 神保四郎右衛門

jinji 人事

Jinson 尋尊

Jirenga awase 自連歌合

Jisankachū 自讃歌注

Jishū 時宗

Jitchū 実中

jitōshiki 地頭職

jitsugen 実言

jittoku 十徳

Jōgyōji 淨業寺

Jōha 紹巴

Jōhō renga 紹芳連歌

jōkō 成劫

(Takeno) Jōō （武野）紹鴎

jōsha hissui 盛者必衰

Jūjūshin'in 十住心院

jukkai 述懐

jūkō 住劫

(Murata) Jukō （村田）珠光

Jukō, Furuichi Harima-hōshi ate no isshi 珠光, 古市播磨法師宛一紙

Jun'a 旬阿

Junsō 馴窓

Juntoku-in 順徳院

kaikyū 懐旧

Kaisō-gun 海草郡

Kaku'a 覺阿

Kamakura ōzōshi 鎌倉大草子

Kamata Mitsusuke 鎌田満助

Kamo no Chōmei 鴨長明

kanjin 閑人

Kanjinshū 閑塵集

Kanrei 管領

Kantan no yume 邯鄲の夢

Kantō hasshū 関東八州

        Kubō 公方

        Kanrei 関領

Kao-t'ang fu 高唐賦

Karanani hyakuin 唐何百韻

karekashike samukare 枯れかしけ寒かれ

karine 仮寝

kari no yado 仮の宿

Kawagoe-jō 河越城

Kawagoe senku 河越千句

Kazuya-kan 糟屋館

Keichō kembunshū 慶長見聞集

Keikandō 景感道

keiki 景気

keikyoku no tai 景曲の体

Keizuian 景瑞庵

Ken'a 兼阿

Kenkō 兼好

Kenninji 建仁寺

Kenten 顕天

Kenzai 兼載

Kenzai zōdan 兼載雑談

Kibe Yoshinori 木戸孝範

kichū no byōshin 羇中の病心

kigandera 祈願寺

Kii 紀伊

kinjū 近習

Kinkaishū 金槐集

Kinokawa 紀川

kisasage 木豇豆・楸

Kitano-sha ichimanku gohokku waki daisan narabi ni jo 北野社一万句御発句脇第三并序

Kiyomizudera 清水寺

Kiyō-shuza 季揚首座

Kiyō-shuza wain no jo 季揚首座和韻序

kochūshaku 古注釈

Koga Kubō 古河公方

Kogamo senku 小鴨千句

Kogamo Yukimoto 小鴨之基

kōin 光陰

Kokemushiro 苔莚

Kokin denju 古今伝授

Kokin rokujō 古今六帖

Kokinshū 古今集

Kokinshū ryōdo kikigaki 古今集両度聞書

kokoro no en 心の艶

kokoro no hana 心の花

Kokoro no shi no fumi 心の師の文

kokoro no tsuki 心の月

kokorozuke 心付

Korai fūteishō 古来風体抄

kōryō issui no yume 黄梁一炊の夢
koto shikarubeki tai 事可然體
Kōyū 高雄
Kōzanji 高山寺
kūgen 空言
kuhon no rendai 九品の連台
kūkanteki na Zen no seishin
　空間的な禪の精神
kūke 空仮
kūkō 空劫
Kumano hōraku senku 熊野法楽千句
kunibome uta 国讃歌
kurayaku 蔵役
Kurihara Ikuhiro 栗原幾弘
Kurodani 黒谷
Kyōshō (or Keisei) 慶政
Kyōshun 興俊
Lu Hsiu-ching 陸修静
Lu-shan 蘆山
maeku 前句
mae-maeku 前々句
Maigetsushō 毎月抄
Makashikan 摩訶止觀
manako no tsukedokoro 眼の付所
Mandokoro 政所
Mansai jugō nikki 満済准后日記
mappō 末法
Masayori 正頼
Meisū goi 名数語彙
mempakutei・omoshiroki tai 面白体
Miidera 三井寺
Minamoto Sanetomo 源実朝
　　　　Toshiyori (or Shunrai) 俊頼
　　　　Tsunenobu 経信
　　　　Yoritomo 頼朝
　　　　Yoshitsune 義経
Minishū 壬二集
Mino senku 美濃千句
minu omokage 見ぬ面影
miraiki 未来記
misogi 禊

misotose no teikin 三十年の庭訓
mitsu no kashiwa 三角柏
miyama 深山
Mōgyū (Ch. *Meng Ch'iu*) 蒙求
mono isshiki ni 物一色に
mono no aware もののあはれ
mononofu no michi 武士の道
muinaru ku 無為なる句
mujō 無常
mumyō chōya 無明長夜
musabetsu 無差別
Musashi 武蔵
Musashi Shinagawa minato no
　senchō 武蔵品川湊船帳
mushikikai 無色界
mushin renga 無心連歌
Myōe 明恵
Myōkokuji 妙国寺
Myōkokuji engi 妙国寺縁起
Myōmanji 妙満寺
Nagusamegusa なぐさめ草
Nakusa 名草
Nanifune hyakuin 何船百韻
Nanihito hyakuin 何人百韻
Naniki hyakuin 何木百韻
Nanimichi hyakuin 何路百韻
Nasu no shinohara 那須の篠原
nayutake 弱竹
Nichimei 日明
Nijō Tameuji 二条為氏
　　　　Yoshimoto 良基
Ninagawa Chikamasa (Chiun)
　蜷川親当
　　　　Chikamoto 親元
Ninzei 忍誓
nioi-zuke 匂付
Nōa (Nōami) 能阿(能阿弥)
Nōin 能因
nori no mizu 法の水
nori no tsuki 法の月
nōtei・komayaka naru tai 濃体

nushi mo nashi 主もなし

Ōan shinshiki 応安新式

Ochiba hyakuin 落葉百韻

Ōgigayatsu 扇谷

Ōgo Norishige 大胡修茂

Ōgo Norishige yoriai 大胡修茂寄合

oi no kazashi 老の挿頭

Oi no kurigoto 老のくりごと

Oi no susami 老のすさみ

oku fukaki michi 奥深き道

Oku no hosomichi 奥の細道

omokage 面影

On'ami 音阿弥

Ōninki 応仁記

Ōnin no ran 応仁の乱

Ōsen Keisan 横川景三

Ōta Dōkan (Sukenaga)
　大田道潅(資長)

Ōta Dōkan-tō utaawase
　大田道潅等歌合

Ōta Dōshin (Sukekiyo)
　大田道真(資清)

Otonashikawa 音無川

Otowayama 音羽山

Ōuchi Masahiro 大内政弘

Ōyama 大山

Po Chü-i 白居易

reitei·uruwashiki tai 麗体

Reizei 冷泉

Reizei Tamesuke 冷泉爲相
　　　　Tameyuki 爲之

Renga entokushō 連歌延徳抄

Renga hajakenshō 連歌破邪顕正

Renga hyakkutsuke 連歌百句付

rengashi 連歌師

renga shichiken 連歌七賢

Renga shinshiki 連歌新式

Renga shogakushō 連歌初學抄

Renga tsukeai no koto 連歌付合の事

Renga yoriai 連歌寄合

Renju gappekishū 連珠合璧集

Renkai 連海・蓮海

rikon naru fūkotsu 利根なる風骨

rikuchin 陸沈

rikugi 六義

(Sen) Rikyū （千）利休

rokudō 六道

Rokuharamitsuji 六波羅密寺

Ryōjin hishō 染塵祕抄

ryokyaku inshi 旅客隠士

sabi さび・寂

Saigyō 西行

Saijun 西順

Saimon no ji 柴門辞

Saishōji 最勝寺

Saitō Myōshun 斉藤妙春

Samboku kikashū 散木奇歌集

samidare 五月雨

sangai no kataku 三界の火宅

Sange gakushōshiki 山家学生式

Sanjōnishi Kin'eda 三条西公条
　　　　Sanetaka 実隆

santai·sandai 三諦

sari kirai 去嫌

Sasamegoto ささめごと

sekisho 関所

Sen'ichi Kengyō 千一検校

Senjun 専順

Shibakusa kunai hokku
　芝草句内発句

Shibakusa kunai Iwahashi
　芝草句内岩橋

Shibakusa-nai renga awase
　芝草内連歌合

shide no yamaji 死出の山路

shigure 時雨

Shihōshō 至宝抄

shikan 止観

shikikai 色界

shikimoku 式目

Shikishi-naishinnō 式子内親王

shikisō no yume 色相の夢

Shikō Shūa hyakuban renga awase
　侍公周阿百番連歌合
shimpen 神変
Shimpen Musashi fūdokikō
　新編武蔵風土記稿
Shinagawa 品川
Shingyokushū 心玉集
Shingyokushū (by Shinkei) 新玉集
Shingyokushū shūi 心玉集拾遺
shinji shugyō 心地修行
Shinkei 心敬
Shinkei dokugin yamanani
　hyakuin 心敬独吟山何百韻
Shinkei kushū kokemushiro
　心敬句集苔莚
Shinkei renga jichū 心敬連歌自注
Shinkei shigo 心敬私語
Shinkei-sōzu hyakku 心敬僧都百句
Shinkei-sōzu hyakushu 心敬僧都
　百首
Shinkei-sōzu jittei waka 心敬僧都十
　体和歌
Shinkei-sōzu kushū 心敬僧都句集
Shinkei-sōzu teikin 心敬僧都庭訓
Shinkei Yūhaku e no hensho
　心敬有伯への返書
Shinkō 心孝
Shinkokin nukigakishō
　新古今抜書抄
Shinkokinshū 新古今集
shinku 親句
Shinsen Tsukubashu 新撰菟玖波集
Shinshiki kin'an 新式今案
Shinzoku Kokinshū 新続古今集
(Kikei) Shinzui (季瓊)真蘂
Shirai 白井
Shirakawa kikō 白河紀行
Shirakawa no seki 白河の関
Shiyōshō 私用抄
shizuya 賤屋
shōdō, shōfū 正道, 正風

Shōgetsuan 松月庵
shogyō mujō 諸行無常
Shōhaku 消柏
Shōjōkōji 清淨光寺
shoki 書記
Shōkō 正広
Shōkokuji 相国寺
Shōtetsu 正徹
Shōtetsu monogatari 正徹物語
Shūa 周阿
Shūbun 周文
shugo daimyō 守護大名
shuhitsu 執筆
Shūi gusō 拾遺愚草
Shun'a 俊阿
Shutsuyō-gyō 出曜經
Sōanshū 草庵集
Sōboku 宗牧
Sōchō 宗長
Sōetsu 宗悦
Sōgen 宗沅
Sōgi 宗祇
Sōgi shūenki 宗祇終焉記
Sōgi-Zenshi e no hensatsu
　宗祇禅師江返札
Sōi (Sugihara Katamori)
　宗伊(杉原賢盛)
Sōkonshū 草根集
soku 疎句
sonkotei 尊古体
Sono no chiri 園塵
Sōseki 宗碩
sōshō 宗匠
Sōyō 宗養
Soyu (Inadoko Motonari)
　宗雄(稲常元成)
Sōzei (Takayama Tokishige)
　宗砌(高山時重)
suki 数寄
Sung Yü 宋玉
Su Tung-p'o 蘇東坡

Suzuki Dōin 鈴木道印
　　Kōjun 幸順
　　Nagatoshi 長敏
Ta'i 田井
T'ai-kung-wang (J. Taikōbō) 太公望
Taikyoku 大極
Tamatsushima-myōjin 玉津島明神
T'ao Yüan-ming 陶淵明
te ni o ha てにをは
tenja 点者
tenka seihitsu 天下静謐
tennin no gosui 天人の五衰
Tōfukuji 東福寺
Tōfū renga hiji 当風連歌秘事
Toganoo 栂尾
toi 問
Tokihide-kyō kikigaki 時秀卿聞書
Tokoro-dokoro hentō 所々返答
tokusei 徳政
Ton'a 頓阿
Tō no Tsuneyori 東常縁
toriawase 取合
Tōshōin 洞昌院
Tōyashū kikigaki 東野州聞書
tōzan kenju 刀山剣樹
tsukeai 付合
tsukeku 付句
Tsukuba mondō 筑波問答
Tsukubashū 菟玖波集
Tsuruwaka 鶴若
Tu Fu 杜甫
Tung-t'ing ch'iu yüeh 洞庭秋月
Tzu-yu (Wang Hui-chih)
　子猷（王徽之）
Uesugi Akisada 上杉顕定
　　Masazane 政真
　　Norizane 憲実
　　Sadamasa 定正
Ungyokushō 雲玉抄
Uraba 宇良葉
ushin renga 有心連歌
ushintei 有心体

utamakura 歌枕
wabicha わび茶・侘茶
waka 和歌
Wakanoura 和歌浦
Wakan rōeishū 和漢朗詠集
waki 脇
Wakuraba 老葉
Wang Chih 王質
warehito no michi 我人の道
Wasuregusa 宣草
Wen hsüan (J. *Monzen*) 文選
wen jen 文人
Yamanani hyakuin 山何百韻
Yamana Noriyuki 山名教之
　　Sōzen 宗全
Yamanouchi 山内
Yamanoue Sōji 山上宗二
Yamanoue Sōji ki 山上宗二記
yariku 遣り句
yasesamuku やせさむく・痩せ寒く
Yasutomi Morinaga 安富盛長
Yodo no watari 淀渡
yojō 余情
Yokawa 横川
yokkai 欲界
yomogi ga shima 蓬が島
yo no ure'e 世の憂・愁
yōon 幽遠
yoriai 寄合
yotsude 四つ手
yūen 優艶
yūgen 幽玄
yūin 幽韻
Yūki Naotomo 結城直朝
　　Ujitomo 氏朝
Yuki no keburi 雪の煙
yume no yo 夢の世
Zeami 世阿弥
(Komparu) Zenchiku （今春）禪竹
zenteki hitei 全的否定
zokugo 俗語

Index of First Lines

With the exception of the verses in the two sequences, "Cuckoo" and "Broken beneath Snow," all waka, hokku, and tsukeku appearing in the book are included in this index. Unless otherwise indicated, the author of the poetry is Shinkei. "Source unknown" indicates that the piece is not to be found in *KT*. The numbers refer to page location in the book, modified by *n* when the entry appears in a note.

Waka

Tsukeku

Subject Index

In this index an "f" after a number indicates a separate reference on the next page, and an "ff" indicates separate references on the next two pages. A continuous discussion over two or more pages is indicated by a span of page numbers, e.g., "pp. 57–58." *Passim* is used for a cluster of references in close but not consecutive sequence.

Library of Congress Cataloging-in-Publication Data

Ramirez-Christensen, Esperanza U.
  Heart's flower : the life and poetry of Shinkei / Esperanza
Ramirez-Christensen.
    p. cm.
  Includes bibliographical references and index.
  ISBN 0-8047-2253-6 (alk. paper) :
  1. Shinkei, 1406–1475. 2. Poets, Japanese—1185–1600—Biography.
3. Priest, Buddhist—Japan—Biography. 4. Shinkei,—1406–1475—
Translations into English. I. Shinkei, 1406–1475. Selections.
1994. II. Title.
PL792.S45Z89 1994
895.6'124—dc20
[B]   93-17305
                                              CIP

♾ This book is printed on acid-free paper